TRAJECTORIES THROUGH THE NEW TESTAMENT AND THE APOSTOLIC FATHERS

Trajectories through the New Testament and the Apostolic Fathers

Edited by

ANDREW F. GREGORY

CHRISTOPHER M. TUCKETT

OXFORD
UNIVERSITY PRESS

OXFORD
UNIVERSITY PRESS

Great Clarendon Street, Oxford OX2 6DP

Oxford University Press is a department of the University of Oxford.
It furthers the University's objective of excellence in research, scholarship,
and education by publishing worldwide in

Oxford New York

Auckland Cape Town Dar es Salaam Hong Kong Karachi
Kuala Lumpur Madrid Melbourne Mexico City Nairobi
New Delhi Shanghai Taipei Toronto

With offices in

Argentina Austria Brazil Chile Czech Republic France Greece
Guatemala Hungary Italy Japan Poland Portugal Singapore
South Korea Switzerland Thailand Turkey Ukraine Vietnam

Oxford is a registered trade mark of Oxford University Press
in the UK and in certain other countries

Published in the United States
by Oxford University Press Inc., New York

First published 2005

British Library Cataloguing in Publication Data
Data available

Library of Congress Cataloging in Publication Data
Trajectories through the New Testament and the Apostolic Fathers
/ edited by Andrew Gregory, Christopher Tuckett.
p. cm.
ISBN 0-19-926783-9 (alk. paper)
1. Bible. N.T.–Criticism, interpretation, etc. 2. Apostolic Fathers.
I. Gregory, Andrew F. II. Tuckett, C. M. (Christopher Mark)
BS2361.3.T73 2005
225'.06–dc22

2005018648

Typeset by SPI Publisher Services, Pondicherry, India
Printed in Great Britain
on acid-free paper by Biddles Ltd, King's Lynn, Nonfolk

ISBN 0–19–926783–9 978–0–19–926783–5

1 3 5 7 9 10 8 6 4 2

Preface

The essays and studies included in these two volumes are intended to update, to develop, and to widen the scope of the issues considered by members of 'A Committee of the Oxford Society of Historical Theology' in their landmark and still valuable reference book, *The New Testament in the Apostolic Fathers*. That volume was published by the Clarendon Press in 1905, and it is to acknowledge the importance of that famous book that these companion volumes are published in its centenary year. The 1905 volume was very much a product of Oxford, albeit by a number of scholars who may have been on the fringes of university life (as John Muddiman explains, in *Trajectories through the New Testament and the Apostolic Fathers*, p. 107); Kirsopp Lake is listed among the contributors as Professor of New Testament Exegesis in the University of Leiden, but he was curate of the University Church of St Mary the Virgin in Oxford until his appointment to that chair in 1904.

Oxford connections remain important in these centenary volumes. Both editors are members of the Oxford Theology Faculty, and these papers represent the first-fruits of an ongoing research project on the New Testament and the second century that is supported by the Theology Faculty. Yet there is also a strong international dimension to the research presented in these volumes, for the contributors are drawn from Belgium, Germany, Canada, the USA, and South Africa, as well as from Oxford and elsewhere in the United Kingdom. Many of the papers were presented and discussed at a conference held at Lincoln College, Oxford, in April 2004; others were written solely for publication. But this collection is by no means just another Conference Proceedings; all the contributions printed here have been through the process of peer review that is customary in academic publishing.

The chapters that appear in *The Reception of the New Testament in the Apostolic Fathers* offer a comprehensive and rigorous discussion of the extent to which the writings later included in the New Testament were known, and cited (or alluded to), by the Apostolic Fathers, and they do so in the light of contemporary research on the textual traditions of both corpora. The chapters in *Trajectories through the New Testament and the Apostolic Fathers* are also sensitive to these issues, but offer a representative sample of a range of issues that arise in the comparative study of these texts. They cannot be comprehensive, because they address wider questions than those addressed in the companion volume, but they advance contemporary discussion and understanding of each of the Apostolic Fathers and much of the New Testament in the wider context of Christian origins and development in the first and second centuries.

Both editors are glad to thank various people for their help in producing these volumes. We are grateful to Hilary O'Shea, who brought the proposal before the Delegates of Oxford University Press, and to Lucy Qureshi, who saw the volumes through from their acceptance by the Press until their publication. Dorothy McCarthy, Enid Barker, Amanda Greenley, Samantha Griffiths, and Jean van Altena each helped us to keep to a tight production schedule and gave valuable advice on many points of detail. Particular thanks are due to the anonymous reader who read a large typescript with great speed and equal care, and offered a number of helpful and incisive suggestions.

OUP provided financial support for our conference, as did the British Academy, the Zilkha Fund of Lincoln College, Oxford, and the Theology Faculty of Oxford University. We are glad to acknowledge the assistance of each. Adam Francisco provided indispensable help in running the conference website, which allowed delegates to read papers in advance, and was of great assistance throughout the planning and administration of the conference, as were Mel Parrott and her colleagues at Lincoln College.

Most importantly, both editors were overwhelmed by the support and interest shown by such a range of international experts in the study of the New Testament and early Christianity, and we are grateful to all who have allowed us to include their work in this publication. We hope that that these volumes will become a standard reference work for many years to come, and that they will provide a useful resource for future researchers in New Testament and Patristics.

AFG
CMT

Contents

List of Contributors

Arthur J. Bellinzoni is Professor Emeritus at Wells College, and Special Assistant to the President for Strategic Initiatives. His publications include *The Sayings of Jesus in the Writings of Justin Martyr* (1967), *The Future of Christianity: Will It Survive in the Third Millennium?* (forthcoming); and, as editor, *The Two Source Hypothesis: A Critical Appraisal* (1985).

Allen Brent, formerly Associate Professor in History, James Cook University of North Queensland, Australia, is a member of the Faculty of Divinity in the University of Cambridge, and a senior member of St Edmund's College. His published work, which explores the interface between classical culture and early Christian history, includes *The Imperial Cult and the Development of Church Order: Concepts and Images of Authority in Paganism and Christianity before the Age of Cyprian* (1999) and several articles on Ignatius.

Carsten Claussen is Lecturer in New Testament Theology at the Protestant Theological Faculty, University of Munich, Germany. He is the author of *Versammlung, Gemeinde, Synagoge: Das hellenistisch-jüdische Umfeld der frühchristlichen Gemeinden* (2002). His other publications include articles about the Gospel of John and the Jewish background to early Christianity.

Boudewijn Dehandschutter is Professor of Church History and the History of Theology at the Catholic University of Leuven. His many publications include *Martyrium Polycarpi: Een literair-kritische Studie* (1979).

Jonathan A. Draper is Professor of New Testament at the School of Theology, University of Kwazulu-Natal, Pietermaritzburg campus. His publications include (with Richard A. Horsley) *Whoever Hears You Hears Me: Prophets Performance and Tradition in Q* (1999), and, as editor, *The Didache in Modern Research* (1996), *The Eye of the Storm: Bishop John William Colenso and the Crisis of Biblical Interpretation* (2003), *Orality, Literacy, and Colonialism in Southern Africa* (2003) and *Orality, Literacy, and Colonialism in Antiquity* (2004).

Andrew F. Gregory is a Research Fellow at Keble College, Oxford. He is a series editor of Oxford Early Christian Gospel Texts and the Oxford Apostolic Fathers, and the author of *The Reception of Luke and Acts in the Period before Irenaeus* (2003). His other publications include articles on the importance of second-century Christian texts for the interpretation of the New Testament.

Paul A. Hartog is an Associate Professor at Faith Baptist Theological Seminary, where he teaches New Testament and Patristics courses. He is the author of *Polycarp and the New Testament* (2002).

Charles E. Hill is Professor of New Testament at Reformed Theological Seminary, Orlando, Florida. He is the author of *Regnum Caelorum: Patterns of Millennial Thought in Early Christianity* (2nd edn., 2001), *The Johannine Corpus in the Early Church* (2004), and several articles on first- and second-century Christianity.

Michael W. Holmes is Professor of Biblical Studies and Early Christianity, and Chair of the Department of Biblical and Theological Studies, Bethel University. An editor of the SBL-sponsored monograph series The New Testament in the Greek Fathers, he is the author or editor of six books, including *The Apostolic Fathers: Greek Texts and English Translations* (3rd edn., 1999), and has also published more than twenty articles, essays, or chapters in books.

Clayton N. Jefford is Professor of Scripture at the Saint Meinrad School of Theology. He is the author of *The Sayings of Jesus in the Teaching of the Twelve Apostles* (1989), editor of *The Didache in Context* (1995), and has published articles and chapters on the New Testament and second-century Christian literature. He is the Secretary/Treasurer of the North American Patristics Society.

John S. Kloppenborg is Professor of Religion at the Centre for the Study of Religion, University of Toronto. He is the author of many articles and books, including *Excavating Q: The History and Setting of the Sayings Gospel* (2000).

Helmut Koester is John H. Morison Research Professor of Divinity and Winn Research Professor of Ecclesiastical History at the Harvard Divinity School. He is the author of many books and articles, including *Synoptische Überlieferung bei den apostolischen Vätern* (1957) and *Ancient Christian Gospels* (1990).

Andreas Lindemann is Professor of New Testament at the Kirchliche Hochschule Bethel (Bielefeld, Germany). He is the author of many books and articles, including *Paulus im ältesten Christentum: Das Bild des Apostels und die Rezeption der paulinischen Theologie in der frühchristlichen Literatur bis Marcion* (1979), *Die Clemensbriefe* (1992), *Der Erste Korintherbrief* (2000) and, as editor (with H. Paulsen), *Die Apostolischen Väter: Griechisch-deutsche Parallelausgabe* (1992), and *The Q Source and the Historical Jesus* (2001).

Harry O. Maier is Professor of New Testament Studies at Vancouver School of Theology in Canada. He is author of *The Social Setting of the Ministry as Reflected in the Writing of Hermas, Clement and Ignatius* (2002), and

Apocalypse Recalled: The Book of Revelation after Christendom (2002), as well as many articles relating to the social world and theology of the New Testament and Early Christianity.

John Muddiman is George Caird Fellow in Biblical Studies, Mansfield College, Oxford, and Lecturer in Theology at Oxford University. His publications include the *Black's New Testament Commentary on Ephesians* (2001).

Peter Oakes is J. G. Greenwood Lecturer in the New Testament at the University of Manchester. His publications include *Philippians: From People to Letter* (2001) and, as editor, *Rome in the Bible and the Early Church* (2002). He also edits the *Journal for the Study of the New Testament Booklist.*

David M. Reis is Assistant Professor of Religion Studies at the College of Santa Fe and a research fellow with the Committee for the Scientific Examination of Religion. He has published articles in *Studies in Religion/Sciences Religieuses, The Journal of Higher Criticism,* and *Cauda Pavonis: Studies in Hermeticism.*

Alistair Stewart-Sykes is vicar of Sturminster Marshall, Kingston Lacy, and Shapwick, Dorset, UK. His publications include *From Prophecy to Preaching: A Search for the Origins of the Christian Homily* (2001) and *The Life of Polycarp: An Anonymous Vita from Third-Century Smyrna* (2002).

Christopher M. Tuckett is Professor of New Testament at the University of Oxford and Fellow of Pembroke College. He is a series editor of Oxford Early Christian Gospel Texts and the Oxford Apostolic Fathers, and the author of many books and articles. These include *Q and the History of Early Christianity* (1996) and *Christology and the New Testament* (2001).

Thomas G. Weinandy, O.F.M. Cap., is Executive Director for the Secretariat for Doctrine and Pastoral Practices at the United States Conference of Catholic Bishops, Washington, DC, and an Honorary Fellow of Greyfriars, Oxford, and sometime Warden. His publications include *The Father's Spirit of Sonship: Reconceiving the Trinity* (1995) and *Does God Suffer?* (2000).

David F. Wright, FRHS, has recently retired as Professor of Patristic and Reformed Christianity at the University of Edinburgh, where he taught for thirty-nine years. His research interests have included Augustine, certain Reformers and their use and abuse of the Fathers, and the strange history of infant baptism. His publications include many articles on infant baptism, 'What has Infant Baptism done to Baptism?' and, as an editor, *New Dictionary of Theology* (1988) and *A Dictionary of Scottish Church History and Theology* (1993).

Frances Young, FBA, OBE, was formerly Edward Cadbury Professor of Theology and Dean of Arts and Pro-Vice-Chancellor of the University of Birmingham, but is now in active retirement. Her books include *From Nicaea to Chalcedon* (1983), *The Making of the Creeds* (1991), *The Theology of the Pastoral Letters* (1994), and *Biblical Exegesis and the Formation of Christian Culture* (1997).

Abbreviations

AB	Anchor Bible
ABD	*Anchor Bible Dictionary*, ed D. N. Freedman, 6 vols. (New York: Doubleday, 1992)
ABR	*Australian Biblical Review*
ACW	Ancient Christian Writers
AGAJU	Arbeiten zur Geschichte des antiken Judentums und des Urchristentums
ANRW	*Aufstieg und Niedergang der römischen Welt*, ed. H. Temporini and W. Haase (Berlin: De Gruyter, 1972–)
ATR	*Anglican Theological Review*
BCH	*Bulletin de correspondance hellénique*
BECNT	Baker Exegetical Commentary on the New Testament
BETL	Bibliotheca Ephemeridum Theologicarum Lovaniensium
BHT	Beiträge zur historischen Theologie
Bib	*Biblica*
BLE	*Bulletin de littérature ecclésiastique*
BNTC	Black's New Testament Commentaries
BR	*Biblical Research*
BTB	*Biblical Theology Bulletin*
BVC	Bible et vie chrétienne
BZNW	Beihefte zur Zeitschrift für die neutestamentliche Wissenschaft
CBQ	*Catholic Biblical Quarterly*
CIG	A. Boeck, *Corpus Inscriptorum Graecarum* (Berlin: George Reimer, 1828–77)
CIL	*Corpus Inscriptionum Latinarum* (Berlin, 1862–)
Comm	*Communio*
CRAI	Comptes rendus de l'Académie des inscriptions et belles-lettres
CRINT	Compendia Rerum Iudaicarum ad Novum Testamentum
CTQ	*Concordia Theological Quarterly*
DR	*Downside Review*
ÉBib	Études Bibliques
EKK	Evangelisch-katholischer Kommentar zum Neuen Testament

EQ	*Evangelical Quarterly*
ET	English Translation
ETL	*Ephemerides Theologicae Lovanienses*
EvTh	*Evangelische Theologie*
ExpT	Expository Times
FC	Fontes Christiani
FRLANT	Forschungen zur Religion und Literatur des Alten und Neuen Testaments
GOTR	*Greek Orthodox Theological Review*
HNT	Handbuch zum Neuen Testament
HTKNT	Herders theologischer Kommentar zum Neuen Testament
HTR	*Harvard Theological Review*
HTS	Harvard Theological Studies
HTS	*Hervormde Teologiese Studies*
ICC	International Critical Commentary
IGRom	R. Cagnat and G. Lafaye (eds.), *Inscriptiones Graecae ad res Romanas Pertinentes* (Paris: Ernest Leroux, 1906)
IGUR	L. Moretti (ed.), *Inscriptiones Graecae urbis Romae* (Rome: G. Bardi, 1968–)
JBL	*Journal of Biblical Literature*
JECS	*Journal of Early Christian Studies*
JEH	*Journal of Ecclesiastical History*
JETS	*Journal of the Evangelical Theological Society*
JHS	*Journal of Hellenic Studies*
JQR	*Jewish Quarterly Review*
JR	*Journal of Religion*
JRH	*Journal of Religious History*
JRS	*Journal of Roman Studies*
JSNT	*Journal for the Study of the New Testament*
JSNTSup	Journal for the Study of the New Testament Supplement Series
JSOTSup	Journal for the Study of the Old Testament Supplement Series
JSPS	Journal for the Study of the Pseudepigrapha Supplement
JTC	*Journal of Theology and the Church*
JTS	*Journal of Theological Studies*
KAV	Kommentar zu den apostolischen Vätern
KD	*Kerygma und Dogma*
KEK	Kritisch-exegetischer Kommentar über das Neue Testament

LCL	Loeb Classical Library
LJ	*Liturgisches Jahrbuch*
LTP	*Laval théologique et philosophique*
Neot	*Neotestamentica*
NHS	Nag Hammadi Studies
NICNT	New International Commentary on the New Testament
NIGTC	New International Greek Testament Commentary
NovT	*Novum Testamentum*
NovTSup	Novum Testamentum Supplements
NTAbh	Neutestamentliche Abhandlungen
NTAF	*The New Testament and the Apostolic Fathers* (Oxford, 1905)
NTOA	Novum Testamentum et orbis antiquus
NTS	*New Testament Studies*
OpMinSel	*Opuscula Minora Selecta*
ÖTKNT	Ökummesicher Taschenbuch Kommentar zum Neuen Testament
PRE	*Pauly's Real-Encylcopädie der classichen Altertumswissenschaft*
QD	Quaestiones disputatae
RAC	*Reallexicon für Antike und Christentum*
RArc	*Revue archéologique*
RDC	*Revue de droit canonique*
RHR	*Revue de l'histoire des religions*
RSR	*Recherches de science religieuse*
SBFLA	*Studii Biblici Franciscani liber annus*
SBLDS	Society of Biblical Literature Dissertation Series
SBS	Stuttgarter Bibelstudien
SBT	Studies in Biblical Theology
SC	Sources Chrétiennes
SC	*Second Century*
SEG	*Supplementum epigraphicum Graecum* (1923–)
SE	*Studia evangelica*
SHAW	Sitzungen der Heidelberger Akademie der Wissenschaften
SJLA	Studies in Judaism in Late Antiquity
SJT	*Scottish Journal of Theology*
SL	*Studia Liturgica*
SNTSMS	Society of New Testament Studies Monograph Series

SNTW Studies of the New Testament and its World
SPAW Sitzungsberichte der preussischen Akademie der Wissenschaften
SR *Studies in Religion/Sciences Religieuses*
STDJ Studies on the Texts of the Desert of Judah
STL Studia theologica Lundensia
StPatr *Studia Patristica*
SUNT Studien zur Umwelt des Neuen Testaments
Syll.[3] W. Dittenberger, *Sylloge Inscriptionum Graecarum*, 3rd edn. (1915–24)
SVTP Studia in veteris testamenti pseudepigrapha
TANZ Texte und Arbeiten zum neutestamentlichen Zeitalter
TDNT *Theological Dictionary of the New Testament*, ed. G. Kittel and G. Friedrich, 10 vols. (Grand Rapids, Mich.: Eerdmans, 1964–76)
THKNT Theologischer Handkommentar zum Neuen Testament
TS Texts and Studies
TS *Theological Studies*
TSAJ Texte und Studien zum antiken Judentum
TU Texte und Untersuchungen
TZ *Theologische Zeitschrift*
UTB Uni-Taschenbücher
VC *Vigilae Christianae*
VCSup Supplements to *Vigiliae Christianae*
WMANT Wissenschaftliche Monographien zum Alten und Neuen Testament
WUNT Wissenschaftliche Untersuchungen zum Neuen Testament
ZAC *Zeitschrift für antikes Christentum*
ZKG *Zeitschrift für Kirchengeschichte*
ZNW *Zeitschrift für die neutestamentliche Wissenschaft*
ZPE *Zeitschrift für Papyrologie und Epigraphik*
ZTK *Zeitschrift für Theologie und die Kirche*
ZWT *Zeitschrift für wissenschaftliche Theologie*

Introduction and Overview

Andrew F. Gregory and Christopher M. Tuckett

The first modern editor to refer to a collection of early Christian writings as the Apostolic Fathers appears to have been J. Cotelier, whose edition was published in 1672. The most recent is Bart D. Ehrman, a contributor to this collection, whose Greek–English edition in the Loeb Classical Library replaces the original and much-used Loeb volumes produced by Kirsopp Lake. Lists of those who are included in the conventional but largely arbitrary collection known as the 'Apostolic Fathers' do vary slightly (Ehrman takes a more inclusive approach than both Lake and the Oxford Committee),[1] but included in *The Reception of the New Testament in the Apostolic Fathers* and in *Trajectories through the New Testament and the Apostolic Fathers* are treatments of the central texts in this category, as found also in the 1905 volumes, *The New Testament in the Apostolic Fathers*: the *Didache*, *1 Clement*, *2 Clement*, the letters of Ignatius, Polycarp's *Letter to the Philippians*, the *Letter of Barnabas*, and the *Shepherd of Hermas*. Also included in the second of these 2005 volumes is the *Martyrdom of Polycarp*, which the Oxford Committee did not consider.

The 1905 volume treated a relatively narrow set of issues: namely, the extent to which the documents of the New Testament were known, and cited (or alluded to), by the Apostolic Fathers. Such issues remain important, so they are the central concern of *The Reception of the New Testament and the*

[1] Lake included the *Letter to Diognetus*, in addition to those named above and discussed in the present volumes; Ehrman includes all these texts, as well as the fragments of Papias and Quadratus. This collection, he notes, is comparable to other similarly arbitrary collections of second- and third-century Christian writings: e.g., the apologists, the heresiologists, and the Nag Hammadi Library. Understood as a collection of writings based only on convention, the Apostolic Fathers, he continues, 'is not an authoritative collection of books, but a convenient one, which, in conjunction with these other collections, can enlighten us concerning the character of early Christianity, its external appeal and inner dynamics, its rich and significant diversity, and its developing understandings of its own self-identity, social distinctiveness, theology, ethical norms, and liturgical practices'. See, further, B. D. Ehrman, 'General Introduction', in *The Apostolic Fathers*, i, LCL 24 (Cambridge, Mass.: Harvard University Press, 2003), 1–14, quotation on pp. 13–14.

Apostolic Fathers. Each Apostolic Father is treated in turn, as in the 1905 volume, but these studies are now prefaced by a careful discussion of methodological issues that must be addressed in seeking to determine what might constitute a reference in the Apostolic Fathers to one of the writings that later became the New Testament, and also a number of investigations of the text and transmission of both the New Testament and the Apostolic Fathers. Thus contemporary scholars continue to ask questions that have remained important and relevant since the publication of the 1905 volume, but they do so in light of manuscript evidence that was not available a century ago (newly discovered papyri of the New Testament and the Apostolic Fathers, as well as of other early Christian writings), and on the basis of a century's continuing work on these texts. Questions of canon and authority are rarely far from the surface, but difficulties in assessing the relative likelihood that individual Apostolic Fathers were drawing on proverbial expressions and free traditions or on contemporary versions or copies of texts that would emerge in the surviving manuscripts of the late second or early third century papyri such as $P^{4-64-67}$, P^{75}, and P^{45} make these questions difficult to answer. Some of these studies reach conclusions not dissimilar to those of the Oxford Committee (see, for example, Gregory on *1 Clement*), whereas others find more (for example, Verheyden on *Hermas*) or less (for example, Foster on Ignatius) evidence for the use of the New Testament in the Apostolic Father whom they discuss than did the authors of the corresponding discussion in 1905. Questions of method are of great consequence, and readers will note how individual contributors, most notably William Petersen, in his essay on the Apostolic Fathers as witnesses to the text of the New Testament in the second century, have chosen to assess the evidence in a way different from that proposed by the editors. Such questions remain controversial and controverted, and we hope to have provided both useful discussion of these methodological issues and also a major reference tool for those who wish to take further the discussion of the New Testament in the Apostolic Fathers.

The contributions contained in *Trajectories through the New Testament and the Apostolic Fathers* are also sensitive to these difficulties. Many of its papers contribute to and advance the discussion of similar questions to those addressed in *The Reception of the New Testament in the Apostolic Fathers* (most obviously Andreas Lindemann's discussion of Pauline influences in *1 Clement* and Ignatius, the discussions of Helmut Koester and Arthur Bellinzoni of gospel traditions in the Apostolic Fathers and other second-century texts, and Boudewijn Dehandschutter's discussion of the *Martyrdom of Polycarp*), but they also range more widely.

One significant development since 1905 has been the renewed recognition that the interpretation of any text can be significantly enriched by considering its 'effect' and its usage in subsequent history, i.e., its *Wirkungsgechichte*, as well as its antecedents. Thus some papers note how distinctive emphases or ideas that are present in certain writings of the New Testament are taken up and developed by certain Apostolic Fathers, and the continuities or discontinuities in the trajectories that are traced cast new light on both the New Testament and the Apostolic Fathers. It is not, of course, that all authors understand development to have taken place in the same way. Frances Young's treatment of the relative absence of terms relating to Wisdom in the Christology of the Apostolic Fathers raises questions about the way in which such language is understood by interpreters who confine themselves largely to the New Testament and the earlier Jewish tradition, on which it draws, whereas Thomas Weinandy argues strongly for clearly discernible continuity from Pauline Christology through that of Ignatius and ultimately to that of the Chalcedonian definition.

Attention is also given to literary as well as theological issues: for example, in Michael Holmes's discussion of how the genre of a 'passion narrative' is developed as one moves away from accounts of the death of Jesus to accounts of the death of later martyrs such as Polycarp. Nor are issues of sociology neglected: Clayton Jefford offers an illuminating account of how an examination of two apparently related texts—the *Didache* and Matthew—may provide some sort of insight into the development of Christianity in one place, as does Peter Oakes in his discussion of the situations that may be reflected in the letters of Paul and of Polycarp to the Philippians. Also significant in this respect is Paul Hartog's discussion of similar concerns found in Polycarp's letter (written from Smyrna) and 1 John (probably associated with nearby Ephesus), not least in the light of what Hartog considers to be the almost certain literary dependence of the former on the latter.

The arrangement of chapters in *The Reception of the New Testament in the Apostolic Fathers* is self-evident and straightforward, but something of the rich interplay between many of the texts considered can be seen in the range of ways in which *Trajectories through the New Testament and the Apostolic Fathers* might have been ordered. Were we to have given greater prominence to the place of the New Testament (or at least some of it) than to that of the Apostolic Fathers, we might have arranged chapters with more emphasis on how they fell (at least primarily) into what might be considered synoptic, Johannine, Pauline, or other trajectories defined by their apparent relationship to New Testament books. Were we to have given greater prominence to the place of the Apostolic Fathers (or at least some of them) than to that of the New Testament, we might have arranged chapters with more emphasis on how they relate (at least primarily) to the study of individual Apostolic Fathers.

Equally, decisions might have been made to arrange these essays primarily on thematic grounds, rather than on the basis of the ancient text or texts with which each is primarily concerned. Jonathan Draper's treatment of prophets and teachers in the *Didache* and the New Testament might have been presented alongside Alistair Stewart-Sykes's discussion of charismatic functionaries and household officers; and the discussions of Paul and Ignatius by David Reis, by Harry Maier, and by Allen Brent might stand alongside the essay by Andreas Lindemann, thus accentuating the interplay between the influence of the apostle and that of the Graeco-Roman world—and in particular the impact of the Second Sophistic—on how early Christians such as 'Clement' and Ignatius presented themselves in their writings.

Similarly, the discussions of Boudewijn Dehandschutter and Michael Holmes of gospel and other New Testament traditions in the *Martyrdom of Polycarp* might have been juxtaposed with the discussions of Arthur Bellinzoni and Helmut Koester, not to mention those of John Kloppenborg and Charles Hill; but, as it is, these different essays emphasize the central place of early Christian reflection on the person of Jesus. Thus discussions of the development and reception of gospel tradition not only book-end the volume, but also appear prominently in the middle.

So fluid and unclear are many of the boundaries between these closely related texts and issues that no neat or definitive boundaries may be drawn. Thus the approach that we have chosen is intended both to reflect the complexity and diversity of these writings and also to be of practical assistance to other researchers who can see at a glance which contributions may be of most use to them.

Some of the Apostolic Fathers receive more attention than others (most notably Ignatius and the *Didache*), but none is neglected. Neither *1 Clement* (strictly speaking) nor *Barnabas* appears in the table of contents for *Trajectories through the New Testament and the Apostolic Fathers*, but the former features prominently in the discussions of Andreas Lindemann and Alistair Stewart-Sykes, and the latter is considered by David Wright. John Muddiman and Alistair Stewart-Sykes each discuss a range of texts (the former, *2 Clement* and the *Shepherd of Hermas*; the latter, the *Didache*, Ignatius, *1 Clement*, and the *Shepherd of Hermas*), and their essays on ecclesiology and church order, together with those of Carsten Claussen and David Wright on the sacraments, help to make valuable connections between individual Apostolic Fathers as well as between the Apostolic Fathers and the New Testament. Their contributions, together with the rest of the papers collected in this volume, serve as important reminders of the benefits to be gained from reading the New Testament in the wider context of other early Christian writings, and show why even later texts are an essential component of what is sometimes referred to as 'New Testament background'. It was only thanks to later Christians, perhaps some of the Apostolic Fathers among them, that the writings that became the New Testament were preserved and transmitted, so—as both these volumes demonstrate—knowledge of their concerns is a useful tool in interpreting both the New Testament and the development of Christianity from the late first to the mid- or late second century. Most, if not all, of the Apostolic Fathers may well have written later than most of the authors whose writings were later included in the New Testament, but almost certainly all of them wrote before even an early form of the canon of the New Testament, such as that witnessed to by Irenaeus, had yet emerged. The extent to which they witness to the existence of earlier collections such as the fourfold Gospel or (perhaps more likely) a Pauline corpus are among the questions that these studies address.

Part I

Paul in the Apostolic Fathers

1

Paul's Influence on 'Clement' and Ignatius

Andreas Lindemann

The writings of the early Christian authors called 'Apostolic Fathers' are different from most of the New Testament texts written during the last decades of the first century and the early decades of the second century: the authors do not hide their identities behind pseudonyms such as 'Paul' or 'Peter' or 'James'. Rather, they try to convince their addressees not by using the authority of famous persons of the past but by the strength of their own theological argumentation. But often they refer to biblical and apostolic authorities, especially to the apostle Paul, as support for their arguments. Since in my view the most important texts in the corpus of the 'Apostolic Fathers' are the *First Letter of Clement* and the seven letters of Ignatius, bishop (ἐπίσκοπος) of Antioch, I will restrict my short study to these writings.

I

1. The epistle usually called *First Clement*[1] was written by the church of Rome (ἡ ἐκκλησία τοῦ θεοῦ ἡ παροικοῦσα Ῥώμην) and was sent to the church of Corinth (τῇ ἐκκλησίᾳ τοῦ θεοῦ τῇ παροικούσῃ Κόρινθον).[2] With regard to the dating of *1 Clement*, the last years of the 90s CE can be assumed as most likely.[3] In this letter to Corinth, the Roman church does not claim any

[1] *1 Clement* does not mention the name of its author but certainly the Roman Christian community did not write it 'collectively'.

[2] The Greek text is taken from A. Lindemann and H. Paulsen (eds.), *Die Apostolischen Väter: Griechisch-deutsche Parallelausgabe auf der Grundlage der Ausgaben von F. X. Funk/K. Bihlmeyer und M. Whittaker, mit Übersetzungen von M. Dibelius und D.-A. Koch* (Tübingen: Mohr Siebeck, 1992).

[3] Cf. A. Lindemann, *Die Clemensbriefe*, HNT 17 (Tübingen: Mohr Siebeck, 1992), 12: 'Eine Datierung des 1 Clem [before 100 CE] wird am ehesten durch die Analyse der vorausgesetzten Kirchenstruktur ermöglicht.' There is no allusion to any persecution of Christians by Domitian, as has often been argued; cf. L. L. Welborn, 'The Preface to *1 Clement*: The Rhetorical Situation and the Traditional Date', in C. Breytenbach and L. L. Welborn (eds.), *Encounters with Hellenism:*

formal authority over the Corinthian church (or any other Christian communities); but the author apparently expects that his critical comment on the actual situation in Corinth will be very important for the future of the Corinthian church. In the context of his argumentation, he makes use of biblical texts (OT) and of Paul and Pauline letters, especially the (first) letter to the Corinthians.[4]

2. For the first time in the letter, Paul is mentioned by name in 5. 5–7. After the prescript, which obviously seems to be very 'Pauline' in its form,[5] the author begins to discuss the *στάσις* which has started in the Corinthian church. As a contrast, he describes the glorious past of his addressees, surprisingly making the statement that 'every sedition and every schism was abominable to you' (2. 6).[6] After a quotation of Deut. 32. 15, LXX ('My beloved ate and drank, and he was enlarged and waxed fat and kicked'), the author concludes that from this came 'jealousy and envy' (3. 2), and then he demonstrates how 'jealousy and envy' are reasons for any wickedness in the past and the present: 'Each goeth after the lusts of his evil heart, seeing that they have conceived an unrighteous and ungodly jealousy, through which also death entered into the world' (3. 4; cf. Wisd. 2. 24). Then he gives several examples drawn first from the scriptures and the history of Israel, then from the most recent past: 'Let us come to those champions who lived very near to our time. Let us set before us the noble examples which belong to our generation. By reason of jealousy and envy the greatest and most righteous pillars of the church were persecuted and contended even unto death' (5. 1–2).

Then, two of these 'pillars' are mentioned by name (5. 3–7), the 'good apostles' (*ἀγαθοὶ ἀπόστολοι*) Peter and Paul. Here the author obviously employs the rhetorical device of 'Achtergewicht'—the most important person is not Peter but Paul.[7] About Peter the author says that he 'endured not one or two but many labours, and thus having borne his testimony went to his

Studies on the First Letter of Clement, AGAJU 53 (Leiden and Boston: Brill, 2004), 197–216: the words *συμφορά* and *περίπτωσις* do not belong to the language of persecution (cf. Lindemann, *Clemensbriefe*, 26).

[4] Paul's first letter to Corinth was well known in Rome as *1 Clem.* 47. 1 clearly shows; we cannot say anything about the knowledge of 2 Corinthians (or its original parts). Cf. *NTAF*, 41 and also 51–2 (comparing *1 Clem.* 36. 2 with 2 Cor. 3. 18: 'It would appear that the phrase (*ἐνοπτριζόμεθα*) is not distinctive enough to enable us to infer that Clement knew this Epistle.'

[5] Cf. Lindemann, *Clemensbriefe*, 25. It is unlikely that the author had 1 Cor. 1. 1–2 in mind (*παροικοῦσα* is not found in the NT).

[6] English translations of the text of *1 Clement* are taken from J. B. Lightfoot, *The Apostolic Fathers*, Part 1, 2: *S. Clement of Rome: A Revised Text with Introductions, Notes, Dissertations, and Translations* (repr. Hildesheim and New York: Georg Olms, 1973 (= London, 1890)).

[7] Against K. Beyschlag, *Clemens Romanus und der Frühkatholizismus: Untersuchungen zu I Clemens 1–7*, BHT 35 (Tübingen: Mohr Siebeck, 1966), 280; he thinks that Paul is put in Peter's shadow, but the opposite interpretation seems to be correct.

appointed place of glory' (5. 4). The description of Paul and his work is much more impressive: 'he had been seven times in bonds, had been driven into exile, had been stoned.' Paul 'had preached in the East and in the West', which means 'everywhere': 'he won the noble renown which was the reward of his faith, having taught righteousness unto the whole world.' And 'having reached the farthest bounds of the West', having 'borne his testimony before the rulers', Paul 'departed from the world and went unto the holy place'—that is, he was put to death. We really are not able to recognize which historical details of Paul's life the author of *1 Clement* was familiar with or which sources he may have used.[8] But it seems clear that in the view of the author of *1 Clement* Paul for the readers in Corinth is a unique pattern of patient endurance, and thus the antitype of those Christians in Corinth who had fallen into στάσις instead of standing firm in ὑπομονή. The word ὑπομονή is not used by Paul in his (first) letter to Corinth, but the verb ὑπομένειν is used in 1 Cor. 13. 7: ἡ ἀγάπη πάντα στέγει, πάντα πιστεύει, πάντα ἐλπίζει, πάντα ὑπομένει. Moreover, in Romans ὑπομονή is used several times in an important way (5. 3–4; 8. 25; esp. 15. 3–5); it is possible that the author of *1 Clement* may have learned about the importance of ὑπομονή from Paul's letter to Rome.

In the following parts of his letter, the author of *1 Clement* stresses in different ways the need for 'obedience and submission'. He draws examples from almost every sphere of life, including the relations of workers and their employers (34. 1) and even the structure of military authority in the army (37. 1–4).[9] Then the principle of right 'order' (41. 1) is carried over into the idea of what in later times was called 'the apostolic succession' (42. 1–4): 'The Apostles received their Gospel for us from the Lord Jesus Christ; Jesus Christ was sent forth from God . . . [The Apostles] preaching everywhere in country and town . . . appointed their first-fruits . . . to be bishops and deacons (ἐπίσκοποι καὶ διάκονοι) unto them that should believe.'[10] The author does not claim that the Corinthian presbyters, now being deposed from their office by a majority (?) of the community, were invested by Paul himself. But apparently he wants to give his addressees the impression that this in fact had been the case. The idea of 'succession' is repeated in 44. 1–4, and here the author emphasizes that the presbyters should not be 'unjustly thrust out from

[8] There are linguistic parallels on the topic in Cynic and Stoic literature; cf. the excursus in Lindemann, *Clemensbriefe*, 40.

[9] There is a discussion as to whether the author refers to the *Roman* army or to a kind of 'messianic' army; cf. H. E. Lona, *Der erste Clemensbrief*, KAV 2 (Göttingen: Vandenhoeck & Ruprecht, 1998), 410–11; T. Schmitt, *Paroikie und Oikoumene: Sozial- und mentalitätsgeschichtliche Untersuchungen zum 1. Clemensbrief*, BZNW 110 (Berlin and New York: Walter de Gruyter, 2002), 26–36, who argues for the latter interpretation.

[10] As a biblical reference the author quotes Isa. 60. 17 (very different from LXX and the Hebrew text).

their ministration'. In support of this rule, in 45. 1–46. 3 the writer cites several biblical passages as well as a statement of the Lord himself (46. 7–8).[11]

In this context we find the second explicit reference to Paul. In 47. 1, the Corinthians are urged to 'take up the epistle of the blessed Paul the Apostle' (*ἀναλάβετε τὴν ἐπιστολὴν τοῦ μακαρίου Παύλου τοῦ ἀποστόλου*). 'Of a truth he charged you in the Spirit' (*πνευματικῶς*), when he was writing about the 'parties' and was criticizing them.[12] What Paul had to say forty years ago is still valid and gives help for the argumentation and for the hoped-for repentance in the present situation. 'Clement' reminds the Corinthian Christians of the recognized value of Paul's apostolic authority from 'the beginning of the gospel' (47. 2)—that is, from the opening chapters of Paul's (first) letter to the Corinthians. Once this reminder is given, no further argumentation is needed: in 48. 1 the writer can call the addressees to repentance: 'Let us fall down before the Master (*προπέσωμεν τῷ δεσπότῃ*), and entreat Him with tears, that He may show himself propitious, and be reconciled unto us.' *1 Clem.* 47 shows that in the last decade of the first century a copy of the first Pauline letter to Corinth was extant in Rome, and that the Roman church could assume that this letter was also 'at hand' in Corinth.[13] This seems to be taken for granted, both in the communities in Corinth and in Rome itself.[14]

Since the church at Rome and the church at Corinth apparently had no theological differences, the only point of dissension was the removal of the Corinthian presbyters from their office. So, we have found references to Paul at two important points in the line of argument in the Roman letter: first, the writer uses the example of Paul to show his addressees the high value of *ὑπομονή* (5. 5–7); second, even more important, he declares that Paul, writing to the Christians in Corinth in former times, had already provided the solution to the present problem. But why is Paul not mentioned by name in the passage on 'apostolic succession' (42. 1–4)? Did the author not count Paul as one of those who had received the gospel from the Lord Jesus Christ? In that case, we would not expect Paul to be called an 'apostle' at all in *1 Clement.*

[11] Cf. *NTAF*, 62: 'We have here the combination of the words spoken by our Lord with regard to Judas, recorded by Matthew [Matt. 26. 24; 18. 6–7] and Mark [Mark 14. 21; 9. 42], with a saying which is recorded in another connexion in the three Synoptic Gospels [cf. Luke 17. 1–2].' It is perhaps probable 'that we have here... a quotation from some form of catechetical instruction in our Lord's doctrine'.

[12] The author here uses the term *προσκλίσεις* (in the NT only 1 Tim. 5. 21) instead of *σχίσμα* (1 Cor. 1. 10). This is 'bewußte Abschwächung (vgl. *ἥττων ἁμαρτία*); immerhin waren die damals von den Adressaten... anerkannten Parteihäupter ausgezeichnete Männer gewesen', which now is not the case (Lindemann, *Clemensbriefe*, 139).

[13] Cf. *NTAF*, 41.

[14] For early collection of Paul's letters cf. A. Lindemann, 'Die Sammlung der Paulusbriefe im 1. und 2. Jahrhundert', in J.-M. Auwers and H. J. de Jonge (eds.), *The Biblical Canons*, BETL 153 (Leuven: Peeters, 2003), 321–51.

It is more likely that, without any discussion, 'Clement' included Paul among the apostles who were authorized for the *εὐαγγέλιον* by Christ. Moreover, the line of argument in 42. 1–4 appears to show the 'apostolic succession' in Corinth started by Paul's missionary activity; in 'Clement's' view this was not a special case, but rather followed the usual way.

3. The author of *1 Clement* knows and makes use not only of Paul's first letter to Corinth but also of the letter to the Romans, though this letter is not mentioned or quoted explicitly.[15] There seems to be an allusion to a Pauline argument in the epistle to the Romans in the passage on 'justification' (or 'righteousness') in *1 Clem.* 31. 1–32. 4.[16] At the beginning we see an indirect reference to Paul's idea that the *imperative* of what Christians have to do is founded in the *indicative* of what has been done for them by God. In 30. 1 already, we find an almost 'classic' sentence: 'Seeing then that we are the special portion of a Holy God (*ἅγια οὖν μέρις ὑπάρχοντες*), let us do all things that pertain unto holiness (*ποιήσωμεν τὰ τοῦ ἁγιασμοῦ πάντα*).'[17] The statement in 30. 3, that Christians are justified 'by works and not by words' (*ἔργοις δικαιούμενοι καὶ μὴ λόγοις*) is not anti-Pauline (or a contradiction of the argument in 32. 3–4; see below), but should be understood in its actual paraenetical context: Christians must realize their status of 'holiness' by doing works, not merely by speaking words. We might remember the words of Paul in 1 Cor. 7. 19: 'Circumcision is nothing, and uncircumcision is nothing, but the keeping of the commandments of God.' The biblical and dogmatic aspect of the doctrine of justification is asserted in *1 Clem.* 31. 2 ('Wherefore was our father Abraham blessed? Was it not because he wrought righteousness and truth through faith'...(*οὐχὶ δικαιοσύνην καὶ ἀλήθειαν διὰ πίστεως ποιήσας;*)) and in 32. 4: 'And so we, having been called through His will in Christ Jesus, are not justified (*δικαιούμεθα*) through ourselves or through our own wisdom or understanding or piety or works which we wrought in holiness of heart, but through faith, whereby the Almighty God justified (*ἐδικαίωσεν*) all men that have been from the beginning.' The use of the verb *δικαιοῦν* clearly indicates Pauline influence. This influence might be present also in the author's definition of the relation between 'righteousness by faith' (32. 4) and 'every good work' (*πᾶν ἔργον ἀγαθόν*) in 33. 1. 'Clement' is here using the style of the diatribe, as Paul had done in the transition from Rom. 5 to

[15] Cf. A. Lindemann, *Paulus im ältesten Christentum: Das Bild des Apostels und die Rezeption der paulinischen Theologie in der frühchristlichen Literatur bis Marcion*, BHT 58 (Tübingen: Mohr Siebeck, 1979), 173 f.

[16] Cf. Lindemann, *Clemensbriefe*, 97–108.

[17] The following catalogue of vices is probably traditional, and not to be read as a picture of reality in the Corinthian community.

Rom. 6.[18] But, unlike Paul, 'Clement' does not put his argument in *christological* but rather in *theological* terms: it is God, called ὁ δημιουργός and ὁ δεσπότης τῶν ἁπάντων (cf. 32. 4: ὁ παντοκράτωρ θεός), who is said to 'rejoice in His works'—that is, in the creation. By comparing God and the righteous 'man' in this way, the author of *1 Clement* shows that he is not a teacher of 'justification by works'. It is the righteous person who produces good works—that is, works according to righteousness (cf. 33. 8: 'let us with all our strength work the work of righteousness'); it is not good works that produce the righteous person.

The main theme of *1 Clement* is the order of the church or, with respect to the Christian individual, his or her submission to God's will, to 'His faultless ordinances' (37. 1). The examples used by the author at this point are the command structure of the army (37. 1–4)[19] and the image of 'the body and its members' (37. 5–38. 1).[20] The term χάρισμα (38. 1) and the allusion to the problem of 'the weak and the strong' suggest dependence on 1 Cor. 12 and especially on Rom. 14.[21] It is rather surprising that 'Clement' in 37. 5 does not employ the (deutero-)Pauline image of Christ as 'the head of the body', though this figure would have suited his ecclesiology very well; thus the conclusion seems certain that the 'Pauline' epistle to the Ephesians was not known to him.[22] 'Clement' is apparently not interested in an ecclesiological theory, but rather in the concrete consequences of the 'body'-image for the life of the church. He seems to assume that the addressees are familiar with that image without reminding them that they should know it from any of Paul's letters. When in 46. 7 he again refers to that image, he once again has no particular Pauline text in mind, but is certainly influenced by the Pauline metaphor of σῶμα. After the reference to the image of 'body and members' ('Wherefore do we tear and rend asunder the members of Christ [τὰ μέλη τοῦ Χριστοῦ], and stir up factions against our own body [τὸ σῶμα τὸ ἴδιον], and reach such a pitch of folly, as to forget that we are members one of another

[18] *NTAF*, 38: 'It seems most probable that Clement is here writing under the impression of the passage in the Romans. It is true that there is little verbal coincidence between the passages, but their thought is closely related.' *NTAF* particularly refers to the respective contexts.

[19] On the problem of which army the author is referring to, see n. 9 above.

[20] Cf. A. Lindemann, 'Die Kirche als Leib: Beobachtungen zur "demokratischen" Ekklesiologie bei Paulus', in *idem*, *Paulus, Apostel und Lehrer der Kirche: Studien zu Paulus und zum frühen Paulusverständnis* (Tübingen: Mohr Siebeck, 1999), 132–57.

[21] The formula ὅλον τὸ σῶμα ἐν Χριστῷ Ἰησοῦ seems to be an allusion to Rom. 12. 4. In 1 Cor. 12, Paul does *not* speak about the 'strong', but uses the term δυνατός only in Rom. 15. 1.

[22] Cf. *NTAF*, 52–3. The committee discusses the possible coincidence of *1 Clem.* 46. 6 and Eph. 4. 4–6, but comes to the conclusion 'that the passages both in Ephesians and in Clement are very possibly founded upon some liturgical forms, and it thus seems impossible to establish any dependence of Clement upon Ephesians' (p. 53).

[μέλη ἔσμεν ἀλλήλων]'), he quotes a saying of the Lord: 'Woe unto that man' who is offending or perverting 'one of Mine elect' (46. 8).[23] Then he applies it to his readers: 'Your division (σχίσμα) hath perverted many; it hath brought many to despair, many to doubting, and all of us to sorrow. And your sedition (στάσις) still continueth' (46. 9). The terms σχίσμα and στάσις are the key words that prompt the reference to 'the blessed Paul the Apostle' and to his letter to the Corinthians (47. 1–3; see above). Thus, it can be observed that in chs. 46 and 47 'Clement' is deliberately appealing both to Jesus and to Paul, the two most important authorities of the church, and at the same time both traditions and texts on which the New Testament canon later will be mainly based.

Almost at the end of *1 Clement*, we read a long prayer (59. 3–61. 3),[24] which includes prayers for 'our rulers and governors upon the earth' (60. 4, τοῖς δὲ ἄρχουσιν καὶ ἡγουμένοις ἡμῶν ἐπὶ τῆς γῆς), the text of the prayer then following in 61. 1–2. It has been argued that those rulers and governors are not Caesar or any Roman authorities but Christian church leaders ('Amtsinhaber der Kirche').[25] But this seems improbable, since neither in the prescript nor at the end of the letter are any 'Amtsinhaber der Kirche' mentioned.[26] The theological basis for the prayer for (political) 'rulers and governors' can be found in texts of Judaism in the Hellenistic diaspora; it reflects the same kind of understanding of the (Roman) state as is evident in Rom. 13, though there is no indication that 'Clement' made use of Rom. 13. 1–7 here. But one may compare this prayer with 1 Tim. 2. 1–3 ('First of all, then, I urge that supplications, prayers, intercessions, and thanksgivings be made for everyone, for kings and all who are in high positions, so that we may lead a quiet and peaceable life in all godliness and dignity. This is right and is acceptable in the sight of God our Savior').[27] Since it seems to be possible that the pastoral epistles were written in Rome, not much earlier or (more probably) later than

[23] See n. 11. Cf. Lindemann, *Clemensbriefe*, 137.

[24] On that text see the important study by H. Löhr, *Studien zum frühchristlichen und frühjüdischen Gebet: Untersuchungen zu 1 Clem 59 bis 61 in seinem literarischen, historischen und theologischen Kontext*, WUNT 160 (Tübingen: Mohr Siebeck, 2003). His conclusion: 'Mit 1 Clem 59 bis 61 besitzen wir das nach dem Unser Vater zweite bedeutende Zeugnis frühchristlicher Frömmigkeit und Gebetssprache vom Ende des 1. Jahrhunderts nach Christus, d.h. aus der Zeit von Mt, Lk und Joh' (p. 531).

[25] Cf. Schmitt, *Paroikie*, 40–60, at p. 58: There is no doubt 'daß das Fürbittgebet am Ende des Briefes um Gottes Unterstützung der ἄρχοντες καὶ ἡγούμενοι allein auf Amtsinhaber der Kirche bezogen werden kann'.

[26] Cf. also the, to this extent, 'traditional' (and in my view correct) exegesis of that prayer by Löhr, *Studien*, 282–301.

[27] NRSV. For contemporary sources cf. Löhr, *Studien*, 334–60 (excursus 'Die Fürbitte für die politischen Herrscher in ihrem frühchristlichen Kontext').

1 Clement, both texts might represent the ecclesiology of the Roman Christian community at the turn of the first and second centuries.[28]

4. The Roman letter to Corinth is certainly not a primarily 'theological' or even 'dogmatic' writing. The author does not present his readers with difficult reflections on theological problems, but is concerned to set out his view (or his community's view) regarding a major error in the Corinthian church: namely, the 'sedition' against the presbyters. Thus for 'Clement', Pauline texts and positions were of interest only in so far as they could serve to refute this 'error'. So, *1 Clement* tells us little about the influence of Pauline *theology* in the Roman church in the last years of the first century. But the letter does show that Paul was of great importance for the church of Rome, both as an apostle and as a teacher of the church, even several decades after Paul's death. One might deplore the fact that only such problems of church order, rather than theological questions, were at the forefront of the discussion. But we must not suppose that the theological concerns of Roman Christians at the end of the first century CE were *exclusively* dominated by problems of this kind. One may ask what we would think about Paul's theology if we had read only his first letter to the Corinthians and nothing else he had written.

II

1. The epistles of Ignatius were written under circumstances quite different from the writing of *1 Clement*. The bishop of Antioch, sending his seven letters to several communities and to his Smyrnean colleague Polycarp,[29] is a prisoner on the way to martyrdom in Rome. His letters are responses to churches whose representatives had visited him, the only exception being the letter to the Christians in Rome. Thus the Ignatian letters might be read

[28] *NTAF*, 54–5, compares 1 Tim. 1. 17 with *1 Clem.* 61. 2: 'The phrase is striking, but Dr. Lightfoot has pointed out in his notes on the passage, that it is probably based upon Jewish liturgical forms.'

[29] The question arises why Ignatius wrote a letter to the Smyrneans *and* to their bishop. Cf. A. Merz, *Die fiktive Selbstauslegung des Paulus: intertextuelle Studien zur Intention und Rezeption der Pastoralbriefe*, NTOA 52 (Göttingen: Vandenhoeck & Ruprecht; Fribourg: Academic Press, 2004), 177: 'Diese Frage wird, wenn sie überhaupt gestellt wird, nur unzureichend beantwortet.' Her own thesis is that Ignatius is imitating Paul's (pseudonymous) letters to Timothy and Titus. 'Das Vermächtnis des Paulus, wie es Ignatius vor Augen stand, setzte sich zusammen aus Briefen an Gemeinden und aus Briefen, die Gemeindeleiter zur rechten Amtsführung anleiten sollten. Ignatius wollte es ihm darin gleich tun, darum schrieb er an Polykarp einen "Pastoralbrief".' Cf. also the literature mentioned ibid. n. 129.

as 'last words' of a bishop facing death,[30] and therefore we should not expect extensive references either to biblical (OT) texts or to Christian literature.[31]

During recent exegesis of the Ignatian letters,[32] a new discussion has started on the date and the authenticity of these letters.[33] One result in my view seems to be that the traditional dating of the letters (going back to Euseb. *HE* 3. 36. 2–4) very early in the second century in the time of the emperor Trajan is probably no longer acceptable. On the other hand, there are no convincing reasons to date the letters late in the second century;[34] moreover, it is not necessary to read them as pseudepigraphical writings.[35] Since a Christian person called Ignatius is otherwise unknown,[36] there is no evidence that any author in the second half of the second century would have been interested in writing such letters under this name as a pseudonym.[37]

2. Ignatius mentions the name of Paul in two of his letters. In *Eph.* 12. 2, he praises the church to which he is sending his letter: 'Ye are the highroad (*πάροδος*) of those that are on their way to die unto God.'[38] The Ephesian Christians are 'associates in the mysteries with Paul' (*Παύλου συμμύσται*); Ignatius speaks of Paul as the one who 'was sanctified (*τοῦ ἡγιασμένου*), who obtained a good report (*τοῦ μεμαρτυρημένου*, sc. from God), who is worthy

30 This corresponds to the (fictional) situation of 2 Timothy. Cf. Merz, *Die fiktive Selbstauslegung*, 145.

31 Cf. W. R. Schoedel, *Ignatius of Antioch: A Commentary on the Letters of Ignatius of Antioch*, Hermeneia (Philadelphia: Fortress, 1985), 7–10, on the literary character of those letters.

32 For discussion of research from 1870 to 1988 see C. Munier, 'Où en est la question d'Ignace d'Antioche?: Bilan d'un siècle de recherches', *ANRW* 2. 27. 1, 359–484.

33 R. M. Hübner, 'Thesen zur Echtheit und Datierung der sieben Briefe des Ignatius von Antiochien', *ZAC* 1 (1997), 44–72; A. Lindemann, 'Antwort auf die Thesen zur Echtheit und Datierung der sieben Briefe des Ignatius von Antiochien', *ZAC* 1 (1997), 185–94; G. Schöllgen, 'Die Ignatianen als pseudepigraphisches Briefcorpus: Anmerkung zu den Thesen von Reinhard M. Hübner', *ZAC* 2 (1998), 16–25; M. J. Edwards, 'Ignatius and the Second Century: An Answer to R. Hübner', *ZAC* 2 (1998), 214–26.

34 Hübner, 'Thesen', dates the letters as late as 170/180. Cf. my critical argumentation against this (see n. 33).

35 See Hübner, 'Thesen', and esp. T. Lechner, *Ignatius adversus Valentinianos? Chronologische und theologiegeschichtliche Studien zu den Briefen des Ignatius von Antiochien*, VCSup 47 (Leiden: Brill, 1999), 64: Polycarp wrote his letter 'um 150', and 'zwischen 165 und 175 wird der *Philipperbrief* vom Verfasser der *Ignatianen* interpoliert'; the texts referring to Ignatius' letters (Pol. *Phil.* 1. 1 and 13) were interpolated by the author of the Ignatian letters. See my review (*ZAC* 6 (2002), 157–61). Cf. also Merz, *Die fiktive Selbstauslegung*, 133–40, esp. 141 n. 1.

36 With exception of the letter of Polycarp to the Philippians (cf. note above).

37 Cf. H. Paulsen, *Die Briefe des Ignatius von Antiochia und der Brief des Polykarp von Smyrna: zweite, neubearbeitete Auflage der Auslegung von Walter Bauer*, HNT 18 (Tübingen: Mohr Siebeck, 1985), 4; Schoedel, *Ignatius*, 5–7.

38 The English translation of the Ignatian letters is taken from J. B. Lightfoot, *The Apostolic Fathers, Part II,2: S. Ignatius, S. Polycarp: A Revised Text with Introductions, Notes, Dissertations, and Translations* (repr. Hildesheim and New York: Georg Olms, 1973 (= 2nd edn., London, 1889)).

of all felicitation (ἀξιομακαρίστου)'. Ignatius wants to be found in his footsteps (ὑπὸ τὰ ἴχνη εὑρεθῆναι), and this expression might remind us of a sentence written by Paul.[39] The epithets given to Paul by Ignatius are without parallel in the Christian literature of the early second century; but this does not indicate special knowledge of the biography of Paul. When Ignatius writes that Paul makes mention of the Ephesians 'in every letter' (ἐν πάσῃ ἐπιστολῇ), he is obviously wrong. But certainly it was not his aim to give his addressees precise information on the frequency of the word *Ephesus* (or *Ephesians*) in Pauline letters known to him; he is simply trying to link Paul and the church of Ephesus together as intimately as possible.[40]

Ignatius mentions Paul again, this time in conjunction with Peter, in *Rom.* 4. 3. After his plea that 'all the churches' should not hinder his martyrdom but let him be given to the wild beasts, he writes to the Roman Christians: 'I do not enjoin (διατάσσομαι) you, as Peter and Paul did. They were Apostles, I am a convict; they were free, but I am a slave to this very hour.' And he continues: 'Yet if I shall suffer, then I am a freed-man of Jesus Christ, and I shall rise free in Him.' This text also shows no specific knowledge of any of Paul's letters, including Romans. But especially the last part of 4. 3 shows influence of Pauline language,[41] and in some way, Ignatius refers implicitly to an authority, though he seems to want to avoid making such a claim explicit.[42] Putting Paul and Peter side by side, Ignatius' argument reminds us of *1 Clem.* 5. 4–7. Of

[39] Merz, *Die fiktive Selbstauslegung*, 152–3, sees a possibility that we have here 'einen gewichtigen intertextuellen Verweis' on 2 Cor. 12. 18. 'Die Frage muss offen bleiben, da über die Kenntnis des 2Kor durch Ignatius keine letzte Sicherheit zu gewinnen ist, aber die Möglichkeit, dass Ignatius sich durch die gewählte Formulierung in die Reihe der unmittelbaren Apostelschüler stellt, ist m.E. nicht von der Hand zu weisen.' The committee of *NTAF*, 70, sees some links with 2 Corinthians; none of them, 'taken singly, is more than a possible allusion; but taken together they make the use of the Epistle by Ignatius fairly probable' (category d). But 2 Cor. 12. 18 is not mentioned.

[40] A different interpretation is given by Merz, *Die fiktive Selbstauslegung*, 143: 'Will man... Ignatius nicht unterstellen, er habe den Ephesern ein rhetorisch ungeschicktes, da unzutreffendes Kompliment gemacht, muss man entweder annehmen, Ignatius und die Epheser hätten Kenntnisse von weiteren Paulusbriefen gehabt, in denen Ephesus erwähnt wurde, oder—naheliegender—auf beiden Seiten mit der Kenntnis der Pastoralbriefe rechnen (1Tim 1,3; 2Tim 1,16–18; 4,12.19).'

[41] *NTAF*, 65, refers to 1 Cor. 7. 22 and 9. 1 (ἀπελεύθερος κυρίου/ἀπελεύθερος Ἰησοῦ Χριστοῦ); moreover, ἐν αὐτῷ ἐλεύθερος resembles the often used Pauline formula ἐν Χριστῷ. Cf. Ign. *Pol.* 4. 3.

[42] Merz, *Die fiktive Selbstauslegung*, 152: 'Indem Ignatius das zweite (ἐλεύθερος) als (zukünftig) auch für sich geltend erweist, rückt er sich selbst deutlich in die Nähe der Apostel.' Ignatius three times stresses that he is not giving any commands to his addressees (*Eph.* 3. 1; *Trall.* 3. 3; *Rom.* 4. 3). Cf. Merz, *Die fiktive Selbstauslegung*, 150: 'Das klingt bescheidener als es ist. Denn man muss sich fragen, warum Ignatius diese Bemerkungen überhaupt für nötig oder angebracht hält.' It seems to be clear that Ignatius 'mit seinen Briefen eine den Aposteln bzw. besonders Paulus entsprechende Vollmacht zur brieflichen Ermahnung und Lehre in Anspruch genommen hat'.

course, Ignatius did not know that letter, but possibly he knew traditions about Peter's and Paul's destinies, and possibly their deaths in Rome.[43]

3. Regarding the question of theological influence of Paul in Ignatius' letters, four texts are important: *Eph.* 18–20, *Magn.* 8–9, *Trall.* 9–10, and *Phld.* 8.

In the first of these texts *Eph.* 18–20, Ignatius is developing the idea of the 'paradox' of revelation. In 17. 2, it is understood as 'the knowledge of God (θεοῦ γνῶσις), which is Jesus Christ'. In the opening sentence of the next passage in 18. 1,[44] Ignatius calls the cross a 'stumbling-block (σκάνδαλον) to them that are unbelievers, but to us salvation and life eternal (σωτηρία καὶ ζωὴ αἰώνιος)'. Then he continues with three rhetorical questions: 'Where is the wise? Where is the disputer?[45] Where is the boasting of them that are called prudent?' It seems to be evident that this passage has been composed in literary dependence on 1 Cor. l. 18–25, although we should remember that Ignatius certainly did not have a copy of l Corinthians with him in prison on the way to Rome.[46] The incarnational christology expressed in *Eph.* 18. 2 seems to be reminiscent of the early christological formula quoted by Paul in Rom. 1. 3–4.[47] But Ignatius calls Jesus 'our God' (ὁ θεὸς ἡμῶν Ἰησοῦς ὁ Χριστός), and this goes beyond any Pauline christology.[48] *Eph.* 19, which is a highly mythological text, in v. 1 contains the so-called *Relevationsschema* ('And hidden from the prince of this world were the virginity of Mary and her

[43] A special connection between both apostles seems to be assumed by the mention of Paul's letters (letter corpus?) in 2 Pet. 3. 14–16.

[44] Lechner, *Ignatius*, 221, referring to K. Berger, 'Hellenistische Gathungen in Neuen Testament', *ANRW* II. 25.2 (1984), 1149–71, argues that Ignatius in *Eph.* 18. 1–20. 1 has used 'das Formschema des hellenistischen Hymnus'. *Eph.* 18 as well as *Eph.* 19 in themselves are built as a 'hymns' after that 'Formschema', and both hymns 'bilden zusammen einen groaen ... "Christushymnus" '. See below.

[45] This traditional translation of the Greek συζητητής (only here and in 1 Cor. 1. 20) should be revised, as has been shown by M. Lautenschlager, 'Abschied vom Disputierer: zur Bedeutung von συζητητής in 1 Kor 1,20', *ZNW* 83 (1992), 276–85; he suggests 'philosophischer Forscher'; cf. A. Lindemann, *Der erste Korintherbrief*, HNT 9.1 (Tübingen: Mohr Siebeck, 2000), 45.

[46] *NTAF*, 64: 'That Ignatius is quoting St. Paul is made more certain by the echo of 1 Cor. 1. 18 in the preceding sentence.' The Oxford Committee rightly thought that Ignatius without doubt made use of 1 Cor. (category A).

[47] Paul is writing about Jesus, the Son of God, τοῦ γενομένου ἐκ σπέρματος Δαυὶδ κατὰ σάρκα, τοῦ ὁρισθέντος υἱοῦ θεοῦ ἐν δυνάμει κατὰ πνεῦμα ἁγιωσύνης ἐξ ἀναστάσεως νεκρῶν. For analysis and interpretation of the pre-Pauline formula see recently E. Lohse, *Der Brief an die Römer*, KEK 4 (Göttingen: Vandenhoeck & Ruprecht, 2003), 64–7.

[48] Lechner, *Ignatius*, 218: Ignatius is arguing against a specific Gnostic—i.e. Valentinian—christology. 'Im Zentrum der Glaubensformel Eph. 18.2 steht das heilsgeschichtliche Ereignis der Jungfrauengeburt'; Ignatius stresses the real pregnancy of Mary (ἐκυοφορήθη ὑπὸ Μαρίας). But if this were an explicit polemic against Gnostic christology, one would expect at least an allusion to the *incarnation*: i.e., the use of the key word σάρξ. Cf. my discussion of Lechner's argumentation (*ZAC* 6 (2002), 160).

child-bearing and likewise also the death of the Lord—three mysteries to be cried aloud—the which were wrought in the silence of God. How then were they made manifest to the ages?'). Paul alludes to that 'Schema' in 1 Cor. 2. 6–9; it became important in the deutero-Pauline literature.[49] The language of the 'christology of epiphany' in *Eph.* 19. 2, 3, however, is different from Paul's thought. At the beginning of *Eph.* 20, Ignatius in v. 1 interrupts his line of thought, announcing the writing of a 'second tract' (ἐν τῷ δευτέρῳ βιβλιδίῳ, ὃ μέλλω γράφειν ὑμῖν) on the christological theme.[50] Whether or not the phrase εἰς τὸν καινὸν ἄνθρωπον Ἰησοῦν Χριστόν resembles 1 Cor. 15. 45, 47 and/or Eph. 2. 15; 4. 24, is very difficult to say.[51] But in *Eph.* 20. 2 Ignatius makes extensive use of Pauline terminology,[52] in particular the 'In Christ' formula (including the idea of 'living in Jesus Christ', ζῆν ἐν Ἰησοῦ Χριστῷ). Thus, the three chapters *Eph.* 18–20 indicate that Ignatius was substantially influenced by Paul; but Pauline theological categories seem to be presumed, rather than made explicit to the epistle's readers.

In *Magn.* 8–9, Ignatius gives a strict warning against life 'after the manner of Judaism' (κατὰ Ἰουδαϊσμόν). Although it is unlikely that Ignatius knew Paul's letter to the Galatians,[53] we can observe that in his discussion with his opponents Ignatius uses arguments similar to those of Paul in his epistle to the churches in Galatia. Moreover, the first sentence in 8. 1 ('Be not seduced by strange doctrines nor by antiquated fables, which are profitless') actually resembles arguments used by the author of the Pastoral Epistles against 'godless and silly myths', 'stupid controversies, genealogies, dissensions, and quarrels over the law' and 'Jewish myths' (1 Tim. 4. 7; Titus 3. 9; 1. 14, 16; cf. 2

[49] Cf. D. Lührmann, *Das Offenbarungsverständnis bei Paulus und in paulinischen Gemeinden*, WMANT 16 (Neukirchen-Vluyn: Neukirchener Verlag, 1965), 124–33. For the interpretation of the Ignatian text see Paulsen, *Briefe des Ignatius*, 43–5, and Schoedel, *Ignatius*, 87–94; cf. also Lechner, *Ignatius*, 234–42, 246–300.

[50] This book or letter was never written. It seems clear that *Eph.* 20. 1 cannot be part of a 'hymn' as Lechner, *Ignatius*, has suggested (see n. 45). Lechner thinks that *Eph.* 18 is the 'Prooimion' of that hymn, *Eph.* 19 'Epischer Mittelteil', and *Eph.* 20. 1 '(Ersatz für ein) Gebet' (ibid. 222). Ign. *Eph.* 20. 1 is no prayer, for Ignatius is addressing the Ephesians themselves.

[51] *NTAF*, 68: 'St. Paul uses the phrase in a slightly different sense; but, as Lightfoot suggests, Ignatius may have taken "to put on the new man" as meaning "to put on Christ", an explanation, we may add, which St. Paul would have not repudiated.' Cf. also 1 Cor. 15. 45 ὁ δεύτερος ἄνθρωπος.

[52] We cannot be sure that the phrase about Christ 'who after the flesh was of David's race' (τῷ κατὰ σάρκα ἐκ γένους Δαυίδ) resembles the formula quoted by Paul in Rom. 1. 3, 4 (see n. 47) or Rom. 9. 5.

[53] *NTAF*, 70–1, compares esp. *Phld.* 1. 1 (ὃν ἐπίσκοπον ἔγνων οὐκ ἀφ' ἑαυτοῦ οὐδὲ δι' ἀνθρώπων) and Gal. 1. 1 (οὐκ ἀπ' ἀνθρώπων οὐδὲ δι' ἀνθρώπου) and four other texts (category d). The conclusion: 'The passage in Philad. is the only one which strongly indicates knowledge of this Epistle [sc. Galatians] by Ignatius; and as it stands almost alone, we cannot claim a very high degree of probability for the reference.'

Tim. 4. 4).[54] Ignatius says that if we live κατὰ Ἰουδαϊσμόν, 'we avow (ὁμολογοῦμεν) that we have not received grace' (8. 1).[55] Life κατὰ Ἰουδαϊσμόν, as Ignatius writes in 9. 1, means 'walking (ἀναστραφέντες) in ancient practices' and 'observing sabbaths' (σαββατίζοντες). Ignatius' problem in *Magn.* 8–9 is the distinction between the sabbath and the Lord's day (κατὰ κυριακὴν ζῶντες).[56] That distinction is not a merely formal one, but from Ignatius' point of view is a part of the Christian confession (ὁμολογεῖν). Writing 'we avow that we have not received grace', Ignatius probably means more than just a failing of an intellectual 'acknowledgement' of the reception of grace. On the contrary, for Ignatius, if a Christian person lives κατά Ἰουδαϊσμόν, that person has made the 'non-reception' of grace the content of his or her confession (ὁμολογοῦμεν χάριν μὴ εἰληφέναι). That is a highly polemical position. But Ignatius' theological argument seems clear: life κατά Ἰουδαϊσμόν, as described in 9. 1, is incompatible with the confession of God's revelation in Jesus Christ.[57] Since the phrase χάριν μὴ εἰληφέναι (8. 1) is reflected in the unique expression ἐλάβομεν τὸ πιστεύειν in 9. 1, grace and faith are closely linked. So, we can see that the details of Ignatius' arguments in *Magn.* 8–9 differ from those of Paul. But the structure of the Ignatian theological thinking in this passage seems to recall Paul, in whose theology it may have originated.

[54] Merz, *Die fiktive Selbstauslegung*, 160–1: 'Auffällig ist neben den offensichtlichen Parallelen der Gebrauch von ὁμολογεῖν am Schluss der Polemiken. Beide Male wird den Gegnern das, was sie für sich in Anspruch nahmen (Gott zu kennen, die Gnade empfangen zu haben), durch ein Wortspiel entrungen.' According to Merz, there is no proof that *here* Ignatius has used the Pastoral Epistles, but in her study she argues with very good reasons that Ignatius knew and used these deutero-Pauline texts.

[55] Cf. Titus 1. 16: The opponents 'profess to know God, but they deny him by their actions' (θεὸν ὁμολογοῦσιν εἰδέναι, τοῖς δὲ ἔργοις ἀρνοῦνται); cf. Merz (n. 54).

[56] Paulsen, *Briefe des Ignatius*, 53: κυριακή zählt 'zu jenen Adjektiven, bei denen das üblicherweise dazugehörende Hauptwort (ἡ ἡμέρα) so allgemein feststeht, daß es auch fehlen kann'. G reads κυριακὴν ζωήν, L has *dominicam*.

[57] Paulsen, *Briefe des Ignatius*, 52: 'Ablehnung des Ἰουδαϊσμός bedeutet keineswegs, wie die Gegner des Ign behauptet zu haben scheinen, die Verwerfung der göttlichen Offenbarung in der Schrift und damit der Gnade, die mit ihr nicht im Widerspruch stehen kann. Denn für Ign deckt sich die prophetische Predigt mit der in Christus erschienenen Gnade, die sie vorausverkündet hat.' For the text-critical problem in *Magn.* 8. 2 concerning Ignatius' statement on Christ's revelation see Lightfoot, *Apostolic Fathers*, 2. 2. 126–8; also Paulsen, *Briefe des Ignatius*. Lechner, *Ignatius*, p. xxiii, without discussion accepts Hübner's thesis that the original text should be read 'Christ ὅς ἐστιν αὐτοῦ λόγος ἀΐδιος οὐκ ἀπὸ σιγῆς προελθών', this being 'Polemik gegen die *valentinianische* Vorstellung vom Hervorgang des *Logos* aus der *Sige*: "Damit kommen wir in jedem Fall in die Zeit nach 155/160".' Paulsen, *Briefe des Ignatius*: 'Jedoch dürfte die Lesart λόγος ἀπὸ σιγῆς προελθών (bezeugt durch A und Severus von Antiochien) als lectio difficilior dem Ign Verständnis entsprechen.'

In *Trall.* 9–10, Ignatius is arguing polemically against a kind of docetic christology.[58] The Christians in Tralles are not to accept any teaching which is 'apart from Jesus Christ' (χωρὶς Ἰησοῦ Χριστοῦ). Ignatius interprets 'Christ' in 9. 1, 2 by quoting a credal formula: 'Jesus Christ, who was of the race (ἐκ γένους) of David, who was [the son] of Mary, who was truly (ἀληθῶς) born and ate and drank, was truly persecuted under Pontius Pilate, was truly crucified and died in the sight of those in heaven and on earth and those under the earth;[59] who moreover was truly raised from the dead, His Father having raised Him (ἀληθῶς ἠγέρθη ἀπὸ νεκρῶν, ἐγείραντος αὐτὸν τοῦ πατρὸς αὐτοῦ).' Ignatius then continues by saying that God 'in the like fashion (κατὰ τὸ ὁμοίωμα) will so raise us also who believe on Him' (9. 2). This way of arguing shows distinct similarities to the train of thought in 1 Thess. 4. 13–18 as well as in 1 Cor. 15; in both texts, Paul moves from the implicitly or explicitly quoted creed (1 Thess. 4. 14a; 1 Cor. 15. 3–5) to its anthropological and ecclesiological consequences regarding the resurrection of the dead (1 Thess. 4. 14b; 1 Cor. 15. 12–20).[60] In this context giving hints of his own destiny (*Trall.* 10), Ignatius seems to recall Paul's similar comments in 1 Cor. 15 (cf. esp. v. 32).[61] But Ignatius does not mention Paul explicitly, as the apostle has written nothing against docetism. Thus, once again it is not so much in the content but in the structure of Ignatius' argument that he took his orientation from Paul.

In *Phld.* 8. 2, Ignatius gives a report of a discussion with some adversaries ('certain persons', τινες). They had said: 'If I find it not in the charters (ἐν τοῖς ἀρχείοις), I believe it not in the Gospel (ἐν τῷ εὐαγγελίῳ οὐ πιστεύω).'[62] The opponents apparently declared that they believe in the Christian gospel only

[58] The polemical character is visible already in the first word used by Ignatius: κωφώθητε ('Be ye deaf...').

[59] The triad ... τῶν ἐπουρανίων καὶ ἐπιγείων καὶ ὑποχθονίων recalls the hymn in Phil. 2. 6–11 (v. 10); this parallel is not mentioned in *NTAF.* Paulsen, *Briefe des Ignatius*, 63: 'Daß die Mächte bei der Passion zuschauen, bleibt bemerkenswert (zumal es sonst eher ein "häretisches" Motiv ist; vgl. NHC VII 55,10ff.).'

[60] Cf. Lindemann, *Paulus*, 207–8.

[61] Merz, *Die fiktive Selbstauslegung*, 156: 'Dass θηριομαχεῖν auch mit Blick auf 1Kor 15,32 gewählt ist, sollte man nicht bestreiten'; cf. 166: 'Am leichtesten erklärt sich das Nebeneinander von Erwartung des realen Tierkampfes (IgnRöm 5,2; IgnEph 1,2; Ign Trall 10) und metaphorischer Verwendung von θηριομαχεῖν (IgnRöm 5,1) durch die Annahme, dass Ignatius sich die Chance nicht entgehen lassen wollte, sich auch in diesem Punkt mit dem verehrten Paulus zu vergleichen.' This seems to be correct (against Lindemann, *Paulus*, 208 n. 240).

[62] The phrase ἐν τῷ εὐαγγελίῳ οὐ πιστεύω should rather be translated 'I do not believe in the gospel'; cf. Lindemann, *Paulus*, 212–14, referring to Mark 1. 15 (πιστεύετε ἐν τῷ εὐαγγελίῳ). Paulsen, *Briefe des Ignatius*, 86: 'glaube ich nicht an das Ev., glaube ich dem Ev. nicht'; this translation better fits the 'Radikalität der gegnerischen Position'. For different argumentation see Schoedel, *Ignatius*, 207: Mark 1. 15 is a 'slim authority'. 'Ignatius could not have accomplished anything by twisting his opponents' words that badly (I take it for granted that they regarded themselves as believers in the gospel).'

in so far as it coincides with 'the charters', which probably means the Bible ('Old Testament').[63] Ignatius' first reply was the assertion: 'It is written (γέγραπται)', this certainly to be understood not just as a reference to a biblical text but as an appeal to the Bible as interpreted in the Christian way. But when he calls into question (πρόκειται) this assertion by the opponents, Ignatius changes and strengthens his response in a different way: 'As for me my charter is Jesus Christ, the inviolable charter is His cross and His death and His resurrection, and faith through Him' (8. 2). This line of christological thought might again be thought to be reminiscent of Paul's own style of theological argumentation. This is shown especially by Ignatius' use of the Pauline key word δικαιοῦσθαι at the very end of *Phld.* 8 (ἐν οἷς θέλω ἐν τῇ προσευχῇ ὑμῶν δικαιωθῆναι).[64]

4. The study of 'Ignatius and Paul' has a long tradition.[65] Both, the ἐπίσκοπος of Antioch and the ἀπόστολος to the Gentiles wrote letters to Christian communities and individuals.[66] As far as we know, Ignatius was the first Christian author after Paul to write such letters under his own name. But, certainly there are important differences: Paul was the organizer of an extensive 'world mission'; most of his letters were addressed to churches founded by himself.[67] He gave responses to questions or commented on information he had received. Writing his letters, Paul knew that in the churches he addressed his authority was recognized, at least in principle. Where this authority seemed to be doubted or even denied, as was apparently

[63] Schoedel (see n. 62) is certainly right that the opponents are Christians. But the special point seems to be the claim for a complete agreement of the gospel (tradition) and the (OT) Bible. So, it is possible to understand Ignatius' further arguments (see text above).

[64] Schoedel, *Ignatius*, 179 (refering to Ign. *Rom.* 5. 1): 'Ignatius speaks of his justification in terms that are directly dependent on 1 Cor 4:4 (echoed again in *Tr.* 5.2); but "justification" for Ignatius is apparently nothing other than becoming a disciple (cf. *Tr.* 5.2) and gaining perfection (cf. *Phd.* 8.2) through martyrdom; Paul's words serve to emphasize the fact that Ignatius' justification is still future and thus to discourage the Roman Christians from interfering with his attaining it.' Cf. Merz, *Die fiktive Selbstauslegung*, 166 (see above n. 29).

[65] See R. Bultmann, 'Ignatius und Paulus', in E. Dinkler (ed.), *Exegetica: Aufsätze zur Erforschung des Neuen Testaments* (Tübingen: Mohr Siebeck, 1967), 400–11; H. Rathke, *Ignatius von Antiochien und die Paulusbriefe*, TU 99 (Berlin: Akademie-Verlag, 1967).

[66] The only authentic letter of Paul to an individual is the epistle to Philemon, certainly unknown to Ignatius; but Ignatius knew the letters to Timothy and Titus, and thus he seemed to have imitated Paul; cf. Merz, *Die fiktive Selbstauslegung*, 145: 'In bewusster Nachahmung der beiden unter dem Namen des Paulus überlieferten Briefformen verfasst Ignatius Briefe an Gemeinden und ein Schreiben an einen Amtsträger.'

[67] The only exception is the letter to the Romans. Colossians is written pseudonymously as an epistle of Paul to a community not founded by Paul himself. Cf. A. Lindemann, 'Die Gemeinde von "Kolossä": Erwägungen zum "Sitz im Leben" eines pseudopaulinischen Briefes', in *Paulus, Apostel und Lehrer* (see n. 20), 187–210.

the case in Galatia and in Corinth in the situation of 2 Cor. 10–13,[68] Paul could be sure that his argument would nevertheless be a factor of considerable weight. Ignatius, by contrast, had no formal authority with respect to the churches to whom he wrote his letters.[69]

III

From this short review of *1 Clement* and Ignatius, we might draw a double conclusion. Neither of these early Christian authors show signs of an intensive interest in an explicit use of Paul, either of his letters or of his theology; nor do they demonstrate a deep interest in a 'critical discussion' of Pauline theology. But this does not mean that Paul was 'forgotten' or had become unimportant in the churches to whom 'Clement' and Ignatius addressed their work. In fact, the letters of the apostle and his theological ideas were employed when and where 'Clement' or Ignatius thought it might be important to call upon the apostolic authority in support of their own arguments. At the end of the first century and during the thirties of the second century, Paul's theological arguments were 'needed' in Rome as well as in Corinth, as *1 Clement* shows, and the same was the case in Asia, as Ignatius' letters (and Polycarp's letter to the Philippians[70]) demonstrate.

[68] 2 Cor. 10–13 was originally an independent letter in my view. Cf. M. Thrall, *The Second Epistle to the Corinthians*, 2 vols., ICC (Edinburgh: T. & T. Clark, 1994, 2000), 5–13, 596. 2 Cor. 10–13 is not the 'painful letter' ('Tränenbrief'), but it is not the latest of the letters now incorporated into 'Second Corinthians' (cf. H. Conzelmann and A. Lindemann, *Arbeitsbuch zum Neuen Testament*, UTB 52, 14th edn. (Tübingen: Mohr Siebeck, 2004), 270–4).

[69] Merz, *Die fiktive Selbstauslegung*, 145: The allusions and quotations of Pauline letters should be interpreted 'im Dienste der Selbstwahrnehmung und Selbstdarstellung des Ignatius als Paulusnachfolger'. But Ignatius could not be sure that this image was accepted by his addressees.

[70] Cf. Lindemann, *Paulus*, 87–91, 221–32.

Part II

Gospel Traditions in the Apostolic Fathers

2

Gospels and Gospel Traditions in the Second Century

Helmut Koester

THE SITUATION A HUNDRED YEARS AGO AND THEREAFTER

At the time of the publication of *The New Testament in the Apostolic Fathers*,[1] the four canonical gospels ruled supreme as the almost exclusive source for the knowledge of Jesus' words and deeds. In some respect, interest in the study of the gospel quotations in the Apostolic Fathers was dictated by the quest for the dating of these gospels: if the dates of the writing of the Apostolic Fathers could be ascertained, their gospel quotations could be used as *terminus ante quem* for the writing of the New Testament gospels.

There was, to be sure, a good deal of knowledge about other, so-called apocryphal gospels. But full texts of such gospels that could possibly be dated before the end of the second century were rare. One could mention here the *Protevangelium Jacobi* and the *Infancy Gospel of Thomas*. The knowledge of other early apocryphal gospels, such as the Jewish-Christian gospels, the *Gospel of Thomas*, the *Gospel of the Egyptians*, and some other Gnostic gospels, was derived mostly from occasional quotations of the Church Fathers (especially Clement of Alexandria, Origen, Hippolytus, Eusebius, Jerome, and Epiphanius). And there was, of course, the elusive search for the *Gospel of the Hebrews*, believed to have been the Hebrew original of the Gospel of Matthew. Only on rare occasions did any of these gospels yield information that could be useful for answering the question of the use of gospels in the Apostolic Fathers. The period of the discovery of new gospel materials had just begun in the last two decades of the nineteenth century. The first fragments with sayings of Jesus from Oxyrhynchus (*P Oxy.* 1, 654, 655) had been published in 1897 and 1904 and had generated considerable interest,

[1] A Committee of the Oxford Society of Historical Theology, *The New Testament in the Apostolic Fathers* (Oxford: Clarendon Press, 1905).

although there was no knowledge at the time that these were in fact fragments of the Greek original of the *Gospel of Thomas.* Rather, the category under which these fragments were classified was 'Extra-canonical Sayings of Jesus', of which Alfred Resch had published a very extensive collection.[2] Manuscripts of larger portions of the extra-canonical gospels were scarcely available, with the exception of a fragment presenting the passion narrative of the *Gospel of Peter,* which had been published in 1892.[3]

Although most of the more important discoveries of the twentieth century were yet to come, the careful, balanced assessment of the evidence by the Oxford Committee was at that time a signal for a fresh understanding in the midst of the battle for an early or a late dating of the canonical gospels on the basis of the evidence to be derived from the Apostolic Fathers.[4] The committee's findings often permit the presence of traditions that are independent of the canonical gospels. At that time, however, a free oral tradition of Jesus' sayings had hardly been widely acknowledged, and form criticism was still in its infancy and had not yet been systematically applied to the study of the New Testament. Major non-canonical gospels or fragments of such gospels were still waiting to be discovered—not to talk of the possibility of dating some of such gospels to the time of the Apostolic Fathers. In what follows, my aim is to survey these recent discoveries, not available in 1905, and to assess their potential significance for our current understanding of the development of gospel tradition both during and after the time of the Apostolic Fathers. The possible witness of the Apostolic Fathers to the use of the canonical gospels has been considered at length elsewhere in this volume and its companion.[5] Here I focus on other gospels that are not considered in such detail elsewhere in these volumes, some or all of which may have their origins in the period in which the Apostolic Fathers were active. In so doing I provide the fuller

[2] A. Resch, *Agrapha: Außerkanonische Schriftfragmente gesammelt und untersucht,* 2nd edn., TU n.s. 15, 3–4 (Leipzig, 1906; repr. Darmstadt: Wissenschaftliche Buchgesellschaft, 1967; 1st edn. published in 1889 as *Agrapha: Außerkanonische Evangelienfragmente,* TU 5, 4)). See also J. H. Ropes, *Die Sprüche Jesu, die in den kanonischen Evangelien nicht überliefert sind: eine kritische Bearbeitung des von D. Alfred Resch gesammelten Materials,* TU 14, 1 (Leipzig: Hinrichs, 1896).

[3] U. Bouriant, 'Fragments du texte grec du livre d'Énoch et de quelques écrits attribués a saint Pierre', in *Mémoirs publiés par le members de la Mission archéologique française au Caire,* 12, 1 (Paris, 1892); H. B. Swete, *The Gospel of Peter: The Akhmim Fragment of the Apocryphal Gospel of St Peter,* 2nd edn. (London: Macmillan, 1893). The so-called 'Fayyum Fragment' had been published in 1887, and the Strasbourg Coptic Papyrus in 1900; although both texts may be fragments of apocryphal gospels, these gospels do not seem to have been written before the year 200.

[4] For some literature see H. Köster, *Synoptische Überlieferung bei den Apostolischen Vätern,* TU 65 (Berlin: Akademie-Verlag, 1957), 1–2.

[5] See the contributions in Andrew Gregory and Christopher Tuckett (eds.), *The Reception of the New Testament in the Apostolic Fathers* (Oxford: Oxford University Press, 2005), and the essays by Bellinzoni, Dehandschutter, Hill, and Holmes in this book.

context in which the analysis of their potential use of Jesus traditions that later became canonical must be conducted.

When I worked on my dissertation in the early 1950s under the guidance of Rudolf Bultmann,[6] a few additional early gospel materials had come to light, most significantly the 'Unknown Gospel' of Papyrus Egerton 2,[7] but the Nag Hammadi Library had not yet seen the light of publication. I also profited, of course, from the pioneering works of gospel form criticism by Rudolf Bultmann and Martin Dibelius and others. This enabled me to argue for the presence of a continuing oral tradition as the source of most of the gospel materials referred to in the Apostolic Fathers. After the publication of my dissertation, I intended to work on a book dealing with the gospels of the second century; but the dream of an early completion of such work was shattered providentially by the publication of the gospel materials from the Nag Hammadi Library, in which I took an active part.

The publication of the gospels from the corpus of the Nag Hammadi Library, as well as a few other discoveries during the past half-century, opened up the possibility of a fresh understanding of the development of gospel literature in the second century. Four different insights seem to me to be most valuable.

1. The *Gospel of Thomas* demonstrated the existence at an early time, possibly as early as the second half of the first century, of written collections of the sayings of Jesus.
2. Numerous fragments of gospels as well as quotations and references in the Church Fathers attest to a proliferation of gospel literature in the second century, whether or not such literature is dependent upon the canonical gospels. Most important is here, among other discoveries, the Papyrus Egerton 2.
3. Several documents attest the development of dialogues of Jesus with his disciples, which are interpretations of traditional sayings of Jesus, also beginning in the second half of the first century. Direct or indirect evidence comes from the *Dialogue of the Saviour*, the *Apocryphon of James (Epistula Jacobi)*, and the *Gospel of Mary*.[8]

[6] Later published as *Synoptische Überlieferung bei den Apostolischen Vätern*.

[7] H. I. Bell and T. C. Skeat, *Fragments of an Unknown Gospel* (London: British Museum, 1935); *idem*, *The New Gospel Fragments* (London: British Museum, 1935). Preceding this important discovery, the fragments of gospel manuscripts *P Oxy.* 840 and 1224 had been published in 1908 and 1914, respectively.

[8] These dialogues and discourses seem to provide the basis for the more extensive 'discussions of Jesus with his disciples', such as the *Pistis Sophia*, which are characteristic of later Gnostic literature; they will not be included in the discussion here.

4. The discovery and publication by Morton Smith of the *Secret Gospel of Mark*[9] provides a fresh insight into the question of the stability of the texts of the canonical gospels during the second century before their eventual canonization.

WRITTEN COLLECTIONS OF THE SAYINGS OF JESUS AND THE ORAL TRADITION

The earliest major collection of sayings of Jesus is, of course, the synoptic sayings gospel Q,[10] which was incorporated into the Gospels of Matthew and Luke. It is not possible to know anything about the continued existence of this common source of these two synoptic gospels. Most likely, it was no longer copied, because it was superseded by the Gospels of Matthew and Luke,[11] just like the Gospel of Mark, which, after its incorporation into Matthew and Luke, left only very few traces in the second century.[12]

Another early written collection of sayings of Jesus underlies the *Gospel of Thomas,* although it cannot be assumed that this collection was identical with the Greek text that was translated into the preserved Coptic text of this gospel. The *Gospel of Thomas,* as it appears in the fourth century in its Coptic translation, reflects the instability of such sayings collections. It would probably prove to be very difficult to reconstruct the history of the text of this gospel from its earliest composition to its latest form. But it would give valuable insight into the factors that influenced the ongoing revisions in the transmissions of such collections of sayings.

Evidence for the continued existence of sayings collections is not easy to obtain. Preserved fragments of 'apocryphal gospels'[13] often do not yield much

[9] M. Smith, *Clement of Alexandria and a Secret Gospel of Mark* (Cambridge, Mass.: Harvard University Press, 1973); *idem, The Secret Gospel: The Discovery and Interpretation of the Secret Gospel of Mark* (New York: Harper & Row, 1973).

[10] J. M. Robinson, P. Hoffmann, and J. S. Kloppenborg (eds.), *The Critical Edition of Q,* Hermeneia Supplements (Minneapolis: Fortress, 2000); see also *idem, The Sayings Gospel Q in Greek and English with Parallels from Mark and Thomas* (Minneapolis: Fortress, 2002).

[11] W. Bousset, *Die Evangelienzitate Justins des Märtyrers* (Göttingen: Vandenhoeck & Ruprecht, 1891) endeavoured to demonstrate that Justin Martyr drew his quotations of sayings of Jesus from Q; this thesis, however, proved to be unconvincing. On Justin Martyr and his use of gospels, see below.

[12] The only trace of the Gospel of Mark before Irenaeus and Clement of Alexandria appears in Justin, *Dial.* 106. 3, where Justin refers to the sons of Zebedee as *βοανεργές*; see Mark 3. 17 (this special name for the sons of Zebedee is missing in Matthew and Luke). The oldest manuscript of the Gospel of Mark appears about half a century later than the first fragments and manuscripts of Matthew, Luke, and John. On Mark and *Secret Mark,* see below.

[13] *P Oxy.* 840 and Papyrus Egerton 2 seem to be portions of gospels that also contained narrative sections.

evidence, and numerous later quotations of non-canonical sayings may derive from the free oral tradition of sayings, from gospels that have perished, or from additions to the canonical gospel manuscripts.[14] In any case, the free oral tradition continues well into later centuries, and influenced both apocryphal and canonical gospel manuscripts. Sometimes the setting for the free transmission of sayings of Jesus is evident. The quotation of the Lord's Prayer in *Did.* 8 derives from the liturgical tradition of the early church.[15] A baptismal setting is evident for the saying about rebirth quoted by Justin Martyr, *1 Apol.* 60. 3.[16] Other free sayings derive from catechetical instructions—for example, the group of sayings quoted in *1 Clem.* 13. 3.

The primary source for the existence of sayings collections in the second century is also Justin Martyr. To be sure, Justin uses the first three canonical gospels, and he utilizes both narrative and sayings materials from these gospels. Both the narrative materials and the sayings appearing in Justin's writings are harmonizations of the parallel texts of the Gospels of Matthew and Luke. It could be argued, however, that in his quotations of groups of sayings, Justin is not quoting from a gospel harmony that included also the narrative sections of the gospels but from compositions of sayings derived from this harmony. Some of these clusters of sayings reveal signs of composition for instruction of the community, especially the sayings in *1 Apol.* 15–16. In another instance, *Dial.* 35. 3, a collection of prophetic sayings drawn from Matthew and Luke, includes the apocryphal saying *ἔσονται σχίσματα καὶ αἱρέσεις*. Also the non-canonical saying *Ἐν οἷς ὑμᾶς καταλαβῶ, ἐν τούτοις καὶ κρινῶ* (*Dial.* 47. 5) may come from such a collection of prophetic sayings.[17]

The existence of written sayings collections that are based on the canonical gospels but also include non-canonical materials is confirmed by *2 Clement.* The sayings quoted in this mid-second century writing show mixtures of readings from Matthew and Luke, just like those that appear in Justin Martyr. Twice, *2 Clement*'s quotations of sayings show the same harmonizations of sayings from Matthew and Luke as the quotations appearing in Justin Martyr. *2 Clem.* 5. 2–4 harmonizes Matt. 10. 28 and Luke 12. 4–5 in a way that is similar to the quotation in Justin, *1 Apol.* 19. 7.[18] An almost identical

[14] This is the case with respect to the famous apophthegm of the worker on the sabbath that appears in Luke 6. 5 in Codex D. The saying 'And only then shall you be glad, when you look on your brother in love' is derived, according to Jerome, from the *Gospel of the Hebrews.*

[15] In spite of some criticism, I am not inclined to abandon my earlier arguments (*Synoptische Überlieferung*, 203–7) for the independence of this quotation from the Gospel of Matthew.

[16] The form of this saying, as quoted by Justin, is more original than the form that appears in John 3. 3, 5. John changes the original *ἀναγεννηθῆτε* to *γεννηθῇ ἄνωθεν*, and *εἰσέλθητε εἰς τὴν βασιλείαν* to *ἰδεῖν τὴν βασιλείαν* (John 3. 3; John 3. 5 still preserves the original *εἰσελθεῖν εἰς τὴν βασιλείαν*).

[17] A. J. Bellinzoni, *The Sayings of Jesus in the Writings of Justin Martyr*, NovTSup 17 (Leiden: Brill, 1967).

[18] On the parallel in *P Oxy.* 4009, most likely a fragment of the *Gospel of Peter*, see below.

harmonization of this saying appears in *Ps.-Clem. Hom.* 17. 5. 2.[19] In the other instance, *2 Clem.* 4. 2, 5, the quotation reflects not only the same harmonizations but also the same combination of sayings from different contexts from Matthew and Luke[20] that appear in the quotations of the same saying in Justin Martyr.[21] At the same time, this harmonized quotation is combined in *2 Clement* with a non-canonical variant that appears as a marginal notation to Matt. 7. 5 in the so-called *Gospel Edition Zion* (MS 1424).[22] The sayings collection used by *2 Clement* reveals the inclusion of non-canonical sayings also in its quotation, 'When the two become one, and the outside like the inside' (*2 Clem.* 12. 2, 6) that is paralleled in the *Gospel of Thomas* (saying 22)[23] and the *Gospel according to the Egyptians*.[24] The latter, written before the middle of the second century, may also have been a collection of sayings, although direct relationships to materials of the synoptic tradition are not visible. There is, however, too little material left in order to make a certain judgement about its character. Though it was written in Greek, it does not seem to have enjoyed a wider distribution.[25]

It is possible to conclude that, while the earlier sayings collection Q soon disappeared in the second century, one or several new sayings collections appeared, which were based on harmonizations of Matthew's and Luke's texts but also included additional free sayings that found their way also into other non-canonical gospels that circulated or were written at that time. It is remarkable that this development does not assign any special dignity to the canonical gospels, but could freely combine materials drawn from these gospels with non-canonical materials.

THE PROLIFERATION OF GOSPELS DURING THE SECOND CENTURY

Of the written gospels composed before the end of the second century, the Gospels of Matthew and Luke, the latter separated from its original companion, the Acts of the Apostles, began to emerge from their original local context

[19] See my analysis of this quotation in *Synoptische Überlieferung*, 94–102.

[20] Matt. 7. 21–3; 13. 42–3; Luke 6. 46; 13. 26–8.

[21] *1 Apol.* 16. 9–12 and *Dial.* 76. 5.

[22] Köster, *Synoptische Überlieferung*, 83–94.

[23] Ibid., 102–5. Of course, I did not yet know the latter parallel at the time of the publication of my earlier book.

[24] Clement of Alexandria, *Strom.* III 4. 63–4.

[25] On the *Gospel according to the Egyptians*, see W. Schneemelcher, 'The Gospel of the Egyptians', in *idem* (ed.), *New Testament Apocrypha*, rev. edn., 2 vols. (Cambridge: James Clarke & Co.; Louisville, Ky.: Westminster/John Knox, 1991), i. 209–15.

and to circulate more widely in Asia Minor and Greece. While Ignatius of Antioch still seemed to be dependent mostly upon oral traditions, his younger colleague Polycarp of Smyrna certainly knew Matthew and Luke. These two gospels were also known well in Rome before the middle of the century, as Justin Martyr and Marcion attest.

On the other hand, the Gospels of Mark, John, and Thomas—all written in their original form before the end of the first century—did not enjoy a more general circulation. That the Gospel of Mark was known in Rome in the middle of the second century is evident from Justin's reference to this gospel, but it remains otherwise hidden until Clement of Alexandria and Irenaeus; the *Secret Gospel of Mark*, however, could indicate that Mark's Gospel was popular in Egypt earlier in the second century.[26] The *Gospel of Thomas* was at first used in eastern Syria as the special gospel of a sectarian group. But it was brought to Egypt some time during the second century, as fragmentary papyri[27] demonstrate.[28] Also the Gospel of John must have remained the property of a small group of churches somewhere in Syria or Palestine for some time. Polycarp of Smyrna, writing some time before the middle of the second century, did not know this gospel,[29] though a generation later Irenaeus, originally from Smyrna, knew and defended it. But these gospels appear in Egypt at an early time. John appears in Egypt early in the second century, as P^{52}[30] attests, as well as its use by Valentinus.

The first decades of the second century thus show that there were a number of older gospels in existence, which were originally used in limited geographical locations by special groups, but found their way into Egypt at an early date. A note of caution must be inserted here. The available evidence is biased towards Egypt. Not only do all the papyri with gospel fragments come exclusively from Egypt, but also the two Church Fathers, Clement and Origen, who give the most valuable evidence for the existence and use of gospels in the second century, were located in Alexandria. Were it not for the single reference to a passage from Mark in Justin Martyr's *Dialogue*, we would not have any evidence for the presence of that gospel in Rome in the middle of the

[26] For further discussion of the *Secret Gospel of Mark*, see below.

[27] *P Oxy.* 1, 654, 655.

[28] H. W. Attridge, 'Appendix: The Greek Fragments', in B. Layton (ed.), *Nag Hammadi Codex II,2–7*, NHS 20 (Leiden: Brill, 1989), i. 95–128.

[29] Whether Ignatius of Antioch knew the Gospel of John is still debated; see the literature in W. R. Schoedel, *Ignatius of Antioch: A Commentary on the Letters of Ignatius of Antioch*, Hermeneia (Philadelphia: Fortress, 1985), 9 n. 52.

[30] A date in the early second century for this papyrus, however, is not as certain as generally believed; see D. Lührmann, *Die apokryph gewordenen Evangelien: Studien zu neuen Texten und zu neuen Fragen*, NovTSup 112 (Leiden: Brill, 2004), 134 (*c.* 170 CE).

second century.[31] Nevertheless, it cannot be doubted that written gospels were in the beginning the property of limited circles of churches or special groups and achieved a more general circulation only during the second and third centuries.

The gospel writings produced in the first century were soon joined by an increasing number of additional writings that claimed to be legitimate presentations of the teachings and works of Jesus. It is doubtful, however, whether they appeared under the title 'gospel' (εὐαγγέλιον), because this term was not yet used for written documents in the first half of the second century.[32] The title 'Gospel according to...'[33] was in most instances added only by later scribes in the colophons—and often for writings that had no real relationship to gospel literature—that is, writings that recorded the words and deeds of Jesus of Nazareth. The often-discussed question, whether or not any of these gospels were dependent on one or several of the canonical gospels, is immaterial for the following survey. What we shall find is a blend of older traditions and sources, free materials, and influence from those gospels that later became canonical.

The *Gospel of Peter*, originating in Syria,[34] was also brought to Egypt before the end of the second century; this is attested by two papyrus fragments (*P Oxy.* 2940 and 4009), which confirm a date before 200 CE.[35] While the first of these fragments (*P Oxy.* 2940) belongs to the passion narrative of this gospel that had become known through the sixth-century Akhmim Codex Papyrus Cairo 10759, the second (*P. Oxy.* 4009)[36] presents a combination of Matt. 10. 16 // Luke 10. 3 and Matt. 10. 28 // Luke 12. 4–5 that resembles the harmonized quotation of these synoptic passages in *2 Clem.* 5. 2–4, although the similarities are not close enough to justify the hypothesis that *2 Clement* is dependent upon the *Gospel of Peter*. If it is correct that this fragment indeed belongs to the *Gospel of Peter*, it is evident that this gospel also contained

[31] I am, of course, aware of the widespread assumption of scholars that the Gospel of Mark was written in Rome. There is, however, no single piece of evidence. Mark was used by Matthew in Syria and by Luke in Antioch or in Ephesus in the last third of the first century. That a gospel written in Rome should have been brought to the East at such an early time seems most unlikely.

[32] See H. Koester, 'From the Kerygma-Gospel to Written Gospels', *NTS* 35 (1989), 361–81.

[33] With Schneemelcher ('Gospels: Non-Biblical Materials about Jesus: Introduction', in *idem* (ed.), *New Testament Apocrypha*, i. 77–85) I disagree with the assumption of M. Hengel, (*Die Evangelienüberschriften*, SHAW, Phil.-hist. Kl. 1984.3 (Heidelberg: Winter, 1984)) that these titles of the canonical gospels were already used at the beginning of the second century.

[34] This is suggested by the claim of Peter as the author and by the report of Serapion of Antioch quoted by Euseb. *EH* 6. 12. 2–6.

[35] *P Oxy.* 4009 may even date from as early as the middle of the second century; Lührmann, *Die apokryph gewordenen Evangelien*, 60–7.

[36] As it was reconstructed with the help of 2 *Clem.* 5. 2–4 by Lührmann, *Die apokryph gewordenen Evangelien*, 74–82.

sayings of Jesus, not just a passion narrative. Should one also consider the story of the transfiguration reported by the 'eye-witness' Peter in 2 Pet 1. 16–18 as possibly derived from this gospel? In that case, the *Gospel of Peter* would have been a gospel writing with narratives and sayings, resembling the synoptic gospels of the New Testament canon.[37]

The *Gospel of the Hebrews* was, according to the *Stichometry of Nicephorus*, almost as long as the Gospel of Matthew. It is now generally accepted that this gospel was a Greek writing that must be distinguished from two other Jewish-Christian gospels, the *Gospel of the Ebionites* and the *Gospel of the Nazareans*.[38] But in spite of numerous references to the *Gospel of the Hebrews* in antiquity, only as few as seven quotations have been assigned to it in recent scholarship, among these also a saying about finding rest, which is paralleled in the *Gospel of Thomas*.[39] Considering the information from the *Stichometry of Nicephorus*, this seems precious little. Recently, Dieter Lührmann[40] has argued persuasively that the story of the woman taken in adultery, quoted by Didymus the Blind in his *Commentary on Ecclesiastes*,[41] may also belong to the *Gospel According to the Hebrews*, although it is introduced by Didymus as coming from 'certain gospels' (ἐν τισιν εὐαγγελίοις). Lührmann demonstrates that this story as reported by Didymus cannot have been derived from John 8. 3–11,[42] but is an independent variant of the same story, which was also known to Papias of Hierapolis as a story that was included in the *Gospel According to the Hebrews* (ἣ τὸ καθ' Ἑβραίους εὐαγγέλιον περιέχει).[43] Whatever is quoted elsewhere from this gospel reveals elements of a gnosticizing wisdom theology. This has led to the conclusion that this gospel was essentially characterized by a mystic piety and shared very little material with the synoptic gospels. One other reference in Didymus the Blind, however, may direct further inquiry in a different direction. In his *Commentary on the Psalms*[44] he says that in the *Gospel of the Hebrews* (ἐν τῷ καθ' Ἑβραίους εὐαγγελίῳ τοῦτο φαίνεται) the Levi of Luke

[37] It must remain doubtful whether also the Fayyum Fragment PapVindob. G 2325, presenting a parallel to Mark 14. 27–30, could be shown to have been a part of the *Gospel of Peter* (Lührmann, *Die apokryph gewordenen Evangelien*, 87–90).

[38] P. Vielhauer and G. Strecker, 'Jewish-Christian Gospels', in Schneemelcher (ed.), *New Testament Apocrypha*, i. 134–78.

[39] Ibid. i. 172–8.

[40] Lührmann, *Die apokryph gewordenen Evangelien*, 191–215.

[41] Tura Papyrus IV 7–7, 18.

[42] The story appears in Greek manuscripts of the New Testament only in the Middle Ages, although it was a part of the text of John in Latin manuscripts much earlier (the Greek version of Codex D may be a translation from Latin; see Lührmann, *Die apokryph gewordenen Evangelien*, 221–8).

[43] Quoted in Euseb. *HE* 3. 39. 16.

[44] Tura Papyrus III, 184. 9–10.

5. 27, 29 is identical not with the tax collector Matthew of Matt. 9. 9 but with the newly appointed twelfth apostle Matthias (Acts 1. 23, 26).[45] This would indicate that the author of this gospel was familiar with materials from the canonical writings and probably included a good deal of material parallel with, or even drawn from, the synoptic gospels. The reference in Papias also gives a firm date of composition before the middle of the second century.

The only other Jewish-Christian gospel that can be dated to the second century is the *Gospel of the Ebionites,* so designated because it was used by a special group calling themselves 'Ebionites' (its actual title may possibly have been *Gospel of the Twelve*). It was a harmonizing Greek composition on the basis of the three synoptic gospels that shows some similarities with the gospel harmony of Justin Martyr. Non-canonical materials do not seem to have been included.[46] The third of the Jewish-Christian gospels, the *Gospel of the Nazareans,*[47] an Aramaic translation of the Greek Gospel of Matthew that was expanded with some extra-canonical materials, is not attested until the late fourth century; it is not likely to have existed much earlier.[48]

The only other, and most important, evidence for the gospels in the second century is the 'Unknown Gospel' of Papyrus Egerton 2. The fragments were first published by Bell and Skeat in the year 1935.[49] A new fragment of this gospel has been identified in Papyrus Köln 255.[50] These gospel fragments preserve the story of the healing of the leper (Mark 1. 40–4 and parallels, including a parallel with John 5. 14), the discussion about paying taxes to Caesar (Mark 12. 13–15 and parallels, with materials also found in Luke 6. 46, Mark 7. 6–7 // Matt. 15. 6–9), and the debate about searching the Scriptures and the authority of Moses (cf. John 5. 39–47), followed by a reference to an attempt to arrest Jesus (cf. John 7. 30; 10. 30, 39). In addition, the fragments of this gospel contain some damaged sentences that seem to introduce materials which have no parallels in other known gospels (apparently a miracle story). The question of whether and to what degree the text of this

[45] D. Lührmann, 'Das Bruchstück aus dem Hebräerevangelium bei Didymus von Alexandrien', *NovT* 29 (1987), 265–79; *idem, Die apokryph gewordenen Evangelien,* 182–91.

[46] Vielhauer and Strecker, 'Jewish-Christian Gospels', in Schneemelcher (ed.), *New Testament Apocrypha,* i. 166–71; H. Koester, *History and Literature of Early Christianity,* 2nd edn. (New York: De Gruyter, 2000), 208–9; Lührmann, *Die apokryph gewordenen Evangelien,* 231–3.

[47] Vielhauer and Strecker, 'Jewish-Christian Gospels', in Schneemelcher (ed.), *New Testament Apocrypha,* i. 154–65.

[48] On the complex history of the search for the original Hebrew Matthew, based largely on Jerome's claims that he had found this original Hebrew in the *Gospel of the Nazareans,* see Lührmann, *Die apokryph gewordenen Evangelien,* 233–58.

[49] Bell and Skeat, *Fragments from an Unknown Gospel*; *idem, The New Gospel Fragments.*

[50] M. Gronewald, 'Unbekanntes Evangelium oder Evangelienharmonie (Fragment aus dem "Evangelium Egerton")', in *Kölner Papyri,* 6 (PapyCol, 7) (Cologne: 1987), 136–45.

gospel is dependent upon the four canonical gospels is a much debated issue. With respect to the three synoptic gospels, one could argue that their text has indirectly influenced the composition of materials in the 'Unknown Gospel'.[51] With respect to the passage paralleling John 5. 39–47; 7. 30; 10. 30, 37, however, there can be little doubt that the 'Unknown Gospel' preserves a text that is more original than the respective passages in the Gospel of John; all characteristic Johannine elements are missing here.[52] Moreover, Papyrus Egerton 2 must date from well before the year 200.[53] That makes it unlikely that the author could have chosen sundry passages from the four canonical gospels and combined them at random to create new units. Rather, we must assume that the composition of this gospel—by all means a full gospel text with narrative materials and sayings—is dependent upon some independent written source (the portion paralleling John 5. 39–47), orally transmitted stories and sayings of Jesus, albeit in wording influenced by the synoptic gospel texts, and apocryphal materials.[54] The 'Unknown Gospel' may therefore stand as a key example of the development of gospel literature in the second century. We find a mixture of written materials, some pre-dating the canonical gospels, memories of sentences from written gospels combined into new units, and oral materials not otherwise attested or paralleled in hitherto known witnesses.

New discoveries during the past 100 years have unveiled fragments of gospel materials existing in the second century that cannot be assigned to any known gospel writing. Here belong the story of the discussion of Jesus with a 'Pharisaic Chief Priest' (*P Oxy.* 840),[55] Pharisees and priests challenging Jesus' participation in a meal with sinners (*P Oxy.* 1224),[56] a fragment discussing Mary's and Joseph's flight to Egypt and Mary's encounter with Elizabeth (Papyrus Cairensis 10735),[57] and a scene at the last meal of Jesus

[51] I am not certain whether my arguments (presented in *Ancient Christian Gospels: Their History and Development* (Harrisburg, Pa.: Trinity Press International; London: SCM, 1990), 211–15) for independence can be upheld. Lührmann (*Die apokryph gewordenen Evangelien*, 125–33) expresses some serious doubts; see also J. Jeremias and W. Schneemelcher, 'Papyrus Egerton 2', in Schneemelcher (ed.), *New Testament Apocrypha*, i. 96–9.

[52] Koester, *Ancient Christian Gospels*, 208–11.

[53] The dates have been debated since its first publication, which put it early in the second century; the present scholarly consensus prefers a later date: cf. Lührmann, *Die apokryph gewordenen Evangelien*, 127; Jeremias and Schneemelcher, 'Papyrus Egerton 2', in Schneemelcher (ed.), *New Testament Apocrypha*, i. 96–8.

[54] See the assessment of P. Vielhauer, *Geschichte der urchristlichen Literatur*, De Gruyter Lehrbuch (Berlin: De Gruyter, 1975), 638.

[55] J. Jeremias and W. Schneemelcher, 'Oxyrhynchus Papyrus 840', in Schneemelcher (ed.), *New Testament Apocrypha*, i. 94–5.

[56] W. Schneemelcher, 'Oxyrhynchus Papyrus 1224', in *idem* (ed.), *New Testament Apocrypha*, i. 100.

[57] *Idem*, 'Papyrus Cairensis 10735', in *idem* (ed.), *New Testament Apocrypha*, i. 101.

(the so-called Fayyum Fragment).[58] Some of these may belong to the second century. All of these, except *P Oxy.* 840, have parallels in the synoptic gospels and may demonstrate some knowledge of these gospels, in whatever way. They attest the fact that memories of gospel texts could be freely expanded, amplified, and joined with 'apocryphal' traditions.

DIALOGUES OF JESUS WITH HIS DISCIPLES

Dialogues of Jesus with his disciples, often including longer monologue-type discourses of Jesus, became an increasingly popular form of gospel literature beginning at the end of the first century. Such dialogues must be already presupposed for the Gospel of John, whose author revised such dialogues in both parts of his gospel. They are not necessarily 'dialogues of Jesus with his disciples *after* the resurrection'. During the second and third centuries, dialogue gospel literature was further developed into what is commonly known as Gnostic gospel literature, where the relationship to older and independent gospel traditions is often no longer visible, and the setting of a discussion of Jesus with his disciples is no more than an artificial framework.[59] I shall present here three dialogues, which are still related to materials of the gospel tradition and deserve to be dated fairly early.

The *Dialogue of the Saviour*[60] is based on an older dialogue of Jesus with his disciples that is composed as a discussion of traditional sayings, possibly closely related to the sayings of the *Gospel of Thomas*. Although external evidence for the dating of this document is lacking, its character and some similarities to the farewell speeches of the Gospel of John argue for a date of the older dialogues no later than the beginning of the second century. The sayings that are interpreted here, as Jesus talks with Mary, Judas (Thomas!), and Matthew, deal with the topics of the light, seeking and finding, marvelling, and finding rest. Sometimes a traditional saying is used to formulate a question of a disciple, at other times a saying is the basis for the answer of Jesus. While in these older dialogue sections no dependence upon extant written gospels can be established, the later editor, who added several longer speeches of Jesus, is clearly dependent upon several letters of Paul.[61]

[58] *Idem*, 'The So-called Fayyum Fragment', in *idem* (ed.), *New Testament Apocrypha*, i. 102.

[59] This is clearly the case in the *Sophia Jesu Christi* (Nag Hammadi Codex III and V) and in the *Book of Thomas* (Nag Hammadi Codex II; see H.-M. Schenke, 'The Book of Thomas', in Schneemelcher (ed.), *New Testament Apocrypha*, i. 232–40).

[60] S. Emmel (ed.), *Nag Hammadi Codex III,5: The Dialogue of the Saviour*, NHS 26 (Leiden: Brill, 1984); see also Koester, *Ancient Christian Gospels*, 173–87.

[61] The preserved writing that incorporated these dialogue materials may have been written at the end of the second century or later; it reveals some knowledge of the Pauline corpus.

The *Apocryphon of James*[62] claims to be a letter of James regarding the transmission of the 'secret book' that was revealed to James and Peter by the Lord. But this is only an external framework for what is essentially a discussion of the meaning of Jesus' sayings and parables.[63] The document was originally written in Greek early in the second century, probably in Syria/Palestine. There are close parallels to the sayings and discourses of the Gospel of John[64] as well as to some sayings[65] and parables[66] of the synoptic tradition, but dependence upon a canonical gospel is unlikely. Remarkably, there is also a list of parables (*Apocr. Jas.* 8. 1–4): the shepherds, the seed, the building, the lamps of the virgins, the wages of the workmen, the didrachmae, and the woman. The author must have had access to a special collection of parables that also included the parable of the palm shoot (*Apocr. Jas.* 7. 22–8), which has no synoptic parallel. The dialogues of the *Apocryphon of James*, like those of the *Dialogue of the Saviour*, are in any case less developed than those of the Gospel of John and can be characterized as precursors of the dialogues of the Fourth Gospel.

The *Gospel of Mary* must also be mentioned among the early dialogue gospels. It was discovered in 1896 as one of four writings of the fifth-century Coptic Papyrus Berolinensis 8502 but was only published for the first time in 1955.[67] Meanwhile, two Greek fragments[68] have come to light, which prove that the Greek original of the *Gospel of Mary* must have been written in the second century. These fragments also prove that the Coptic translator made some not insignificant changes.[69] Unfortunately, the Coptic translation as well as the two Greek papyri are very fragmentary. The first six pages are missing completely in the Coptic text, and there is a major lacuna from page 11 to page 14. Thus much of the initial dialogue is lost. Only the end, with a question of Peter, Jesus' answer, and the farewell of Jesus, is left from the first

[62] H. W. Attridge (ed.), *Nag Hammadi Codex I (The Jung Codex)*, 2 vols., NHS 22–3 (Leiden: Brill, 1985), i. 13–35, ii. 7–37. This writing is also known as the *Epistula Iacobi*.

[63] R. Cameron, *Sayings Traditions in the Apocryphon of James*, HTS 34 (Philadelphia: Trinity Press International, 1984); Koester, *Ancient Christian Gospels*, 187–200; D. Kirchner, 'The Apocryphon of James', in Schneemelcher (ed.), *New Testament Apocrypha*, i. 285–91.

[64] Cf. John 12. 35–6; 14.9; 16. 23, 26, 29; 20. 29.

[65] Matt. 5. 11 (Q).

[66] The parable of the sower (cf. Mark 4. 3–8) is quoted in *Apocr. Jas.* 8. 16–23, introduced with an allegorical interpretation (8. 10–15), which is completely different from the allegorical interpretation in the synoptic gospels.

[67] W. C. Till, *Die gnostischen Schriften des koptischen Papyrus Berolinensis 8502*, TU 60 (Berlin: Akademie-Verlag, 1955; 2nd edn. by H.-M. Schenke, 1972).

[68] *P Oxy.* 3525 and P. Rylands 463, published in 1983 and 1938 respectively; only the latter papyrus was available for Till's edition. For a reconstruction of the Greek texts with help of the Coptic version, see Lührmann, *Die apokryph gewordenen Evangelien*, 107–20. A very helpful English translation with the Coptic and Greek parallels side by side can be found in K. L. King, *The Gospel of Mary of Magdala: Jesus and the First Woman Apostle* (Santa Rosa, Calif.: Polebridge, 2003), 13–18. I am indebted to King's book for my comments.

[69] Lührmann, *Die apokryph gewordenen Evangelien*, 107–20.

part of this writing. While the question of Peter and Jesus' answer are probably based on Rom. 7,[70] Jesus' farewell speech includes several allusions to sayings of the gospel tradition. The preserved text consists mostly of a dialogue between Mary and the disciples. Mary consoles the disciples, who are distressed because of Jesus' departure, and tells them what Jesus had revealed to her in a vision. While Andrew and Peter object, saying that Jesus could not have revealed all this to a woman, Levi (= Matthew!) sides with Mary and, according to the older Greek version of Papyrus Rylands 463, goes alone to fulfil the command of Jesus to go out and to preach the good news. The later Coptic translator says that all the disciples went out to teach and to preach. Whatever appear as gospel tradition are free sayings of Jesus that can hardly be traced back to an origin in the canonical gospels.[71]

THE GOSPELS THAT LATER BECAME CANONICAL IN THE SECOND CENTURY

The fluid state of gospels and gospel traditions in the second century that is evident in a number of so-called apocryphal gospels raises the question of whether the gospels that later became canonical were not also subject to changes, additions, and new editions. Except for the small fragment of the Gospel of John in p^{52}, no gospel manuscript written in the second century or fragments of such gospel manuscripts have survived. All earliest manuscripts of the canonical gospels date from around the year 200, mostly John and Luke, while Matthew appears less often, and Mark only 50 years later. What happened to these gospels in the time from their autographs to the earliest manuscript evidence? This does not concern the changes in the texts of the canonical gospels that are evident in the later manuscript tradition, such as the addition of the secondary endings of the Gospel of Mark and the addition of the story of the woman taken in adultery in John 7. 53–8. 11.

The question is made even more urgent because of what we know about the use in the second century of the four gospels that later became canonical. Marcion radically edited the Gospel of Luke for his new authoritative scriptures. Justin Martyr composed a harmony of the synoptic gospels, for the most part neglecting the Gospel of Mark. A bit later his student Tatian composed a harmony of all four canonical gospels, including the Gospel of John. Gospels and some non-canonical materials that were later called

[70] King, *Gospel of Mary of Magdala*, 119–27.

[71] See King's careful analysis, ibid. 93–118.

'apocryphal' liberally used materials from the gospels that later became canonical and often combined their borrowings freely with surviving older sources and free 'apocryphal' materials. Other gospels expanded sayings of Jesus to form dialogues of Jesus with his disciples—a process that had apparently begun already in the last decades of the first century, as is evident in the dialogues and discourses of the Gospel of John. Moreover, the memory of Jesus, especially in his sayings, was alive as the voice of the Saviour that spoke again in new pronouncements through prophets and speakers of wisdom.

There are a number of indications that the earliest manuscripts of the canonical gospels do not represent the text of the original that circulated right after they were first distributed. The Gospel of John was originally circulated without chapter 21, which contains the narrative of Jesus' appearance at the lake,[72] and without the several corrections of John's radically realized eschatology[73] and the eucharistic interpolation in chapter 6.[74] Moreover, the question of the original order of some chapters in the Gospel of John has been discussed repeatedly. Did John 15–17 originally stand after John 13. 34–5, and did chapter 6 originally follow directly upon chapter 4?[75] Even if such suggestions for the reordering of the sequence of some chapters are not generally accepted, it must be conceded that the extant manuscripts do not present the Gospel of John in its original form.

While the text of the Gospel of Matthew, as far as can be known, seems to have been quite stable throughout the second century,[76] the work of Luke has survived in two different versions, the Alexandrian text and the so-called Western text. As the differences of these two text forms persist throughout the Gospel of Luke and the Book of Acts, both versions must have been circulated before the separation of Luke's work into two different books. While the Alexandrian text is preferred by most scholars as the original version, the Western text is also known to have been used in the middle of the second century.[77] That the text of Luke's gospel (as also that of the Gospel of Matthew!) was by no means sacrosanct is evident not only in Justin Martyr's free expansions of Lucan materials in his harmonizations of the texts of the

[72] The beginning of a variant of this story stands at the end of the Akhmim fragment of the *Gospel of Peter.*

[73] John 5. 27b–29 and the phrase 'and I shall raise him on the last day' (6. 39b, 40b, 44b).

[74] John 6. 51b–59; see G. Bornkamm, 'Die eucharistische Rede im Johannesevangelium', *ZNW* 47 (1956), 161–9; R. E. Brown, *The Gospel according to John*, 2 vols., AB 29–29A (Garden City, NY: Doubleday, 1966, 1970), i. 289–94, 303–4.

[75] R. Bultmann, *The Gospel of John: A Commentary* (ET Philadelphia: Westminster, 1971), 459–60, 209–10.

[76] Matthew appears later in a revised version, supplemented with apocryphal sayings, in Aramaic translation, known as the *Gospel of the Nazareans.*

[77] See my essay 'The Text of the Synoptic Gospels in the Second Century', in W. L. Petersen (ed.), *Gospel Traditions in the Second Century: Origins, Recensions, Text, and Transmission,*

synoptic gospels;[78] it is also evident in Marcion's radical new edition of that gospel.

With respect to the Gospel of Mark, it has long been suspected that the text of Mark preserved in the manuscript tradition may not be identical with the text of this gospel that was used by Matthew and Luke. This suggestion is based on the observation of many 'common agreements' of the texts of Matthew and Luke, whenever both are dependent upon the text of Mark. Many of these common agreements could perhaps be explained without assuming a different Marcan text as Matthew's and Luke's common source.[79] There is also the possibility that the extant text of Luke may have been influenced by the better-known text of Matthew.[80] These possible explanations, however—even if seemingly persuasive—call for a re-evaluation in the light of the publication of a fragment of a letter of Clement of Alexandria, which quotes and discusses two passages from a *Secret Gospel of Mark*.[81] In spite of some doubts regarding the authenticity of the letter,[82] what these references to the *Secret Gospel of Mark* might suggest for the history of the text of Mark's Gospel should be given some serious consideration.[83] I have observed that in a number of instances of the canonical text of Mark there are special Marcan features that are absent in the Gospels of Matthew and Luke but fit very well with the tendency and wording of the story of the raising of a young man that is told in the *Secret Gospel*.[84] That story of the raising of the young man, though no longer present in the canonical text of Mark, is itself remarkable as form-critically much older than the version of this story in John 11. The version of the story of the epileptic boy in Mark 9. 14–29 must be the product of a later editor, who changed the much simpler account

Christianity and Judaism in Antiquity, 3 (Notre Dame, Ind.: University of Notre Dame Press, 1989), 19–37, as well as other contributions in this volume.

78 See Koester, *Ancient Christian Gospels*, 360–402.

79 F. Neirynck, *The Minor Agreements of Matthew and Luke against Mark*, BETL 37 (Leuven: Leuven University Press, 1979).

80 This possibility is repeatedly discussed in F. Bovon, *Luke 1: A Commentary on the Gospel of Luke 1:1–9:50*, Hermeneia (Minneapolis: Fortress, 2002), *passim*.

81 Smith, *Clement of Alexandria and a Secret Gospel of Mark*; English translations of the two quotations from Clement's letter and a listing of relevant literature can be found in H. Merkel, 'Appendix: The "Secret Gospel" of Mark', in Schneemelcher (ed.), *New Testament Apocrypha*, i. 106–9.

82 See the above-mentioned contribution of Merkel to Schneemelcher (ed.), *New Testament Apocrypha*, where the relegation of this text to an 'Appendix' already indicates the gratuitous negative judgement. See also C. W. Hedrick, G. G. Stroumsa, and B. D. Ehrman, 'The Secret Gospel of Mark: A Discussion', *JECS* 11 (2003), 133–63.

83 H. Koester, 'History and Development of Mark's Gospel (From Mark to *Secret Mark* and "Canonical" Mark)', in Bruce Corley (ed)., *Colloquy on the New Testament* (Macon, Ga.: Mercer University Press, 1983), 35–57.

84 See also Koester, *Ancient Christian Gospels*, 275–84, 293–303.

of an exorcism, still well preserved in both Matt. 18. 14–21 and Luke 9. 37–42a, into a much more elaborate story of the raising of the boy from the dead. This rewriting thus forms a parallel to the raising of the young man that was inserted in the *Secret Gospel* after Mark 10. 34. Closely related is the note in Mark 14. 51–2 about a young man at the arrest of Jesus letting his linen cloth go and fleeing naked, which is missing in both Matthew and Luke. It recalls the appendix to the story of the young man who was raised from the dead, of whom the *Secret Gospel* tells that he went to Jesus to be initiated into the mystery (μυστήριον) of the kingdom of God 'dressed with a linen cloth over his naked body'. Finally, there is the use of the term 'mystery' in the singular in Mark 4. 11, where both Matthew (13. 11) and Luke (8. 10) use the much more appropriate plural. There are thus several passages in the extant text of the canonical Gospel of Mark which reveal changes and additions introduced by the author of *Secret Mark*.[85] The story of Mark's Gospel may thus be a paradigm of the instability during the second century of a text of a Gospel that later became canonical.

A CONCLUDING REMARK

The time-honoured division of canonical gospels and apocryphal gospels falsifies the actual story of gospel literature in the second century. The extant witnesses attest, rather, that there were multiple gospels in circulation that were not distinguished at the time with respect to their authority and authenticity. Nor were their texts considered to be inviolable. On the contrary, their texts could be reused freely in new forms of writing, be expanded by new materials, and be shaped otherwise according to the demands of the community. All these gospels were primarily produced not as 'literature' but as writings destined for oral performance; memory of texts heard and interpreted could also find its way into the copying of texts. Some of these gospels seem to have been restricted in their usage geographically or as the special property of one or another group of a very diversified Christianity, while others circulated freely.

[85] There are other instances, not related to the text of the *Secret Gospel*, where the question can be raised, whether the extant text of Mark is identical with the text of Mark used by Matthew and Luke. The most striking example is the expansion of the question of the Great Commandment in Mark 12. 28–31 with the quotation of Deut. 6. 4 ('Hear, O Israel...') and Jesus' debate with the scribe who is not far from the kingdom of God. See G. Bornkamm, 'Das Doppelgebot der Liebe', in W. Eltester (ed.), *Neutestamentliche Studien für Rudolf Bultmann*, BZNW 21 (Berlin: Töpelmann, 1954), 85–93.

The process that eventually resulted in the production of the four-gospel canon at the end of a hundred years of a very rich proliferation of gospel literature cannot be pursued here. It is most likely related to the fact that those gospels became canonical which were the property of Christian groups committed to the building of socially viable communities and whose central ritual was the Eucharist interpreted by the memory and reading of the story of Jesus' suffering and death. Only gospels with a passion narrative were authorized for use in the emerging early catholic church.

3

The Gospel of Luke in the Apostolic Fathers: An Overview

Arthur J. Bellinzoni

I. INTRODUCTION

In an article published in 1992, I traced the use of the Gospel of Matthew in second-century Christian literature from the Apostolic Fathers through Irenaeus.[1] Such a study, I maintained, is central to an understanding of the origin and development of the church's fourfold gospel canon.

Then, in 1998, in a *Festschrift* in honour of Joseph B. Tyson, I examined the use of the Gospel of Luke in writers from the middle of the second century, specifically Marcion, Justin Martyr, and Tatian, all three of whom clearly knew, used, and substantially reworked the Gospel of Luke.[2] In that article, I argued that it was clearly in Rome that the process of canonization began, with Marcion (who created a new edition of Luke as his *one* gospel), with Justin (who harmonized texts or perhaps created a full-blown harmony of Matthew and Luke as his *one* gospel, for reading, along with the 'writings of the prophets', in Christian worship services in Rome), and with Tatian (who wrote the *Diatessaron*, a harmony of Matthew, Mark, Luke, and John as his *one* gospel). Marcion, Justin, and Tatian apparently all agreed that there could be only *one* gospel. They disagreed, however, on the nature and the content of that single gospel.

Inasmuch as Marcion, Justin, and Tatian all took steps in the process of creating a single gospel to serve as the core of what would later become a New Testament canon, even if unwittingly so, it is important to look more closely at the decades between the initial composition of the gospels and the

[1] Arthur J. Bellinzoni, 'The Gospel of Matthew in the Second Century', *SC* 9 (1992), 197–259. The present article draws freely on the 1992 study.

[2] Arthur J. Bellinzoni, 'The Gospel of Luke in the Second Century CE', in R. P. Thompson and T. E. Phillips (eds.), *Literary Studies in Luke–Acts: Essays in Honor of Joseph B. Tyson* (Macon, Ga.: Mercer University Press, 1998), 59–76.

decisions to identify one or more gospels as authoritative. The period of the Apostolic Fathers was undoubtedly crucial, as it seemingly laid the foundation for these striking mid-second-century developments. It is, consequently, imperative once again to revisit the question of the New Testament in the Apostolic Fathers.

In what follows I examine the knowledge and use of the Gospel of Luke in the Apostolic Fathers. This study is but an overview, a prolegomenon, a contribution to a foundation for future and more detailed studies of the early use of all four of what later became the canonical gospels. By focusing on only one text later included in the New Testament—namely, Luke—it complements both my own earlier work on the use of the third canonical gospel in the period after that of the Apostolic Fathers and the discussions of possible references to all the writings later included in the New Testament that are collected together in the companion volume to this work.

As in my previous studies on gospel tradition in the second century, I use as my points of departure the foundational studies of Édouard Massaux[3] and Helmut Koester,[4] together with Andrew Gregory's recent study of the reception of Luke and Acts in the period before Irenaeus.[5]

II. METHODOLOGICAL CONCERNS

In my 1992 article, I indicated that there are methodological concerns that complicate any study of the use of gospel tradition in the second century. First, there are enormous difficulties involved in reconstructing the textual histories of both Luke and the Apostolic Fathers, especially during the first century(ies) of their transmission. Such difficulties make it virtually impossible to know to what extent the third-century archetypes of our best manuscript families conform either to the autograph of Luke or to the text(s) of Luke that were available to writers in the early second century. Neither, of course, do we have the autographs of the writings of the Apostolic Fathers.

[3] Édouard Massaux, *Influence de l'Évangile de saint Matthieu sur la littérature chrétienne avant saint Irénée* (Louvain: Publications Universitaires de Louvain, 1950, repr. 1986), Eng. trans. by Norman J. Belval and Suzanne Hecht, *The Influence of the Gospel of Saint Matthew on Christian Literature before Saint Irenaeus*, 3 vols., ed. with an introduction by Arthur J. Bellinzoni (Macon, Ga.: Mercer University Press, 1990–3). All references to and quotations from Massaux in this paper are from the English version.

[4] Helmut Koester, *Synoptische Überlieferung bei den apostolischen Vätern*, TU 65 (Berlin: Akademie Verlag, 1957).

[5] Andrew Gregory, *The Reception of Luke and Acts in the Period before Irenaeus: Looking for Luke in the Second Century*, WUNT 2.169 (Tübingen: J. C. B. Mohr (Paul Siebeck), 2003).

Second, to the extent possible, we must attempt to determine the dates and the places of composition of the Apostolic Fathers in whose writings we hope to identify possible citations of or allusions to Luke. And third, scholars must continue to try to establish and refine the criteria that serve to determine what constitutes 'use' of the Gospel of Luke by these early Christian writers. I will address briefly each of these methodological issues.

1. The Textual Histories of Luke and of the Apostolic Fathers

In a study of the text of the synoptic gospels in the second century, Helmut Koester observed that for the period before the third century, 'we have no manuscript evidence at all, and text types can be identified only by that evidence that comes from those who used Gospels', such as the Apostolic Fathers and early Christian apologists.[6] Koester further indicated that 'a text, not protected by canonical status, but used in liturgy, apologetics, polemics, homiletics, and instruction of catechumens is most likely to be copied frequently and is thus subject to frequent modifications and alterations'.[7] Koester also observed that:

> All of that evidence... points to the fact that the text of the Synoptic Gospels was very unstable during the first and second centuries.... With respect to Matthew and Luke, there is no guarantee that the archetypes of the manuscript tradition are identical with the original text of each Gospel. The harmonizations of these two Gospels demonstrates that their text was not sacrosanct and that alterations could be expected, even if they were not always as radical as in the case of Marcion's revision of Luke, the *Secret Gospel*'s revision of Mark, and Justin's construction of a harmony.[8]
>
> New Testament textual critics have been deluded by the hypothesis that the archetypes of the textual tradition which were fixed ca. 200 CE—how many archetypes for each gospel?—are (almost) identical with the autographs. This cannot be confirmed by any external evidence. On the contrary, whatever evidence there is indicates that not only minor, but also substantial revisions of the original texts have occurred during the first hundred years of the transmission.[9]

[6] Helmut Koester, 'The Text of the Synoptic Gospels in the Second Century', in William L. Petersen (ed.), *Gospel Traditions in the Second Century* (Notre Dame, Ind.: University of Notre Dame Press, 1989), 19.

[7] Ibid. 2.

[8] To add to Koester's list of radical revisions to the gospels, I would call attention to the fact that scholars who subscribe to the priority of Mark could certainly consider the Gospels of Matthew and Luke as radical editorial revisions of Mark's Gospel.

[9] Koester, 'The Text of the Synoptic Gospels', 28. So too François Bovon, *Luke 1: A Commentary on the Gospel of Luke 1:1–9:50*, Hermeneia (Minneapolis: Fortress, 2002), 1: 'Copyists in the second century worked on the text [of Luke] with the best of intents, but thus concealed the original shape of the text. Theologians either tried to purify the work by abridgment (like Marcion) or to harmonize it with other Gospels (like Tatian).... The variant readings within

The issues raised by Koester make it abundantly clear that we cannot simply assume that our best reconstruction of the text of Luke, the text which we must compare to the writings of the Apostolic Fathers, is the same as the autograph of Luke or the same as the text or texts of Luke that were available to and used by our second-century writers. To compound the problem, manuscript evidence for the Apostolic Fathers is scant, often late, and sometimes in a language other than the original Greek.[10]

We can, therefore, never be confident that we are comparing the texts that demand comparison. Specifically, we can never be sure that we are comparing the autograph of Luke or the text(s) of Luke available to the Apostolic Fathers with the autograph of each of the Apostolic Fathers. We must resign ourselves instead to comparing later witnesses to such texts, with all of the hazards that such comparisons involve.

2. The Dates and Places of Composition of the Relevant Documents

Establishing the dates and places of composition of New Testament and extra-canonical Christian writings is exceedingly difficult. Some writings are easier to date and place than others. Specific internal and/or external evidence may make the task less difficult, but sometimes there is little or no such evidence, or the significance of the evidence is equivocal and disputed by equally reputable scholars. Yet, in order to study the use of the Gospel of Luke in the Apostolic Fathers, we must endeavour within the limits of historical reason to place the relevant documents in their historical and geographical contexts.[11]

the manuscript tradition have various causes: copyists' mistakes, the influence of oral tradition or of the other Gospels (esp. Matthew), recensions, and tendencies in theological development or ecclesiastical sensibilities.' See also William L. Petersen's 'What the Apostolic Fathers Tell Us about the Text of the New Testament in the Second Century,' in the companion volume, ch. 2. Petersen finds 'profoundly flawed' the view that the text of the New Testament was fixed, for the greater part, in the form known to us today. Petersen asks poignantly: are we 'to presume that in the period when the text was the *least* established, the *least* protected by canonical status, and the *most* subject to varying constituencies . . . vying for dominance within Christianity, the text was preserved in virginal purity, magically insulated from all those tawdry motives? To assent to this thesis not only defies common sense, but mocks logic and our experience with the texts of other religious traditions. . . . The text of the documents which would later be included in the New Testament was neither stable nor established' (ibid., pp. 45–6).

[10] The Codex Sinaiticus (fourth century) included texts of *Barnabas* and *Hermas*; Codex Alexandrinus (fifth century) included texts of *1* and *2 Clement*; and the Bryennios manuscript (a codex from 1052) included texts of *Barnabas*, *1* and *2 Clement*, the *Didache*, and the long recensions of the letters of Ignatius of Antioch.

[11] The placing of documents in their historical and geographical contexts is a matter with which Massaux seems to have been largely unconcerned.

According to François Bovon, the Gospel of Luke is usually dated 'between 80 and 90 CE, after the death of Peter and Paul, and definitely after the fall of Jerusalem'.[12] The place of composition is more difficult to fix. Bovon places it in Macedonia (Philippi), an area apparently familiar to the author of Luke–Acts, with Rome as the next best alternative.[13] Raymond Brown agrees with the early church tradition that Luke 'was written in and to an area of Greece', and that 'the best date would seem to be 85, *give or take five to ten years*'.[14] Joseph Fitzmyer dates the composition of Luke *c.*80–5, and maintains that 'As for the place of composition of the Lucan Gospel, it is really anyone's guess. The only thing that seems certain is that it was not written in Palestine. Ancient tradition about the place of composition varies greatly: Achaia, Boetia, Rome. Modern attempts to localize the composition elsewhere are mere guesses.'[15] Helmut Koester locates the place of composition as 'somewhere in the geographical realm of... Antioch, Ephesus, or Rome', and argues that 'the time of the gospel's writing... cannot have been any later than ca. 125'.[16]

It is evident that the second century was critical for the formation of the fourfold gospel canon. The canon at the beginning of that century was the scriptures that the church had inherited from Judaism (the Old Testament); but by the end of the second century the Gospels of Matthew, Mark, Luke, and John, largely through the efforts of Irenaeus, began to achieve a status equal to that of the Jewish scriptures.[17] To trace developments over that critical century, we need to know, whenever possible, which documents were written when and where.

The status and the use of the gospels were, of course, not the same throughout the second century, and were certainly not the same in every region of the Christian world. What were regarded in Rome by 150 CE as authoritative writings were not necessarily the same as what were so regarded

[12] Bovon, *Luke 1*, 9.

[13] Ibid.

[14] Raymond E. Brown, *An Introduction to the New Testament* (New York: Doubleday, 1997), 273–4.

[15] Joseph A. Fitzmyer, *The Gospel of Luke (I–IX)*, AB 28 (Garden City, NY: Doubleday, 1981), 57.

[16] Helmut Koester, *Introduction to the New Testament*, ii (Philadelphia: Fortress, 1982), 310.

[17] Irenaeus, bishop of Lyons in Gaul, writing at the end of the second century, essentially created the core of the New Testament canon of Holy Scripture. It was he who placed side by side with the Old Testament a New Testament canon consisting of the Pauline letters, some of the Catholic epistles, and the four separate gospels of Matthew, Mark, Luke, and John. Many Fathers of the Church, beginning apparently with Marcion in the middle of the second century and continuing with Justin, Tatian, and others, appear to have adhered to *one* exclusive gospel authority. On the basis of a curious cosmological argument that there were four winds and four ends of the earth, Irenaeus argued against the apparently widespread belief that there could be only *one* gospel (*Adv. Haer.* 3. 11. 1–11).

in Alexandria, or Ephesus, or Antioch. The virtually universal agreement of the various regions of the Christian world regarding the fourfold gospel canon came late in the second or more probably early in the third century. To understand the regional issues and to trace their development, we must endeavour to determine whether a particular text was written in Rome, or Ephesus, or Antioch, and when and for what purpose it was written. Without such information, the picture is incomplete. In this regard, scholarly arguments tend at times to be circular. With writings that are less easy to identify by date and/or place of composition, scholars are sometimes tempted to make material fit where it best suits an already working hypothesis. In so doing, however, we must then avoid using that new information as evidence to confirm the hypothesis. Stated simply, we must avoid circular reasoning entirely, or at least recognize such reasoning for what it is and for what it is not.

3. Criteria that Constitute 'Use'

In looking for evidence of the 'use' of Luke in the Apostolic Fathers, scholars must develop and refine the criteria required to determine that it is, in fact, Luke that has been used and not some non-Lucan pre-synoptic oral or written tradition that simply resembles Luke.[18] In that regard I have identified three criteria for detecting what might constitute knowledge or use of one or more of the gospels in second-century Christian literature.[19]

First, the criterion of *accessibility* asks whether an author could have had physical access to the document or documents in question. In that regard the dates and places of composition of the respective documents are of foremost

[18] In a response to my 1992 study on the Gospel of Matthew in the second century, H. Edward Everding, jun. ('A Response to Arthur J. Bellinzoni', *SC* 9 (1992), 259–60) observed that the word 'use' has various meanings throughout my paper: 'use' as 'allusion'; 'use' as 'knowledge of the gospel'; 'use' as 'freely used'; 'use' as 'clear citation from the text'; 'use' as 'reworked harmonizations'; 'use' as an 'authoritative source' or as 'sacred scripture' or 'canonical'; 'use' *not* as interpretation. In fact, ancient Christian authors 'used' the Gospel of Luke quite differently, especially from the beginning as compared to the end of the second century. Having said that, it is important to recognize that Everding has identified the heart of the methodological dilemma: what constitutes 'use'?

[19] In his recent study, *Reception of Luke*, 7–15, Andrew Gregory has provided an excellent discussion of methodology, specifically the earlier debate as to what constitutes 'use' of synoptic tradition in the writings of the second century. Gregory's discussion focuses primarily on the work of Massaux, Koester, and Köhler (Wolf-Dietrich Köhler, *Die Rezeption des Matthäusevangeliums in der Zeit von Irenäus*, WUNT 2.24 (Tübingen: Mohr Siebeck, 1987). See also the insightful essay by Gregory and Christopher Tuckett in the companion volume: 'What Constitutes the Use of the Writings that later formed the New Testament in the Apostolic Fathers? Reflections on Method' (ch. 4).

importance. I submit that this criterion is a *sine qua non* in considering the question of use. Second, the criterion of *textual distinctiveness* implies that it is essential to identify and distinguish specific redactional characteristics of a prospective source and then to look for clear evidence of the presence of those redactional characteristics in our second-century writings.[20] This criterion is critical to the analysis of every passage in question; but, as we shall see, it is generally the most difficult criterion to apply to the passages in question. Third, the criterion of *rate of recurrence* asks how often there appear to be parallels between the texts in question. Numerous parallels indicate more probable knowledge and/or use of a source, whereas a single isolated allusion may signify something other than knowledge or use of a known written source. The fact that there may be only one passage in which a writer appears to cite one of the gospels does not disqualify the possibility that the gospel itself was the actual source of a citation or allusion. Nevertheless, more instances of possible use obviously strengthen the case. Only by employing such criteria rigorously and in concert can we conclude that we have good evidence for the use of Luke by an Apostolic Father. Alternatively, obviously non-Lucan material mixed with what may seem like Lucan tradition should alert us to the possible use of a source other than the gospel itself, perhaps a post-synoptic harmony of Luke and one or more other gospels.

In his 1986 preface to the reprint of Édouard Massaux's *The Influence of the Gospel of Saint Matthew on Christian Literature before Saint Irenaeus*, Franz Neirynck notes that since its appearance in 1950 'Massaux's book was destined to become one of the classical works on the acceptance of New Testament writings in primitive Christianity'.[21] Neirynck remarks that 'Massaux's basic thesis of the influence of the canonical gospels and of the preponderance of Matthew found a formidable opponent in the book of Helmut Koester, *Synoptische Überlieferung bei den apostolischen Vätern*',[22] which was written without knowledge of Massaux's work. These two studies are in sharp conflict with respect to their interpretation of the evidence regarding gospel tradition, particularly Matthean tradition, in the Apostolic Fathers. When it comes to finding citations of or allusions to the synoptic gospels in the writings of the Apostolic Fathers, Massaux is a maximalist, Koester a minimalist.

In this time of renewed interest in the use of gospel tradition in the second century, the contributions of Koester and Massaux are still invaluable, not only for their very different assessments of the same evidence, but also for

[20] Koester expresses this requisite thus: 'Hängt die Frage der Benutzung davon ab, ob sich in den angeführten Stücken Redaktionsarbeit eines Evangelisten findet' (*Synoptische Überlieferung*, 3).

[21] F. Neirynck, in Massaux, 'Preface to the Reprint', *Influence of the Gospel*, i, p. xiv.

[22] Ibid.

their exhaustive collection of relevant texts.[23] The studies of Koester and Massaux, therefore, serve once again as the focus of this study, although I will draw other relevant secondary sources into the discussion as appropriate, most especially Andrew Gregory's recent comprehensive monograph.[24]

The studies of Massaux and Koester are very different, not only in their conclusions, especially with respect to the Gospel of Matthew, but even more significantly in their approach to the evidence, which is to say in their methodology. Massaux's study was first published in Belgium more than fifty years ago at a time when Roman Catholic scholarship outside Germany had taken little note of form criticism, and before the emergence of redaction criticism. Accordingly, Massaux predictably explains virtually all similarities between the gospels and second-century Christian writings as evidence of direct literary dependence on the gospels themselves. More specifically, Massaux assumes that the Apostolic Fathers not only knew, but also frequently quoted from, the Gospel of Matthew. Oral tradition is not an option for Massaux.

Since the publication of Koester's *Synoptische Überlieferung*, however, many scholars maintain with Koester that, in citing dominical sayings, Christian writers in the first half of the second century borrowed either from oral tradition or from a pre-synoptic collection, such as has been postulated by those scholars who claim the existence of the so-called Q source. This position nuances the work of Massaux, who simply did not ask with sufficient rigour whether the second-century writings reflect a tradition that has clear and characteristic redactional features of the gospel for which he argues literary dependence.[25]

[23] In addition to the studies of Koester and Massaux, the collection of gospel parallels that are relevant to second-century Christian literature in *Biblia Patristica: Index des citations et allusions bibliques dans la littérature patristique*, i: *Dès origines à Clément d'Alexandrie et Tertullien* (Paris: Editions du Centre National de la Recherche Scientifique, 1975) is invaluable. I have provided relevant information from *Biblia Patristica*, and from other studies as well, about possible use of Matthew in the second century in appendices to the individual chapters in the English translation of Massaux's 3-vol. work.

[24] Gregory, *Reception of Luke*. Although Gregory provides a comprehensive discussion of the literature and a careful analysis of the data for most of the writings from the second century, I am puzzled as to why he devotes virtually no attention to two of the Apostolic Fathers, the *Shepherd of Hermas* and the *Epistle of Barnabas*. There are passing references to both works in Gregory's book, but no examination of how Luke was 'received' by the authors of these two presumably second-century writings.

[25] This problem is admittedly more problematic in Massaux in the case of the Gospel of Matthew than in the case of the Gospel of Luke. That portion of Massaux's work on Matthew that examines *1* and *2 Clement*, Ignatius, Polycarp, *Barnabas*, the *Shepherd of Hermas*, and the *Didache* (which Massaux dates after 150), has, in my opinion, been superseded by Koester's work. Massaux's study on Matthew continues to be valuable, especially for its examination of Christian writings from the second half of the second century.

III. LUKE AND THE APOSTOLIC FATHERS

Before embarking on our journey through the Apostolic Fathers, it is essential to state at the outset that there is no possible way in the pages allotted to this paper to examine and analyse in detail each and every possible citation of or allusion to the Gospel of Luke. Rather, I intend in the pages that follow to make brief reference to the studies of Massaux, Koester, Gregory, and others in those instances in which they substantially agree in their understanding of the evidence. I will present details of evidence only in those few instances when Massaux, Koester, or Gregory concludes that one of the Apostolic Fathers knew or actually used the Gospel of Luke.[26]

In addition, at the end of the sections on each of the Apostolic Fathers, I will provide with regard to the Gospel of Luke the information from *Biblia Patristica*, which purports to be totally inclusive, of all possible Lucan citations and allusions in the Apostolic Fathers.

1 Clement

1 Clement was written to the church at Rome probably between 90 and 100. Koester dates it to 96–7.[27] This letter is possibly our oldest extra-canonical Christian writing and pre-dates several canonical books. Assuming that Luke was written in the mid to late 80s, *1 Clement* may have been written just a few years later.

Already in 1832 Karl August Credner rejected the view that *1 Clement* made use of the synoptic gospels and maintained that the author was dependent rather on oral tradition.[28] So too Massaux maintains that 'No text of Lk. seems to have exercised a definite literary influence on 1 Clement'.[29] Massaux notes that there are a few passages in *1 Clement* in which some scholars find possible reminiscences of Luke; however, Massaux himself finds no evidence of literary dependence on Luke. Yet, he obviously equivocates when he states that 'No text of Clement... seems to have been under the literary influence of

[26] In this section I borrow freely material from my earlier paper on the use of the Gospel of Matthew in the second century, especially with regard to contextual information about the various writings under consideration.

[27] Koester, *Introduction*, ii. 288. Likewise Laurence L. Welborn ('Clement, First Epistle of', in *ABD* i. 1060) states: 'The epistle is customarily dated to the end of the reign of Domitian (95 or 96 C.E.).'

[28] Karl August Credner, *Beiträge zur Einleitung in die biblischen Schriften* (Halle, 1832), 27.

[29] Massaux, *Influence of the Gospel*, i. 33.

the Gospel of Lk. or of the Acts of the Apostles. But it could be said that the similarity of vocabulary comes from a certain familiarity of Clement with these writings.'[30]

Koester is confident that *1 Clement* never used any of the written gospels. The only authority that *1 Clement* recognized apart from the Old Testament (the only scripture known to the earliest Christian communities) was 'What the Lord said'.[31] According to Koester, the author of *1 Clement* knew none of our synoptic gospels.[32]

Gregory concurs that the few passages in which possible parallels between Luke and *1 Clement* have been noted 'provide no strong evidence for the reception of *Luke*'.[33]

Indeed, if Luke was written about 85 (or even later) somewhere in Greece, and if *1 Clement* was written in Rome just a few years later (or at about the same time), we should not be surprised if the author of *1 Clement* was unfamiliar with the Lucan gospel (the criterion of *accessibility*). The author of *1 Clement* might conceivably have been familiar with the Gospel of Mark, assuming that Mark was written in Rome two to three decades earlier than *1 Clement*, but that issue is beyond the scope of this paper.

Although the case for *1 Clement*'s use of Luke is exceedingly weak based on all three criteria (*accessibility*, *textual distinctiveness*, and *rate of recurrence*), *Biblia Patristica*, nevertheless, lists six citations or allusions to Luke in *1 Clement*:

1 Clement	Luke
13. 2	6. 31
13. 2	6. 37–8
24. 5	8. 5
7. 7	11. 32
46. 8	17. 1–2
23. 4	21. 29–33

30 Massaux, *Influence of the Gospel*, i. 35.

31 Koester, *Introduction*, ii. 291.

32 Koester, *Synoptische Überlieferung*, 23. Donald A. Hagner ('The Sayings of Jesus in the Apostolic Fathers and Justin Martyr', in D. Wenham (ed.), *The Jesus Tradition Outside the Gospels*, Gospel Perspectives, 5 (Sheffield: JSOT Press, 1985), 239) likewise maintains that 'The data of Clement taken together are best explained as the result of dependence upon oral tradition similar to, but separate from, the written Synoptic Gospels'.

33 Gregory, *Reception of Luke*, 125–9, esp. 128–9.

Didache

Massaux dates the *Didache* after 150 CE based on what he mistakenly assumes is *Didache*'s use of the 'Two Ways' tradition in *The Epistle of Barnabas*.[34] Although Koester also proposed a relatively late date for the *Didache* in his *Synoptische Überlieferung*,[35] in his *Introduction* Koester places the writing in Syria toward the end of the first century.[36] In his recent commentary on the *Didache*, Kurt Niederwimmer locates the place of composition probably in 'Syria or the borderland between Syria and Palestine', and states that 'In sum, the date of the *Didache* is a matter of judgment. An origin around 110 or 120 C.E. remains hypothetical, but there are as yet no compelling reasons to dismiss this hypothesis.'[37]

Massaux maintains that 'Other than those passages in the first section [*Influence*, iii. 144–76] in which I pointed out a literary influence [viz., *Did.* 1. 4d // Luke 6. 29b and *Did.* 1. 5a // Luke 6.30], the third gospel seems to have exerted no literary influence on any other text of the Teaching'.[38] In these few instances, Massaux at best picks up a word here and a word there to prove use of Luke. Specifically, with regard to *Did.* 1. 4d, Massaux gives preference to Luke 6. 29b over Matt. 5. 40 because 'contrary to Mt., the Didache mentions the cloak (ἱμάτιον) in the first part of the sentence, and the tunic (χιτῶνα) in the second, thus following the order of Luke. Moreover, Mt. uses the verb λαμβάνω, whereas the Didache and Lk. use the word αἰρεω.'[39] With regard to *Did.* 1. 5a, Massaux states that 'the text is even closer to Lk. 6:30 than to Mt. 5:42. In fact, only Lk. has, like the Didache, the adjective πάντι in the first part of the sentence, and ἀπαίτει in the second part, as opposed to ἀποστραφης in Mt.'[40]

[34] Massaux, *Influence of the Gospel*, iii. 160–1. See also Gregory, *Reception of Luke*, 18–19, who likewise rejects Massaux's thesis.

[35] Koester, *Synoptische Überlieferung*, 159.

[36] Koester, *Introduction*, ii. 158. Robert A. Kraft ('Didache', in *ABD* ii. 195–6) states that 'assigning firm dates and locations to this type of material has been especially challenging', and remarks that although most commentators have opted for Syria, or Syria-Palestine, as the place of origin of the *Didache*, Egypt and Asia Minor also have their supporters.

[37] Kurt Niederwimmer, *The Didache* (ET Minneapolis: Fortress, 1998), 53. Niederwimmer is admittedly tentative in his position regarding both the date and the place of composition ('Such argumentation, placing the *Didache* in Syria-Palestine, is not very strong but has some things in its favor,' 54). The fact that some portions of the *Didache* have an archaic flavour (the prayers in *Did.* 9–10 and the references to itinerant apostles and prophets in *Did.* 11–15) does not necessarily indicate an early date for the *Didache*; it may mean that the author of the *Didache* incorporated earlier traditional material into his work (Kraft, 'Didache', 197).

[38] Massaux, *Influence of the Gospel*, iii. 177.

[39] Ibid. 151.

[40] Ibid.

With regard to the question of the *Didache*'s knowledge of our synoptic gospels, Koester maintains that if the author of the *Didache* knew the synoptic gospels, he certainly did not use them. Rather the material in the *Didache* stems from the same oral traditions from which the compilers of the synoptic gospels drew their material.[41]

Regarding *Did.* 1. 4d and 1. 5a, the two passages in which Massaux observed a literary influence from Luke, Niederwimmer, in agreement with Koester, states that 'Verse 4d is again close to Luke (6:29b)', and that 'v. 5a is more strongly reminiscent of the Synoptic tradition (and particularly Lk. 6:30)'.[42] Nevertheless, Niederwimmer concludes: 'For the whole pericope it is again easy to suppose that we have before us an oral tradition parallel to that of the synoptics, or (better) the use of the same apocryphal sayings collection that was already suggested for [*Didache*] 1:3b–5a.'[43]

Hagner examines eleven sayings of Jesus in the *Didache* and concludes that 'Although the *Didache* contains an abundance of material similar, and related in some way, to the Gospels, it is very interesting that the case for dependence upon the Gospels is so particularly weak. The phenomenon can be readily explained as the result of dependence upon oral tradition.'[44]

Christopher Tuckett maintains that the *Didache* may have drawn material from Luke in *Did.* 16. 1 (// Luke 12. 35, 40) and in *Did.* 1. 3–2. 1 (// Luke 6. 27–8, 32–5),[45] although, Gregory maintains, there may be other explanations.[46] Indeed, if Luke was written about 85 (or even later, as several scholars, including Koester[47] and Gregory,[48] seem to argue), somewhere in Greece (which is by no means certain), and if the *Didache* was written in Syria just a few years later (which is also not certain), then we should not be surprised that the author of the *Didache* was likely unfamiliar with Luke

41 Koester, *Synoptische Überlieferung*, 239–41.

42 Niederwimmer, *The Didache*, 79.

43 Ibid. 80.

44 Hagner, 'Sayings of Jesus', 241–2. See also Richard Glover ('The Didache's Quotations and the Synoptic Gospels', *NTS* 5 (1958), 12–29), who argues that the sources used by the author of the *Didache* are the same as the sources used by Matthew and Luke; and Bentley Layton, 'The Sources, Date and Transmission of *Didache* 1.3b–2.1', *HTR* 61 (1968), 343–83.

45 Christopher M. Tuckett, 'Synoptic Tradition in the *Didache*', in J.-M. Sevrin (ed.), *The New Testament in Early Christianity: La réception des écrits néotestamentaires dans le christianisme primitif*, BETL 86 (Leuven: Peeters, 1989), 197–230, esp. 212–14, 217, 219–20, 228.

46 Gregory, *Reception of Luke*, 120, 124. In fact, Gregory states that 'it is not possible to adduce the *Didache* as a firm witness to the reception and use of *Luke*' (p. 124).

47 Helmut Koester, *Ancient Christian Gospels: Their History and Development* (Harrisburg, Pa.: Trinity Press International; London: SCM, 1990), 334. See also Koester, *Introduction*, ii. 310.

48 Although Gregory does not assign a firm date to the composition of the Gospel of Luke, he says that 'the earliest external evidence for *Luke* can be dated no earlier than the activity of Marcion and Justin in the mid second-century, which means that it must have been written in some form by c140' (*Reception of Luke*, 353).

(the criterion of *accessibility*). The author of the *Didache* would more likely have been familiar with the Gospel of Matthew, assuming Matthew was written in Syria a few years earlier, but that issue too is beyond the scope of this paper. Clearly the application of the criterion of *accessibility* depends on too many variables in the case of the Didachist's knowledge and use of the Gospel of Luke. Yet, as in the case of *1 Clement* and based on at least two criteria (*textual distinctiveness* and *rate of recurrence*), and possibly on all three, there is no convincing evidence that the author of the *Didache* either knew or used Luke.

Nevertheless, *Biblia Patristica* lists seven citations or allusions to Luke in the *Didache*:

Didache	Luke
1. 3	6. 27–33
1. 4	6. 29
1. 4	6. 30
1. 7	6. 31
13. 1+	10. 7
8. 2	11. 2–4
16. 1	12. 35

Ignatius of Antioch

The writings of Ignatius, bishop of Antioch in Syria, include letters to the Ephesians, Magnesians, Trallians, Romans, Philadelphians, Smyrneans, and to Polycarp, bishop of Smyrna. They were written between 110 and 117, when Ignatius was being taken to Rome as a prisoner.

One passage, *Smyrn.* 3. 2, dominates the debate among scholars as to whether Ignatius knew and used the Gospel of Luke. Massaux maintains that a comparison of *Smyrn.* 3. 2 and Luke 24. 39 initially suggests a literary dependence.[49] However, Origen connects these words to the *Doctrina Petri*;[50] Eusebius says that he does not know the source of Ignatius' text;[51] and Jerome states that the passage in Ignatius is drawn from the *Gospel of the Hebrews*.[52] In the end, Massaux concludes that the tradition of these Church Fathers makes literary dependence on Luke doubtful.[53]

[49] Massaux, *Influence of the Gospel*, i. 98. [50] Origen, *De princ.* 8. praef.
[51] Euseb. *HE* 3. 36. [52] Jerome, *Vir. Ill.* 2.
[53] Massaux, *Influence of the Gospel*, i. 99.

The larger context of this verse in *Smyrn.* 3. 1–3 concerns Ignatius' discussion of the reality of Christ's passion and resurrection. In his commentary on Ignatius, William Schoedel maintains that the tradition in *Smyrn.* 3. 2[54] 'is closely related to Luke 24. 39 ("see my hands and my feet that it is I; handle me and see that a spirit does not have flesh and bones as you have"). Yet, Ignatius is probably not simply presenting a loose version of the Lukan text since further evidence for dependence on Luke is virtually absent in Ignatius'[55]—the criterion of *rate of recurrence.*

Koester's analysis of Ignatius leads him to conclude that there is no citation drawn decidedly from the synoptic gospels;[56] he is unequivocal in stating that use of the synoptic gospels by Ignatius is out of the question. What little evidence has been advanced is unconvincing.[57] Hagner also cites the similarities between *Smyrn.* 3. 2 and Luke 24. 39, and between *Pol.* 2. 1 and Luke 6. 32; however, he summarizes his observations by saying that 'in every instance it is impossible to deny the possibility that oral tradition rather than dependence upon the Gospels may explain the words'.[58]

Gregory concurs that 'there is no compelling reason to suggest that Ignatius drew on *Luke*, and there are strong, if not compelling, reasons that he may not have done'.[59]

As in the case of *1 Clement* and *Didache*, and using the same criteria, there is no convincing evidence that Ignatius either knew or used the Gospel of Luke. If Ignatius of Antioch knew any of our canonical gospels, he would likely have known and used the Gospel of Matthew, if, indeed, Matthew was written in Antioch, or elsewhere in Syria.

Biblia Patristica lists the following five citations or allusions to Luke in Ignatius:

Ignatius	Luke
Eph. 11. 1	3. 7
Poly. 2. 1	6. 32
Eph. 14. 2	6. 44
Eph. 6. 1	12. 42
Smyrn. 3. 2	24. 39

54 Which reads: 'And when he came to those about Peter, he said to them: "Take, handle me, and see that I am not a bodiless demon." And immediately they touched him and believed, being intermingled with his flesh and spirit. Therefore they despised even death and were found to be above death.'

55 William R. Schoedel, *Ignatius of Antioch: A Commentary on the Letters of Ignatius of Antioch* (Philadelphia: Fortress, 1985), 226.

56 Koster, *Synoptische Überlieferung*, 24, 61.

57 Ibid. 61.

58 Hagner, 'Sayings of Jesus', 239–40.

59 Gregory, *Reception of Luke*, 69–75, esp. 74.

Polycarp of Smyrna

Polycarp, bishop of Smyrna at the time of Ignatius' martyrdom, left a document (not well preserved) known as his *Letter to the Philippians.*

It is the view of Percy Harrison that Polycarp's letter, as we know it, is actually two different letters that were addressed to the church at Philippi at very different times. The earlier of the two writings consisted of chapter 13, and possibly chapter 14, and served as a cover letter from Polycarp to accompany the letters of Ignatius that the church at Philippi had requested of him. This early letter can be dated to 110–17. *Phil.* 1–12, on the other hand, reflects a totally different situation, and was probably written toward the end of Hadrian's reign (which extended from 117 to 138), two or more decades later than the first letter.[60] Harrison's thesis may provide an important key to the question of Polycarp's knowledge and use of the Gospel of Luke.

In examining the relationship between Polycarp and Luke, Massaux states: 'No passage in the letter of Polycarp bears a trace of a definite literary dependence on the Gospel of Mk. or Lk.'[61] Unlike Massaux, however, Koester finds contact between Polycarp and Luke (*Phil.* 2. 3a // Luke 6. 38) in the single word ἀντιμετρηθήσεται, a word that occurs nowhere else in the New Testament.[62] Koester specifically cites Harrison in claiming that Polycarp, at *Phil.* 2. 3a, is familiar with *1 Clem.* 13. 14, as well as with the gospels of Matthew and Luke.[63] Koester concludes that if his understanding and analysis of this text is correct, then Polycarp must have known the Gospel of Luke.[64] In his *Introduction*, looking at a different passage in *1 Clement*, Koester again notes that Polycarp 'corrects the quotations of sayings of Jesus in 1 Clem. 13:2 according to the text that had been established by the Gospels of Matthew and Luke (Phil. 2:3); a knowledge of the text of those gospels is also shown elsewhere (Phil. 7:2)'.[65] Gregory finds no 'decisive element for Polycarp's knowledge and use of *Luke*'.[66]

The question of the use of Luke in Polycarp's *Letter to the Philippians* is simplified somewhat by Harrison's thesis, because it is not in the earlier letter

[60] Percy N. Harrison, *Polycarp's Two Epistles to the Philippians* (Cambridge: University Press, 1936), 286. See also Koester, *Introduction*, ii. 306.

[61] Massaux, *Influence of the Gospel*, ii. 34. Hagner also concludes that any similarity between Polycarp and the Gospels of Matthew and Luke may 'derive equally well from oral tradition as from the written Gospels' ('Sayings of Jesus', 240). Hagner further maintains that Harrison's thesis of two distinct letters 'has no bearing on our study' (ibid. 263 n. 34), and Gregory effectively agrees with Hagner's comment in this regard (*Reception of Luke*, 136).

[62] Koester, *Synoptische Überlieferung*, 117.

[63] Ibid.

[64] Ibid. 118. Koester, of course, argues for Polycarp's knowledge and use of both Matthew and Luke.

[65] Koester, *Introduction*, ii. 306.

[66] Gregory, *Reception of Luke*, 129–36, esp. 136.

of 110–17 that we find possible use of Matthew, Luke, and *1 Clement*. Rather, if there is knowledge and use of these writings, it appears in the second letter from 135 or later. These results confirm our conclusions about the other early Apostolic Fathers: that they reflect no knowledge of Luke or, for that matter, any of the canonical gospels. If there is a reference to Luke in Polycarp, it comes in the later letter written approximately twenty years after Polycarp's original letter. Even then the case for the use of Luke in the letter from 135 or later is not convincing. Koester's argument hangs largely on the single word ἀντιμετρηθήσεται in the six-word sequence ἐν ᾧ μέτρῳ μετρεῖτε ἀντιμετρηθήσεται ὑμῖν (the absence of γὰρ in *Philippians* is, of course, inconsequential).[67] The striking differences in the rest of the texts of *Phil.* 2. 3a and Luke 6. 38 make it difficult to conclude that there is, indeed, clear evidence of Polycarp's use of Luke:

Phil. 2. 3a	Luke 6. 38
μνημονεύοντες δὲ ὧν εἶπεν ὁ κύριος διδάσκων· Μὴ κρίνετε, ἵνα μὴ κριθῆτε· ἀφίετε, καὶ ἀφεθήσεται ὑμῖν· ἐλεᾶτε, ἵνα ἐλεηθῆτε· ᾧ μέτρῳ μετρεῖτε, ἀντιμετρηθήσεται ὑμῖν·	δίδοτε, καὶ δοθήσεται ὑμῖν· μέτρον καλὸν πεπιεσμένον σεσαλευμένον ὑπερεκχυννόμενον δώσουσιν εἰς τὸν κόλπον ὑμῶν· ᾧ γὰρ μέτρῳ μέτρεῖτε ἀντιμετρηθήσεται ὑμῖν.

Polycarp's second letter clearly meets the criterion of *accessibility*. It is not entirely clear, however, that it meets the criterion of *textual distinctiveness*, because the only textual distinctiveness between Polycarp and Luke (as opposed to Matthew) lies in the prefix ἀντι before the verb μετρηθήσεται. The total dissimilarity of the material immediately preceding the saying in the texts of Polycarp and Luke makes one wonder whether it is the Gospel of Luke that Polycarp was using rather than an oral saying that happened, perhaps coincidentally, to match the Lucan version.[68] In addition, it is clear that Polycarp does not meet the criterion of *rate of recurrence* with regard to use of Luke, as this is the only passage in which there is, perhaps, distinctive verbal agreement between them. But how much importance should be assigned to that criterion alone? I conclude that the evidence for Polycarp's use of Luke (in either the earlier or the later letter, assuming Harrison's thesis) is decidedly 'underwhelming'.

[67] The parallel in Matt. 7.2 reads : ἐν ᾧ μετρῳ μετρεῖτε μετρηθήσεται ὑμῖν.

[68] Yet, according to Moulton's concordance, the verb ἀντιμετρηθήσεται is not found in the LXX or in other Greek versions of the OT, including the Apocrypha, nor is it found in Greek writers earlier than the NT (W. F. Moulton and A. S. Geden (eds.), *A Concordance to the Greek Testament according to the Texts of Westcott and Hort, Tischendorf and the English Revisers* (Edinburgh: T. & T. Clark, 1957), pp. viii, 80).

Biblia Patristica lists the following citations or allusions to the Gospel of Luke in Polycarp:

Polycarp	Luke
2. 3	6. 20
12. 3	6. 27
2. 3	6. 36–8
7. 2	11. 4
2. 1	11. 50–1
7. 2	22. 46

The Epistle of Barnabas

It is particularly difficult to establish the date and place of composition of *The Epistle of Barnabas.* Suggestions range from *c.* 100 to 132–5; however, the truth of the matter is that we know virtually nothing about the author of *Barnabas* or its place and date of composition.[69]

Massaux states that 'neither the Gospel of Mk. nor the Gospel of Lk. seems to have exercised a literary influence on the Epistle of Barnabas'.[70] Koester observes that although use of Matthew, Luke, and an apocryphal gospel has sometimes been argued, generally judgement is either withheld or denied, or else use of the Gospel of Matthew alone is argued.[71] According to Koster, all that can be said for certain is that *Barnabas* and the synoptic gospels both used the same oral tradition.[72] If gospels were in circulation during the time of *Barnabas*, Koester maintains, they were apparently of little or no interest to the author. In fact, the failure of *Barnabas* to use the gospels may possibly be because the epistle was written close to the turn of the first century rather than later.[73] *Barnabas* fails on all three criteria.

Biblia Patristica lists the following citations or allusions to the Gospel of Luke in Barnabas:

[69] Jay Curry Treat, 'Barnabas, Epistle of', in *ABD* i. 611–13. Treat indicates that scholars have variously suggested Alexandria, Palestine, Syria, and Asia Minor as the place of composition. The date of composition is sometime before 135.

[70] Massaux, *Influence of the Gospel*, i. 74.

[71] Koester, *Synoptische Überlieferung*, 124–5.

[72] Ibid. 126.

[73] Ibid. 158. Hagner too sees no direct dependence on the synoptic gospels ('Sayings of Jesus', 242). For reasons that are not clear to me, Gregory does not discuss the reception of Luke in the *Epistle of Barnabas.*

Barnabas	Luke
14. 9	4. 18–19
5.9	5. 32
6. 13	13. 30
12. 11	20. 44
15. 5	21. 25–7

The *Shepherd of Hermas*

According to the reference in the Muratorian Canon, the *Shepherd of Hermas* was written in Rome toward the middle of the second century.[74] Massaux maintains that the Gospel of Luke does not seem to have afforded much inspiration to the *Shepherd*.[75] He claims that there may be a slight reminiscence of Luke in *Mand.* 9. 8 just after he states that 'as for the Gospel of Lk., Hermas seems to have drawn very little from it'.[76]

Koester confirms the absence of any clear references to synoptic tradition in the *Shepherd.* He notes that although external evidence requires a date of composition no later than the middle of the second century, it is impossible to establish a more exact dating.[77] He observes that at best the *Shepherd* contains material that agrees only very faintly with passages in the synoptic gospels. There is not a single passage that reflects clear use of synoptic material.[78] Koester argues that the *Shepherd*'s failure to quote from early Christian writings does not necessary mean that the author did not know them, because

[74] Graydon F. Snyder, ('Hermas' The Shepherd,' in *ABD* iii. 148) proposes 'a preferred date' of 140. Carolyn Osiek (*Shepherd of Hermas*, Hermeneia (Minneapolis: Fortress, 1999), 18–20) notes that 'There are three pegs upon which all theories regarding of the dating [of Hermas] hang: 'the Hermas of Rom 16:14, the reference to Clement in *Vis.* 2.4.3, and the *Muratorian Canon*'. All three 'pegs' cannot be correct, because they range over a period of eighty years. Osiek concludes that 'The best assignment of date is an expanded duration of time beginning perhaps from the very last years of the first century, but stretching through most of the first half of the second century' (p. 20).

[75] Massaux, *Influence of the Gospel*, ii. 130, and again on 132.

[76] Ibid. 132. The Oxford Committee refers *Mand.* 1. 9. 8 to Luke 18. 1 and points out that 'the idea of Hermas' is related to that of Luke, and that the texts bear enough similarity to suggest literary dependence (*NTAF*, 120).

[77] Koester, *Introduction*, ii. 258.

[78] Koester, *Synoptische Überlieferung*, 254–6; *idem*, *Introduction*, ii. 258. Hagner observes: 'Since the Shepherd of Hermas may date as late as the middle of the second century, the probability that the written Gospels would be quoted seems proportionately higher than for the earlier Apostolic Fathers. It is all the more striking, then, to observe that the quotations do not yield any high degree of confidence that Hermas used the written Gospels. Instead, tradition can adequately account for the data examined. It is worth noting that this is true despite the probability that Hermas knew the Gospels' ('Sayings of Jesus', 243–4).

the *Shepherd* also does not quote from the Old Testament.[79] Although Koester is technically correct, the lack of citations or allusions to any of the gospels may be because the *Shepherd* was written earlier, rather than later, in the second century. It meets none of the criteria to establish knowledge or use of the Gospel of Luke.[80]

Nevertheless, *Biblia Patristica* lists two citations or allusions to the Gospel of Luke in the *Shepherd of Hermas*:

Hermas		Luke
98. 1	(*Sim.* 9. 21. 1–4)	8. 13
6. 8	(*Vis.* 2. 2. 8)	12. 9

2 Clement

2 Clement was written sometime between 120 and 160. It is generally located in Rome because of its association with *1 Clement*; however, Koester suggests Egypt before the middle of the second century.[81]

With respect to *2 Clement*'s knowledge and use of Luke, Massaux states: 'The author of 2 Clement certainly knew the Gospel of Lk. He does not refer to it explicitly, he does not quote from it word for word, but he is at times very close to it, demonstrating clearly that he is inspired by it. Yet, the texts are few where the literary dependence on the third gospel is certain; in most instances, the dependence is very probable and does not exclude the hypothesis of the use of an apocryphal source.'[82]

Koester's conclusions with respect to *2 Clement*'s use of Luke and the other synoptic gospels are more detailed than Massaux's and reflect a better appreciation of the role of oral tradition in the early church: (1) many of the *logia* of Jesus cited in *2 Clement* display a form that they could have had in the oral tradition before being taken over into our written gospels; (2) several citations reflect a revisional reworking of the Gospel of Luke (*2 Clem.* 6. 1; 13. 4a; and possibly 8. 5); (3) several citations reflect revisional reworking of the Gospel

[79] Koester, *Introduction*, ii. 258.

[80] For reasons that are not clear to me, Gregory does not discuss the reception of Luke in the *Shepherd of Hermas*.

[81] Koester, *Introduction*, ii. 236.

[82] Massaux, *Influence of the Gospel*, ii. 17. Massaux discusses the following passages that in his opinion reflect definite or probable use of the Gospel of Luke: (1) *2 Clem.* 4. 5 //Luke 13. 27; (2) *2 Clem.* 5. 2–4 //Luke 13. 3; 12. 4–5 and Matt. 10. 16, 28, possibly in combination, although Massaux believes that use of an apocryphal source is more likely; (3) *2 Clem.* 6. 1 //Luke 16. 13; (4) *2 Clem.* 8. 5 //Luke 16. 10–12; and (5) *2 Clem.* 13. 4 //Luke 6. 27, 32–5 (*Influence of the Gospel*, ii. 12–16).

of Matthew (*2 Clem.* 2. 4; 3. 2; 6. 2); (4) in many citations in *2 Clement* parallel passages in Matthew and Luke have clearly been harmonized and bear striking similarities to harmonizations of Matthew and Luke found in the writings of Pseudo-Clement and Justin Martyr (*2 Clem.* 9. 11; 4. 2, 5; 5. 2–4); (5) other departures from or variations of the texts of Matthew or Luke go back to the author of *2 Clement*; (6) there is, in addition, clear evidence of the use of extra-canonical apocryphal tradition (*2 Clem.* 12. 2, 6). Koester concludes that the author of *2 Clement* did not use the gospels of Matthew and Luke directly. Rather, he used a written collection of sayings of Jesus that was similar to the collection known to us in the Oxyrhynchus papyri. The specific collection known to the author of *2 Clement* was based on the gospels of Matthew and Luke and contained, in addition, apocryphal material as well as further development of synoptic sayings. The collection known to the author of *2 Clement* was probably designated as a collection of sayings of the Lord 'from the Gospel'.[83]

Koester makes much the same claim in his *Introduction*:

> There is clear evidence that *2 Clement* cannot have been written at the earliest period of Christianity. The sayings of Jesus that are quoted in the writing presuppose the NT gospels of Matthew and Luke; they were probably drawn from a harmonizing collection of sayings which was composed on the basis of these two gospels. *2 Clem.* 8:5 refers to the written 'gospel' as a well-established entity (though it is not necessary to understand the reference to the 'apostles,' *2 Clem.* 14:2, as a reference to writings under apostolic authority).[84]

On the basis of Koester's detailed analysis of the evidence, I would argue that the similarity of the gospel harmonies available to *2 Clement* and Justin Martyr make Rome a likely place of origin for the letter.[85]

Gregory is particularly guarded in his conclusions regarding *2 Clement*'s knowledge and reception of Luke. He finds possible Lucan redaction in *2 Clem.* 9. 11 in one of its three sayings, implying possible use of Matt. 12. 49–50 and Luke 8. 21 or of a post-synoptic harmony of these two gospels. In addition, Gregory observes that *2 Clem.* 2. 7 may paraphrase Luke 19.10, although he states that this is by no means certain. In summary, Gregory finds little evidence to support *2 Clement*'s use of Luke.[86]

[83] Koester, *Synoptische Überlieferung*, 110–11. See also *idem*, *Ancient Christian Gospels*, 349–60.

[84] Koester, *Introduction*, ii. 235.

[85] I have argued elsewhere that Justin Martyr, writing in Rome in the middle of the second century, had available to him a text (or texts) that harmonized the gospels of Matthew and Luke (and possibly Mark), that this harmony was known to other Fathers in substantially the same form as that used by Justin, and that texts in 2 *Clement* prove the existence of this harmonization of Matthew and Luke prior to Justin (Arthur J. Bellinzoni, *The Sayings of Jesus in the Writings of Justin Martyr*, NovTSup 17 (Leiden: Brill, 1967), 25, 108–11).

[86] Gregory, *Reception of Luke*, 136–49.

The evidence indicates that *2 Clement* likely meets all three criteria: *accessibility, rate of recurrence*, and *textual distinctiveness*. Yet, it is likely that *2 Clement* did not use Luke itself, but instead used a post-synoptic harmony that combined elements of Matthew and Luke and, in at least two instances (*2 Clem.* 12. 2, 6) extra-canonical apocryphal tradition.

Biblia Patristica lists the following citations or allusions to the Gospel of Luke in *2 Clement*:

2 Clement	Luke
17. 7	3. 17
2. 4	5. 32
13. 4	6. 32
13. 4	6. 35
9. 11	8. 21
6. 2	9. 25
5. 2	10. 3
3. 4	10. 27
5. 4	12. 4–5
3. 2	12. 8
4. 5	13. 27
8. 5	16. 10–12
6. 1	16. 13
2. 7	19. 10
8. 5	19. 17
14. 1	19. 46
11. 2	21. 29–33

IV. CONCLUSIONS

This study of the Gospel of Luke in the Apostolic Fathers reveals little difference between the positions of Édouard Massaux, Helmut Koester, and Andrew Gregory. When I examined the use of the Gospel of Matthew in the Apostolic Fathers in my 1992 study, I found Massaux and Koester in sharp disagreement. Whereas Massaux found substantial use of Matthew by the Apostolic Fathers, Koester found very little use of Matthew. The difference of opinion between Massaux and Koester is minimal on the question of the use

Table 3.1 Summary overview

Author or writing	Date	Place of composition	Use of the Gospel of Luke
1 Clement	90–100	Rome	none
Didache	95–120	Syria or Palestine-Syria	none
Ignatius of Antioch	110–17	Syria (Ignatius' place of origin)	none
Polycarp of Smyrna	#1 110–17	Asia Minor	none
	#2 post-135	Asia Minor	at most one example of use
Epistle of Barnabas	100–35	Alexandria?	none
Shepherd of Hermas	100–50	Rome	none
2 Clement	120–60	Rome (or Egypt?)	used material harmonized from Matthew and Luke, etc.

of the Gospel of Luke: both find little use of Luke by the Apostolic Fathers. Andrew Gregory concurs in this assessment. It is only as we approach the Apostolic Fathers toward the middle of the second century, specifically *2 Clement*, and possibly the later writing included in Polycarp's *Letter to the Philippians*, that there may be evidence of use of Luke (see table 3.1). Even then, it is not entirely clear that it is Luke itself that was actually used.

In the course of this paper I have attempted to trace the use of the Gospel of Luke in the Apostolic Fathers. Specifically, I have looked at seven writers or writings covering the period from the end of the first century to the middle of the second century.[87]

Among these writings, there appears to have been little or no use of the Gospel of Luke *per se*, but rather use of pre-synoptic oral and/or written tradition. This literature from the first half of the second century reflects use not of the synoptic gospels but of the same tradition that underlies the synoptic gospels. The source of that tradition was individual Christian communities, which, based on their practical needs, handed down and made use of synoptic-like oral and written tradition.

Exceptions to the use of pre-synoptic tradition among the Apostolic Fathers appear possibly in the latter portion of Polycarp's *Letter to the Philippians*, probably written in Smyrna after 135, and more clearly in *2 Clement*, probably written in Rome toward the middle of the second century.

[87] I have limited my study to these seven writers/writings and have not examined the question of the Gospel of Luke in Papias, the *Martyrdom of Polycarp*, Diognetus, or Quadratus. Scholars have for centuries debated which works properly belong to the collection of Apostolic Fathers. In fact, many scholars, including myself, wonder whether the category 'Apostolic Fathers' is itself meaningful.

Polycarp's second letter may reflect use of the Gospel of Luke, but even that is not entirely clear, and I very much doubt it. However, *2 Clement* unmistakably reflects knowledge and use of Luke or, more accurately, use of a post-Lucan harmony of material from the Gospels of Matthew and Luke, combined perhaps with extra-canonical apocryphal tradition.

Quite obviously, none of the Apostolic Fathers had an understanding of the Gospel of Luke as sacred scripture. Such an understanding of Luke, or of any of the gospels, as Scripture likely occurred first with Marcion, who was active in Rome in the mid-second century. In fact, it was Marcion, Justin Martyr, and Tatian who apparently set the stage and laid the foundation for the initial formation of the Christian canon a half-century later.[88]

Other second-century Christian writings, mostly later than the Apostolic Fathers, reflect knowledge and use of Luke. Writings from the second half of the second century reflect circumstances in which writers continued to modify Luke freely, often making significant alterations and changes to the text of the gospel, sometimes harmonizing it with Matthew and/or other gospels.[89] There is nothing in the literature before Irenaeus to suggest that Church Fathers in the second century might have felt obligated to preserve the Gospel of Luke in its original form.

Although my primary focus in this paper has been the Gospel of Luke in the Apostolic Fathers, this study has, I believe, important implications for an understanding of the development of the New Testament canon and serious ramifications for textual criticism and for the study of the synoptic problem.[90]

What does this study tell us about the status of the Gospel of Luke during the first half of the second century? Can we reasonably assume that there were Christian scribes who faithfully copied the autographs of the Gospel of Luke and the other gospels at a time when many, apparently most, second-century Christian writers obviously treated these same texts quite freely? What are the long-term implications of this study for textual criticism and for proposed

[88] Bellinzoni, 'Gospel of Luke in the Second Century'.

[89] E.g., Justin Martyr and Tatian, probably reacting against Marcion's proto-canon of Luke and ten Pauline letters, developed collections of authoritative writings of their own in the mid second-century. Justin used harmonized texts of Matthew and Luke (and possibly Mark), perhaps even a full-blown harmony of these gospels. Tatian created his one harmonized Gospel, the *Diatessaron*, based on Matthew, Mark, Luke, and John. The *Protevangelium of James*, written sometime after 150, presupposes knowledge of both Matthew and Luke. Athenagoras of Athens, writing *c.* 175, echoes passages from Matthew, apparently in harmony with related material from Luke; and according to Jerome (*Ep.* 121. 6. 15), Theophilus of Antioch, writing shortly after 180, composed a harmony of the gospels.

[90] See in this connection Joseph B. Tyson, 'Source Criticism of the Gospel of Luke', in C. H. Talbert (ed.), *Perspectives on Luke–Acts* (Macon, Ga.: Mercer University Press, 1978), 24–39.

solutions to the synoptic problem?[91] Obviously, I cannot address these questions here, but I have uncovered a number of concerns that clearly need further consideration and deliberation in light of my findings.

I mentioned at the outset that this study is but a first step, an overview, a prolegomenon to the question of the Gospel of Luke in the Apostolic Fathers. By focusing on one text later included in the New Testament, it complements the rigorous and systematic re-examination of possible references to all the writings later included in the New Testament that are collected together in the companion volume to this work. Those studies confirm and illustrate the need to give critical attention to questions of method, and the need for scholars to continue to work diligently to develop and refine criteria to determine what constitutes the use of one or more of the gospels.

Édouard Massaux, Helmut Koester, Wolf-Dietrich Köhler, Andrew Gregory, and others have made a good start in their respective monographs, and each has built on the foundational and lasting work of the committee of the Oxford Society of Historical Theology whose results were published 100 years ago. Yet fresh insights and fresh discoveries may continue to call for rigorous reassessments of gospel traditions in all of the Apostolic Fathers, and beyond that narrow corpus to all of the Christian writings of the second century.

[91] E.g., are not the so-called minor agreements of Matthew and Luke against Mark explained most easy as second-century developments that reflect a tendency on the part of Christian scribes to rework the gospels in light of one another, rather than evidence for a particular solution to the synoptic problem (i.e. the Griesbach hypothesis)?

Part III

Christology in the New Testament and the Apostolic Fathers

4

The Apostolic Christology of Ignatius of Antioch: The Road to Chalcedon

Thomas G. Weinandy, O.F.M. Cap.

What New Testament teachings Ignatius of Antioch (d. *c.*107–10) was acquainted with, either in their written form or through the oral traditions that gave rise to them, has caused a great deal of debate. For example, did Ignatius have access to some or all of the written Gospels of Matthew, Luke, and John, or was he merely acquainted with their various oral traditions, or even traditions parallel to them? Which, and how many, of Paul's letters did he possess or had he read? There is no scholarly consensus concerning these issues. Some authors offer a positive assessment, and affirm that Ignatius did possess some of the writings later canonized as the New Testament, the most likely being Matthew, John, and 1 Corinthians, and that he was acquainted with various oral traditions, the most likely being Lucan and Pauline traditions. Others scholars are more or less sceptical.[1] At present, it is very difficult, and in the end most likely impossible, to ascertain exactly which Christian writings Ignatius either had read or knew simply from the various oral traditions that he had received. I would cautiously affirm that Ignatius did

[1] For a careful recent survey see Paul Foster, Ch. 7 in the companion volume. Other discussions include W. Burghart, 'Did Saint Ignatius of Antioch Know the Fourth Gospel?', *TS* 1 (1940), 130–56; R. M. Grant, 'Scripture and Tradition in St. Ignatius of Antioch', *CBQ* 25 (1963), 322–35; *idem*, *The Apostolic Fathers*, iv: *Ignatius of Antioch* (London: Thomas Nelson & Sons, 1966), 1–24; C. E. Hill, 'Ignatius and the Apostolate: The Witness of Ignatius to the Emergence of Christian Scripture', in M. Wiles and E. Yarnold (eds.), *StPatr* 36 (Leuven: Peeters, 2001), 226–48; D. L. Hoffman, 'The Authority of Scripture and Apostolic Doctrine in Ignatius of Antioch', *JETS* 28 (1985), 71–9; L. W. Hurtado, *Lord Jesus Christ: Devotion to Jesus in Earliest Christianity* (Grand Rapids, Mich.: Eerdmans, 2003), 235–40; S. E. Johnson, 'Parallels between the Letters of Ignatius and the Johannine Epistles', in E. W. Conrad and E. G. Newing (eds.), *Perspectives on Language and Text* (Winona Lake, Ind.: Eisenbrauns, 1987), 327–38; H. Koester, 'History and Cult in the Gospel of John and in Ignatius of Antioch', *JTC* 1 (1965), 111–23; C. C. Richardson, *The Christianity of Ignatius of Antioch* (New York: AMS Press, 1935), 60–75; J. Smit Sibinga, 'Ignatius and Matthew', *NovT* 8 (1966), 263–83; C. M. Trevett, 'Approaching Matthew from the Second Century: The Under-Used Ignatian Correspondence', *JSNT* 20 (1984), 59–67.

have access to Matthew and to 1 Corinthians in written form, as well as to much of the Pauline corpus, or at least of the Pauline tradition; and that he was at least very familiar with Lucan and Johannine traditions, and may even have known the latter in written form.[2]

None the less, what is most significant within this discussion, and what is often overlooked, is that whatever specific writings Ignatius did or did not have access to, or whatever specific traditions he was or was not aware of, when one reads Ignatius' seven letters, one finds oneself in substantial continuity with a number of the theological concerns of those texts and traditions that came to be canonized in the New Testament and that may be considered as apostolic.[3] Although Ignatius moulded such tradition as he had received as apostolic in order to address contemporary issues that he faced, the basic Christian Gospel that he espoused and defended is nevertheless recognizably the same Christian gospel as that found in at least some of the writings of the New Testament. Some of the apostolic traditions that became embodied in the New Testament are the very same apostolic traditions that are found in Ignatius' seven brief letters. Ignatius, I would argue, is by no means a doctrinal innovator, for it is precisely this composite apostolic tradition, which he regarded as the already given authoritative tradition, that he wanted to defend. Ignatius endorsed and fostered a high theology of the bishop, one that he believed to have arisen from within the apostolic tradition itself,

[2] While this essay will highlight some of the similarities between Ignatius' Christology and that of various New Testament writings, there are other elements of his writings that also bear a likeness to New Testament documents. For example, Ignatius' emphasis on Christians being Christ's 'temples' and on living 'in Christ' and so composing 'the body of Christ' are substantially Pauline (see *Eph.* 4; 10. 3; 11. 1; 12. 2; 15. 3; *Magn.* 12, 15; *Trall.* 7. 1; 11. 1; *Pol.* 8. 3). Richardson, *Christianity of Ignatius of Antioch*, 61, notes that there are at least five clear parallels between Ignatius' letters and 1 Corinthians: *Eph.* 16. 1 // 1 Cor. 6. 9; *Eph.* 18. 1 // 1 Cor. 1. 18–23; *Rom.* 5. 1 // 1 Cor. 4. 4; *Rom.* 9. 2 // 1 Cor. 15. 8–10; *Magn.* 10. 3 // 1 Cor. 5. 7. Of the references noted in n. 1 see esp. Grant, 'Scripture and Tradition'. He finds parallels between Ignatius' letters and the Pauline corpus, plus Matthew, Luke, and the Johannine tradition.

[3] Throughout this essay I use the terms 'apostolic tradition', 'apostolic traditions', and 'apostolic writings', and I will argue that Ignatius espoused an 'apostolic Christology'. By 'apostolic' I mean that tradition or those traditions that made up the kerygma of the first generation of Christians as it arose from within the proclamation of the apostles. These various oral 'apostolic traditions' ultimately took written form in what would become the New Testament. The New Testament, then, is composed of the various apostolic traditions, and so embodies the complete apostolic tradition. It is within these apostolic traditions, both as distinct parts and as a composite whole, whether oral or written, that I want to situate Ignatius' seven letters and the Christology articulated therein.

W. Schoedel argues that there is evidence not only of Ignatius' employment of New Testament material, but also of the use of semi-credal patterns. See W. R. Schoedel, *Ignatius of Antioch: A Commentary on the Letters of Ignatius of Antioch*, Hermeneia (Philadelphia: Fortress, 1985), 7–8. Grant recognizes three passages in Ignatius' letters that are credal: *Eph.* 18. 2; *Trall.* 9. 1–2; and *Smyrn.* 1. 1–2 (*Ignatius*, 10).

because he was convinced that it is specifically the bishop who is now the appointed apostolic custodian and guardian of this apostolic gospel.[4]

I have concerned myself with these preliminary issues because I want to argue in this essay that Ignatius' Christology is an apostolic Christology—that is, a Christology that originated from within, and gave expression to, the various apostolic traditions that were later canonized within the New Testament. Thus there is a fundamental continuity, I will argue, between the apostolic Christology as recounted and proclaimed within New Testament Christianity and as found in Ignatius' letters. Some may think that this in itself is a rather dubious enterprise, but the more controversial aspect of this essay is my claim that Ignatius' apostolic Christology, and so New Testament Christology, is the first step along the road that leads to Chalcedon. My thesis is that Ignatius of Antioch forged the first of many links that historically and doctrinally established the fundamental continuity that is to be found between between the Christology of the New Testament and the Christology of the Council of Chalcedon.[5]

My argument is composed of four parts. The first examines how Ignatius conceived Jesus' relationship to the Father, and in so doing establishes his apostolic foundation for discerning the Son's divine status. The second examines Ignatius' understanding of Jesus' humanity in relation to the apo-

[4] While it could be argued that Ignatius' understanding of the threefold ecclesial order of deacons, priests, and bishops was innovative, since it does not appear as such within the New Testament, I would argue that even here he was not the originator of such an ecclesial notion. Ignatius did stress the centrality of the monarchical bishop within the local Christian community, but he did so not as one attempting to establish an ecclesial order that was controversial or one that was yet to be fully recognized. Rather, he was merely clarifying and expounding what to him were the evident implications and consequences of an ecclesial order that was already recognized to be in place. How this ecclesial order, historically and theologically, derived from the various ministries found within the New Testament is another question.

[5] In saying this I do not imply, as will become clear, that Ignatius already employed the technical theological concepts and vocabulary of Chalcedon. Rather, I merely want to demonstrate that for both it is one and the same Son who existed as God and as man, so both divine and human attributes can properly be predicated of one and the same Son.

For other studies of Ignatius' Christology see the following: E. de Bhaldraithe, 'The Christology of Ignatius of Antioch', in M. Wiles and E. Yarnold (eds.), *StPatr* 36 (Leuven: Peeters, 2001), 200–6; W. F. Bunge, 'The Christology of Ignatius of Antioch' (Th. D. diss., Harvard University, 1966); V. Corwin, *St. Ignatius and Christianity in Antioch* (New Haven: Yale University Press, 1960), 91–115; M. D. Goulder, 'A Poor Man's Christology', *NTS* 45 (1999), 332–48; Hurtado, *Lord Jesus Christ*, 635–40; M. Rackl, *Die Christologie des heiligen Ignatius von Antiochien*, Freiburger Theologische Studien, 14 (Freiburg im Breisgau: Herdersche Verlagshandlung, 1914); E. Robillard, 'Christologie d'Ignace d'Antioche', in R. Laflamme and M. Gervais (eds.), *Le Christ hier, aujourd'hui et demain* (Quebec: Les Presses de L'Université, 1976), 479–87; I. Saliba, 'The Bishop of Antioch and the Heretics: A Study of a Primitive Christology', *EQ* 54 (1992), 65–76; G. F. Snyder, 'The Historical Jesus in the Letters of Ignatius of Antioch', *BR* 8 (1963), 3–12; C. Story, 'The Christology of Ignatius of Antioch', *EQ* 56 (1984), 173–82; R. D. Young, 'Ignatius of Antioch, "Attaining the Father" ', *Comm* 26 (1999), 333–43.

stolic traditions. The third articulates how Ignatius perceived the unity between the divinity and humanity of Jesus as found primarily within his use of the communication of idioms. Lastly, what has been garnered from all of the above is marshalled to argue that Ignatius' apostolic or New Testament Christology is an initial step down the theological road that will ultimately arrive at the Council of Chalcedon.

THE DIVINITY OF JESUS CHRIST

Ignatius' whole Christology is conceived and articulated from within a soteriological setting.[6] Correctly acknowledging who Jesus is and what he did all bears upon the genuine effecting of human salvation, and to propose a counterfeit Christology completely nullifies, for Ignatius, the reality of that salvation. Thus, the nature of Jesus' divine status is articulated from within the historical and earthly economy, for it is the historical and earthly Jesus, not some ethereal transcendent divinity, such as found in the Gnostics, who secures human salvation. 'For our God, Jesus the Christ, was conceived by Mary according to God's plan (*κατ' οἰκονομίαν θεοῦ*), both from the seed of David and of the Holy Spirit' (*Eph.* 18. 2; see *Eph.* 20. 1).[7] Ignatius articulated his understanding of Jesus' divine status primarily by elucidating descriptively what it means for him to be the Son of the Father and the Word of God.[8]

In harmony with the Pauline corpus Ignatius frequently aligned the Father and Jesus Christ together in such phrases as: '[G]reetings in God the Father and in Jesus Christ' (*Magn.* prol.; see also *Magn.* 1. 2) or 'Farewell in God the Father and in Jesus Christ' (*Eph.* 21. 2). This close configuration is founded upon their singular relationship. Throughout his letters Ignatius highlighted that the Father is uniquely the Father of Jesus Christ (see *Eph.* 2. 1; *Magn.* 3. 1; *Trall.* prol.; 9. 2), and therefore he is the Father's 'only Son (*τοῦ μόνου υἱοῦ αὐτοῦ*)' (*Rom.* prol.).[9] As the only Son, he not only 'came

[6] For some examples of the soteriological setting of Ignatius' Christology see *Eph.* 3; 19; 20; *Magn.* 5. 2; 9; *Trall.* prol.; 2; 13; *Phld.* 5; 11; *Smyrn.* 2; 4; 6. 2; *Pol.* 3. For studies of Ignatius' soteriology see e.g. Corwin, *St. Ignatius*, 154–88, and D. F. Winslow, 'The Idea of Redemption in the Epistles of St. Ignatius of Antioch', *GOTR* 11 (1965), 119–31.

[7] I am employing the Greek text as found in J. B. Lightfoot and J. R. Harmer (eds.), *The Apostolic Fathers: Greek Texts and English Translations of the Writings*, ed. and rev. M. W. Holmes 2nd edn. (Grand Rapids, Mich.: Baker Book House, 1992).

[8] For an excellent study of Ignatius' 'God language' see D. Trakatellis, 'God Language in Ignatius of Antioch', in B. A. Pearson (ed.), *The Future of Early Christianity: Essays in Honor of Helmut Koester* (Minneapolis: Fortress, 1991), 422–30.

[9] This name 'Jesus' conjoined with this title 'Christ' is Ignatius' almost universal manner of referral (112 times).

forth from the one Father (τὸν ἀφ' ἑνὸς πατρὸς προελθόντα)'; he also 'remained with the One and returned to the One (καὶ εἰς ἕνα ὄντα καὶ χωρήσαντα)' (*Magn.* 7. 2). This was an eternal coming forth, for the Son was 'before all ages with the Father (ὃς πρὸ αἰώνων παρὰ πατρὶ ἦν) and appeared at the end of time' (*Magn.* 6. 1). It is not surprising, then, that Ignatius emphasized, within his overarching theme of unity, the unity between the Father and Jesus Christ. Christians are to be united to the bishop as the church is united to Christ and 'as Jesus Christ is with the Father (καὶ Ἰησοῦς Χριστὸς τῷ πατρί)' (*Eph.* 5. 1; see *Smyrn.* 3. 3). Therefore, Christians must be subject to their bishop, 'as Jesus Christ in the flesh was to the Father' (*Magn.* 13. 2).

This intimate relation between the Father and Jesus Christ, in keeping with the Johannine tradition, finds its ultimate expression, for Ignatius, precisely in his being subject to the Father within the economy of salvation. Jesus, 'as the Lord did nothing without the Father either by himself or through his apostles for he was united with him (ἡνωμένος ὤν)' (*Magn.* 7. 1). Again, Christians are to be 'imitators of Jesus Christ, just as he is of his Father' (*Phld.* 7. 2), and all must follow the bishop, 'as Jesus Christ followed the Father' (*Smyrn.* 8. 1).

This doing of the Father's salvific will, for Ignatius, is chiefly witnessed in Jesus being the Word and Wisdom of the Father, and so the revealer and teacher of the Father. Here (I think) Ignatius appears to be both following the Johannine tradition and creatively exploiting it. For Ignatius, there 'is one God who revealed himself through Jesus Christ his Son, who is his Word which came forth from silence (ἀπὸ σιγῆς προελθών), who in every respect pleased him who sent him' (*Magn.* 8. 2). Ignatius' notion is that silence would have prevailed within the world, and so human beings would have been deprived of divine knowledge, if the Word had not come forth from the Father and been sent by the Father into the world to reveal the Father; and it is the Son's revelation of the Father which specifically pleased him. As the Word of the Father, 'Jesus Christ [is] the unerring mouth (ὑμῖν ταῦτα φανερώσει ὅτι ἀληθῶς λέγω τὸ ἀψευδὲς στόμα) by whom the Father has spoken truly' (*Rom.* 8. 2). Moreover, Jesus Christ 'is the mind of the Father (τοῦ πατρὸς ἡ γνώμη)' (*Eph.* 3. 2), and 'all become wise by receiving God's knowledge, which is Jesus Christ' (*Eph.* 17. 2). Jesus Christ is, therefore, 'our only teacher' (*Magn.* 9. 1), who is so powerful that he 'spoke and it happened' and yet 'even the things which he has done in silence are worthy of the Father' (*Eph.* 15. 1). Echoing the Johannine tradition and in harmony with the Letter to the Hebrews, Ignatius stated that Jesus Christ is 'the High Priest entrusted with the Holy of Holies', and he 'alone has been entrusted with the hidden things of God, for he himself is the door of the Father (αὐτὸς ὢν θύρα τοῦ πατρός)', through whom all must enter (*Phld.* 9. 1).

Ignatius' understanding of the relationship between the Father and Jesus Christ, his Son and Word, possesses the authentic ring of the apostolic tradition as found in the New Testament. Even when he is articulating something that is particularly his own, he does not depart significantly from New Testament motifs; rather, his creativity arises specifically from within these various traditions, such as his notion of the Word coming forth from the silence of the Father and so becoming his mouthpiece.

Moreover, while descriptive and functional, Ignatius' apostolic conception of the singular relationship between the Father and the Son/Word confirmed for him that the earthly and historical Jesus Christ as the Son and the Word, unlike other human beings, is divine.[10] Thus, Ignatius effortlessly and spontaneously wove within his understanding of the relationship between the Father and the Son the simple and unequivocal proclamation that Jesus Christ is God. For Ignatius, Jesus Christ is 'our God (*τοῦ θεοῦ ἡμῶν*)' (see *Eph.* prol.; 18. 2; *Rom.* prol.; 3. 3; 6. 3; *Smyrn.* 1. 1; *Pol.* 8. 3). The Lord dwells within Christians, and therefore they are 'his temples and he may be in us as our God (*ἐν ἡμῖν θεὸς ἡμῶν*)' (*Eph.* 15. 3). It has often been noted that, unlike the New Testament, in which *ὁ θεός* is used almost exclusively for the Father, Ignatius unhesitatingly, as the above references testify, effortlessly and, again, spontaneously applied this designation to the Son.[11] Here I would argue that Ignatius is both faithful to the apostolic tradition as witnessed within the New Testament and also accentuates, intensifies, and exploits what is often implicitly, though at times explicitly, contained within that tradition. Moreover, I would equally argue, as I did at the onset, that in this he was not an

[10] Grant states: 'Ignatius is insisting upon the divine function, and also upon the divine nature, of the incarnate Lord, just as certain New Testament writers also insist upon it (John 1:1, 20:28; Heb. 1:8–9; Tit. 2:13; 2 Pet. 1:1)' (*Ignatius*, 8).

[11] Ignatius designates Jesus as 'God' on at least eleven occasions. M. P. Brown states: 'Ignatius does not make a theological issue of this usage; the epithet (i.e., God) is applied casually, for the most part, and apparently without fear of being misunderstood. . . . Thus, it is difficult to avoid the conclusion that the peculiar assignment of *ὁ θεός* to Jesus Christ is unselfconscious' (*The Authentic Writings of Ignatius* (Durham, NC: Duke University Press, 1963), 22). Trakatellis insists that Ignatius' designation of Jesus as God was not 'unselfconscious'; rather, while 'Ignatius "does not make an issue of this usage," he does make a clear statement' ('God Language', 426). Or again, he states: 'Ignatius makes no effort to prove that Jesus Christ is God or to develop apologetic strategies in that direction. He simply issues his high christological statement as a matter of fact, as a truth taken for granted and fully shared by the recipients of his letters' (ibid. 427).

While the New Testament almost always reserves the term *ὁ θεὸς* for the Father, there are a few instances where it could be argued that it refers to Jesus Christ. See Titus 2. 13 (*τοῦ μεγάλου θεοῦ καὶ σωτῆρος ἡμῶν Χριστοῦ Ἰησοῦ*); 1 John 5. 20 (*ἐν τῷ υἱῷ αὐτοῦ Ἰησοῦ Χριστῷ. Οὗτός ἐστιν ὁ ἀληθινὸς θεὸς*); 2 Pet. 1. 1 (*τοῦ θεοῦ ἡμῶν καὶ σωτῆρος Ἰησοῦ Χριστοῦ*); Heb. 1. 8 (*ὁ θρόνος σου ὁ θεὸς*); and John 20. 28 (*ὁ κύριός μου καὶ ὁ θεός μου*). For a discussion of these and other similar passages see R. E. Brown, *An Introduction to New Testament Christology* (New York: Paulist Press, 1994), 171–89.

innovator—that is, that he was not the first to do so. Rather, the very spontaneity with which Ignatius designated Jesus Christ as 'our God', without strained argument or embarrassed defence, bears witness that Christianity, at least as Ignatius knew it, now embraced a fuller appreciation of the apostolic proclamation that Jesus Christ, as Son and Word, is indeed the God of Christians.[12] He has exploited this affirmation in order to refute clearly what he considered to be false perceptions of who Jesus Christ is. *Contra* the Jews, who wish to deny the divinity of Jesus, and *contra* the Gnostics, who acknowledge a whole host of deities, and the Docetists, who refuse to acknowledge Jesus' authentic humanity, Ignatius designates the human Jesus to be *ὁ θεός* of Christians, and thereby shrewdly counters them all.

In closing this section on Ignatius' understanding of the divinity of Jesus Christ, I want to draw one conclusion that is pertinent to my present thesis. By articulating his conception of Jesus Christ's divinity within the apostolic tradition(s) as found within the New Testament, and by exploiting the present interpretation of that tradition by unequivocally affirming that 'Jesus Christ is our God', Ignatius has both intrinsically linked his Christology to that apostolic tradition and simultaneously nudged it vigorously down the doctrinal road to Nicaea and, ultimately, to Chalcedon.

THE HUMANITY OF JESUS CHRIST

As stated previously, the full soteriological significance of Jesus Christ being 'our God' lies specifically, for Ignatius, within the economy—that is, in the authentic reality of the Incarnation, and thus in Jesus' genuine humanity—for it is what he actually underwent as man and the deeds he actually performed as man that are salvific. Our salvation was procured 'when God appeared in human form (*θεοῦ ἀνθρωπίνως φανερουμένου*) to bring the newness of eternal life' (*Eph.* 19. 3). This is articulated primarily in response to the Docetists, who denied the genuineness of the Jesus' humanity, and also, to some extent,

[12] Ignatius frequently calls Jesus Christ 'Lord', which could also be seen, given the New Testament evidence, as a divine title. See *Eph.* 6. 1; 7. 2; 10. 3; 15. 2; 17. 2; *Magn.* 9. 1; 13. 1; *Trall.* 10; *Rom.* 4. 2; *Phld.* 1. 1; 11. 1; *Smyrn.* 1. 1; 4. 2; 5. 2; and *Pol.* prol.; 4. 1; 5. 1; 8. 3.

There are also a few passages in Ignatius' letters which are trinitarian in nature and thus, equally, manifest his belief in the full divinity of Jesus Christ as the Son and the Word of the Father. See *Eph.* 9. 1; *Magn.* 13. 1; and *Phld.* 7.

One might also argue that Ignatius' designation of both God the Father and Jesus Christ as Polycarp's bishop equally affirms Jesus' divine status: *μᾶλλον ἐπισκοπημένῳ ὑπὸ θεοῦ πατρὸς καὶ κυρίου Ἰησοῦ Χριστοῦ, πλεῖστα χαίρειν* (*Pol.* 1. prol.). See also *Eph.* 1. 3 and *Magn.* 3. 1.

against the Gnostics, who separated the Christ from the man Jesus.[13] In keeping with 1 John 2. 22 and 4. 2, Ignatius accused both parties of blasphemy 'by not confessing that he (the Lord) was clothed in flesh (*μὴ ὁμολογῶν αὐτὸν σαρκοφόρον*). Anyone who does not acknowledge this thereby denies him completely and is clothed in a corpse' (*Smyrn.* 5. 2). Thus, Ignatius, while never addressing theologically or philosophically the issue of how God could actually become truly man, consistently, with almost repetitious monotony, asserted the reality of Jesus' humanity, and so the reality of those human experiences undergone within that humanity and the reality of those human deeds performed within that humanity.

Ignatius affirmed, then, Jesus' full humanity, not by constructing an anthropology, but by insisting upon the historicity and physicality of his salvific experiences and actions. For Ignatius, as for Paul, while the cross 'is a stumbling block to unbelievers, [it is] salvation and eternal life to us' (*Eph.* 18. 1). Ignatius himself has 'taken refuge in the gospel as the flesh of Jesus (*ὡς σαρκὶ Ἰησοῦ*)' (*Phil.* 5. 1). For Ignatius, 'the "archives" (*ἀρχεῖά*) are Jesus Christ, the inviolable archives are his cross and death and his resurrection and the faith that comes through him' (*Phld.* 8. 2). The suffering and resurrection were but a part of 'the divine plan with respect to the new man Jesus Christ' (*Eph.* 12. 3, see *Smyrn.* 7).

Within these affirmations, the Magnesians were warned 'not to get snagged by the hooks of worthless opinions'. Rather, they must be fully 'convinced about the birth and the suffering and the resurrection, which took place during the time of the governorship of Pontius Pilate. These things were truly and most assuredly done by Jesus Christ, our hope (*πραχθέντα ἀληθῶς καὶ βεβαίως ὑπὸ Ἰησοῦ Χριστοῦ τῆς ἐλπίδος ἡμῶν*) (*Magn.* 11). Equally, the Trallians were to 'keep away from every strange plant, which is heresy', for such people 'mix Jesus Christ with poison' (*Trall.* 6), and the Philadelphians were not to align themselves with schismatics, for such 'are not the Father's planting', because they have dissociated themselves 'from the Passion' (*Phld.* 3; see *Trall.* 11). He exhorted the Trallians:

> Be deaf, therefore, whenever anyone speaks to you apart from Jesus Christ, who was of the family of David, who was the son of Mary, who really (*ἀληθῶς*) was born, who both ate and drank, who really (*ἀληθῶς*) was persecuted under Pontius Pilate, who really (*ἀληθῶς*) was crucified and died while those in heaven and on earth and under the earth looked on; who, moreover, really (*ἀληθῶς*) was raised from the dead when his Father raised him up, who—his Father, that is—in the same way will likewise

[13] This is probably why Ignatius consistently joined the two together. In speaking of 'Jesus Christ', Ignatius was constantly designating that it was the earthly man Jesus who was the Christ, and not some transcendent deity apart from him.

also raise us up in Christ Jesus who believe in him, apart from whom we have no true life. (*Trall.* 9)

For Ignatius it was ludicrous that he should to be in real chains and on the verge of actual death, if 'these things were done by our Lord in appearance only' (*Smyrn.* 4. 2). It is actually the unbelievers, Ignatius believed, who 'exist in appearance only', who assert that Jesus Christ 'suffered in appearance only (τὸ δοκεῖν πεπονθέναι)' (*Trall.* 10; see also *Smyrn.* 2). Ignatius, like Paul, glorified in 'Jesus Christ, the God who made you [the Smyrnaeans] wise', for they too, in faith, have been nailed to the cross of their Lord Jesus Christ (*Smyrn.* 1. 1). Ignatius was convinced that Jesus was not only in the flesh prior to his death, but that he was also 'in the flesh even after the resurrection'. In accordance with the Lucan and Johannine traditions, the risen Jesus 'ate and drank' with his disciples 'like one who is composed with flesh' and urged them to touch him (*Smyrn.* 3. 3).

Ignatius' insistence upon the human flesh of Jesus found its termination in the Eucharist. Those who refuse to acknowledge Jesus' physical humanity 'abstain from the Eucharist and prayer, because they refuse to acknowledge that the Eucharist is the flesh (σάρκα) of our Saviour Jesus Christ, which suffered for our sins and which the Father by his goodness raised up' (*Smyrn.* 6. 2). What Ignatius desired most is 'the bread of God, which is the flesh of Christ (σὰρξ τοῦ Χριστοῦ) who is of the seed of David, and for drink I want his blood, which is incorruptible love' (*Rom.* 7. 3).[14]

In closing this section I again want to draw a couple of conclusions. First, it is evident that Ignatius' understanding of Jesus' humanity is the same as that expressed in the New Testament. One clearly perceives echoes of (or similarities with) Matthew, Luke, John, and 1 John, as well as phrases and ideas that bear the voice of Paul. Even if Ignatius was acquainted merely with their various apostolic traditions, yet the traditions that he was defending were theirs. Thus, Ignatius' Christology, when it bears upon Jesus' authentic physical reality and the actual historicity of his life, is genuinely apostolic in origin, content, and expression. Secondly, as with his understanding of the divinity of Jesus Christ, Ignatius did not merely repeat the apostolic tradition; he also moulded it so as to affirm it against erroneous tenets.[15] It is here, more than in his clear affirmation that Jesus Christ is 'our God', that Ignatius has become, I believe, truly an innovator, in that he has made an original contribution that is particularly his own. While the apostolic tradition

[14] For further references and allusions to the Eucharist and the physical reality of Jesus' presence, see *Eph.* 20. 2; *Trall.* 8. 1; *Smyrn.* 12. 2; and *Phld.* 4.

[15] Trakatellis states that Ignatius 'evidently did not invent his Christology... What Ignatius did was to interpret the Johannine and the Pauline christological traditions or formulas in a way that could serve the immediate and pressing needs of the church' ('God Language', 430).

provided him with his faith in the historical and physical Jesus, it was Ignatius who now clearly articulated that it is precisely the historical events (*contra* the Gnostics) of Jesus' fleshly birth, death, and resurrection (*contra* the Docetists) that are salvific. For Ignatius, the authenticity, the genuineness, the efficaciousness, and the reality of humankind's salvation is predicated, intrinsically and necessarily, upon the authenticity, the genuineness, the efficaciousness, and the historical reality of Jesus' incarnation, life, death, and resurrection. While this causal connection is embedded within the apostolic tradition of the New Testament—for example, in Rom. 5–8 and the Letter to the Hebrews—it was Ignatius who unearthed it for all to see. Thirdly, what is equally evident again is that, while he was clearly tethered to the Christology of the apostolic tradition as found within the New Testament, Ignatius has tugged it further along the road to Chalcedon. Already within Ignatius' stress upon the reality and historicity of the Incarnation one finds some of the foundational principles and central arguments later employed by Irenaeus in his refutation of the Gnostics.[16] Moreover, the whole soteriological setting of Ignatius' Christology, whereby the human experiences and historical actions of 'our God' effect a newness of life with the Father, foreshadows the Irenaean and Athanasian tenet that God came in the likeness of man that man might become the likeness of God.[17] Likewise, incubating within his Christology is the theological refutation of Apollinarius' denial of Christ's human soul and the prophetic clue to Gregory of Nazianzus' maxim that 'what is not assumed is not healed/saved'.[18]

THE ONENESS OF JESUS CHRIST

Thus far I have argued that Ignatius' Christology bears the indelible imprint of the apostolic tradition as witnessed within the New Testament in a twofold manner. (1) He affirmed that Jesus Christ, as the Son and the Word of the Father, is 'our God'. (2) He equally affirmed the reality of Jesus Christ's physical humanity and all that authentically pertains historically to such a humanity. Moreover, in confirming and, most of all, in defending these two christological truths of apostolic origin against what he considered to be the counterfeit gospels of the Judaizers, the Gnostics, and the Docetists, Ignatius advanced the authentic understanding and interpretation of the apostolic

[16] See, e.g., Irenaeus, *Adv. Haer.* 3. 18. 6–7 and 4. 20. 4.
[17] See ibid. 5. praef., and Athanasius, *De Incarn.* 54.
[18] See Gregory of Nazianzus, *Ep.* 101. 4.

christological tradition. Now where all this finds its cumulative effect, and in so doing proceeds to a new depth of meaning and insight, is in Ignatius' employment of what came to be termed 'the communication of idioms'.[19] For Ignatius it is one and the same Jesus Christ who *is* both 'Son of God' and 'Son of man'; thus he instinctively recognized that the authentic attributes of each are properly and necessarily predicated of that one and the same Jesus Christ (see *Eph.* 20. 2). Moreover, these passages have the feel of being part of an already existing tradition, for Ignatius employed them spontaneously and effortlessly without providing any intimation of their needing to be defended or displaying any symptoms of embarrassment at their use. While he used them to address his immediate concerns, they are, then, not entirely his own creations. In other words, Ignatius was not the originator of such theological linguistic expressions; rather, he was utilizing a manner of speaking that was readily available to him.[20]

Ignatius thus assured the Ephesian Christians that they had assumed a new life 'through the blood of God (ἐν αἵματι θεοῦ)' (*Eph.* 1. 1). This is a striking and even scandalous phrase. First, God can only truly possess human blood if he has actually become a human being. What the communication of idioms does linguistically, then, is to conjoin the two christological truths of Jesus Christ's divinity and humanity so as to express the ontological oneness of who Jesus is as the Son or the Word of God existing as man. This phrase, as are all instances of the communication of idioms, is an arresting alignment of seemingly clashing words with their seemly irreconcilable meanings ('blood' and 'God') that accentuates the reality of the Incarnation; that is, only if the divine Son of God did actually become man and so exist as man, does such an alignment make theological sense and possess any literal meaning. Thus the communication of idioms testifies to the truth that the incarnational 'becoming' actually terminates in an incarnational 'is'. Secondly, this particular

[19] The term 'communication of idioms' was first used in its Greek form in the sixth century by those who wanted to defend the definition of the Council of Chalcedon. The Latin form, taken from the Greek, was not in use until sometime in the Middle Ages.

[20] The scriptural basis for the communication of idioms might be found in such Pauline passages as Rom. 1. 2–4; 2 Cor. 8. 9; Gal. 4. 4; Phil. 2. 5–11; Col. 1. 15–20. A. Grillmeier holds that the communication of idioms became popular around the time when the Christian books (particularly book 6) were added to the *Sibylline Oracles*, which was sometime in the second century (see *Christ in Christian Tradition*, i (London: Mowbrays, 1975), 63). In book 6 is found the proclamation: 'O blessed tree, on which God was hung!'

I have argued elsewhere that 'the whole of orthodox patristic Christology, including the conciliar affirmations, can be seen as an attempt to defend the practice and to clarify the use of the communication of idioms' (*Does God Suffer?* (Edinburgh: T. & T. Clark, 2000), 175). See also my 'Cyril and the Mystery of the Incarnation', in T. Weinandy and D. Keating (eds.), *The Theology of St. Cyril of Alexandria: A Critical Appreciation* (London: T. & T. Clark/Continuum, 2003), 31.

phrase also alludes to the shedding of God's blood, which would scandalize the Docetists, but which, for Ignatius, would strikingly portray the grandeur of the Christian gospel. Moreover, for Ignatius, Christians derive their true existence from Jesus' 'divinely blessed suffering (θεομακαρίστου αὐτοῦ πάθους)' (*Smyrn.* 1. 2). This phrase too attests that what makes Jesus' suffering blessed, and so salvific, is precisely that it was the divine Son of God who endured it; but he could only have endured such suffering if he had truly existed as a human being. Ignatius himself desired to imitate 'the suffering of my God (τοῦ πάθους τοῦ θεοῦ μου)' (*Rom.* 6. 3). Again, God could humanly suffer only if he actually became a man, and Ignatius desired to imitate 'the suffering of my God' so as to achieve precisely what that human suffering endured by God attained—eternal life.

Besides these phrases that accentuate the reality of the Incarnation, and so the ontological unity of the divinity and humanity in the one Jesus Christ, Ignatius also employed a couple of what might be termed rhythmical or poetic semi-credal proclamations the purpose of which is to accentuate this incarnational oneness. Thus, he exhorted Polycarp to 'wait expectantly for him who is above time: the Eternal, the Invisible (τὸν ἄχρονον, τὸν ἀόρατον), who for our sake became visible (ὁρατόν); the Intangible, the Unsuffering (τὸν ἀψηλάφητον, τὸν ἀπαθῆ), who for our sake suffered (παθητόν), who for our sake endured in every way' (*Pol.* 3. 2).[21] Clearly there is here present only one subject, one 'who', who is eternal, invisible, intangible, and unsuffering, but who, equally, because of the Incarnation, became visible and suffered for our sake. Here divine and human attributes are predicated of one and the same subject, and such an attribution finds it legitimacy in the reality of the Incarnation.

Moreover, for Ignatius 'there is only one physician, who is both flesh and spirit, born and unborn, God in man, true life in death, both from Mary and from God, first subject to suffering and then beyond it, Jesus Christ our Lord (ἕις ἰατρός ἐστιν, σαρκικὸς καὶ πνευματικός, γεννητὸς καὶ ἀγέννητος, ἐν ἀνθρώπῳ θεός, ἐν θανάτῳ ζωὴ ἀληθινή, καὶ ἐκ Μαρίας καὶ ἐκ θεοῦ, πρῶτον παθητὸς καὶ τότε ἀπαθής, Ἰησοῦς Χριστὸς ὁ κύριος ἡμῶν)' (*Eph.* 7. 2). This is the most celebrated example of Ignatius' use of the communication of idioms.[22] There is one subject, in that there is 'one physician' who is 'Jesus Christ our Lord'. Yet, the physician Jesus Christ possesses both 'flesh' in so far as he actually is man and 'spirit' in so far as he actually is God. He is actually 'born', in that he is from Mary as man, and he is actually 'unborn' in that he is

[21] For scriptural, philosophical, and early patristic parallels to this passage, see Schoedel, *Ignatius*, 267–8.

[22] Schoedel sees once again some semi-creedal formulae in this passage. See Schoedel, *Ignatius*, 60.

eternally from God the Father. He is 'true life' even 'in death', because the one who died as man is the living God. While Jesus Christ was 'first subject to suffering' as a human being like us, he has now passed beyond it as a risen man. Ignatius' ontological basis for this juxtaposition of divine and human attributes lies precisely in that Jesus is 'God in man'—that is, in the authentic reality of the Incarnation.

IGNATIUS AND THE COUNCIL OF CHALCEDON

The above demonstrates that Ignatius employed the communication of idioms, as would his descendants, to ensure the reality of the Incarnation, and in so doing to ensure the reality of the salvific events associated with the Incarnation. The fact that Ignatius did have descendants is of the utmost significance for my thesis. He anticipated and even embodied within his own Christology later controversies and doctrinal development. In light of the subsequent christological history, what Ignatius did was to lift the apostolic christological tradition of the New Testament upon his shoulders and carry it, being joined along the way by many Fathers, especially Athanasius and Cyril of Alexandria, to the very doorstep of the Council of Ephesus, and then by way of Ephesus into the very inner sanctum of the Council of Chalcedon.[23]

On one level the above statement may be an anachronistic exaggeration. Ignatius did not display, philosophically or theologically, the christological refinements of the later Fathers and Councils. Nowhere did he speak of one *prosopon* or of one *hypostasis*; nor did he employ the concepts of *ousia* and *phusis*. None the less, I am convinced that Ignatius would not have felt out of place or out of his depth either at Nicaea or at Ephesus or Chalcedon. His understanding of the singular relationship between the Father and the Son, which found its most concise formulation in the simple truth that 'Jesus Christ is our God', would have allowed him to give his immediate assent to the

[23] Significant for my thesis is Schoedel's statement: 'In Ignatius . . . flesh and spirit represent two spheres or two dimensions that refer to human and divine reality respectively. We have here the kernel of the later two-nature christologies' (*Ignatius*, 60). He also writes with respect to this passage: 'When Ignatius refers to Christ as "both fleshly and spiritual, he has in mind the union of the divine and human in the God-Man and thus anticipates the classical two-nature-christology" (ibid. 20). Likewise, Hurtado states: "His [Ignatius'] letters are also noteworthy for expressions of faith that anticipate, and perhaps influenced, subsequent developments in formative orthodox doctrine about Jesus' (*Lord Jesus Christ*, 635). Or again he writes: "[I]t is fairly clear that he [Ignatius] represents the profound commitment to Jesus' divinity and real human existence that demanded those efforts toward the distinctive Christian idea of God, and especially toward the idea of Jesus' "two natures," doctrinal efforts that heavily occupied the developing orthodox/catholic tradition well through the fourth century' (ibid. 640).

Nicene Creed's declaration that the Son is 'God from God, Light from Light, true God from true God, begotten not made, one in being with the Father', even if he, along with many others, might have struggled hard to explain the exact meaning of the term *homoousios*. His adamant defence of the historical and physical humanity of Jesus would have easily allowed him to champion the constituency that condemned Apollinarius. Moreover, he would have had no doubt that Mary was *Theotokos*, for he himself had asserted that the Son, who was eternally with the Father and so unborn, was the same Son who was born of Mary. Ignatius would have eagerly taken up arms over the issue surrounding the christological legitimacy of the communication of idioms, for he was present on the field of battle long before Nestorius and Cyril had sounded the trumpets of war. Lastly, while I am sure that he would have been awed by the christological sophistication of Chalcedon's Creed, yet Ignatius would have felt very comfortable in professing it, for it bears the imprint of his own faith—one and the same Son is truly God and truly man, and thus both divine and human attributes can properly be predicated of that one and the same Son. Equally, Ignatius' employment of the communication of idioms demonstrates that, while the attributes pertaining to God and man are united in the one and the same subject of Jesus Christ, and so are not separated and divided, neither the divinity nor the humanity is changed or confused.

Now it is the one and the same Ignatius of Antioch, whom I believe concluded his journey, by way of the christological tradition, at the Council of Chalcedon who is the one and the same Ignatius of Antioch who began his journey within the apostolic christological tradition of the New Testament. Thus it is this same Ignatius, along with many subsequent Fathers, who pioneered the route between the faith of the apostles and the faith of the Fathers at Chalcedon. Obviously, while it is a significant milestone in the history of Christology, Chalcedon is not Land's End. The history of christological development continues through the centuries up to the present and beyond, and with it the same continuity of faith continues its apostolic journey as well. Thus Ignatius, whose Christology takes its departure from within the earliest apostolic tradition, continues to be a fellow apostolic pilgrim.

5

Wisdom in the Apostolic Fathers and the New Testament

Frances Young

In many and various ways wisdom appears to be a key concept in the early church. By the time of Augustine, it has spiritual and intellectual connotations, as well as christological significance,[1] both of these aspects of wisdom having roots in the Bible and earlier tradition. The figure of personified Wisdom, as described in Proverbs 8, was at the centre of the doctrinal controversy initiated by Arius in the fourth century.[2] From the second century on, wisdom figured in Gnostic myths, and so, being contested, was ripe for reclamation or resistance by those claiming to be orthodox. Scholarly literature suggests that in various ways wisdom is important in the New Testament. So it seemed a natural research question to ask: what about wisdom in the texts known as the 'Apostolic Fathers'? The results were a surprise. It may be that they demand a reassessment of some classic scholarly assumptions.

THE VIRTUAL ABSENCE OF *SOPHIA*

The word σοφία ('wisdom') is absent from the *Didache*, and its absence from *2 Clement*, the *Martyrdom of Polycarp*, and the *Epistle to Diognetus* is also worth noting if, as convention would dictate, we count them among the Apostolic Fathers. Σοφία is almost entirely absent from the letters of Ignatius. Virtually the only occasion when he uses a form of the word is in *Smyrn.* 1, where God is described as τὸν οὕτως ὑμᾶς σοφίσαντα—the one who has thus

[1] See my paper, 'Wisdom in Augustine's *De Doctrina Christiana*', forthcoming in *St Patr* Also, Carol Harrison, 'Augustine, Wisdom and Classical Culture', in S. C. Barton (ed.), *Where shall Wisdom be Found?* (Edinburgh: T. & T. Clark, 1999), 125–37.

[2] See my article, 'Proverbs 8 in Interpretation (2): Wisdom Personified. Fourth Century Readings: Assumptions and Debates', in D. F. Ford and G. N. Stanton (eds.), *Reading Texts, Seeking Wisdom* (London: SCM Press, 2003), 102–15.

made you wise. The proof of this is said to be their firm faith 'as if nailed to the cross of the Lord Jesus Christ'. One is tempted to wonder whether the expression is not reminiscent of 1 Cor. 1. 18 ff., where God's wisdom is associated with the foolishness of the cross. In *Eph.* 18, Ignatius certainly alludes to this passage: 'Where is the wise? (ποῦ σοφός;) Where is the debater? Where is the boasting of those who are said to have understanding?'

Polycarp's *Epistle to the Philippians* provides only one instance. He claims (3. 2) that he is writing at their invitation, because neither he nor any other like him is able to follow τῇ σοφίᾳ τοῦ μακαρίου καὶ ἐνδόξου Παύλου—the wisdom of the blessed and glorious Paul, who when present taught the word of truth and when absent wrote letters, 'from the study of which you will be able to build yourselves up into the faith given you'. Hermas likewise provides only one instance (*Vis.* 1. 3): remembering the last words the lady read to him, he describes God as the one who by his mighty power and understanding created the world, and by his own wisdom (σοφία) and foresight created his Holy Church.

There is a little more in *1 Clement.* In urging humble-mindedness, he wrote: 'Let not the wise man boast in his wisdom, nor the strong in his strength, nor the rich in his riches; but let the one who boasts boast in the Lord' (13. 1), so quoting Jer. 9. 23–4 and recalling Paul in 1 Cor. 1. 31 and 2 Cor. 10. 17. In assembling a list of exemplary humble characters (*1 Clem.* 18), the author mentions David (18. 2–17) and quotes Ps. 51. 1–17, which includes 'you revealed to me the secrets of your wisdom'. So far, then, wisdom appears incidentally in scriptural quotations which are actually focusing on other things. In *1 Clem.* 32 we find a statement again reminiscent of Paul:

> And so we, who have been called by his will through Jesus Christ, are not justified by ourselves, nor by our wisdom or understanding or piety or the works we do in holiness of heart, but through faith, by which Almighty God has justified all from the beginning.

And in *1 Clem.* 38, in a series of exhortations, we read: 'Let the wise display his wisdom not in words but in good deeds.' Such statements put wisdom, or rather the wise, in their place—so too, in *1 Clem. 48*, where a person who is faithful, or who has the power to speak knowledge, or is wise in debating with words, or pure in deeds, is expected to be the more humble-minded the more great he seems. On the other hand, in *1 Clem.* 39, a long quotation from Job includes the comment that 'they died for lack of wisdom'; and eventually *1 Clem.* introduces a long quotation from Proverbs, spoken by what he calls ἡ πανάρετος σοφία—the all-perfect wisdom, which includes: 'The evil will seek and not find me. For they hated wisdom, and did not choose the fear of the Lord' (*1 Clem.* 57. 5, quoting Prov. 1. 23–33). Overall, it almost seems as if this long passage from Proverbs provides the 'text' for the whole of the exhortation in this epistle. Clement goes on: Let us be obedient to his most holy and glorious name, so escaping the threats spoken by wisdom to the unfaithful...(58. 1). In *1 Clement*, wisdom is the fear of the Lord, and it is found in humility.

Barnabas also refers to wisdom a number of times. He suggests (5. 3) that we should give great thanks to the Lord, because he has made known to us what has happened, made us wise (ἐσόφισεν) for the present, and we are not without understanding for the future. Later (6. 10) he proclaims: 'Blessed be our Lord who lays within us the foundation of wisdom (σοφία) and understanding of his secrets.' It would seem that this is insight into the prophetic, or christological, meaning of the scriptures, as he goes on: 'For the prophet speaks a parable of the Lord—"Who shall understand, except the one who is wise (σοφός) and understanding and loving of his Lord?" ' Right at the end, however, wisdom is associated with faithfulness and obedience, as the author signs off with a prayer that God might give the readers wisdom (σοφία), understanding, shrewdness, knowledge of his commandments, and patience. This echoes words near the beginning, where fear and patience, together with long-suffering and continence, are described as helpers of our faith, with the added comment that as long as these stay focused on the Lord in purity, wisdom (σοφία), understanding, learning, and knowledge rejoice.

A WIDER SAPIENTIAL VOCABULARY?

These latter lists of words associated with wisdom are important, and they alert us to pursue our researches further than mere use of the word conventionally translated 'wisdom'. The opening of the book of Proverbs associates with 'wisdom' a range of more or less synonymous words and ideas, and some of these are more prolific in the Apostolic Fathers than the sparse usage we have found by confining attention to σοφία. Daniel Harrington has noted the importance for understanding Qumran wisdom of what he calls the 'sapiential vocabulary' provided by Proverbs, and lists from Prov. 1. 2–7 the following: 'wisdom, instruction, understanding, wise dealing, righteousness, justice, equity, shrewdness, knowledge, prudence, learning, skill and so forth'. In addition he notes the importance of 'fear of the Lord'.[3] The LXX version of these verses in Proverbs alerts us to look for παιδεία (education or training),

[3] Daniel J. Harrington, *Wisdom Texts from Qumran* (London and New York: Routledge, 1996), 8.

φρονῆσις (intellect), δικαιοσύνη (righteousness), κρίμα (judgement, in the sense of assessment that is straight and true), πανουργία (cleverness), αἴσθησις (perception), ἔννοια (thought), σύνεσις (understanding), and εὐσέβεια (godliness, piety). In addition, one might highlight again the definition of wisdom as 'fear of the Lord', and note that the wise person grasps the sense of a proverb or parable (παραβολή in the Greek of the LXX, while the book of Proverbs is called παροιμίαι), a dark word (σκοτεινὸς λογός), and sayings of the wise and their riddles (αἰνίγματα). Pursuing all this in the Apostolic Fathers, we might find that the wider characterization of wisdom in Proverbs informs these texts, as it does those found at Qumran. For clearly the ethical dimension is paramount, and so is the discernment of the real intention of metaphorical and parabolic speech, at least in *Barnabas*.

1 Clement and *Barnabas*, however, remain the only significant texts for our enquiry. We find a few more hints where we found little or no reference to wisdom as such. *Σύνεσις* (understanding) appears in Hermas (*Sim.* 9. 22) as the opposite of foolishness, and in Ignatius it is something Polycarp should pray for (*Pol.* 1. 3), as well to be φρόνιμος (clever) as a serpent (clearly an allusion to the saying also found in the gospels at Matt. 10. 16). Both Hermas and the *Didache* address their advice Proverbs-like to 'my child', and the *Didache* links acceptable teaching to δικαιοσύνη (righteousness) and γνῶσις (knowledge) of the Lord. This draws on the lists of presumed synonyms we noted in *Barnabas*, though the constellation of words in Proverbs omits γνῶσις (knowledge) and includes παιδεία rather than διδαχή (teaching). We find occasional quotations and allusions to Proverbs and other wisdom texts in Hermas, as well as Ignatius, the letter of Polycarp, and the *Didache*. Hermas is clear that 'fear of the Lord' is fundamental: *Mand.* 7 develops the idea that there are two sorts of fear: fear of the devil and fear of the Lord, which is 'powerful and great and glorious', enabling you to avoid evil and do good. But overall there is very little apart from the presumption that the Two Ways in the *Didache*, not to mention other paraenetical collages, may owe something to sapiential traditions, and a few other marginal features which parallel things we shall note in 1 Clement.

1 Clement

The opening paragraphs of *1 Clement* associate 'perfect and secure knowledge (γνῶσις)' with a piety (εὐσέβεια) that is sober (σώφρων) and modest (ἐπιεικής), having the commandments (προστάγματα) and ordinances (δικαιώματα) of the Lord written on the tablet of their hearts. That last phrase comes from Prov. 7. 3, and the words used overlap with those in Prov. 1. 1–3, without reproducing the exact list. The recipients of the letter are told that once they were like that, but now the foolish have risen against the *φρονίμοι* (intelligent), and because of this, righteousness is absent, and each has deserted the 'fear of God' (*1 Clem.* 3, 7). The foolish (*ἄφρονες*) and mindless (*ἀνοήτοι*) are exalted and boast in the pride of their words rather than in God. They should display a pure life-style, with modesty in speech. So material similar to the Proverbs constellation is followed by a contrast between the wise and foolish such as characterizes chapters 1–9 of that biblical book.

The polarization of foolishness and fear of the Lord recurs in *1 Clem.* 21, where we also find the warning, so characteristic of the Pastorals and the Apostolic Fathers, that God is a searcher of thoughts and desires, a point grounded in a quotation from Prov. 20. 27: 'The Spirit of the Lord is a lamp searching the inward parts.' God is so near that nothing of our thoughts or inner discussions escapes him. Gentleness of tongue is to be evident in silence. *Παιδεία* (instruction) is to form children in the ways of humility and pure love before God, as well as fear of him. This letter focuses on instruction and training in the right way, again reflecting the thrust, if not the text, of Proverbs. In the following paragraph, for example, we are told that God calls us in these words: 'Come, children, listen to me and I will teach you fear of the Lord'—and the rest of Ps. 34. 11–17 follows, with the addition of Ps. 32. 10—psalm material that mirrors the characteristics of the 'wisdom' of Proverbs in its suggestion that life and prosperity follow from fear of the Lord, which involves keeping the tongue from evil, doing good, and seeking peace, aware that the eyes of the Lord are on the righteous and his ears open to their prayers, while the face of the Lord is against those who do evil. The slip into Psalm 32 reinforces this by paralleling the quotation,

> Many are the torments of the wicked
> But mercy surrounds those who hope in the Lord,

with the verse from Psalm 34,

> The righteous has called to the Lord, and the Lord heard.
> And rescued him from all his troubles.

The explicit references to the Psalms are a clue to the source of another pervasive emphasis in this and other texts among the Apostolic Fathers, especially the *Shepherd*: namely, the insistence on a 'single mind' (*ἁπλῆ διανοία*) and the avoidance of double-mindedness (*μὴ διψυχῶμεν*). Yet it seems at first sight probable that the overall tradition of 'wisdom' is what informs the notion of the mind being fixed on God, seeking the things that are well-pleasing and acceptable to God, following in the way of his truth, and casting away all unrighteousness and wickedness, greed, strife, bad habits and trickery, gossip and malice, pride and arrogance, hatred of God and love of empty glory, with lack of hospitality (*1 Clem.* 35). Through a check on where scriptural quotations come from, the presence of this 'wisdom' character seems the more apparent: Proverbs, Job, Sirach, and Wisdom of Solomon are all utilized. However, the fact is that both the Psalms and the Law and the Prophets are quoted more frequently. The extent to which so many of the quotations seem to serve this overall 'wisdom' outlook is interesting. You might say the Scriptures are read for a *paraenesis* shaped by the wisdom traditions. Or is it rather that the generic distinctions so beloved of modern scholars were not explicit for the early Christians?[4] Anything that supported the ethical advice was exploited—the biblical narratives becoming models of good behaviours like repentance, or bad characteristics like jealousy and envy, alongside the use of maxims and commandments, and all exploited without differentiation.

The overall perspective we have explored in *1 Clement* has a theological dimension (*1 Clem.* 33, 60). It was by his infinite power that the Creator fixed the heavens, and by an understanding (*σύνεσις*) beyond our grasp that he set them in order. As for humankind, he shaped it in the stamp of his own image, as the best and greatest of his creatures according to his intellect (*κατὰ διάνοιαν*). God is wise (*σοφός*) in his creating and understanding (*συνετός*) in establishing what has come into being, as well as faithful, righteous, and gracious. The *paraenesis* seeks to form divine qualities in believers, the object being to please God with lives lived in holiness, righteousness, faith, repentance, love, self-control, truth, patience, long-suffering, concord, peace, gentleness, humility. The basis of due order in worship and service is the fact that 'we have looked into the depths of divine knowledge (*τὰ βάθη τῆς θείας γνώσεως*)' (*1 Clem.* 40). It is through Christ that 'we fix our gaze on the heights of heaven', through him that 'the eyes of our heart have been opened', through him that 'our foolish and darkened mind (*ἡ ἀσύνετος καὶ ἐσκοτωμένη διάνοια*) blossoms towards the light', through him that 'the Master wished us to taste immortal knowledge (*ἡ ἀθάνατος γνῶσις*)' (*1 Clem.* 36). The way to salvation is through Jesus Christ.

[4] Cf. S. Weeks, 'Wisdom in the Old Testament' in Barton (ed.), *Where shall Wisdom be Found?*, 19–30. He deconstructs the idea of the wisdom literature as a distinct biblical genre, suggesting that the 'wisdom tradition' is a 'modern construct' (p. 21). We should also note, perhaps, the fact that the 'sapiential texts' from Qumran, as well as those from Hellenistic Judaism, appear to conflate wisdom with Torah or Halakah, while wisdom elements appear in the community 'rule-books'. (See the essays by G. J. Brooke, D. J. Harrington, and C. Hempel in C. Hempel, A. Lange, and H. Lichtenberger (eds.), *The Wisdom Texts from Qumran and the Development of Sapiential Thought*, BETL 159 (Leuven: Peeters, 2002). It is also well known that wisdom elements appear in apocalyptic. (See, e.g., the essays in the same volume by P. S. Alexander and L. T. Stuckenbruck, as well as those by L. T. Stuckenbruck and C. C. Rowland in *Where shall Wisdom be Found?*)

The strange thing is, however, that there is no trace of a Wisdom Christology in this letter.[5] Christ is a model of the humble-mindedness the author wishes to encourage, and Isa. 53 is quoted at length to show that (*1 Clem.* 16). Soon after (*1 Clem.* 18), David fulfils the same role with a long quotation from Ps. 51, and between these two passages, the examples of Elijah, Elisha and Ezekiel, Abraham, Job, and Moses are called in to make the same point, though all of these are said to be heralding the coming of Christ (*1 Clem.* 17). Mostly, the author appeals simply to the blood of Christ, poured out for our salvation (*1 Clem.* 7, 21, 49), to Christ as the defender and helper of our weakness (*1 Clem.* 36), or as our High Priest and guardian (*1 Clem.* 36, 59), through whom God chose us to be his own people (*1 Clem.* 64). God's 'beloved child', Jesus Christ, called us from darkness to light, from ignorance to full knowledge (ἐπίγνωσις) of the glory of his name (*1 Clem.* 59); through him, God taught us and sanctified us. Allusion to the teaching of Jesus is occasionally made, notably in *1 Clem.* 13:

> Be merciful that you may obtain mercy; forgive that you may be forgiven; as you do, so it will be done to you; as you give, so it will be given you; as you judge, so you will be judged; as you do good, so good will be done to you; by what measure you measure, it will be measured to you.

To this is added an exhortation to walk in obedience; and a quote from Isaiah is introduced with the words, 'for the holy word says', clearly meaning the Scriptures. The Christology of *1 Clement* gets nowhere near a Wisdom or Logos Christology—and this despite the evident knowledge of at least some Pauline Epistles, and the clear knowledge of Proverbs.

So, among the Apostolic Fathers, *1 Clement* is one of only two texts which use the 'wisdom' word, σοφία, a certain amount. A wider trawl of sapiential vocabulary and characteristics increases the sense that *1 Clement* is indebted to wisdom traditions. Yet the collages of scriptural allusions suggest that wisdom may not be identified as a particular genre, and there is no development of Christology in terms of the divine Wisdom.

The Epistle of Barnabas

As we have already noted, *Barnabas* associates σοφία (wisdom), σύνεσις (understanding), ἐπιστήμη (learning), and γνῶσις (knowledge). Furthermore, this author links all of these virtually synonymous qualities with

[5] For fuller discussion of *1 Clement's* Christology, see Harold Bertram Bumpus, *The Christological Awareness of Clement of Rome and its Sources* (University Press of Cambridge, 1972). This study draws attention to the narrowing of the range of christological titles in *1 Clement* compared with the New Testament, and focuses on Clement's use of κύριος, together with the blood theme, the servant theme and the High Priest theme. Overall, Clement's Christology is characterized as functional.

knowing the meaning of things, past, present, and future. Much of his treatise is engaged in interpreting what he identifies as prophetic words and signs. In the midst of this process, he inserts comments like 'I write to you more simply so that you may understand (συνιῆτε)' (*Barn.* 6. 5), or 'Learn what knowledge (γνῶσις) says' (6. 9), or 'Blessed be our Lord, brothers, who has placed in us wisdom (σοφία) and understanding (νοῦς) of his secrets' (6. 10). Later certain Mosaic laws (called δόγματα by the author) are given allegorical interpretations, and in introducing them the author asserts that David was given knowledge (γνῶσις) of these three teachings, and proceeds to quote texts to show this. This is the way in which this author fulfils Proverbs' interest in understanding the dark sayings of the wise. It would seem not to differentiate scriptural genres into law, prophecy, and wisdom.

On the whole, scriptural allusions and references in this text are to the Law and the Prophets, and to the Psalms. There are a few quotations from Proverbs and possible allusions to the Wisdom of Solomon, but Isaiah is quoted against those who trust in their own understanding and learning. There is exhortation to practise the fear of the Lord, but to this is added the need to strive to keep his commandments—for he will judge without respect of persons (*Barn.* 4. 11–12). Again, then, as in the case of *1 Clement*, one must ask whether there is any conscious awareness of 'wisdom' as a distinct genre.

The Two Ways tradition would seem to confirm the sense that scripture is used in undifferentiated ways. The Way of Light (*Barn.* 19) clearly enjoins a pattern of life very similar to that recommended in *1 Clement*, drawing upon a range of scriptural sources: in a rapid survey, we note that it covers the following ground—to love and fear one's Creator, to glorify one's Redeemer, and not to take the Lord's name in vain; to be simple in heart and not double-minded, to hate what is not pleasing to God, and to refuse to desert the commandments; to be humble-minded and not exalt oneself, avoid specified sexual sins, not bear malice, love one's neighbour more than one's own soul, not practice infanticide or covet one's neighbours' goods, not cause quarrels, and remember that God's judgement is to be faced. The Way of the Black One is the converse—idolatry, for example, hypocrisy, double-heartedness, adultery, murder, pride, self-sufficiency, lack of fear of God. True, the Two Ways (both here and in the *Didache*) reflect the kind of moral dualism found in the wisdom texts of the Dead Sea Scrolls and adumbrated by the Proverbs contrast between Wisdom and Folly.[6] True, it is Proverbs that speaks of walking in the way of the good and keeping to the paths of righteousness

[6] Harrington, *Wisdom Texts*, 34–5, 52 ff.

(2. 20), and *Barnabas* sums up by saying 'It is good to learn all the written ordinances (δικαιώματα) of the Lord and walk in them... May God who rules the whole earth, give you wisdom, understanding, learning, knowledge of his ordinances, patience.' But surely it is the whole scriptural picture of God's providential plans, prophetic utterances, and commandments that *Barnabas* has in mind. Furthermore, both the Dead Sea Scrolls and these texts from the Apostolic Fathers put their wisdom injunctions into an eschatological framework,[7] which is not characteristic of the sapiential literature of the Bible, and implies a conflation of many genres.

As in the case of *1 Clement*, we find little trace of a Wisdom or Logos Christology in this text. The only hint is a reference to the 'glory of Jesus, for all things are in him and for him' (*Barn.* 12. 7), which is a statement very similar to those taken to imply a cosmic 'wisdom' idea in the New Testament. However, there is no mention of wisdom, and the question is: to what does the phrase 'all things' refer? It could be all the riches of salvation in Christ. The following statement focuses on the fact that he is not to be seen 'as son of man but as Son of God manifested in a type in the flesh'; but here and elsewhere in this epistle, the emphasis is on 'types' of the cross. He endured corruption, so that we might be sanctified through his sprinkled blood and become heirs of the covenant (*Barn.* 5, *passim*; note the elaborate development of 'types' of his sacrificial death, etc.). He is the Son of God, destined to judge the living and the dead, one who could not suffer except for our sakes (*Barn.* 7, *passim*; here the types of Isaac, the sin offering, and the Day of Atonement are developed, leading to the red heifer in *Barn.* 8). This elaborates the message stated from the beginning: that our Lord Jesus Christ abolished sacrifice and brought a new law (2. 6), a new covenant, sealed in our hearts (4. 8). The people of the new covenant celebrate not on the sabbath but on the eighth day, when 'Jesus rose from the dead, was made manifest and ascended to heaven' (15. 9). When we received the remission of sins, we became new, created again from the beginning, and God truly dwells in us, as in a spiritual temple. In explaining how this happens, the author speaks of 'his word of faith, the calling of his promise, the wisdom (σοφία) of his ordinances, the commandments of his teaching (διδαχή)', adding also the fact of his prophesying and dwelling in us, of his opening the door of the temple to those enslaved to sin and giving us repentance (*Barn.* 16). As elsewhere in the Apostolic Fathers, it is the saving work of Christ which takes centre stage, in a work that has ethical interest at its heart.

[7] Ibid., 51–2, 70–3. See also material cited in n. 4.

WISDOM IN THE APOSTOLIC FATHERS: CONCLUSION

To sum up: even broadening our enquiry, wisdom seems a less than central interest in the Apostolic Fathers. There is little hint of any kind of Wisdom Christology. There is widespread use of sapiential vocabulary, some quotations and allusions to the wisdom literature, and the predominant interest is ethics. But 'wisdom' is not the sole contributor to this. Where Scripture is an important quarry, the Psalms and the Law and the Prophets are at least equally important, and in Ignatius, Scripture, like wisdom, features little, even in one place being played down: Christ is more important than the ancient texts (*Phld.* 8). In the light of this we might ask: Is it possible that, with regard to wisdom, too much has been read back into the New Testament from later perspectives?

WISDOM IN EARLY CHRISTIANITY

Before we turn to the New Testament, it is worth asking a little more about those later perspectives. At what date can we trace a Wisdom Christology? Is there any evidence that wisdom as a genre was recognized, or even produced, by Christian authors?

To take the second question first, two texts are significant: the *Sentences of Sextus* and the *Teachings of Silvanus.* Interestingly, both are to be found in the Nag Hammadi library, but whereas the *Teachings of Silvanus* is a new discovery, fuller versions of the *Sentences of Sextus* were already known in the original Greek, and in Latin, Syriac, Armenian, and Georgian translations.[8] Neither has characteristics generally associated with Gnosticism, so both reinforce the point that the Nag Hammadi library is not to be regarded as a Gnostic library as such; rather, it seems to be a collection of texts found spiritually congenial by Pachomian monks.[9] Both texts resemble the wisdom literature in being collections of wise sayings or proverbs. However, parallels can also be cited with collections of maxims attributed to Pythagoras and other philosophers in the Greek tradition. Both works have been influenced

[8] For full discussion, see Henry Chadwick, *The Sentences of Sextus*, TS 5 (Cambridge: Cambridge University Press, 1959); and R. L. Wilken, 'Wisdom and Philosophy in Early Christianity', in *idem* (ed.), *Aspects of Wisdom in Judaism and Early Christianity* (Notre Dame, Ind.: University of Notre Dame Press, 1975), 143–68.

[9] J. M. Robinson, Introduction, in *The Nag Hammadi Library in English* (Leiden: Brill, 1977), 1–25.

by a blend of Stoicism and Platonism, but then the same could be said of the Wisdom of Solomon. The *Sentences of Sextus* is clearly a reworking of an earlier collection; its Christian character is somewhat veiled, though Origen and others seem to have known it as a Christian work. The *Teachings of Silvanus* show many remarkable parallels to Clement of Alexandria.[10] Both would seem to have begun to circulate in the late second century, and both presuppose the view that Christianity is a philosophy, teaching the right way of life.

Despite close parallels to Proverbs, Sirach, and the Wisdom of Solomon, there is not necessarily a direct dependence on the biblical wisdom books. Wilken points out that 'pithy and pointed sayings about fame or loquacity are as old as the human race...(They) are familiar in most cultures and are amply attested from Greek and Latin antiquity.'[11] Their existence suggests the development of Christian 'wisdom literature' as the second century progressed—though probably under the influence of Hellenistic philosophy rather than conscious imitation of a recognized, distinct biblical genre.

As for Wisdom Christology, we might presume that the Logos theology of Justin Martyr has Wisdom features. Interestingly, there is no explicit trace of this in the *Apologies*. However, in the *Dialogue with Trypho* 61, Prov. 8. 21–36 is quoted in full, to justify the claim that, before all creatures, God begat a Beginning, and this is named by the Holy Spirit in Scripture, now the Glory of the Lord, now the Son, now Wisdom, now an Angel, then God, and then Lord and Logos. This is confirmed by appeal to Genesis (*Dial.* 62): 'Let us make man in our own image' and 'Behold, Adam has become as one of us'. Clearly there were at least two involved in the act of creation, and it was the one Solomon calls Wisdom, begotten as a Beginning before all creatures, whom God addressed. The Son of God, who is God's Logos, is similarly identified with personified Wisdom in other apologists—Athenagoras and Theophilus, for example. It then becomes standard in the work of Clement of Alexandria, Origen, and Tertullian, eventually being an unquestioned assumption at the time when the Proverbs text was catapulted into the centre of controversy because Arius took the words 'The Lord created me as a beginning of his ways' literally, and argued that this so-called 'Begotten' One was the first and greatest of the creatures.[12]

Wisdom Christology of a sort is present, then, from the mid-second century. We might note, however, that it arises explicitly from the process of searching the Scriptures—prior to the development of a New Testament

[10] See J. Zandee, *"The Teachings of Silvanus" and Clement of Alexandria: A New Document of Alexandrian Theology* (Leiden: Ex Oriente Lux, 1977).

[11] Wilken, 'Wisdom and Philosophy', 149.

[12] See my article 'Proverbs 8 in Interpretation'.

canon and without any obvious cross-reference to the texts that would eventually make up the New Testament—for passages illuminating the person of Christ. Furthermore, it is an element in building up a picture of the pre-existent Logos out of undifferentiated prophetic texts, rather than a discrete Christological tradition. On the other hand, it must have been at about the same time as Justin made this connection with Wisdom that Valentinus began to develop (or perhaps inspire the development of)[13] the myth of Sophia, which has such a central place in his version of Christian Gnosticism. Both imply recognition of Wisdom as a pre-existent heavenly being. Despite the negative evidence of the Apostolic Fathers, one might imagine that such notions did not spring up *de novo* in the mid-second century.

REASSESSING WISDOM IN THE NEW TESTAMENT

It is time to ask the question whether there needs to be a reassessment of wisdom in the New Testament as a result of these explorations.[14]

There are undoubtedly more uses of *σοφία* and related words in the New Testament than there are in the Apostolic Fathers. But before we turn to work through these in detail, a general comment seems apposite. As in the Apostolic Fathers, there are long passages of *paraenesis* in the New Testament. At one time it almost seemed appropriate to suggest that, since the Law no longer applied to Christians, the Christian way of life was shaped by collections of wisdom sayings. 'Wisdom' seemed to explain the character of, for example, the Epistle of James. In the light of our findings concerning the Apostolic Fathers, I would like to suggest that this is too hasty a judgement, and this is confirmed by a quick glance at the range of scriptural allusions in the example already mentioned: James may contain quotations and allusions to Proverbs and Sirach, but there are just as many to Psalms, and indeed to the Law. The same could be said about the ethical teaching at the end of Romans.

[13] This caveat arises from the fact that the myth of Sophia does not appear in the *Gospel of Truth* and is attributed to Ptolemaeus by Irenaeus in *Adversus Haereses*.

[14] For the current position, and corollaries drawn from it, see the essays by J. D. G. Dunn, 'Jesus: Teacher of Wisdom or Wisdom Incarnate?', and S. C. Barton, 'Gospel Wisdom', in Barton (ed.), *Where shall Wisdom be Found?*, 75–92, 93–110 resp. A few sentences may be quoted here: 'In [John's] Gospel there is no doubt that Jesus is presented as Wisdom Incarnate' (p. 77). '[I]n his use of this material [Q sayings] Matthew seems consciously to have edited it to present Jesus more in the person of or as the embodiment of divine Wisdom' (p. 78). 'At the heart of [Matthew's] portrayal, Jesus' identity as the wisdom of God is revealed uniquely and powerfully in a prayer-cum-invitation [= Matt. 11. 25–30], itself analogous to the words about wisdom in Sir. 6. 23 ff and 51. 2 ff' (pp. 95–6). 'If in Matthew, Jesus teaches the way of wisdom, in John much more explicitly he is the Way' (p. 104).

Besides this, we should take account of the relatively recent reassessment of the Pauline literature, suggesting that it was the applicability of the ethnic marks of a Jew to Gentiles, rather than the commandments as such, that was at issue. Like that of the Apostolic Fathers, the *paraenesis* of the New Testament is taken from right across the Scriptures, and it is as much to be regarded as divine commandments as moral advice, for obedience is expected. My first conclusion, then, is that, as in the Apostolic Fathers, so in the New Testament, there is no explicit recognition of a distinct wisdom genre.

We should now examine the actual use of *σοφία* and its cognates.

The Pauline Epistles

It is, of course, the Pauline material which provides us with the most frequent usage, and most notably 1 Corinthians. In chapters 1–3[15] Paul protests that he was not sent to preach the Gospel *ἐν σοφίᾳ λόγου* (with eloquent wisdom), quotes Isa. 29. 14: 'I will destroy the wisdom of the wise', and asks 'Where is the wise one? . . . Has not God made foolish the wisdom of the world?' As we have seen, this negative evaluation of wisdom is taken up in the Apostolic Fathers—in Ignatius and especially *1 Clement*. Paul goes on to say that God decided to save those who believe through the foolishness of preaching, because in the wisdom of God, the world did not know God through wisdom. Not many wise are called, and the wise are shamed by what is foolish. The foolishness of preaching is about Christ crucified—foolishness to the Gentiles, yet, according to Paul, Christ the Wisdom of God. For God's foolishness is wiser than human wisdom. Hays suggests that this is clearly irony, yet a few verses later Paul affirms that Christ Jesus became for us Wisdom from God.

Now it is very easy to read a Wisdom Christology into such a direct identification of Christ with wisdom, especially in the light of later developments. But given that this does not happen in the Apostolic Fathers, yet there are there clear allusions to Paul's perspectives in this epistle, is this justified? Maybe we need to bracket out our awareness of Colossians as we proceed with the Corinthian correspondence.

As we move into chapter 2, Paul continues to affirm that it was not with lofty words or wisdom that he proclaimed God's mystery. His word or preaching was not characterized by the persuasive words of wisdom. The reason for this was to ensure that it was not on human wisdom that the listeners' faith rested. Yet he did speak wisdom among the mature, wisdom

15 For a full discussion of this passage, see R. B. Hays, 'Wisdom according to Paul', in Barton (ed.), *Where shall Wisdom be Found?*, 111–23. Hays emphasizes the irony in this passage, and argues against there being a Wisdom Christology here.

not of this world, the wisdom of God in a mystery. So what is this wisdom? He says it was secret and hidden, decreed before the ages for our glory. He has already identified it as Christ crucified. So far from being a Wisdom Christology, this would seem to be reflection on the mysterious fact that the Messiah died, a foolish fact, an unexpected fact, but now affirmed to be within the divine foreknowledge and gracious provision for human salvation. Paul's apostrophe to wisdom in Romans (11. 33: 'O the depth of the riches and wisdom and knowledge of God!') also occurs in a context where the inscrutability of God's judgements and providential plans are in question. The association of wisdom and foresight that we noticed in Hermas (*Vis.* 1. 3) may confirm this reading.

No wonder Paul has to speak of these things in words taught by the Spirit, rather than in words taught by human wisdom (2. 13). Human wisdom, which finds these things incomprehensible, is foolishness with God: Job and the Psalms are called in to confirm this: 'He catches the wise in their cleverness (πανουργία[16])' and 'the Lord knows the thoughts of the wise that they are futile' (1 Cor. 3. 19–20). In 2 Corinthians 'fleshly wisdom' is contrasted with single-mindedness, sincerity, and God's grace (1. 12). Yet, among the gifts given by the Spirit (1 Cor. 12. 8), Paul includes the word of wisdom and the word of knowledge. His interest in wisdom is highly paradoxical, because the cross is distinctly paradoxical, and God's ways are beyond human comprehension. Yet the paradox of human wisdom is already to be found in the Scriptures, and Paul exploits this, referring not only to the Psalms and wisdom literature but to the prophet Jeremiah: 'Let him who boasts, boast in the Lord' alludes to a verse which begins 'Do not let the wise boast in their wisdom' (Jer. 9. 23).[17]

So in the unquestionably authentic Pauline epistles, where wisdom is explored explicitly, it is within the same range of use as that found in the Apostolic Fathers, and, as in their case, informed by the Scriptures, Psalms and Prophets, as well as wisdom literature. One other passage, however, we cannot overlook, even though wisdom is not mentioned: namely 1 Cor. 8. 6: 'But for us there is one God the Father, from whom are all things and we are for him, and one Lord Jesus Christ through whom are all things and we are through him.' This statement is often interpreted as if the relationship between God and Christ is being patterned on the personified Wisdom who is God's instrument of creation (Prov. 8). The cryptic use of prepositions means

[16] All uses of πανουργία in the NT are negative in meaning—besides this, see 2 Cor. 4. 2; 11. 3; Eph. 4. 14; Luke 20. 23. Cf. πανοῦργος in 2 Cor. 12. 16.

[17] For the development of this ambivalence about wisdom in apocalyptic and the NT, see Christopher Rowland, ' "Sweet Science Reigns": Divine and Human Wisdom in the Apocalyptic Tradition', in Barton (ed.), *Where shall Wisdom be Found?*, 61–74.

that the meaning can be teased out only by importing assumptions, and maybe 'all things' (τὰ πάντα) is not as transparent as is often assumed. Reading in the light of *1 Clement* rather than Colossians, we might suggest that the one God the Father is the source of all (possibly all the riches of salvation, as I suggested in relation to *Barnabas*) and our goal, while the one Lord Jesus Christ is the means whereby all God's purposes of salvation are effected and the one through whom we are called into those benefits.

If the obscurities of 1 Cor. 8. 6 are discounted, it is clear that the references to wisdom in Ephesians and Colossians give us rather different material from that examined so far. Σοφία appears almost entirely in a positive light in Colossians. So 1. 9: in prayers for the recipients, the request has been made that they be 'filled with knowledge (ἐπίγνωσις) of God's will in all spiritual wisdom and understanding (σύνεσις); 1. 28: preaching Christ involves teaching everyone in all wisdom; 3. 16: it is hoped that the word of Christ may dwell in them richly and that they will teach one another in all wisdom; 4. 5: they are to 'walk in wisdom' with respect to outsiders. Only in one context does the word of wisdom appear as negative, identified with human commands and teachings (2. 22–3).[18] Christ is explicitly said to be the one 'in whom all the treasures of wisdom and knowledge are hidden' (2. 3). In an earlier passage,[19] which does not actually mention wisdom, it is suggested that 'he is the image of the invisible God, the first born of all creation, for in him all things in heaven and on earth were created ... he is before all things and all things hold together in him' (1. 15–17). This certainly seems to express the content of Prov. 8 in an allusive way, and it attributes this creative pre-existence to God's 'beloved Son' (1. 13), who is 'the head of the body, the church', and the 'first-born of the dead' (1. 18). It would seem, then, that we have here the makings of an explicit Wisdom Christology, though we should perhaps take note of Robert Morgan's caveat: '[T]hese Wisdom passages in the New Testament probably originated in liturgical contexts ... This wisdom idea is *mythos* not *logos*, and therefore not, strictly speaking, a Christology which expresses conceptually what the myth narrates pictorially. The phrase "Wisdom Christology" is therefore potentially misleading, a product of a one-sidedly doctrinal emphasis in New Testament theology.'[20]

In Ephesians σοφία is apparently identified with revelation: 1. 8 tells of the grace 'which overflows on us, with all wisdom and insight (φρόνησις), making

[18] This passage seems to owe something to Gal. 4. 3, and shares some of the same difficult features for interpretation: e.g., to what does the phrase 'elements of the world' refer?

[19] For a full discussion of this passage, see M. D. Hooker, 'Where is Wisdom to be Found? Colossians 1. 15–20 (1)', in Ford and Stanton (eds.), *Reading Texts, Seeking Wisdom*, 116–28.

[20] R. Morgan, 'Jesus Christ, the Wisdom of God (2)', in Ford and Stanton (eds.), *Reading Texts. Seeking Wisdom*, 29.

known (γνωρίσας) to us the mystery of his will'; 1. 17 prays that God may give the addressees the spirit of wisdom and (the spirit of) revelation in knowing (ἐπίγνωσις) him, so that the eyes of the heart, being enlightened, may know what is the hope of his calling (etc.); 3. 10 wants the wisdom of God to be known to the rulers and powers in the heavens through the church—apparently picking up the notion in 1 Cor. 2. 8 that the rulers of this world did not know God's wisdom. All of these statements could be interpreted in the same terms as 1 Corinthians (see above). Explicit Wisdom Christology is less evident than in Colossians, but the same generally positive use of σοφία distinguishes both from the Corinthian correspondence and the Apostolic Fathers. Perhaps we have stumbled on further evidence suggesting that Colossians and Ephesians are post-Pauline.[21] In any case, they seem not to be known to Ignatius, Polycarp, and Clement, even though these authors knew the Corinthian letters. Whatever their provenance, they apparently anticipate the development of Logos theology later in the second century, as well as the interest in *Sophia* found among Gnostics.

Other New Testament Material

So what about the rest of the New Testament? The cluster of sapiential vocabulary is scattered around the New Testament texts: σύνεσις and συνετός, φρόνησις and φρόνιμος, σοφία and σοφός, together with a fairly widespread assumption that 'instruction' (παιδεία) is needed, and righteousness the goal. Thus, 2 Tim. 2. 7 suggests that the Lord will give Timothy understanding (σύνεσις) in all things, and that the scriptures are able to make you wise (σοφίσαι) for salvation, because they are useful for the instruction (παιδεία) that leads to righteousness (3. 15). According to Titus 2. 12, the grace of God has appeared with salvation, 'training (παιδεύουσα) us to renounce impiety and worldly passions' (cf. 1 Tim. 1. 20: to train not to blaspheme; 2 Tim. 2. 25: correcting (παιδεύων) opponents with gentleness). James encourages the reader to ask for wisdom if it is lacking (1. 5). The question is posed (3. 13): who is wise (σοφός) and understanding (ἐπιστήμων) among you? The answer lies in the advice, 'Let him show by a good life that his works are done with gentleness born of wisdom'. This is contrasted with ambition, boastfulness, and being false to the truth, which are attributed to a wisdom that does not come down from above, but is earthly, natural (ψυχική), and 'demonic' (δαιμονιώδης). Wisdom from above is, first, pure,

[21] I should acknowledge that prior to this investigation I accepted Colossians as authentic, though doubted whether Ephesians was.

then peaceable, gentle, willing to give way, full of mercy and good fruits, without partiality or hypocrisy. It is associated with a harvest of righteousness. These ethical characteristics are reminiscent of what we have found in the Apostolic Fathers, and are equally indebted to the whole range of scriptural material.

2 Pet. 3. 15 suggests that Paul wrote 'according to the wisdom (*σοφία*) given him', but denies following 'cleverly devised (*σεσοφισμένοις*) myths' in making known the coming of Jesus Christ (1. 16). Acts indicates that those selected to be deacons were men full of the spirit and wisdom (*σοφία*), and that those who tried to argue with Stephen could not stand up to the wisdom and the spirit with which he spoke (6. 3, 10). In Stephen's speech, Joseph is said to have been enabled to win favour and show wisdom before Pharaoh (7. 10), and Moses is said to have been instructed (*ἐπαιδεύθη*) in all the wisdom of the Egyptians (7. 22). Interestingly, Acts has no other passages which are of interest to our enquiries about wisdom, and apart from the gospels this virtually exhausts our enquiry, though we should perhaps note that Revelation finds wisdom necessary in order to understand the number of the beast (13. 18) and to interpret the seven heads (17. 9), while including wisdom in its hymns: 'Blessing and glory and wisdom ... be to our God! (7. 12); 'Worthy is the Lamb ... to receive power and wealth and wisdom ...' (5. 12). In this apocalyptic work, wisdom is both attributed to God and also associated with unpacking riddles, rather as it is in *Barnabas*. On the whole, these scattered references suggest a positive view of wisdom, and a link between wisdom and the Scriptures. But again there is no hint of awareness of a distinct wisdom genre or indeed of Wisdom Christology.

The one possible hint of a Wisdom Christology is to be found in Heb. 1. 3. Wisdom is again not explicitly mentioned (as in the cases already reviewed in 1 Cor. 8. 6 and Col. 1. 15–20), but language used of the all-pervading cosmic wisdom described in Wisd. 7 is transferred to 'the Son', through whom God made the ages, and who holds all things by the word of his power. This probably needs to be regarded, alongside Colossians, as an early expression of Wisdom Christology. Yet it is an intriguing observation that most of the passages which potentially articulate a Wisdom Christology fail to mention wisdom.

The Gospels

In the synoptic gospels people wonder about the *σοφία* given to Jesus (Mark 6. 2; Matt. 13. 54); Luke suggests that Jesus grew in wisdom (2. 40, 52), and people were amazed at Jesus understanding (*σύνεσις*) as a child (2. 47).

The queen of the south travelled far to listen to Solomon's wisdom, but something greater than Solomon is here (Matt. 12. 42; Luke 11. 31). Jesus promises to give 'words and wisdom' to the disciples when they experience persecution (Luke 21. 15). He advises people to be cunning (*φρόνιμος*) as serpents (Matt. 10. 16), and tells parables: about the cunning person who built his house on a rock, contrasted with the foolish who built on sand (Matt. 7. 24); about cunning and foolish virgins (Matt. 25. 1–12); about faithful and cunning slaves or stewards (Matt. 24. 45; Luke 12. 42). Jesus also teaches in parables, which need interpretation and whose meaning is esoteric (Mark 4. 10–13 and parallels), a reminder of the Proverbs assumption that wisdom involves perception of the meaning of parables and the dark sayings of the wise. Yet wisdom is hardly a discrete element in the complexity of the Jesus tradition. He is seer as well as sage.[22]

There are two perplexing statements in these gospels: (1) 'Wisdom is justified by her works' (Matt. 11. 19) or 'by her children' (Luke 7. 35); and (2) 'For this reason even the Wisdom of God said, "I will send them prophets and apostles, some of whom they will kill and persecute" ' (Luke 11. 49). In the case of the latter, to posit a saying from a lost wisdom book seems wide of the mark, as also to suggest that Christ is identified without explanation as Wisdom. I would like to suggest that this text is best explained in the light of 1 Corinthians: the puzzle of the persecuted Messiah, put to death on a cross, is again in the background. Paul had suggested that this unexpected outcome was to be seen as the wisdom of God, as something deep in the divine foreknowledge. Luke now relates it to the perennial persecution of the prophets evidenced in the Scriptures, attributing to Jesus the thought we found in Paul—that God's wisdom foresaw and foretold the crucifixion. If that explanation is right, then the other saying probably coheres with it. The oddity of Jesus' behaviour if he is a holy man, and his difference from John the Baptist, is like the peculiarity of the crucified Messiah. The outcome—namely, the redemption realized as the outworking of God's providential plan—justifies the notion that it all happened according to God's wisdom.

As far as the gospels are concerned, there remain only the questions raised by the Prologue of John's Gospel and its precursor, the so-called Johannine Thunderbolt in the synoptic material (Matt. 11. 25–30; Luke 10. 21–2). Both are again cases where wisdom is not explicit, but scriptural parallels have made an implicit association an attractive supposition. In the case of the passage in Matthew, attention is drawn to Sir. 51, a chapter which opens with

[22] Ben Witherington III, *Jesus the Sage* (Minneapolis: Fortress, 1994); *idem, Jesus the Seer* (Peabody, Mass.: Hendrickson, 1999). Note the discussion in Dunn, 'Jesus: Teacher of Wisdom or Wisdom Incarnate?', where the 'eschatological plus' modifies the widespread acceptance of the Third Quest that Jesus was simply a teacher of wisdom.

thanksgiving similar to the words of Jesus, 'I thank you, Father, Lord of heaven and earth', and later enjoins those who lack instruction to come to the author's school, put on the yoke, and be willing to learn. This is taken to illuminate the words, 'Come to me ... Take my yoke upon you and learn of me', and to imply that Jesus takes the place of Wisdom. This conflation of Wisdom with the Son of God presumably then informs the Logos Christology of the Johannine Prologue.

However, in the synoptic passage, there is, first, an emphasis very similar to that in 1 Corinthians—the revelation is denied to the wise and given to the humble-minded—and, secondly, even if there is an allusion to Sir. 51, the invitation is to the teacher of wisdom, not Wisdom itself. True, that may be read in by associating it with Sir. 24, where Wisdom is personified as in Prov. 8 and is then identified both with the creative Word of God and with Torah, but the point of the passage is surely that the Son is the best teacher available. The next question is how far the author of the Johannine Prologue might have made all the supposed associations. To which the answer may be: as much as, and no more than, the other passages we have noted which seemed to attach a creative and cosmic role to the pre-existent Christ but without mentioning wisdom. Already the Psalms had affirmed that 'By the word of the Lord the heavens were made' (Ps. 33. 6), and the prophets spoke by the word of the Lord. If the thrust of the passage as a whole is to show that it was the mind and intention of God from the very beginning which was enfleshed in Jesus, then what the Prologue is about is much the same as what we found in 1 Corinthians. Perhaps the apocalyptic notion of God's plan being laid up in heaven to be revealed in God's good time is more pertinent than 'wisdom'.

CONCLUSION

For many theologians and New Testament scholars, what I have offered will seem an extraordinarily minimalist reading of the New Testament material. To some extent it is true that I have sought to play down long-held scholarly assumptions as a kind of experiment. Of course, the New Testament texts had a future, where maximal intertextual associations would make a full-bodied notion of the embodiment of God's Wisdom in Jesus a core component in a richly layered Christology, and maybe the fact is that the Apostolic Fathers fall short of the depth already reached at an earlier date by Paul and other theologians such as the author of John's Gospel. But, somewhat to my own astonishment, this exploration of wisdom in the Apostolic Fathers has provoked the question: to what extent do we owe this maximalist reading to later developments? Do we still too easily read back later doctrines into the earliest texts, even when overtly espousing the historico-critical method? Maybe we do. My minimalist reading is offered as a way of testing this possibility.

Part IV

Church, Ministry, and Sacraments in the New Testament and the Apostolic Fathers

6

The Church in Ephesians, *2 Clement*, and the *Shepherd of Hermas*

John Muddiman

INTRODUCTION

The ground-breaking volume, *The New Testament in the Apostolic Fathers*, published by a committee of the Oxford Society for Historical Theology[1] in 1905, whose centenary this volume and its companion celebrate, introduced into the discussion of the delicate question of the earliest attestation to the New Testament documents some necessary distinctions. The committee categorized possible allusions on a four-point scale: a = 'no reasonable doubt'; b = 'a high degree of probability; c = 'a lower degree of probability; and d = 'too uncertain to allow any reliance', with other very slight allusions noted but left unassessed or 'unclassed'. Although some of the committee's assessments are questionable, and certain of them involving Ephesians will be questioned below, the importance of this refinement of criteria and careful distinctions as to degrees of probability was an important advance in critical scholarship.

The detection of allusions to the New Testament in the earliest Christian writings has a direct bearing on many of the central issues in the history of the early church, such as the dating, provenance, and dissemination of the NT documents; textual criticism before actual manuscript evidence becomes available; the persistence of oral tradition alongside written texts; evidence for lost documents such as Q; the formation of the four-gospel canon and the Pauline letter collection; and highly controversial issues like the date and sources of the *Didache* (and indeed apocryphal works like the *Gospel of Thomas* and the *Gospel of Peter*). Depending on the results of such studies,

[1] The Committee consisted of scholars who were somewhat on the fringe of the university establishment, including dissenters like Professor J. Vernon Bartlet, of the Congregational Mansfield College, and Dr Drummond, Principal of the Unitarian Manchester College, along with Professor Kirsopp Lake, who moved to Leiden in 1904. This may explain a certain distancing in the Preface: 'The Society has no responsibility whatever for the work' (p. iii).

very different reconstructions of the origins and early development of Christianity are proposed.

To illustrate just how important *The New Testament in the Apostolic Fathers* was and still remains, I will give a recent example of what can happen when its cautionary judgements are ignored. In his recent commentary on Ephesians, Harold Hoehner begins his sixty-page defence of Pauline authorship, with this statement: 'Ephesians has the earliest attestation of any New Testament book. Already in the first century or very early second century Clement of Rome (fl. 96), when mentioning "one God and one Christ and one Spirit", may be a reference to Eph 4:4–6.'[2] It is not just the grammar but also the logic of this statement that are confused. Although *The New Testament in the Apostolic Fathers* is footnoted at this point, no mention is made of its judgement that the likelihood of an allusion to Ephesians at *1 Clem.* 46. 6 is no better than d. The reasons the Committee gave deserve to be quoted:

> At first sight it would appear probable that Clement has the passage in Ephesians in his mind; but we must remember that the passages both in Ephesians and in Clement are very possibly founded upon some liturgical forms, and it thus seems impossible to establish any dependence of Clement upon Ephesians.[3]

When Hoehner comes to comment on Eph. 4. 4–6, he claims that it is entirely Paul's free composition, noting that it 'revolves around the three persons of the Trinity' (!) and rebukes the 'many New Testament scholars' who are 'much too eager to designate hymns those portions that seem to have some sort of meter'. But it is not a matter of metre; it is rather the string of verbless nominatives that calls for some kind of liturgical, quasi-credal explanation. Hoehner refers to three other passages in *1 Clement*, as follows: 59. 3: 'the eyes of the heart', which is deemed 'most likely an allusion to Eph 1:17–18'; 36. 2: 'darkened in understanding', which is 'probably an allusion to Eph 4.18'; and 38. 1: 'let each be subject to his neighbour', which is 'reminiscent of Eph 5:21'. Of these the Oxford Committee noted only the first, which it rated d. It is precisely this kind of overstatement of the evidence that *The New Testament in the Apostolic Fathers* was seeking to challenge.[4]

[2] H. Hoehner, *Ephesians—An Exegetical Commentary*, BECNT (Grand Rapids, Mich.: Baker Academic, 2002), 2.

[3] *NTAF*, 53. Cf. H. E. Lona, *Der erste Clemensbrief*, KAV 2 (Göttingen: Vandenhoeck & Ruprecht, 1998), 9: 'Only knowledge of 1 Corinthians and Romans can be demonstrated with certainty', quoted in M. Hengel, *The Four Gospels and the One Gospel of Jesus Christ* (London: SCM Press, 2000), 285 n. 510; see also 285 n. 511 on Lona's unreasonable doubts about *1 Clement*'s use of Hebrews.

[4] The treatment of the NT allusions in *1 Clement* by D. A. Hagner, *The Use of the Old and New Testaments in Clement of Rome*, NovTSup 34 (Leiden: Brill, 1973), to which Hoehner refers approvingly, begins with the key parallel *1 Clem.* 46. 6 // Eph. 4. 4–6 and admits the probability

It is hardly necessary to add that Clement does not attribute any of these phrases to Paul, let alone identify them as coming from his letter to the Ephesians. So, this evidence could only be reckoned 'Attestation of Pauline Authorship of Ephesians'—the heading of the opening section of the commentary—if the mere fact of its use implied the highest apostolic authority for the source. On that showing, with equal cogency, one could argue for early attestation to the Pauline authorship of Hebrews, which is beyond any reasonable doubt employed by Clement! In what follows I shall look briefly at the material on the church in Ephesians, then in subsequent parts examine the textual evidence for the use of Ephesians by *2 Clement* and the *Shepherd of Hermas*. That evidence is inconclusive, but I shall also consider conceptual similarities between these texts at key points, which, I suggest, raise the likelihood of dependence to a higher level of probability.

I. EPHESIANS

The development of Paul's ecclesiology by the pseudonymous author of Ephesians is too large and complex a topic for this short paper. It is sufficient for our present purposes to refer to certain points in the letter relevant to the discussion of the possible relationships, literary and conceptual, between Ephesians, *2 Clement*, and the *Shepherd*.

The priority of Ephesians in terms of date of composition over these other two documents is a reasonable but unprovable assumption. Its use by *1 Clement* is not beyond dispute, as we have seen above. The echoes in Ignatius, not least in his own letter to the Ephesians (see Ign. *Eph.* 1. 3–14; 12. 2), are more compelling.[5] And the parallels between Ephesians and 1 Peter may also be relevant to this issue; but the date of the latter and the direction of the dependence, if any, are uncertain. The earliest part of the date range for the *Shepherd* and *2 Clement* (see below) could in principle precede the dates of Ignatius and 1 Peter.

that both passages 'depend on a primitive confession of faith'. He then withdraws the admission: 'Nevertheless, it is easier to suppose that Clement has derived the passage from Ephesians, since from the following, it seems that he was acquainted with the epistle', and the inconsequential echoes listed above are cited. But to appeal to an accumulation of negligible examples to confirm influence in the one instance where a case, albeit weak for the reason stated, might be made is a very dubious methodology.

[5] See P. Foster, 'The Epistles of Ignatius of Antioch and the Writings that later formed the New Testament', Ch. 7 in the companion volume.

Apart from the dating, there is a second factor affecting the likelihood of the possible influence of Ephesians on the other texts, which is the nature of its association with the other Pauline letters. For instance, if we adopt the Goodspeed–Knox[6] hypothesis that Ephesians was intended from the start as a preface to the collected ten-letter edition, then it is more plausible to argue that demonstrable dependence on any one letter is evidence of acquaintance with them all. But there are good reasons for resisting that hypothesis.[7] If, as seems more likely, Ephesians was at first meant to be read on its own in and around the place of its composition, and was circulated further afield perhaps in conjunction with the other Asiatic letters, Colossians and Philemon, then it is conceivable that it may not have spread to every part of the Christian world (and to Rome in particular[8]) until quite a late date. This is speculation of course. All options remain open.

Before the Pauline letters began to be treated as Scripture, the convention seems to have been not to quote them verbatim—after all, 'the letter kills, the Spirit alone gives life' (2 Cor. 3. 6)—but to continue, as it were, 'the living voice' of the Apostle.[9] While this could be used to argue that very minor similarities in wording might be evidence of knowledge of the letters, equally the preference for oral tradition could mean that these are the common idioms of apostolic preaching and do not require explanation in terms of literary dependence. More important, therefore, are the distinctive underlying patterns of thought in a New Testament text when they reappear in the Apostolic Fathers. It is these aspects of the thought of the author of Ephesians concerning the church to which we now turn.

All the references to ἐκκλησία in Ephesians are to the universal, indeed cosmic church. The word is not used of the local congregation as it regularly is in Paul.[10] The features of the ecclesiology of Ephesians that are relevant are the following. (They are numbered for (1) to (10) for ease of later reference.)

(1) 1. 4: That God the Father has elected us in him before the foundation of the world. (Note the idea of the predestination/pre-existence of the church.)

[6] E. J. Goodspeed, *The Meaning of Ephesians* (Chicago: University of Chicago Press, 1933); J. Knox, *Philemon among the Letters of Paul* (Chicago: University of Chicago Press, 1935).

[7] See J. Muddiman, *The Epistle to the Ephesians*, BNTC (London: Continuum, 2001), 12–14. All subsequent references to this commentary are indicated by *Eph: BNTC*.

[8] The lack of clear evidence that Clement of Rome knew other 'Pauline' letters apart from Hebrews, 1 Corinthians, and Romans might imply that even the Roman church at the end of the first century lacked a full set.

[9] See L. C. A. Alexander, 'The Living Voice: Scepticism towards the Written Word in Early Christianity and Graeco-Roman Texts', in D. J. A. Clines, S. E. Fowl, and S. E. Porter (eds.), *The Bible in Three Dimensions*, JSOTSup 87 (Sheffield: JSOT Press, 1990), 221–47.

[10] And even in Colossians: e.g., 4. 16.

(2) 1. 22 f.: That God appointed Christ head over all things for the Church which is his body, the fullness of the all-filling Christ. (Note the combination of the ideas of the universal lordship of the risen Christ both over creation (combining Ps. 110. 1 and Ps. 8. 7) and also over the church.)

(3) 2. 6: That Christians are already raised with Christ and even seated with him in heaven. (The strongly realized eschatology is noteworthy.)

(4) 2. 20 ff.: That Christ is the corner-stone of a spiritual temple founded on the apostles and prophets. (The church, then, is a building with foundations already laid, but one that is still under construction and with its members like stones, 'fitted together': cf. 4. 16.)

(5) 3. 9: That the church is the means by which the long hidden mysterious plan of God the Creator is now revealed to the principalities and powers in the heavenly places. (The revelatory function of the church is here emphasized, even though the exact means by which it is accomplished are left obscure.)

(6) 3. 21: That glory is due to God in the church and in Christ Jesus. (Note that the parallel implies a certain equality between the two.)

(7) 4. 11: That the ascended Christ is the source of the original apostolic ministry and its successors. (By implication, the church's ministry exercises the authority of the glorified Christ.)

(8) 5. 23: That Christ is the head of the church and himself the saviour of the body.

(9) 5. 25 f.: That Christ loved the church and gave himself for her, cleansing her with the word through the water bath, in order to present her to himself in all her glory without spot or wrinkle.

(10) 5. 31 f.: That Gen. 2. 24 is an allegory of the union between Christ and the church.[11]

There are many other passages which are relevant to an analysis of the teaching on the church in Ephesians, but these remarkable assertions allow us to make a general point: there is no other book in the New Testament where the emphasis on the transcendent character of the church is so explicit and so marked. And when we encounter this same emphasis in certain of the Apostolic Fathers, there is a presumption in favour of some kind of influence, direct or indirect, from Ephesians. In the passages listed above, there are in most cases good reasons, linguistic and contextual, for supposing that the writer himself is formulating these ideas and not just borrowing them from

[11] The last three points will be taken up in slightly more detail below, but for a fuller discussion of the distinctive ecclesiology of Ephesians, see *Eph: BNTC*, 18 f., and *ad loc.*

the source(s) he was using. But it would be wrong to think of this development of Paul's teaching as the distortion of an originally functional, low ecclesiology. Rather, the author of Ephesians is intent on exposing and articulating the deeper roots in Jewish apocalyptic of Paul's thought on the church. Fidelity to the latter is surely implied by the very genre of a pseudepigraphical letter written in Paul's name. Gal. 4 is particularly instructive in this connection, the 'pre-existence' of the redeemed community being made clear in the allegory of Sarah ('the other woman corresponds to the Jerusalem above: she is free and she is our mother', Gal. 4. 26), and the images of heavenly woman and heavenly city being combined.

A few more comments on the last three items in the above list are in order. These all appear in the so-called household code. The author's use of this conventional form derives from his source (whether Colossians or something very like Colossians), but he has completely transformed the first section on husbands and wives. The code sought to endorse family values by placing them in the context of faith 'in the Lord', but the author of Ephesians has a very different purpose: to describe the glorious destiny of the Church.

I have recently argued the case that Eph. 5. 22 incorporates an earlier tradition: 'Just as Man is the head of Woman so Christ is the head of the Church and himself the Saviour of the Body.'[12] The man and woman in question were not just any Ephesian married couple but the primeval pair, Adam and Eve. Just as Adam was the head (source) and head (ruler) of Eve, so Christ is both head and ruler of the church. The pre-existence/foreordination of the church is implied in this appeal to the creation story of Gen. 2–3. The church is allegorically speaking older even than Sarah; she is as old as Eve. Secondly, Eph. 5. 27 refers to the preparation of the bride-church for union with Christ as the washing away not, as one might expect, of the dirt of sin, but of every disfiguring skin blemish (σπίλος) or wrinkle/sign of ageing (ῥυτίς). Whether the author consciously intended by this unusual imagery a reference to baptismal rejuvenation (see John 3. 5), it was open to someone like Hermas to pick up and extensively develop the image in his visions of the woman-church gradually becoming younger in appearance. Thirdly, the creation typology appears again with the citation of Gen. 2. 23 f.,[13] but its literal sense is decidedly secondary to the allegorical interpretation of the text in reference to Christ and the church.[14] We shall observe the same move in *2 Clement* and the *Shepherd*.

[12] *Eph: BNTC*, 259.

[13] Reading the longer text at Eph. 5. 30.

[14] Notice the emphatic ἐγω and the strong adversative, πλήν, at 32 f.: '*I* [the author himself here, rather than Paul] take it to mean Christ and the Church. *However*, if you insist on being literal, then husbands love your wives etc.'

II. *2 CLEMENT*

2 Clement is a written sermon intended for someone other than the author to read aloud to the assembly (19. 1). Its authorship, date, and provenance are not known. Perhaps by the accident of its being copied alongside *1 Clement* in the manuscripts (A C syr), it came to be attributed to Clement of Rome, but the style and content betray a different hand. Harnack famously conjectured that it was a sermon by Soter of Rome sent as a letter to Corinth.[15] Bishop Dionysius in acknowledging its receipt (his reply is preserved in Euseb. *HE* 4. 23. 11) assured the Pope that it would be preserved and reread 'as also the former epistle which was written to us through Clement'. The date then would be very late (AD 166–74), and knowledge of most of the New Testament books almost certain. However, there are problems with this conjecture. It is difficult to see what the point of sending a sermon such as *2 Clement* from Rome to Corinth might have been, and Dionysius is clearly referring to a letter from Soter, not a sermon. The way in which *2 Clement* quotes or paraphrases Jewish scripture and the New Testament, especially the sayings of Jesus, is one of the few clues we have to go on in locating this text, and points perhaps to an earlier date, in the first half of the second century.[16]

The Oxford Committee detected no certain or probable New Testament allusions (a or b), but put Matthew and Hebrews into category c, and relegated Ephesians and Luke, with some other epistles, to d, with two further references marked 'unclassed'. This is a surprisingly negative judgement.[17] Before we look at the possible parallels with Ephesians, there is a relevant similarity between *2 Clement* and Galatians, not discussed by the Committee, which is worthy of note. At the beginning of chapter 2, after referring to conversion as a kind of new *creatio ex nihilo*, the author, rather suddenly, breaks into a quotation from Isaiah (54. 1), the same one used by Paul in his allegory on the two wives of Abraham. Each part of the quotation is explained in the manner of *pesher*.

In saying, 'Rejoice thou barren one that bearest not,' he meant us, for our church was barren before children were given her. And in saying, 'Cry thou that travailest not', he means . . . that we should offer our prayers in sincerity to God, and not grow weary as

[15] See J. Quasten, *Patrology*, i (Westminster, Md.: Newman Press, 1950), 53.

[16] H. Koester, *Ancient Christian Gospels* (London: SCM Press, 1990), 347–60, discusses the gospel material only. He admits traces of Matthean and Lucan redaction, but nevertheless concludes that the author is quoting from a collection of Jesus' sayings, and was writing 'after the middle of the second century'.

[17] Cf. Gregory and Tuckett, Ch. 10 in companion volume.

women that give birth. And in saying, 'For the children of the deserted are many more than hers that hath a husband', he meant that our people seemed to be deserted by God, but that now we who have believed have become many more than those who seemed to have God (τῶν δοκούντων ἔχειν θεόν).

Although there is no direct verbal echo of Galatians here, the way the same Old Testament proof-text is understood may yet argue for some kind of connection. Thus, Paul also implies the barrenness of the old covenant compared with the present fruitfulness of the Christian life (Gal. 5. 22; cf. Rom. 7. 4). He says explicitly: 'Let us not grow weary in doing good' (Gal. 6. 9), and the persecution of the church ('once we seemed to be deserted') for Paul too was both the seal on Christian faithfulness and the stimulus towards missionary growth. The polemic is very faint in *2 Clement* ('more numerous than those who seemed to have God' presumably refers to the Jews), but the interpretation of the text from Isaiah is remarkably similar, and it prepares the way for the later passage on the church, which is of special interest here.

2 Clem. 14. 2 reads: 'Now I imagine that you are not ignorant that the living "Church is the body of Christ." For the scripture says: "God made man male and female"; the male is Christ, the female is the Church. And moreover the books and the Apostles declare that the Church belongs not to the present, but has existed from the beginning.'

The Committee compared this with Eph. 1. 22, 5. 23, and 1. 4. It acknowledged three points of similarity: the church as body, as bride, and as predestined points (2), (8) and (1) in our list above), but it was evidently not impressed by them, giving the passage a d rating. Two other slight allusions are 'unclassed'.[18]

However, there are some other, neglected factors which might give us more confidence that Ephesians was in the preacher's mind as he wrote chapter 14. First, he is alluding in passing to ideas that he thinks his audience will be familiar with from elsewhere—'I imagine you are not ignorant etc.'—so he does not need to spell them out at length. Secondly, this is the one place in *2 Clement* where there is an explicit reference not just to scripture (γραφή or τὰ βιβλία), but also to the apostles. Although that could mean apostolic

[18] The first is *2 Clem.* 19. 2; cf. Eph. 4. 18 and Rom. 1. 21. The Pauline texts are referring to the pagan past from which Christians have now been delivered, whereas *2 Clement* sees this as a possible present threat: sinning through ignorance 'sometimes when we do wrong we do not know it'. The second is 'manpleasers': *2 Clem.* 13. 1; cf. Eph. 6. 6 (and Col. 3. 22). The word is unprecedented in Greek apart from Ps. 52. 6, LXX, and it refers to the false servility that the Christian slave is to avoid. The context in *2 Clement* is different, and the thought of not pleasing others seems immediately to be corrected with that of pleasing outsiders by our uprightness 'in order that the name may not be reproached because of us.' On this point the author sides with Col. 4. 6 over against Eph. 5. 4 in a minor but remarkable point of flat contradiction between the two epistles! No weight can be placed on these elusive parallels.

tradition orally transmitted, in context it more naturally implies acquaintance with apostolic writings.

Thirdly, the immediately preceding verse should be taken together with 14. 2, for it functions as an introduction to the whole section. It reads: 'If we do the will of our Father, God, we shall belong to the first church, the spiritual one, which was created before the sun and the moon; but if we do not do the will of the Lord, we shall fall under the scripture which says: "My house became a den of brigands".' The reference to the first, spiritual church might seem to imply that there is also a second, unspiritual church, but there is nothing elsewhere in the sermon to suggest that sort of ecclesiastical puritanism; the author is candid about his own and his audience's deficiencies. It is more likely, then, that 'first' means earliest, and signifies the divine intention from the very beginning of creation 'before the sun and the moon'. So, although Gen. 1. 27 is about to be quoted, the event to which it allegorically refers *preceded* the creation of the sun and the moon at Gen. 1. 16. The themes of the pre-existence of Wisdom in Jewish sapiential literature and the pre-existence of Israel in Jewish apocalyptic are here being reapplied to the church. This appropriation may be the church's response to the charge, whether from the imperial authorities or from its Jewish competitors that it is a recent upstart with no credentials. On the contrary, the church is older than the universe!

Fourthly, the alternative to membership in the first church is to belong to the house of God which has been turned in a 'den of brigands'. An allusion here to the cleansing of the Temple is hard to deny, and it may imply the positive affirmation that the first church, as well as being the body and bride of Christ, is God's true temple and house of prayer.[19]

Finally, there is the wider context to be taken into account. Already in chapter 12 the male–female contrast has been used in a moral, rather than ecclesiological, sense, with the citation of the notorious agraphon: 'When the two shall be one and the outside like the inside and the male with the female neither male nor female.' *2 Clement* interprets this saying to refer to personal integrity and sexual abstinence, 'that a brother when he sees a sister should not think of her at all as female nor she think of him at all as male. When you do this, the Lord himself says, my Father's kingdom will come.' Thus, having disposed of the literal sexual connotation of the male–female contrast in chapter 12, the way is cleared for a purely allegorical interpretation of the Genesis allusion in chapter 14. The spiritual Christ and the spiritual church

[19] Cf. also the references to the temple of God at 9. 3, when read in the light of 14. 3; and the palace of God at 6. 9. Admittedly, *2 Clement* does not develop this theme in the elaborate way that Hermas does, for whom the destruction of the Jerusalem Temple 'stone by stone' is now being reversed by the reconstruction of the new Temple stone by stone; see further below.

united from the beginning are made manifest in the flesh—that is to say, in history. Without explicitly quoting Gen. 2. 24, he seems to have it in mind, when in apparent contradiction of his opening statement that the church is spiritual, he says 14. 4: 'Now if we say that the flesh is the Church and the Spirit is Christ [i.e. flesh and spirit making one whole body] then he who has abused the flesh has abused the Church.' I suggest that this is very much how a sexual ascetic like our preacher would have read the household code of Eph. 5.[20]

Of course, there are a lot of other references in *2 Clement* to the gospels and various epistles.[21] He is not, after all, writing a commentary on Ephesians. But the number of echoes we have noted[22] is sufficient to increase considerably the probability of his having read it.

III. THE *SHEPHERD OF HERMAS*

The *Shepherd of Hermas* is untypical in many ways among the Apostolic Fathers. It seems to inhabit a world of its own. Its language is remarkably free of quotations or even identifiable allusions to (Jewish) scripture. There are probable echoes of the Psalms here and there, but the only quotation signified as such is from the lost apocryphal work, *Eldad and Modat* (*Vis.* 2. 3. 4). The author's free, not to say unrestrained, method of composition also makes it difficult to identify the extent of influence from New Testament books.[23] As a former slave and once successful business man, he would have had neither the leisure nor the education for serious study. But more importantly perhaps, his belief in his own prophetic gift and special inspiration made cross-reference to sources redundant. In these circumstances, we need perhaps to distinguish between slight verbal echoes that may result from memory of liturgical reading of New Testament texts and the basic concepts with which Hermas is working.

[20] So also J. Daniélou, *The Theology of Jewish Christianity* (ET London: Darton, Longman and Todd, 1964), 307: 'II Clement quotes Gn 1:27 on the distinction between man and woman; but when it recalls that the Church is the Body of Christ, it alludes by implication to 2:24: "They two shall be one flesh", and this is the verse quoted by Paul.'

[21] On which see Gregory and Tuckett, Ch. 10 in companion volume.

[22] Not only (1), (2), and (9) in our list, but also (4), (10), and possibly (7), see *2 Clem.* 17. 5. Note also the reference to the seal of baptism: e.g., 7. 4, cf. Eph. 1.13.

[23] See J. Verheyden, 'The *Shepherd of Hermas* and the Writings that later formed the New Testament', Ch. 11 in companion volume.

The date of the *Shepherd* is a matter of controversy. If the author is identified with the Hermas of Rom. 16. 14,[24] then it can be no later than the end of the first century. But it is not even certain that Rom. 16 was originally addressed to Rome. And the romantic tendency to identify anybody with the same name as someone who appears in Scripture is to be resisted. Support for a late first-century date could be drawn from the reference to Clement in *Vis.* 2. 4. 3, but the same caution is applicable. The Muratorian Canon, on the other hand, attributes the work to the brother of Pope Pius 'more recently in our times'—i.e., *c.*135—and accordingly rejects it from the canonical list. Even if the Muratorian Canon is itself to be dated much later,[25] it is difficult to explain its evidence away. Osiek concludes that 'the best assignment of date is an extended duration of time beginning perhaps from the very last years of the first century, but stretching through most of the first half of the second'.[26] However, this compromise solution does not seem to do justice to the urgency that the author feels (see *Vis.* 2. 4. 3) to send his message abroad. Better perhaps to suppose that it was written at some time within this range, but to refuse greater precision. If the date is towards the end of the time frame, then the likelihood of acquaintance with the Pauline letter collection including Ephesians increases considerably, and correspondingly decreases towards the beginning.

The New Testament in the Apostolic Fathers claimed that Ephesians, along with 1 Corinthians, are category b sources, but the evidence does not quite bear out the Committee's confidence. It is based on two parallels. First, *Mand.* 10. 2 verses 1, 2, 4, and 5 and Eph. 4. 30 on 'grieving the spirit'. But it should be noted that in the *Shepherd* it is grief in the believer that wearies and saddens the spirit.[27] In other words, he does not mean the Holy Spirit of God, as in Ephesians. In any case, the Ephesians text is itself an allusion to Isa. 63. 10 (MT): 'they grieved his Holy Spirit' (the LXX has 'they provoked'), and the Old Testament text in a more literal translation than that of the LXX may be the source of the wording at least in both passages.

The second b-rated parallel is *Sim.* 9 // Eph. 4. 3–6. The *Shepherd* reads (9. 13. 5): 'Those who believe in the Lord through his Son, and clothe themselves with these spirits will be one spirit, one body and one colour of garment' (cf. 9. 13. 7: 'one spirit, one body and one clothing'). Reference is also made to 9. 17. 4: 'one mind, one faith, one love', a triplet repeated at 9. 18. 4 in

[24] So, Origen, *Comm. in Rom.* 10. 3.

[25] With G. Hahnemann, *The Muratorian Fragment and the Development of the Canon*, Oxford Theological Monographs (Oxford: Clarendon Press, 1992).

[26] C. Osiek, *The Shepherd of Hermas*, Hermeneia (Minneapolis: Fortress, 1999), 20.

[27] 'The holy spirit that is within you' is, so Osiek, *Shepherd of Hermas*, 137, argues, to be understood as 'the vulnerable good spirit... oppressed by a person under its influence'.

the longer formulation: 'After these [the double-minded, etc.] are thrown out, the church of God will be one body, one thinking, one mind, one faith, one love.' But this hardly warrants a b grade. In the context of 9. 13 it is the same coloured clothing (the white robes of righteousness) that is the dominant motif; the 'one spirit, one body' phrase is merely introductory and conventional. Similarly, at 9. 17–18, it is the same moral values that are emphasized. Indeed, there is no real similarity of thought between the *Shepherd* and Eph. 4. 4–6. The Ephesians passage is basically doctrinal, the passages in the *Shepherd* basically paraenetic. The most distinctive features of Ephesians—namely, 'one hope, one Lord, one baptism, one God'—are missing from the *Shepherd*, and the most distinctive features of the latter, 'one thinking, one mind, one love', are missing from Ephesians. Moreover, it is likely, as noted in the Introduction, that Eph. 4. 4–5 reflects a liturgical credal formula which could fully explain the superficial similarity at one or two points.

Three further parallels were adjudged d by the Oxford Committee. *Mand.* 3. 1: 'Let all truth proceed out of your mouth'; cf. Eph. 4. 25: 'Speak the truth. Let no rotten speech proceed out of your mouth.' Apart from the Semitic idiom of the verbal phrase, there is no similarity and no need to suppose a literary source for such a commonplace. Secondly, *Sim.* 9. 4, 3 refers to the building of the tower with four courses of stones, ten, twenty-five, thirty-five, and forty, respectively, which are later explained at 9. 15. 5: 'the ten are the first generation, the twenty five the second, the thirty five are the prophets and ministers of God and the forty are apostles and teachers of the proclamation of the Son of God.' The author of Ephesians, by contrast, reserves the titles 'apostles and prophets' for the first, founding generation at 2. 20 and 4. 11 f. Finally, *Sim.* 16. 2 refers to being 'made alive' (Ephesians uses the same verb compounded with *συν-*), and continues: 'Before bearing the name of the [Son of] God a person is dead.' The Ephesians parallel at 2. 1: 'you being dead to trespasses' is remote, especially if this is the correct translation,[28] in which case the phrase is to be taken in the opposite positive sense, comparable with Rom. 6. 11. However, the ambiguous character of these verbal echoes, hardly detectable to the human ear, should not necessarily lead us to the conclusion that Ephesians and the *Shepherd* are unrelated because there are at the same time large-scale conceptual similarities that the close textual method fails to capture.

First, the aged woman, whom Hermas at first mistakes for the Sybil, is finally revealed as the pre-existent and predestined church for whose sake, like Israel's in Jewish texts, the world was created (*Vis.* 2. 4. 1). The woman's age is partly the negative effect of the apathy and withered spirit of Christians

[28] See *Eph: BNTC ad loc.*

(*Vis.* 3. 11. 2), but partly also a positive attribute, denoting antiquity and venerability: this is clear from the fact that although the wrinkles have disappeared by the time of the last vision, she retains her white hair (*Vis.* 4. 2. 1). So it is possible to remove wrinkles by the process of sanctification: that is what Ephesians also claims (point (9) above). The pre-existent church is not a pure idealization: she also mirrors back to her members the consequences of their actions. As Carolyn Osiek comments: 'The Church is both ideal and real at the same time... an eschatological mystery, it is also a community of people of mixed spiritual quality, with need for improvement.'[29]

Secondly, the nuptial motif is present at *Vis.* 4. 2. 1: 'A girl met me dressed as if she were coming from the bridal chamber all in white', picking up the imagery of Eph. 5 and Rev. 21, but it is not really developed in the *Visions.* Indeed, they notably lack reference to the figure of Christ, which the marriage motif inevitably entails. The Christology of the *Shepherd* becomes explicit only later in the book, in which female imagery for the church fades into the background.

Thirdly, and more definitively, the Church as a building (or temple) is common in Paul and certain sayings in the gospels. The Qumran community, another dissident Jewish group, also saw itself as a spiritual temple.[30] The image is fully developed in the *Shepherd* in the third *Vision* and in *Sim.* 9. The emphasis is on placing stones together into a single construction, rejecting, permanently or temporarily, those that are defective and chipping away at those that are too round and smooth (i.e., the rich). The very same emphasis is found in Eph. 2. 21 f. (point (4) above), where Christ is the one 'in whom a whole building *fitting together* grows into a holy temple in the Lord in whom you also are being built up together for a dwelling place of God in the Spirit'. The obligation to collaborate in the joint enterprise of being the church reappears in Ephesians later at 4. 16, where Christ is the one 'from whom the whole body, being constructed and assembled, achieves bodily growth and builds itself up in love'. This latter passage in context (see 4. 11 and point (7) above) emphasizes the basic layer of apostles and prophets, evangelists, pastors, and teachers, who, to change the metaphor, are the supplying joints in the body of Christ. The correlation of the church as woman with the church as building harks back to Jewish roots, Old Testament images for Israel and Jerusalem.[31] As we have seen, it is present already in

[29] Osiek, *Shepherd of Hermas*, 36. To the same effect, she quotes the splendid study of E. Humphrey, *The Ladies and the Cities*, JSPS 17 (Sheffield: Sheffield Academic Press, 1995), which, however, unfortunately nowhere mentions Ephesians.

[30] See B. Gärtner, *The Temple and the Community in Qumran and the New Testament*, SNTSMS 1 (Cambridge: Cambridge University Press, 1965).

[31] See also Humphrey, *Ladies and the Cities*, on Joseph and Asenath and 4 Ezra.

Gal. 4, and of course in Rev. 21–2. These traditions may have played their own part in Hermas's imaginative development of the themes, but Ephesians is highly relevant too.

Fourthly, we have noted in the cases of Ephesians and *2 Clement* the importance of the Genesis creation story for this early Christian doctrine of the transcendent church. Is this the case also with the *Shepherd*? Perhaps it is to some extent. Admittedly, there is no mention of Adam and Eve, but the creation of the world and the creation of the church are linked together. In the first vision, the last words of the woman's reading from her book, and the only ones Hermas could remember (*Vis.* 1. 3. 4), are these: 'Behold, the God of hosts, who has by his mighty power and his great understanding created the world and by his glorious design clothed his creation with beauty, and by his potent word fixed the heavens and founded the earth upon the waters, and by his own wisdom and foresight formed his holy Church.' The link between creation and the church appears again in the building of the tower which, like the universe, is 'built upon water', representing the saving waters of baptism. The six angels doing the construction are identified as those who 'were created first of all, to whom the Lord delivered his creation' (*Vis.* 3. 4. 1). Compare points (2) and (10) in our list of features in Ephesians.

Fifthly, the first and third visions of the woman church envisage a seated figure: in the first, on a great white chair of snow-white wool (*Vis.* 1. 2. 2); later on an ivory couch covered with fine linen and a cushion (*Vis.* 3. 1. 4), an image for heavenly session. The fact is carefully noted (*Vis.* 3. 10. 3–5), and its explanation is given at *Vis.* 3. 1. 9, where Hermas is hurt that he is not yet worthy to sit on her right side on the couch, but she nevertheless 'took me by the hand and raised me up, and made me sit on the couch on the left'. That Christians are already raised and seated in the heavenly realms is the most striking expression of the realized eschatology of Ephesians (2. 6, point (3) above). The image occurs also in Rev. 3. 21, as a future hope for the victorious Christian, and at Rev. 4. 4, of the twenty-four elders already seated in heaven. But Ephesians is nearer to the *Shepherd* in applying it to a present possibility for the Christian, all the necessary qualifications notwithstanding.

Lastly, the woman-church in the *Shepherd* is both the content and the agent of revelation. She exposes Hermas's secret sins and failures as a husband and father, and, more importantly, after that rather trivial beginning, discloses God's grand design for the construction of the tower and the salvation of the universe. In *Sim.* 9, she is identified as 'the Holy Spirit, or the Son of God'; in context these are terms denoting an angel. The church therefore has a revelatory function, which is the highly distinctive feature of the teaching of Ephesians at 3. 9 f. (point (5) above). There the Wisdom of God, which is manifested through the church, is said to be manifold or multi-faceted (ποικίλος)—an attribute well illustrated by the polymorphic appearances of the church in the *Shepherd*.[32]

So, almost all the points that we claimed were highly distinctive of the ecclesiology of Ephesians appear centrally or on the margins of the *Shepherd*. No doubt other texts fed into the author's imagination as well. He may have known Jewish and Jewish-Christian apocalypses like *4 Ezra* and the book of Revelation, but there is a notable independence of imagination, which means that any sources are buried deep in his mind. It may not be insignificant that the reading of the book in the first vision almost entirely washes over him; perhaps he felt much the same when lections were read in worship.

CONCLUSION

This paper has attempted to assess the influence of Ephesians on two of the Apostolic Fathers, who have a similarly exalted view of the church, *2 Clement* and the *Shepherd*. At the level of verbal correspondences, which preoccupied the Committee of the Oxford Society of Historical Theology, it seems more likely that *2 Clement* reflects a direct knowledge and was consciously using Ephesians; and less likely that the *Shepherd* did. But the paper has argued also that exact similarity in wording may not in itself be a satisfactory criterion for establishing a literary relation. *2 Clement* is the product of an official teacher who is obliged to cross-reference his sources. Hermas is an amateur, idiosyncratic visionary, who is not so obligated. However, I hope to have shown that the similarities in the concept of the transcendent church between these three texts is very striking.

In the later second century, Gnostic groups took up this concept with enthusiasm: in the Valentinian system, for example, Ecclesia is one of the pre-existent aeons. This may be one of the reasons why the idea, so strong in Ephesians, *2 Clement*, and the *Shepherd*, soon begins to fade. Another reason may be that some of the aspects of this early high ecclesiology were drawn into and overshadowed by christological and trinitarian debates in the later patristic period, and by the Mariological debates of the medieval period.

[32] Cf. L. Pernveden, *The Concept of the Church in the Shepherd of Hermas*, STL 27 (Lund: Gleerup, 1966). On p. 23 he writes: 'A similar view of the role of divine wisdom appears in Eph. 3.10, where God's manifold wisdom is said to be made known through the Church. This may mean that even if the background to this theme is Jewish, it has nevertheless been absorbed into a Christian tradition, which in this case *undoubtedly* has an offshoot in Hermas' (my emphasis).

7

The Apostolic Fathers and Infant Baptism: Any Advance on the Obscurity of the New Testament?

David F. Wright

The hugely influential Faith and Order Paper on *Baptism, Eucharist and Ministry*, published in 1982, put the issue as follows:

> While the possibility that infant baptism was also practised in the apostolic age cannot be excluded, baptism upon personal profession of faith is the most clearly attested pattern in the New Testament documents.[1]

A dozen years later the massive *Catechism of the Catholic Church* struck a similar note:

> There is explicit testimony to this practice [of infant baptism] from the second century on, and it is quite possible that, from the beginning of the apostolic preaching, when whole 'households' received Baptism, infants may also have been baptized.[2]

The phrases 'cannot be excluded' and 'quite possible' are a far cry from the maximalist certainties of Joachim Jeremias and of the Church of Scotland's Special Commission on Baptism in the 1950s and 1960s.[3] Ever since the sixteenth century, the *onus probandi* has probably rested on those affirming the first-century or apostolic origins of infant baptism, rather than on those who reject this claim. For more than one reason, the position which Jeremias espoused so stalwartly has within the last few decades become more difficult

[1] *Baptism, Eucharist and Ministry*, Faith and Order Paper 111 (Geneva: World Council of Churches, 1982), 4 ('Baptism', 11).

[2] *Catechism of the Catholic Church* (London: Geoffrey Chapman, 1994), 284 (§ 1252).

[3] J. Jeremias, *Infant Baptism in the First Four Centuries* (London: SCM Press, 1960). The German original appeared in 1958. The Scottish Special Commission laboured during 1953–63 under the convenorship of Thomas F. Torrance, who wrote most of the voluminous reports. It remains probably the most comprehensive investigation of baptism, especially in its theological aspects, ever undertaken. For details see D. F. Wright, 'Baptism', in Nigel M. de S. Cameron *et al.* (eds.), *Dictionary of Scottish Church History and Theology* (Edinburgh: T. & T. Clark, 1993), 57–8.

to vindicate.[4] The aim of this paper is to enquire whether the works of the Apostolic Fathers throw any light on the obscurity which envelops the issue in the New Testament writings. It will proceed by asking a series of questions, and, as so often in intellectual enquiry, the validity of the outcome will depend on the appropriateness of the questions.

1. Are there any explicit references to infant baptism in the Apostolic Fathers?

The first is likely to prove the easiest to answer, since no scholar known to me now answers in the affirmative.

2. Are there any indirect references or implicit allusions to infant baptism in the Apostolic Fathers?

We are immediately into trickier territory, in which Polycarp's declaration to the proconsul of Asia, 'Eighty and six years have I served [Christ]', deserves priority treatment, if only because of the prominence it receives in arguments like that of Jeremias.[5] Is there anything new to be said to resolve what I judge to be an impasse? It may be highly probable, although it falls short of certainty, that the number of years denotes Polycarp's age.[6] The text belongs, of course, to a group of similar statements in early Christian literature attesting Christian identity or service from birth or childhood or lifelong Christian discipleship. Kurt Aland contributed to the debate, with a particular relish, since Jeremias had overlooked it, the only other such assertion in the Apostolic Fathers. *1 Clement* tells the Corinthian church that the letter is being carried to them by men who 'have passed blameless lives among us from youth (ἀπὸ νεότητος) until old age'.[7] Aland is keen to emphasize the indefiniteness of 'youth'.

[4] I note that the article 'Baptism 1. *Early Christianity*' by Maxwell E. Johnson in P. Bradshaw (ed.), *The New SCM Dictionary of Liturgy and Worship* (London: SCM Press, 2002), 35–7, mentions infant baptism first in connection with third-century sources.

[5] *Mart. Pol.* 9. 3; Jeremias, *Infant Baptism*, 59–63; K. Aland, *Did the Early Church Baptize Infants?* (London: SCM Press, 1963), 70–3 (German original, 1961); J. Jeremias, *The Origins of Infant Baptism* (London: SCM Press, 1963), 58 (German original, 1962).

[6] It is so assumed by H. König in S. Döpp and W. Geerlings (eds.), *Dictionary of Early Christian Literature* (New York: Crossroad, 2000), 494 (German original, 1998).

[7] Aland, *Did the Early Church Baptize Infants?*, 71, citing *1 Clem.* 63. 3.

There is little point in retracing here the lines of a familiar, and perhaps tedious, discussion. This clutch of testimonies may or may not hang together, but one comment is worth making before we move on. Insufficient attention has been given to the possibility of other non-baptismal markers of Christian belonging in the first three centuries. The fourth and fifth centuries furnish varied evidence of dedication or consecration or enrolment in the catechumenate soon after birth of individuals baptized only in responsible years. The fact that none of the pre-Constantinian texts explicitly identifies baptism as the starting-point of long-lasting or whole-life Christian discipleship at least leaves open the possibility that there may have been at hand some other way, even liturgical in form, of marking a child of Christian parents as intended for Christ. Jeremias and Aland disputed the import of two passages in the *Apology* of Aristides to this effect, but their exchanges focused rather myopically on the presence or absence of infant baptism, with not even Aland entertaining other possibilities.[8]

Statements like Polycarp's when facing martyrdom may not dispel the obscurity of the New Testament, but they do add a new category of evidence to be taken into account, or at least, in instances specifying span of life, evidence of greater precision. The closest parallel in the New Testament must be Timothy, who is declared to have 'known the holy scriptures from infancy (ἀπὸ βρέφους)', within a family in which grandmother and mother were, at least eventually, believers.[9] Jeremias's silence on the case of Timothy no doubt reflects the difficulty of fitting his Christian, rather than Jewish, discipleship from infancy into a credible chronology. In the nature of the case, the New Testament corpus only marginally allows for the elapse of time sufficient to accommodate generational transmission of the faith.

I doubt if any other alleged implicit references to infant baptism in the Apostolic Fathers are clear enough to merit discussion or add anything to the evidence of the New Testament—that is to say, they do not serve to resolve the uncertainties of the New Testament writings. Jeremias cites Ignatius' greeting in *Smyrn.* 13. 1 'to the families (οἴκους) of my brethren with their wives and children' as showing what—better, who—was or were 'commonly understood' by the word οἶκος in the well-known texts in 1 Corinthians and Acts, 'i.e., father and mother of the household and children of all ages'.[10] Ignatius

[8] See my essay 'Infant Dedication in the Early Church', in S. E. Porter and A. R. Cross (eds.), *Baptism, the New Testament and the Church: Historical and Contemporary Studies in Honour of R. E. O. White*, JSNTSup 171 (Sheffield: Sheffield Academic Press, 1999), 352–78, on 362–4.

[9] 2 Tim. 3. 15; 1. 5; cf. Acts 16. 1.

[10] Jeremias, *Infant Baptism*, 19–20. On p. 20 n. 1 Jeremias discusses Ign., *Pol.* 8. 2, where the household(s) of grown-up children seem to be in view, but appears to want both to have his cake and to eat it in claiming that even in this case 'οἶκος does not refer to the household without children'. In *Vis.* 3. 1. 6, Hermas is instructed to 'ask also concerning righteousness,

certainly provides an element of detail lacking in the New Testament references, but without, I judge, making the so-called *οἶκος* formula any more persuasive in the case for infant baptism than it is in its own terms in the New Testament. There is no direct evidence of any kind in the Apostolic Fathers of a household baptism. In *Did.* 4. 9–11, part of the pre-baptismal instruction is suggestive of household inclusiveness, with children and slaves within the family of Christian nurture, but how this relates to the baptismal order of *Did.* 7 is wholly obscure.

3. Do references to baptism in the Apostolic Fathers throw any light on the inclusion of infants among its recipients?

The directions for baptism in the *Didache* envisage responsible participants as its subjects. There is no provision for young children, but nor are they explicitly excluded.[11] If we recall that only one small paragraph betrays the place for infants in the lengthy baptismal order in the Hippolytan *Apostolic Tradition*, such that most questions about their inclusion are left unanswered, we should hesitate to regard the *Didache* as debarring them. Its text does contribute, however, to the general picture which emerges from all the patristic sources, that the rite of baptism developed throughout the era as a rite for believing respondents, into which non-responding babies when they came to be baptized were accommodated with adaptation minimal to the point of being often near invisible.

that you may take a part of it to your family (*οἶκον*)'. Hermas's children (*τέκνα*) and wife are depicted as sinful and in need of repentance (*Vis.* 1. 3. 1–2; 2. 2. 2–4; 2. 3. 1), but the children are by now probably adult (so Carolyn Osiek, *The Shepherd of Hermas: A Commentary*, Hermeneia (Minneapolis: Fortress, 1999), 49), and nothing can be inferred concerning the time of their baptism.

[11] *Did.* 7. Willy Rordorf, 'Baptism according to the Didache', in J. A. Draper (ed.), *The* Didache *in Modern Research*, AGAJU 37 (Leiden: Brill, 1996), 212–22, mentions infant baptism only in connection with the use of warm water and only to dismiss it summarily from consideration (p. 219). There is no mention of infants in Nathan Mitchell, 'Baptism in the *Didache*', in Clayton N. Jefford (ed.), *The* Didache *in Context*, NovTSup 77 (Leiden: Brill, 1995), 226–55. Neither Rordorf (pp. 221–2) nor Mitchell (pp. 226–7) includes provision for infants among the *Didache*'s notable omissions. In 1949 Jeremias still related warm water to the baptism of children, in *Hat die Urkirche der Kindertaufe geübt*, 2nd edn. (Göttingen: Vandenhoeck & Ruprecht, 1949), 29, but no longer in *Infant Baptism* (1958/60). Cf. André Benoît, *Le Baptême chrétien au second siècle: la théologie des pères*, Études d'histoire et de philosophie religieuses, 43 (Paris: Presses Universitaires de France, 1953), 31: 'Rien dans la *Didaché* n'apporte d'argument positif en faveur du baptême des enfants.'

The *Epistle to Barnabas* also furnishes an explicit discussion of baptism, from the perspective of its Old Testament foreshadowing. Not only does the writer with unmistakable purposefulness trace no connection between baptism and circumcision (see section 7 below), but what he does say about baptism clearly has responsible agents in view. They go down into the water (καταβαίνω, 11. 8, 11) 'with their hopes set on the cross' (11. 8), and ascend out of it 'bearing the fruit of fear in [their] hearts and having hope in Jesus in [their] spirits' (11. 11). How instinctively Barnabas avoided envisaging infants as subjects of Christian initiation appears earlier in his work.

> So we are the ones whom [God] brought into the good land. What then do 'milk and honey' mean [in Exod. 33. 3]? That a child is brought to life first by honey and then by milk. So accordingly we too are brought to life by faith in the promise and by the word, and will then go on to live possessing the earth. (6. 16–17)

When Ignatius through Polycarp exhorts the Smyrnaean Christians, 'Let your baptism remain as your weapons, your faith as a helmet, your love as a spear, your endurance as your panoply' (Ign. *Pol.* 6. 2),[12] is it fair comment that baptism fits better with faith, love, and endurance in this context as a recognizable feature of their conscious Christian experience? The assumption would be similar to that made by Paul in Rom. 6. 3–4.

2 Clement's interest in baptism is restricted to keeping it 'pure and undefiled' (6. 9). Twice 'seal' is used of the baptism to be preserved at all costs. (*2 Clem.* 7. 6; 8. 6). Nothing can be confidently inferred from these references.

Hermas was given the explanation of the stones which fell away from the tower near water, yet could not be rolled into the water: 'These are those who have heard the word and wish to be baptized into the name of the Lord,' but subsequently return to their former wickedness (*Vis.* 3. 7. 3). The author's preoccupation with repentance as the prerequisite for baptism is writ large throughout the work, as is the necessity of baptism ('water') for salvation (*Vis.* 3. 3. 5; *Sim.* 9. 16. 2–4). Yet in all of Hermas's elaborate symbolism, no category appears which might specifically accommodate those originally baptized in early infancy.

This survey has not touched on every reference to baptism in the Apostolic Fathers, but only on those which might be pertinent to our enquiry. No baptismal reference is identifiable which envisages other than responding penitents or believers as candidates.

[12] The plural τὸ βάπτισμα ὑμῶν makes clear that no specific reference to Polycarp's baptism is intended.

4. Do statements about children in the Apostolic Fathers throw any light on the possibility of their having been baptized?

The *Didache*, Polycarp, *1 Clement*, and *Barnabas* all instil the Christian duty of bringing up children in the nurture of the Lord.[13] *1 Clement* depicts God's creative love preparing 'his blessing for us before we were born' (38. 3). Yet when Ignatius advises Polycarp on the care of the church of Smyrna, he urges attention to widows, slaves, wives and husbands, but not to children (*Pol.* 4–5). *Barnabas*'s version of the sacrifice of a heifer in Numbers 19 includes among its extra-biblical elements boys (παιδία, παῖδες) who sprinkle all the people, whom he interprets as those who preached the gospel of forgiveness of sins to his own generation. There were three boys, standing for Abraham, Isaac, and Jacob (*Barn.* 8. 1, 3–4). Again *Barnabas* shows his instinctive lack of interest in Christian children.

Hermas provides the fullest and clearest parallel to the strain in the teaching of Jesus which set forth children as models of discipleship. From the twelfth mountain, the white one, came believers who are

> like innocent babies (βρέφη), and no evil rises in their heart nor have they known what wickedness is, but have remained always in innocence. Such believers shall undoubtedly dwell in the kingdom of God, because in none of their conduct did they defile the commandments of God, but remained in innocence all the days of their life with a single mind. All of you who will persevere and be as babies, having no evil, shall be more glorious than all of those mentioned before, for all babies (βρέφη) are glorious before God and come first with him. (*Sim.* 9. 29. 1–3)[14]

What it means for contemporary church practice that very young children—if 'babies' is not merely symbolic—have primacy of honour before God is not so much as hinted at. The message of Hermas (so the passage continues) is blessing on all who reject evil and assume freedom from wickedness, 'for you will live first of all people with God'. Such an exposition surely creates a presumption that the new-born belong to God's people, but it does nothing to dispel the uncertainty inherent in New Testament parallels. In sum, refer-

[13] *Did.* 4. 9; Poly., *Phil.* 4. 2; *1 Clem.* 21. 6; *Barn.* 19. 5. Herm., *Vis.* 1. 3. 2, is told to persevere in correcting his children.

[14] Cf. *Sim.* 9. 31. 2. For Osiek, *Shepherd*, 252, Hermas has in view a 'strictly ideal' group. Cf. *Barn.* 6. 11, explaining the bringing of God's people into the land of milk and honey: 'When he made us new people by the remission of sins, he fashioned us into another pattern (τύπον), that we should have the souls of children (παιδίων) as though he were creating us afresh.' At several places in the Apostolic Fathers, Christians are addressed as children: e.g., *1 Clem.* 22. 1; *Barn.* 7. 1; *Did.* 3. 1, 3, 4, 5, 6; 4. 1.

ences of this type in the Apostolic Fathers fall some way short of the picture that may be drawn from the New Testament writings on the presence of young children in the church community.

5. Are there general theological statements or emphases in the Apostolic Fathers which might suggest that baptism was given to infants?

The History of Infant Baptism by the Anglican writer William Wall, published in 1705, retains its value today as an assemblage of patristic sources. 'It has remained the English classic on the subject.'[15] From the Apostolic Fathers he cites *1 Clement*'s quotation of Job 14. 4: 'No one is clean from defilement, not even if his life be but one day old,' which would become in later Fathers a proof-text for the necessity of baptism to deal with original sin in the new-born.[16] Wall also adduces passages from Hermas which show the necessity of baptism for salvation, passages which bear all the greater authority because Hermas wrote, so Wall believes, before John compiled his gospel, including the standard proof-text among the Fathers for the necessity of baptism, John 3. 5.[17] Such arguments are likely to weigh less heavily with modern students of the Fathers, not least because of the uncertain relationship between baptism and original sin in the Greek patristic tradition.

In an entirely different direction, Ignatius' proto-credal summaries are notable in twice including the baptism of Jesus between his birth and his passion. The anti-Docetic thrust is obvious in the letter to Smyrna. Jesus Christ was 'truly born of a virgin, baptized by John, in order that all righteousness might be fulfilled by him' (*Smyrn.* 1. 1: γεγεννημένον . . . βεβαπτισμένον). The perfect tense of 'baptized' may point to the lasting significance of his submission to John. Writing to the Ephesians, Ignatius' concern is not so patently anti-heretical: 'Jesus Christ our God was conceived by Mary both of the seed of David and of the Holy Spirit. He was born and was baptized, so that τῷ πάθει he might purify the water' (*Eph.* 18. 2: ἐγεννήθη καὶ ἐβαπτίσθη).[18] If τῷ πάθει is translated 'by his passion', then lurking here is a suggestively profound yet undeveloped parallel to Jesus' own anticipation

[15] F. L. Cross (ed.), *Oxford Dictionary of the Christian Church*, 3rd edn., ed. E. A. Livingstone (Oxford: Oxford University Press, 1997), 1717.

[16] *1 Clem.* 17. 4; W. Wall, *The History of Infant Baptism*, 3 vols., 4th edn. (London: Griffith, Farran, Browne & Co., 1819), i. 23.

[17] Wall, *History*, i. 24–7.

[18] Cf. W. R. Schoedel, *Ignatius of Antioch: A Commentary on the Letters of Ignatius of Antioch*, Hermeneia (Philadelphia; Fortress, 1985), 84–6.

of his death as a 'baptism' (cf. Mark 10. 38–9; Luke 12. 50). Less plausible, however, is a reference to his undergoing baptism at John's hands as an act of submission. Nevertheless, Ignatius' understanding of the baptism of Jesus, and of his death as a baptism, is insufficiently developed to have any bearing on our enquiry concerning paedo-baptism.

A theological topic of obvious baptismal reference is that of the church as the body of Christ. Clement's deployment of this imagery is at times less than Pauline, but he maintains the interdependence of small and great, strong and weak, within the one body, yet without indicating how children might fit in (*1 Clem.* 37. 4–5).

It is not possible, then, to identify in any of the Apostolic Fathers theological developments of a non-baptismal character which bear on the question of the baptismal inclusion of infants. The emphasis on faith is pervasive enough, but is never spelt out in such a manner, so I judge, as to exclude youngsters not yet of age to believe.

6. Do the Apostolic Fathers throw any light on the interpretation of contested New Testament texts?

We may leave aside all questions of which New Testament writings the Apostolic Fathers severally may have known, and in which form, since our interest is in whether they help us to clear away any of those writings' obscurities about baptism given to infants. To this question only a confident negative can be given. None, I think I am right in saying, of the New Testament verses commonly in contention with reference to the apostolic origins of paedo-baptism is quoted or alluded to by any of the Apostolic Fathers. By such disputed texts I mean Acts 2. 39; 1 Cor. 7. 14; Col. 2. 11–12; and several mentions of household baptisms, in 1 Cor. 1. 16; Acts 16. 15, 33; 18. 7, and also 11. 14, together with the synoptic accounts of Jesus' blessing of the children, in Matt. 19. 13–15; Mark 10. 13–16 (cf. 9. 36b); and Luke 18. 15–17.[19] On none of these does the corpus of the Apostolic Fathers help to resolve their controverted bearing on the beginnings of infant baptism.

In section 2 above, note was taken of Ignatius' greeting to 'the families of my brothers with their wives and children' at Smyrna (13. 1), but this cannot

[19] On the subsequent fortunes of this pericope, see my paper 'Out, In, Out: Jesus' Blessing of the Children and Infant Baptism', in S. E. Porter and A. R. Cross (eds.), *Dimensions of Baptism: Biblical and Theological Studies*, JSNTSup 234 (Sheffield: Sheffield Academic Press, 2002), 188–206.

be treated as evidence of his, or any other Apostolic Father's, understanding of the supposed 'household baptism' texts listed in the previous paragraph. Remember that establishing how these texts should rightly be read is not part of my remit.

Even if we enlarge the circle of putatively relevant New Testament texts to encompass verses such as Acts 21. 21[20] and the occurrences of κωλύειν in baptismal contexts in Matt. 3. 14 and Acts 8. 36, 10. 47, and 11. 17, which helped Oscar Cullmann and others after him read Jesus' blessing of the children baptismally (the Greek verb occurs in all three synoptics),[21] we still draw a blank among the Apostolic Fathers. This holds also for John 3. 3–5, perhaps echoed in the *Shepherd* (*Sim.* 4. 15. 3),[22] Matt. 18. 10,[23] and for that matter the other places where Jesus commends the child as a model for his followers, such as Matt. 18. 3.[24]

It is not inappropriate here, although the point might well have been made in section 3 above, to state that none of the other baptismal texts in the New Testament which are not normally cited specifically in support of the primitive status of infant baptism is used or alluded to by any of the Apostolic Fathers in a manner which suggests a link between baptism and infants. Most of them have left no trace at all, including [Mark 16. 16]; Acts 1. 5; 8. 36, 38; 19. 3–4, etc.; 1 Cor. 1. 13–16; 10. 2; 12. 13; and Gal. 3. 27. A non-baptismal phrase from Rom. 6. 3–4 may be found in Ign. *Eph.* 19. 3 (καινότης ζωῆς). In passages of plausible dependence on Eph. 4. 4–6, 'one baptism' is missing from *1 Clem.* 46. 6, but has become 'the seal' in the *Shepherd* (*Sim.* 9. 17. 4), while in *Sim.* 9. 13. 7 'one clothing' may stand proxy for one baptismal identity. Hermas at *Vis.* 3. 3. 5 has probably got 'saved through water' from 1 Pet. 3. 20–1, but the 'washing' or 'bath' of Titus 3. 5 (λουτρόν) has not been preserved in a probable borrowing in *Barn.* 1. 3.[25] The only possible indebtedness of the baptismal section in *Did.* 7 is the threefold name from Matt. 28. 19, while *Barn.* 11 on baptism betrays none at all. This is in sum a meagre

[20] Cf. Jeremias, *Infant Baptism*, 48.

[21] Cf. O. Cullmann, *Baptism in the New Testament*, SBT 1 (London: SCM Press, 1950), 71–80 (German original, 1948); Jeremias, *Infant Baptism*, 48–55.

[22] Cf. Jeremias, *Infant Baptism*, 58: 'The Gospel of John could scarcely have formulated in so unqualified a manner the proposition that only those begotten by water and the spirit can enter the kingdom of God (John 3. 5), if in its time baptism had been withheld from children of Christian parents.' Cf. the highly cautious comments in *NTAF*, 123.

[23] Cf. Jeremias, *Infant Baptism*, 65; J. Héring, 'Un texte oublié: Mathieu 18:10. A propos des controversies récentes sur le pédobaptisme', in *Aux sources de la tradition chrétienne: Mélanges offerts à M. M. Goguel* (Neuchâtel and Paris: Delachaux & Niestlé, 1950), 95–102.

[24] On Matt. 18. 3, cf. Jeremias, *Infant Baptism*, 49–52. There may be an echo in Hermas, *Sim.* 9. 29. 1–3; cf. *NTAF*, 122.

[25] On these texts see *NTAF*, 69, 53, 106 (with reference also to *Sim.* 9. 13. 5; 9. 18. 4), 115, 14.

harvest, which must be borne in mind in evaluating the absence of any influence of New Testament texts which later generations have judged pertinent to the paedo-baptism debate.

7. Do any of the Apostolic Fathers support a parallelism between circumcision and baptism?

This larger issue was no more than alluded to in the previous section's reference to Col. 2. 11–12 as a contested text. According to Jeremias, 'Paul here names baptism "the Christian circumcision" (ἡ περιτομὴ τοῦ Χριστοῦ) and describes it thereby as the Christian sacrament which corresponds to Jewish circumcision and replaces it.'[26] This sentence aptly summarizes what had become a common attitude in Cyprian's time in the mid-third century. It is certainly not attested in the Apostolic Fathers. Apart from Ignatius' Delphic utterance to the Philadelphians that 'it is better to hear of Christianity from a man who is circumcised than of Judaism from one who is uncircumcised' (6. 1) and a polemical dismissal of the Jews' 'pride in circumcision' as mere 'mutilation of the flesh' in *Ep. Diogn.* 4. 1, 4, all of the uses of the verb περιτέμνω and the noun, and of ἀκροβυστία, 'uncircumcision', appear in the *Epistle of Barnabas.* None of these is found in section 11 on baptism, and Everett Ferguson is warranted in asserting that 'one thing baptism did not mean to Barnabas: it was not associated with circumcision. The counterpart of circumcision in the flesh is circumcision of the ears and heart by the Holy Spirit (9. 1–9; 10. 11).'[27] Not only did the author devote a full section (9) to circumcision, in which he apparently denies that it was for the people of Israel a seal of their covenant (9. 6), but his discussion of baptism explicitly sets out at the beginning to ascertain whether the Lord gave any Old Testament foreshadowing of it (11. 1). The deliberateness of his failure to relate circumcision to baptism could scarcely be more unequivocal.

8. Concluding reflections: any advance on New Testament obscurity?

To focus an enquiry of this nature on the writings known since at least the seventeenth century as the Apostolic Fathers cannot escape the limitations of

[26] Jeremias, *Infant Baptism*, 39–40.

[27] E. Ferguson, 'Christian and Jewish Baptism according to the *Epistle of Barnabas*', in Porter and Cross (eds.), *Dimensions of Baptism*, 207–23, at 222–3.

this conventional designation. It must not be seen as synonymous with an investigation of a particular span of years, such as 90–170, since I have not pursued other possible sources within the era. The earliest Apostolic Father(s) may pre-date one or more New Testament texts, and the latest, presumably the *Epistle to Diognetus* (if it still deserves to be included), is certainly later than a handful of other patristic texts meriting consideration.

Nevertheless, the enquiry is not pointless—unless it is pointless to perpetuate the category of Apostolic Fathers. In this paper I have not set myself a task which ignores these limitations, but have modestly asked whether any of these writings helps to dispel the obscurity surrounding the baptism of infants in the New Testament. The answer must be that none of them does so. What has been quite widely regarded as evidence supporting infant baptism—the eighty-six-years-long Christian service of Polycarp—does not take us beyond uncertainty at best. The statement itself has no obvious baptismal connotations, though it has been thought to imply one.

In reality, in contrast to the New Testament, the Apostolic Fathers of themselves barely sustain a picture even of obscurity concerning infant baptism. So far are they from dispersing the shadows of the New Testament that, if one started from the Apostolic Fathers and not the New Testament, one could scarcely claim that the baptizing of infants was even obscurely in view. The Apostolic Fathers do not, therefore, present us with any advance on the indeterminate evidence of the New Testament; nor do they leave us with a similarly uncertain *status quaestionis*. Rather, for those who seek dissipation of the darkness, they mark a move backwards rather than forwards, or perhaps sideways into a more uniform blankness concerning the practice of paedo-baptism.

If it is right to continue, with much earlier commentary, to discern among the Apostolic Fathers in general a shared concern with the internal ordering of the life of congregations, with domestic affairs rather than apologetic or doctrinal engagement with the external world, what bearing does this perspective have on our enquiry? Perhaps it allows us to deduce merely that the baptizing of the new-born was not a cause of discord in any of the Apostolic Fathers' churches. On the other hand, the primitive church order in the *Didache* betrays no hint that it was uncontroversial routine practice. Where it might have left some impress, in the chapters in *Barnabas* on baptism and on circumcision, the silence may be more eloquent than in the *Didache*.

The overall conclusion must be that the Apostolic Fathers do not strengthen the case for judging that infant baptism was practised in the New Testament churches. If anything, they weaken the case. A critical question remains as to how we should interpret their silence.

8

The Eucharist in the Gospel of John and in the *Didache*

Carsten Claussen

Unlike the synoptic gospels and Paul's First Letter to the Corinthians, the Gospel of John does not give a narrative account of the Last Supper of Jesus.[1] However, there seem to be a number of possible allusions to the Eucharist[2] in the Fourth Gospel. Since the middle of the twentieth century, these have led scholars to mainly three rather different conclusions:[3]

1. For quite some time many scholars regarded John 6. 51c–58 as clearly eucharistic, but as an interpolation by a later ecclesiastical redactor.[4] However, this view has meanwhile lost most of its influence.[5]

[1] Matt. 26. 17–30; Mark 14. 12–26; Luke 22. 7–38; 1 Cor. 11. 23–6.

[2] When we use terms like 'Eucharist' and 'eucharistic', we do so because they represent the original εὐχαριστία and its derivatives, not because of any dogmatic or denominational implications.

[3] For a survey of the history of research regarding the question of the Eucharist in John, see H. Klos, *Die Sakramente im Johannesevangelium*, SBS 46 (Stuttgart: Katholisches Bibelwerk, 1970); R. E. Brown, 'The Johannine Sacramentary Reconsidered', *TS* 23 (1962), 183–206; *idem*, *The Gospel According to John I–XII*, AB 29 (Garden City, NY: Doubleday, 1966), pp. cxi–cxiv; R. Schnackenburg, *Das Johannesevangelium: Dritter Teil: Kommentar zu Kapitel 13–21*, HTKNT 4/3 (Freiburg: Herder, 1957), 38–53; M. Roberge, 'Le discours sur le pain de vie, Jean 6, 22–59: problèmes d'interpretation', *LTP* 38 (1982), 265–99; L. Wehr, *Arznei der Unsterblichkeit: Die Eucharistie bei Ignatius von Antiochien und im Johannesevangelium*, NTAbh, n.s. 18 (Münster: Aschendorff, 1987), 9–17; M. J. J. Menken, 'John 6:51c–58: Eucharist or Christology', in R. A. Culpepper (ed.), *Critical Readings of John 6*, Biblical Interpretation Series 22 (Leiden: Brill, 1997), 183–204, esp. 183–5.

[4] See R. Bultmann, *The Gospel of John* (ET Philadelphia: Westminster, 1971), 218–19: 'These verses refer without any doubt to the sacramental meal of the Eucharist, where the flesh and blood of the "son of Man" are consumed, with the result that this food gives "eternal life", in the sense that the participants in the meal can be assured of the future resurrection. . . . This not only strikes one as strange in relation to the Evangelist's thought in general, and specifically to his eschatology, but it also stands in contradiction to what has been said just before. . . . Thus, we must inevitably conclude that vv. 51b–8 have been added by an ecclesiastical editor.' Cf. also E. Lohse, 'Wort und Sakrament im Johannesevangelium', *NTS* 7 (1960), 110–25; G. Bornkamm, 'Die eucharistische Rede im Johannesevangelium', *ZNW* 47 (1956), 161–9; repr. in *idem*, *Geschichte und Glaube*, i: *Gesammelte Aufsätze* 3 (Munich: Kaiser, 1968), 60–7; the problems of the Johannine *Literarkritik* are discussed extensively in J. Frey, *Die johanneische Eschatologie*, i: *Ihre Probleme im Spiegel der Forschung seit Reimarus*, WUNT 96 (Tübingen: J. C. B. Mohr (Paul Siebeck), 1997), 429–45.

[5] See the fine collection of essays by R. A. Culpepper (ed.), *Critical Readings of John 6*, Biblical Interpretation Series 22 (Leiden: Brill, 1997), and in particular the editor's summary

2. Others interpret terms like 'bread', 'flesh', and 'blood' as christological and sometimes anti-Docetic references to the person of Jesus, and not in terms of the elements of the Eucharist.[6] In both the above cases one ends up with a non-sacramental (or perhaps even an anti-sacramental) Gospel of John.[7]
3. Some recent contributors to the debate view this passage as genuinely Johannine but nevertheless as eucharistic and as a logical continuation of the preceding passage with its christological message.[8] There are even exegetes who try to interpret as many symbolic references in John's Gospel as possible as referring to the sacraments.[9] Accordingly, among other passages, John 6. 51c–58 is interpreted as 'decidedly, even stridently, eucharistic'.[10] This tendency is one of deliberate sacramentalism (and perhaps ultra-sacramentalism).

(pp. 247–57, esp. 253): 'One of the chief contributions of this collection of essays, therefore, is to reverse the long-held view that John 6:51c–58 is a later redactional insertion that jarringly introduces a eucharistic interpretation of the bread of life theme. The continuities of theme and language are much stronger than was previously assumed, meaning that these verses should now be read as an integral part of the discourse.'

[6] Menken, 'John 6: 51c–58', 201–3; cf. already E. Schweizer, 'Das johanneische Zeugnis vom Herrenmahl', *EvTh* 12 (1953), 341–63; repr. in *idem*, *Neotestamentica: deutsche und englische Aufsätze 1951–1963* (Zürich: Zwingli Verlag, 1963), 371–96, doubts the redactional character of the three sacramental passages, but does not see the sacraments in any way as central to Johannine thought.

[7] See, e.g., P. N. Anderson, 'The *Sitz im Leben* of the Johannine Bread of Life Discourse and its Evolving Context', in Culpepper (ed.), *Critical Readings*, 1–59, esp. 5: '*The "eucharistic interpolation" in John 6 is neither*' (italics original); cf. *idem*, *The Christology of the Fourth Gospel: Its Unity and Disunity in the Light of John 6* (Valley Forge, Pa.: Trinity Press International, 1997), esp. 110–36; Menken, 'John 6: 51c–58', 183–204; cf. already W. Wilkens, 'Das Abendmahlszeugnis im vierten Evangelium', *EvTh* 18 (1958), 354–70, regards John 6. 51c–58 as truly Johannine, but argues in favour of an anti-docetic tendency and a peripheral character of the sacraments in John; H. Köster, 'Geschichte und Kultus im Johannesevangelium und bei Ignatius von Antiochien', *ZTK* 54 (1957), 56–69, plays down the sacraments in John by contrasting them with the metaphysical viewpoint of the sacraments held by Ignatius of Antioch.

[8] See for a very balanced interpretation, e.g., U. Schnelle, *Das Evangelium nach Johannes*, THKNT 4, 2nd edn. (Leipzig: Evangelische Verlagsanstalt, 2000), 140: 'Das gesamte Kapitel läßt sich als eine wohlüberlegte Komposition durch den Evangelisten Johannes verstehen und interpretieren, so daß sich die Annahme einer post-evangelistischen Schicht erübrigt. Auch das Speisungswunder und der Seewandel sind transparent für das eucharistische Mahl.'

[9] A classic statement of this view is O. Cullmann, *Early Christian Worship*, SBT 10 (London: SCM Press, 1953), 58: 'John's Gospel ... treats the two sacraments as expressions of the whole worship life of the early community and correspondingly sets forth the relation between the Lord of the community *present especially in these two sacraments* and the life of Jesus' (italics original). Cf. L. Bouyer, 'Les sacraments dans l'évangile johannique', *BVC* 1 (1953), 121–2; B. Vawter, 'The Johannine Sacramentary', *TS* 17 (1956), 151–66; A. Corell, *Eschatology and Church in the Gospel of St John* (London: SPCK, 1958; translation of *Consummatum est: Eskatologi och kyrka i Johannesevangeliet* (Stockholm: Svenska kyrkans diakonistyrelses bokförlag, 1950)); J. M. Perry, 'The Evolution of the Johannine Eucharist', *NTS* 39 (1993), 22–35.

[10] Perry, 'Evolution', 22.

To sum up, dealing with the question of the sacraments in John seems to be particularly in danger of being affected by dogmatic preconceptions. Modern interpreters know what baptism and the Eucharist are today, and what they should have been in their very beginning. Most would argue that the words of institution are constitutive for a real Eucharist.[11] But this view does not leave much room to look for different liturgical forms in the ancient sources, which may then in turn help us to understand later developments. Before looking at ancient eucharistic passages, it may, therefore, come as a welcome surprise to realize that 'there is no firm evidence at all for the liturgical use of an institution narrative until the fourth century'.[12]

Looking at the eucharistic passages of the Fourth Gospel through the lenses of the synoptic and Pauline passages surely results in the assessment of supposed shortcomings or even over-interpretations on the Johannine side. The authors of *The New Testament in the Apostolic Fathers* took a different path.[13] By comparing the Apostolic Fathers to the New Testament, they greatly enlarged our visual ability to see things that we would not have seen otherwise. A particularly fascinating example for this is the synoptic comparison between the Eucharist in the *Didache* and in John.

THE *DIDACHE* OF THE TWELVE APOSTLES

Modern research on the *Didache*[14] began only in 1883 when Philotheos Bryennios, later the metropolitan of Nicomedia, finally published the *editio princeps* of the text he had found ten years earlier in the library of the patriarch of Jerusalem at Constantinople.[15]

[11] For a recent ecumenical discussion regarding the validity of a Eucharist without the words of institution, see P. M. Lugmayr, 'Die "Anaphora von Addai und Mari" und die Dogmatik', *Una Voce-Korrespondenz*, 33 (2003), 30–47; *idem*, 'Anaphoren ohne "direkte" Wandlungsworte bereits unter Pius XI. (1922–1939): ein Beitrag zu einer aktuellen Diskussion', *Una Voce-Korrespondenz*, 33 (2003), 227–44; see also Pontifical Council for Promoting Christian Unity 'Guidelines for Admission to the Eucharist between the Chaldean Church and the Assyrian Church of the East', *L'Osservatore Romano*, 26 Oct. 2001, p. 7, where members of the Chaldean Church, which is in full communion with the Roman Catholic Church are granted admission to the Eucharist administered by the Assyrian Church of the East, i.e. a Eucharist without words of institution like the Anaphora of Addai and Mari, in situations of pastoral necessity.

[12] P. F. Bradshaw, *The Search for the Origins of Christian Worship: Sources and Methods for the Study of Early Liturgy*, 2nd edn. (New York and Oxford: Oxford University Press, 2002), 62.

[13] Hereafter referred to as *NTAF.*

[14] A second title at the beginning of the document reads: '*Didache* of the Lord through the Twelve Apostles to the Gentiles.'

[15] P. Bryennios, *Διδαχὴ τῶν δώδεκα ἀποστόλων* (Constantinople: S. I. Boutura, 1883).

Although a number of ancient Christian authors like Eusebius and Athanasius of Alexandria, among others,[16] referred to the so-called *Teaching of the Twelve Apostles*, its text had been lost, probably since the fourth or fifth century.

As the document is composed of very different traditional items and redaction, neither a precise dating nor a consensus regarding its place of origin has yet been reached. The teaching of the Two Ways (*Did.* 1–6) may be as early as the mid-first century. Wandering charismatics (*Did.* 11–13) *and* elected deacons and bishops (*Did.* 15) may point to a transitional phase from mainly charismatic beginnings to a more institutionalized church order in the second half of the first century. The separation from Judaism (cf. *Did.* 8. 1–2)[17] may indicate a time late in the first century. Overall, a final redaction around 100 CE seems quite probable.[18]

The early circulation of the document in Egypt may indicate its origin there. However, the wandering charismatics (*Did.* 11–13) as heirs of the Jesus movement would probably fit better into a Syrian or Palestinian environment. Of course, different sections may stem not just from different times but also from a variety of localities. Thus there is at present no certainty in dating or locating the *Didache.*

By 1905, only 22 years after the first modern edition of the *Didache*, when *The New Testament in the Apostolic Fathers* was published, there was already an extensive number of editions, commentaries, and articles dealing with this early church order.[19] Only one year after Bryennios, Adolf Harnack published

[16] K. Niederwimmer, *The Didache: A Commentary* (ET Minneapolis: Fortress, 1998; German original: *Die Didache*, KAV 1 (Göttingen: Vandenhoeck & Ruprecht, 1989, 2nd edn. 1993)), 4–6. Cf. also his summary of possible quotations of the *Didache* in early Christian literature on pp. 6–13, its use in later church orders on pp. 13–17, and by Byzantine authors of the twelfth to fourteenth centuries on pp. 17–18. A Georgian version now appears to be a relatively modern translation. Cf. B. Ehrman, 'Didache: The Teaching of the Twelve Apostles', in *idem, The Apostolic Fathers*, i, LCL 24 (Cambridge, Mass.: Harvard University Press, 2003), 403–43, on pp. 412–13.

[17] This is indicated by the exhortation in *Did.* 8. 1–2: 'And do not keep your fasts with the hypocrites. For they fast on Monday and Thursday; but you should fast on Wednesday and Friday.' Cf. Matt. 6. 16.

[18] For a possible reconstruction of the origin of the *Didache*, see Niederwimmer, *Didache*, 42–54. There is also here a detailed discussion of the 'Time and Place of the Writing' (pp. 52–4).

[19] The early literature prior to 1900 was summarized by A. Ehrhard, *Die altchristliche Literatur und ihre Erforschung von 1884–1900*, i: *Die vornicäische Literatur*, Straßburger Theologische Studien, Supplementband 1 (Freiburg im Breslau: Herdersche Verlagshandlung, 1900), 37–68.

Greek editions with English, French, and German translations are by J. B. Lightfoot, *The Apostolic Fathers: Revised Greek Texts with Introductions and English Translations* (London: Macmillan, 1891; repr. Grand Rapids, Mich.: Baker Book House, 1984, 2nd edn. 1992; rev. edn. 1999); K. Lake, 'The Didache, or Teaching of the Twelve Apostles', in *idem, The Apostolic Fathers*, i, LCL 24 (London: William Heinemann Ltd.; Cambridge, Mass.: Harvard University

his edition in 1884 with a commentary, which soon became fundamental for the subsequent history of research.[20] Harnack was also the first to observe numerous similarities between the Gospel of John and the eucharistic prayers in *Did.* 9 and 10.[21] He cites twelve passages where he finds parallels, almost all of them in John 6 and 17,[22] and concludes: 'Therefore, the assumption of a real literary relationship here is more obvious than in all similar cases.'[23]

Kirsopp Lake (1872–1946), then Professor of New Testament Exegesis at the University of Leiden, took responsibility for investigating the relationship of the New Testament and the *Didache* in the *NTAF*.[24] The 'composite character of the document'[25] was responsible for the major difficulties of such an undertaking. Therefore, Lake divided the document into four sections:

1. 'The *Two Ways*', *Did.* 1–6;
2. 'The ecclesiastical section', *Did.* 7. 1–15. 3;

Press, 1912), 303–33; G. Schöllgen, 'Didache: Zwölf-Apostel-Lehre: Einleitung, Übersetzung und Kommentar', in *idem* and W. Geerlings, *Zwölf-Apostel-Lehre: Apostolische Überlieferung: Lateinisch, Griechisch, Deutsch*, FC 1 (Freiburg: Herder, 1991), 23–139; A. Lindemann and H. Paulsen (eds.), *Die apostolischen Väter: Griechisch–deutsche Parallelausgabe auf Grundlage der Ausgaben von F. X. Funk, K. Bihlmeyer und M. Whittaker, mit Übersetzungen von M. Dibelius und D.-A. Koch* (Tübingen: J. C. B: Mohr (Siebeck, 1992); A. Cody, 'The *Didache*: An English Translation', in C. N. Jefford (ed.), *The* Didache *in Context: Essays on its Text, History and Transmission*, NovTSup 77 (Leiden: Brill, 1995), 3–14 (English trans., pp. 5–14); Ehrman, *Apostolic Fathers*. The last-named edition was mainly used for preparing this paper, although I have taken the liberty of changing parts of Ehrman's translations at times.

More recent editions and commentaries on the *Didache* are by J.-P. Audet, *La Didachè: Instructions des Apôtres* (Paris: Gabalda, 1958); R. A. Kraft, *Barnabas and the Didache*, iii (New York: Thomas Nelson, 1965); K. Wengst, *Didache (Apostellehre), Barnabasbrief, Zweiter Klemensbrief, Schrift an Diognet*, Schriften des Urchristentums 2 (Darmstadt: Wissenschaftliche Buchgesellschaft, 1984); Niederwimmer, *Didache*; W. Rordorf and A. Tuilier, *La Doctrine des douze apôtres (Didachè): Introduction, texte, traduction, notes, appendice et index*, SC 148 (Paris: Cerf, 1978, 2nd edn. 1998); H. van de Sandt and D. Flusser, *The Didache: Its Jewish Sources and its Place in Early Judaism and Christianity*, CRINT 3.5 (Assen: Royal van Gorcum; Minneapolis: Fortress, 2002), includes the edition of Cody; A. Milavec, *The Didache: Faith, Hope, and Life of the Earliest Christian Communities, 50–70 C.E.* (New York and Mahwah, NJ: Newman Press, 2003).

Extensive bibliographies and numerous essays can be found in Jefford (ed.), *The* Didache *in Context*; J. A. Draper (ed.), *The* Didache *in Modern Research*, AGAJU 37 (Leiden: Brill, 1996); *idem*, 'The Didache in Modern Research: An Overview', in *idem* (ed), Didache *in Modern Research*, 1–42, also provides an excellent survey of research regarding the *Didache* from the beginning until the middle of the 1990s.

[20] A. Harnack, *Die Lehre der zwölf Apostel nebst Untersuchungen zur ältesten Geschichte der Kirchenverfassung und des Kirchenrechts*, TU 2 (Leipzig: J. J. Hinrichs'sche Buchhandlung, 1884).

[21] Ibid. 79.

[22] Ibid. 79–80.

[23] Ibid. 81 (my trans.).

[24] K. Lake, 'The Didache', in *NTAF*, 24–36.

[25] *NTAF*, 24.

3. 'The eschatological section', *Did.* 16;
4. 'The interpolation in the "Two Ways" ', *Did.* 1. 3–2. 1.

On comparing relevant sections of the *Didache* with New Testament passages, it becomes quite obvious that, according to Lake's judgement, there is only one instance where there is 'a lower degree of probability'[26] for some connection: The 'Trinitarian baptismal formula' appears both in *Did.* 7. 1 and in Matt. 28. 19.[27] However, as a liturgical formula, it was probably used by many largely independent early Christian communities, and cannot prove literary dependence between the two texts. In several other cases of similarities his grading reaches only a rather low possibility of any dependence.

However, when it comes to comparing the *Didache* with the Fourth Gospel, Lake opts for 'unclassed'.[28] As passages 'which seem reminiscent of Johannine ideas and terminology',[29] he quotes the following texts:

Did. 9. 2: *ὑπὲρ τῆς ἁγίας ἀμπέλου Δαυεὶδ τοῦ παιδός σου* ('for the holy vine of David, thy child');[30]

Did. 9. 3: *Εὐχαριστοῦμέν σοι . . .*[31] *ὑπὲρ τῆς ζωῆς καὶ γνώσεως, ἧς ἐγνώρισας ἡμῖν διὰ Ἰησοῦ τοῦ παιδός σου.* ('We give thee thanks . . . for the life and knowledge which thou didst make known to us through Jesus thy child');

Did. 10. 3: *ἡμῖν δὲ ἐχαρίσω πνευματικὴν τροφὴν καὶ ποτὸν καὶ ζωὴν αἰώνιον διὰ τοῦ παιδός σου.* ('but us hast thou blessed with spiritual food and drink and eternal light through thy child').

Lake noticed similarities of these references to John 15. 1; 17. 3; and 6. 45–55. All of these had already been included in Harnack's list.[32] But altogether the latter's earlier list of twelve similarities in wording was now reduced to merely three passages, and Lake seemed to be a lot less enthusiastic about the relationship between the *Didache* and John. Nevertheless, he also touched upon a common difference of these two sources compared to the synoptics:

It is noticeable that the distinctive ideas of the manna and the identification of the bread with the body of Christ, are not found in the *Didache*. The point of closest resemblance is that the *Didache*, like the Fourth Gospel, does not connect the spiritual food with the specific ideas of the institution, as is done in the Synoptic narrative.[33]

[26] The classification used by the authors of *NTAF* is given on p. iii.
[27] *NTAF*, 27. [28] *NTAF*, 31. [29] *NTAF*, 31.
[30] The translations are inserted from Lake's own edition in the LCL.
[31] Lake omits *πάτερ ἡμῶν*. [32] Harnack, *Lehre*, 79–81. [33] *NTAF*, 31.

This overall impression supports the notion that the *Didache* may somehow be close to the Gospel of John,[34] and has led some scholars over the years to postulate some common ground for the Eucharist between John and the *Didache.*[35] As we find a rather different treatment of the Eucharist in these two texts, compared to what we find in the synoptics and in Paul, we first need to deal with the basic question of the very nature of the eucharistic allusions in the *Didache* and in the Fourth Gospel.

What kind of 'eucharist' do we find in the *Didache*?[36] Or what makes passages like the prayers in *Did.* 9 and 10 and the verses in *Did.* 14. 1–3 'eucharistic', as they include neither an institution narrative nor the words of institution? And on top of it there is a blessing of the wine *before* the bread. First of all, the identification of these passages is corroborated by the composition of the *Didache.* After the text has dealt with baptism (*Did.* 7. 1–3), and closely linked to this with fasting (7.4–8.1) and prayer (8. 2–3), it comes as no surprise: following these presuppositions (9. 5) and identity markers of a Christian life-style, the Didachist now turns to the eucharistic ritual.[37]

However, the most obvious indication for this is the rubric in *Did.* 9. 1: 'And concerning the thanksgiving meal / eucharist (*εὐχαριστία*), you shall give thanks / hold the eucharist (*εὐχαριστέω*) as follows.'[38] This line serves as the title for what follows. It is parallel to the rubric at the beginning of *Did.*

[34] J. Schmid, 'Didache', *RAC* iii. 1009–13, at p. 1012: 'Eben diese Gebete [d.h. die Abendmahlsgebet in *Did.* 9, 10] sind aber auch von einer Mystik inspiriert, die eine gewisse Verwandtschaft mit der johanneischen aufweist.'

[35] For a summary of older contributions, see A. Greiff, *Das älteste Paschrituale der Kirche, Did. 1–10 und das Johannesevangelium*, Johanneische Studien 1 (Paderborn: Schöningh, 1929); J. A. Robinson, *Barnabas, Hermas and the Didache* (London: SPCK; New York: Macmillan, 1920); *idem*, 'The Problem of the Didache', *JTS* 13 (1912), 339–56. Later contributions include E. R. Goodenough, 'John a Primitive Gospel', *JBL* 64 (1945), 145–82, esp. 174–5; C. F. D. Moule, 'A Note on *Didache* IX.4', *JTS* 6 (1955), 240–3; L. Cerfaux, 'La multiplication des pains dans la liturgie de la Didachè', *Bib* (1959), 943–58. Perry, 'Evolution', 28, sums up: 'The various liturgical and theological similarities between the Fourth Gospel and the *Didache* suggest that the Johannine community and that of the Didachist may once have shared a purely eschatological eucharistic tradition, and that at some intersection in their histories the latter community had been influenced by the theology of the former. We may suspect that the influence occurred before the passion-oriented modification of the Eucharist was adopted by the Johannine community, for any reference thereto is lacking in the *Didache*.' Even more recently, K. Berger, *Im Anfang war Johannes: Datierung und Theologie des vierten Evangeliums* (Stuttgart: Quell Verlag, 1997), 216–17, while discussing the question of the Eucharist in John 6 quotes *Did.* 9. 3 as supporting the tradition of a metaphorical relationship between 'bread' and 'word'.

[36] For a summary of the history of research see Draper, 'Didache', 26–31.

[37] For a very convincing treatment of *Did.* 7–10 as an 'integrated block of ritual material', see J. A. Draper, 'Ritual Process and Ritual Symbol in Didache 7–10', *VC* 54 (2000), 121–58, on p. 121.

[38] *Did.* 9. 1: *Περὶ δὲ τῆς εὐχαριστίας, οὕτως εὐχαριστήσατε.*

7. 1 concerning baptism—'And concerning baptism, baptise as follows'[39]—and other rubrics in the *Didache* as well.[40] The clause in *Did.* 9. 5—'But let no one eat or drink from your thanksgiving meal / eucharist unless they have been baptised in the name of the Lord.'[41]—signals the end of this section. The ritual is expressly described by the term εὐχαριστία. Although εὐχαριστία appears in the New Testament altogether fifteen times, mainly in the Pauline and deutero-Pauline literature, it is never used as a *terminus technicus* for the Eucharist or the eucharistic elements.[42] The situation is very different in the Apostolic Fathers. In Ignatius' letters to the Ephesians (13. 1), the Philadelphians (4) and the Smyrnaeans (7. 1, (twice), 8. 1), εὐχαριστία is used in a clearly eucharistic context, sometimes for the ritual act of the Eucharist (*Eph.* 13. 1; *Smyrn.* 7. 1 (first instance), 8. 1) or for the eucharistic elements (Ign. *Phld.* 4; *Smyrn.* 7. 1 (second instance)). The same applies to Justin Martyr, who uses εὐχαριστία for the eucharistic elements.[43] Thus there is no need to doubt that at least *Did.* 9 refers to a eucharistic ritual. But what about the prayer in *Did.* 10?

The structure of *Did.* 9 and 10 is largely parallel,[44] which may count as an important argument that the latter prayer is also about the Eucharist. In addition to this, the formulation in *Did.* 10. 3 offers a clue to the identification of this passage:

> You, Lord Almighty, created all things for the sake of your name, and gave both food and drink to humans for their refreshment, that they might give you thanks. But you graced us with spiritual food and drink and eternal life through your child.

The purpose of general food and drink is obvious: basically it is for the refreshment or enjoyment (εἰς ἀπόλαυσιν) of all human beings. There is no indication that this kind of food is in any way limited to a certain type of

[39] *Did.* 7. 1: *Περὶ δὲ τοῦ βαπτίσματος, οὕτω βαπτίσατε.*

[40] Cf. also the rubrics with περί in *Did.* 6. 3 ('food'), 9. 2 ('cup'), 9. 3 ('broken bread'), and 11. 3 ('apostles and prophets').

[41] μηδεὶς δὲ φαγέτω μηδὲ πιέτω ἀπὸ τῆς εὐχαριστίας ὑμῶν, ἀλλ' οἱ βαπτισθέντες εἰς ὄνομα κυρίου.

[42] However, cf. ἔφαγον τὸν ἄρτον εὐχαριστήσαντος τοῦ κυρίου in John 6. 23. This may be regarded as an anticipation of the later eucharistic usage.

[43] Justin, *1 Apol.* 66. 1: *καὶ ἡ τροφὴ αὕτη καλεῖται παρ' ἡμῖν εὐχαριστία.*

[44] This was already noticed by E. Freiherr v. d. Goltz, *Das Gebet in der ältesten Christenheit* (Leipzig: J. C. Hinrichs'sche Buchhandlung, 1901), 211; L. Clerici, *Einsammlung der Zerstreuten: Liturgiegeschichtliche Untersuchung zur Vor-und Nachgeschichte der Fürbitte für die Kirche in Didache 9,4 und 10,5*, Liturgiewissenschaftliche Quellen und Forschungen, 44 (Münster: Aschendorffsche Verlagsbuchhandlung, 1966), 5–6, provides a synopsis of the prayers in German. Niederwimmer, *Didache*, 139–40, gives a synopsis of the prayers in Greek; E. Mazza, 'Didache 9–10: Elements of a Eucharistic Interpretation', in Draper (ed.), Didache *in Modern Research*, 276–7, includes a synopsis in English.

people. As we shall see in greater detail later on, it shows a close resemblance to Jewish after-meal prayers.[45]

In contrast (δέ) to such food and drink in general, there is also 'spiritual food and drink', which are mentioned together with 'eternal life'. The eucharistic cup (singular!), which is closely connected to the 'holy vine of David' (*Did.* 9. 2) and the broken bread (singular!), is clearly singled out. This special kind of wine and bread is not consumed for the purpose of being fed until one would have had 'enough to eat' (*Did.* 10. 1).[46]

For this eucharistic meal admission is limited to those who are baptized, who have confessed their trespasses (*Did.* 4. 14; 10. 6; 14. 1b), and who live in peace with their fellow Christians (*Did.* 14. 2; cf. 15. 3). Thus there is no evidence whatsoever that candidates for baptism and catechumens would *per se* be excluded from the communal meals.

Although there can be no doubt about the eucharistic context in *Did.* 9 and 10, the precise nature of such a ritual meal is still a matter of dispute. Or, to address the matter more accurately, the question is: does *Did.* 9–10 refer to the Eucharist or to a common meal later called *agapē*?[47]

[45] The *Birkat ha-mazon* begins with the words: 'Blessed art Thou, O Lord, our God, King of the Universe, Who feedest the whole world with goodness, with grace and with mercy'.

[46] The contrast between 'earthly' and 'spiritual' can also be found in Ign. *Rom.* 7. 3 (φθορά/ἄφθαρτος); Justin, *1 Apol.* 66. 2; Irenaeus, *Adv. Haer.* 4 (SC 100, 610 ff.).

[47] It needs to be stressed that the *Didache* does not use the term ἀγάπη in this later sense (cf. however, *Did.* 10. 5; 16. 3). What is meant by this term is a communal meal of the early Christian community. It is obvious that any answer to the above question is in danger of falling victim to anachronistic reconstructions or of being influenced by dogmatic preconceptions. A detailed overview of the different views on the type of ritual in *Did.* 9–10 is provided by Niederwimmer, *Didache*, 141–2. From Harnack, *Lehre*, 58–60, on, many scholars believe that *Did.* 9–10 represent the Eucharist. H. Lietzmann, *Mass and Lord's Supper: A Study in the History of the Liturgy: With Introduction and Further Inquiry by Robert Douglas Richardson* (ET Leiden: Brill, 1979); German original of part 1, i.e. pp. xxv–xxvi, 1–215: *Messe und Herrenmahl—Eine Studie zur Geschichte der Liturgie* (Berlin: Verlag Walter de Gruyter, 1926), offers a similar view: while he sees *Did.* 9–10 and 14. 1–3 as referring to the Eucharist (p. 189), he describes the course of the ceremony as an 'agape introduced by a eucharistic celebration'. However, his reconstruction is based on the assumption that *Did.* 10. 6 had its original place 'before the prayer x.1–5, and the injunction ix.5'. There is no hint in the text for such an operation!

In favour of an *agapē* are, among others (cf. Niederwimmer, *Didache*, 141), R. H. Connolly, 'Agape and Eucharist in the Didache', *DR* 55 (1937), 477–89; F. E. Vokes, *The Riddle of the Didache: Fact or Fiction, Heresy or Catholicism?* (London: SPCK, 1938), 197–207; G. Dix, *The Shape of the Liturgy* (Westminster: Dacre, 1945), 90. P. Drews, 'Untersuchungen zur Didache', *ZNW* 5 (1904), 53–79, on pp. 78–9, opts for *Did.* 9–10 as a Eucharist in the form of a communal meal ('ein Herrenmahl, gefeiert in der Form einer einheitlichen, vollen Gemeindemahlzeit', p. 79) while *Did.* 14 refers to the Eucharist on a Sunday, led by a bishop. A number of scholars argue that *Did.* 9–10 are prayers for the *agapē*, while the Eucharist follows after *Did.* 10. 6; see, e.g., T. Zahn, *Forschungen zur Geschichte des neutestamentlichen Kanons und der altkirchlichen Literatur*, iii: *Supplementum Clementinum* (Erlangen: A. Deichert, 1884), 193 ff.; A. D. Nock, 'Liturgical Notes', *JTS* 30 (1929), 381–95, on pp. 390–1; M. Dibelius, 'Die Mahl-Gebete der Didache', *ZNW* 37 (1938), 32–41, 126–7. Some see them as prayers of the *agapē*, which the

The above examination of the prayers in *Did.* 9 and 10 has made it quite obvious that the whole section follows the rubric in *Did.* 9. 1 which describes what follows as *εὐχαριστία*. Nevertheless, the prayers refer to a ritual unit with expressly eucharistic parts (*Did.* 9. 2–3), with access limited to the baptized (*Did.* 9. 5; cf. *Did.* 10. 6), and with parts of a meal to satisfy hunger (*Did.* 10. 1, 3) for everybody. Although there was an obvious understanding of the difference between these, so that one was able to distinguish the cup and the broken bread from the rest of the meal, both parts still belong together. Thus, there is simply no reason to regard this meal as an *agapē* without the Eucharist.[48] A deeper understanding of this peculiar combination of common meal and Eucharist can be gained by looking into the Jewish background of these prayers.

THE EUCHARISTIC PRAYERS IN THE *DIDACHE* AND JEWISH MEAL-PRAYERS

Already very early, scholars recognized similarities between ancient Jewish and early Christian liturgies, and later on also between the eucharistic prayers in *Did.* 9 and 10 and Jewish prayers. The Dutch Protestant theologian Campegius Vitringa (1659–1722) may have been the first to point out the Jewish roots of the Christian liturgy, and many others followed his line.[49] The scientific study of the history of Jewish liturgy began with the monumental work of Leopold Zunz: *Die gottesdienstlichen Vorträge der Juden,*

Lord's Supper then follows. Cf. R. Bultmann, *Theologie des Neuen Testaments,* UTB 630, 9th edn. (Tübingen: J. C. B. Mohr (Paul Siebeck), 1984), 153; J. Jeremias, *The Eucharistic Words of Jesus* (London: SCM Press, 1966), 134; Rordorf and Tuilier, *Doctrine,* 40–1. A. Vööbus, *Liturgical Traditions in the Didache,* Papers of the Estonian Theological Society in Exile, 16 (Stockholm: Estonian Theological Society in Exile, 1968), 63–83, regards *Did.* 9–10 as belonging to the Eucharist, which had not yet been divided from the *agapē.* Wengst, *Didache,* 45–6, argues that the Eucharist of the *Didache* is nothing but a meal meant to satisfy the hunger of the participants (= 'Sättigungsmahl'). Wengst clarified, but basically defended, his view later on in a dialogue with Lothar Wehr. See Wehr, *Arznei,* 376–7.

[48] This is rightly stressed already by Goltz, *Das Gebet,* 210: 'Gemeinsame Mahlzeit und Herrenmahl und ἀγάπη waren dasselbe'; cf. Vööbus, *Liturgical Traditions,* 70.

[49] C. Vitringa, *De synagoga vetere libri tres: quibus tum de nominibus, structurā, origine, præfectis, ministris, & sacris synagogarum, agitur; tum præcipue, formam regiminis & ministerii earum in ecclesiam christianam translatam esse, demonstratur: cum prolegomenis* (Franeker: Typis & impensis J. Gyzelaar, 1696); abbreviated translation by J. L. Bernard, *The Synagogue and the Church: Being an Attempt to Show that the Government, Ministers and Services of the Church were Derived from those of the Synagogue* (London: B. Fellowes, 1842).

published in 1832.[50] His method was marked by the attempt to reconstruct a single archetype, an *Urtext*, by comparing the different manuscripts.[51] Paul Sabatier, in the earliest French commentary on the *Didache* in 1885, was the first to compare the blessing of the cup (*Did.* 9. 2) and the broken bread (*Did.* 9. 3) to blessings at the beginning of Jewish meals.[52] He tried to show analogies between the *Kiddush*—a simple blessing over the wine at the beginning of each sabbath or feast-day[53]—and *Did.* 9. 1–3. The tenth benediction of the *Amidah*[54] and *Did.* 9. 4–5 also seemed to show some parallels.[55] Nevertheless, in both cases the similarities surely do not outweigh the significant differences.

It was not until 1928 that Louis Finkelstein published his ground-breaking essay on the *Birkat ha-mazon*, the Jewish grace after meals, comparing it to the prayer in *Did.* 10.[56] Finkelstein followed Zunz's methodology, and tried 'to establish the original form of the benedictions'[57] of the grace after meals. His careful reconstruction presents a prayer with three benedictions:[58]

[50] L. Zunz, *Die gottesdienstlichen Vorträge der Juden, historisch entwickelt: ein Beitrag zur Alterthumskunde und biblischen Kritik, zur Literatur-und Religionsgeschichte* (Berlin: Asher, 1832; 2nd edn. von Nehemias Brüll nach dem Handexemplar des Verfassers berichtigte und mit einem Register vermehrte Auflage, Frankfurt am Main: J. Kauffmann, 1892; repr. Hildesheim: Olms, 1966).

[51] For a short overview see Bradshaw, *Search for the Origins*, 25–6.

[52] P. Sabatier, *La Didachè, ou l'Enseignement des douze apôtres, texte grec retrouvé par Mgr Philotheos Bryennios . . . publié pour la première fois en France, avec un commentaire et des notes* (Paris: Fischbacher, 1885), 100. Cf. Drews, 'Untersuchungen', 74; Goltz, *Das Gebet*, 210; *idem*, *Tischgebete und Abendmahlsgebete in der altchristlichen und in der griechischen Kirche*, TU n.s. 14 (Leipzig: Hinrichs, 1905); G. Klein, *Der älteste christliche Katechismus und die jüdische Propaganda-Literatur* (Berlin: Reimer, 1909), 214–19, pointed to the influence of sabbath *Kiddush* prayers on *Did.* 9. Cf. also more recently J. W. Riggs, 'From Gracious Table to Sacramental Elements: The Tradition-History of Didache 9 and 10', *SC* 4 (1984), 83–101, esp. 91–2.

[53] Cf. also *m. Ber.* 6. 1: '(Blessed are you, O Lord, our God, King of the world,) who creates the fruit of the vine . . . . (Blessed are you, O Lord, our God, King of the world,) who brings forth bread from the earth.'

[54] 'Blow a blast upon the great shofar for our freedom and raise a banner for the gathering of our exiles. Blessed art thou, O Lord, who gatherest the dispersed of thy people Israel.' Quoted according to L. H. Schiffman, *Texts and Traditions: A Source Reader for the Study of Second Temple and Rabbinic Judaism* (Hoboken, NJ: KTAV Publishing House, 1998), 658, who reproduces a translation by J. Heinemann and J. J. Petuchowski, *Literature of the Synagogue* (New York: Behrman, 1975), 33–6.

[55] See G. Klein, 'Die Gebete in der Didache', *ZNW* 9 (1908), 132–46, on pp. 134–5; R. D. Middleton, 'The Eucharistic Prayers of the Didache', *JTS* 36 (1935), 259–67, esp. 261–2; Vööbus, *Liturgical Traditions*, 162–9; Riggs, 'Gracious Table', 91–2 n. 30.

[56] L. Finkelstein, 'The Birkat-Ha-Mazon', *JQR* 19 (1928/9), 211–62.

[57] Ibid. 211.

[58] Ibid. 215–16. The threefold pattern 'blessing'—'thanksgiving'—'supplication' was added to the text. For this pattern cf. Thomas Talley, 'The Eucharistic Prayer of the Ancient Church according to Recent Research: Results and Reflections', *SL* 11 (1976), 138–58; *idem*, 'From Berakah to Eucharistia: A Reopening Question', *Worship*, 50 (1976), 115–37; repr. in K. Seasoltz

Birkat ha-mazon	*Did.* 10. 2–5
A. Blessing	B. (*Did.* 10. 2)
Blessed art Thou, O Lord, our God, King of the Universe, Who feedest the whole world with goodness, with grace and with mercy.	We give you thanks, holy Father, for your holy name which you have made reside in our hearts, and for the knowledge, faith, and immortality that you made known to us through Jesus your child.
Blessed art Thou, O, Lord, Who feedest all.	To you be the glory forever.
B. Thanksgiving	A. (*Did.* 10. 3–4)
We thank Thee, O Lord, our God, that Thou hast caused us to inherit a goodly and pleasant land, the covenant, the Torah, life and food. For all these things we thank Thee and praise Thy name forever and ever.	You, Almighty Master, created all things for the sake of your name, and gave both food and drink to humans for their refreshment, that they might give you thanks. But you graced us with spiritual food and drink and eternal life through [Jesus][59] your child. B. Above all we thank you because you are powerful.
Blessed art Thou, O, Lord, for the land and for the food.	To you be the glory forever.
C. Supplication	C. Supplication (*Did.* 10. 5)
Have mercy, O Lord, our God, on Thy people Israel, and on Thy city Jerusalem, and on Thy Temple and Thy dwelling-place and on Zion Thy resting-place, and on the great and holy sanctuary over which Thy name was called, and the kingdom of the dynasty of David mayest Thou restore to its place in our days, and build Jerusalem soon.	Remember your church, O Lord, save it from all evil, and perfect it in your love. And gather it from the four winds into your kingdom, which you prepared for it.
Blessed art Thou, O, Lord, who buildest Jerusalem.	For yours is the power and the glory forever.

(ed.), *Living Bread, Saving Cup: Readings on the Eucharist* (Collegeville, Minn.: Liturgical Press, 1987), 80–101. A fourth benediction of the *Birkat ha-mazon* was added later. It is reflected neither in the *Didache* nor in *Jubilees*. Cf. Finkelstein, 'Birkat', 221–2; Sandt and Flusser, *Didache*, 317 n. 139.

[59] The Coptic fragment Br. Mus. Or. 9271 adds the name 'Jesus'. Cf. *Did.* 10. 2.

The hypothesis of the dependency of the prayer in *Did.* 10 on this supposedly earliest version of the *Birkat ha-mazon* is widely accepted.[60] In fact, Finkelstein's reconstruction became a starting-point even for those scholars who otherwise acknowledged the fluidity in Jewish first-century liturgies.[61]

The problems in arguing in favour of such a close connection between *Did.* 10 and the *Birkat ha-mazon* are nevertheless not minor. Although verbal parallels are clearly visible, these are outnumbered by far by the very significant differences. The same applies to the structure: whereas the Jewish grace after meals starts with a blessing (A) that mentions the feeding by God, a thanksgiving (B) precedes the reference to food in *Did.* 10. 2. Another thanksgiving, as a kind of summary, follows in *Did.* 10. 4. Thus one may argue that the thanksgiving unit (*Did.* 10. 2, 4) is now disrupted by the blessing.[62] As a result the sequences of the *Birkat ha-mazon* and *Did.* 10. 2–5 are not really parallel.

Other issues of concern arise from Finkelstein's methodology, as he follows the dating of the origin of the grace after meals given in the Babylonian

[60] Middleton, 'Eucharistic Prayers'; Dibelius, 'Mahl-Gebete', 32–41; K. Hruby, 'La "Birkat Ha-Mazon" ', in *Mélanges liturgiques offerts au R. P. Dom B. Botte O.S.B. de l'Abbaye du Mont César à l'occasion du cinquantième anniversaire de son ordination sacerdotale (4 Juin 1972)* (Louvain: Abbaye du Mont César, 1972), 205–22; Jeremias, *Eucharistic Words*, 110, who cites Finkelstein's version of the *Birkat ha-mazon* at full length; Talley, 'From Berakah to Eucharistia' (German trans.: 'Von der Berakah zur Eucharistia: Das eucharistische Hochgebet der alten Kirche in neuerer Forschung: Ergebnisse und Fragen', *LJ* 26 (1976), 93–115; French translation: 'De la, berakah' à l'eucharistie, une question à réexaminer', *La Maison-Dieu*, 125 (1976), 11–39); *idem*, 'The Eucharistic Prayer: Tradition and Development', in K. Stevenson (ed.), *Liturgy Reshaped* (London: SPCK, 1982), 48–64; *idem*, 'The Literary Structure of Eucharistic Prayer', *Worship*, 58 (1984), 404–20; Riggs, 'Gracious Table'; Niederwimmer, *Didache*, 155: 'The model for this long prayer is (as has long been acknowledged) the Jewish prayer after meals, the *Birkat Ha-Mazon*.' The judgement of Mazza is still representative for the majority of scholars. See E. Mazza, *The Origins of the Eucharistic Prayer* (Collegeville, Minn.: Liturgical Press, 1995), 17: 'Since the studies of L. Finkelstein, M. Dibelius, and K. Hruby the connection between the *Birkat ha-mazon* and *Didache* 10 no longer requires demonstration.' So too Sandt and Flusser, *Didache*, 312.

[61] This is rightly observed by Bradshaw, *Search for the Origins*, 140. As more recent examples see Niederwimmer, *Didache*, 156: 'The text of the Jewish table prayer was expanded in the course of time, so that it would be difficult to attempt to re-create its original wording.' Sandt and Flusser, *Didache*, 312: 'Admittedly, one must be careful about Finkelstein's reconstruction of the Hebrew text since the exact phraseology of the meal blessing may not yet have been fixed in the first century CE.' Those who dissent from Finkelstein's view are comparatively rare. See Vööbus, *Liturgical Traditions*, 166; Draper, 'Didache', 29; Milavec, *Didache*, 416–21; cf. B. Spinks, 'Beware the Liturgical Horses! An English Interjection on Anaphoral Evolution', *Worship*, 59 (1985), 211–19, who questions the view that Jesus made use of the *Birkat ha-mazon* at the Last Supper.

[62] Sandt and Flusser, *Didache*, 318.

Talmud.[63] No serious scholar would take this at face value today. The final editing of the Babylonian Talmud took place at the end of the sixth or the beginning of the seventh century, and dating the original composition of its passages is notoriously difficult. Even worse, when Finkelstein turns to his reconstruction of the supposed original form, he analyses versions of the *Birkat ha-mazon* which stem more likely from the ninth century. Thus the likelihood that such a comparison of much later versions may reveal the precise wording of the first century CE Jewish grace after meals seems to be extremely limited.[64]

Nevertheless, we can be quite certain that at least some rather fluid pattern of meal-prayers existed during the first century.[65] The *Mishnah* does not give its text, but in *m. Ber.* 6. 8 it refers to such a prayer as 'the three benedictions'.[66] More insights into the early structure may be gained from the second century BCE Book of *Jubilees.* In *Jub.* 22. 6–9 Abraham is portrayed as pronouncing *his* grace after meals:

6. And he (Abraham) ate and drank and blessed God Most High who created heaven and earth and who made all the fat of the earth and gave it to the sons of man so that they might eat and drink and bless their Creator:

[63] *b. Ber.* 48b: 'Moses formulated the first benediction when the manna came down from Heaven; Joshua the second when Israel entered the Land; David composed the prayer for Jerusalem; Solomon added to it the prayer for the Temple; while the fourth benediction was established by the Sages at Jabneh when permission was granted to bury those slain at Bether.' Quoted from Finkelstein, 'Birkat', 212.

[64] One may want to be more cautious than Jeremias, *Eucharistic Words*, 110, who introduces Finkelstein's version with the words: 'At the time of Jesus this grace was probably worded as follows.'

[65] M. Weinfeld, 'Grace after Meals in Qumran', *JBL* 111 (1992), 427–40, argues that 4Q434a is a 'Grace after Meals in the Mourner's House'. See recently also J. R. Davila, *Liturgical Works*, Eerdmans Commentaries on the Dead Sea Scrolls, 6 (Grand Rapids, Mich.: Eerdmans, 2000), 174–6. However, this identification is far from clear. Cf. the criticism by D. K. Falk, 'Prayer in the Qumran Texts', in W. Horbury, W. D. Davies, and J. Sturdy (eds.), *The Cambridge History of Judaism*, iii: *The Early Roman Period* (Cambridge: Cambridge University Press, 1999), 852–76, on p. 865. See J. Neusner, *A History of Jews in Babylonia*, i (Leiden: Brill, 1965), 161 n. 3: a somewhat different meal-prayer from the synagogue at Dura-Europos. If anything may be concluded from these texts, it is that they indicate a broad variety of ancient meal-prayers. Josephus and the Qumran literature report that the Essenes pray before and after eating: Joseph. *BJ* 2. 8. 5; 1QS 6. 3–8; 1QSa 2. 17–18. Unfortunately, they do not provide the content of the prayers. *Ep. Arist.* 185 includes a prayer before a meal which, however, is more a petitionary prayer for the king.

[66] *m. Ber.* 6. 8: 'If a man ate figs, grapes or pomegranates, he should say the three Benedictions after them. So Raban Gamaliel. But the sages say: One Benediction, the substance of the three. R. Akiba says: Even if he ate but boiled vegetables for his meal he must say the three Benedictions after them' (English trans. by H. Danby, *The Mishnah: Translated from the Hebrew with Introduction and Brief Explanatory Notes* (Oxford: Oxford University Press, 1933), 7).

7. 'And now I thank you, my God, because you have let me see this day. Behold, I am one hundred and seventy-five years old, and fulfilled in days. And all of my days were peaceful for me.

8. The sword of the enemy did not triumph over me in anything which you gave to me or my sons all of the days of my life until this day.

9. O my God, may your mercy and your peace be upon your servant and upon the seed of his sons so that they might become an elect people for you and an inheritance from all of the nations of the earth from henceforth and for all the days of the generations of the earth forever.'[67]

The example of this grace after meals is particularly important for two reasons: on the one hand it clearly follows the three-part structure that can be observed in much later prayers.

Jub. 22. 6 reflects the first benediction of God as the creator and the provider of food. Then *Jub.* 22. 7–8 as a thanksgiving for long life, protection, and sustenance corresponds to the second benediction for the gift of the land. Finally, the third benediction, the supplication, is reflected in *Jub.* 22. 9 where Abraham prays for himself, his offspring, and all generations of the earth. *Jubilees* clearly shows that the original three-part structure of the grace after meals goes back at least to the second century BCE.

On the other hand, this 'personal' prayer of Abraham reveals an enormous degree of fluidity and variation. The continuity with later versions goes hardly beyond the basic threefold pattern.[68] Therefore, one can be absolutely certain that the *Birkat ha-mazon* did not exist in one fixed, original, and widely used form at this early time.

This observation fits together well with a major shift that occurred in Jewish liturgical studies through the work of Joseph Heinemann.[69] Following the insights of form criticism, he pays special attention to the particular stylistic features of the liturgical texts, and thus tries to locate their origin. As to the question of an *Urtext*, he chooses the opposite direction compared to Zunz and Finkelstein:

The Jewish prayers were originally the creations of the common people.... Since the occasions and places of worship were numerous, it was only natural that they should give rise to an abundance of prayers, displaying a wide variety of forms, styles and

[67] English trans. by O. S. Wintermute, 'Jubilees: A New Translation and Introduction', in J. H. Charlesworth (ed.), *The Old Testament Pseudepigrapha*, ii (New York: Doubleday, 1985), 97.

[68] Cf. however Sandt and Flusser, *Didache*, 317, who carefully point to some similar wording.

[69] See esp. his doctoral dissertation: J. Heinemann, *ha-Tefilah bi-tekufat-ha-Tana'im veha-Amora'im* (= *Prayer in the Period of the Tanna'im and the Amora'im* (Jerusalem: Hebrew University Press, 1964; 2nd edn. 1966; ET *Prayer in the Talmud: Forms and Patterns*, Studia Judaica, 9 (Berlin and New York: Walter de Gruyter, 1977)), quoted according to the English version).

patterns. Thus, the first stage in the development of the liturgy was characterized by diversity and variety.[70]

Accordingly, he develops his methodology:

Therefore, we must lay down as a fundamental axiom for liturgical studies which would examine developmentally the texts of the various prayers that from the first no single 'original' text of any particular prayer was created, but that originally numerous diverse texts and versions existed side by side. It follows, then, that the widely accepted goal of the philological method—viz., to discover or to reconstruct the one 'original' text of a particular composition by examining and comparing the extant textual variants one with the other—is out of place in the field of liturgical studies. We must not try to determine by philological methods the 'original' text of any prayer without first determining whether or not such an 'original' text ever existed. For we are dealing with materials which originated as part of an oral tradition and hence by their very nature were not phrased in any fixed uniform formulation—which at a later stage came to be 'revised' and expanded—but rather were improvised on the spot; and, subsequently, 're-improvised' and reworded in many different formulations in an equally spontaneous fashion.[71]

After Heinemann it is no longer feasible to search for an original form of the *Birkat ha-mazon* in the first century. His methodology opens up the possibility of a broad variety and fluidity of ancient prayers. Such diversity is hardly surprising when we realize that first-century Judaism found its venues for religious gathering not only in the pre-70 CE Temple and more or less official synagogues, but mainly within the setting of the Jewish family and house synagogues.[72] However, this does not mean that comparing early Christian prayers like those in *Did.* 9–10 to ancient Jewish prayers should be regarded as futile. Heinemann also provides abundant evidence that the people who formulated these prayers made use of specific forms, which are far from arbitrary. Thus earlier reconstructions can still serve as helpful contributions to identify *Did.* 9 with confidence as a prayer at the beginning of a meal and *Did.* 10 as grace after meals. But after Heinemann, research is no longer limited to the comparison of one supposed original with one or more later adaptations.[73]

[70] Heinemann, *Prayer,* 37.

[71] Ibid. 43. His critique of Finkelstein's method follows on p. 44. Cf. the already much earlier rejection of Finkelstein's methodological assumptions by I. Elbogen, *Der jüdische Gottesdienst in seiner geschichtlichen Entwicklung,* 3rd edn. (Frankfurt am Main: J. Kauffmann, 1931), 41–2, 583. For a very recent adoption of Heinemann's insights see Milavec, *Didache,* 416–21.

[72] See C. Claußen, *Versammlung, Gemeinde, Synagoge: Das hellenistisch-jüdische Umfeld der frühchristlichen Gemeinden,* SUNT 27 (Göttingen: Vandenhoeck & Ruprecht, 2002), esp. 37–9 and 294–304.

[73] But see also the criticism regarding Heinemann's form criticism by T. Zahavy, *Studies in Jewish Prayer* (Lanham, Md.: University Press of America, 1990), 4–5.

Consequently, if we are no longer limited to looking for a simple Christianizing adaptation of earlier Jewish material, analysing the particularities of wording and composition become even more valuable.[74]

THE TERMINOLOGICAL BACKGROUND OF *DIDACHE* 9–10

A number of expressions in *Did.* 9–10 clearly reveal their Old Testament or Hellenistic Jewish background. However, many other references are more likely of Christian origin, as the following examples show.[75]

Did. 9. 1—*εὐχαριστία* with cup before bread

Philo uses the verb *εὐχαριστεῖν* for the grace or thanksgiving before meals (*Spec.* 2. 175).[76] And under his influence theologians of the second and third centuries used *εὐχαριστία* and *εὐχαριστεῖν* for the Eucharist.[77] *Did.* 9. 1 could be a very early example of such a more specific Christian usage. Maybe there were already forms of grace in Hellenistic Judaism that began with *εὐχαριστεῖν*.[78]

One of the stumbling-blocks that nevertheless keep some interpreters from identifying *Did.* 9–10 with the Eucharist—although the rubric in *Did.* 9. 1 clearly mentions *εὐχαριστία*—is the sequence of the blessing of the cup *before* the bread.

Although the benefits of comparing these blessings to the Jewish *Kiddush* are limited, it is still important to keep in mind that this prayer starts with the blessing over the cup as well. *Mishnah Berakoth* also testifies to the sequence wine–bread.[79] Thus we may conclude that the *Didache* here follows the normal Jewish custom. That this should not be taken to disqualify us from

[74] M. Klinghardt, *Gemeinschaftsmahl und Mahlgemeinschaft: Soziologie und Liturgie frühchristlicher Mahlfeiern*, TANZ 13 (Tübingen and Basel: A. Francke Verlag, 1996), describes the most common view on the relationship between the prayers of the *Didache* and Jewish prayers as follows: 'Die Ansicht, die sich weitestgehend durchgesetzt hat, besagt, daß in der Didache jüdische Mahlbenediktionen (1.) spiritualisiert und (2.) nur geringfügig durch die *παῖς*-Formel 'verchristlicht' worden seien.' He is right to call this view problematic.

[75] Cf. also the extensive collections of parallels in Clerici, *Einsammlung*; J. Laporte, *Eucharistia in Philo* (New York: Mellen, 1983); K.-G. Sandelin, *Wisdom as Nourisher: A Study of an Old Testament Theme, its Development within Early Judaism and its Impact on Early Christianity*, Acta Academia Aboensis, ser. A, 64/3 (Åbo: Åbo Akademi, 1986), esp. 190–219.

[76] See Laporte, *Eucharistia in Philo*.

[77] H. Conzelmann, '*εὐχαριστέω κτλ.*', *TDNT* ix. 407–15, on p. 415.

[78] Laporte, *Eucharistia in Philo*, 53–5; Bradshaw, *Search for the Origins*, 45.

[79] *m. Ber.* 6. 1, 5. Cf. also *b. Pesaḥ* 101a, 106a, 107a; *m. Ber.* 8. 1.

interpreting these prayers in *Did.* 9–10 as eucharistic is underlined by the evidence of the New Testament: the institution narrative in Luke 22. 14–20 includes blessings first over the cup (Luke 22. 17) and only second over the bread (Luke 22. 19). Only the longer version of the Lucan text then goes on to include another reference to the cup in Luke 22. 20.[80] And although the words of institution in 1 Cor. 11. 23–8 show the normal order bread–cup several times, the apostle Paul can also refer to the Eucharist with the sequence of cup–bread (1 Cor. 10. 16; cf. 10. 21). This observation must not lead to the conclusion that *Did.* 9. 2–3 should be taken as evidence for a different Eucharist altogether.[81] But it surely supplements our understanding of the diversity of eucharistic forms in early Christianity. In *Did.* 9 we find a Eucharist which seems to be a lot closer to ordinary Jewish meals.

Did. 9. 2, 3; 10. 2, 3—Jesus, the παῖς of God, our father

Above all the reference to Jesus clearly indicates that *Did.* 9–10 are Christian prayers. To designate God as father is, of course, possible in a Jewish text.[82] However, as the Lord's Prayer precedes the treatment of the Eucharist in *Did.* 8, the phrase πάτερ ἡμῶν equally belongs to the early Christian environment already. This is even more so for the expression πάτερ ἅγιε (cf. John 17. 11). Again, it is not possible to identify the origin more clearly. In the present context, calling God 'father' correlates with the Christian expression 'through Jesus your servant / child' (*Did.* 9. 2, 3; 10. 2, 3).

Did. 9. 2—The holy vine of David

The first benediction in *Did.* 9. 2 is obviously similar to the usual Jewish blessing over wine: 'over wine a man says: (Blessed are you, O Lord, our God, King of the world,) who creates the fruit of the vine.'[83] More important

[80] For a helpful discussion of the textual evidence, see Jeremias, *Eucharistic Words*, 139–59. That the sequence struck ancient translators of the text as odd can be seen in the Old Latin MSS b and e, where the order is vv. 19a, 17, 18. This is clearly a modification to change the order to bread and cup.

[81] Against Audet, *Didachè*, 406, who calls the meal in *Did.* 9 a 'fraction du pain' (cf. Acts 2. 42, 46; 20. 7); cf. also Lietzmann, *Mass*, who distinguishes between two different types of the Eucharist: the Pauline type with its sacramental emphasis on sharing the body and blood of Christ (pp. 172–87, 204–8) on the one hand and the Egyptian tradition with a strong emphasis on eschatological expectations but no mention of the death of Jesus or any institution narrative (pp. 152–60).

[82] See Isa. 63. 16; 64. 7; Sir. 23. 1, 4; Wisd. 2. 16; 1QH^{a}17. 36 (=Sukenik 9. 35); Philo, *Opif.* 46, 89, 156.

[83] *m. Ber.* 6. 1.

are the differences. The very common Jewish ברוך אתה[84] is replaced by *εὐχαριστοῦμέν σοι*. A more natural rendering would have been *εὐλογητὸς εἶ/σύ*,[85] but the Didachist probably wants to allude to the Eucharist.

But what is it precisely that '(God) our Father... made known to us through Jesus your child' (*Did.* 9. 2)? The phrase 'the holy vine of David' has always been a puzzling one.[86] Any interpretation needs to take into account the well-established meaning of the 'vine' as a simile for Israel as the elect people.[87] 'David' may be read as a qualifying reference to the messianic expectations now fulfilled in Jesus.[88] Sandelin[89] points to the 'close relationship between David and personified Wisdom'[90] and Wisdom described as a vine in Philo.[91] This may indicate a Hellenistic Jewish background for the phrase. Although the meaning still remains cryptic, it seems most likely that the Jewish-Christian community who prays it thanks God for being part of his elected people through Jesus and through the wisdom which they have received through him.

Did. 9. 3—Life and knowledge; *Did.* 10. 2—Knowledge, faith, and immortality

The concepts of life and knowledge are central in sapiential texts of the Old Testament.[92] In *Did.* 10. 2 *ἀθανασία* replaces *ζωή* in the parallel *Did.* 9. 3. Since *ἀθανασία* never appears in those parts of the LXX which are translated from the original Hebrew, one can already suspect a Hellenistic Jewish environment.[93] This is confirmed by Philo's frequent use of the term[94] and by a number of occurrences in *Wisdom of Solomon* and *4 Maccabees*.[95] The word

[84] See 1QH^a 18. 16 (= Sukenik 10. 14); 13. 22 (= Sukenik 5. 20); 4Q414 frg. 2 2. 6; 4Q512 frgs. 42–44 2. 3.

[85] That *εὐχαριστεῖν* and *εὐλογεῖν* are not simply synonymous has been shown convincingly by R. J. Ledogar, *Praise Verbs in the Early Greek Anaphoras* (Rome: Herder, 1968); Talley, 'From Berakah to Eucharistia'; J. A. Draper, 'A Commentary on the Didache in the Light of the Dead Sea Scrolls and Related Documents' (unpublished Ph.D. diss., Cambridge University, 1983), 182–8.

[86] See already Harnack, *Lehre*, 29. For an overview of the history of research see Klinghardt, *Gemeinschaftsmahl*, 432–3.

[87] Cf. Ps. 80. 9–17 or *4 Ezra* 5. 23, where the election of the vine from all trees of the earth is mentioned.

[88] Greiff, *Pascharituale*, 61–9.

[89] Sandelin, *Wisdom as Nourisher*, 195.

[90] Cf. Ps. 154 (cf. 11Q5); Sir. 51.

[91] Philo, *Somn.* 2. 190; *Fug.* 176.

[92] Prov. 1–9, esp. 2. 6, 10, 12, 20; 3. 13–18; 9. 1–6; Sir. 4. 11–12.

[93] See Dibelius, 'Mahl-Gebete', 37.

[94] *Plant.* 37–8, 45; *Conf.* 7; *Migr.* 37, 189, etc.

[95] Wisd. 3. 4; 4. 1; 8. 13, 17; 15. 3; *4 Macc.* 14. 5; 16. 13.

πίστις could also stem from a Hellenistic Jewish background.[96] But in Philo and in the LXX there is no close connection between πίστις and γνῶσις, but this is very common in the New Testament.[97] Thus a Christian background is more likely.

Did. 9. 4—Scattered and gathered; *Did.* 10. 5—from the four winds into your kingdom

The terms διασκορπίζω and συνάγω belong to the terminology of the Jewish diaspora.[98] In the parallel *Did.* 10. 5, the plea to 'remember your church, O Lord' (μνήσθητι, κύριε, τῆς ἐκκλησίας σου) sounds almost like a Christian adaptation of Ps. 73. 2, LXX: 'Remember your congregation, which you acquired long ago' (μνήσθητι τῆς συναγωγῆς σου ἧς ἐκτήσω ἀπ' ἀρχῆς). The closest parallel to this in the New Testament is John 11. 51–2, where the high priest is said to prophesy that Jesus would die in order 'to gather into one the dispersed children of God (τὰ τέκνα τοῦ θεοῦ τὰ διεσκορπισμένα συναγάγῃ εἰς ἕν)'. That the elect will be gathered by the angels 'from the four winds' is stated in the synoptic eschatological discourse (Mark 13. 27; cf. Matt. 24. 31). But similar usage also appears in the Old Testament[99] and in the Qumran literature.[100]

Did. 9. 4, 10. 5—your church; *Did.* 10. 5—save it from all evil, and perfect it in your love

In the Old Testament we do not find the idea that God perfects (τελειόω) his people or an individual. But in Wisd. 4. 7 the righteous man who died is described as 'being made perfect (τελειωθείς)'. And according to Philo, God leads human beings to perfection.[101]

As a result of this analysis, it has become obvious that it is not possible to view *Did.* 9–10 just as a Jewish text with Christian adaptations. While a

[96] *4 Macc* 15. 24; 16. 22; 17. 2; Philo, *Abr.* 262.

[97] 1 Cor. 12. 8–9; 13. 2; 2 Cor. 8. 7; Phil. 3. 8–9.

[98] Deut. 30. 1–4; Isa. 11. 12; Ezek. 28. 25; 37. 21. Especially Clerici, *Einsammlung*, 65–92, has collected and analysed the relevant material. But for the same view see also Moule, 'Note', 240–1; H. Riesenfeld, 'Das Brot von den Bergen; Zu Did. 9, 4', *Eranos*, 54 (1956), 142–50, on p. 146; Vööbus, *Liturgical Traditions*, 143; Sandelin, *Wisdom as Nourisher*, 202–3.

[99] Jer. 49. 36; Ezek. 37. 9.

[100] E. Main, 'For King Joshua or Against? The Use of the Bible in 4Q448', in M. Stone and E. G. Chazon (eds.), *Biblical Perspectives: Early Use and Interpretation of the Bible in Light of the Dead Sea Scrolls: Proceedings of the First International Symposium of the Orion Center for the Study of the Dead Sea Scrolls and Associated Literature, 12–14 May 1996*, STDJ 28 (Leiden, Boston, and Cologne: Brill, 1998), 113–35, esp. 115–17.

[101] Philo, *Agr.* 169, 173; *Fug.* 172; *Mut.* 270.

number of expressions point to Philo, the Old Testament and especially wisdom literature seem to provide equally important insights into the background of the Didachist and his community. That they may be designated as part of Jewish Christianity is obvious. However, as we do not have Jewish meal-prayers from the first century, it is not possible to reconstruct the history of composition of *Did.* 9–10. Nevertheless, these prayers are very different from most other early Christian accounts of the Eucharist. This is particularly true with regard to the relationship between the *Didache*'s eucharistic expressions and the sacrifice of Christ on the cross.

THE EUCHARIST IN THE *DIDACHE* AND THE IDEA OF SACRIFICE

The words of institution in the New Testament emphasize the connection between Christ's atoning death as sacrifice and the Lord's Supper.[102] However, the *Didache*'s understanding of the Eucharist does not concern the death of Jesus.[103] Unlike the Pauline epistles[104] or the Letter to the Hebrews,[105] there is no indication that the author of the *Didache* has any interest in the atonement. He does not make use of the Passover tradition, which for many scholars is crucial for understanding the origins of the Eucharist.[106] This is even more surprising given that this document is heavily influenced by Jewish tradition.

Thus, it comes as another surprise that *Did.* 14. 1–3 uses the term 'sacrifice' (ἡ θυσία) in a eucharistic context.

Did. 14. 1–3

1. On the Lord's day, when you gather together, break bread and give thanks *[Or: celebrate the Eucharist]* after you have confessed your transgressions (τὰ παραπτώματα ὑμῶν), that your sacrifice may be pure.

[102] Matt. 26. 28; Mark 14. 24; Luke 22. 20; 1 Cor. 11. 25–6.

[103] H.-W. Kuhn, 'The Qumran Meal and the Lord's Supper in Paul in the Context of the Graeco-Roman World', in A. Christophersen, C. Claussen, J. Frey, and B. Longenecker (eds.), *Paul, Luke and the Graeco-Roman World: Essays in Honour of Alexander J. M. Wedderburn*, JSNTSup 217 (London: Sheffield Academic Press, 2002), 221–48, on p. 237 n. 57, points out: 'There are traces of a meal, without mention of the soteriological aspect of the death of Jesus, in Mk 14. 25 (following the ritual words) and in Lk. 22. 15–17 (before the ritual words).'

[104] Cf. Rom. 3. 25; 5. 8; 8. 31–2; 2 Cor. 5. 17–21.

[105] Heb 9. 26–8; 10. 10.

[106] See the classic study of Jeremias, *Eucharistic Words*.

2. Let no one quarrelling with his neighbour join you until they are reconciled, that your sacrifice may not be defiled.

3. For this is the sacrifice mentioned by the Lord: 'In every place and time, bring me a pure sacrifice. For I am a great King, says the Lord, and my name is considered marvelous among the Gentiles (Mal 1. 11, 14)[107]

There is no reference to sacrifices in the rest of the text, not even in the eucharistic prayers of *Did.* 9–10, where one could expect them, too. What does 'sacrifice' refer to in *Did.* 14. 1–3?

Of course, it is tempting to identify the Eucharist in *Did.* 14. 1–3 as the *θυσία*. Around 150 CE Justin Martyr calls 'the bread of the eucharist, and also the cup of the eucharist' sacrifices.[108] This interpretation would make *Did.* 14. 1–3 the earliest instance of the later common understanding of the Eucharist as a sacrifice.[109] But such an identification is far from certain. The later tradition saw a connection between the Eucharist and sacrifice precisely because the Pauline and the synoptic traditions connect the Eucharist with the passion of Jesus. However, as the passion tradition does not surface in the *Didache*, one should be careful not to see the same connection implied here as well.[110]

It is much more likely that the prayers of thanksgiving for the cup and the bread which appear in *Did.* 9–10 may be viewed as 'sacrifices'.[111] The literature of ancient Judaism provides many examples of prayers as spiritualized sacrifices. Numerous passages in the Dead Sea Scrolls speak of prayer in connection with sacrifice.[112] In Philo we find prayers described as part of the sacrifices for sins in general.[113] In the early Christian tradition, Justin

[107] The translation follows Ehrman, *Didache*. However, he translates *παραπτώματα* as 'unlawful deeds'.

[108] Justin, *Dial.* 41. 3 (Goodspeed, 138). Interestingly enough he also quotes Mal. 1. 10–12: 'I have no pleasure in you, saith the Lord; and I will not accept your sacrifices at your hands: for, from the rising of the sun unto the going down of the same, My name has been glorified among the Gentiles, and in every place incense is offered to My name, and a pure offering: for My name is great among the Gentiles, saith the Lord: but ye profane it.' Cf. *Did.* 14. 3. Harnack, *Lehre*, 55–6, quotes a number of early Christian sources which quote Mal. 1. 11, 14, in relation to the Eucharist. *Dial.* 117. 1 refers to the eucharistic prayers as sacrifices.

[109] Possibly 1 Cor. 10. 14–22 already implies an interpretation of the Eucharist as sacrifice. Cf. Niederwimmer, *Didache*, 197 n. 22.

[110] Wengst, *Didache*, 53.

[111] Ibid. 53–7; Rordorf and Tuilier, *Doctrine*, 70–1; W. Rordorf, 'L'eucharistie selon la *Didachè*', in *idem et al.* (eds.), *L'eucharistie des premiers chrétiens*, Le point theologique, 17 (Paris: Beauchesne, 1976), 7–28; J. Neijenhuis, *Das Eucharistiegebet—Struktur und Opferverständnis: Untersucht am Beispiel des Projekts der Erneuerten Agende*, Arbeiten zur Praktischen Theologie, 15 (Leipzig: Evangelische Verlagsanstalt, 1999), 43–5.

[112] CD 11. 20–1; 1QS 9. 4–5, 26; 10. 6, etc.

[113] See J. Leonhardt, *Jewish Worship in Philo of Alexandria*, TSAJ 84 (Tübingen: Mohr Siebeck, 2001), 132.

Martyr in *Dial.* 117. 2, 4 refers to prayers and thanksgivings as sacrifices, following a quotation of Mal. 1. 11 (!).

None of the above interpretations seems to be impossible. However, one still wonders whether they fit well with the *Didache*'s overall intention to instruct catechumens and also baptized members of a Christian community in general.

For the author of the *Didache*, confessing one's transgressions is not just a preparation for the Eucharist or for Sunday worship as a whole. For him, confessing sins is a necessary preparation for 'the path of life' (*Did.* 4. 14). Without confession of sins, there is no prayer and no good conscience (*Did.* 4. 14), no Lord's Prayer (*Did.* 8. 2), no baptism of catechumens (*Did.* 7. 1), no holiness (*Did.* 10. 6), no participation in the Sunday worship and its Eucharist (*Did.* 14. 1–3). One 'who has committed a sin against his neighbour' is to be shunned until he repents (*Did.* 15. 3).

One can easily imagine that the *Manual of the Two Ways* (*Did.* 1–6) with all its ethical instructions and its long listing of sins may have served for the examination of conscience (*Did.* 4. 14). Therefore, it seems quite likely that 'your sacrifice' (*Did.* 14. 1–2) refers to the sacrifice that every individual member and the local Christian community as a whole offers by choosing and pursuing the 'path of life' (*Did.* 4. 14).[114] That this interpretation of 'sacrifice' is quite likely in a Jewish-Christian context is supported by Heb. 13. 15–16:

> Through him [i.e. Jesus Christ], then, let us continually offer a sacrifice (θυσία) of praise to God, that is, the fruit of lips that confess his name. Do not neglect to do good and to share what you have, for such sacrifices (θυσία) are pleasing God.

Here it is quite obvious that 'to do good' in connection with sharing one's belongings (cf. *Did.* 4. 8) is understood in terms of a Christian sacrifice.[115]

Nevertheless, the culminating point of such a radical way of life in terms of a sacrifice to God would still be the eucharistic worship service when the consequences of confession and reconciliation are put to the test.

The social reasons for such strictness should not be underestimated. If people quarrelling with their neighbour were not prepared to seek forgiveness and reconciliation, this could easily divide a small house church community like the ones the author of the *Didache* had in mind. Finally, it must have been unbearable to petition the Father 'to gather the members of the community together into his kingdom at the end of time' (*Did.* 9. 4; 10. 5) if someone did

[114] Cf. Heb. 13. 16.

[115] Perhaps Heb. 6. 4–5; 9. 20; 10. 29 and 13. 9–10 (!) even refer to the Eucharist. For the question of the Eucharist in Hebrews, cf. H.-F. Weiß, *Der Brief an die Hebräer*, KEK 13 (Göttingen: Vandenhoeck & Ruprecht, 1991), 726–9.

not even 'want to see or encounter, much less to eat with' his or her neighbour on earth.[116] What can we learn from the *Didache*'s understanding of the Eucharist for interpreting the Fourth Gospel?

THE 'EUCHARIST' IN JOHN IN LIGHT OF THE *DIDACHE*

The *Didache* reveals parallels to the Eucharist in the Gospel of John in several areas. First of all, we find a number of nearly verbal parallels, which are especially frequent in John 6 and 17 but also in John 15.[117] Words and formulations like the vine (ἄμπελος in *Did.* 9. 2 and John 15. 1–2), the plea to be saved from all evil (πονηρός in *Did.* 10. 5 and John 17. 15), the importance of God's name (ὄνομα in *Did.* 10. 2 and John 17. 6, 11, 26), and the reference to God's love (τελειῶσαι αὐτὴν ἐν τῇ ἀγάπῃ σου in *Did.* 10. 5 and ἠγάπησας αὐτοὺς καθὼς ἐμὲ ἠγάπησας in John 17. 23[118]) already give the impression of some closeness. Some verbal parallels between *Did.* 9–10 and John 17 are partly due to these texts being prayers. Thus both address God as πάτερ ἅγιε (*Did.* 10. 2; John 17. 11).

For some scholars a corner-stone of the proposed connection between these two texts is the term κλάσμα, which really means 'fragment'. It is used in *Did.* 9. 3, 4, to describe the eucharistic bread. In the New Testament it appears in all four gospel accounts of the feeding of the multitudes.[119] Erik Peterson has pointed out that κλάσμα is a technical term for the particle of the host.[120] It is common in the eucharistic language of Egypt. A number of exegetes want to see this as a late emendation of the text.[121] The original word would have been ἄρτος, as in similar patristic contexts.[122] Although ἄρτος would probably make better sense in *Did.* 9. 3, such a changing of the present text is highly unlikely because of κλάσμα in *Did.* 9. 4. Since both instances would have to be replaced, ἄρτος would have to make sense in *Did.* 9. 4 as well.

[116] A. Milavec, 'The Purifying Confession of Failings Required by the Didache's Eucharistic Sacrifice', *BTB* 33 (2003), 64–76.

[117] See the lists in Harnack, *Lehre*, 79–81; J. Betz, 'The Eucharist in the *Didache*', in Draper (ed.), Didache *in Modern Research*, 255.

[118] Cf. 1 John 2. 5; 4. 12, 17, 18.

[119] Matt. 14. 20, 15. 37; Mark 6. 43; 8. 8, 19, 20; Luke 9. 17; John 6. 12, 13.

[120] E. Peterson, 'Μερίς: Hostienpartikel und Opferanteil', in *idem*, *Frühkirche, Judentum und Gnosis: Studien und Untersuchungen* (Rome: Herder, 1959), 97–106, esp. 99–100.

[121] Peterson, 'Μερίς', 100; Vööbus, *Traditions*, 89, 146–48; Wengst, *Didache*, 97–8 n. 71.

[122] The evidence is gathered in J. Magne, 'Klasma, sperma, poimnion: le vœu pour le rassemblement de Didachè IX,4', in *Mélanges d'histoire des religions offerts à Henri-Charles Puech* (Paris: Presses universitaires de France, 1974), 197–208, esp. 199–201.

But why should 'bread' (= ἄρτος) be more likely than 'broken bread' (= κλάσμα in the sense of 'crumbs or fragments of bread') to be 'scattered upon the mountains'? This clearly does not make any sense.[123] As Jewish Christians, the Didachist and the members of his community were accustomed to the breaking of bread at every meal. So only a fragment would have been lifted up for the benediction, which makes perfect sense in *Did.* 9. 3. Probably they also knew about the regulations for meal offerings where κλάσματα were used.[124]

In John 6. 12 κλάσματα is used when Jesus commands his disciples to 'gather up (συνάγειν) the fragments, so that nothing may be lost', which eventually filled up twelve baskets (John 6. 13). One needs to take into account the strong Johannine emphasis in John 6. 39; 17. 2, 24, that none of those that were given (δίδωμι) to Jesus by his father should be lost, which always has an eschatological aspect,[125] and the number 'twelve'[126] as a reference to the disciples as representing the complete people of God. These thoughts come very close to the expectation of a gathering (συνάγειν) of the ἐκκλησία into God's kingdom (*Did.* 9. 4; 10. 5; cf. 14. 1; 16. 2), which God prepared (ἑτοιμάζω) for them (*Did.* 10. 5; cf. John 14. 2–3). Both *Did.* 10. 3 and John 6. 27 refer to a special kind of—eucharistic—'food' (βρῶσις in John 6. 27, 55; cf. 4. 32; 6. 35, 51–8; πνευματικὴ τροφὴ καὶ ποτός in *Did.* 10. 3) in connection with eternal life.[127]

Also striking is the connection between knowledge (γνῶσις in *Did.* 9. 3; 10. 2; γινώσκω in John 17. 3) and eternal life (ζωὴ αἰώνιος in *Did.* 10. 3 and John 6. 27, 40, 47, 54, 68; 17. 2; cf. 17. 3 etc.; ἀθανασία in *Did.* 10. 3; cf. ζωή in *Did.* 9. 3 and John 6. 33, 53, etc.), both given through Jesus (*Did.* 10. 3; cf. *Did.* 9. 3; John 6. 40, 51, 54; 17. 2, etc.).[128] The phrase 'bread of life' and Jesus' self-identification with it in the eucharistic context of John 6. 35, 48, make this connection in the Fourth Gospel even clearer than in the *Didache.* However,

[123] Milavec, *Didache*, 8.

[124] Lev. 2. 6, LXX = פִּתִּים in Lev. 2. 6, MT; Lev. 6. 14, LXX = פִּתִּים in Lev. 6. 14; פִּתִּים in *m. Menaḥ* 3. 2. This is not to say that the Eucharist in the *Didache* is a meal offering, but to provide evidence that the use of κλάσμα neither has to be a *late* emendation nor points to a late origin for the *Didache.* The later was argued by C. Bigg, 'Notes on the Didache', *JTS* 6 (1905), 411–15, esp. 414. However, later authors drawing on the *Didache* may no longer have been aware of this background. Thus *Ap. Const.* 7. 25. 3 presents the reading ἄρτος.

[125] John 6. 39: resurrection on the last day; 17. 2: eternal life; 17. 24: prayer that the disciples may be with Jesus in his glory.

[126] For the first time the disciples are referred to as 'the twelve' in this chapter: John 6. 67, 70; cf. 20. 24.

[127] Cf. Ign. *Rom.* 7. 3; *Eph.* 20. 3.

[128] Jesus as the one who gives (eternal) life: *Did.* 10. 3; cf. *Did.* 9. 3; John 6. 40, 51, 54; 17. 2, etc., and the one through whom things are made known (γνωρίζω): *Did.* 9. 2, 3; 10. 2; John 15. 15; 17. 26.

there is no connection between the Eucharist and the death of Jesus in the *Didache*. This is different from the Fourth Gospel: especially in John 6. 51 where Jesus identifies 'bread' and 'flesh' with himself, which he will give (δώσω—future!) 'for the life of the world' it clearly points to Jesus death on the cross and thus links the Eucharist with it.[129]

Neither the *Didache* nor the Gospel of John include the words of institution, and there is no definite evidence that their authors knew them.[130] As a result, one can assume that both texts belong to a liturgical tradition which did not use the institution narrative in the eucharistic liturgy. Such eucharistic prayers of ancient origin like the early East Syrian Anaphora of Addai and Mari (AM) are well known, and still in use in some eastern churches up to the present day.[131] As in *Did.* 14. 1–3, sacrifice in the Anaphora of Addai and Mari is referred to not in terms of the atonement but as something which the priest representing the church offers to God: 'in the commemoration of the body and blood of thy Christ, which we offer to thee upon the pure and holy altar, as thou hast taught us'.[132] While the death of Christ is mentioned only once, the resurrection appears several times: 'celebrating this great and awesome mystery of the passion and death and resurrection of our Lord Jesus Christ'.[133]

[129] See also σάρξ in John 6. 51–6. Cf. Ign. *Smyrn.* 7. 1; *Rom.* 7. 3; *Phld.* 4; *Trall.* 8. 1, who also uses σάρξ instead of σῶμα for a eucharistic element. Cf. Schnelle, *Johannes*, 131–2.

[130] Although ἔλαβεν οὖν τοὺς ἄρτους ὁ Ἰησοῦς καὶ εὐχαριστήσας διέδωκεν shows some similarities to 1 Cor. 11. 23b–24 and Luke 22. 19, the verbs εὐχαριστεῖν and δίδωμι also appear in the synoptic feeding miracles. See the synopsis of the passages in Brown, *Gospel according to John*, 243. However, there is good reason to argue that the Fourth Evangelist knew at least the Gospel of Mark, perhaps even the Gospel of Luke. Cf. M. Lang, *Johannes und die Synoptiker: Eine redaktiongeschichtliche Analyse von Joh 18–20 vor dem markinischen und lukanischen Hintergrund*, FRLANT 182 (Göttingen: Vandenhoeck & Ruprecht, 1999), 61–206; J. Frey, 'Das Vierte Evangelium auf dem Hintergrund der älteren Evangelientradition: Zum Problem: Johannes und die Synoptiker', in T. Söding (ed.), *Johannesevangelium—Mitte oder Rand des Kanons? Neue Standortbestimmungen*, QD 203 (Freiburg: Herder, 2003), 60–118. Thus one may *assume* that the Fourth Evangelist knew the words of institution.

[131] E. C. Ratcliff, 'The Original Form of the Anaphora of Addai and Mari: A Suggestion', *JTS* 30 (1928), 23–32, the most significant early study on the Anaphora of Addai and Mari, called them 'εὐχαριστία pure and simple'. A. Gelston, *The Eucharistic Prayer of Addai and Mari* (Oxford: Clarendon Press, 1992); St. B. Wilson, 'The Anaphora of the Apostles Addai and Mari', in Paul F. Bradshaw (ed.), *Essays on Early Eastern Eucharistic Prayers* (Collegeville, Minn.: Liturgical Press, 1997), 19–37. For the relevance of the question of the validity of a Eucharist without the words of institution, see Lugmayr, 'Anaphora von Addai und Mari'; *idem*, 'Anaphoren'. For similarities between the Anaphora of Addai and Mari and the *Birkat ha-mazon*, see G. Rouwhorst, 'Jewish Liturgical Traditions in Early Syriac Christianity', *VC* 51 (1991), 72–93, esp. 79–80.

[132] AM E 39–40, cf. A 7. The translation here and further on follows Gelston, *Eucharistic Prayer*, 48–55.

[133] AM G 54–5; cf. D 24: 'thou mightest restore us to life by thy divinity'; D 27: 'resurrect our mortality'; H 58: 'for the great hope of the resurrection from the dead'.

This leaves us with a picture of early eucharistic prayers in *Did.* 9–10 and in the Anaphora of Addai and Mari and allusions to the Eucharist mainly in John 6 and 17 for which the celebration of the resurrection of Jesus and the hope for the resurrection of his followers were much more central than the memory of his death.[134] Consequently, the early Christians did not meet on the Friday but on the Sunday as the day of the Lord (*Did.* 14. 1)—i.e., the day of Jesus' resurrection.[135]

The connection between the *Didache* and John may, however, be most obvious as one tries to address the question of self-identity of their authors and the communities around them. Both groups view themselves as being set apart from the rest of mankind on the one hand and as being very close to God on the other hand. Although this may to some degree be true for every Christian group, the consequences for these two communities' understanding of the Eucharist are remarkably close. As we have seen above, *Did.* 10. 3 makes a distinction between God's provision of food in general for everyone and 'spiritual food and drink, and eternal life through your child'. Just the same distinction is obviously at work in John 6: While there is more than enough food for everybody present (John 6. 12–13)—as with the manna in the desert (John 6. 49)—only very few have faith (John 6. 47)—i.e., receive spiritual food in terms of Jesus himself (John 6. 48–51, 56–7) and are given eternal life (6. 58). In both contexts we end up with a picture where in the very middle of a meal,[136] which—according to the benediction (*Did.* 9–10; John 6. 11) is not really very different from a normal Jewish meal—something special happens to the elect. These few are in return prepared to worship and live their life as sacrifice (*Did.* 14. 1–3). In John 6. 68 Simon Peter is portrayed as having sacrificed everything with the words on his lips: 'Lord, to whom can we go? You have the words of eternal life' (NRSV).

However, there is a crucial difference regarding the 'process' of how the group of the elect is created in the two contexts. In the Fourth Gospel a 'eucharistic experience' is possible only through the spiritual interpretation of Jesus' words (John 6. 53–8). Only for those who receive Jesus, not just ordinary (or even special) food, can an ordinary meal suddenly become something special as the eucharistic colouring of the terminology in John 6 reveals. The preaching of Jesus provides the organizing force which selects the followers. By contrast, the *Didache* employs clear-cut criteria for admission to the Eucharist. As we have already mentioned, only those who have been

[134] Cf. O. Cullmann, 'The Meaning of the Lord's Supper in Primitive Christianity', in *idem* and F. J. Leenhardt (eds.), *Essays on the Lord's Supper* (Atlanta: John Knox, 1958), 8–16, esp. 22 n. 1.

[135] Cullmann, *Early Christian Worship*, 10–12.

[136] Cf. Mark 14. 22: ἐσθιόντων states that the words of institution were spoken within the framework of a meal. Cf. Kuhn, 'Qumran Meal', 237.

baptized (*Did.* 9. 5) and who are prepared to confess their trespasses in church (*Did.* 4. 14), who seek reconciliation with their neighbour if necessary (*Did.* 14. 1–3)—but otherwise are to be shunned (*Did.* 15. 3)—may come to the Eucharist. The ones who have not followed the ethical advice of *Did.* 1–6 need to repent before the Eucharist (*Did.* 10. 6).

While the Fourth Gospel is interested only in the centrality of receiving Jesus, the *Didache* reveals a much more developed stage of institutionalization. Nevertheless, the goal for the authors of both the Fourth Gospel and the *Didache* and also of the communities who pray with them is unity. The Didachist prays for the church 'to become one' and to 'be gathered together from the ends of the earth into your kingdom' (*Did.* 9. 4). For John's Gospel this unity among the disciples is based on the unity between Jesus and his father (John 17. 11, 21–2). This is certainly more than early Christians like those of the *Didache* would have been able to express in their eucharistic prayers.

CONCLUSION

This paper first described the eucharistic prayers of *Did.* 9–10. Comparing them with ancient Jewish meal-prayers led to the conclusion that there must have been a broad variety and thus great fluidity in wording of these texts in the first century CE. In addition to the above-mentioned prayers of the *Didache*, a further eucharistic passage in *Did.* 14. 1–3 has shown that the worship of the Christian community behind this text and practically the whole life of its members are understood as sacrifice. However, there is no understanding of Christ's death as a sacrifice.

Comparison of the terminology of *Did.* 9–10 has revealed clear parallels in the Old Testament and especially in Hellenistic Jewish texts like the writings of Philo and in wisdom literature. A significant number of words and phrases are, however, best understood against a Christian background. This fits well with the identification of the Didachist and his community as Jewish Christian. Although there is a rather large number of verbal parallels between *Did.* 9–10 on the one hand and especially John 6 and 17 on the other hand, they are not close enough to allow a conclusion of textual dependence in one or the other direction.[137] Similarities in wording and theology make it quite likely

[137] The parallels between other sections of the *Didache* and the Gospels of Matthew and Luke seem to be much closer. See C. M. Tuckett, 'Synoptic Tradition in the *Didache*', in J.-M. Sevrin (ed.), *The New Testament in Early Christianity*, BETL 86 (Leuven: Peeters, 1989), 197–230; repr. in Draper (ed.), Didache *in Modern Research*, 92–128. For a very recent study of the relationship

that the Fourth Gospel and the *Didache* may be seen as belonging to the same liturgical tradition. They may date from roughly the same time, around the end of the first century, with the *Didache* probably a bit later because of its more developed ecclesiology.

Thus the *Didache* provides significant insights for our understanding of an early type of Eucharist without an institution narrative and a strong emphasis on resurrection and eternal life that can also be seen behind the eucharistic allusions in John's Gospel.

between Matthew and the *Didache*, cf. A. J. P. Garrow, *The Gospel of Matthew's Dependence on the* Didache, JSNTSup 254 (London and New York: T. & T. Clark International, 2004); however, such an early dating of the *Didache* before the Gospel of Matthew seems to be rather unlikely.

9

Prophecy and Patronage: The Relationship between Charismatic Functionaries and Household Officers in Early Christianity

Alistair Stewart-Sykes

During the nineteenth century, and throughout the twentieth, a consensus was built that office as such did not exist in early Christianity but developed at a later stage. This consensus has been described at length by Burtchaell and by Brockhaus,[1] and for this reason there will be no attempt to repeat the description at any length. In essence the consensus holds not only that the earliest generation of Christians knew no office and that the emergence of offices was a later development, but that in the absence of any office, congregations were ordered by the Spirit in an unmediated manner. Of course there is great variety of detail amongst exponents of the consensus, but this brief statement will suffice for the present.

The consensus has recently received thoroughgoing critiques from Burtchaell, basing himself on the assumption that the structures of early Christianity must have derived from the synagogue, and thus that they could not have emerged later but must have been present from the beginning,[2] and from Campbell, who bases himself on the Pauline and deutero-Pauline evidence, again suggesting that office was present in the church's organization from the beginning.[3] Whereas these are adequate critiques of the more extreme forms of the consensus, as represented, for instance, by von Campenhausen and Käsemann,[4] they do not deal with the question of potential conflict between these offices and those exercising charisma, except in so far as Burtchaell

[1] J. T. Burtchaell, *From Synagogue to Church: Public Services and Offices in the Earliest Christian Communities* (Cambridge: Cambridge University Press, 1992), 61–179; U. Brockhaus, *Charisma und Amt: die paulinische Charismenlehre auf dem Hintergrund der frühchristlichen Gemeindefunktionen* (Wuppertal: Rolf Brockhaus, 1972), 7–94.

[2] Burtchaell, *From Synagogue to Church.*

[3] R. A. Campbell, *The Elders* (Edinburgh: T. & T. Clark, 1994).

[4] H. von Campenhausen, *Ecclesiastical Authority and Spiritual Power in the Church of the First Three Centuries* (ET Stanford, Calif.: Stanford University Press, 1969); E. Käsemann, 'Ministry

suggests that such a conflict none the less may have taken place.[5] Brockhaus confronts this issue, but deals solely with the Pauline evidence.[6] Burtchaell's critique, moreover, is highly contentious as a result of his dependence upon the synagogue as the sole source of Christian office. Thus Campbell, who joins him in critique of the consensus, will not, for instance, accept a synagogal origin of Christian presbyters,[7] but bases his theory on the widely recognized domestic origin of early Christianity. Since early Christian communities were based on the household, he suggests, they took their structures likewise from the household. This, more widespread, understanding of the origins of Christian office is what is assumed in this paper. Length precludes any deeper engagement with this debate, or indeed with many other aspects of church order in early Christianity such as the origin of the titles employed for officers in the churches and their significance. Thus the starting-point of the essay is broad agreement with Campbell that there was office in the earliest church, that such office was based on the household, and therefore that extreme forms of the consensus are invalid. However, alongside the more extreme statements, there are exponents such as von Harnack, who argued that local offices existed uneasily alongside those who claimed charisma.[8] It is the interplay of these which is the subject of our investigation. Although most of the study of the phenomenon of the interplay between charisma and office has been based on the Pauline literature, the same assumptions have marked studies of the literature of the second century. The critique of the consensus, however, has not been extended specifically to the Apostolic Fathers, and therefore the focus of this essay will be the extension of the critique to later documents, taken by the consensus as representing the betrayal of the charismatic ideal.

In doing so I am indebted to the typology of domination produced by Weber, and will begin by expressing the thesis of this paper in Weberian terms. Whereas it is generally assumed that there was a conflict in early Christianity between charismatically legitimated leadership and rationally legitimated leadership, I suggest that there was no such conflict. There was no conflict because those concerned with charisma were not concerned with leadership. Weber's typology concerned domination, which has led to the assumption that those who *acted* charismatically must have been concerned to *govern* charismatically. This does not follow. The conflict which can be traced in the

and Community in the New Testament', in *idem*, *Essays on New Testament Themes* (ET London: SCM Press, 1964), 63–94.

[5] Burtchaell, *From Synagogue to Church*, 335.

[6] Brockhaus, *Charisma und Amt*, 203–18.

[7] Campbell, *Elders*, 203–4.

[8] A. von Harnack, *The Constitution and Law of the Church in the First Two Centuries* (ET London: Williams and Norgate, 1910).

New Testament and the Apostolic Fathers is between rationally legitimated leadership and traditionally legitimated leadership. Charisma enters into the equation only marginally, and does so only when a rational type of domination is established, which hardly occurred in the period under discussion.

Although Burtchaell claims Weber as a follower of the consensus,[9] and although it is true that Weber's understanding of early Christianity was largely derived from Harnack and Sohm, his typology was not based solely upon early Christian evidence but upon a far broader reading of history; so his typology continues to have heuristic value in the examination of this question.[10] Broadly, he identifies three modes by which leadership may be legitimated. His three modes are charismatic leadership, traditional leadership, and rational leadership. Charismatic leadership derives from the force of the personality of the individual leader alone, and claims no legitimation beyond the leader except perhaps some supernatural legitimation. Weber's typology has been extended more recently to suggest that charismatic leaders arise within traditional societies when these societies are breaking down as a result of external stresses such as urbanization or colonization.[11] Traditional leadership is derived from custom and is exercised through the maintenance of traditional values. So, for instance, feudal societies and gerontocracies are traditionally legitimated forms of authority. Finally, rational-legal leadership is that known in most modern states and institutions, by which the leader exercises leadership on the basis of an appeal to law and competence, rather than custom or a particular gift of the leader.[12]

The utility of Weber's typology lies in its analysis of the manner in which charisma can be routinized in traditional or rational societies, and in providing categories for classifying forms of domination. It also enables us to comprehend tension between traditionally and rationally legitimated structures of leadership. This is not the place to enter into a full-scale critique of Weber, but two points must be made regarding the category of charismatic leadership as it may apply to early Christianity. First, that whereas we may assume that prophets exercised charisma on the grounds that they claim supernatural revelation, the prophets of early Christianity do not meet all the criteria of Weber's charismatic leader. In particular, whereas Weber's

[9] Burtchaell, *From Synagogue to Church*, 138–40.

[10] J. H. Elliott, in 'Elders as Honored Household Heads and not Holders of "Office" in Earliest Christianity: A Review Article', *BTB* 33 (2003), 77–82 (a review of Campbell's *Elders*), has recently suggested that NT scholars have made insufficient use of Weber.

[11] A. F. C. Wallace, 'Revitalization Movements', *American Anthropologist*, 58 (1956), 264–81, on pp. 268–70.

[12] For further discussion and examples of the typology employed here and its terminology, see especially M. Weber, *Economy and Society*, i (ET Berkeley: University of California Press, 1978), 213–71.

leader plays no part in any institution, but rather seeks to overthrow existing norms, we find prophets participating in the worship of early Christian communities. Secondly, whereas charismatic leaders along the lines of Weber's typology have existed, this does not mean that every society has known a charismatic leader. Thus it has been assumed that prophets exercised leadership in early Christianity, but there is no evidence that such was the case. This will be explored further below, but the point is made at the beginning because the assumption that charismatics are leaders can skew our reading of the evidence. The confusion has come about because the general term 'charisma', which has meaning within the sociology of religion as referring to one who has a particular gift or revelation, has been confused with the charismatic leader of the sociology of domination.[13] Early Christian prophets were charismatic in the former sense, but this does not necessitate their being charismatic leaders.

Although the focus of this paper is the second century, I must begin with Paul, in order that the fundamental flaw in the consensus may be identified. For whatever may be wrong with the consensus, it does at least have some initially plausible basis in the Pauline writings. Thus, whereas Paul speaks frequently of function, he says little of formal ministries, and he suggests, moreover, that functions are bestowed on members of the congregation by the Spirit. It is this Pauline vision of charisma which leads to the effective negation of ministries by the consensus.

This, however, is to make the illegitimate assumption that, because Paul discusses charisma and not office when listing functions within the congregation, he intends thereby to denigrate official ministries, or even to deny their existence. Again, a complete discussion of the consensus and the arguments raised against it is beyond the scope of this paper, but there is one major point which must be raised: namely, that the assumption is based partly on an argument from silence, the silence being the relative absence of officials from the lists of charismatic functions to be found in Paul's writings.[14] The silence may be explained, however, not by presupposing the absence of officials, but their irrelevance to any discussion concerning the liturgy, which is the context of the Pauline lists of functions.

We may begin by noting Brockhaus's contention that the context of Paul's discussion of charisma is charisma alone, and not charisma and office, and particular issues relating to the exercise of charisma in Corinth. 1 Cor. 12,

[13] See, similarly, the brief discussion of B. Malina, 'Was Jesus a Charismatic Leader?', in *idem*, *The Social World of the Gospels* (London: Routledge, 1996), 123–42.

[14] We may note as an example a relatively recent version of the consensus: D. L. Bartlett, *Ministry in the New Testament* (Minneapolis: Fortress, 1993), 46–8.

which contains two lists of *charismata*, is part of a wider treatment of congregational life in general. Two broad points are made: first, that it is the Spirit which appoints gifts and directs them to different individuals, and second, that, just as a body is made up of a number of functioning parts, so the body of Christ needs the performance of a number of distinct spiritual functions in order to be healthy. As such, the passage does not concern itself with office, but purely with particular charismatic functions. Brockhaus observes that not only is the whole point of the passage an exhortation to unity within the congregation, and thus that he is not describing an actual order but setting out an ideal, but, moreover, that Paul is acquainted with the congregation and that individuals are indeed intended by the different groups which are described. Paul's point, in this context, is that gifts should lead to unity, not division and strife, within the congregation. The context in which the unity is expressed, moreover, is the worship of the church, for which reason the discussion in 1 Corinthians goes on to the conduct of prophecy.[15]

None the less, the relative absence of official ministries is seized upon by proponents of the consensus. Yet Brockhaus recognizes, as Theissen and Chow more recently have made very clear, that there was abuse of positions of leadership by many who exercised them within the Corinthian congregation.[16] I therefore suggest that the relative downgrading of positions of leadership is deliberate. The whole context of the passage is not only an exhortation to unity, but also a treatment of those gifts which are of the highest significance: principally love and, as far as utility within congregational life is concerned, prophecy. As such, the charisma of prophecy is being opposed not to any leadership, but to the alternative charisma of glossolalia. Part of this discussion concerns women prophets, who are directed not to teach in church and not to prophesy with uncovered head.[17] But whereas this is a conflict with a charismatic party, it is once again not a conflict between charisma and office as such, but a conflict regarding what Weber would recognize as the process of routinization which must occur on the departure of the charismatic leader. As Weber notes, the problem with any charismatic leader is the problem of succession; charisma operates fully only when a movement begins, and in time it must be either traditionalized or

[15] Brockhaus, *Charisma und Amt*, 142–92.

[16] Gerd Theissen, *The Social Setting of Pauline Christianity* (ET Philadelphia: Fortress, 1982); J. K. Chow, *Patronage and Power: A Study of Social Networks at Corinth*, JSNT Sup 75 (Sheffield: JSOT Press, 1992).

[17] See the discussion and reconstruction of A. C. Wire, *The Corinthian Women Prophets: A Reconstruction through Paul's Rhetoric* (Minneapolis: Fortress, 1990). Recognition that women prophets were one of the parties involved in opposition to Paul's appointees is not to accept the entirety of Wire's reconstruction.

rationalized, a process that has potential for conflict.[18] Paul has designated Stephanas as his effective successor in Corinth, and Stephanas may claim leadership on the basis of his householding, but because of the lack of established structure, his claims are not accepted. As Weber notes, pure patrimonialism depends upon the acceptance of authority by others.[19] Thus Stephanas is opposed by others who claim traditional legitimation (other householders), just as Paul, who is simply temporarily absent and therefore unable personally to exercise his charismatic authority, is opposed by other charismatics (women and glossolalists.) It is even possible that the householders and the charismatics are the same people.[20]

The discussion in which the relative absence of officials occurs is, as has been noted, a discussion of functions within the worshipping assembly. However, bound up to the consensus recognition of the absence of office-holders is an assumption that were these ministries not being carried out through charisma, they would fall to office-holders; for this reason the relative absence of office-holders is noted. However, the assumption that office-holders would have a liturgical role, the assumption which in turn makes the relative absence of office-holders noticeable, is the assumption which, more than anything else, leads in turn to the assumption of conflict. If prophets were concerned with leadership, and if leaders were concerned with the communication of the word of God in the assembly (which is properly the task of the prophet), then there is potential for conflict. But there is no evidence of the leadership of communities by prophets, or indeed of a liturgical role in the assembly for officers such as bishops or elders. We are used to the Christian leader being the person who is responsible for teaching and preaching as part of leadership, but we must recognize that this was not the case in the earliest centuries.

One point which may indicate some confusion of roles is the *Didache*'s prescription that prophets might offer the Eucharist using whatever words they wish (*Did.* 10. 7). This has universally been taken as implying that they would do so instead of bishops. However, it is to be noted that the *Didache* is here concerned solely to regulate the words used, not the person who says them: 'Now regarding the thanksgiving, give thanks thus... but allow the prophets to give thanks just as they wish' (9. 1; 10. 7).

One might anticipate that the bishop was eucharistic president on the assumption that the Didachist's community is based on a household, in that the *episkopos*, as patron, might reasonably be expected to preside in his own house, and indeed that the provision of the community meal might be

[18] Weber, *Economy and Society*, 246. [19] Ibid. 231.

[20] As suggested by Chow, *Patronage and Power*, 184–5.

part of his (or her) benefaction. All that the *Didache* actually says about this, however, is that prophets are allowed to give thanks in whatever manner they deem fitting, rather than using the standardized graces provided. Thus, although the *episkopos* might be the community president, this does not necessitate his presiding at the Eucharist. We may note that in Jewish custom, to which the graces of the *Didache* are acknowledged as proximate, certain graces were said individually, others by the president, and one is entitled to ask whether the *Didache* is referring to individual graces. In other words, far from seeing the president as either the bishop or a prophet, it is possible that we should see the same informality with regard to the speaker in the act of thanksgiving that has been perceived in the liturgy of the word. The regulation leaves this possibility open, as it regulates only the words that are to be used by those who are not prophets, but does not regulate who is permitted to give voice to the graces it prescribes. However, Audet links the instructions regarding the appointment of *episkopoi* and *diakonoi* to the preceding instructions regarding the gathering of the community, suggesting that the link is the role of these officers in the worship of the community.[21] Although he is mistaken, in view of the argument above, in assuming that this reflects a proper concern that the bishop should have a part in the eucharistic liturgy, the link might not be altogether without logic. *Did.* 14 regards the Eucharist as an offering; is it not possible that the direction for the appointment of *episkopoi* and *diakonoi* follows because these are the officials who are to receive, and distribute, offerings made at the Eucharist? Thus, seeing the bishop as eucharistic president is an assumption which is reasonable, but unsupported by the text, whereas there is absolutely nothing which would support the assumption that the bishop has any role beyond presidency, and in particular that he has any role in teaching or preaching.[22]

Another point at which a liturgical role for officials has been identified is *1 Clem.* 40, in which it is stated that God commanded the offering of προσφοράς and λειτουργίας. On this von Campenhausen writes: 'In what the essential work of the bishops consists is made clear in *1 Clement*; like the priests of the old covenant they "present the gifts", that is to say, they are the leaders of worship, and at the celebration of the eucharist they offer prayer on behalf of the congregation.'[23] In response to such assertions, Bowe

[21] J.-P. Audet, *La Didachè: Instructions des Apôtres*, ÉBib (Paris: Gabalda, 1958), 464–7; similarly Harnack, *Constitution*, 79.

[22] G. Schöllgen, 'The *Didache* as a Church Order', in J. A. Draper (ed.), *The* Didache *in Modern Research*, AGAJU 37 (Leiden: Brill, 1996), 43–71, on p. 61 and at n. 109 comes close to the interpretation offered here, but is unable to conceive of bishops who have no liturgical role whatever.

[23] Von Campenhausen, *Ecclesiastical Authority*, 85.

marshalls impressive arguments for not overemphasizing 'the cultic aspects of... *leitourgia*'.[24] She notes that Lightfoot's suggestion that the offerings were as much alms and offerings for the ἀγάπη as prayers or thanksgivings. Moreover, Bowe notes that the adverbs used in *1 Clem.* 44 of the service of the presbyters in offering, ἀμέμπτως and ὁσίως, are part of the vocabulary of moral conduct rather than of ritual purity, and finally that, in *1 Clem.* 44, the presbyters are said to have given good service (καλῶς πολιτευμένους), which is, she notes, language not used of cultic officials but of public servants. We may thus suggest that Clement's *leitourgia* is a public office, and that the offering of gifts to which he refers in the same context is in no sense a sacrifice, but refers to the gifts which are made through the *leitourgia*. This point is so vital that we may pause to illustrate the fact that *leitourgia* and its cognates continue to be employed in the ancient sense of public service. We shall note below that the same misunderstanding has bedevilled interpretation of the *Didache*. The meaning of *leitourgia* may be illustrated both from literature and from the Oxyrhynchus papyri. Thus *P Oxy.* 1119 is concerned with the *leitourgia* of tax collection; *P Oxy.* 1412 uses the term λειτουργήματα for public responsibilities; and *P Oxy.* 82 concerns a fair and even distribution of λειτουργῶν. In the second century, Dio Chrystostom frequently refers to *leitourgiai* as the responsibility of wealthy citizens,[25] and Strabo, in describing the system of poor-relief at Rhodes, states that the provision of food for the poor was considered a *leitourgia*.[26] This usage may still be found in some of Eusebius' sources, when succession lists imply that the bishop's role was considered a *leitourgia*.[27]

Next we may turn to the suggestions of Jefford. Jefford is arguing that the reason why presbyters are not mentioned in the *Didache* is that they are the addressees of the document. They, he assumes, are those who are to instruct, baptize, and celebrate the Eucharist in conformity with the directions given. But the evidence which he presents for liturgical functions is weak indeed, being restricted to Polycarp, *Phil.* 6. 1, and *1 Clem.* 40. *1 Clement* has already been discussed; Poly., *Phil.* 6. 1, concerns the social duties of *presbuteroi*, but would seem here to mean older men, as the prior instruction is addressed to *neōteroi*.[28] More to the point, there is no mention here of a liturgical role, but solely of charity.

[24] B. E. Bowe, *A Church in Crisis* (Minneapolis: Fortress, 1988), 150–2.

[25] Dio Chrys. *Or.* 7. 26. 2–4; 20. 2. 2; 34. 1. 4; 46. 6; 46. 14.

[26] Strabo, *Geog.* 14. 2. 5.

[27] Euseb. *HE* 3. 22; 5. 28. 7; 6. 11. 1; 6. 29. 1.

[28] Though neither J. B. Bauer, *Die Polykarpbriefe*, KAV 5 (Göttingen: Vandenhoeck & Ruprecht, 1995), 55, nor W. Schoedel, *Polycarp, Martyrdom of Polycarp, Fragments of Papias* (London: Nelson, 1967), 21, appear to countenance the possibility.

Next we may note that, in asserting that the duty of the bishop according to Ignatius is teaching and preaching, Lohse is able to adduce only one passage which is a proverbial use of the term *μαθηταί*, which tells us nothing about a bishop's responsibilities, and a much adduced passage which is often taken to refer to preaching, but actually concerns conversation:[29] *τὰς κακοτεχνίας φεῦγε, μᾶλλον δὲ περὶ τούτων ὁμιλίαν ποιοῦ* (*Pol.* 5. 1). That the speech here is not teaching or public proclamation, but conversation, I have argued at length elsewhere.[30] Anyone might speak at the dinner table of the Ignatian communities, as perhaps at that of the *Didache*, but none, not even the *episkopos*, is under obligation to speak. There may be an expectation that teachers and prophets will speak, but not that bishops, deacons, and presbyters will do so. So it is that in Ignatius' letter to the Ephesians we meet the silent bishop Onesimus, whose silence Ignatius defends (*Eph.* 6. 1). If Onesimus lacked eloquence, this would lead to an implicit defence of Onesimus' silence, but a defence would be impossible on any terms were a bishop's fundamental role to teach in the assembly. Clearly there is some expectation that Onesimus should be refuting heresy, but this is to be undertaken in the same way that Polycarp refutes *κακοτεχνίαι*: namely, in discussion among the members of the household. In the event, according to Onesimus at least, this is not necessary (*Eph.* 6. 2).[31] This implies, in turn, that, whatever the competence of the Ignatian bishop, his role did not extend to teaching in the assembly.[32]

Ignatius' direction of duties addressed to Polycarp, whom he assumes to be the *episkopos*, is particularly interesting; it is the most comprehensive list of the duties of a bishop within the literature under examination, yet nowhere is any liturgical role in the assembly envisaged. Apart from refuting heresy with individuals (*Pol.* 2. 1–3), Polycarp is to care for widows (4. 1), ensure that slaves do not purchase manumission from the funds of the church (4. 3), and to oversee the marriage of individuals (5. 2). His principal concern is therefore with the financial management of the church, for although this latter duty might not appear at first sight to be related to the funds and finance of the church, this would inevitably be bound up with the question of a dowry

[29] E. Lohse, 'Die Entstehung des Bischofamtes in der frühen Christenheit', *ZNW* 71 (1980), 58–73, on p. 59.

[30] A. Stewart-Sykes, *From Prophecy to Preaching*, VCSup 59 (Leiden: Brill, 2001), 20–2, 77, 90–1, 276–8.

[31] See, however, the discussion below.

[32] So von Campenhausen candidly admits: 'it is part of this man's duty to instruct his congregation . . . but . . . it is astonishing how little weight is put upon this side of his work' (*Ecclesiastical Authority*, 101). In fact, the only references to instruction which von Campenhausen is able to quote are references to converse (*Pol.* 1. 2; 5. 1).

and the disposition of funds;[33] it is for the same reason that the *mebaqqer* has oversight of marriage and divorce within the Essene community.[34]

The same is true if one examines the qualifications laid down. Bishops and deacons should be ἀφιλαργύροι and πραεῖς, states the Didachist; meekness is, as de Halleux observes, linked in *Did.* 5. 2 to a proper concern for the poor.[35] It is thus close in significance to the concern that the bishop and the deacon should be free of avarice, in that it indicates that the function for which qualification is being sought is the handling of money. A similar concern for an absence of avarice is exhibited in Onasander's treatise on the general.[36] Here the rationale is given that a general should not be corrupt in management. Beyond this, bishops and deacons should be honest (ἀληθεῖς) and tested (δεδοκιμασμένους, probably meaning that they are long-standing members of the community). We may thus note that nothing here equips the bishop to speak in the assembly, but rather that the qualifications given are those of an economic administrator.

Although there has been some attempt to justify the notion that officials had a liturgical role, for all the frequent assertions of charismatic leadership in early Christianity no example of a charismatic leader in a stable community has yet been adduced, with the exception of Hermas, who will be discussed shortly. Certainly Paul was a charismatic leader, but Paul did not have charge of a community. This is because of the inherent instability of charismatic leadership, which depends solely upon the personality of the leader.

It thus seems that there is no overlap between the functions of bishops and of prophets, and thus no basis for conflict between them. As already noted, alongside the older consensus, a new and different consensus has emerged in recent years, that church order in the first two centuries, the period covered by the New Testament and the Apostolic Fathers alike, is a development from the household. The frequent references to churches meeting in houses, the adoption of domestic rituals, the frequent statement of the requirement that Christian leaders should offer hospitality, and the architectural adaptation of households all support this. In this instance one would expect that the leader and patron of the community, the presbyter or bishop, would be the householder. But, to turn to Weber's typology again, we should note that in this instance the leader is legitimated not on the basis of a rational-legal

[33] Cf. M. Y. MacDonald, 'The Ideal of the Christian Couple: Ign. *Pol.* 5.1–2 Looking Back to Paul', *NTS* 40 (1994), 105–25.

[34] CD-A 13. 16–17.

[35] A. de Halleux, 'Ministers in the *Didache*', in Draper (ed.), Didache *in Modern Research*, 300–20, on p. 313.

[36] Onasander, *De Imperatoris officio* 1. 2, 1. 8. See B. S. Easton, 'New Testament Ethical Lists', *JBL* 51 (1932), 1–12.

occupation of an office, but on the basis of the traditional legitimation of a patron, a wealthy householder who offers social support to others. So when von Campenhausen, observing the presence of *kubernēsis* in the list of functions at 1 Cor. 12, denies that this means governance, 'for an office of governor on the lines of the presbyterate or of the later monarchical episcopate there was no room at Corinth either in practice or in principle',[37] and suggests instead that these terms refer to the giving of social support, he is failing to observe that whereas social support is indeed part of what is intended here, patronage can hardly be separated from governance in the ancient world, but that governance by patrons is no block to the exercise of charisma in the context of worship and in the communication of the word of God.

Having suggested that there is no theoretical basis for a conflict between charismatic functionaries and church officers in the period of the Apostolic Fathers, we may go on to examine in detail the points at which conflict has been determined by exponents of the consensus, in order principally to refute the suggestion that a conflict between office and charisma was occurring, and secondly to discover what was actually occurring. For the reasons outlined above, we concentrate on evidence provided by the Apostolic Fathers.

We begin with a discussion of the *Shepherd of Hermas*. This is because a case can be made for seeing Hermas as a charismatic leader in conflict with traditional modes of domination. Hermas has much to say about leaders of the churches in Rome, and much of it is critical.

> You shall say to the leaders of the churches that they should reform their ways. (*Vis.* 2. 2. 6)

> I speak now to you leaders of the church, and those who preside. Do not be like sorcerers, for sorcerers carry their potions in boxes, but you carry your potion and poison in your heart. (*Vis.* 3. 9. 7)

> Those with spots are those deacons who served ill and devoured the living of widows and orphans and served themselves through the ministry which they received to administer. (*Sim.* 9. 26. 2)

It is also true that Hermas was a prophet. As Young points out, not only is he the recipient of revelations which he communicates to his *oikos* and to the church at large (the whole context of Hermas's book), but the depiction of his prophetic activity is the exact opposite of that of the false prophet depicted in *Mand.* 11: that is to say, he is careful to give way to the elders, he makes his prophecy a public, rather than a private, affair, and is not concerned with divination but with proclaiming the message as he has received it.[38]

[37] Von Campenhausen, *Ecclesiastical Authority*, 65.

[38] So S. Young, 'Being a Man: The Pursuit of Manliness in the *Shepherd of Hermas*', *JECS* 2 (1994), 237–55.

Given that Hermas is a prophet who is critical of those in leadership positions, does this therefore mean that Hermas is a charismatic leader? This is the manner in which Jeffers seeks to characterize Hermas, contrasting him as such with the traditionally legitimated Clement of *1 Clement* and claiming that Hermas holds a social locus relatively low in Roman Christianity and represents a revival of charismatic leadership in Roman Christianity responding to the wealth of the circle of leaders around Clement.[39] However, even if Hermas's prophetic charism contributed to his position of leadership, charisma is certainly not the sole basis of his leadership. For in a church led by householders, he himself is a householder, and head of his household (*Sim.* 7. 3), for this is the clear implication of his address to his children. His *oikos* (*Mand.* 12. 3. 6; *Sim.* 5. 3. 9) is his church.[40] Thus we may note that Hermas owns land (*Vis.* 3. 1. 2–4), and is knowledgeable concerning business matters (*Sim.* 4. 5); these are indications that his social status, although not that of the decurionate, is relatively high.[41] This of itself is enough to disqualify Hermas as a charismatic leader in the pure sense, in that he holds office not simply on the basis of charisma but through being a member of the traditional class of leaders. Moreover, even if Hermas's prophetic charisma contributes to his performance of his office, and even though he criticizes the conduct of many leaders, there is no critique of leadership *per se* and no suggestion that the leader should be other than a householder, for unless the leader were a householder, he would not be in a position to exercise the hospitality and the charity that Hermas believes are essential marks of Christian leadership (*Sim.* 9. 27. 2). Similarly he encourages the wealthy within the Christian church of Rome to exercise patronage (*Vis.* 3. 9. 3);[42] he thus supports the traditional structures of society, and wishes to see them exercised within the church. In so far as the house churches are, as Maier demonstrates, already based on a traditional model,[43] his prophetic call is to maintain the tradition. There is no dispute with leadership as such, and so Hermas speaks of the bishops and deacons alongside apostles and teachers, some of whom are still alive, who serve in holiness and who agree among themselves (*Vis.* 3. 5. 1).

[39] J. S. Jeffers, *Conflict at Rome: Social Order and Hierarchy in Early Christianity* (Minneapolis: Fortress, 1991), 145–59.

[40] H. O. Maier, *The Social Setting of the Ministry as Reflected in the Writings of Hermas, Clement and Ignatius* (Waterloo, Ont.: Wilfred Laurier University Press, 1991), 63–5, argues for a household arrangement for Hermas's church without making it explicit that Hermas is himself such a leader.

[41] For further discussion of Hermas's household, and his economic status, see M. Leutzsch, *Die Wahrnehmung sozialer Wirklichkeit im Hirten des Hermas* (Göttingen: Vandenhoeck & Ruprecht, 1989), 50–62.

[42] The point that this is patronage is observed by Maier, *Social Setting*, 61.

[43] Ibid. 59–65.

What is interesting about Jeffers's discussion is his explicit use of Weber, and his identification of Clement as representing, and recommending to the Corinthians, a traditionally legitimated mode of leadership. However, although Hermas represents some of the characteristics of the charismatic leader, he is himself a traditionally legitimated person, and supports the traditional structures of leadership. Hermas is a charismatic in the sense employed in the sociology of religion, but not a charismatic leader; he is humble and self-deprecating, not one who demands leadership, and whilst he criticizes the social conduct of some, he accepts the social order.[44] Jeffers is led to characterize Hermas as he does, not via Weber, but via the weight of the consensus which sets up charisma in opposition to office, which understands all office effectively to be of a rational-legal type, and reckons charismatic leadership to be more primitive.

Although there is no dispute regarding leadership *per se*, there is a critique of certain individuals. In the eleventh Mandate there appears one seated on a chair who is a false prophet. It is noteworthy that the false prophet is seated on a chair, as this was the normal position of the teacher in the ancient world. That the listeners are seated on a learners' *sumpsellion* is further indication of the scholastic setting intended. The point is that it is a teacher, rather than a bishop, who is characterized as a false prophet. Thus we may characterize this dispute as one between one who holds his position by virtue of patronage, a traditional form of legitimation, and one who seeks position on the basis of competence as a teacher (that is to say, on a rational basis). If we turn to the Ignatian correspondence, we find the same conflict. Ignatius' insistence on the claims of the bishop are taken as implying opposition from a charismatic party, in particular by Meinhold.[45] It is the suggestion of this essay that the opposition comes not from charisma, but represents a conflict between rational and traditional legitimation.

We may begin with Ignatius' letter to the Philadelphians, since here at least a case can be made for charismatic opposition to the bishop on the grounds of Ignatius' use of charismatic speech to reinforce his message of unity with, and submission to, the bishop. This may be read as an indication that those who oppose the bishop are claiming charisma, and that their point is being countered with their own weaponry.

While I was with you I cried out. I spoke in a great voice, the voice of God: 'Give heed to the bishop and to the presbytery and deacons. Some suspected me of saying this having foreknowledge of the schism of certain persons. He, on whose account I am in chains, is witness to me that I had no knowledge from any human flesh. The spirit

[44] Cf. Jeffers, *Conflict at Rome*, 156–8.

[45] P. Meinhold, *Studien zu Ignatius von Antiochen* (Wiesbaden: Franz Steiner, 1979), 19–36.

proclaimed this, saying: 'Do nothing separately from the bishop, keep your flesh as the temple of God, love unity, flee divisions, be imitators of Jesus Christ, as was he of his Father.' (Ign. *Phld.* 7. 1)

Ignatius' subsequent comment that some suggested that he had prior knowledge of the situation, and that this therefore invalidated his prophecy, has likewise been seen as opposition from a charismatic party, on the grounds that they do not recognize his speech as genuinely prophetic or charismatic.

Apart from this, however, there is no indication within the letter of any 'charismatic' opposition. Rather, there appear to be issues arising from Jewish Christianity and the interpretation of the first Testament, as Ignatius urges the Philadelphians to give no heed to anyone 'who expounds Judaism to you' (Ign. *Phld.* 6.1).

There is certainly opposition to the bishop, but this opposition might come as much from the 'Judaizing' party as from any charismatic group. According to Trevett, there is no link between the opponents of the bishop and the 'Judaizing' party, but the anti-episcopal activity is a third error, alongside Judaizing and Docetism.[46] However, both Trevett and Meinhold make the simple assumption that opposition to the bishop must derive from those opposed to office in any form, a charismatic group. This is an assumption only. Ignatius suggests that the bishop had his office from God and from Christ, and not from vainglory or through human election (*Phld.* 1. 1), but in doing so is implying an opposition that would claim leadership on the basis of human election, not a group that would not have leadership at all.

The report of Ignatius' prophecy is peculiar, but we should note that if charismatic speech is employed in favour of the bishop, this implies that the charisma of prophecy is recognized by the episcopal party, which in turn indicates that they would hardly oppose those who exercise charisma on principle, or be opposed in turn. The failure of Ignatius' prophecy to pass the test in some quarters is not a necessary indication that the opposition is charismatic, as the testing of spirits is widespread and normal; we do not know, however, who undertook the testing and on what criteria, and therefore we can hardly attribute the testing to a party of charismatics. Moreover, the reading of the opposition as charismatic, and as such opposed to the investment in office of the Ignatian party, is not the only possible reading of the situation. It is quite possible that teachers independent of the bishop and presbytery have formed the opposition, and are organizing their households separately from that of the bishop. Indicative of this is the issue regarding the use of the Old Testament, for if the opposition is representative of some kind

[46] C. Trevett, 'Prophecy and Anti-Episcopal Activity: A Third Error Combatted by Ignatius?', *JEH* 34 (1983), 1–18.

of Judaizing Christianity, then it is possible in turn that their church order is based entirely on synagogal models, with the evolving role of the authoritative teacher and interpreter, which thus has no room for an episcopate. As such, there is no third error at Philadelphia, but rather a single party of opponents who are influenced by a Jewish form of Christianity and are organizing households as schools teaching a Christianity distinct from that of the bishop.

If this is adopted as a hypothesis, then it makes sense of Ignatius' response to the opponents of the bishop: Ignatius urges *χριστομαθία*, and denies any demand to find any point expressed in Scripture. Teaching in Christ, and Christ as the true *ἀρχεῖα*, thus oppose any other teaching and any dependence upon written documents (*Phld.* 8. 2). Ignatius' response is an answer to those who teach from Scripture, subordinating Scripture to the more urgent claim of the Spirit speaking in the assembly. Ignatius is the charismatic, and not the opponents. It is in this light, moreover, that we may read Ignatius' statement that the bishop did more through being silent than those who employ words, which implies that the use of speech is the preserve of the opposition. Certainly it is possible that the speech is prophecy, and that the expectation is that the bishop should be prophesying,[47] but it is more likely that the speech in question is ordered teaching from the Scriptures of the old covenant, for Ignatius joins the prophets in his love together with the bishop and the presbytery (*Phld.* 5. 2).

Not at Philadelphia alone, but at Ephesus, Meinhold sees opposition to the bishop from a charismatic party, characterizing the opponents specifically as *Wanderprediger.*[48] Certainly the opposition has come from outside Ephesus, for Ignatius states that they had arrived at Ephesus (*Eph.* 9. 1), but this need not mean that they are wandering charismatics, as the reason for their travel is not stated and, as Draper rightly reminds us, not all travellers are wandering charismatics;[49] yet their supposed itinerant status is the sole basis on which charismatic legitimation might be attributed to them. The two main points which may be gathered are that the opponents of the *episkopos* held their own eucharistic celebration, and that they criticized the silence of the bishop (*Eph.* 5. 3–6. 2). These are the very same points which are at issue in Philadelphia. For Meinhold the criticism of Onesimus' silence indicates that those who opposed the bishop claimed inspired speech.[50] However, whereas this is a possible reconstruction of the situation, it is not the only possible reconstruction. Is it not possible that other households had separated themselves from

[47] So Meinhold, *Studien*, 27.

[48] Ibid. 20–1.

[49] J. A. Draper, 'Weber, Theissen, and Wandering Charismatics of the *Didache*', *JECS* 6 (1998), 541–76, on pp. 565–8.

[50] Meinhold, *Studien*, 21–2.

the household represented by the bishop, in order to form schools in which they might hold their own eucharistic celebrations? Is it not possible that the bishop is expected not to speak prophetically, but to speak anti-prophetically, or to teach, and that failure on the part of the bishop to act as a teacher is causing those households of scholastic character to break away? Moreover, the silence of the bishop may be held as a mark of respect for those who prophesy, in that the bishop is allowing prophecy, whilst making no claim himself to the prophetic charism. Meinhold explains the separate eucharistic celebrations by noting the provisions of *Did.* 10. 7, which allow the prophets to say the eucharistic prayer, and suggests that the same situation had previously obtained in the communities addressed by Ignatius, but that prophets had separated because their right to offer the Eucharist had been effectively usurped by the bishop.[51] However, as we have already noted, the eucharistic president is nowhere named in the *Didache*; the *Didache* does not state who the eucharistic president should be, but simply lays down the words to be used by those who are not prophets, and the assumption that otherwise the eucharistic president should be the bishop is an assumption only. There is therefore more than a simple choice between bishop and prophet as regards the person who says the eucharistic words. Similarly, in the case of Ignatius, we must note that he nowhere states that the bishop is to say the eucharistic words, simply that a eucharistic celebration should not take place unless the bishop is present. A silent bishop is not offering the Eucharist, and if the bishop is not doing so, then perhaps the prophets are!

Not only do the cohesion with Philadelphia and the internal coherence of the hypothesis sketched above indicate that the issue is with teachers, but Ignatius' comments about the opposition point in this direction. The visitors have 'wicked teaching' (*Eph.* 9. 1), they are *μεγαλορημοσύνας* (*Eph.* 10. 2), whereas it is better to be silent than to speak of what is not real, for teaching is good only if the teacher acts in accordance with what is taught, and there is but one true teacher (*Eph.* 15. 1).

We may deal more briefly with Meinhold's reading of the situation at Magnesia and Smyrna.[52] In Magnesia, Meinhold detects opposition on the basis of his understanding of Ignatius' defence that the episcopate is an office independent of the personality of the office-holder. This rational-legal legitimation (to employ the terms of Weber), he suggests, must therefore be opposed to a charismatic legitimation. However, once again, the only certain

[51] Ibid. 21.

[52] Ibid. 25–6. Meinhold finds no charismatic opposition at Tralles, and so his discussion of this letter is not noted here.

thing about the situation in Magnesia, other than opposition to the bishop, is that there is difficulty with Judaizing practices, such as keeping the sabbath (*Magn.* 9. 1). It is possible that the same situation that was discerned in Philadelphia is prevailing, though the evidence from Ignatius' language is less strong, the only indication of opposition from a scholastic party being Ignatius' comment that the only title worth having is that of pupil (*Magn.* 10. 1). This is not of itself convincing, but it is more convincing than any a priori conviction that the opposition is charismatic. Finally, in the letter to Smyrna, we meet a party opposed to the bishop, whom Ignatius loudly upbraids. But once again, as Meinhold recognizes, the fundamental issues are not charisma and office, but the content of the opponents' teaching,[53] which once again indicates a pattern of opposition on the basis not of legitimation but of emerging orthodoxy.

Thus, in so far as it is possible to derive a coherent picture of opposition to the *episkopos* from the Ignatian correspondence, there is no correlation between claims of charisma and opposition to the bishop. It seems overall most probable that opposition to the bishop comes from teachers. It may be objected, however, that the teachers were themselves charismatic functionaries and that on these grounds the existence of a conflict between charisma and office may continue to be maintained. Harnack noted the appearance of 'apostles, prophets and teachers' as a triad at 1 Cor. 12. 28 and, given that this group appeared in the context of a discussion of charisma, concluded that 'They are all charismatics, i.e. their calling rests on a gift of the Spirit, which is a permanent possession for them'.[54] Yet he had already noted that the reason why the triad was placed at the head is that they are each principally concerned with the proclamation of the word of God, and so their position here is unrelated to any claim of charisma. To return to the observations of Brockhaus, the focus of the chapter is the discussion of the communication of the word of God within the assembly, and for this reason the teacher finds a position with the prophets. It is the same rationale—namely, their common task of speaking the word of God—which places the teachers alongside the prophets in the *Didache*. For although Niederwimmer[55] and Stempel[56] assert that the teacher in the *Didache* is a charismatic figure, no evidence is produced for this assertion beyond the close association between teacher and prophet. Rather, Ignatius is the charismatic and, in exhorting submission to the bishop, the presbytery, and the deacons, has some of the qualities of the charismatic

[53] Ibid. 31. [54] Harnack, *Constitution*, 24.

[55] K. Niederwimmer, *The Didache* (ET Minneapolis: Fortress, 1998), 189–90.

[56] H.-A. Stempel, 'Der Lehrer in der "Lehre der zwölf Apostel"', *VC* 34 (1980), 209–17.

leader.[57] The charisma may be undergoing routinization, but is real none the less.[58]

At this point we may turn again briefly to the *Didache*. At *Did.* 15 a new topic appears to be introduced in the instruction that bishops and deacons should be appointed. The common reading of this passage in line with the consensus is that no bishop or deacon had previously been appointed, and that theretofore the community was either under the governance of a charismatic hierarchy or was completely without hierarchy, and that the appointment of officers is an entirely new departure.[59] But as de Halleux points out, and as we may point out here more forcibly, to see the appointment of *episkopoi* and *diakonoi* as a new departure is completely to misread the text. The *Didache* does not say *tout court* that ministers should be appointed, but that the ministers who are appointed should demonstrate certain qualities,[60] those qualifications for office examined above. This leaves open the question of the origin of officers in this community, but even if this chapter is an addition to the work of the original Didachist,[61] it means that *episkopoi* and *diakonoi* are already established offices in the community. There is no sudden take-over by bishops from prophets. Given that *Did.* 15 is not about the appointment of officers *de novo* but concerns the qualifications such officers should have, we may turn to the following statement:

for they themselves liturgize for you the liturgy (*ὑμῖν γὰρ λειτουργοῦσι καὶ αὐτοὶ τὴν λειτουργίαν*) of the prophets and teachers. Therefore do not despise them. For they are honoured among you alongside the prophets and teachers (*Did.* 15. 1–2)

The statement that the officials should not be despised has been interpreted as stating that the officers appointed should not be despised at the expense of charismatic officers,[62] which would be an indication that they are indeed being despised. But the point, given the argument above that officers such as bishops exercised no liturgical ministry, is that they are to be honoured alongside prophets and teachers, even though they exercise no public ministry, which is the preserve of prophets and teachers.

[57] So, perceptively and with due reservations, Maier, *Social Setting*, 158–63.

[58] So A. Brent, 'Pseudonymity and Charisma in the Ministry of the Early Church', *Augustinianum*, 27 (1987), 347–76, on pp. 352–4, in response to Schillebeeckx's statement of the consensus.

[59] So, notably, W. Rordorf and A. Tuilier, *La Doctrine des douze apôtres*, 2nd edn. (Paris: Cerf, 1998), 63–4, 73–7.

[60] De Halleux, 'Ministers', 313.

[61] As Rordorf and Tuilier, *Doctrine*, 63, suppose.

[62] So Niederwimmer, *Didache*, 200; J. A. Kleist, *The Didache*, ACW (Westminster: Newman Press, 1948), 165.

Rather, as the *Didache* says, they 'liturgize . . . the liturgy of the prophets'. It might be suggested that just as in *1 Clement* the *leitourgia* of the presbyters was a public office undertaken at one's own expense, so the term 'liturgize' is here likewise used in its ancient sense—that is to say, the bishops provide financial support for the teachers and prophets, and enable them to carry out their ministry. Thus, just as the requirement for meekness and the concern for lack of avarice indicate that the concern of the bishop and deacons is financial, so the reason for these qualifications is explained by their function: namely, the support of those who do exercise a ministry in the assembly. The liturgizing of the liturgy of the prophets and teachers is not the performance of the office of prophets and teachers, as is generally assumed,[63] but is social and economic support for those who do exercise this office. It is this misunderstanding of the term in this text which has bedevilled interpretation from Harnack on. The bishops and deacons should be honoured, states *Did.* 15. 1–2, because they provide the means by which the prophets and teachers exercise their ministry, and should therefore receive like respect.

These bishops and deacons are therefore patrons of the Didachist's community, householders who are in a position to offer support to the charismatics. There is thus no conflict between the groups;[64] nor have the bishops and deacons been obliged to take over from the 'charismatic' functionaries due to their decline and disappearance,[65] but rather a position of mutual support is envisaged. The situation is rather as Burtchaell puts it: the office-holders were present in the church, but, compared to those who exercised more public ministries, were relatively insignificant.[66] Burtchaell argues that offices begin entirely in the synagogue, and suggests that office-holders come to prominence because of the failure of the charismatic functionaries, whereas I have argued elsewhere that borrowing from the synagogue is something which marks the second or third generation of the Pauline communities[67] and that the offices of early Christian communities are transformed in their nature so that the functions previously performed by individuals become attached to offices; but in his assessment of the fundamental state of affairs in the earliest stratum of Christianity, Burtchaell is surely correct. The one thing which *Didache* says about bishops and deacons is that their responsibility is a

[63] A. von Harnack, *Die Lehre der zwölf Apostel nebst Untersuchungen zur ältesten Geschichte der Kirchenverfassung und des Kirchenrechts,* TU 2 (Leipzig: Hinrichs'sche Buchhandlung, 1884), 140–1; Niederwimmer, *Didache,* 201; Rordorf and Tuilier, *Doctrine,* 73.

[64] As presupposed by Niederwimmer, *Didache,* 200–1.

[65] So Harnack, *Lehre,* 153–8; H. Lietzmann, 'Zur altchristlichen Verfasssungsgeschichte', in *Kleine Schriften,* i, TU 67 (Berlin: Akademie, 1958), 141–85, on p. 169; Rordorf and Tuilier, *Doctrine,* 76–7.

[66] Burtchaell, *From Synagogue to Church,* 188, 310–12, 348–51.

[67] Stewart-Sykes, *From Prophecy to Preaching,* 79–87, 170–4.

leitourgia, and involves the financial support of those who teach and prophesy, and that the qualifications demanded for this post indicate those prepared to offer such a *leitourgia*. If this point seems to have been somewhat laboured, it is because of the significance lent to the text in the past. There is no decline of prophecy leading to the necessity of bishops stepping in to fill the role, and no conflict between these functionaries and their patrons.

A conflict between functionaries and their patrons may, none the less, be the conflict in Corinth which occasioned *1 Clement*. This characterization of the conflict is different from the widespread assumption that *1 Clement* is the result of a conflict between emerging office and continuing, or resurgent, charismatic activity,[68] for if the suggestion of this paper that the assumption of a conflict between office and charismatic activity derives from a flawed methodology has any validity, then even a relatively cautious statement of the consensus such as that of Lona, who suggests that the transfer from the charismatically orientated community described by Paul in 1 Corinthians to one in which office is known would hardly occur without difficulty,[69] is without ground. We need not therefore repeat the argument and deal in detail with the various versions of the consensus which have been brought to bear on *1 Clement*, but may set about seeking a new solution. The solution suggested, in line with the argument of the essay so far, is that functionaries were no longer content to accept the *leitourgia* of patrons, but sought leadership on their own account. The situation has thus moved on significantly from that described in the *Didache*.

Although I have suggested that the consensus is wanting, none the less there is a prima-facie case for seeing the conflict in Corinth as in some way relating to the emergence of office, not simply in that the occasion of the dispute was the removal of presbyters, but also in Clement's statement that the apostles knew that there would be strife over the episcopate (*1 Clem.* 44. 1). However, although the removal of presbyters is a vital issue, we must note that *some* presbyters had been removed, which does not indicate that there was general dissatisfaction with the presbyteral system, since it equally implies that some presbyters were left in place. Moreover, when Clement states that the Lord himself knew that there would be strife as to who bore the office of oversight, he is implying that, far from wanting to avoid all fixed order in the congregation, the group of opponents themselves desire to hold office. The same is implied in Clement's indication that certain individuals had brought about the strife through their failure to observe their proper

[68] See the references at O. M. Bakke, '*Concord and Peace*': *A Rhetorical Analysis of the First Letter of Clement with an Emphasis on the Language of Unity and Sedition*, WUNT 2.143 (Tübingen: Mohr Siebeck, 2001), 282–3.

[69] H. E. Lona, *Der erste Klemensbrief*, KAV 2 (Göttingen: Vandenhoeck & Ruprecht, 1998), 81.

station (*1 Clem.* 14. 1). We may thus begin to see that the conflict might not be so much about office itself as about legitimation.

Before suggesting that the issue at Corinth was the same as that addressed by Ignatius, particularly in Philadelphia, we may recall the domestic basis of the Corinthian church, in line with the newer consensus observed above which aligns office with status within a household. The emphasis that Clement assigns to hospitality implies that the household is still the essential unit in the Corinthian church (*1 Clem.* 1. 2; 11. 1; 12. 1), on which basis we may assume that the leading householders would take the place of presbyters.[70] The word consistently used by Clement to describe the situation is *stasis* (*1 Clem.* 1. 1; 2. 6; 14. 2); in political discourse this was classically applied to factionalism within a state, being defined by Aristotle as the desire of individuals to be self-governing;[71] as such it implies that the factionalism is taking place within households. Secondly we should note Clement's statements that a few individuals only are the cause of the strife (*1 Clem.* 1. 1; 47. 6). Again this implies that the *stasis* is occurring within households, rather than being more generalized (although we must recognize that the minimization of the numbers involved may serve some rhetorical effect). Finally, we may recall again Clement's statement that there would be strife among those who would claim the office of bishop, which is why a system of succession was set up. Whereas this might mean that a single householder is attempting to exercise *episkopē* over other households, *episkopē* would be found within households; thus I suggest that the strife was taking place within individual households, and that presbyters have been deposed within certain households.

In this light we may turn to the interesting explanation of the situation addressed by *1 Clement* offered by Bakke, who suggests that the cause of stasis is economic inequality.[72] He points to the relative lack of economic homogeneity which marked the Christian households known in the Corinth of Paul, and suggests that the poor in the congregations were seeking office instead of the existing presbyters in order to obtain a better division of wealth, which leads to dishonour as the rules of patronage are not obeyed by those below. Competition for the honour of leadership is thus the basis of the tension in Corinth, and the competition results from economic factors. Certainly this fits with what is otherwise known of conflict in Corinth in an earlier period, and coheres with some of the thematic statements of *1 Clem* 3. 3[73] by explaining the opposition to presbyters as opposition to a

[70] So Bowe, *Church in Crisis*, 11–16.

[71] Arist. *Pol.* 5. 6. 1; *Eth. Nic.* 9. 1167A.

[72] Bakke, '*Concord and Peace*', 289–317.

[73] E.g., the statement that 'The worthless rose up against those in honour, those of no reputation against the renowned, the foolish against the prudent, the young against the elders

patronal system—as opposition, in other words, to a traditionally legitimated form of leadership.

A relative lack of economic homogeneity may have led to the situation of *stasis* within these households, and this would explain the characterization by Clement of the opponents of the presbyters as motivated by ζῆλος and φθόνος (*1 Clem.* 3. 2; 4. 7; 5. 2), as well as the exhortations of Clement to submissiveness and obedience. But if Bakke is correct in pointing to economic inequality as the motivation for the activity of the opponents, then a closer characterization of the opponents is still required. Economic revolutions do not occur within traditional societies, which are always marked by economic stratification, without leaders opposed to the traditionally legitimated leadership. We should not see the *stasis* here as generalized popular revolution, but rather as a leadership bid by some class which is relatively economically disadvantaged by comparison with the patrons, but which has a reasonable claim to the honour and status enjoyed by the patrons, though on a basis different from patronage. This class could be that of the teachers; a teacher may hold a subservient position in an ancient household, and need not be a person of social status, may indeed be a slave or a freedman, and may accept the patronage of a householder as, we have suggested, teachers, alongside prophets, accepted patronage in the Didachist's community.[74] Teachers, who were the recipients of patronage, might be those who are disturbing the accepted order of patronage.

But some more positive argument than this is needed. In providing one, we may turn to an exponent of the older consensus, namely Meinhold, as there is much to commend his view that the opponents were charismatics who based their case on superior spiritual gifts, and in particular glossolalia.[75] The spiritual gifts which Clement praises are fundamentally concerned with wisdom, knowledge, and speech. *1 Clem.* 15 is a series of citations which concern true speech: *1 Clem.* 17. 5, in using the example of Moses as one of humility,

(*presbuterous*)'. Whereas we might be excused for thinking that *presbuterous* here simply refers to older men, we must recall that both sender and recipients were aware of the issue, and therefore would not need to have matters spelt out. The language recalls Isa. 3. 5, but as Bakke, '*Concord and Peace*', 291–2, points out, this is a clever rhetorical adoption of the language of Scripture.

[74] U. Neymeyr, *Die christlichen Lehrer im zweiten Jahrhundert*, VCSup 4 (Leiden: Brill, 1989), 218–20, notes the various ways in which teachers in the ancient world might support themselves. The other option apart from the charging of fees or dependence upon patronage would be an officially endowed chair, which is clearly out of the question here. For a satirical treatment of the situation of a teacher, dependent on patronage, who gradually finds himself dropping down the social scale, see Lucian, *De Mercede conductis potentium familiaribus*, esp. 14–18, 26. Such loss of status within a patronal system might lead to the questioning of the social order within the Christian households of Corinth.

[75] Peter Meinhold, 'Geschehen und Deutung im ersten Clemensbrief', *ZKG* 58 (1939), 82–129.

points out that he is a person of simple speech; at 31. 5 Clement suggests that the opponents take pride in their words rather than in God, and at 30. 3 and 38. 2 Clement contrasts good works with fine words as the sign of one who is truly wise. A similar view is proposed by Opitz.[76] Apart from the passages observed already, Optiz notes the exhortation of Clement at 57. 2: 'Learn to be submissive, putting aside the boastful and haughty effrontery of your tongue!'

Although Meinhold and Opitz, in reliance on the older consensus, assume that the opponents are charismatic, and are therefore opposed to office in principle, whereas we have already seen that, far from being the work of those who seek a charismatic order and do not recognize office, the factionalism results from those who seek office for themselves, none the less they point to an important issue: namely, that the opponents claim a superiority of speech and a superiority of teaching. There is no reason, however, to assume that this is charismatic speech. For all Meinhold suggests that the charismatic party appeals to Paul,[77] when Clement cites 1 Cor. 12, he does not cite the discussion of glossolalia, which would have helped his case had this been in his purview, but encourages fidelity and wisdom and notes the parallel factionalism between the households.[78]

The strength of Meinhold's case lies in his identification of speech as a central issue, and the weakness is that there is no indication that the speech was charismatic. But if the speech is not charismatic, then we point once again to the possibility that there are teachers who are providing the focus of opposition within some households. They too may claim a wisdom of speech, but their speech is not charismatic. As such, they may claim a greater wisdom than the householders, and it is their wisdom which in turn is characterized as foolishness by Clement (*1 Clem.* 39. 1); the wise should manifest their wisdom in good deeds (38. 2). They are supported by the householders, and may receive the fruit of their labour with the Stoic freedom of *parrhēsia*, but a true *parrhēsia* is in Christ, as the position of those in receipt of patronage is that of the angels who serve God (34. 1–6). Clement's answer to the claims of the teachers is to point to the *diadochē* of leadership received from the apostles; since *diadochē* is a concept deriving from the philosophical schools, we may see Clement's use of the idea as directly countering the claims of those claiming a *diadochē* along scholastic lines.[79]

[76] H. Opitz, *Ursprünge frühkatholischer Pneumatologie* (Berlin: Evangelische Verlaganstalt, 1960), 13–15. Opitz, however, presses the case too far by suggesting that the presbyters are seeking control over an entirely glossolalist congregation.

[77] Meinhold, 'Geschehen und Deutung', 100–1.

[78] So Bakke, '*Concord and Peace*', 288, with reference to *1 Clem.* 47–8; see also Maier, *Social Setting*, 89.

[79] On *diadochē* as a scholastic concept transferred to the Christian realm, note A. Brent, 'Diogenes Laertius and the Apostolic Succession', *JEH* 44 (1993), 367–89.

Office at Corinth, as already argued, was not a bureaucratically legitimated office which was in the process of emergence at the expense of religious charisma, but a traditionally legitimated office which had always existed alongside the exercise of charismata in the assembly. The challenge made is to these traditionally legitimated officers, and the basis of the challenge is superiority in speech and wisdom. This is not charismatic speech, for charismatic speech coexisted at the time of Paul with a system of traditional leadership, but the very ordered speech which Paul encouraged. Herein may be the basis of an appeal to Paul: not to Paul the charismatic, but to the Paul who would rather speak a few words of edification than a thousand in tongues (1 Cor. 14. 19). For this reason, in citing 1 Cor. 12, Clement makes no allusion to the discussion of glossolalia, because the fundamental thrust of Paul's discussion would lead to a discussion of the place of teachers in a Christian community.

The point has been reached at which a summary is possible. In exploring the consensus that office in Christian communities had in some way supplanted the exercise of charisma, it was observed that one of the reasons why a conflict between office and charisma has been assumed is the assumption, in turn, that officers exercised functions in the assembly. As far as is possible, it has been shown that they did not, and so there were no grounds for conflict. A second confusion in the consensus was identified: that charismatic leadership has been identified with the exercise of charismatic functions. Rather, it has been suggested, charismatic functions could be exercised within a society with traditionally legitimated leadership. This occurs in the Didachist's community and in the community of Hermas, as well as in the Corinth addressed by Paul. Rather than representing a conflict between charisma and office, as the older consensus assumed, an examination of the relevant material has shown either that there was no conflict, or that the conflict which occurred was between teachers and householder-bishops. I suggest that the conflict comes about because teachers may threaten the traditionally legitimated bishop, in that they are capable of acting outside the structures of the household through becoming self-supporting. At the time of the *Didache*, no conflict has appeared, and the teachers appear content to accept patronage from the bishops and deacons, but we may deduce that there was criticism of the bishop, presbytery, and deacons from various teachers in several of the communities addressed by Ignatius, that teachers had adopted the position of presbyters in the Corinth addressed by Clement, and that Hermas, a householder, is suspicious of a teacher whom he characterizes as a false prophet.

This essay leaves many questions unanswered, such as the origin of bishops, deacons, and presbyters, the precise extent and scope of their duties (as part of which we should pose the, as much unasked as unanswered, question of how bishops and/or presbyters come to have the exclusive right of presidency at the Eucharist), the fate of the teacher in the second century, and the manner in which, despite the opposition of such figures as Clement, Hermas, and Ignatius, the episcopate takes on an intellectual role in the second century.[80] By escaping from the assumptions of the consensus, however, the way is cleared for a fresh examination of these issues.

[80] A term borrowed from L. W. Countryman, 'The Intellectual Role of the Early Catholic Episcopate', *Church History*, 48 (1979), 261–8.

Part V

The *Didache*

10

Didache 1. 1–6. 1, James, Matthew, and the Torah

John S. Kloppenborg

The topic of the *Didache* and James is perhaps an odd choice for this conference commemorating the 1905 publication of *The New Testament in the Apostolic Fathers*, whose purpose it was to inquire into the likelihood that the Apostolic Fathers displayed some acquaintance with books of the New Testament.[1] Kirsopp Lake found no reason to mention James in his chapter on the *Didache*; James is in fact discussed only in the chapters on the *Shepherd* and *2 Clement*.[2] Even in the more recent index, *Biblia patristica*, which adopts generous definitions of 'citation' and 'allusion', there are no entries for the *Didache* in the section that compiles early patristic citations of James.[3] There are indeed no good grounds for believing that James and the *Didache* enjoyed any direct literary relationship.

The question of the relationship between the *Didache* and Matthew is, of course, a much livelier subject of debate, with scholars defending the Didachist's knowledge of the first gospel,[4] others denying any direct

[1] Committee of the Oxford Society of Historical Theology, *The New Testament in the Apostolic Fathers* (Oxford: Clarendon Press, 1905).

[2] *NTAF*, 108–13 (the *Shepherd*), 127–8 (*2 Clement*).

[3] *Biblia Patristica: Index des citations et allusions bibliques dans la littérature patristique*, i: *Des origines à Clément d'Alexandrie et Tertullien*, ed. J. Allenbach (Paris: Editions du Centre National de la Recherche Scientifique, 1975).

[4] E. Massaux, *Influence de l'Évangile de saint Matthieu sur la littérature chrétienne avant saint Irénée* (Louvain: Publications Universitaires de Louvain, 1950), 604–46; B. C. Butler, 'The Literary Relations of *Didache*, Ch. XVI', *JTS* 11 (1960), 265–83; *idem*, 'The "Two Ways" in the *Didache*', *JTS* 12 (1961), 27–38; F. E. Vokes, *The Riddle of the Didache* (London: SPCK, 1938), 92–119; S. E. Johnson, 'A Subsidiary Motive for the Writing of the Didache', in M. H. Shepherd and S. E. Johnson (eds.), *Munera Studiosa: Studies Presented to W. H. P. Hatch on the Occasion of his Seventieth Birthday* (Cambridge, Mass.: Episcopal Theological School, 1946), 107–22, on p. 112; C. C. Richardson, *Early Christian Fathers*, The Library of Christian Classics, 1 (Philadelphia: Westminster Press, 1953), 161–79, esp. 163, 165–6; B. Layton, 'The Sources, Date and Transmission of *Didache* 1.3b–2.1', *HTR* 61 (1968), 343–83; L. W. Barnard, 'The Dead Sea Scrolls, Barnabas, the *Didache* and the Later History of the "Two Ways"', in *idem*, *Studies in the Apostolic Fathers and their Background* (New York: Schocken Books; Oxford: Basil Blackwell,

relationship,[5] and still others advocating the use of a common source[6] or even Matthew's knowledge of the *Didache.*[7] With respect to the Two Ways document (1. 1–2; 2. 2–6. 1), it is much more difficult to find defenders of Matthaean dependence; the case for dependence on Matthew is normally made from the uses of εὐαγγέλιον in *Did.* 8. 2; 11. 3; 15. 3, 4, from the convergence between the sayings in *Did.* 16. 3–8 and Matt. 24–5, and from the similarities between the catena of sayings interpolated into the Two Ways section (1. 3b–2. 1) and sayings of Jesus in Q, Matthew, and Luke.

The third pair in this literary triangle, the relationship between James and Matthew, has also received some attention. A few scholars defended a direct relationship between James and Matthew,[8] but such a hypothesis demands too high a degree of ingenuity to command much assent. Nevertheless, the numerous contacts between James and the Jesus tradition suggest that even if there is not a direct literary relationship between James and either Matthew or

1966), 99 n. 2; E. Schweizer, *Matthäus und seine Gemeinde*, SBS 71 (Stuttgart: Verlag Katholisches Bibelwerk, 1974), 141 n. 12, 164–5; C. M. Tuckett, 'Synoptic Tradition in the *Didache*', in J. M. Sevrin (ed.), *The New Testament in Early Christianity: La Réception des Écrits Néotestamentaires dans le Christianisme Primitif*, BETL 86 (Leuven: Peeters, 1989), 197–230; K. Wengst, *Didache (Apostellehre), Barnabasbrief, Zweiter Klemensbrief, Schrift an Diognet, eingeleitet, herausgegeben, übertragen und erläutert*, SUC 2 (Darmstadt: Wissenschaftliche Buchgesellschaft, 1984), 19, 24–31.

[5] J.-P. Audet, *La Didachè: Instructions des apôtres*, ÉBib (Paris: Gabalda, 1958), 166–86; W. Rordorf, 'Does the Didache Contain Jesus Tradition Independently of the Synoptic Gospels?', in H. Wansbrough (ed.), *Jesus and the Oral Gospel Tradition*, JSNTSup 64 (Sheffield: JSOT Press, 1991), 394–423; W. Rordorf and A. Tuilier, *La Doctrine des douze apôtres (Didachè): introduction, texte, traduction, notes, appendice et index*, 2nd edn. rev. et augmentée, SC 248 (Paris: Cerf, 1998), 91, 232. K. Niederwimmer, *The Didache: A Commentary*, Hermeneia (ET Minneapolis: Fortress, 1998), 48–51) argues that if there is any influence of the NT, it is only at the level of the redactor of the *Didache*. The Two Ways documents (*Did.* 1. 1–2; 2. 2–6. 1), the liturgical section (7. 1–10. 7), the church order (11. 1–15. 4), and probably the apocalypse (16. 3–8) display no dependence on the NT at all.

[6] E.g., R. Glover, 'The Didache's Quotations and the Synoptic Gospels', *NTS* 5 (1958), 12–29.

[7] A. J. P. Garrow, *The Gospel of Matthew's Dependence on the* Didache, JSNTSup 254 (London: T. & T. Clark International, 2004).

[8] One of the first to defend James's use of Matthew was W. Brückner, 'Zur Kritik des Jakobusbriefes', *ZWT* 17 (1874), 530–41, on p. 537: 'So ist es auch leichter in allen Stellen, an die hier gedacht werden kann, die unmittelbare Abhängigkeit vom Matthäusevangelium vorauszusetzen.' The case was taken up by M. H. Shepherd, 'The Epistle of James and the Gospel of Matthew', *JBL* 75 (1956), 40–51; he divided James into eight didactic discourses, each of which, he argued, was built around a central macarism or gnomic saying that had striking parallels with Matthew. Similarly, C. N. Dillman, 'A Study of Some Theological and Literary Comparisons of the Gospel of Matthew and the Epistle of James' (Ph.D. diss., University of Edinburgh, 1978). Shepherd explained the lack of verbal agreement between Matthew and James on the theory that James was acquainted with the first gospel through its oral use in the liturgy. But F. Gryglewicz, 'L'Épitre de St. Jacques et l'Évangile de St. Matthieu', *Roczniki Theologicano-Kanoniczne* 8, no. 3 (1961), 33–55, later argued that James knew the written text of Matthew.

Luke, there may be some indirect relationship, either via the Sayings Gospel Q or oral Jesus tradition.[9]

Although it is difficult to make a case for direct literary dependence among the Two Ways document, James, and Matthew, conceptual similarities exist, similarities that point to origins in a common intellectual milieu. The thesis of this paper, stated briefly, is that the conceptual similarities that exist among these three documents exist not so much at the level of literary relationships—relationships of dependence—as at the level of shared assumptions, shared *topoi*, and shared argumentative strategies. The three documents, taken together, point to a sector of the Jesus movement which held Torah observance to be a mark of identity, and which therefore found itself at some variance with Paul, and later with Barnabas and Ignatius. This sector of the Torah-observant Jesus movement eventually lost ground to those sectors represented by Paul and Ignatius.

The working assumption of this paper is that not only can we isolate the contours of the Two Ways document (TW) employed by the *Didache*, but that a history of editorial development can be reconstructed.

A synoptic analysis of the available 'Two Ways' documents (1QS 3. 13–4. 26; *Barn.* 18–20; *Did.* 1–6; *Doctrina* 1. 1–5. 2; the *Canons of the Holy Apostles* (or *Apostolic Church Order*) 4. 1–13. 4, the *Epitome of the Canons of the Holy Apostles*, and the *Ap. Const.* 7. 2. 2–6) permits us to work out a rough genealogy of the Two Ways tradition (see Fig. 1). This involves three basic forms: (α) a recension used by Barnabas, displaying a rather loose topical organization and having many conceptual affinities with 1QS 3. 13–4. 26; (β) a second recension with a greater degree of topical organization and betraying an effort to assimilate the list of prohibitions in *Did.* 2 / *Doctrina* 2 to those of the Decalogue. This version was used independently by the Greek *Vorlage* of the *Doctrina* (δ) and the *Didache*, which was in turn used in the *Didache*'s successor, book 7 of *Apostolic Constitutions*; and finally, (γ) a slightly attenuated version used by the *Canons* and the *Epitome* closely paralleling β but missing the Way of Death and sharing a few elements with α that are missing in β.[10]

[9] See the surveys of the question by D. B. Deppe, *The Sayings of Jesus in the Epistle of James* (D.Th. diss., Free University of Amsterdam; Ann Arbor: Bookcrafters, 1989); P. J. Hartin, *James and the 'Q' Sayings of Jesus*, JSNTSup 47 (Sheffield: Sheffield Academic Press, 1991); J. S. Kloppenborg, 'The Reception of the Jesus Tradition in James', in J. Schlosser (ed.), *The Catholic Epistles and the Tradition*, BETL 176 (Leuven: Peeters, 2004), 93–141.

[10] See J. S. Kloppenborg, 'The Transformation of Moral Exhortation in *Didache* 1–5', in C. N. Jefford (ed.), *The* Didache *in Context: Essays on its Text, History and Transmission*, NovTSup 77 (Leiden: Brill, 1995), 88–92. This agrees closely with, and is indebted to, the analyses of Stanislaus Giet, *L'Énigme de la Didachè*, Publications de la faculté des lettres de l'université de Strasbourg, 149 (Paris: Éditions Ophrys, 1970), 71; Niederwimmer, *Didache*, 30–41. Barnard

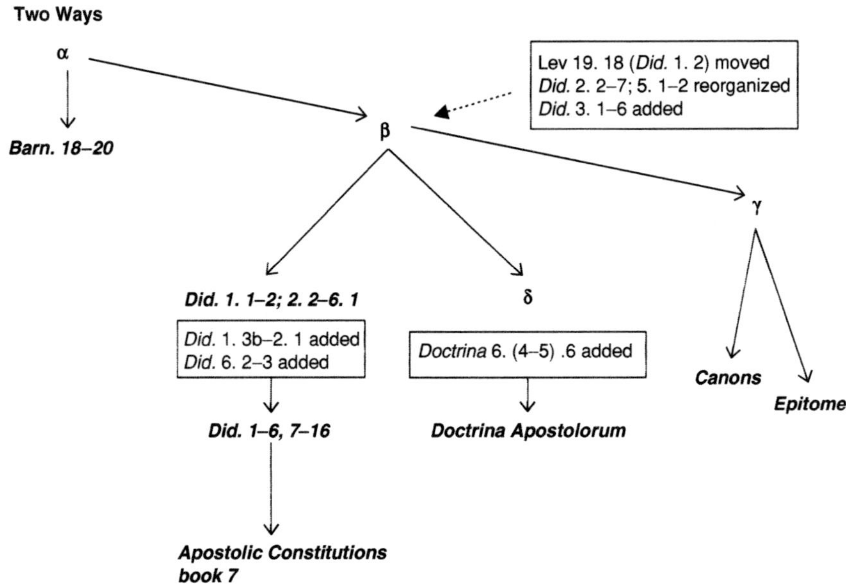

Figure 1 The Two Ways Tradition

Several developments within the β-recension are worthy of mention. In addition to an assimilation of its prohibitions to the Decalogue, this recension also contains the so-called τέκνον section (*Did.* 3. 1–6 / *Doctrina* 3. 1–6), missing in *Barnabas*. This section, characterized by the repetitive address, τέκνον μου, is a separate sapiential composition apparently inserted into the Two Ways document at this point.[11] This series of admonitions, which Audet calls 'une adapatation sapientielle du décalogue',[12] is formulated around key terms of the Decalogue (φόνος, μοιχεῖα, εἰδωλολατρία, κλοπή, βλασφημία), and takes the form of admonitions against lesser vices (anger, passion, augury,

("Dead Sea Scrolls', 107) proposes a similar stemma, but, following Goodspeed ('The Didache, Barnabas and the Doctrina', *ATR* 27 (1945), 228–47), places the Greek original of the *Doctrina* as the direct source of *Barnabas* and the *Didache*.

[11] R. H. Connolly, 'The Didache in Relation to the Epistle of Barnabas', *JTS* 33 (1932), 241–2 observes that of the twenty-five terms used for vices or faults in 3. 1–6, fully nineteen do not appear elsewhere in the *Didache*. Audet (*Didachè*, 299–300) observes that whereas *Did* 2. 2–7 uses οὐ with the future indicative, in imitation of the Decalogue, in 3. 1–6, 'on a... l'imperatif, beaucoup plus intime, plus enveloppé aussi de chaleur humaine, et à mon sens, plus <relatif>, de la tradition des sages'.

[12] Audet, *Didachè*, 301. Niederwimmer, *Didache*, 95 n. 6, thinks that this characterization goes too far.

mendacity, and grumbling), on the grounds that these inevitably 'lead' (ὁδηγεῖ) to the vices named in the Decalogue.[13]

The *Didache*'s branch of the β-recension also contained a catena of Jesus' sayings (*Did.* 1. 3b–6) dependent on at least the Gospel of Luke and probably added in the mid-second century CE.[14] This catena is not present in the *Doctrina* (or presumably in its Greek *Vorlage*), but was taken up by the *Apostolic Constitutions*. The interpolation of 1. 3b–6 necessitated the addition of δευτέρα δὲ ἐντολὴ τῆς διδαχῆς in *Did.* 2. 1, serving as a transition back to the earlier Two Ways document (β).[15]

Limiting the investigation to the Two Ways (TW) portion of the *Didache*, i.e., 1. 1–2; 2. 2–6. 1, a number of general convergences with James and Matthew can be noted.

1. SPEECH ETHICS

a. The Two Ways (TW)

The editing of the TW document has paid particular attention to speech ethics. This is especially clear in the expanded Decalogue in 2. 1–7 and in the τέκνον section (3. 1–6). To the Decalogue's οὐ ψευδομαρτυρήσεις (2. 3), the *Didache* adds οὐκ ἐπιορκήσεις and οὐ κακολογήσεις. The expansion continues by dwelling in particular on ambivalence in speech and thought:

[13] Several have suggested that *Did.* 3. 1–6 might be understood on the analogy of 'building a fence' around the Torah (*m. 'Abot* 1. 1): C. Taylor, *The Teaching of the Twelve Apostles: With Illustrations from the Talmud* (Cambridge: Deighton Bell, 1886), 1–17, on p. 23; Vokes, *Riddle*, 76; R. M. Grant, 'The Decalogue in Early Christianity', *HTR* 40 (1947), 9; C. N. Jefford, *The Sayings of Jesus in the Teachings of the Twelve Apostles*, VCSup 11 (Leiden: Brill, 1989), 63–4. Audet (*Didachè*, 301), however, rightly points out that 'elle [the fence] est constituée, non par exhortations du genre de celles que nous avons ici, mais par des décisions et des décrets tranchant une question d'observance, visant généralement soit à adapter la loi ancienne aux conditions nouvelles, soit à redresser une situation jugée irrégulière ou simplement périlleuse'. In addition, I have observed that whereas 'the "hedge" in *m. 'Abot* 1. 1 and elsewhere entails the formulation of precautionary extensions to the Torah that function to ensure that there will be no violations of the commandments', the logic of the *Didache / Doctrina* instead 'implies the fundamental *unity* of the Law, which now includes not only the Decalogue but numerous other admonitions, and warns that violation of an apparently lesser admonition, if it is not tantamount to violation of one of the commandments of the Decalogue, tends inevitably in that direction' ('Transformation of Moral Exhortation', 105–6).

[14] See J. S. Kloppenborg, 'The Use of the Synoptics or Q in Did. 1.3b–2.1', in H. van de Sandt (ed.), *The Didache and Matthew: Two Documents from the Same Jewish-Christian Milieu?* (Assen: Van Gorcum; Minneapolis: Fortress, 2005), 105–29.

[15] Thus, among others, Niederwimmer, *Didache*, 86–7; Jefford, *Sayings of Jesus*, 53.

4 οὐκ ἔσῃ διγνώμων οὐδὲ δίγλωσσος· παγὶς γὰρ θανάτου ἡ διγλωσσία. 5 οὐκ ἔσται ὁ λόγος σου ψευδής, οὐ κενός, ἀλλὰ μεμεστωμένος πράξει

(Do not be 'double-minded' or 'double-tongued', for *diglossia* is the snare of death. Your speech shall not be false or empty, but shall be completed in action) (2. 4–5)

A comparison of the *Didache*'s Two Ways with *Barn.* 19 indicates that the warning against *dignomon*[16] and *diaglossia* in 2. 4 belonged to the tradition common to the *Didache* and *Barnabas.*[17] The contribution of the TW's editor was twofold: first, to associate the warnings concerning improper speech with the Decalogue, and thereby to bring such prohibitions under the aegis of the Torah, and second to expand the admonition against ambivalence in 2. 5 by a second admonition on empty promises (2. 6), also 'Torahized' by association with the Decalogue.

This association of speech ethics with the Decalogue continues in the *τέκνον* section. There the Decalogue's prohibitions of murder (3. 2), adultery (3. 3), idolatry (3. 4), theft (3. 5), and blasphemy (3. 6) are linked to lesser offences, including lying (3. 5), which the TW connects with theft, and grumbling (3. 6), linked to idolatry.

Finally, the TW concludes the 'way of life' with an admonition to communal confession of sins, which suggests that a clear 'consciousness' is a condition for efficacious prayer:

ἐν ἐκκλησίᾳ ἐξομολογήσῃ τὰ παραπτώματά σου, καὶ οὐ προσελεύσῃ ἐπὶ προσευχήν σου ἐν συνειδήσει πονηρᾷ

In the assembly confess your sins, and do not approach in your prayer with a defiled consciousness. (4. 14)

b. James

The convergences of the TW with James are clear and relatively numerous. It is well known that James displays a particular interest in control of speech. James has exhortations on control of the tongue (3. 1–12), slander (4. 11–12), boasting (4. 13–17), oath-taking (5. 12), and prayer and confession of sins (5. 13–18). William Baker notes that twenty-three of James's fifty-four imperatives directly concern speech ethics, and a further six are indirectly

[16] The term *δίγνωμος* is rare, though not unattested prior to the first century CE: Dorotheus (1st century BCE), *Fragmenta Graeca* 413. 21; Diogenianus [2nd century CE] *Paroemiae* 4. 32 (meaning 'vacillating').

[17] *Barn.* 19. 7: *οὐκ ἔσῃ διγνώμων οὐδὲ δίγλωσσος· παγὶς γὰρ θανάτου ἐστὶν ἡ διγλωσσία. ὑποταγήσῃ κυρίοις ὡς τύπῳ θεοῦ ἐν αἰσχύνῃ καὶ φόβῳ. Barn.* 19. 8: *παγὶς γὰρ στόμα θανάτου.*

concerned with speech.[18] James's view of oath-taking goes well beyond that found in the TW: like Matthew's (5. 33–7), James's view is that oaths should not be taken at all. Like the *Didache*, James shows special interest in ambivalence: the concern for 'double mindedness' is found in 1. 6–7 in connection with petitions for wisdom, and especially in 3. 9–12, where James argues that the tongue ought not to be a simultaneous source of blessing and cursing.

At 4. 11–12 James includes a brief argument against slander (*καταλαλεῖν*), concluding that whoever slanders or judges a brother slanders and judges the Law—an argument which takes as its intertext Lev. 19. 15–16, the Holiness Code's prohibition of slander:

Μὴ καταλαλεῖτε ἀλλήλων, ἀδελφοί· ὁ καταλαλῶν ἀδελφοῦ ἢ κρίνων τὸν ἀδελφὸν αὐτοῦ καταλαλεῖ νόμου καὶ κρίνει νόμον· εἰ δὲ νόμον κρίνεις, οὐκ εἶ ποιητὴς νόμου ἀλλὰ κριτής. εἷς ἐστιν ὁ νομοθέτης καὶ κριτὴς ὁ δυνάμενος σῶσαι καὶ ἀπολέσαι· σὺ δὲ τίς εἶ ὁ κρίνων τὸν πλησίον;

Do not slander one another, brothers. Whoever slanders a brother or judges his brother slanders the Law and judges the Law. Now if you judge the Law, you are not a doer of the Law but a judge. The Lawgiver and the judge are One; who is able to save and to destroy. But who are you, judging your neighbour? (Jas. 4. 11–12)

As Luke Timothy Johnson has argued, James begins with an allusion to Lev. 19. 16, *οὐ πορεύσῃ δόλῳ ἐν τῷ ἔθνει σου*, representing the MT's לֹא-תֵלֵךְ רָכִיל בְּעַמֶּיךָ, 'do not go around as a slanderer among your people'.[19] But the logic of the second clause, *ὁ καταλαλῶν ἀδελφοῦ ἢ κρίνων τὸν ἀδελφὸν αὐτοῦ καταλαλεῖ νόμου καὶ κρίνει νόμον*, which pairs slander with judgement, suggests that the author treats slander as a species of (false) judgement. For this reason it seems likely that not only Lev. 19. 16 is in view, but also Lev. 19. 15: *οὐ ποιήσετε ἄδικον ἐν κρίσει . . . , ἐν δικαιοσύνῃ κρινεῖς τὸν πλησίον σου*. It is this intertext that supplies the rationale for the conclusion, *εἰ δὲ νόμον*

[18] W. R. Baker, *Personal Speech-Ethics: A Study of the Epistle of James against its Background*, WUNT 2.68 (Tübingen: J. C. B. Mohr (Paul Siebeck), 1995), 6. These include *αἰτείτω* (1. 5); *αἰτείτω* (1. 6); *καυχάσθω* (1. 9); *λεγέτω* (1. 13); *ἔστω . . . βραδὺς εἰς τὸ λαλῆσαι* (1. 19); *ἔχετε τὴν πίστιν* (2. 1); *λαλεῖτε καὶ οὕτως ποιεῖτε* (2. 12); *μὴ πολλοὶ διδάσκαλοι γίνεσθε* (3. 1); *μὴ κατακαυχᾶσθε καὶ ψεύδεσθε* (3. 14); *κλαύσατε* (4. 9); *μὴ καταλαλεῖτε* (4. 11); *κλαύσατε* (5. 1); *μὴ στενάζετε* (5. 9); *μὴ ὀμνύετε* (5. 12); *ἤτω δὲ ὑμῶν τὸ ναὶ ναί* (5. 12); *προσευχέσθω . . . ψαλλέτω* (5. 13); *προσκαλεσάσθω . . . προσευξάσθωσαν* (5. 14); *ἐξομολογεῖσθε . . . εὔχεσθε* (5. 16).

[19] L. T. Johnson, 'The Use of Leviticus 19 in the Letter of James', *JBL* 101 (1982), 391–401, on pp. 395–6, points out that in both the LXX and the NT, *καταλαλεῖν* came to mean 'slander' (Ps. 100. 5: *τὸν καταλαλοῦντα λάθρα τὸν πλησίον αὐτοῦ*; Ps. 49. 20: *καθήμενος κατὰ τοῦ ἀδελφοῦ σου κατελάλεις καὶ κατὰ τοῦ υἱοῦ τῆς μητρός σου ἐτί θεις σκάνδαλον*; Wisd. 1. 11: *Φυλάξασθε τοίνυν γογγυσμὸν ἀνωφελῆ καὶ ἀπὸ καταλαλιᾶς φείσασθε γλώσσης*). M. Dibelius (*James: A Commentary on the Epistle of James*, rev. by H. Greeven, Hermeneia (Philadelphia: Fortress, 1976), 228) demurs: 'The author does not have in mind some specific commandment against slander found in the law—for then the statement would contain simply a truism—, but rather the commandment of love in Lev 19. 18 (notice "neighbor" (*πλησίον*) in v. 12 and cf. Jas 2. 9–11).'

κρίνεις, οὐκ εἶ ποιητὴς νόμου ἀλλὰ κριτής, for slander viewed as unjust judgement clearly violates the Law (Lev. 19. 15) and constitutes the slanderer as what James earlier calls κριτὴς διαλογισμῶν πονηρῶν (2. 4). The second part of James's argument appeals to the unity of God, as it did at 2. 11, and argues that the slanderer has arrogated to himself the role of God, who is both lawgiver and judge.

Many authors see Lev. 19. 18 as supplying the essential logic to Jas. 4. 11–12, pointing to the use of the word πλησιός.[20] But πλησίος also occurs in Lev. 19. 15, and hence the conclusion that the law of love (Lev. 19. 18) supplies the logical basis for Jas. 4. 11–12 is unnecessary. It seems more likely that the prohibitions of false judgement and deceit taken from the Holiness Code (Lev. 19. 15–16) have been coupled with the Jesus saying found in Q 6. 37 (Matt. 7. 1) to form an argument that slander not only violates the Holiness Code but also represents an arrogation of divine prerogatives. What is worth noting is that while James's argument against slander adopts a more elaborate argumentative form than the simple prohibitions of the TW, both expressly connect their prohibitions with the commandments of the Torah.

James also concludes with an exhortation on the practice of communal confession of sins which seems to make the same assumptions as *Did.* 4. 14—that confession of sins renders prayer more efficacious:

καὶ ἡ εὐχὴ τῆς πίστεως σώσει τὸν κάμνοντα, καὶ ἐγερεῖ αὐτὸν ὁ κύριος· κἂν ἁμαρτίας ᾖ πεποιηκώς, ἀφεθήσεται αὐτῷ.
ἐξομολογεῖσθε οὖν ἀλλήλοις τὰς ἁμαρτίας καὶ εὔχεσθε ὑπὲρ ἀλλήλων, ὅπως ἰαθῆτε.
πολὺ ἰσχύει δέησις δικαίου ἐνεργουμένη.

The prayer of faith will save the sick, and the Lord will raise them up; and anyone who has committed sins will be forgiven. Therefore confess your sins to one another, and pray for one another, so that you may be healed. The prayer of a righteous person is powerful and effective. (5. 15–16)

c. Matthew

Matthew's interest in speech ethics is perhaps not so pronounced as that in the TW or James, but is nonetheless present.[21] Famously, Matt. 5. 33–7 forbids not only perjury, but, like James, oath-taking in general. The prohibition

[20] Dibelius, *James*, 228; F. Mussner, *Der Jakobusbrief: Auslegung*, HTKNT 13.1, 3rd edn. (Freiburg, Basel, and Vienna: Verlag Herder, 1975), 187; S. Laws, *A Commentary on the Epistle of James*, BNTC (London: A. & C. Black, 1980), 187; P. H. Davids, *The Epistle of James: A Commentary on the Greek Text*, NIGTC (Grand Rapids, Mich.: Eerdmans, 1982), 170.

[21] E.g., various injunctions concerning greeting others (5. 47), prayer (6. 5–6, 7; 7. 7–11), fraternal correction (7. 1–5; 18. 15–20), and acclamations of Jesus (7. 21–3; 10. 32–3).

which Matthew takes as his point of departure, *οὐκ ἐπιορκήσεις*, is not from the Decalogue or any other biblical book,[22] but is a piece of Second Temple Jewish *paraenesis* presented as if it were one of the prohibitions of the Torah, i.e., precisely in the way that it appears in the TW's extended Decalogue.[23] In considering the relationship between *Did.* 2. 5 and Matt. 5. 33, Jefford points out that since the *Didache* lacks the prohibition of oaths distinctive of Matthew (and James), there is no reason to posit a literary dependence of the TW on Matt. 5. 33 at this point. Indeed, if there is any relationship at all, Matthew is more likely dependent on an expanded Decalogue of which *Did.* 2. 3–5 is an instance.[24] Matthew also 'Torahizes' his prohibition of angry and insulting speech by associating it with the Decalogue's prohibition of murder (5. 22).[25] The TW stands remarkably close to Matthew at this point, for while the TW uses the trope of one vice 'leading to' (*ὁδηγεῖ*) another instead of Matthew's equation of one vice with another, the TW expressly connects anger and quarrelsomeness with murder, and does so in the context of an exhortation structured around the Decalogue.[26]

All three documents display concern over teaching. Comparison of *Barn.* 19. 9b–10 indicates that the redaction of the *Didache*'s Two Ways has accentuated the importance of attending to teaching. Whereas *Barnabas* exhorts his audience to 'love as the apple of your eye all who speak the word of the

[22] The closest biblical parallels are the prohibitions of invoking the divine name in Exod. 20. 7: *οὐ λήμψῃ τὸ ὄνομα κυρίου τοῦ θεοῦ σου ἐπὶ ματαίῳ*; Lev. 19. 12: *καὶ οὐκ ὀμεῖσθε τῷ ὀνόματί μου ἐπ ἀδίκῳ καὶ οὐ βεβηλώσετε τὸ ὄνομα τοῦ θεοῦ ὑμῶν*; and Deut. 23. 22–4: *ἐὰν δὲ εὔξῃ εὐχὴν κυρίῳ τῷ θεῷ σου, οὐ χρονιεῖς ἀποδοῦναι αὐτήν, ὅτι ἐκζητῶν ἐκζητήσει κύριος ὁ θεός σου παρὰ σοῦ, καὶ ἔσται ἐν σοὶ ἁμαρτία: ²³ ἐὰν δὲ μὴ θέλῃς εὔξασθαι, οὐκ ἔστιν ἐν σοὶ ἁμαρτία. ²⁴ τὰ ἐκπορευόμενα διὰ τῶν χειλέων σου φυλάξῃ καὶ ποιήσεις ὃν τρόπον εὔξω κυρίῳ τῷ θεῷ σου δόμα, ὃ ἐλάλησας τῷ στόματί σου*. The final phrase in Matt. 5. 22, *ἀποδώσεις δὲ τῷ κυρίῳ τοὺς ὅρκους σου*, seems to be an adaptation of Ps. 49. 14: *θῦσον τῷ θεῷ θυσίαν αἰνέσεως καὶ ἀπόδος τῷ ὑψίστῳ τὰς εὐχάς σου.*

[23] E.g., Ps-Phocylides 16–17: *μὴ δ' ἐπιορκήσῃς μήτ' ἀγνὼς μήτε ἑκοντί· ψεύδορκον στυγέει θεὸς ἄμβροτος ὅστις ὀμόσσῃ* ('Do not commit perjury, neither ignorantly nor willingly; the immortal God hates the perjurer, whosoever it is who has sworn'); *Sib. Or.* 2. 68: *μήδ' ἐπιορκήσῃς μήτ' ἀγνὼς μήτε ἑκοντί : ψεύδορκον στυγέει θεός, ὅττι κεν ἄν τις ὀμόσσῃ* ('Do not commit perjury, either ignorantly or willingly; God hates the perjurer, whatever it is he has sworn'); *Did.* 2. 5. Philo's elaboration of the Decalogue in *Spec. Leg.* 2. 224 interprets the third commandment (against invoking the Divine Name in vain) as a prohibition of perjury: *τὸ περὶ τοῦ μὴ ψευδορκεῖν ἢ συνόλως μάτην ὀμνύναι* ('[the prohibition] concerning perjury or vain oath-taking in general'). For parallels in Theognis, Hesiod, and Menander, see P. W. van der Horst, *The Sentences of Pseudo-Phocylides: With Introduction and Commentary*, SVTP 4 (Leiden: Brill, 1978), 123.

[24] Jefford, *Sayings of Jesus*, 57–8.

[25] W. D. Davies, *The Setting of the Sermon on the Mount* (Cambridge: Cambridge University Press, 1966), 237–8, points to a similar prohibition of angry speech in 1QS 6. 25–7, which, however, is not framed as an elaboration of the Torah.

[26] *Did.* 3. 2: *μὴ γίνου ὀργίλος, ὁδηγεῖ γὰρ ἡ ὀργὴ πρὸς τὸν φόνον, μηδὲ ζηλωτὴς μηδὲ ἐριστικὸς μηδὲ θυμικός· ἐκ γὰρ τούτων ἁπάντων φόνοι γεννῶνται.*

Lord to you', but then shifts to an exhortation to 'remember the day of judgment, day and night, and seek each day the face of the saints' (19. 9b–10a), the TW offers a more sustained exhortation on the honouring of teachers and the pursuit of their words in a communal context:

τέκνον μου, τοῦ λαλοῦντός σοι τὸν λόγον τοῦ θεοῦ μνησθήσῃ νυκτὸς καὶ ἡμέρας, τιμήσεις δὲ αὐτὸν ὡς κύριον· ὅθεν γὰρ ἡ κυριότης λαλεῖται, ἐκεῖ κύριός ἐστιν. ἐκζητήσεις δὲ καθ ἡμέραν τὰ πρόσωπα τῶν ἁγίων, ἵνα ἐπαναπαῇς τοῖς λόγοις αὐτῶν. οὐ ποιήσεις σχίσμα, εἰρηνεύσεις δὲ μαχομένους· κρινεῖς δικαίως, οὐ λήψῃ πρόσωπον ἐλέγξαι ἐπὶ παραπτώμασιν. οὐ διψυχήσεις, πότερον ἔσται ἢ οὔ.*

My child, remember day and night the one who speaks the word of God to you, honouring him as the Lord. For wherever the Lord's nature is spoken of, there the Lord is. Then seek daily the face of the saints so that you might find rest in their words. Do not create schisms, but reconcile those who strive; judge with righteousness, not showing favouritism in reproving transgressions. Do not be of two minds, whether it shall be so or not. (*Did.* 4. 1–4)

The focus of James's and Matthew's discourse on teaching and teachers is not so much an exhortation to attend to teachers as warnings to teachers. Whereas the *Didache*'s admonitions appear to be aimed at the congregation generally, Matt. 18. 1–35 has in view those in roles of leadership, presumably teachers. Nevertheless, the two display a common interest in reconciliation and reproof in a communal context (cf. also *Did.* 4. 14). And the TW's justification of the role of teachers by invoking the Divine Presence resembles Matthew's strategy for justifying the community's role in the forgiveness of sins (Matt. 18. 20).[27]

Though the TW does not betray much anxiety about the dangers of teaching, both Matthew and James do. James warns that teachers are judged by more stringent standards (3. 1), proposing a behavioural test based on the way of life (ἀναστροφή) of those claiming to be wise (3. 13–18). Such concerns are even more pronounced in Matthew, who is anxious to

[27] Compare *m. 'Abot* 3. 6: 'R. Halafta of Kefar Hanania said: [When there are] ten sitting together and occupying themselves with Torah, the Shekinah rests among them, as it is said: "God stands in the congregation of God" [Ps. 82. 1]. And whence [do we infer that the same applies] even [when there are] five? [From] that which is said: "And he founded his band upon the earth" [Amos 9. 6]. And whence [do we infer that the same applies] even [when there are three?] [From] that which is said: "In the midst of the judges he judges" [Ps. 82. 1]. And whence [do we infer that the same applies] even [where there are] two? [From] that which is said: "Then they who fear the Lord spoke one with another, and the Lord listened and heard" [Mal. 3. 16]. And whence [do we infer that the same same applies] even [when there is] one? [From] that which is said: "In every place where I cause my name to be mentioned I will come unto thee and bless you" [Exod. 20. 21].'

warn teachers of the dangers of teaching that is contrary to the Torah (5. 19–20). And Matthew, of course, also proposes a similar behavioural test for teachers (7. 15–20).[28]

2. PARTIALITY AND *DYPSYCHIA*

A second set of convergences, at least between the TW and James, has to do with partiality towards the rich and powerful and concern over ambivalence (*dipsychia*). In the TW the topic of partiality appears twice, once in 4. 3b–4, where the author counsels against partiality in judgement as this pertains to reproof of fellow members,[29] and a second time in 5. 2. The appearance of the Septuagintalism[30] *πρόσωπον λαμβάνειν* (4. 3) in the context of an exhortation concerning reproof (*ἐλέγξαι ἐπὶ παραπτώμασιν*) strongly suggests that the Holiness Code (Lev. 19. 15–17) is the intertext here.[31] The same conclusion suggests itself when it comes to *Did.* 5. 2 and its list of vices, which concludes by condemning those who are merciless to the poor, exploit labourers, turn away the needy, serve as advocates for the rich, and are 'lawless judges of the poor (*πενήτων ἄνομοι κριταί*)' (cf. Lev. 19. 10–15).[32]

Although James does not raise the issue of partiality in the context of communal reproof, he too is concerned with partiality (*προσωπολημψία*) in Jas. 2. 1–13. That the Holiness Code is in view is clear from the fact that

[28] See also Matt. 12. 31–7, which makes speech (blasphemy) a criterion of judgement (12. 36–7), since speech flows from the heart. Matthew's appeal to the relation of trees to fruit (12. 34–5) can be compared to James's similar argument in 3. 9–12.

[29] Again there is a partial parallel in *Barn.* 19. 4, but *Barnabas*'s exhortation (*οὐ λήμψῃ πρόσωπον ἐλέγξαι τινὰ ἐπὶ παραπτώματι*) appears in a rather rambling and disorganized list of prohibitions.

[30] Cf. Lev. 19. 15: *οὐ λήμψῃ πρόσωπον πτωχοῦ οὐδὲ θαυμάσεις πρόσωπον δυνάστου*; 1 Esd. 4. 39: *καὶ οὐκ ἔστιν παρ αὐτῇ λαμβάνειν πρόσωπα*; Mal. 1. 8: *εἰ προσδέξεται αὐτό εἰ λήμψεται πρόσωπόν σου*; 2. 9: *ἐλαμβάνετε πρόσωπα ἐν νόμῳ*; Job 42. 8: *εἰ μὴ πρόσωπον αὐτοῦ λήμψομαι*; Ps. 81. 2: *ἕως πότε κρίνετε ἀδικίαν καὶ πρόσωπα ἁμαρτωλῶν λαμβάνετε διάψαλμα*; Sir 4. 22: *μὴ λάβῃς πρόσωπον κατὰ τῆς ψυχῆς σου*; 4. 27: *καὶ μὴ λάβῃς πρόσωπον δυνάστου*; 35. 13: *οὐ λήμψεται πρόσωπον ἐπὶ πτωχοῦ καὶ δέησιν*; 42. 1: *καὶ μὴ λάβῃς πρόσωπον τοῦ ἁμαρτάνειν*.

[31] Lev. 19. 17: *οὐ μισήσεις τὸν ἀδελφόν σου τῇ διανοίᾳ σου ἐλεγμῷ ἐλέγξεις τὸν πλησίον σου καὶ οὐ λήμψῃ δι αὐτὸν ἁμαρτίαν*. Cf. also *Did.* 2. 7 (*οὐ μισήσεις πάντα ἄνθρωπον, ἀλλὰ οὓς μὲν ἐλέγξεις*).

[32] Cf. Lev. 19. 10–15: *καὶ τὸν ἀμπελῶνά σου οὐκ ἐπανατρυγήσεις οὐδὲ τοὺς ῥῶγας τοῦ ἀμπελῶνός σου συλλέξεις : τῷ πτωχῷ καὶ τῷ προσηλύτῳ καταλείψεις αὐτά . . .*[13] *οὐκ ἀδικήσεις τὸν πλησίον καὶ οὐχ ἁρπάσεις, καὶ οὐ μὴ κοιμηθήσεται ὁ μισθὸς τοῦ μισθωτοῦ παρὰ σοὶ ἕως πρωί . . .*[15] *οὐ ποιήσετε ἄδικον ἐν κρίσει : οὐ λήμψῃ πρόσωπον πτωχοῦ οὐδὲ θαυμάσεις πρόσωπον δυνάστου, ἐν δικαιοσύνῃ κρινεῖς τὸν πλησίον σου*.

James cites Lev. 19. 18 (Jas. 2. 8) and alludes to Lev. 19. 15 (Jas. 2. 1, 9),[33] and that he invokes the *topos* of the powerful oppressing the poor with the co-operation of the courts (Jas. 2. 6; cf. Lev. 19. 15). According to James, those who defer to the rich and ignore the poor are κριταὶ διαλογισμῶν πονηρῶν (Jas. 2. 4), apparently not too different from the *Didache*'s πενήτων ἄνομοι κριταί.

The use of δίψυχος and διψυχεῖν by James and the TW is also of great interest, especially if the thesis of Stanley Porter can be sustained, that James coined the term.[34] James uses the adjective twice, and, as Porter shows, there are differences in connotation. At Jas. 1. 8 (ἀνὴρ δίψυχος, ἀκατάστατος ἐν πάσαις ταῖς ὁδοῖς αὐτοῦ) James's focus is on the practical and subjective issue of those who 'may be divided in their belief about God's faithfulness to answer a prayer for wisdom'.[35] At Jas. 4. 8. (καθαρίσατε χεῖρας, ἁμαρτωλοί, καὶ ἁγνίσατε καρδίας, δίψυχοι) the issue has to do with objective divisions among the addressees, where James is concerned with those who display loyalties to values or institutions outside the group—which he lumps together under the rubrics of the world and the devil (4. 4, 7).

The appearance of διψυχεῖν in *Barn.* 19. 5 (οὐ μὴ διψυχήσῃς πότερον ἔσται ἢ οὔ) and *Did.* 4. 4 (οὐ διψυχήσεις πότερον ἔσται ἢ οὔ) in virtually the same phrase indicates that this admonition belongs to the TW tradition used by both the *Didache* and *Barnabas.* Although Porter treats both as second-century CE documents, and therefore (presumably) later than James, this is unlikely.[36] The final redactions of *Barnabas* and the *Didache* may indeed belong to the second century, but the TW document is now generally regarded as earlier. The agreement between *Barnabas* and the *Didache* in their use of διψυχεῖν suggests that this detail in fact belongs to the earliest strata of the TW tradition. Hence it is doubtful that James provides the first attestation of

[33] Cf. also Ps.-Phocylides 10–11: μὴ ῥίψῃς πενίην ἀδίκως, μὴ κρῖνε πρόσωπον· ἢν σὺ κακῶς δικάσῃς, σὲ θεὸς μετέπειτα δικάσσει ('Cast not the poor down unjustly, nor judge with partiality [Lev. 19. 15]. If you judge evilly, God will judge you thereafter').

[34] S. E. Porter, 'Is *Dipsuchos* (James 1,8; 4,8) a "Christian" Word?', *Bib* 71 (1991), 469–98, argues that James provides the earliest attestation of δίψυχος (1. 8; 4. 8) and suggests that James may have coined the term (p. 498). He does allow that James's usage might depend on *Did.* 4. 4 or *1 Clem.* 11. 2; 23. 3, but even in this case it stands that 'δίψυχος is a Christian word' (p. 497). Sophie Laws argued earlier that the term was a local Roman term on the basis of its use in James, *1 Clement, 2 Clement,* and *Hermas* (S. S. C. Marshall, 'Δίψυχος: A Local Term?', *SE* 6 (1973), 348–51; Laws, *James,* 60–1).

[35] Porter, '*Dipsuchos*', 484. Cf. *1 Clem.* 11. 2, which uses the adjectives in relation to Lot's wife, who is said to have changed her mind and was punished for this vacillation: 'she became a pillar of salt until this day, to make known to all that those who are double-minded (δίψυχοι) and have doubts (διστάζοντες) concerning the power of God incur judgment and become a warning to all generations'. Similarly, *2 Clem.* 19. 2, where διψυχία is paired with ἀπιστία.

[36] Porter, '*Dipsuchos*', 487.

the term.[37] The conjunction of James and the TW in using the same (probably newly coined) term nevertheless points to a common linguistic environment.

The precise connotation of *διψυχεῖν* in *Barn.* 19. 5 is difficult to determine, because it appears in a string of rather miscellaneous injunctions, sandwiched between admonitions not to bear malice towards one's fellows and not to use the divine name in vain. The use of *ἔσται* suggests that the ambivalence in question has something to do with expectations about the future, but this interpretation does not cohere with the immediate context, which concerns behaviour in the present, rather than attitudes or beliefs about the future. In the *Didache*'s TW, however, what was a rather miscellaneous set of admonitions in *Barnabas* has been reframed as a set of sayings which have to do with the inner cohesion of the group: the recognition of the authority of teachers, the importance of group solidarity, the dangers of schism, and high value placed on reconciliation. Reproof of members is an important value, but reproof must not be equivocal or display partiality:

> [3] *οὐ ποιήσεις σχίσμα, εἰρηνεύσεις δὲ μαχομένους· κρινεῖς δικαίως, οὐ λήψῃ πρόσωπον ἐλέγξαι ἐπὶ παραπτώμασιν.* [4] *οὐ διψυχήσεις, πότερον ἔσται ἢ οὔ.* (*Did.* 4. 3–4)

As argued above, the idiom *πρόσωπον λαμβάνειν* recalls the prohibition of judicial partiality in the Holiness Code (Lev. 19. 15). Given this context, *διψυχεῖν* appears to connote equivocation and partiality when it comes to reproof, probably based on the fear of reproving one of higher social status.

Porter thinks that the vagaries in the usage of *διψυχεῖν* in *Barnabas* and the *Didache* are best explained if the TW is conflating the various senses attested in James.[38] But the TW's usage has nothing to do with ambivalence in prayer (cf. Jas. 1. 8). Nor does it converge with the usage in Jas. 4. 8, which concerns allegiances divided between the Jesus group and 'the world'. Rather than attesting semantic borrowing from James, the TW tradition as it is attested in *Barnabas* and revised in the *Didache* and Jas. 1. 8 and 4. 8 instances a certain fluidity and experimentation with a term newly coined in one sector of the Jesus movement. Later documents such as the *Shepherd* and the *Apostolic Constitutions* use the term with much greater consistency.[39]

The TW is, of course, concerned not only with ambivalent behaviour or attitudes (*διψυχία*), but *διγλωσσία*, *διγνώμων* (2. 5; above p. 198) and

[37] Whether the *δίψυχος* and its cognates are 'Christian' terms, as Porter avers, begs the question as to whether it is meaningful to distinguish 'Christian' from 'Jewish' in a (say) early to mid-first-century CE tradition or document.

[38] Porter, '*Dipsuchos*', 487.

[39] *1 Clem.* 23. 3; *2 Clem.* 11. 2, 5; and the *Apostolic Constitutions*, 7. 11, apply the term *διψυχία* to doubts as to the veracity of oracles. Hermas's use in *Vis.* 2. 2. 4, 7; 3. 2. 2; 3. 3. 4; 3. 7. 1; 3. 10. 9; 3. 11.2; 4. 1. 4; 4. 2. 4, 6; *Man.* 5. 2. 1; 9. 1, 5, 6, 8, 9, 10, 11, 12; 10. 1. 1; 10. 2. 2, 4; 11. 1–2; 12. 4. 2; *Sim.* 6. 1. 2; 8. 7. 1–2; 8. 8. 3, 5; 8. 9. 4; 8. 10. 2; 8. 11. 3; 9. 18. 3; 9. 21. 1–2 is close to that of Jas. 1. 8

διπλοκαρδία (5. 1). This array of terms is probably rooted in the conceptual world of such literature as the *Testament of Asher* 1–2. *T. Ash.* 2. 2–3 uses διπρόσωπον rather than δίψυχος, and lays out the problem of ambivalence in some detail.

Two ways has God appointed for humanity and two dispositions (διαβούλια), two types of action (πράξεις), two courses (τόπους) and two ends (τέλη).... So, if the soul is inclined towards the good (θέλῃ ἐν καλῷ), each of its acts will be just, and even if it sins, it will immediately repent.... But if its disposition is towards what is evil, each of its acts will be evil. (*T. Ash.* 1. 3, 6, 8)[40]

T. Ash. 2 offers several examples of morally ambivalent situations—of someone who loves an evil-doer, of a thief who gives alms to the poor, and of an adulterer who observes *kashrut.* In each instance, the judgement is the same: τὸ ὅλον πονηρόν ἔστι (2. 2). The assumption of the *Testament of Asher* is that while such actions seemingly have two aspects (διπρόσωπον, 2. 2, 3, 7, 8), one evil and the other good, the fundamental unity of intention (διβούλιον, 1. 5) and the unity of God who gives the commandments (τόν ἐντολέα τοῦ νόμου κύριον, 2. 6) requires that seemingly ambiguous actions be judged as wholly evil.[41]

The TW's simple injunction οὐ διψυχεῖς becomes part of a sustained argument of James. James contrasts God's simplicity (ἁπλῶς) as a giver (1. 5) with the ambivalence of the 'unstable' person who 'is divided' (ὁ ... διακρινόμενος) in prayer, and compares the 'divided person' with the waves of the sea (1. 6). It is perhaps significant that James uses the same verb, διακρίνειν, when condemning the 'evil judges' of 2. 4 who are 'divided' (διεκρίθητε) in so far as they defer to the wealthy and dishonour the poor (2. 1–6). The partiality condemned by James in 2. 1–13 is for him related to the inability to act 'simply'—that is, in a manner that grasps the basic unity of moral law and the unity of the Lawgiver.[42] Indeed, this is exactly what James argues in 2. 8–11 (see below, p. 210), and what *T. Asher* had argued in regard to ambivalent behaviour.

It is worth observing again that what appears as a simple imperative in the TW is made the subject of sustained argument by either James or Matthew, or both. This is as true in the case of διψυχεῖν as it is in the case of the topics of

[40] Cf. the similar view expressed in *T. Jud.* 20. 1: ἐπίγνωτε οὖν, τέκνα μου, ὅτι δύο πνεύματα σχολάζουσι τῷ ἀνθρώπῳ, τὸ τῆς ἀληθείας καὶ τὸ τῆς πλάνης· καὶ μέσον ἐστὶ τὸ τῆς συνέσεως τοῦ νοός, οὗ ἐὰν κλῖναι.

[41] See the discussion of this point in H. C. Kee, 'The Ethical Dimensions of the Testaments of the XII as a Clue to Provenance', *NTS* 24 (1978), 259–70, on p. 266.

[42] I have argued elsewhere that James's description of God in 1. 5 as μὴ ὀνειδίζοντος already anticipates his argument against patronage in 2. 1–13. See J. S. Kloppenborg, 'Patronage Avoidance in the Epistle of James', *HTS* 55 (1999), 755–94, on pp. 768–70.

slander (above, p. 199), perjury (above, p. 201), and teaching and teachers (above, p. 202). What the TW enjoins in a single imperative is found in a more elaborated and articulated argument in James (slander, teaching, ambivalence) and Matthew (perjury, teaching).

3. LEV. 19. 18 AND THE ROLE OF THE TORAH

Both the TW and James elevate Lev. 19. 18 to a position of special prominence in their respective arguments.

a. The TW Document

The *Didache* deploys Lev. 19. 18 programmatically as the second of two principal commandments which preface the TW document: *πρῶτον ἀγαπήσεις τὸν θεὸν τὸν ποιήσαντά σε, δεύτερον τὸν πλησίον σου ὡς σεαυτόν* (1. 2). That this positioning of Lev. 19. 18 at the head of the TW section is the result of deliberate redaction is clear from a comparison of the *Didache* and *Doctrina Apostolorum* with *Barn.* 18–20.

Like the *Didache* and the *Doctrina* (and hence, presumably, *β*), *Barnabas* prefaced his TW instruction with an elaboration of Deut. 6. 5 (*ἀγαπήσεις τὸν ποιήσαντά σε, φοβηθήσῃ τόν σε πλάσαντα, δοξάσεις τόν σε λυτρωσάμενον ἐκ θανάτου*, 19. 2). To be sure, Barnabas quotes Lev. 19. 18, but it lies buried in the middle of a string of prohibitions that appear later in his list of commandments (19. 5).[43] By contrast, both the *Didache* and the *Doctrina* have moved Lev. 19. 18 to the head of the document, where it sits beside a version of Deut. 6. 5. Since a comparison of the *Doctrina* with *Did.* 1. 1–6. 1 indicates that the two represent parallel, rather than sequential, developments of the TW tradition, we must conclude that the promotion of Lev. 19. 18 in the structural hierarchy of the TW tradition is not the work of the framer of the *Didache*'s TW, but was already a characteristic of *β*, the *Vorlage* on which *Did.* 1. 1–6. 1 and the *Doctrina* are dependent.

The promotion of Lev. 19. 18 in the *β*-recension of the TW is part of a larger editorial strategy which included the assimilation of the prohibitions in *Did.* 2 / *Doctrina* 2 to those of the Decalogue. While *Barnabas*'s list of more

[43] Barn. 19. 5: *οὐ μὴ διψυχήσῃς πότερον ἔσται ἢ οὔ. οὐ μὴ λάβῃς ἐπὶ ματαίῳ τὸ ὄνομα κυρίου. ἀγαπήσεις τὸν πλησίον σου ὑπὲρ τὴν ψυχήν σου. οὐ φονεύσεις τέκνον ἐν φθορᾷ, οὐδὲ πάλιν γεννηθὲν ἀνελεῖς. οὐ μὴ ἄρῃς τὴν χεῖρά σου ἀπὸ τοῦ υἱοῦ σου ἢ ἀπὸ τῆς θυγατρός σου, ἀλλὰ ἀπὸ νεότητος διδάξεις φόβον κυρίου.*

than forty imperatives in *Barn.* 19 contains only adultery and covetousness from among the Ten Words,[44] the *Didache* and the *Doctrina* include the entire second register of the Decalogue: murder, adultery, theft (omitted by the *Doctrina*), covetousness, and false witness. Moreover, as Clayton Jefford has noted, the *sequence* of the *Didache*'s prohibitions also corresponds to that of the MT and Codex Alexandrinus of Exod. 20. 13–16 (and, we should add, Codex Alexandrinus of Deut. 5. 17–21).[45]

There are three other aspects of 'Torahizing' in the β-recension. The first is the TW's repetitive use of asyndetic future indicatives (*οὐ φονεύσεις. οὐ μοιχεύσεις, οὐ παιδοφθορήσεις, οὐ πορνεύσεις, οὐ κλέψεις*, etc.), matching the characteristic syntactical form of Deut. 5. 17–21 / Exod. 20. 13–16 in LXX^{A}: *οὐ φονεύσεις, οὐ μοιχεύσεις, οὐ κλέψεις*, etc. This contrasts with *Barnabas*'s more varied usage, which combines *οὐ* with the future indicative and *οὐ μή* with the subjunctive. Second, just as the β-recension assimilated 2. 2–7 to the Decalogue, so too has the Way of Death in 5. 1–2 been modified to include items of the Decalogue missing in *Barn.* 20. 1: *κλοπαί* / *furta*, and *ψευδομαρτυρίαι* / *falsa testimonia*. And the list of vices has been restructured so that elements corresponding to those of the Decalogue appear in six of the first ten positions on the list: *φόνοι, μοιχεῖαι, ἐπιθυμίαι, πορνεῖαι, κλοπαί, εἰδωλολατρίαι, μαγεῖαι, φαρμακίαι, φαρμακίαι, ἁρπαγαί*, and *ψευδομαρτυρίαι*.[46] By contrast, the overlap with the Decalogue is less noticeable in *Barnabas*, which has only *εἰδωλολατρεία* (in the first position), *μοιχεία* (in sixth position), and *φόνος* (in seventh position). Finally, as pointed out above, the interpolated *τέκνον* section in 3. 1–6 is constructed around five prohibitions of the Decalogue, and presents an argument according to which lesser vices are related by their inherent tendencies to the vices of the Decalogue. In these significant ways, then, the TW has been edited and restructured so as to make it clear that the ethical instruction of the TW flows from, and is grounded in, the Torah.

Given the Torahizing transformation of the TW document, the relocation of Lev. 19. 18 to the head of the list of imperatives is not at all surprising. For,

[44] *Barn.* 19. 4: *οὐ μοιχεύσεις*; 19. 6: *οὐ μὴ γένῃ ἐπιθυμῶν τὰ τοῦ πλησίον σου*.

[45] Jefford, *Sayings of Jesus*, 55–6. The order of the first two prohibitions varies. The MT of both Exod. 20. 13–14 and Deut. 5. 17–18 placed murder before adultery, which agrees also with Codex A for Exod. 20. 13–14 and Deut. 5. 17–18, and with Matthew's sequence of verbs: *οὐ μοιχεύσεις, οὐ κλέψεις, οὐ ψευδομαρτυρήσεις* (19. 18). The sequential agreement between *Did.* 2. 2–3 and the Decalogue is not perfect, however: the *Didache* uses the order *ψευδομαρτυρήσεις-ἐπιθυμήσεις*, while the MT / LXX^{A} have the reverse. Moreover, the *Doctrina* agrees with LXX^{B} against the *Didache* by placing *non moechaberis* (= *οὐ μοιχεύσεις*) before *non homocidium facies* (= *οὐ φονεύσεις*).

[46] The sequence of vices in the *Doctrina* displays greater variance from that of the *Didache* and the Decalogue: *moechationes* (2 in the *Didache*), *homicidia* (1), *falsa testimonia* (10), *fornicationes* (4), *desideria mala* (3), *magicae* (7), *medicamenta iniqua* (8), *furta* (9), *vanae superstitiones* (6).

as is well known, in Second Temple Judaism the command to love one's fellow, coupled with the injunction to love God, came to be treated as a summary of the two registers of the Decalogue. This pairing of the injunctions to love God and to love one's fellows can be seen in a number of documents of the Second Temple period.[47]

The promotion of Lev. 19. 18 to the head of the β-recension, by the *Didache* and the *Doctrina*, is appropriate in another respect. While the TW opens with ἀγαπήσεις τὸν θεὸν τὸν ποιήσαντά σε, and while the τέκνον section and the Way of Death include warnings against εἰδωλολατρία (3. 4; 5. 1) and βλασφημία (3. 6), corresponding to the commands in the first register of the Decalogue against idolatry and misuse of the divine name, it is clear that the centre of gravity of β's interest is the second register, which is richly elaborated. Given this manifest interest in the 'philanthropic' side of the Decalogue, the use of Lev. 19. 18 as a κεφαλαῖον for the list is perfectly apt.

[47] *T. Iss.* 5. 2: ἀλλ' ἀγαπᾶτε κύριον καὶ τὸν πλησίον. πένητα καὶ ἀσθενῆ ἐλεᾶτε ('But love the Lord and your neighbour, show mercy to the poor and the weak'); *T. Iss.* 7. 1: τὸν κύριον ἠγάπησα ἐν πάσῃ τῇ ἰσχύι μου· ὁμοίως καὶ πάντα ἄνθρωπον ἠγάπησα. ὡς τέκνα μου ('I loved the Lord with all my strength; likewise I loved every human as my own child'); *T. Dan.* 5. 3: ἀγάπατε τὸν κύριον ἐν πάσῃ τῇ ζωῇ ὑμῶν καὶ ἀλλήλους ἐν ἀληθινῇ καρδίᾳ ('Love the Lord with all your life, and (love) each other with a true heart'); *T. Benj.* 3. 3: φοβεῖσθε κύριον, καὶ ἀγάπατε τὸν πλήσιον ('Fear the Lord, and love your neighbour'); Josephus, *Bell.* 2. 139 (of the Essenes): πρὶν δὲ τῆς κοινῆς ἅψασθαι τροφῆς ὅρκους αὐτοῖς ὄμνυσι φρικώδεις, πρῶτον μὲν εὐσεβήσειν τὸ θεῖον. ἔπειτα τὰ πρὸς ἀνθρώπους δίκαια φυλάξειν ('Before touching the common food, they [candidates for the Essenes] must swear tremendous oaths, first to show piety towards the divinity, and then to observe just actions in respect to people') (cf. *Ant.* 15. 375); Philo, *Prob.* 83 (of the Essenes): παιδεύονται δὲ εὐσέβειαν ... ὅροις καὶ κανόσι τριττοῖς χρώμενοι, τῷ τε φιλοθεῷ καὶ φιλανθρώπῳ ('They are trained in piety... taking for their standard these three: love of God, love of virtue, and love of humankind'); Philo, *Spec.* 2. 63: ἔστι δ' ὡς ἔπος εἰπεῖν τῶν κατὰ μέρος ἀμυθήτων λόγων καὶ δογμάτων δύο τὰ ἀνωτάτω κεφάλαια, τό τε πρὸς θεὸν δι' εὐσεβείας καὶ ὁσιότητος καὶ τὸ πρὸς ἀνθρώπους διὰ φιλανθρωπίας καὶ δικαιοσύνης, ὧν ἑκάτερον εἰς πολυσχιδεῖς ἰδέας καὶ πάσας ἐπαινετὰς τέμνεται ('Among the large number of particular truths and principles studied there [in synagogues], two main heads stand out high above the others: the (duty) toward God, (expressed) through piety and holiness, and the (duty) towards humans (expressed) through humanity and justice. Each of these is further subdivided into numerous ideas, all equally praiseworthy'; Mark 12. 29–31: πρώτη ἐστίν, ἄκουε, Ἰσραήλ, κύριος ὁ θεὸς ἡμῶν κύριος εἷς ἐστιν.[30] καὶ ἀγαπήσεις κύριον τὸν θεόν σου ἐξ ὅλης τῆς καρδίας σου καὶ ἐξ ὅλης τῆς ψυχῆς σου καὶ ἐξ ὅλης τῆς διανοίας σου καὶ ἐξ ὅλης τῆς ἰσχύος σου.[31] δευτέρα αὕτη, ἀγαπήσεις τὸν πλησίον σου ὡς σεαυτόν. μείζων τούτων ἄλλη ἐντολὴ οὐκ ἔστιν ('The first (command) is: "Hear Israel, the Lord your God is one, and you shall love the Lord your God with your entire heart and your entire life and your entire mind and your entire strength." This is the second (command): "You shall love your neighbour as yourself." No commandment is greater than these'). See K. Berger, *Die Gesetzesauslegung Jesu: ihr historischer Hintergrund im Judentum und im Alten Testament*, WMANT 40 (Neukirchen-Vluyn: Neukirchener Verlag, 1972), 99–136. According to P. W. Skehan and A. A. Di Lella, *The Wisdom of Ben Sira: A New Translation with Notes*, AB 39 (Garden City, NY: Doubleday, 1987), 383, by the time of Sirach the Decalogue itself was viewed as divisible into two parts, the first pertaining to God and the second to one's 'neighbors' (see Sir. 17. 14).

b. James

James likewise promotes Lev. 19. 18 to the role of a κεφαλαῖον for the second register of the Decalogue. The text is given special prominence in the rhetorical organization of the argument against προσωπολημψία (2. 1–13):

[8] *εἰ μέντοι νόμον τελεῖτε βασιλικὸν κατὰ τὴν γραφήν, ἀγαπήσεις τὸν πλησίον σου ὡς σεαυτόν, καλῶς ποιεῖτε·* [9] *εἰ δὲ προσωπολημπτεῖτε, ἁμαρτίαν ἐργάζεσθε, ἐλεγχόμενοι ὑπὸ τοῦ νόμου ὡς παραβάται.*

If indeed you fulfil the royal law, in accordance with the Scripture, 'You shall love your neighbour as yourself', you do well. But if you act with partiality, you are committing sin, being convicted under the Law as a wrongdoer.

Two interpretive problems beset this text. First, scholars are divided over whether for James Lev. 19. 18 is the 'royal law' itself, such that fulfilling the love command amounts to fulfilling the entire Law[48] or whether it is a summary or epitome of the Law.[49] The latter view seems preferable, given the structure of James's argument in 2. 8–11. The *νόμος βασιλικός* of verse 8 is parallel to *ὅλος ὁ νόμος* in 2. 10, and both phrases are then elaborated with reference to individual commandments: Lev. 19. 18 in the case the 'royal Law', and the prohibitions of adultery and murder in the case of the 'entire Law'. Moreover, the structure of James's argument in 2. 8–11 is parallel to that in 2. 18–19. At 2. 8 James addresses the imaginary interlocutors who claim to be fulfilling the Law, summarized by Lev. 19. 18, congratulating them with *καλῶς*

[48] Laws, *James*, 107–10 argues that Jas. 2. 1–9 does not treat Lev. 19. 18 as one commandment among others; rather, the warning against partiality in Lev. 19. 15 (which is not even directly cited) is comprehended within Lev. 19. 18, which James dignifies with the honorific 'royal'. R. P. Martin, *James*, Word Biblical Commentary, 48 (Waco, Tex.: Word Books, 1988), 67–8, argues that Lev. 19. 18 is treated as a 'new law', the observance of which fulfils the entire will of God. Mussner, *Jakobusbrief*, 107: 'Den Wesensinhalt des "vollkommenen Gesetzes der Freiheit" sieht Jak sicher ausgesprochen in dem "königlichen Gesetz gemäß der Schrift: Du sollst deinen Nächsten lieben wie dich selbst," das auch Jesus dem Gebot der Gottesliebe gleichgeordnet hat.' Later, however, he says of 2. 8–10, 'im folgenden geht es nicht um das "Hauptgebot" und das Verhältnis der anderen Gebote zu ihm, sondern um die These, daß die Verletzung eines einzigen Gebotes eine unteilbare Totalverletzung des ganzen Gesetzes ist.... Darum scheint mit dem Ausdruck "königlichen Gesetz" nur gesagt zu sein, daß das Gebot von Lv 19,18 *königlichen Rang* under den anderen Geboten hat' (124, emphasis original).

[49] J. H. Ropes, *A Critical and Exegetical Commentary on the Epistle of St. James*, ICC (New York: Charles Scribner's Sons, 1916), 198; Dibelius, *James*, 142; Davids, *Epistle of James*, 114; H. Frankemölle, *Der Brief des Jakobus*, ÖTKNT 17 (Gütersloh: Gütersloher Verlag-Haus; Würzburg: Echter Verlag, 1994), 402; L. T. Johnson, *The Letter of James: A New Translation with Introduction and Commentary*, AB 37A (Garden City, NY: Doubleday, 1995), 230; C. Burchard, *Der Jakobusbrief*, HNT 15.1 (Tübingen: J. C. B. Mohr (Paul Siebeck), 2000), 103–5; M. A. Jackson-McCabe, *Logos and Law in the Letter of James: The Law of Nature, the Law of Moses, and the Law of Freedom*, NovTSup 100 (Leiden: Brill, 2001), 153; P. J. Hartin, *James*, Sacra Pagina, 14 (Collegeville, Minn.: Liturgical Press, 2003), 121.

ποιεῖτε. At 2. 19 the author addresses other imaginary interlocutors who affirm the monotheistic confession that heads the first register of the Decalogue, *εἶς ἐστιν ὁ θεός* (cf. Deut. 6. 4), again congratulating them with *καλῶς ποιεῖτε*. But in both instances, as the argument makes clear, the violation of *other commandments* subverts the claim to be Torah-observant. The structure of James's argument thus suggests that James treats Deut. 6. 4 and Lev. 19. 18 as summaries of the Torah, but rejects the notion that fulfilment of the two commandments, however important, amounts to fulfilling the whole Law.

The second question has to do with the logic of the argument in 2. 8–9. The majority view hold that the act of partiality in 2. 9 constitutes a violation of the Law because it violates the love command (Lev. 19. 18).[50] M. Jackson-McCabe has recently urged, cogently in my view, that the correspondence between 2. 8 (*εἰ μέντοι νόμον τελεῖτε βασιλ ικὸν . . .*) and 2. 10a (*ὅστις γὰρ ὅλον τὸν νόμον τηρήσῃ*), and between 2. 9 (*εἰ δὲ προσωπολημπτεῖτε, ἁμαρτίαν ἐργάζεσθε, ἐλεγχόμενοι ὑπὸ τοῦ νόμου ὡς παραβάται*) and 2. 10bc (*πταίσῃ δὲ ἐν ἑνί, γέγονεν πάντων ἔνοχος*) indicates that James is positing 'simultaneous rather than opposite conditions'.[51] That is, in spite of the summarizing functions that Deut. 6. 4–5 and Lev. 19. 18 have with respect to the rest of the Law, the violation of any of the other commandments—Lev. 19. 15 on partiality, or the prohibitions of murder or adultery—constitutes the agent as a lawbreaker and belies the claim to be Torah-observant.

In both the Two Ways and James, then, Lev. 19. 18 is treated as a *κεφαλαῖον* for the second register of the Decalogue, and the Law is also treated as an essential unity, since violation of one commandment compromises one's claim to be Torah-observant (James)[52] and lesser commandments not originally included in the Decalogue are related by their inherent *Tendenz* to those named in the Decalogue (*Didache*).

[50] Thus Mussner, *Jakobusbrief*, 124; Laws, *James*, 110; Davids, *Epistle of James*, 115; L. T. Johnson, *Letter of James*, 235–6; Burchard, *Jakobusbrief*, 105; W. H. Wachob, *The Voice of Jesus in the Social Rhetoric of James*, SNTSMS 106 (Cambridge and New York: Cambridge University Press, 2000), 95–6. Martin, *James*, 68, considers the possibility that James has Lev. 18. 15 in view, but adds: 'it may be that James also is speaking of the new law of 2. 8, since one cannot fulfill the "supreme law" and still discriminate against the poor'.

[51] Jackson-McCabe, *Logos and Law*, 170.

[52] Compare various *halakôt*: *t. Dem.* 2. 4–7: 'A proselyte who took upon himself all the obligations of the Torah and is suspected with regard to one of them—even with regard to all the Torah, behold he is deemed to be like an apostate Israelite.[5] An "*am ha-'aretz* who took upon himself all the obligations of the *haberut* except for one item—they do not accept him. A proselyte who took upon himself all the obligations of the Torah except for one item—they do not accept him. R. Yosé b. R. Judah says, "Even if it be a minor item from among the stipulations of the scribes" [2. 6–7 use the same formula for a priest and a Levite].' *b. Bek.* 30b ascribes the first opinion to R. Meir: 'R. Meir, as it has been taught: An "*am ha-'aretz* who accepted the obligations of a *haber* and who is suspected of ignoring one item is suspected of disregarding the whole Torah. But the Sages say: He is only suspected of ignoring that particular

c. Matthew

The importance of Lev. 19. 18 for Matthew is clear from his redaction of Mark 12. 29–31, where Matthew not only enumerates the commandments of Deut. 6. 4–5 and Lev. 19. 18 as *πρώτη ... δευτέρα*, but also redactionally adds *ἐν ταύταις ταῖς δυσὶν ἐντολαῖς ὅλος ὁ νόμος κρέμαται καὶ οἱ προφῆται* (22. 40). The same attention to the Decalogue and Lev. 19. 18 is seen in Matthew's redaction of Mark 10. 17–22, where Matthew not only assimilates Mark's list of commandments to the second register of the Decalogue (omitting *μὴ ἀποστερήσῃς*) and substituting *οὐ* with the future for Mark's subjunctives, but also adding *ἀγαπήσεις τὸν πλησίον σου ὡς σεαυτόν* (19. 19b).

There is no indication in Matthew that the Torah has been 'reduced' to Lev. 19. 18, any more than in James. On the contrary, Matt. 5. 17–20 makes clear that the Torah remains valid in its details,[53] and the logic of the 'antitheses' in 5. 21–48 take for granted that individual commandments remain in force.

d. Paul

The view of Lev. 19. 18 and of the Law developed in the TW, James, and Matthew is in stark contrast to that articulated by Paul in Gal. 5. 14 and Rom. 13. 8–10. Lev. 19. 18 is cited by Paul at Gal. 5. 13–15:

ὑμεῖς γὰρ ἐπ' ἐλευθερίᾳ ἐκλήθητε, ἀδελφοί· μόνον μὴ τὴν ἐλευθερίαν εἰς ἀφορμὴν τῇ σαρκί, ἀλλὰ διὰ τῆς ἀγάπης δουλεύετε ἀλλήλοις. ὁ γὰρ πᾶς νόμος ἐν ἑνὶ λόγῳ

item'; *Sifra* Parashat Qedoshim 8. 5 agrees with *t. Dem.* 2. 5, but adds, following the statement of R. Yosé b. R. Judah, ' "... shall be to you as a native among you" [Lev. 19. 34], and you shall love him as yourself, just as it is said to Israel, "You will love your neighbour as yourself" [Lev 19. 18]'; *Sifre* Num. 112 to 15. 31: 'Whoever says, I will take upon me the whole Torah except for this one word, of him it is true, For he has despised the word of the Lord.' H. van de Sandt and D. Flusser (*The Didache: Its Jewish Sources and its Place in Early Judaism and Christianity*, CRINT 3.5 (Assen: Royal Van Gorcum; Minneapolis: Fortress, 2002), 164 n. 84) cite Mekhilta d'Rabbi Sim'on b. Yochai on Exod. 20. 14: "You might have thought that a person is not guilty unless he transgresses all these commandments; therefore does the Torah say: "You shall not murder, You shall not commit adultery, You shall not steal, you shall not bear false witness, you shall not covet" (Exod. 20. 13), in order to make one liable for each commandment separately. That being so, why does Deuteronomy join all these commandments together, saying, "You shall not murder *and* you shall not commit adultery *and*... covet." It is to teach us that they are all interrelated. When a person breaks one of them, he will end up by breaking them all.'

[53] See G. Barth, 'Matthew's Understanding of the Law', in G. Bornkamm *et al.*, *Tradition and Interpretation in Matthew* (ET Philadelphia: Westminster; London: SCM Press, 1963), 58–164, esp. pp. 64–73, 92–5; W. D. Davies and D. C. Allison, *A Critical and Exegetical Commentary on Matthew*, 3 vols., ICC (Edinburgh: T. & T. Clark, 1988–97), i. 482, 492–3, 496; A. J. Saldarini, *Matthew's Christian-Jewish Community* (Chicago and London: University of Chicago Press, 1994), 124–64.

πεπλήρωται, ἐν τῷ ἀγαπήσεις τὸν πλησίον σου ὡς σεαυτόν. εἰ δὲ ἀλλήλους δάκνετε καὶ κατεσθίετε, βλέπετε μὴ ὑπ' ἀλλήλων ἀναλωθῆτε.

For you were called to freedom, brothers; only do not use your freedom as an opportunity for self-indulgence, but through love become slaves to one another. For the whole law is fulfilled in a single word, 'You shall love your neighbor as yourself'. If, however, you bite and devour one another, take care that you are not consumed by one another. (Gal. 5. 13–15)

Paul continues with a list of the 'works of the flesh and the works of the spirit' analogous to the *Tugend- und Lasterkataloge* of *Did.* 2. 2–7 and 5. 1–2:

φανερὰ δέ ἐστιν τὰ ἔργα τῆς σαρκός, ἅτινά ἐστιν πορνεία, ἀκαθαρσία, ἀσέλγεια, εἰδωλολατρία, φαρμακεία, ἔχθραι, ἔρις, ζῆλος, θυμοί, ἐριθεῖαι, διχοστασίαι, αἱρέσεις, φθόνοι, μέθαι, κῶμοι, καὶ τὰ ὅμοια τούτοις, ἃ προλέγω ὑμῖν καθὼς προεῖπον ὅτι οἱ τὰ τοιαῦτα πράσσοντες βασιλείαν θεοῦ οὐ κληρονομήσουσιν. ὁ δὲ καρπὸς τοῦ πνεύματός ἐστιν ἀγάπη, χαρά, εἰρήνη, μακροθυμία, χρηστότης, ἀγαθωσύνη, πίστις, πραΰτης, ἐγκράτεια· κατὰ τῶν τοιούτων οὐκ ἔστιν νόμος.

Now the works of the flesh are plain: fornication, impurity, licentiousness, idolatry, sorcery, enmity, strife, jealousy, anger, selfishness, dissension, party spirit, envy, drunkenness, carousing, and the like. I warn you, as I warned you before, that those who do such things shall not inherit the kingdom of God. But the fruit of the Spirit is love, joy, peace, patience, kindness, goodness, faithfulness, gentleness, self-control; against such there is no law. (Gal. 5. 19–23)

Although superficially it might seem that Paul is using Lev. 19. 18 as it is employed in Jas. 2. 8 or *Did.* 1. 2, there are profound differences. First, the list of vices Gal. 5. 19–21 shows no strong affinities with the Decalogue—only *εἰδωλολατρία* finds a counterpart in the Ten Words. More important is the difference in the argumentative context. In Gal. 5 Paul argues against the practice of circumcision on the basis of a claim that *τῇ ἐλευθερίᾳ ἡμᾶς Χριστὸς ἠλευθέρωσεν· στήκετε οὖν καὶ μὴ πάλιν ζυγῷ δουλείας ἐνέχεσθε* (5. 1). The claim is remarkable for its use of *ζυγός* and for the assertion, articulated in Gal. 5. 3, that one who is circumcized *ὀφειλέτης ἐστὶν ὅλον τὸν νόμον ποιῆσαι*. The phrase *ζυγὸς δουλείας* in Gal. 5. 1 seems to be a deliberate and ironic use of 'yoke' as a metaphor for the commandments of the Torah.[54] What *Did.* 6. 2 considers as a yoke to be embraced, Paul treats as a

[54] See Sir. 51. 26: *τὸν τράχηλον ὑμῶν ὑπόθετε ὑπὸ ζυγόν, καὶ ἐπιδεξάσθω ἡ ψυχὴ ὑμῶν παιδείαν*; Matt. 11. 29–30; Acts 15. 10: *νῦν οὖν τί πειράζετε τὸν θεὸν ἐπιθεῖναι ζυγὸν ἐπὶ τὸν τράχηλον τῶν μαθητῶν ὃν οὔτε οἱ πατέρες ἡμῶν οὔτε ἡμεῖς ἰσχύσαμεν βαστάσαι*; *Did.* 6. 2: *εἰ μὲν γὰρ δύνασαι βαστάσαι ὅλον τὸν ζυγὸν τοῦ κυρίου, τέλειος ἔσῃ*; *Barn.* 2. 6: *ταῦτα οὖν κατήργησεν, ἵνα ὁ καινὸς νόμος τοῦ κυρίου ἡμῶν Ἰησοῦ Χριστοῦ, ἄνευ ζυγοῦ ἀνάγκης ὤν, μὴ ἀνθρωποποίητον ἔχῃ τὴν προσφοράν*; *m. 'Abot* 3. 5: 'R. Nehunia B. Hakkanah said: Whoever takes upon himself the yoke of the Torah, they remove from him the yoke of government and the yoke of worldly concerns, and whoever breaks off from himself the yoke of the Torah, they place upon him the

yoke of bondage. At Gal. 5. 3 Paul shifts from irony to the recollection of a well-known *halakah*, according to which embracing the Torah entails embracing all of its individual commandments.[55] As commentators often observe, this *halakah* is also adduced in Jas. 2. 10. But Paul uses the *halakah contra sensum* by construing it in the light of the argument he had made at Gal. 3. 10. There, Jews stand under a curse if they do not 'do' (ποιῆσαι) *all* the Law (Deut. 27. 26). The implication of Gal. 5. 3, then, is that acceptance of circumcision ought to imply acceptance of the entire Torah, which in turn obligates the agent to full performance and places the agent under the curse of Deut. 27. 26. It is debated whether Paul believes the Law to be inherently unfulfillable,[56] or whether Paul's problem with the Law is that it manifestly rests not on faith but on performance (ποιῆσαι) and therefore cannot be the basis of salvation, even if one could achieve a perfect observance of the Torah.[57] The latter view seems to me to be preferable. This debate notwithstanding, it is clear that when in Gal. 5. 14 Paul declares that 'the whole law is fulfilled in a single word', citing Lev. 19. 18, this 'law' has undergone a *de facto* reduction, since circumcision, sabbath, and *kashrut* are no longer part of it.[58]

Although Paul's citation of Lev. 19. 18 in Rom. 13. 8–10 differs from that in Gal. 5. 14 in so far as it lacks the polemical context of Gal. 5 and in fact lists

yoke of government and the yoke of worldly concerns.' On 'yoke' as a metaphor for the Torah, see C. Deutsch, *Hidden Wisdom and the Easy Yoke: Wisdom, Torah and Discipleship in Matthew 11.25–30*, JSNTSup 18 (Sheffield: JSOT Press, 1987). On Gal. 5. 1 as an allusion to the yoke of the Torah, see H. D. Betz, *Galatians: A Commentary on Paul's Letter to the Churches in Galatia*, Hermeneia (Philadelphia: Fortress, 1979), 258.

[55] P. J. Tomson, *Paul and the Jewish Law: Halakah in the Letters of the Apostle to the Gentiles*, CRINT 3. 1 (Minneapolis: Fortress, 1990), 88–9, points out that Paul's use of μαρτύρομαι ('I testify') (5. 3) finds parallels in the Hebrew העיד ('testify'), which means to quote formally an oral tradition, usually a *halakah*: e.g., *m. 'Ed.* 1.3: 'But when two weavers from the dung gate which is in Jerusalem came and testified (והעידו) in the name of Shemaiah and Abtalion, "Three logs of drawn water render the miqweh unfit," the sages confirmed their statement' (see also 2. 1, 3).

[56] See, e.g., H. Räisänen, *Paul and the Law* (Philadelphia: Fortress, 1986), 94–6.

[57] E. P. Sanders, *Paul, the Law, and the Jewish People* (Philadelphia: Fortress, 1983), 27–9.

[58] So, in various ways, H. Hübner, *Law in Paul's Thought: A Contribution to the Development of Pauline Theology*, SNTW (Edinburgh: T. & T. Clark, 1984), 37: Gal. 5. 14 is described rightly as a reduction of the content of the Mosaic Law, 'but reduction means conscious abrogation of essential elements of the content of the Torah so that we can speak of the "whole" Law only in the critical and ironical way just described'; Sanders, *Paul, the Law, and the Jewish People*, 101: Paul is engaged in a *de facto* reduction of the Law, but offers no theoretical basis for this reduction. Betz, *Galatians*, 260, speaks of rabbinic attempts 'to reduce the number of demands to their common denominator, in order to make it possible to keep the whole Torah', appealing to *b. Sabb.* 31a. But this seems to be a misreading of the text, which does not dispense with the commandments other than Lev. 19. 18, but instead construes them as pointing to Lev. 19. 18 as their epitome. Betz (*Galatians*, 275) argues that Paul distinguishes between 'doing' the Law and 'fulfilling' it: the Jew 'does' the works of the Torah; the Christian 'fulfils' the Torah through the act of love, to which he or she is freed by the acts of Christ. Thus the 'whole Law' (ὁ πᾶς νόμος) is here not the Law quantitatively with its 613 commandments.

four commandments from the Decalogue, it is none the less clear that Paul does not employ Lev. 19. 18 in the way James or the *Didache* did:

μηδενὶ μηδὲν ὀφείλετε, εἰ μὴ τὸ ἀλλήλους ἀγαπᾶν· ὁ γὰρ ἀγαπῶν τὸν ἕτερον νόμον πεπλήρωκεν. [9] *τὸ γὰρ οὐ μοιχεύσεις, οὐ φονεύσεις, οὐ κλέψεις, οὐκ ἐπιθυμήσεις, καὶ εἴ τις ἑτέρα ἐντολή, ἐν τῷ λόγῳ τούτῳ ἀνακεφαλαιοῦται, [ἐν τῷ] ἀγαπήσεις τὸν πλησίον σου ὡς σεαυτόν.* [10] *ἡ ἀγάπη τῷ πλησίον κακὸν οὐκ ἐργάζεται· πλήρωμα οὖν νόμου ἡ ἀγάπη.*

Owe nothing to anyone except to love one another; for the one who loves another has fulfilled the Law. For 'you shall not commit adultery, you shall not murder, you shall not steal, you shall not covet' and if there is any other commandment, are summed up in one word, 'love your neighbour as yourself'. (Rom. 13. 8–10)

The citation of the four prohibitions from the Decalogue makes clear that Paul is here speaking of the Mosaic Torah. But since Paul almost immediately moves to dismiss *kashruth* in Rom. 14. 14, 20, it is equally clear that, just as in Gal. 5. 14, there is a reduction of the Torah rather than a summation.[59]

Where Jas. 2. 8–11 accepts the principle that one who is Torah-observant can claim to be so only if one is fully observant, on the principle of the indivisibility of the Torah and the unity of the Lawgiver, and whereas the TW holds the view that observation of *ἡ ὁδὸς τῆς ζωῆς* involves adherence to the Decalogue and to various prohibitions which are seen either to flow from those of the Decalogue (2. 2–7) or which might lead the agent to the transgressing of the Decalogue (3. 1–7), Paul argues *against* the embracing of circumcision as an element in the 'yoke' precisely because it obligates the agent to the full observance of the Torah. The Torah clearly does not provide the framework for salvation for Paul. At Gal. 6. 13 Paul accuses those who had been circumcised of being lawbreakers. The grounds for this accusation are unclear; but perhaps Paul is here employing a radicalized form of the logic of Gal. 5. 3 and Jas. 2. 10, that *any* transgression of the Torah by Jews or would-be Jews makes one guilty of breaking the whole Law.[60]

The comparison of James and the TW with Galatians shows that these documents engage a very similar issue with the same set of texts and arguments in mind, but from opposite perspectives. This *issue* has to do with the general framework for salvation. That the Torah as it is epitomized in the Decalogue and summarized by Lev. 19. 18 is conceived of as the framework for salvation is clear from the Two Ways' designation of its expanded

[59] Hübner, *Law in Paul's Thought*, 85; Sanders, *Paul, the Law, and the Jewish People*, 100–1.

[60] In this case Paul's use of the maxim would ignore the fact that the covenant provides means of expiation of sin. Sanders is right to point out that the force of halakic principles such as Gal. 5. 3 and Jas. 2. 10 is not that perfect obedience is required by the Law, but that full *acceptance* is required. See Sanders, *Paul, the Law, and the Jewish People*, 28.

Decalogue as ἡ ὁδὸς τῆς ζωῆς (1. 1; 4. 12), from the 'Torahizing' of the Two Ways in 1. 2; 2. 2–7; 3. 1–6; and 5. 1–2, and from the Two Ways' allusions to the preface to the Deuteronomic Torah in its summation of the Way of Life (4. 13–14).[61]

In like manner, James seems to be thinking of the Torah when he refers to *νόμος τέλειος ὁ τῆς ἐλευθερίας* at 1. 25 and 2. 12 and *νόμος βασιλικός* at 2. 8. This is a controversial assertion, since such commentators as Mussner, Laws, and Martin hold that for James the 'royal law' is *restricted* to Lev. 19. 18, thus implying a dramatic reduction of the Law.[62] Other commentators argue that the qualifier 'of perfect freedom' implies that the 'law' in question lacks various portions of the Torah—normally the so-called ceremonial portions,[63] or conclude from James's concentration on Lev. 19. 18 as a summary of the Law and his silence concerning the 'ritual laws' that the full Mosaic Torah is no longer in view.[64]

[61] Cf. *Did.* 4. 13–14: *οὐ μὴ ἐγκαταλίπῃς ἐντολὰς κυρίου, φυλάξεις δὲ ἃ παρέλαβες, μήτε προστιθεὶς μήτε ἀφαιρῶν . . . αὕτη ἐστὶν ἡ ὁδὸς τῆς ζωῆς* with Deut. 4. 1–2: *καὶ νῦν, Ισραηλ, ἄκουε τῶν δικαιωμάτων καὶ τῶν κριμάτων, ὅσα ἐγὼ διδάσκω ὑμᾶς σήμερον ποιεῖν, ἵνα ζῆτε καὶ πολυπλασιασθῆτε καὶ εἰσελθόντες κληρονομήσητε τὴν γῆν,* [cf. *Did.* 3. 7] *ἣν κύριος ὁ θεὸς τῶν πατέρων ὑμῶν δίδωσιν ὑμῖν.* [2] *οὐ προσθήσετε πρὸς τὸ ῥῆμα, ὃ ἐγὼ ἐντέλλομαι ὑμῖν, καὶ οὐκ ἀφελεῖτε ἀπ᾽ αὐτοῦ· φυλάσσεσθε τὰς ἐντολὰς κυρίου τοῦ θεοῦ ὑμῶν, ὅσα ἐγὼ ἐντέλλομαι ὑμῖν σήμερον.*

[62] Mussner (*Jakobusbrief*, 107) concludes 'daß es beim "vollkommenen Gesetz der Freiheit" weder nur um das alt. Gesetz (im jüdischen Verstande) noch nur um das "Evangelium" (im Sinn der Bergpredigt oder gar des Apostel Paulus) geht, sondern um den Willen Gottes, der sowohl nach atl. wie nach ntl. Ethik fordert, dem Nächsten Gutes zu tun. Das Gebot Gottes ise für Jak eines'; similarly, Martin, *James*, 51. Laws (*Epistle of James*, 14) argues that 'Law' in James is limited to Lev. 19. 18 and the Decalogue, and does not include the ceremonial law; she later contends that while James cites Lev. 19. 18 as the 'royal law', 'it is not a governing principle, but rather one commandment which has, however, a certain primacy of importance' (p. 28).

[63] E.g., Dibelius, *James*, 18, asserts that 'the expression "law of freedom" (1. 25 and 2. 12) is also a clear indication the author does not have the Mosaic Law in mind at all'; pp. 119–20: 'that Ja[me]s completely ignores the question of the Law—it is not even dealt with in 2:14ff.—, that he pays no attention to even the possibility of ritual commandments, can be explained only if this law is actually perceived as the perfect moral law; in other words—to use Stoic terms—, if it is perceived as a law of those who are truly free, or—to use the expression of our letter—as a "perfect law of freedom." ' Dibelius (p. 119) makes much of the fact that James is not concerned with 'ritualism', and concludes from this that James, along with *Did.* 1–6 and *Barn.* 18–21, exemplifies a form of Christianity which took its lead from a Hellenistic Jewish 'tendency toward simplifying and concentrating the requirements of the Law' and eventually eliminating 'the burden of ritualism'. See also M. Tsuji, *Glaube zwischen Vollkommenheit und Verweltlichung: Eine Untersuchung zur literarischen Gestalt und zur inhaltlichen Koharenz des Jakobusbriefes*, WUNT 2.93 (Tübingen: J. C. B. Mohr (Paul Siebeck), 1997), 110–15.

[64] According to R. Hoppe, *Jakobusbrief*, Stuttgarter kleiner Kommentar. Neues Testament, n.s. 15 (Stuttgart: Verlag Katholisches Bibelwerk, 1989), 47, early Christianity did not regard the obligation to fulfil the law as meritorious ('Verdienstlichkeit'), and 'der Jak kommt deshalb nicht auf dem Gedanken, dem Gesetz heilbedeutsame Kraft zuzusprechen; dies ist allein die Sache Gottes (4,11f.).... Jakobus versteht das Gesetz nicht als Ritualgesetz palästinischer Denkart, sondern als das Liebesgebot, das wir auch aus der synoptischen Tradition kennen und das als die Zusammenfassung des ganzen Gesetzes gilt... und das zusammengebunden ist mit dem Gebot

While it is precarious to draw strong inferences from silence, it seems to me a defensible view that James continues to embrace the Torah in its fullest form and regards it as the framework for salvation. First, it has already been argued above (p. 210) that the 'royal law' of 2. 8 is not simply Lev. 19. 18, but the Torah as epitomized by Lev. 19. 18. This conclusion is supported by Jackson-McCabe's observation that the argument of 2. 1–13 against partiality presupposes that the author has in view the *written text* of Lev. 19, where the prohibition of partiality (19. 15) stands beside the love command (19. 18), and the text of the LXX^{B} Decalogue where the prohibition of murder immediately follows the prohibition of adultery (cf. Jas. 2. 11).[65] Second, as Ropes pointed out, the description of the Law as 'perfect' or 'of freedom' hardly implies a reduction: Ps. 19. 7 calls the Torah 'perfect'; Philo contrasts the Torah with other law codes described as *ὡς οὐκ ἐλευθέροις ἀλλὰ δούλοις* (*Moses* 2. 9); and *m. 'Abot* 6. 2[66] declares that the truly free person is one who devotes himself to the study of Torah.[67] James's characterization of the law as 'the law of perfect freedom' may well be an answer to Paul's reference to the 'yoke of slavery'. It can be added that Philo contrasts the 'slaves' who lived under the domination of the passions with 'the free' who lived by the Law.[68]

der Gottesliebe (vgl. Jak 2, 5–7).' L. T. Johnson, *Letter of James*, 30, notes the influence of Lev. 19 on James, but concludes that 'whatever James means by *nomos*, it cannot be connected with any recognizable program for Jewish ethnic identity, still less any "Judaising" tendency in early Christianity'. Commenting on the lack of mention of circumcision, purity, food, marriage, sabbath, and festival-day commands, Burchard (*Jakobusbrief*, 89) suggests that 'vieles davon seinen Adressaten beschwerlich gewesen sein muß; also galt es nicht, weil er davon schweigt', admitting that this conclusion is not entirely secure.

65 Jackson-McCabe, *Logos and Law*, 176.

66 *m. 'Abot* 6. 2: 'R. Joshua B. Levi said: Every day a *Bath Qol* goes forth from Mount Horeb, and makes proclamation and says: "Woe unto men on account of [their] contempt towards the Torah", for whoever occupies himself not with the Torah is called: "[The] rebuked [one]", as it is said, "As a ring of gold in a swine's snout, so is a fair woman that turns away from discretion" [Prov. 11. 22], and it says, "and the tables were the work of God, and the writing was the writing of God, graven (...) upon the tables' [Exod. 32. 16]. Do not read *harut* (חָרוּת) [graven] but *herut* (חֵרוּת) [freedom]. For there is no free man for you but he that occupies himself with the study of Torah.'

67 Ropes, *James*, 178: 'These references show that there is no ground for the common affirmation that this phrase ["law of freedom"] implies a sublimated, spiritualized view of the Jewish law, which, it is said, would have been impossible for a faithful Jew.... It is also evident that the words *τέλειον* and *τῆς ἐλευθερίας* are not introduced in order thereby to mark the law which James has in mind as distinguished from, and superior to, the Jewish law.' Ropes nevertheless argues that James conceives of the Torah as an old law to be fulfilled along with 'Christianity as a new law'. But not only is there no basis for a distinction in James between an 'old' and a 'new' law, but there is no basis for a distinction between 'Judaism' and 'Christianity'.

68 *Prob.* 45–6: *τῶν ἀνθρώπων, παρ' οἷς μὲν ὀργὴ ἢ ἐπιθυμία ἤ τι ἄλλο πάθος ἢ καὶ ἐπίβουλος κακία δυναστεύει, πάντως εἰσὶ δοῦλοι, ὅσοι δὲ μετὰ νόμου ζῶσιν, ἐλεύθεροι* ('people, among whom anger or lust or some other passion or treacherous evil hold power, are in all respects slaves, but as many as live by the Law are free').

Philo, of course, rejects neither circumcision nor *kashrut* nor purity laws, even if his principal focus was the Law as a means of moral transformation. Finally, that the Torah is in view is suggested by the fact that in his exhortation on slander in 4. 11–12 James alludes to Lev. 19. 15–16, arguing that slander strikes at both the Law and the Lawgiver. In brief, all of James's references to νόμος are consistent with the supposition that he has the Torah in view, and at 2. 8–11 and 4. 11–12 he cites specific commandments of the Decalogue and the Holiness Code as part of the Law.[69]

The *halakic principle* that in James has been employed to guard against a reductive attitude toward the Torah is also used by Paul to dissuade full acceptance of the Torah and its commandments. Both James and the Two Ways document understand Lev. 19. 18 as a summary of the Torah, but 'summary' that does not imply a reduction; Paul, by contrast, cites Lev. 19. 18 as 'summing up' the Law, but his argument indicates that he has a dramatic reduction in view. Although Matthew does not employ the same halakic principle as Jas. 2. 10, the logic of Matt. 5. 19 (and 23. 23) leads to the same conclusion: the Law is a unity such that neither the 'light' nor the 'heavy' commandments can be ignored.[70]

[69] R. J. Bauckham, *James: Wisdom of James, Disciple of Jesus the Sage* (London and New York: Routledge, 1999), 142–7 argues that in Jas. 2. 8–12 'James can hardly be speaking of anything other than the whole law of Moses' (p. 142). This Law is 'understood as the law of the rule of God over his Messianically renewed people', and is transformed by 'internalization'—God's inward renewal—, 'concentration'—the content of the Law is understood through the lens of Lev. 19. 18—, and 'intensification'—the Law is interpreted via Jesus' teaching on specific commandments (e.g., Jas. 5. 12) (p. 147). R. W. Wall (*The Community of the Wise* (Valley Forge, Pa.: Trinity Press International, 1997), 86–8) likewise takes 'law' in James to refer to the whole of the biblical Torah. 'The status of law in Jacobean Christianity is different [from that in Pauline Christianity], since divine approval (2. 8) and judgment (2. 12–13) are conditioned upon observance of the law' (p. 87). Nevertheless, Wall avers that, like 'Jesus and other Jewish contemporaries who reduced the extensive rules of right conduct and ritual purity to a few principles, James defines the Torah's moral code in terms of the Decalogue and the "royal law" of neighborly love (2. 8)'. 'Clearly James does not take "whole law" literally, as a reference to the 600+ laws that make up the Torah's legal code' (p. 315). Hartin (*James*, 111–15) holds that the 'perfect law of liberty' in James is the 'biblical Torah'. Hartin notes that James pays no attention to the 'ceremonial law', but refrains from concluding that this implies that James does not treat these provisions as part of the Law. Davids (*Epistle of James*, 48–50) observes that while James is interested primarily in ethical commandments, other aspects of the Torah (circumcision, etc.) may or may not have been practised. Nevertheless, Davids insists on introducing a notion of the 'new law', constituted by Jesus' words (p. 50).

[70] Cf. *m. 'Abot* 2. 2: 'And be careful with a light precept as with a heavy one, for you do not know the grant of reward [for the fulfilment] of precepts' [cf. *b. Ned.* 39b]; 4. 2: 'Ben "Azzai said: Run to [perform] a light precept, as [you would] in [the case of] a heavy one, and flee from transgression; for [one] precept draws [in its train another] precept, and [one] transgression draws [in its train another] transgression.'

e. Barnabas

The apogee of the Pauline trajectory can be seen in *Barnabas*, which begins by arguing that the covenant cannot belong to both Jews and Christians, pointing to Moses' breaking of the tablets of the Law in reaction to idolatry (4. 6–7). In *Barn.* 9 the author declares that circumcision, in which the Jews trusted, 'has been abolished' and was in fact at the instigation of an evil angel (9. 4). Although the use of καταργεῖν might suggest that Barnabas is implying that circumcision was once valid, he immediately points out that it is irrelevant, since Syrians, Arabs, and pagan priests are also circumcised (9. 7). Instead, the true significance of circumcision (ch. 9) and *kashruth* (ch. 10) is moralizing.[71]

It is, then, not surprising that when Barnabas reproduces the Two Ways teaching in chapters 19–21, Lev. 19. 18, though present in a slightly modified form (19. 5), is in no way raised to the status of a κεφαλαῖον of the Decalogue, as it is in the *Didache*'s TW document. In fact, the Decalogue is hardly recognizable in Barnabas's string of imperatives in chapter 19.

CONCLUSION

The argument of this paper has been that the Two Ways document of the *Didache* displays significant convergences with other documents representative of the Torah-observant Jesus movement: namely, James and Matthew. Comparison of the Two Ways section of *Barnabas* with that in the *Didache* allows us to track some of the redactional transformations that contributed to the final form of the TW, just as comparison of Matthew with Mark allows us to notice Matthew's distinctive contributions.

In all three documents, the TW, James, and Matthew, the Decalogue is given special prominence, and Lev. 19. 18 is featured as a κεφαλαῖον of the second register of the Decalogue. Other commandments from the Holiness Code figure as important intertexts for both the TW and James. Further, we find various convergences in discussions of teaching and the role of teachers (TW, James, Matthew), oath-taking (James, Matthew), communal confes-

[71] Cf. *Barnabas*'s typological interpretation of the scapegoat (ch. 7) and red heifer (ch. 8). See Räisänen, *Paul and the Law*, 220: 'Barn thus consistently reduces the God-given law to a moral law. The moral law remains in force, as is shown by the detailed description of the "way of light" in ch. 19.... The Jewish Law is divided into two parts; of these one is a Jewish misunderstanding, the other is divine and valid.'

sion (TW, James), slander (TW, James), *dipsychia* (TW, James), and partiality (TW, James), and in each of these documents there is a pronounced tendency to 'Torahize' lesser commandments such as the prohibitions of perjury or slander by associating them directly with the Decalogue or the Holiness Code.

In several instances it was possible to observe that simple imperatives found in the TW, on perjury, slander, teaching, partiality, and ambivalence were subject to detailed elaboration and argument in either James or Matthew (or both):

2. 3 *οὐκ ἐπιορκήσεις*	Matt. 5. 33–7; Jas. 5. 12
2. 3 *οὐ κακολογήσεις*	Jas. 4. 11–12
4. 1 *τοῦ λαλοῦντος σοι τὸν λόγον . . . μνησθήσῃ*	Matt. 18. 1–35; Jas. 3. 1–12
4. 3 *οὐ λήψῃ πρόσωπον*	Jas. 2. 1–13
4. 4 *οὐ διψύχεις*	Jas. 1. 5–8; 4. 1–8

This could imply either that the TW tradition as it is embodied in the *Didache* served as a basis for elaboration, much as gnomic sentences and chriae serve as the starting-point for rhetorical elaboration in Greek education,[72] or the TW might represent a condensation of the moralizing traditions found in James and Matthew. The former seems more likely, given the fact that the TW does not betray knowledge of any of the specific developments of the latter two (e.g., the prohibition of oath-taking). In either case, however, the convergences of these three documents in *topoi* and in argumentative assumptions suggest that the three come from a common intellectual milieu.

It is of course true that the TW underwent redaction through the addition of *Did.* 6. 2–3. It is disputed what this addition signifies. Niederwimmer, following Rordorf and Tuilier, argues that *ὅλος ὁ ζυγὸς τοῦ κυρίου* now relates to the law of Christ as laid out in the sayings of Jesus interpolated by the redactor into the TW.[73] If this is so, it would imply that the rigorism of the earlier TW has been relaxed. More likely, in my view, is the contention of Draper and others that 6. 2–3 calls on Gentiles to observe the entire Torah; that is, it imagines two levels of observance, an absolute minimum that includes the avoidance of idol-meat and an ideal level that embraces the Torah.[74] In this case the *Didache* continues to represent a markedly different

[72] See G. A. Kennedy, *Progymnasmata: Greek Textbooks of Prose Composition and Rhetoric* (Atlanta: Society of Biblical Literature, 2003).

[73] Niederwimmer, *Didache*, 122–3. Rordorf and Tuilier, *Doctrine*, 32–3, had argued that 6. 2–3 was an original part of the Jewish TW, but that, as it stands, refers to 1. 3–2. 1.

[74] J. A. Draper, 'Torah and Troublesome Apostles in the *Didache* Community', *NovT* 33 (1991), 347–72; *idem*, 'A Continuing Enigma: The "Yoke of the Lord" in *Didache* 6: 2–3 and Early Jewish–Christian Relations', in P. J. Tomson and D. Lambers-Petry (eds.), *The Image of the Judaeo-Christians in Ancient Jewish and Christian Literature*, WUNT 158 (Tübingen: Mohr

pole in the Jesus movement than that represented by Paul and post-Pauline developments, which ignored the restrictions on idol-meat and advocated practices of table-fellowship and views of the Torah that effectively excluded Jewish Christians from participation.

Siebeck, 2003), 106–23, on p. 113; C. N. Jefford, 'Tradition and Witness in Antioch: Acts 15 and Didache 6', in E. V. McKnight (ed.), *Perspectives on Contemporary New Testament Questions: Essays in Honour of T. C. Smith* (Lewiston, Me.: Edwin Mellen Press, 1992), 408–19; D. Flusser, 'Paul's Jewish-Christian Opponents in the Didache', in S. Shaked (ed.), *Gilgul: Essays on Transformation, Revolution and Permanence in the History of Religions, Dedicated to R. J. Zwi Werblowsky*, Studies in the History of Religions, Supplements to Numen 50 (Leiden: Brill, 1987), 71–90; repr. in Draper (ed.), *The* Didache *in Modern Research*, 195–211; Michelle Slee, *The Church in Antioch in the First Century CE*, JSNTSup 244 (London and New York: T. & T. Clark International, 2003), 83–91.

11

First-fruits and the Support of Prophets, Teachers, and the Poor in *Didache* 13 in Relation to New Testament Parallels

Jonathan A. Draper

1. INTRODUCTION

Few today would pronounce with as much confidence as Adolf Harnack, in his pioneering commentary *Die Lehre der Zwölf Apostel*,[1] on the saying found twice in slightly different forms in *Did.* 13. 1–2, 'The labourer is worthy of his food': 'Der Verfasser fusst auch hier auf einem Herrnwort in der Fassung des Matthäus.' For one thing, scholarly opinions on the dependence of the *Didache* on Matthew's Gospel remain deeply divided,[2] and therefore an opinion on a particular logion will partly depend on one's judgement on the situation as a whole. For another, the possibility that individual logia set by the evangelists on the lips of Jesus may have originated from more general Jewish tradition is more widely accepted. So, on this saying, Rudolf Bultmann remarks that it is 'evidently a proverb which has been turned to use by the Church for the instructional material it provided'.[3] It is indeed a saying which is found not only in Q (Matt. 10. 10 = Luke 10. 7) but also in 1 Tim. 5. 18, and it probably also underlies the argumentation of Paul in 1 Cor. 9. 1–18 as well as the *Gospel of Thomas*, 88. In such a case, it seems that the balance of the evidence must favour caution, so that Helmut Köster's conclusion is probably right in this case: 'Ergebnis der zu Did. 13,1f gemachten Erwägung ist, dass hier ein Maschal verwendet wird, das schon früh als Herrenwort in der freien Überlieferung bekannt war. Da in der Did. jede Zitationsformel an dieser

[1] A. von Harnack, *Die Lehre der zwölf Apostel nebst Untersuchungen zur ältesten Geschichte der Kirchenverfassung und des Kirchenrechts*, TU 2 (Leipzig: Hinrichs' sche Buchhandlung, 1884), 50.

[2] See, e.g., C. M. Tuckett, 'Synoptic Tradition in the *Didache*', in J. A. Draper (ed.), *The* Didache *in Modern Research*, AGAJU 37 (Leiden: Brill, 1996), 92–128, *contra* J. A. Draper, 'The Jesus Tradition in the *Didache*', in Draper (ed.), Didache *in Modern Research*, 72–91.

[3] R. Bultmann, *The History of the Synoptic Tradition* (ET Oxford: Basil Blackwell, 1963), 103.

Stelle fehlt, ist es noch nicht einmal sicher, ob sie diesen Maschal als Herrenwort überkommen hatte oder nur also profanes Sprichwort.'[4] To this must be added the overwhelming evidence provided by Peter Tomson that this proverbial saying is rooted in Jewish *halakah*.[5]

I do not, therefore, intend in this paper to reopen the question of the dependence of the *Didache* on Matthew, which I have already opposed on numerous occasions.[6] In almost every instance where the *Didache* shows direct points of contact with the gospel tradition, it is with Q. It never occurs in an identical form to either Matthew or Luke, sometimes closer to one, sometimes to the other, though usually closest to Matthew. An exception is the eucharistic prayer, where traditions found also in the Johannine corpus surface.[7] It simply seems inconceivable that the Didachist could have known the extant gospels Matthew and/or Luke, yet used only the Q material in them, never the Marcan material.[8] I would go further. One of the consequences of the formation of the Christian canon is that the question is usually posed in the fashion, 'Is an early Christian writing dependent on the New Testament?' The question is rarely asked the other way round. In the case of a writing such as the *Didache*, this raises important issues. Most scholars today concur that its final form should be dated no later than the end of the first century or perhaps the beginning of the second century CE. Many, myself included, would date it much earlier.[9] Even if we were to accept the later end of the scale, most scholars would also agree that it contains much material that must be dated considerably earlier than its final form.[10] The same kind of

[4] H. Köster, *Synoptische Überlieferung bei den Apostolischen Väter*, TU 65 (Berlin: Akademie-Verlag, 1957), 213.

[5] P. Tomson, *Paul and the Jewish Law: Halakah in the Letters of the Apostle to the Gentiles*, CRINT 3.1 (Assen and Maastricht: Van Gorcum; Minneapolis: Fortress, 1990), 122–31.

[6] Most recently J. A. Draper, 'A Continuing Enigma: The "Yoke of the Lord" in *Didache* 6:2–3 and Early Jewish–Christian Relations', in P. J. Tomson and D. Lambers-Petry (eds.), *The Image of Judaeo-Christians in Ancient Jewish and Christian Literature*, WUNT 158 (Tübingen: Mohr Siebeck, 2003), 106–23; *idem*, 'Does the (Final) Version of the Didache and Matthew Reflect an "Irrevocable Parting of the Ways" with Judaism', in H. van de Sandt (ed.), *The Didache and Matthew: Two Documents from the same Jewish-Christian Milieu?* (Assen: van Gorcum Press, 2005), 217–41.

[7] J. Betz, 'The Eucharist in the *Didache*', in Draper (ed.), Didache *in Modern Research*, 244–75.

[8] Cf. J. S. Kloppenborg, 'Didache 16:6–8 and Special Matthean Tradition', *ZNW* 70 (1979), 54–67, for a similar argument.

[9] Most recently A. Milavec, *The Didache: Faith, Hope, and Life of the Earliest Christian Communities, 50–70 C.E.* (New York and Mahwah, NJ: Newman Press, 2003); M. Slee, *The Church in Antioch in the First Century CE*, JSNTSup 244 (London and New York: T. & T. Clark International, 2003), 54–116; A. J. P. Garrow, *The Gospel of Matthew's Dependence on the* Didache, JSNTSup 254 (London and New York: T. & T. Clark International, 2004).

[10] E.g., Enrico Mazza argues that Paul knows and is influenced by the eucharistic prayers prior to 1 Corinthians (i.e., prior to 50–2 CE): E. Mazza, '*Didache* 9–10: Elements of a Eucharistic

inconclusive result comes with regard to the dating of Matthew itself: while a few argue for a date as early as 80 CE, rather more opt for the period 85–95 CE, and many, like Saldarini, play safe with 'the last two decades of the first century'.[11] Essentially, this places Matthew and the *Didache* in the same time frame, especially if one adopts the concept of the latter as 'evolving literature'.[12] Many place either or both of Matthew and the *Didache* in the same milieu as well: namely, Antioch.[13] The question of influence, then, could legitimately be posed the other way round, particularly if the *Didache* is a genuine community rule of such an important Christian community. In that case, those familiar with the practice of the community would be formatively influenced in their writing directly and indirectly by their community's rule. I have already argued the possibility of such a scenario.[14]

In the case of the 'first fruits' in *Did.* 13, the question I would ask is not, 'Is the *Didache* dependent on Matthew?' but, 'Is there an internal coherence and authenticity in the use of the logion in *Didache*, which might shed light on the origin of the use of the saying in the New Testament in general and in Matthew in particular?' Historically speaking, the Jesus tradition probably emerged in concrete settings in life prior to its incorporation in more systematic and theologically ordered works such as the gospels.

2. THE UNDERLYING STRUCTURE OF THE *DIDACHE* AS JEWISH-CHRISTIAN CATECHESIS

Despite the recent attempt of Aaron Milavec[15] in his massive new commentary on the *Didache* to see a seamless and intentional 'pastoral genius' behind the work, it seems clear that it is a many-layered text, which has been

Interpretation', in Draper (ed.), Didache *in Modern Research*, 276–99; also *idem*, *The Origins of the Eucharistic Prayer* (Collegeville, Minn.: Liturgical Press, 1999), 36–41.

[11] A. J. Saldarini, *Matthew's Christian-Jewish Community* (Chicago and London: University of Chicago Press, 1994), 4. For a summary of the evidence, see D. C. Sim, *The Gospel of Matthew and Christian Judaism: The History and Social Setting of the Matthean Community* (Edinburgh: T. & T. Clark, 1998), 33–40.

[12] R. Kraft; *Barnabas and the Didache: The Apostolic Fathers, A New Translation and Commentary*, iii (New York: Thomas Nelson, 1965); S. Giet, 'Coutume, évolution, droit canon, à propos de deux passages de la "Didachè" ', *RDC* 16 (1966), 118–32.

[13] See esp. the recent work of Slee, *Church in Antioch*.

[14] J. A. Draper, 'Christian Self-Definition against the "Hypocrites" in *Didache* 8', in Draper (ed.), Didache *in Modern Research*, 223–43; also *idem*, 'Continuing Enigma'; and *idem*, 'Does the (Final) Version?'. See also the arguments for the late dating of Matthew *vis-à-vis* the *Didache* in P. Tomson, 'Halakhic Elements in Didache 8 and Matthew 6', H. van de Sandt (ed.), *Didache and Matthew*, 131–41; Slee, *Church in Antioch*, 118–55; Garrow, *Matthew's Dependence.*

[15] Milavec, *Didache*, pp. vii–xiii.

repeatedly redacted in the course of the evolution of the community which used it as a rule of life. On the other hand, there is a logic and coherence to the *Didache*, when it is taken seriously as an integral composition, however long the process took. At the heart of the work lies its orientation as 'teaching of the twelve apostles' towards 'the gentiles (τοῖς ἔθνεσιν)', as its (to my mind) original *titulum* has it. Its concerns and argumentation reveal it to be a Jewish-Christian work, designed to integrate Gentile converts into the Jewish-Christian community(ies) which were striving to remain faithful to the Torah.[16] These communities were under pressure particularly from the growing rabbinic ascendancy over Jewish people inside and outside Palestine (*Did.* 8) and from those Christian groups in the Pauline tradition which had abandoned the Torah (*Did.* 11. 1–2; 16. 1–4).

The Two Ways teaching of *Did.* 1–6 provides the basic catechesis for the Gentiles joining the community, based on halakic development of the ethical second table of the Ten Commandments and the so-called Noachic Covenant. Acceptance of this teaching and strict avoidance of *eidolothuton*, food offered to idols (6. 3), provided the minimum basis for a common life between Jewish and Gentile believers. However, this was only a minimum, and the hope or even expectation of the community was that converts would eventually take on themselves the 'whole yoke of the Lord' and become observant Jews (*Did.* 6. 2). The baptismal procedure, with its emphasis on grades of water (7. 1–3), and the initiatory meal, with its concern to exclude those who had not been baptized as unclean like dogs (9. 5; 10. 6; cf. 14. 1), which follows, shows a major concern with ritual purity.

Since the teaching is understood to be mediated by the apostles, it is no surprise that the instructions on initiation are followed by hospitality rules concerning apostles (11–12). In the nature of things, apostles are those sent on a particular mission by a particular person or community and carry the authority of that person or community, indeed stand in the place of that person or community: 'the *shaliach* is as the one who sent him/ her'.[17] Hence,

[16] This was the hypothesis defended in my doctoral dissertation (J. A. Draper, 'A Commentary on the Didache in the Light of the Dead Sea Scrolls and Related Documents', unpublished Ph.D. diss., Cambridge University, 1983), and it has undergirded my research since. See esp. J. A. Draper, 'Ritual Process and Ritual Symbol in Didache 7–10', *VC* 54 (2000), 1–38. A similar thesis is developed by Slee, *Church in Antioch*, except that she envisages it as written in its entirety in mid-first-century Antioch to regularize the table-fellowship of Gentile Christians with Jewish Christians after the incident mentioned by Paul in Gal. 2. 11–14.

[17] See, e.g., *m. Ber.* 5. 5; *b. Ned.* 72b; *b. Kidd.* 41b; *b. Hag.* 10b; *b. Nazir.* 12b; *b. B.M.* 96a; *b. Men.* 93b; *Mekh. Ex.* 12. 4, 6. For a more detailed argument see J. A. Draper, 'Weber, Theissen and the Wandering Charismatics of the Didache', *JECS* 6 (1998), 541–76. It is important to bear in mind that Christian apostles might be both male and female, sometimes in partnership, as in the case of Prisca and Aquila. This has been clearly argued by Elizabeth Schüssler Fiorenza, *In Memory of Her: A Feminist Reconstruction of Christian Origins* (New York: Crossroad, 1989),

they are *en route* somewhere and carry letters of authorization. Unless their letters of commission specify that particular community receiving them as its target, setting out their authority and their business, they may only expect accommodation on the way and must leave the next day or two if need be, to take account of the prohibition on travelling on the sabbath, with enough provisions to reach their next stop on the way. To ask for more would reveal that they are not on a genuine embassy at all and would expose them as frauds. Takaaki Haraguchi comments that the word ἐργάτης became a *terminus technicus* for the early Christian missionary, and argues that it points in two directions: to the duty of the communities to support them and also to the duty of the missionaries to undertake an itinerant life-style.[18] In my own understanding, 'the duty to undertake a wandering lifestyle without protection' to which he points is an invention of modern scholars. I would argue that it simply points to the obligation of hospitality towards an extensive network of travelling emissaries connecting the various centres of the early Christian movement.[19]

This instruction on apostles has attracted instruction on prophets as well, since they were clearly, at some stage in the history of the community, liable to arrive in the community from outside also, but without any letters or authorization, and to make claims for sustenance. It would appear that this happened at a later stage in the development of the tradition, in view of the elaborate nature of the rules designed to correct abuse of hospitality. The Spirit, of course, cannot be tested, but prophets can be tested by their conduct. Rules are provided for this purpose (11. 7–12). My own hypothesis is that this section is an interpolation into the earlier rules, where instruction concerning apostles was originally followed by brief instructions concerning those arriving in the community who were not apostles and did not claim to be (12. 1–5). They may also be supported on their travel, but only after their genuineness has been tested. If they want to stay, the rule is 'let them work and let them eat (ἐργαζέσθω καὶ φαγέτω)' (12. 3). Any refusal to live by this rule reveals them to be frauds out to exploit the community.

160–175; cf. A. Wire, *The Corinthian Women Prophets: A Reconstruction through Paul's Rhetoric* (Philadelphia: Fortress, 1991).

[18] T. Haraguchi, 'Das Unterhaltsrecht des frühchristlichen Verkündigers', *ZNW* 84 (1993), 178–95, esp. 178, 181–2, 190, where he cites the many scholars who advocate the same position, particularly the influential work of G. Theissen, 'Legitimation und Lebensunterhalt: ein Beitrag zur Soziologie urchristlicher Missionäre', *NTS* 21 (1975), 192–221; *idem, The First Followers of Jesus: A Sociological Analysis of Earliest Christianity* (London: SCM Press; Philadelphia: Fortress, 1978).

[19] R. A. Horsley and J. A. Draper, *Whoever Hears You Hears Me: Prophets, Performance, and Tradition in Q* (Harrisburg, Pa.: Trinity Press International, 1999), 29–45.

Did. 13. 1–2 is really a part of this instruction, and rests on the same principle, 'let them work and let them eat', as Audet has also argued.[20] In this instance, prophecy and teaching are deemed to be work, so they are to be supported by the community who benefit from their work. However, it is, in my opinion, an interpolation into the earlier schema deriving from the same period as 11. 7–12 and 15. 1–2. The earliest material is marked above all by the use of the second person singular form of address; the redaction is marked by a second person plural form of address, as I have argued elsewhere.[21] However, since the giving of first fruits was probably originally connected logically with the instructions concerning apostles who were to receive them and take them back to Jerusalem in the form of money, there is a logical connection with what follows also.

Did. 13. 3–7 belongs to the underlying schema, since the giving of tithes and first-fruits was probably required for the food used by the Gentile members of the community, in order for them to share table-fellowship with Jewish members. Food rules concerning eating tithes and first-fruits originating in the Holiness Code for priests seem to have been extended by many Jewish groups, including Christian Jews, by the end of the Second Temple period to all their members on the basis of Exod. 19. 5–6.[22] In addition, Jewish communities in the Diaspora were particularly anxious about pollution from food offered to idols.[23] If they were in danger of eating contaminated food, then table-fellowship would be broken, and the unity of the community compromised. Thus these instructions are a development of *Did.* 6. 3: *περὶ δὲ τῆς βρώσεως ὃ δύνασαι βάστασον*. Space is left for conscience in keeping Jewish food laws (*ὡς ἂν σοι δόξῃ*), but there is nevertheless a minimum requirement: namely, a strict prohibition on food offered to idols (*ἀπὸ δὲ τοῦ εἰδωλοθύτου λίαν πρόσεχε*). The later Jewish tractate on proselytes, *Gerim*, requires newly circumcized and baptized converts to give 'gleanings, forgotten sheaves, the corner of the field and tithes' (1. 3). Hence it is probably part of the earliest substructure of the *Didache* also.[24] It is interesting to note, furthermore, that the discussion of the rights of an apostle to support from the Gentile Christian community at Corinth (1 Cor. 9. 1–4) comes in the context of Paul's discussion of food offered to idols. Tomson[25] has seen the

[20] J.-P. Audet, *La Didachè: Instructions des Apôtres*, ÉBib (Paris: Gabalda, 1958), 453–7.

[21] J. Draper, 'A Continuing Enigma', esp. 115–18.

[22] P. Seidensticker, *Die Gemeinschaftsform der religiösen Gruppen des Spätjudentums und der Urkirche* (Jerusalem: Studium Biblicum Franciscanorum Liber Annus, 1959), 94–198.

[23] The evidence is set out by Tomson, *Paul and the Jewish Law*, 151–258; also Slee, *Church in Antioch*, 17–23.

[24] Draper, 'A Continuing Enigma', 118–20.

[25] Tomson, *Paul and the Jewish Law*, 125.

discussion as a 'digression' from the latter, but perhaps it might indicate that the question of εἰδωλοθύτον and the question of support of apostles might have been linked by the allocation of first-fruits in the earliest Christian communities.

3. PROPHETS, TEACHERS, AND ENTITLEMENT TO SUPPORT FROM FIRST-FRUITS

Perhaps I should start by setting out schematically my understanding of the redactional layers of the text. The earliest layer is in bold type, marked by second person singular, concerned with the requirement to give first-fruits. The second layer is in italics, marked by second person plural, concerned above all with the income of prophets and secondarily of teachers. The third layer is underlined, and represents a further halakic development,[26] to cover the case of the absence of prophets (and teachers?) in the community:

1a Πᾶς δὲ προφήτης
ἀληθινός, θέλων καθῆσθαι πρὸς ὑμᾶς,
ἄξιός ἐστι
τῆς τροφῆς αὐτοῦ.
1b Ὡσαύτως διδάσκαλος
ἀληθινός
ἐστιν ἄξιος καὶ αὐτὸς ὥσπερ ὁ ἐργάτης
τῆς τροφῆς αὐτοῦ.
2a Πᾶσαν οὖν ἀπαρχὴν γεννημάτων ληνοῦ καὶ ἅλωνος,
βοῶν τε καὶ προβάτων
λαβῶν
δώσεις τοῖς προφήταις·
αὐτοὶ γάρ εἰσιν οἱ ἀρχιερεῖς ὑμῶν.
2b Ἐὰν δὲ μὴ ἔχητε προφήτην,
δότε τοῖς πτωχοῖς.

2c **Ἐὰν σιτίαν ποιῇς,**
τὴν ἀπαρχὴν λαβὼν
δὸς κατὰ τὴν ἐντολήν.
2d **Ὡσαύτως κεράμιον οἴνου ἢ ἐλαίου ἀνοίξας,**
τὴν ἀπαρχὴν λαβὼν
δὸς τοῖς προφήταις.

[26] G. Alon, 'Halakah in the Teaching of the Twelve Apostles (*Didache*)', in Draper (ed.), Didache *in Modern Research*, 165–94., esp. 191–4.

2e Ἀργυρίου δὲ καὶ ἱματισμοῦ
καὶ παντὸς κτήματος
λαβὼν τὴν ἀπαρχήν, ὡς ἄν σοι δόξῃ,
δὸς κατὰ τὴν ἐντολήν.

The teaching is carefully composed and formulaic,[27] but fluctuates, as we have observed, between the first and second person plural. This could be the result, as some have argued, of a move in the sense from cultic to personal obligations.[28] However, since this feature is a mark of redactional activity throughout the *Didache*, it seems more likely to be a sign of revision here also.[29]

3.1 The Worker is Worthy of Her/His Food

Since the instructions regarding the prophets and teachers are almost exactly parallel, nothing suggests that they were not composed at the same time. In the first case, as the schema shows, the question is what happens when the prophet wishes to settle (θέλων καθῆσθαι πρὸς ὑμᾶς). If the prophet is genuine, then she or he speaks with the authority of the Spirit, and so there can be no further question of her or his right to support. In the second case, the question concerns whether the teacher is really engaged in full-time work for the community (καὶ αὐτὸς ὥσπερ ὁ ἐργάτης). In both cases, the community is required to test their genuineness (ἀληθινός). It is true that the second citation of the pericope, in the case of teachers, is somewhat clumsy, but this demonstrates that their status was disputed rather than that the instruction is a later addition. The teachers do not come, it seems, from outside the community but from inside it, since no mention is made of any desire to settle. If there were many claimants to be teachers in the community, it would have posed a financial problem had their support been automatically guaranteed. The criterion for support in this case would be that they had been designated as full-time workers by the community. In both cases, the same logion is used to support the claim: 'The worker is worthy of her or his food.'

This saying is directly cited three times in the New Testament, as we have already noted, in Matt. 10. 10, Luke 10. 7, and 1 Tim. 5. 18. Matthew and the *Didache* use τροφῆς, while Luke and 1 Timothy use μισθοῦ:

[27] For an analysis, see G. Schille, 'Das Recht der Propheten und Apostel—gemeinderechtliche Beobachtungen zu Didache Kapitel 11–13', in P. Wätzel and G. Schille (eds.), *Theologische Versuche*, i (Berlin: Evangelische Verlag-Anstalt, 1966), 84–103; M. del Verme, 'The Didache and Judaism: The ἀπαρχή of *Didache* 13:3–7', *SP* 26 (1993), 113–39, on p. 114.

[28] E.g. Schille, 'Das Recht'.

[29] See, e.g., the same fluctuation in *Did.* 6–7: Draper, 'A Continuing Enigma', 115–17. I agree with del Verme, 'Didache and Judaism', 114, that Schille's argument is unconvincing.

Did. 13. 1–2	Matt. 10. 8–10	Luke 10. 7–8	1 Tim. 5. 17–18
1 *Πᾶς δὲ προφήτης ἀληθινός, θέλων καθῆσθαι πρὸς ὑμᾶς,* ***ἄξιός εστι τῆς τροφῆς αὐτὸῦ.*** 2 *Ὡσαύτως διδσκαλος ἀληθινός* ***ἐστιν ἄξιος καὶ αὐτὸς ὥσπερ ὁ ἐργάτης τῆς τροφῆς αὐτοῦ.***	8 *δωρεὰν ἐλάβετε δωρεὰν δότε.* 9 *Μὴ κτήσησθε χρυσὸν μηδὲ ἄργυρον μηδὲ χαλκὸν εἰς τὰς ζώνας ὑμῶν,* 10 *μὴ πήραν εἰς ὁδὸν λμηδὲ δύο χιτῶνας μηδὲ ὑποδήματα μεηὲ ῥάβδον·* ***ἄξιος γὰρ ὁ ἐργάτης τῆς τροφῆς αὐτοῦ.***	7 *’Εν αὐτῇ δὲ τῇ οἰκίᾳ μένετε ἐσθίοντες καὶ πίνοντες τὰ παρ’ αὐτῶν* ***ἄξῖος γὰρ’ ὁ ἐργάτης τοῦ μισθοῦ αὐτοῦ*** *μὴ μεταβαίνετε ἐξ οἰκίας εἰς οἰκίαν.* 8 *καὶ εἰς ἣν ἂν πόλιν εἰσέρχησθε καὶ δέχωνται ὑμᾶς ἐσθίετε τὰ παρατιθέμενα ὑμῖν.*	17 *Οἱ καλῶς προεστῶτες πρεσβύτεροι διπλῆς τιμῆς ἀξιούσθωσαν μάλιστα οἱ κοπιῶντες ἐν λόγῳ καὶ διδασκαλίᾳ* 18 *λέγει γὰρ ἡ γραφή, Βοῦν ἀλοῶντα οὐ φιμώσεις καί* ***Ἄξιος ὁ ἐργάτης τοῦ μισθοῦ αὐτοῦ.***

In the first place, when we examine these texts, it is striking that the Q texts (Matt. and Luke) refer the logion to apostles and not to prophets. Matthew has combined Mark's account of the mission of the twelve apostles with Q's account of the mission of the seventy apostles, which is preserved separately in Luke. While Paul does not cite this logion, he clearly knows it and its use in the early Christian communities:[30]

Οὐκ εἰμὶ ἐλεύθερος;
οὐκ εἰμὶ ἀπόστολος;
οὐχὶ Ἰησοῦν τὸν κύριον ἡμῶν ἑώρακα;
οὐ τὸ ἔργον μου ὑμεῖς ἐστε ἐν κυρίῳ;
εἰ ἄλλοις οὐκ εἰμὶ ἀπόστολος
ἀλλά γε ὑμῖν εἰμι.
ἡ γὰρ σφραγίς μου τῆς ἀποστολῆς ὑμεῖς ἐστε ἐν κυρίῳ
Ἡ ἐμὴ ἀπολογία τοῖς ἐμὲ ἀνακρίνουσίν ἐστιν αὕτη.
μὴ οὐκ ἔχομεν ἐξουσίαν φαγεῖν καὶ πεῖν; (1 Cor. 9. 1–4)

Clearly the work of an apostle is regarded by the addressees as binding the communities which receive her or him to give provisions. The problem he faces is not that the community does not recognize the rights of an apostle, but that he himself is not accepted as an apostle because he does not carry letters of authorization from Jerusalem.[31] By refusing his right to support, he

30 For a good account and an analysis of the halakic basis of the saying, see Tomson, *Paul and the Jewish Law*, 125–31.

31 Cf. Haraguchi, 'Unterhaltsrecht', 183: 'Die Korinther interpretieren seinen Verzicht auf das Lebensunterhaltsrecht als Zeichen des Mangels an apostolischer Autorität.' However, the

makes a virtue out of necessity and defuses the crisis. His apologia is another indication that the right originally belonged to the apostle and not to the prophet.

Luke presents the saying in the context of the requirement that the apostle should stay in one house and not go from one house to another. Since no time limit for the stay is given, this might lead to the kind of abuse which the *Didache* sets out to avoid by limiting the stay to one or two days at most. In any case, the logion is introduced to support the apostle's right to be provisioned during her or his stay in a town or village. In return, the household receives the peace pronounced upon it by the apostle as its reward. The use of the term *μισθός* makes it clear that the proclamation of the gospel by the apostle is regarded as labour earning a wage. The logion is obviously well known, and probably proverbial, regardless of whether or not Jesus himself used it, since it is introduced simply by *γάρ*. However, as Haraguchi has rightly pointed out, the practice already belongs to an ideal past for Luke, as 22. 35–6 shows.[32] Luke's version makes it clear that what is to be expected is 'eating and drinking', but the language of 'wages' might be open to misunderstanding if taken out of context. Tomson[33] argues that 'food' is more ancient, since it depends on extending the rights of the ox (Deut. 25. 4) to eat while threshing, *qal wa-homer*, to humans, and the rights of labourers in the fields to eat from the produce they are reaping (Deut. 23. 24 f.), *qal wa-homer*, to spiritual labour. Haraguchi argues, to the contrary, that Luke's form is more ancient, since he brings the saying in its original Q setting, while Matthew has mixed it in with Marcan material.[34] However, the argument from the ordering of the material, where Luke clearly preserves the more original sequence, does not necessarily apply to the *wording* of the material, in which Matthew often seems to preserve the more ancient form.

Matthew attaches the logion to Jesus' prohibition to the apostles of taking money, any begging bag for food, or clothing (spare tunic, sandals, or staff). The logion provides the rationale for taking no provision for the journey: food will be provided along the way by those who receive the proclamation. The logic of the saying is that clothes, including tunic, sandals, and staff, will also be provided if needed by those along the way. In addition, it is striking

sequence may have been the reverse of this. Haraguchi, pp. 183–4, points to the interesting difference in *content* between Paul and the Q saying: viz., that Paul bases the right on preaching, while Q bases the right on travelling. This significant shift reflects also a difference in their respective understandings of apostleship.

[32] Ibid. 190–1.

[33] Tomson, *Paul and the Jewish Law*, 126–8.

[34] Haraguchi, 'Unterhaltsrecht', 186, 189; though he does acknowledge that Paul's usage is derived from the earliest Palestinian missionary discourse (p. 179).

that the passage is introduced by the saying found only in Matthew: δωρεὰν ἐλάβετε δωρεὰν δότε. This amounts to a prohibition on demanding money for services rendered. In other words, the labourer is worthy of food (τροφή) and provisions, but not of a wage (in money)! This caution fits with Matthew's warning concerning false prophets who come from outside the community (7. 19–23), which may show that his community, like that of the *Didache*, was more used to prophets than to apostles, who had, perhaps, disappeared in practice from the life of the church after the destruction of Jerusalem.[35]

In 1 Timothy, it is the πρεσβύτεροι who are the objects of the logion's provision. All elders are worthy of honour; those (patrons) who administer the community well are worthy of double honour, but those who labour in 'word' and teaching should receive financial reward. I disagree with Dibelius[36] that the word τιμή implies of itself financial remuneration for all elders in the community, and would instead give it its literal meaning: honour accorded to those who perform voluntary service for the community (λειτουργία; cf. *Did.* 15. 1–2).[37] 'Liturgy', or public service, is an obligation for those who have the means, and its due reward is the public honour so coveted in the ancient world. Failure to perform patronage on the part of the wealthy results in shame.[38] It is only the performance of the teaching function that occasions the mention of entitlement to material support.

When the use of the logion concerning ἐργάτης in Q is compared with that in the *Didache*, it is remarkable, first, that it is applied to prophets and teachers.[39] This is particularly so, given that the text knows of apostles who are passing through the community on their way to other destinations, or, as I would argue, sent with letters to this particular community. Q would suggest that the logion applies originally to them, and not to the teachers and prophets. This is my suggestion, based on my redaction-critical analysis. In other words, what was originally the right of the apostles coming from Jerusalem to the communities which recognize its authority has been transferred to the new class of travellers which emerged after the destruction of

[35] Cf. ibid. 192–3.

[36] M. Dibelius and H. Conzelmann, *The Pastoral Epistles: A Commentary*, Hermeneia (Philadelphia: Fortress, 1972), 78; so too Haraguchi, 'Unterhaltsrecht', 185, regards it as a clear reference to money (*eindeutig*).

[37] Cf. W. Michaelis, *Pastoralbriefe und Gefanenschaftsbriefe: zur Echtheitsfrage der Pastoralbriefe* (Gütersloh: Bertelsmann, 1930; n.s. 1,6]) 1961), cited by Dibelius; cf. J. A. Kirk, 'Did "Officials" in the New Testament Church Receive a Salary?', *ExpT* 84 (1973), 105–8.

[38] See B. Malina, 'Patron and Client: The Analogy behind Synoptic Theology', *Forum*, 4 (1988), 2–32; K. C. Hanson and D. E. Oakman, *Palestine in the Time of Jesus: Social Structures and Social Conflicts* (Minneapolis: Fortress, 1998), 63–97.

[39] Haraguchi, 'Unterhaltsrecht', 180, rightly observes that ἐργάται and ἀπόστολοι are two synonymous self-designations of Paul's opponents in Corinth and Philippi, and one would expect the same thing to be true in the *Didache*, which also knows travelling apostles.

Jerusalem: the prophets and, alongside them, the teachers (as in 1 Timothy).[40] Apostles as an institution seem to have retreated in the face of prophets in this community. The latter have the right to preside at the Eucharist (10. 7) and to preach and give instructions in the Spirit in the assembly (11. 7–12), and these instructions in the final form of the text show that the community of the *Didache*, like that of Matthew, is experiencing instances of abuse from prophets, and not from apostles.

Secondly, it is noteworthy that, as so often, the *Didache* is closer to Matthew than to Luke or 1 Timothy. Matthew, like the *Didache*, avoids the abuse of the apostolic commission to get money as a μισθός, allowing only food and necessities for the journey. Yet the use of τροφή in the *Didache* has a logic to it which is not present in Matthew: namely, the way it couples the right to food to the duty to give first-fruits.

Finally, the saying occurs in the *Gospel of Thomas*, which has a form of the apostolic commission dominated by concern with the purity of the food that is provided:

> When you go into any country and walk from place to place, when the people receive you, eat what they serve you and heal the sick among them. For what goes into your mouth will not defile you; rather, it is what comes out of your mouth that will defile you. (Saying 14b)

Here again, there is an underlying assumption of a right of angels / messengers and prophets to provision rather than to a wage:

> Jesus said, 'The angels (ἄγγελοι) and the prophets (προφῆται) will come to you and give to you those things you (already) have. And you too, give them those things which you have, and say to yourselves, 'When will they come and take what is theirs'. (Saying 88)

It seems to echo Matthew's linking of the saying,' You have freely received, so freely give', with the saying, 'The worker is worthy of her or his food'.

3.2 The First-fruits

The development and integration of the agricultural offerings, linked to the priestly and temple offering system, is complex and contested terrain. What originated as different systems for offering the first-fruits and tithes, presented variously by Num. 18. 8–32; Exod. 22. 28–31; Deut. 18. 1–5, was synthesized somewhat differently by different groupings in Israel into a whole system.

[40] Cf. J. A. Draper, 'Torah and Troublesome Apostles in the *Didache* Community', in Draper (ed.), Didache *in Modern Research*, 340–63.

The various rabbinic tractates in the division *Zeraim* seek to clarify, differentiate, and harmonize the different obligations incumbent on an Israelite with respect to offerings, tithes, and taxes.[41] However, it is not entirely clear what the exact circumstances were prior to the destruction of the Temple in 70 CE. According to Freyne,[42] the peasantry in the birthplace of the Christian movement in Galilee remained loyal to the Temple festivals and paid first-fruits, probably because of their perceived link to the fertility of the holy land, but did not pay tithes or the half-shekel tax. Beyond this, Sanders is probably right in saying that 'We cannot, however, be sure who tithed what!'[43] The tithe may have been collected by Herod locally, since he would have been responsible for the payment of the tribute from Galilee to Rome.

Fortunately, for our purposes, it seems fairly certain that the agricultural laws of first-fruits of the land were not considered valid outside Palestine, since they were understood as giving back to God a token of what belonged to God: namely, the land of Israel.[44] The ruling is made with regard to *bikkurim* by R. Jose the Galilean (T2): 'They may not bring First-fruits from beyond Jordan since that is not a land flowing with milk and honey.'[45] A Gentile who owns land in Palestine may bring them, but not make the avowal in the temple (unless his mother was a Jew), since he cannot make the declaration from Deut. 26. 3, 'Which the Lord swore unto our Fathers to give us' (*m. Bik.* 1. 4). This rabbinic understanding that first-fruits are due only on the produce of *Eretz Israel* is confirmed independently by Philo of Alexandria in *de Somniis* 2. 75, where Lev. 23. 10 is restricted to the land of promise (πλὴν οὐ παντί ἀλλὰ τῷ ἀπὸ τῆς γῆν ἣν ἐγὼ δίδωμι ὑμῖν).

On the other hand, the variable distance from Jerusalem, even during the time when the Temple still stood, made the offering of first-fruits a problem. Some things just could not last the time it took to get there.[46] Hence, it was

[41] See, e.g., G. Alon, *The Jews in their Land in the Talmudic Age (70–640 CE)* (ET Cambridge, Mass.: Harvard University Press, 1989), 254–60; S. Safrai and M. Stern, *The Jewish People in the First Century: Historical Geography, Political History, Social, Cultural and Religious Life and Institutions* (Assen: Von Gorcum; Philadelphia: Fortress, 1976), 817–33; and the somewhat polemical description of E. P. Sanders, *Judaism: Practice and Belief 63 BCE–66 CE* (London: SCM Press; Philadelphia: Trinity Press International, 1992), 146–69.

[42] S. Freyne, *Galilee from Alexander the Great to Hadrian 323 BCE to 135 CE: A Study of Second Temple Judaism* (Edinburgh: T. & T. Clark, 1980), 259–304.

[43] Sanders, *Judaism*, 149.

[44] E. Schürer, G. Vermes, F. Millar, and M. Black, *The History of the Jewish People in the Age of Jesus Christ (175 B.C.–A.D. 135)*, ii (Edinburgh: T. & T. Clark, 1979), 269.

[45] H. Danby, *The Mishnah Translated from the Hebrew with Introduction and Brief Explanatory Notes* (Oxford: Oxford University Press, 1933), 95.

[46] E.g. *m. Ter.* 2. 4, in Danby, *Mishnah*, 54: 'Where there is a priest Heave-offering must be given from the choicest kind; but where there is no priest [it should be given] from the kind that best endures'. See Schürer *et al.*, *History of the Jewish People*, 2. 269; Sanders, *Judaism*, 147.

normal to take the produce of the first-fruits, where appropriate, rather than the fruits straight from the field. Chief among these were olive oil, wine, and fleece (Num. 18. 12; Neh. 10. 35, 37; Deut. 18. 4).[47] In other words, there was in effect a double first-fruits offering: once direct from the field, which could usually only be eaten by a local priest if available, and once from the produce of the field, which could be taken to the Temple on pilgrimage if possible. Another two aspects of the first-fruits already processed but owed to the priest were the three pieces of an edible animal slaughtered for food, and the dough or loaf of bread. These were not taken to Jerusalem, but offered to the local priest if such a person existed. Then again, the second tithe seems early on to have been redeemed by conversion into money for offering rather than carried to Jerusalem and consumed there.[48] All of these offerings of first-fruits in both kinds fell away as an obligation outside the land of Israel, but one might ask whether they continued in the Diaspora as a free-will offering for locally resident priests, Levites, and/or the poor (based on Deut. 14. 27–9; 26. 12–15).

The situation with regard to the tithe, or *ma'aseroth*, is not so clear. It was designed, not for the specific benefit of the priest, but for the maintenance of the whole Temple state. Its status after the destruction of the Temple was disputed for that reason, although the rabbis attempted to maintain it.[49] It is not clear whether Jews outside Palestine felt themselves obligated to pay it or not. They certainly paid the half-shekel Temple tax in the Diaspora.[50] It is likely that they felt themselves obligated to pay the offering for firstlings, at least of their own children, since their own fruit was not limited to the Holy Land. The Mishnah, at least, recognizes this difference by placing the tractate *Bekhoroth* in the division *Kodashim*, and not under *Zeraim*. We have little else to go by, except for the precious piece of evidence offered by Philo concerning the position in Rome, which he himself knew at first hand from his embassy there. Writing of Augustus Caesar, he says:

> He knew therefore that they have houses of prayer and meet together in them, particularly on the sacred sabbaths when they receive as a body a training in their ancestral philosophy. He knew too that they collect money for sacred purposes from their first-fruits (*ἀπὸ τῶν ἀπαρχῶν*) and send them to Jerusalem by persons who would offer sacrifices. Yet nevertheless he neither ejected them from Rome nor deprived them of their Roman citizenship because they were careful to preserve their Jewish citizenship also, nor took any violent measures against the houses of

[47] Cf. Sanders, *Judaism*, 152.

[48] *M. Ma'as Sh.* 5. 7; *t. Ma'as Sh.* 3. 18; *y. Ma'as* 4. 54d and 3. 54b. See Alon, *Jews in their Land*, 258.

[49] Alon, *Jews in their Land*, 256–7.

[50] The evidence is cited in Sanders, *Judaism*, 156.

prayer, nor prevented them from meeting to receive instructions in the laws, nor opposed their offerings of the first-fruits. (Philo, *Leg.* 156–7, LCL)

Since Philo has already said that first-fruits are not payable outside *Eretz Israel*, one can reasonably suppose that pious Diaspora Jews made a communal collection of the tithes and the price of the redemption of their first-born in cash and sent it to Jerusalem, while the Temple still stood.

3.3 The Offering of the First-fruits in the *Didache*

On the basis of what we have observed, it is possible to understand the instructions concerning the first-fruits in the *Didache* as carefully thought-through *halakah*. This is an observant Jewish community(ies) in the Diaspora, which wishes to remain a part of the broader Jewish society in its location.[51] We have to move away from the anachronistic understanding of Judaism in the first century as a religion. It is 'embedded religion', but not religion in our modern sense. It is a whole ethnic, cultural, economic, and social grouping, which includes, of course, at its centre a religious world-view. Buildings for communal gatherings, synagogues, were not only religious buildings, but social centres and foci of Jewish identity. The Jewish way of life, especially in the Diaspora, would have required special markets to make possible the observation of Jewish dietary laws. Then there was the question of making sure that children were able to marry within the community. Just as there was diversity, disagreement, and competition in Palestine around how one should live out one's social and cultural identity as a member of God's covenant people, which would be related to one's geographical location, class, and ideological position, so there was in the Diaspora. However, the need to maintain a Jewish identity under the pressure of living among Gentiles would have resulted in compromises and a grudging acceptance of a common identity in spite of these divisions. On this point I am entirely in agreement with Sanders's trenchant observation:

My basic assumption—here as throughout the book—is that other people besides the rabbis wanted to obey the law and that they considered how best to do so. A priest who lived in Upper Galilee would have seen the problem and offered some kind of advice. What we should not assume is what most scholars do assume: people either obeyed the rabbis (or Pharisees), or they were non-observant. We must always remember the very large number of people who, when push came to shove, were ready to die for the law, and who kept most of it in ordinary circumstances.... Just as

[51] Hence I agree with del Verme, 'Didache and Judaism', esp. 113, that the *Didache* 'reflects an ongoing process of interaction with Judaism and Jewish institutions'.

later they would fight and die for Jerusalem, the temple and the law, so during the heyday of the temple they tried to fulfil their scriptural obligations. In the case of first fruits, we cannot know just how they did so. We should assume, however, intention and effort to observe the law.[52]

I would argue that the community of the *Didache* was no different in its desire to fulfil the Law as best it could, despite its ambiguities when applied outside Palestine. The repeated phrase *κατὰ τὴν ἐντολήν* indicates, in my understanding, a genuine belief that the community arrangements were a faithful and appropriate interpretation of Jewish Torah, rather than a Christian instruction developed *analogously*, as suggested by del Verme.[53] They were, in other words, Christian *halakah*.[54] The point has rightly been made by del Verme,[55] that the Greek word *ἀπάρχη* is ambiguous in first-century Hellenistic Jewish usage, and covers both first-fruits of the harvest, or *reshith*, and also agricultural offerings more generally, or *terumoth*. In what follows, I argue that the *Didache* has in mind the technical usage of first-fruits of the harvest, both primary and secondary (i.e., processed), *per se*.

For those who 'bore the whole yoke of the Lord' as observant Jews, an essential part of maintaining their position in Jewish society would have been sharing in the communal collection and dispatch of the half-shekel tax, the tithes, and the firstlings (the five shekels to redeem the first-born son, or *bekhoroth*) to Jerusalem before the fall of the Temple (opinion was divided on the continuance of the practice after that event; see *y. Sheq*. 8. 51b: 'In this age, one does not dedicate, nor evaluate, nor make sacrosanct nor set aside *terumot* and *ma'aserot*'[56]). Even after 70 CE, however, Christian Jewish members of the *Didache* community would have been obliged to fall in with the decisions of the local community concerning the disposal of these things, if they wished to stay a part of it. Gentiles who were initiated into the community, on the other hand, were not obligated to pay any of these things. In fact, they may even have been prohibited from doing so (in the case of firstlings, at least), unless they became full converts and adopted the Torah. Even then, opinion in the Jewish community as a whole was divided on whether or not they qualified.

[52] Sanders, *Judaism*, 153–4.

[53] Del Verme, 'Didache and Judaism', 115.

[54] Cf. Kraft, *Barnabas and the Didache*, 173; del Verme, 'Didache and Judaism', 116–18, argues for the necessity of examining Jewish *halakhah* of the period for understanding the background to the *Didache*, but does not seem to consider that the latter is itself *halakhah*, as I would argue.

[55] Del Verme, 'Didache and Judaism', 116–18; cf. Milavec, *Didache*, 508–25.

[56] Cited in Alon, *Jews in their Land*, 257.

First-fruits (*bikkurim*), on the other hand, were a different matter. They were to be paid only by Jews, not Gentiles, and on produce of *Eretz Israel*, but not of land outside it. First-fruits from the Holy Land were due to the priests in the Temple, but perishable goods were to be consumed by priests in the local communities where these were far from the Temple. Christian Jewish members of the *Didache* community would have required an assurance that the food eaten or provided for communal meals was in some sense uncontaminated by idol offerings, and had in some sense been offered to God in accordance with the Torah. The same concern is evidenced in the later rabbinic tractate on proselytes, *Gerim* 1. 3. This instructs converts being circumcized and baptized to give 'gleanings, forgotten sheaves, the corners of the fields and tithes'. Gentiles in the *Didache* community, on the other hand, were not full converts to Judaism. Hence they could not, and should not, pay tithes or firstlings, but they could, and should, offer first-fruits to God. As Milavec[57] rightly points out, first-fruits were an accepted and universal feature of pagan life, but the pagan practice of offering them to the gods rendered them *eidolothuton* according to the Jewish understanding. As we have already observed, the *Didache* demands that *eidolothuton* must be strictly avoided, in order to allow Gentile converts and Christian Jews to live together. *Did.* 13. 3–7 solves this legal question in *halakic* fashion.

Thus Gentile members of the community were to offer the first-fruits of primary agricultural and secondary processed products to the Lord, including *hallah* and *hullin*, the dough and parts of the slaughtered beast offered to the priests. They could not send tithes and offerings to the Temple in Jerusalem through the local Jewish community structures, as Christian Jews did. Their offerings would be unlikely to have been accepted by the broader Jewish community based around the synagogue, because of the danger of contamination from idol offerings, particularly since the local Jewish communities appear to have been dominated by the Pharisaic party in the areas where the *Didache* communities were located, as *Did.* 8 shows.[58]

In terms of my broader redactional hypothesis, I believe that the original practice of the *Didache* community, at its earliest redactional layer, was to convert the first-fruits into money, where possible, to send to Jerusalem, except for the perishable things, which would have been disposed of locally, possibly to local priests (though they might have worried about its state of purity) or more likely to the poor, in line with Jewish custom if there was a

[57] Milavec, *Didache*, 504–5.

[58] At least by the time of the final redaction of the text. See Draper, 'Christian Self-Definition', 223–43.

surplus or there were no priests.[59] These offerings would have been dispatched to Jerusalem in the hands of the apostles—either delegates from Jerusalem visiting or passing through, or the community's own nominated apostles sent to Jerusalem for the purpose (who would themselves have the right to hospitality in Christian communities along the way by virtue of letters they carried). In the logic of this Christian Jewish community, the 'pillars' in Jerusalem (Paul's term in his polemic in Gal. 2. 9) had taken the place of the high priests, at least with respect to the first-fruits, and were deemed the proper objects of their support. While Gentile members of the *Didache* community contributed first-fruits to the apostles, Christian Jews continued to contribute along with the rest of the local Jewish community their obligatory taxes, tithes, and redemption of firstlings, which are excluded from the list in the *Didache* for this reason. I believe that this Gentile offering of first-fruits was what lay behind the saga of Paul's collection for Jerusalem, which he had agreed to (Gal. 2. 10). But his insistence that the Gentile converts did not have to keep even minimal purity with regard to *eidolothuton* would lie behind his (fully justified) anxiety as to whether the offering would be accepted by the 'pillars' in Jerusalem (Rom. 15. 30–3).

After the fall of Jerusalem in 70 CE, and the departure of the Christian leadership from the city—whenever that might have been and whether or not the leaders went to Pella in 68 CE—there were no more apostles coming from Jerusalem and no further possibility of sending the monetary value of the first-fruits there either. The place of Jerusalem and its apostles was taken by a newly emerging class of Christian prophets. I have argued[60] that this phenomenon was probably partly a feature of the dislocation experienced in Palestine during the Jewish War of 68–70, in which Christian Jewish refugees would have sought shelter in communities in Syria and elsewhere, taking their traditions of Jesus with them. Not unnaturally, many of them would have wished to settle in the communities they visited, particularly in light of probable loss of land and income in Judaea and Galilee. For most that would have meant finding employment, 'Let them work and let them eat'; but for those with deep knowledge of the Jesus tradition and for those who were prophets, the rule was that they earned their keep by their work of prophecy and teaching. The first-fruits, which had previously been taken by the apostles to Jerusalem for the support of the 'poor saints' (i.e., the

[59] At least, that was the custom in Jerusalem with the surplus, as indicated in *m. Maaser Sheni* 3. 5. See Safrai and Stern, *Jewish People in the First Century*, 823; Sanders, *Judaism*, 157.

[60] J. A. Draper, 'Social Ambiguity and the Production of Text: Prophets, Teachers, Bishops, and Deacons and the Development of the Jesus Tradition in the Community of the *Didache*', in C. N. Jefford (ed.), *The* Didache *in Context: Essays on its Text, History, and Transmission*, NovTSup 77 (Leiden: Brill, 1995), 284–312.

Christian equivalent of the righteous poor, the scholars of Torah, among the Pharisees), were now diverted to the prophets and teachers settling (as refugees and migrants) among the communities of the *Didache.*

Even in non-Christian Jewish communities, the problem of what to do with tithes, taxes, and first-fruits was forced on them by the destruction of the Temple. Whereas the custom had been for first-fruits in the Holy Land, which could not be sent to Jerusalem, to be consumed locally by the priesthood, this seems gradually to have been replaced by payment to the synagogue and the rabbis. The local community was now seen to have an obligation to support their full-time teachers, and the formulation of this obligation often sounds remarkably like the saying 'The labourer is worthy of his hire'. So in the saying from *Tanhuma* 119a, 'He who busies himself with Torah gets his sustenance from it'.[61] There is an even more interesting saying attributed to R. Abin (A4) in *Leviticus Rabbah* 34. 13, where support for the rabbis, as righteous poor, is connected with the offering of first-fruits. Among various explanations of Isa. 58. 7 ('Thou shalt bring the poor *merudim* to thy house'), there is a discussion of the role of the righteous poor, which concludes:

> Whoso entertains a scholar in his house is regarded by Scripture as though he had offered first-fruits, for it says here, '*Thou shalt bring*' and it says elsewhere, '*The choicest first-fruits* thou shalt bring *into the house of the Lord thy God*' (Ex. XXIII, 19); as in the latter context it applies to firstfruits so here also it applies to first-fruits.[62]

This late saying indicates a continuing tradition which probably goes back to an earlier time. Although in its present formulation, *Did.* 13. 4 represents the latest stage in the redaction of the text, it is likely that the obligation to the poor and the presentation of the perishable first-fruits were part of the tradition from the beginning. This would be the way in which the community satisfied its obligations in terms of *Did.* 1. 5–6. The temptation to take from the community's store of first-fruits, even when one was not really in dire need, would have occasioned the kind of instructions and warnings given there. The community needs to test the poor also, to make sure that they too are ἀληθινός!

On the basis of this analysis, one can see the logic of the *halakah* in *Did.* 13. 3–6. The community sets aside only the first-fruits which are not part of the general collection of the whole Jewish community, because they are not applicable to produce outside *Eretz Israel.* While the Christian Jewish members were not obligated to pay them and were already paying tithes and taxes, they could perhaps offer them as a free-will offering beyond what was required by the Law. Of these, the interest is not in the token first head of corn or first ripe olive, but in the processed produce that could serve the needs of the community for the support of those who taught in the community, the

[61] Quoted in Strack-Billerbeck i 569. [62] Soncino Edition, 439.

prophets and teachers and the poor. It would be only among Gentile Christian communities, and, later perhaps, Christian Jews after they had been expelled from the synagogue, that the offering of the tithe proper, or *ma'aseroth*, could be used in this way. The expression *ἀπαρχὴν γεννημάτων ληνοῦ καὶ ἅλωνος* is clearly meant to be exemplary, rather than exclusive: the word *ληνός*, for example, refers in my opinion to what is produced by the press and so is gathered in the vat. It could refer to oil, as well as to wine, for which it is more normally used. Likewise, the word *ἅλων* could refer to any grain threshed on the threshing floor, barley as well as wheat. So too *βοῶν τε καὶ προβάτων* refers to the first-fruits of all 'clean' animals, without raising the question of the first-fruits of unclean animals. It also leaves open the question of whether it refers to the redemption of the animals by a cash payment, or to provision of the priests' portion of sacrificed animal ('shoulder and two cheeks and maw', Deut. 18. 3–4). Perhaps both options are deliberately left open. The offering of bread or dough, or *hallah*, is a well-known and much-discussed right of the priest in rabbinic writings, and the extension of this right of 'second first fruits' to wine and oil is not without parallels. Certainly the offering of fleece is attested, and may underlie the gift of *ἱματισμός* to the prophets as high priests. The inclusion of money and every possession (*παντὸς κτήματος*) is surprising, especially in view of the reservations concerning apostles and prophets and money in *Did.* 11. It is not based on any specific Old Testament law, but on a general extension of the rule to give first-fruits to everything. However, the provision that all is subject to the conscience of the individual (*ὡς ἂν σοι δόξῃ*) is important, and is in line with the practice throughout the *Didache*, especially in chapters 6–7. Presumably the elders and deacons, who were appointed by the community itself (15. 1–2) and served in the fashion of the ancient world for *τιμή* and not for financial gain (which is why they must be *ἀφιλάργυροι*, 15. 2),[63] would have control of the allocation of the first-fruits, rather than the prophets and teachers themselves (11. 6, 12). They were given first to the 'religious poor' (i.e., those engaged full time in prophecy and teaching) and then, finances permitting, to the 'secular poor', the needy in general.

4. CONCLUSION

We have seen that the passage concerning first-fruits in *Did.* 13 has a coherence and a logic, which fits well with the text as a whole. The passage found not only here but also in Q and 1 Timothy, *ἄξιος ὁ ἐργάτης τοῦ μισθοῦ/τῆς*

[63] Draper, 'Social Ambiguity'.

τροφῆς αὐτοῦ is probably a free-floating proverb or midrash, which was known not only in the Christian communities but also more generally in early Judaism as well. The *Didache* is closest in its use of the saying, however, to Matthew, not just in the wording, but also in the concerns and the framework it provides. Matthew is concerned to avoid the idea of the apostle as working for a monetary wage: 'freely receive, freely give', while at the same time according the apostle the right of support on his or her travel. The *Didache* seems originally to have been concerned also with the right of apostles and the poor to support, both those travelling and also the apostles of the Lord in Jerusalem (both the 'poor saints' and the local poor). However, by the time of the final redaction, the right of support is given to prophets, teachers, and the poor. The support is given in terms of the first-fruits, which is primarily a matter of perishable food (*τροφή*), but which extends also to secondary production. While money and other durable goods (such as fleece or clothes) are likely to have been destined for Jerusalem, they remain on the list of first-fruits and are, potentially, in conflict with the prohibition on the apostles (11. 6) or prophets (11. 12) asking for money: *ὃς δ' ἂν εἴπῃ ἐν πνεύματι : δός μοι ἀργύρια ἢ ἕτερά τινα οὐκ ἀκούσεσθε αὐτοῦ.* However, it leaves room for the 'redemption' of materials which might be deemed liable to first-fruits, but which, for one reason or another, might not easily be given in kind.

In my opinion, the kind of situation underlying the instructions in the *Didache* on the first-fruits is presupposed by the Q tradition. It could not have been constructed from either Matthew or Luke's version as a source, but rather forms essential background material, together with the information from Paul in this case, for an understanding of that tradition. The *Didache* presents us with the kind of community practice in which a Q saying originated, prior to its incorporation into the gospel tradition, here as in many other instances. It is a form of Christian Jewish *halakah* designed to enable Jewish believers to admit, coexist, and share table-fellowship with Gentile believers, in one and the same community of faith, without severing their connection with the wider Jewish *ethnos.*

12

Social Locators as a Bridge between the *Didache* and Matthew

Clayton N. Jefford

Numerous studies have appeared since the rediscovery of the *Didache* which have sought to explain the historical or literary relationships between that text and the Gospel of Matthew. Such efforts have provided various solutions that, under the assumption that there was indeed some relationship between the two writings, may be classified into three broad possibilities.[1]

The first solution, and among the earliest suggestions toward a solution to the problem, is that the author of the *Didache* (i.e., the Didachist) both knew and used some form of the Gospel of Matthew. This approach typically dates the text no earlier than the second century, and assumes that parallels between the two writings are evidence that the Didachist has quoted from Matthean materials. A distinct advantage to this position is that the author of Matthew and the Didachist need not have worked within a single setting.[2]

A second, more recent view offers that the author of Matthew both knew and used materials that came to form the *Didache* and perhaps, as has been recently suggested, may have actually borrowed passages from the written version of the text itself.[3] This tack must necessarily date the *Didache* quite early in the evolution of early Christian literature, and even if one is unwilling to attribute some formalized version of the text to a 50–70 CE date, recognizes that the traditions of the text were quite ancient in their origins and in their

[1] For a broader survey of positions on the literary (in)dependence of the *Didache*, see J. D. Crossan, *The Birth of Christianity* (New York: HarperSanFrancisco, 1998), 363–406, and J. A. Draper, 'The Didache in Modern Research: An Overview', in J. A. Draper (ed.), *The* Didache *in Modern Research*, AGAJU 37 (Leiden: Brill, 1996), 16–24.

[2] This view has dominated the history of *Didache* research from the early writings of F. W. Farrar, 'The Bearing of the "Teaching" on the Canon', *Expositor*, 8 (1884), 81–91, to the more recent scholarship of C. M. Tuckett, 'Synoptic Tradition in the *Didache*', in J.-M. Sevrin (ed.), *The New Testament in Early Christianity*, BETL 86 (Leuven: Leuven University Press, 1989), 197–230.

[3] Thus the recent volume of A. J. P. Garrow, *The Gospel of Matthew's Dependence on the* Didache, JSNTSup 254 (London: T. & T. Clark International, 2004).

usage within the nascent church. An advantage of this perspective is that the late first-century author of Matthew must have come into contact with the *Didache* or its materials relatively quickly within the development of the New Testament, though most other canonical authors did not.[4]

A third position holds that the two texts arose more or less simultaneously, with the respective authors maintaining an awareness of materials and traditions that were incorporated into their counterpart's work. Adherents of this view are perhaps fewer than those of either of the other positions for various reasons, not the least of which is the difficulty that arises in efforts to offer conclusive proof for the likelihood of this solution. An advantage to this argument is that it sees the *Didache* and its materials as quite old; a disadvantage is that it strains to explain the specifics of the relationship between the author of Matthew and the Didachist, who presumably worked within a single community setting.

With the present essay I offer an additional argument in support of this third position that is directed toward the view that Matthew and the *Didache* contain common situational elements. Reflected in each work are historical moments and social indicators that characterize their evolution and vaguely define familiar community issues. Indeed, if some relationship between the two writings is to be seen as viable, then at least some such overlap should be expected.[5]

THE POSITION OF STEPHENSON H. BROOKS ON MATTHEW

In the 1987 publication of his dissertation,[6] Stephenson Brooks offers a relatively clear and concise summation of previous historical-critical examinations of Matthew that have taken two specific elements into consideration: the special nature of unique Matthean materials—that is, the so-called

[4] For a historical reconstruction that may also support this position, see M. Slee, *The Church in Antioch in the First Century CE*, JSNTSup 244 (London: T. & T. Clark International, 2003), 54–76, 118–25.

[5] This essay is my third approach to this topic in recent years, with previous efforts appearing in my 'Reflections on the Role of Jewish Christianity in Second-Century Antioch', in S. C. Mimouni and F. S. Jones (eds.), *Actes du colloque international: Le judéo-christianisme dans tous ses états* (Paris: Éditions du Cerf, 2001), 147–67, and 'The Milieu of Matthew, the Didache, and Ignatius of Antioch: Agreements and Differences', in H. van de Sandt (ed.), *Matthew and the Didache: Two Documents from the Same Jewish-Christian Milieu?* (Assen: Van Gorcum, 2005), 35–47.

[6] S. H. Brooks, *Matthew's Community: The Evidence of his Special Sayings Material*, JSNTSup 16 (Sheffield: Sheffield Academic Press, 1987). I have previously offered a brief summary of the Brooks hypothesis in my own published dissertation; see C. N. Jefford, *The Sayings of Jesus in the Teaching of the Twelve Apostles*, VCSup 11 (Leiden: Brill, 1989), 130–2.

M source—and the distinct likelihood that the Gospel of Matthew is the product of an evolutionary development through separate literary stages. Building on the work of B. H. Streeter, T. W. Manson, and G. D. Kilpatrick, Brooks seeks to identify through systematic analysis those materials within Matthew that can be identified as unique to the author of the gospel. He then employs these materials to reconstruct the historical steps of the evolving Matthean community.

In the summary of his research, Brooks settles upon three primary stages of development underlying the text of Matthew.[7] The first stage represents a community of Jewish Christians prior to 70 CE who were faithful to the synagogue but a challenge to its leadership. These messianic Jews anticipated the return of the Son of Man and focused their beliefs upon Palestine and the sayings of Jesus. The second stage is characterized by a time when this group found itself in conflict with the synagogue, having become somewhat well developed with respect to Christology and firm in its recognition of the authority of Jesus as the legitimate, eschatological lawgiver of God. The final stage represents the time of the evangelist himself, who, fixed firmly within the history of the broader community, incorporated the Gospel of Mark and the Q source into the broader M tradition in order to produce the gospel that we have today.

Brooks is convinced that the author of Matthew knew the M source materials in their oral form only, and that the construction of the gospel text ultimately broke the cycle of their oral transmission. With this acknowledgement in mind, he appeals to the observation of Werner Kelber that 'oral transmission is controlled by the law of *social identification* rather than by the technique of verbatim memorization',[8] by which he seeks to group the various sayings of the M materials into five separate traditions, the first three of which contain certain social locators of the developing community. The resulting traditions are identified as follows:

1. Matt. 5. 19, 21–2, 27–8, 33–5, 37; 12. 36–7; 18. 18; 19. 12 (?); 23. 8–10
2. Matt. 6. 1–6, 16–18; 23. 2–3, 5
3. Matt. 5. 23–4 (?); 23. 15, 16–22, 24, 33
4. Matt. 10. 5b–6, 23b
5. Matt. 6. 7–8; 7. 6[9]

Brooks assigns each grouping to a specific stage in the community's evolution. The collections of sayings in groups 2 and 4 are 'sayings representative of

[7] Brooks, *Matthew's Community*, 119–23.

[8] W. H. Kelber, *The Oral and the Written Gospel* (Philadelphia: Fortress, 1983), 24 (emphasis original).

[9] Brooks, *Matthew's Community*, 109–10.

a tradition coming from a Christian Jewish group'; groups 3 and 5 are 'sayings from an interim period'; and group 1 is 'sayings representative of a tradition coming from a Jewish Christian community'.[10] Through his analysis of 'social indicators' for each grouping, he thus concludes that the Matthean community was composed of several parties of divergent Christians, who maintained oral traditions that were preserved and reinterpreted—a process that was interrupted to some extent by the composition of the Gospel of Matthew. It is the 'historicizing' element of the gospel that ultimately served to bind these various oral traditions together into a literary unity.

Based upon his analysis of Matt. 10 and 23, Brooks describes the specific view of Christian history that was shared by the Matthean redactor and the community from which the M tradition was derived.[11] One finds in these chapters the gradual removal of the authority of the Jewish leaders from their influence upon the faith community of the evolving messianic consciousness of the Matthean community. These leaders were judged for their false interpretations of the Jewish tradition, for their behaviour with respect to that tradition, and for their persecution of the 'Christian prophets' who had criticized their shortcomings. According to Brooks, one finds within these materials 'four distinct historical stages in the relationship between the contemporary readers of specific sayings and the Jewish community':

> (1) the reader's religious life is circumscribed by the authority of the Jewish synagogue leaders; (2) in antithesis to this circumscribed position, the reader is subject only to the authority of Jesus as teacher and Christ, and God as Father; (3) the reader is given an explanation of the new position firstly with reference to the invalid interpretation and religious behavior of the synagogue rulers, and secondly with reference to their overt persecution of members of the community of Jesus; (4) finally, the reader's ties with Judaism/Israel are severed.[12]

In the final analysis of this development, the separation between the Jews and the Matthean community occurred because the Christians were rejected by the synagogue leaders.

STAGES IN THE HISTORY OF THE *DIDACHE*

In a little over a century of research upon the text of the *Didache*, a variety of opinions have been raised with respect to the formation and editing of the text. These views vary widely, and reflect a growing understanding of the

[10] Brooks, *Matthew's Community*, 120–3, 188–91.
[11] Ibid. 115–19. [12] Ibid. 117.

nature of the work and its function within the apostolic and post-apostolic church. In certain respects, particularly with reference to the suggestions and influence of Jean-Paul Audet,[13] the second half of the twentieth century witnessed the rise of a belief that the *Didache* itself represents the product of various stages of compilation. The secondary literature of the period reflects the academic efforts that have been undertaken to identify these stages and the sources of their formative materials. And while there has certainly been some disagreement in this process, one might safely offer a general understanding of the divisions of the text according to such a process.[14]

In general, those students of the text who have argued for literary divisions have accepted that the so-called evangelical materials of 1. 3b–2. 1 are not original to the text. Numerous arguments have been set forth that the unique quality of these sayings within the materials of the *Didache*, together with their more obvious dependence upon sayings that are known in similar form from Matthew and Luke, suggest their presence within the text as an addition.[15]

Similar arguments have been offered with respect to the concluding collection of apocalyptic materials in the final chapter of the *Didache*, though the situation is somewhat more complicated there. On the one hand, the sayings of chapter 16 seem to reflect some awareness of the synoptic tradition, as with 1. 3b–2. 1 above. Yet, as Paul Drews suggested a century ago,[16] there may be some reason to speculate that these apocalyptic materials originally formed the conclusion of an even longer series of collected sayings, a collection that can now be identified within the rough parameters of *Did.* 1–5 (6). Indeed, the original framework of the traditions that composed the sayings trajectory underlying the *Didache* could easily have included chapters 1–6 and 16 together without any essential change in the nature of the materials that appear there.

[13] J.-P. Audet, *La Didachè: Instructions des Apôtres*, ÉBib (Paris: Gabalda, 1958).

[14] I hasten to add here that a focus upon the literary construction of the text according to historical stages has not been unanimously supported. Indeed, the work of Kurt Niederwimmer suggests instead that the *Didache* is the product of separate source traditions, though not the evolution of historical editing; see, e.g., his *Die Didache*, 2nd edn. (Göttingen: Vandenhoeck & Ruprecht, 1993; ET Minneapolis: Fortress, 1998), and his subsequent article, 'Der Didachist und seine Quellen', in C. N. Jefford (ed.), *The* Didache *in Context*, NovTSup 77 (Leiden: Brill, 1995), 15–36. One must also take into account the question of the oral nature of the text, arguments for which have been undertaken in recent years through the work of I. H. Henderson; see, e.g., his '*Didache* and Orality in Synoptic Comparison', *JBL* 111 (1992), 283–306, and 'Style-Switching in the *Didache*: Fingerprint or Argument?', in Jefford (ed.), Didache *in Context*, 177–209.

[15] The best-known argument based upon this view was offered by B. Layton, 'The Sources, Date, and Transmission of *Didache* 1.3b–2.1', *HTR* 61 (1968), 343–83.

[16] P. Drews, 'Untersuchungen zur Didache', *ZNW* 5 (1904), 53–79. See also the later discussion of E. Bammel, 'Schema und Vorlage von *Didache* 16', in F. L. Cross (ed.), *StPatr* 4, TU 79 (Berlin: Akademie-Verlag, 1961), 253–62.

This brings us, then, to the question of the sayings that lie within *Did.* 1–5. These materials are clearly different from what appears in chapters 7–15, which have been identified as either liturgical or ecclesiastical in form. Parallels to the sayings of chapters 1–5 are found in *Barn.* 18–20 and in the Latin *Doctrina Apostolorum*, which may suggest that these materials evolved from a teaching tradition that circulated separately from the remaining chapters at some early stage in the development of the *Didache.*[17] Various arguments have been offered during the last century to explain how these texts have intertwined in the literary history of the tradition, but most scholars now agree that they represent a diverse source (either oral, written, or mixed) that was used by multiple church communities in one context or another.

Apart from this collection of teachings in chapters 1–5, the liturgical and ecclesiastical traditions of chapters 7–15 seem to form a separate unit, at least by genre. Contained within these chapters is a collection of diverse traditions associated with various liturgical matters: namely, baptism, prayer, ritual food events, and public worship. Also found here are ecclesiastical instructions that offer directions on how to receive travelling apostles, how to evaluate the quality of a teacher's spirit, how to appoint worthy community leaders, and how to engage prophets of the Lord.

Between the materials of chapters 1–5 and 7–15 falls a brief segment that serves to conclude the opening materials and provide a bridge to the latter section. This is a particularly interesting chapter, which clearly reflects the issues addressed in the famous 'apostolic decree' from the Jerusalem council that is portrayed in Acts 15. The primary concern here is the question of foods that are acceptable for responsible Christians to eat. And the answer is the same as in Acts: that the true believer should refrain from eating food that has been offered to false gods as actions of piety.[18]

In summary, then, we might say that students of the *Didache* have often identified a variety of possible layers behind the text that may suggest differing historical milieus or developments within a single community. These include the materials of 1. 1–3a with 2. 2–5. 1 (and perhaps some or all of 6. 1–3), the passages in 6. 1–3, 7. 1–15. 4, 16. 1–8 (perhaps combined with 1. 1–5. 1), and the addition of 1. 3b–2. 1. While scholars have often agreed upon some of

[17] Certainly this is suggested by their usage in the later *Rule of Benedict* and book 7 of the *Apostolic Constitutions.*

[18] See D. Flusser, 'Paul's Jewish-Christian Opponents in the *Didache*', in S. Shaked, D. Shulman, and G. G. Stroumsa (eds.), *Gilgul: Essays on Transformation, Revolution and Permanence in the History of Religions, Dedicated to R. J. Zwi Werblowsky*, Studies in the History of Religions, supplements to Numen, 50 (Leiden: Brill, 1987), 71–90; J. A. Draper, 'Torah and Troublesome Apostles in the *Didache* Community', *NovT* 33 (1991), 347–72; Slee, *Church in Antioch*, 83–90.

these divisions, more often there is considerable debate about the limits that should be assigned to individual sections and whether the identification of divisions suggests literary evolution.

DEVELOPING THE BROOKS HYPOTHESIS BESIDE THE VIEW OF AN EVOLVING *DIDACHE*

It must be observed from the outset that the historical strata that Brooks reconstructs for the community of Matthew based on the M source find little parallel with corresponding materials in the *Didache*. Indeed, his M materials from groups 2 and 4 ('sayings representative of a tradition coming from a Christian Jewish group') find a parallel only in *Did.* 8. 2a (Matt. 6. 1–6) and 15. 4 (Matt. 6. 16–18). His M materials from groups 3 and 5 ('sayings from an interim period') find a parallel only in *Did.* 2. 2–3 (Matt. 5. 23–4), 9. 5 (Matt. 7. 6), and perhaps 15. 4 again (Matt. 6. 7–8). His M materials from group 1 ('sayings representative of a tradition coming from a Jewish Christian community') find a parallel only in *Did.* 2. 2–3 (Matt. 5. 27–8). Furthermore, the few materials that may be included here are primarily traditional in scope and include passing references to the Decalogue, the nature of prayer, and the need to keep holy items from dogs. As a surface comparison of sources, this is hardly impressive.

A more pronounced development of the Brooks hypothesis leads us in a somewhat more positive direction, however. In a paper delivered at Tilburg University in 2003, Wim Weren combined the efforts of Brooks with the work of Antony Saldarini and David Sim to advance a similar reconstruction of the Matthean situation.[19] Like Brooks, Weren distinguished three stages in the evolution of the Matthean community, but with more of a focus upon the details of the tradition. Weren's first stage includes sayings of Jesus that circulated prior to the year 70, that were profoundly Jewish in character, and that find no parallel in either Mark or Q. His second stage is best represented by the editorial work of the Matthean redactor who, working in the 80s, incorporated the influence of Mark and Q upon the unique tradition of the Matthean community's materials. Finally, his third stage reveals the last redactional level of Matthew at the end of the 80s, a time when the community had separated from its original Jewish context to form a separate, unique

[19] This paper has now been published: W. Weren, 'The History and Social Setting of the Matthean Community', in H. van de Sandt (ed.), *The Didache and Matthew: Two Documents from the Same Jewish Christian Milieu?* (Assen: Van Gorcum, 2005), 31–62.

identity. A consideration of Weren's extension of the Brooks hypothesis reveals a ready foundation for similar materials in the *Didache*. And it is here that we encounter materials that, while not included by Brooks as strata of the M source, are clearly unique to Matthew's cache of resources.[20]

The Matthean materials that find close parallels in the *Didache* may be grouped into a variety of forms. In the first instance there are materials that could easily have circulated freely in the early Christian tradition as isolated sayings.[21] While they have been attributed to the historical Jesus in most cases, they could have been associated with any Jewish sage or prophet. For the purposes of reconstruction, we should focus upon those materials that find obvious parallels only in Matthew among the New Testament gospels. Most noticeable here are sayings such as 'be meek, for the meek shall inherit the earth' (3. 7), and 'do not give anything holy to dogs' (9. 5). Of second consideration are liturgical elements that find specific parallels in Matthew. These include materials such as the instruction to 'baptize in the name of the Father and of the Son and of the Holy Spirit' (7. 1, 3) and the so-called Lord's Prayer in its Matthean form (8. 2). Finally, there are general instructions in the *Didache* whose application finds parallels in Matthew. Specifically, here we discover instructions about community correction in 15. 3 that are clearly reflected in Matt. 18. 15–35. There is also a general call to conduct prayers and give alms in 15. 4 that may be joined with a critique of the fasting of the hypocrites in 8. 1, texts that are likewise clearly reflected in content, if not in context, in Matt. 6. 1–18.

What is particularly distressing about this consideration of the Brooks hypothesis is the suggestion that there are in reality only a limited number of true, specific parallels between actual sayings that appear both in Matthew and in the *Didache*. Yet, as any good student of early Christian literature knows, there is more to textual comparison than simple quotations that exist in common between documents. Indeed, it is within the background of the remaining material that the glue between the *Didache* and Matthew becomes most readily apparent.[22]

[20] Though further developed in later studies, a clear list of parallels in addition to those suggested by Brooks may be found in J. M. Court, 'The Didache and St. Matthew's Gospel', *SJT* 34 (1981), 109–20. Also now, see Garrow, *Matthew's Dependence*, 243.

[21] So the premiss of H. Köster, *Synoptische Überlieferung bei den Apostolischen Vätern*, TU 65 (Berlin: Akademie-Verlag, 1957), 159–241.

[22] It is specifically in this respect that the present essay seeks to address the weaknesses of the basic text-critical approach to the relationship of the New Testament and the Apostolic Fathers that the current volume seeks to celebrate: i.e., A Committee of the Oxford Society of Historical Theology, *The New Testament in the Apostolic Fathers* (Oxford: Clarendon Press, 1905).

The clearest indication of additional texts that must be considered occurs with respect to the question of sayings. Thus, to the specific parallels that have been cited above, we must certainly add the opening lines of the *Didache*: namely, 'there are two ways, one of life and one of death' (1. 1), 'love the God who made you' (1. 2a), 'love your neighbor as yourself' (1. 2b), and 'whatever you would not have done to you, do not do to another' (1. 2c). These sayings are widespread throughout the common traditions of Judaism, with prominent parallels to be found in Deut. 30. 19; 6. 5, Lev. 19. 18; and Tobit 4. 15, respectively. There are, of course, parallels to these sayings in Matthew, specifically at 7. 13–14, 22. 37 and 39, and 7. 12. But attempts to assign a connection between the *Didache* and Matthew here tend to fall prey to two objections: first, that the first and last materials are from the Q source (see Luke 13. 23–4 and 6. 31); second, that the middle materials are from the Marcan source (see Mark 12. 29, 31; Luke 10. 27). For those who desire to maintain a strict dependence upon literary traditions, this does indeed seem to present a major problem. But here we should recall that sayings circulated in antiquity in numerous forms and were collected in different locales in various contexts. Indeed, I have attempted to demonstrate elsewhere that the so-called 'two ways' saying of *Did.* 1. 1 is actually found only in Matthew within the New Testament literature, since the Lucan parallel is not concerned with the same concept: that is, two distinct choices in life. So too, and in the same place, I have argued that the author of Matthew was aware of the sayings of love of God and neighbour from a source other than that which is represented in Mark. Furthermore, the Matthean conclusion to each saying ('for this is the law and the prophets') suggests that the author of the gospel text may have recognized that these three sayings together represented the complete teaching of a specific tradition, at least for the Matthean community.[23]

From the beginning of the *Didache* we may easily move to the conclusion of the work. Further sayings are evident in the final chapter of the writing, materials that find a clear parallel in the apocalyptic section of Matthew. It is certainly true that the author of Matthew appears to be heavily dependent upon the Gospel of Mark for his basic framework, and this would seem to hold true as well of Matthew's dependence upon Mark 13 for the structure of materials in Matthew 23–5. But, as John Kloppenborg convincingly argued some twenty-five years ago,[24] the apocalyptic material that appears in the *Didache* 'shows no dependence upon either Mark (or his source) or Matthew,

[23] For the extended discussion, see Jefford, *Sayings of Jesus*, 22–9, 146–59.

[24] J. S. Kloppenborg, 'Didache 16: 6–8 and Special Matthean Tradition', *ZNW* 70 (1979), 54–67. See, however, Tuckett, 'Synoptic Tradition', and V. Balabanski, *Eschatology in the Making: Mark, Matthew and the Didache*, SNTSMS 97 (Cambridge: Cambridge University Press, 1997), 210.

but rather seems to represent a tradition upon which Matthew drew'.[25] Indeed, it would thus seem that the evidence of materials within the *Didache* itself suggests the presence of both sapiential and apocalyptic sayings that find clear and true parallels within the M materials of Matthew.

From the beginning to the end of the *Didache*, therefore, we discover a tendency to incorporate specific sayings that are in some sense unique to, or typical of, the Matthean M tradition. That is to say, there are certain materials that are common to both writings, and these materials reflect tendencies that are unique among the New Testament gospels. The question that follows, then, is whether we might attribute these materials to a common source that was shared by both authors. If this is in fact true, we must question the nature of that source.

Typical of the materials that appear in *Did.* 1. 1–2 and 16. 3–8 is a heavy dependence upon Old Testament texts and Jewish traditions. This holds true not only for the opening lines and concluding chapter of the text, materials that may originally have derived from the same early layer of the *Didache* construction, but for sayings that stem from other divisions of the work as well. For example, in 1. 3b we find the saying on love of enemies that is attributed to the Q source (Matt. 7. 12 // Luke 6. 31), but that may find its ultimate roots in Tobit 12. 8. And in 1. 6 we find a saying on alms that is clearly dependent upon Sir. 12. 1. These materials come from what is widely recognized as the latest addition to the text of the *Didache*, that is, 1. 3b–2. 1, which would mark a general tendency throughout the text to draw from Old Testament-based materials, a propensity that thus spans the earliest layer of the writing to its most recent addition.

Similar tendencies occur throughout the remaining materials of the *Didache*: namely, the dependence upon the Decalogue of Exod. 20. 13–16 (in *Did.* 2. 2–3; 3. 2–6; and 5. 1), a command not to hate based upon Lev. 19. 17–18 (in 2. 7), the blessing of the meek from Ps. 37. 11 (in 3. 7), and some instruction for those who come in the name of the Lord from Ps. 118. 26 (in 12. 1). Such sayings, dependent upon Old Testament traditions, span both the so-called catechetical materials of *Did.* 1–5 and the ecclesiastical materials of *Did.* 11–15. Their presence argues that use of such traditions within the *Didache* extends not only from the earliest to the latest layers of the text, but across the boundaries of the different genres of literature that appear throughout.

Into this mix one may add a variety of traditions that reflect specific Jewish traditions that seem to have been in evidence within the early church. Scholars have traditionally focused much of their research energy in

[25] Kloppenborg, 'Didache 16', 66.

these areas.[26] Most apparent among these traditions are materials that include comments upon the nature of baptism in *Did.* 7,[27] considerations of the role of fasting and prayer within the community as found in *Did.* 8,[28] and especially use of early Jewish meal-prayers and food rituals in *Did.* 9–10.[29] One may easily find countless examples of research into the Jewish nature of materials in the *Didache*, studies that focus upon specific relationships of the text with the Gospel of Matthew, contemporary Jewish sects, and the Dead Sea Scrolls. Ultimately, it appears that evidence of Jewish links between the situation and concerns of the Didachist and those of the author of Matthew are irrefutable. And the basis of those links is the concern with Jewish sources and traditions that appear in both works, somewhat uniquely among the documents of early Christian literature.

What is suggested here is that, if one can actually identify evolving stages of Matthew based upon the community's relationship to Judaism, and, if one can accept developmental stages of the *Didache* based upon editorial adaptation, then there must be some commonality of elements that can be seen to unite the works, provided that they stem from the same community situation. The clearest associations are indicated through the dependence upon Old Testament sources in uniquely shared materials, on the one hand, and the preponderance of concern for Jewish traditions of training, liturgy, and community structure, on the other. What is perhaps most remarkable about these links, at least with respect to the *Didache*, is that they are apparent throughout the entire work, regardless of whether the materials appear in those chapters that are sometimes associated with the earlier stages of the writing or with the later stages. So too, they are found throughout the writing, regardless of the genre of materials that is employed, whether sapiential, liturgical, ecclesiastical, or apocalyptic. If we are to accept the development of the Brooks hypothesis, particularly as illustrated by the argument of Weren, and to apply it to some proposal for the developmental stages of the *Didache*,

[26] For a brief, general review, see Draper, 'Didache in Modern Research', 24–31.

[27] See W. Rordorf, 'Le Baptême selon la *Didaché*', in *Mélanges liturgiques offerts au R. P. Dom Bernard Botte O.S.B.* (Louvain: Abbaye du Mont César, 1972), 499–509; ET 'Baptism according to the Didache', in Draper (ed.), *The* Didache *in Modern Research*, 212–22.

[28] See J. A. Draper, 'Christian Self-Definition against the "Hypocrites" in *Didache* 8', in E. H. Lovering (ed.), *Society of Biblical Literature 1992 Seminar Papers* (Atlanta: Scholars Press, 1992), 362–77.

[29] See J. M. Robinson, 'Die Hodajot-Formel in Gebet und Hymnus des Früchristentums', in *Apophoreta, Festschrift für E. Haenchen*, BZNW 30 (Berlin: Alfred Töpelmann, 1964), 194–235; J. Betz, 'Die Eucharistie in der Didache', *Archiv für Liturgiewissenschaft*, 11 (1969), 10–39; ET 'The Eucharist in the *Didache*', in Draper (ed.), *The* Didache *in Modern Research*, 244–75; and E. Mazza, 'Didaché IX–X: Elementi per una interpretazione Eucaristica', *Ephemerides Liturgicae*, 92 (1979), 393–419; ET 'Didache 9–10: Elements of a Eucharistic Interpretation', in Draper (ed.), *The* Didache *in Modern Research*, 276–99.

then we must somehow explain the consistency of these materials throughout the text of the *Didache*.

It is proposed here that the most favourable solution to these circumstances can be found in recognizing that the segment of the community that produced the *Didache* remained consistent in its ancient understanding of Christianity alongside the evolving perspective of the author of Matthew, who represented a progressive movement within the same community. In other words, while the author of Matthew produced a gospel of ideological progression, the Didachist produced a reactionary text of ideological regression. It is to that divide that we now turn.

THE SOCIOLOGY OF JEWISH–CHRISTIAN RELATIONS IN FIRST-CENTURY ANTIOCH

In his recent book on the rise of Christianity in first-century Antioch, Magnus Zetterholm has offered some intriguing socio-political insights into the situation of that ancient city, whose setting could have offered the occasion for significant links between Matthew and the *Didache*.[30] These insights are related to the role of Judaism within the city during the rise of our texts, evidence for interaction between Jews and Christians there, and the politics of persecution that drove that interaction.

Zetterholm notes what others have observed before him as the foundation for his analysis of the Antiochean situation: that is, that there was a strong Jewish community within the city, perhaps from its foundation, and that the influence of the synagogue remained prevalent at least until the end of the first century.[31] The city was certainly capable of supporting a number of synagogues,[32] much like the numerous parallel situations in other large cities throughout the Diaspora. These synagogues would have served as the centres of Jewish life and culture, having as their primary purpose the support of 'prayers, study and the teaching of scripture on the Sabbath'.[33] At the same time, of course, there would have been a thriving non-religious dimension to life within the synagogue, whose function as an organization was to support

[30] See M. Zetterholm, *The Formation of Christianity in Antioch* (London and New York: Routledge, 2003).

[31] Ibid. 31–42.

[32] So M. Hengel and A. M. Schwemer, *Paul between Damascus and Antioch: The Unknown Years* (London: SCM Press, 1997), 186.

[33] Zetterholm, *Formation*, 38. Zetterholm offers this perspective based upon the work of D. D. Binder, *Into the Temple Courts: The Place of the Synagogue in the Second Temple Period* (Atlanta: Society of Biblical Literature, 1999), 449.

community activities, including the collection of funds for charity, opportunities for shared meals, and the settlement of legal disputes. The presence of synagogues would have served both a religious and a civic function for local Jews.

Zetterholm presses forward in his reconstruction of the Antiochean situation through an adaptation of M. M. Gordon's analysis of cultural assimilation in modern American culture.[34] While he admits that there are few sources for knowledge of the Jewish cultural situation in Antioch, he suggests three general patterns that were probably at work within the community: religion became optional to a limited degree; some individuals intensified their religious identity, while others chose to assimilate into the majority society; and religious institutions assumed new formations.[35] The primary factor for those who assimilated to the broader society around them was the availability of structural compatibility: that is, the convenient opportunity to intermesh familiar structures with models that were more broadly recognized within the wider community. At the same time, there would have been many Jews who would have reacted negatively to such 'opportunities', choosing instead to reform the boundaries of their traditional faith and culture into a more Torah-obedient perspective. Zetterholm observes that such opposing tendencies within the wider Jewish community were more likely to have been divided and scattered among different synagogues, with the result that a single ideology tended to dominate individual locations.

What becomes a paramount issue, then, is the likely interaction between the Jews of Antioch and the broader non-Jewish society. Zetterholm offers an intriguing investigation into the various aspects of cultural, religious, and political struggle that ensued, and observes that a key element in the early churches that arose within such a setting was the need to address the question of self-identification, either pro-Jewish or anti-Jewish.[36] In the midst of this interaction and struggle, he argues that the Gospel of Matthew reflects the movements of this very location and its times.[37] Matthew stands between the original setting of Jewish Christianity in Antioch and the social movement that Bishop Ignatius led in an effort to separate the church from its Jewish roots. As Zetterholm states:

> It would not be too bold a hypothesis to assume that the presence of the Jewish Gospel of Matthew in the hands of the Gentile non-Jewish and even anti-Jewish community of Ignatius in some way represents a culmination of the process of transition from a Jewish to a Gentile setting.[38]

[34] Zetterholm, *Formation*, 67–100. See M. M. Gordon, *Assimilation in American Life: The Role of Race, Religion, and National Origins* (New York: Oxford University Press, 1973 [1964]).

[35] Zetterholm, *Formation*, 97.

[36] Ibid. 112–224. See also Slee, *Church in Antioch*, 12–35.

[37] Zetterholm, *Formation*, 211–16.

[38] Ibid. 212.

On the one hand, the Gospel of Matthew reflects the early Antiochean church's conflict with formative Judaism. At the same time, the text was employed by Ignatius as the launching point from which to break from the very Matthean community that produced it. Thus the gospel became an 'ideological resource' for the Matthean community, which believed heavily in the teachings of Jesus. But the gospel's inherent conflict with Pharisaic Judaism and its successors became the basis for the Ignatian rejection of any Judaic influence within the developing church.

In the summary and implications of his findings, Zetterholm brings a number of interesting conclusions to his analysis of the first-century situation of the church in Antioch.[39] He finds in Antioch that there was principally a division between 'Jesus-believing Jews' and 'Jesus-believing Gentiles'. The position of Paul regarding this division—that is, that non-Jews should be included within the covenant of Judaism—would have been seen as 'an attractive solution' to the latter group, but 'a serious threat' to the former. The 'Jesus-believing Gentiles' who associated with their Jewish counterparts, in an effort to avoid their legal obligations to the cultic religion of the state, most likely pretended to be Jews. The struggles that resulted within the Antiochean church, then, became a complicated effort to define the role of this group of believers and to develop an understanding of the relationships that could make them an acceptable part of the local Christian setting. Ultimately, as he concludes,

> In this study we have found evidence of Jews who wanted to become Gentiles, and of Gentiles who wanted to become Jews. We have found evidence of other Jews who, by becoming Jesus-believers, found a way *to cease being Jewish.* While some Gentiles originally joined the Jesus movement because of a profound interest in Judaism, other Gentiles within the same movement later *wanted to separate from Judaism and establish a non-Jewish religion.*[40]

THE *DIDACHE* AND MATTHEW AT WORK IN THE SAME COMMUNITY

The analysis that Zetterholm offers to our study is most interesting in that it provides a contextual framework for the evolution of first-century Christianity at Antioch that permits a sociological explanation for the role of the

[39] Zetterholm, *Formation*, 231–5.

[40] Ibid. 234 (emphasis original). The gravity of 'faith switching' is particularly acute with the recognition that Rome's persecution of illegal religions in the late first century often revolved around the issue of paying specific religious taxes; see M. Sordi, *The Christians and the Roman Empire* (ET London and Norman, Okla.: University of Oklahoma Press, 1986), 38–54, esp. 48–9.

Didache within the city. Strictly speaking, Zetterholm himself does not entertain this idea, yet he provides the method that I wish to utilize here.

If it is indeed true that the religious situation in Antioch was one in which Christianity evolved from strict Jewish roots through the influence of Pauline theology and the addition of non-Jewish believers who were attracted in various ways to messianic Judaism, then the response to that non-Jewish attraction would have been most significant. Zetterholm argues that the Jewish response would have varied throughout the city according to individual synagogues, each of which would have been motivated by a general ideology that would have either accepted the presence of non-Jews ('God-fearers') or rejected them.[41] So too, one might expect to see a similar process at work among the evolving house churches of the city, religious centres of Jesus-believing Jews whose response to the presence of non-Jews would have varied from one location to another. As Zetterholm reconstructs the resulting situation, he notes that the portion of the Antiochean church that produced the Gospel of Matthew found itself at the centre of two points of tension: first, in forming an identity in conflict with formative Judaism; secondly, as a tool for those who wished to free Christianity from its Jewish roots altogether.

What is not discerned in this reconstruction is any recognition that those Jews who were attracted to Christianity, yet who wished to maintain their Jewish identity, may have compiled their own collection of Antiochean traditions, including the sayings of Jesus and the unique liturgical and ecclesiastical practices of local Christianity. One might expect these materials to be composed of ancient traditions that were somewhat unique, either in form or in substance, to the Christian situation in Antioch, of course.[42] And if we can already place Matthew within the Antiochean setting, then we might assume that the majority of those local traditions would be reflected in the so-called M source materials of that gospel text. There need not be any assumption that the other sources for the Gospel of Matthew would be present within that collection of materials, sources such as Mark and Q, though their presence might indeed be noticed, depending upon the date of the collection and editing of the text itself. Nor should we assume that the Antiochean materials that appear in this collection would necessarily be used in the same manner or context as Matthew might have used them. In fact, because the interpretation of such materials was in dispute, one would expect them to

[41] Indeed, the popularity of Judaism among 'proselytes' in the city was likely a strong motivation for the anti-Semitism that arose there in the late first century; so E. M. Smallwood, *The Jews under Roman Rule*, SJLA 20 (Leiden: Brill, 1981), 360–2.

[42] Hence the conclusions of Slee, *Church in Antioch*, 158 ('whenever the Didachist utilizes the same tradition as the Evangelist he preserves it in its more primitive form').

appear in somewhat different contexts, used for divergent purposes.[43] Finally, while it would be nice to be able to point to a primary list of sayings and traditions that appear both in this hypothetical source and in Matthew's own M materials, there need not be too much of an explicit, extensive connection to suggest an association between the writings. The overt connections may justifiably be minimal. For while the author of Matthew incorporated local materials and traditions into a gospel structure, modelled upon the Gospel of Mark and supplemented by the Q source for the specific purpose of identifying Christianity apart from Judaism (but within the light of Judaism), the Didachist marshalled those same materials and traditions as a conservative backlash against the rising trend of Matthew's progressive understanding of the faith.

The socio-political situation that Zetterholm describes and the appearance and relationship of materials common to Matthew that would be suggested for our source, seems to apply precisely to the situation that occurs with respect to the *Didache*. While Zetterholm does not address the question of a second literary development of source materials that may have existed within the Antiochean church, apart from those that are now preserved in Matthew, his community reconstruction certainly leaves room for such a text. Indeed, the parameters of such materials might easily fit those that are now identified in the *Didache*, if that writing may be attributed to some specific segment of the church community that wanted to preserve specific local Jesus-oriented traditions within their Jewish context. It is certainly conceivable that many local Christian Jews would have seen the imposition of outside sources and traditions as a disruption of the original practices of the religious community, and their efforts to resist that influence would have been a natural response.

The situation that I propose for the placement of the *Didache* with relation to the Gospel of Matthew and within the Antiochean setting seems to fit the following scenario, at least as it might be presented in the light of the speculation of Brooks, Weren, and Zetterholm specifically. If we can accept the premiss of Brooks that the evolution of the Matthean community may be understood through the author/editor's use of materials that were specific to the community (the so-called M source), then we have a framework by which to understand that the community grew into its ultimate Matthean form as it struggled to identify itself apart from the synagogue. The use of specific M materials provides some sort of framework for understanding the stages by which this occurred. As this applies to the *Didache*, and the hypothesis that it too is the product of an evolutionary process, there is little specific content

[43] *Contra* the conclusions of A. Milavec, 'Synoptic Tradition in the *Didache* Revisited', *JECS* 11 (2003), 478–80.

that is shared between what Brooks identifies as M materials in Matthew and what is preserved throughout the layers of the Didachist's own text. Admittedly, Brooks is somewhat restrictive in his identification of M materials, preferring to focus upon sets of materials rather than upon isolated aphorisms.

With these limitations in mind, we may turn to the adaptations that Weren makes to the Brooks hypothesis. A primary contribution is the recognition that the M materials are heavily Jewish in form and orientation. In other words, it is not sufficient simply to identify the M materials as the delimiters of the stages that the Matthean community underwent in its separation from Judaism. Instead, it is necessary to recognize that those materials were most at home within the context of their Jewish setting. As Weren offers in his conclusions, 'Matthew tried to stimulate the social cohesion in his community by uniting the various subgroups around the interpretation of the Torah offered by Jesus and further cultivated by the community's local leaders.'[44] Such an attempt to rally around the Torah could not have been seen as a feasible project except to the extent that the author of Matthew recognized that the Torah remained a legitimate authority for the gospel's hearers. The development of the Matthean community, therefore, is not to be viewed strictly as an evolution away from Judaism itself, though it was interpreted as such by Ignatius and his followers. Instead, the Gospel of Matthew offers a transition moment away from what its author viewed to be the 'false' leadership of Judaism and the religious perspectives that such leadership endorsed, perspectives that did not condone the recognition of Jesus of Nazareth as the promised messiah of Israel.

Finally, we turn to the work of Zetterholm and its implications for the role of the *Didache*. Here we find that the Antiochean situation was one in which Jews who believed in Jesus came into contact with non-Jews with the same basic beliefs. These believing Jews found themselves in the midst of an anxious situation, with a choice to become 'less Jewish' in their orientation toward their gathering Christian convictions. So too, the believing non-Jews were in a similar struggle, with a choice to become 'more Jewish' in their own orientation. For various social and political reasons, the members of both groups made decisions in either direction. The Gospel of Matthew represents the literary understanding of one segment of that Christian community that stood somewhere in the middle of the debate. Ignatius offers slightly later materials that indicate the direction that he intended to pull the church in his effort to break with Judaism altogether, indicating the path that Christianity was ultimately destined to take.

[44] Weren, 'History and Social Setting', 62.

At the same time, if there were Jews in Antioch who constructed ideological defences against the rising tide of messianic fervour that swept the city in the first century, then it is also very likely that there were Jewish Christians who took a similar stance against the influence of non-Jewish Christians. These more conservative churches would have held fast to a principle that was represented by the Jewish teachings and traditions that characterized Christianity, at least as they had always known it. Their Jesus was thoroughly Jewish, defined in a low christological sense by the teachings of the Torah that appeared in the Pentateuch, Psalms, and Proverbs. Traditional forms of prayer, concerns for fasting and proselyte baptism, questions regarding the giving of the first-fruits of their labours to the righteous prophets and leaders of God characterized their rituals. They would have maintained a sense of Jewish identity that would have exceeded that which is represented by the Gospel of Matthew. At the same time, however, they may have purposefully chosen to break with many traditional trappings of the synagogue in an effort to give concrete definition to their messianic consciousness. This would undoubtedly have represented more of an institutional transition than an ideological one, and would surely have characterized the very type of perspective against which Paul objected in Galatians.

The *Didache* offers a number of suggestive elements to this type of historical reconstruction. In the first instance, we see that the elements of the source tradition that the Didachist has utilized extend beyond the minimal definition of M source materials that appear in Matthew. The M source materials are highly Jewish in character, are easily identified with the ministry of any rabbinic teacher, are represented in both the sapiential and apocalyptic genres of the text, and are scattered broadly among the liturgical and ecclesiastical segments of the work.

Secondly, we find that, even if the text of the *Didache* may be broken up into historical layers that found their way into the original *Vorlage* of the work, these layers need not have extended over a particularly long period of time. Indeed, if the Gospel of Matthew represents a transition within the Antiochean church from pre-70s traditions to a final phase between the years 80 and 90, as Weren and others suggest, then the evolution of the *Didache* itself could have easily fallen within that same period. Most noticeably in this regard, while the *Didache* seems to pay little attention to the materials of Mark or Q that were used by the author of Matthew to shape both the framework (= Mark) and the teachings (= Mark/Q/M) that now characterize the Matthean gospel, this does not mean that the Didachist was unaware of those separate sources. On the contrary, the Didachist undoubtedly represented a segment of the Antiochean church that knew, yet rejected, such 'outside sources' of inspiration, while Matthew actually preferred them to the local M materials in most cases. At the same time, it was ultimately possible for the Didachist's community to acknowledge the validity of a source tradition like Q, as appears to be evident from the editorial addition at *Did.* 1. 3b–2. 1.

Finally, many of the traditional issues that have scandalized those who have sought to link the *Didache* and Matthew are no longer valid. For example, the acknowledged fact that the author of Matthew and the Didachist employed the same materials in different contexts now seems reasonable on the assumption that both authors cherished the materials, but in different ways. It is true that their views of the materials were radically different. But this divergent use of familiar traditions is what one might expect from competing factions within the same community. Further, it also makes sense that the liturgical rituals that appear in the *Didache* for observing the Eucharist are not those that appear in Matthew. Matthew represents the tradition of Mark in an almost wooden sense, whereas the *Didache* may have preserved the ritual as originally observed among the first Jewish congregations of the city. It is certainly possible that the prayers of the *Didache* and the words of institution of the Markan/Matthean tradition were used together within the community at some point. Indeed, as has been demonstrated by Paul in 1 Cor. 11, there were early Christian communities who came to know more than one form of the Eucharist ritual. Finally, the occasional references to 'the Gospel' that appear throughout the *Didache* (see 8. 2; 11. 3; 15. 3–4) need not be seen as an indication of the late nature of the work as a whole, but may be a reflection of the fact that the Didachist knew of the composition and use of Matthew within the Antiochean church, and constructed his own text in the light of that rising literary reality.

Despite the differences between Matthew and the *Didache*, the similarities that have traditionally been recognized between the two works indicate a core perspective that bound the writings together within a single metropolitan situation. These include the familiar words of the Lord's Prayer, the presentation of Jesus as a teacher of wisdom and Torah from the perspective of Moses at Mt Sinai, and the concern for correct ritual behaviour. In addition, both texts reflect a concern about pseudo-prophets and false teachers and for the structuring of community life and ethics, tendencies that are typical of Christian literature from the latter part of the first century.

Both Matthew and the *Didache* bear the definite marks of Christian theology as viewed from a Christian perspective, though the directions in which their authors lean are opposed: progressive versus conservative. Ultimately, it is certainly possible, if not probable, that these two writings could have evolved and served useful purposes for different Christian congregations within the same broad church milieu, especially in a city with such a diverse and changing population as Antioch. Indeed, it seems more useful to consider these writings and their authors in the same historical situation than to imagine their creation in separate circumstances.

Part VI

Ignatius

13

Ignatius, 'the Gospel', and the Gospels

Charles E. Hill

INTRODUCTION

The conclusions drawn by Inge for the Oxford Committee a century ago with regard to the question of Ignatius' use of the canonical gospels were very measured, though generally positive. While careful not to claim certainty, Inge wrote that the parallels supported the probability of Ignatius' knowledge of Matthew, Luke, and John.[1] His assessment was more optimistic than many later ones would be, particularly after the publication in 1957 of Helmut Köster's landmark book, *Synoptische Überlieferung bei den Apostolischen Vätern*,[2] which argued that Ignatius' synoptic parallels do not signify his knowledge of any of our written gospels, but only his use of (usually older) 'free tradition'. Not only did this book establish a method for approaching synoptic parallels in the Apostolic Fathers, it also gave an authoritative interpretation of Ignatius' use of the term 'gospel', which Koester has maintained ever since, now with many others. When Ignatius uses the term 'gospel', Koester concludes, it 'certainly does not refer to any written text enumerating the basic topics of Jesus' appearance. It is rather the message of salvation in general of which the center is Christ's death and resurrection.'[3]

[1] W. R. Inge, 'Ignatius', in A Committee of the Oxford Society of Historical Theology, *The New Testament in the Apostolic Fathers* (Oxford: Clarendon Press, 1905), 63–83. 'Ignatius was certainly acquainted either with our Matthew, or with the source of our Matthew, or with a Gospel very closely akin to it... the indications on the whole favour the hypothesis that he used our Greek Matthew in something like its present shape' (p. 79); 'The balance of probability seems to be slightly in favour of a knowledge of the Third Gospel' (p. 80); 'Ignatius's use of the Fourth Gospel is highly probable, but falls some way short of certainty' (p. 83). Inge found no strong Marcan parallels. For a more recent assessment, see P. Foster, 'Ignatius of Antioch and the Writings that later formed the New Testament', Ch. 7 in the companion volume.

[2] H. Köster, *Synoptische Überlieferung bei den Apostolischen Vätern*, TU 65 (Berlin: Akademie-Verlag, 1957).

[3] H. Koester, *Ancient Christian Gospels* (Harrisburg, Pa.: Trinity Press International; London: SCM Press, 1990), 8; 'Ignatius never implies that he is speaking of a written text when he uses this term' (p. 7); 'Ignatius employs the term exclusively... as a designation of the proclamation

As we approach the question of Ignatius' use of the term gospel, several preliminary matters seem to call for attention.

PRELIMINARY CONSIDERATIONS

First, it is virtually certain that by the time Ignatius wrote (AD 107 or 108, possibly as late as 118), all four of the ecclesiastical gospels (leaving aside for the moment the question of other gospels) were in existence, perhaps for decades, and known to at least some part of the Christian reading public. The circulation of these gospels would not, of course, have rendered all surviving oral tradition about Jesus superfluous; we cannot assume that it would have immediately displaced other written accounts which might have been in circulation. We can say, however, that Ignatius, being both a literate person and a Christian bishop, who held to the pre-eminence of 'the coming of the Saviour, our Lord Jesus Christ, his passion, and the resurrection' (*Phld.* 9. 2), is just the kind of person we would expect to have been interested in any written accounts of the life, death, and resurrection of the Saviour. Judging from his view of the apostolate, transparent throughout his letters,[4] his interest in such written accounts would have been particularly acute in the case of any which he might have believed were associated with the witness of any of the apostles of Jesus.

Second, at this time there was apparently no standard way of referring to writings now customarily designated 'gospels'. For instance, besides 'gospels', Justin used the phrase 'memoirs of the apostles' (twelve times in *Dial.* 98–107), and this had precedents in Papias's elder, who characterized Mark as the reminiscences of Peter (Euseb. *HE* 2. 15. 1; 3. 24. 5;[5] 3. 39. 15; cf. *Apoc. Jas.* 2. 7–16). Papias's elder also referred to the gospels as containing 'the Lord's sayings' (*HE* 3. 39. 15, 16), 'the acts of Jesus' (*HE* 3. 24. 10, 11), or 'the things said or done by the Lord' (*HE* 3. 39. 15). None of these modes of referring to

of Christ's death and resurrection' (p. 15); cf. *Synoptische Überlieferung*, 8. W.-D. Köhler, *Die Rezeption des Matthäusevangeliums in der Zeit vor Irenäus*, WUNT 2.24 (Tübingen: Mohr Siebeck, 1987), 73–7, believes that the word designates the content of the message, Jesus Christ, the question of oral or written being inappropriate. He concludes from the parallels that Ignatius did know the Gospel according to Matthew.

[4] See C. E. Hill, 'Ignatius and the Apostolate: The Witness of Ignatius to the Emergence of Christian Scripture', in M. F. Wiles and E. J. Yarnold (eds.), *StPatr* 36 (Leuven: Peeters, 2001), 226–48.

[5] For the relationship of the traditions in *HE* 3. 24. 3–15 to Papias's elder, see C. E. Hill 'What Papias Said about John (and Luke): A "New" Papian Fragment', *JTS* 49 (1998), 582–629, on pp. 614–16.

the gospels—including the word 'gospel'—is in the first instance the title of a book. Each is based on the content or the character of the writings. By themselves, none of them necessarily indicates anything written, though each might. Thus, it would also be quite possible for the word 'gospel' to function at an early stage not exactly as a title, but as a reference to the content[6] of a written work or works.[7] Moreover, with forms of reference such as those mentioned demonstrably in use, it is possible that Ignatius might refer to written gospels or their contents with some other locution besides the word 'gospel'.

Third, as invaluable as Ignatius' letters are for testing such a priori considerations, we must not forget that at best they are capable of furnishing only very partial answers. It was not on Ignatius' agenda to list all his textual authorities for his readers. As a prisoner in transition, he probably did not have any, let alone all, of these with him as he wrote,[8] and thus had to rely upon memory, as seems evident even from his Old Testament parallels and citations.[9] And, in all probability, when it came to literary borrowings, the ideals of exact verbal duplication and contextual fidelity were not his own ideals, or not his only ideals.[10]

Fourth, perhaps the chief reason why some have concluded that Ignatius did use the word 'gospel' to designate one or more written gospels[11] is that he uses it in conjunction with other apparent designations of scriptural books. We may observe that his eight uses of the term εὐαγγέλιον appear in the following striking combinations:

Phld. 5. 1–2: gospel . . . apostles . . . prophets . . . gospel . . . gospel
Phld. 8. 2: archives . . . gospel
Phld. 9. 1–2: prophets . . . apostles . . . gospel . . . gospel
Smyrn. 5. 1: the prophecies . . . the Law of Moses . . . the gospel
Smyrn. 7. 2: prophets . . . gospel

6 Cf. the use of the term 'law' in John 1. 17; Acts 7. 53; Rom. 6. 14, 15; 10. 4; Gal. 3. 17; Eph. 2. 15; Heb. 9. 19.

7 The singular 'gospel' was often used to denote plural written works throughout the second century (*Ep. Apost.* 1; Justin, *Dial.* 10. 2; 100. 1; *2 Clem.* 8. 5; Theophilus, *Ad Autol.* 3. 12; Irenaeus, e.g., *Adv. Haer.* 1. 7. 4; 3. 5. 1; 4. 34. 1).

8 C. C. Richardson, *The Christianity of Ignatius of Antioch* (New York: AMS Press, 1935), 66.

9 Inge (*NTAF*, 64), observed that 'Ignatius always quotes from memory', whether from the Old or the New Testament, and that 'he is inexact even as compared with his contemporaries'.

10 See J. Whittaker, 'The Value of Indirect Tradition in the Establishment of Greek Philosophical Texts or the Art of Misquotation', in John N. Grant (ed.), *Editing Greek and Latin Texts: Papers given at the Twenty-Third Annual Conference on Editorial Problems, University of Toronto, 6–7 November 1987* (New York: AMS Press, 1989), 63–95.

11 E.g., R. Joly, *Le Dossier d'Ignace d'Antioche* (Brussels: Éditions de l'Université de Bruxelles, 1979), 66; J. P. Meier, 'Matthew and Ignatius: A Response to William R. Schoedel', in D. L. Balch (ed.), *Social History of the Matthean Community: Cross-Disciplinary Approaches* (Minneapolis:

Thus we see that four of the five passages lay the gospel alongside either the prophets or the prophecies; the remaining instance has 'archives' instead. One, *Smyrn.* 5. 1, has alongside the prophecies, the law of Moses. Two of the five passages contain also a mention of 'apostles'. A total of five apparent categories are used: the law of Moses, the prophets or prophecies, the archives, the gospel, and the apostles. In each passage at least one designation is used which represents the Old Testament scriptures, and at least one is used which pertains to the new revelation in Christ (always 'the gospel', sometimes 'the apostles' as well), designations which correspond to those used by other second-century authors to denote portions of the New Testament. (See Appendix.)

These certainly have the appearance of 'canonical categories', but are they? The 'archives' mentioned alongside the gospel in *Phld.* 8. 2 is acknowledged to be a reference to the OT[12] (or possibly to the place where the OT books are kept in the church's library),[13] but what about the others? Ignatius mentions 'the prophets', to be sure, in *Phld.* 5. 1; 9. 1; *Smyrn.* 7. 2, but according to Köster he means the prophets 'as persons and not as texts'.[14] What about *Smyrn.* 5. 1, where Ignatius mentions 'the prophecies', and 'the law of Moses'? These certainly represent written texts, but Köster finds in this passage a closer co-ordination of 'gospel' with Ignatius' own human sufferings, also mentioned. Therefore, 'the gospel' is not a text here either.[15] In examining Ignatius' letters, then, attention must be given to both the 'textual' and the 'non-textual' terms with which the word 'gospel' is associated.

One final question which has not received adequate attention is this: why is it that all the texts in which Ignatius uses the term εὐαγγέλιον, and all the texts in which he uses two or more of the quasi-canonical terms, occur in the letters to the Philadelphians and the Smyrnaeans, two of his last three letters, written from Troas? Remarkably, Ignatius wrote to the Magnesians, the Romans, the Trallians, and the Ephesians (and his last, personal letter to Polycarp) without ever using the term εὐαγγέλιον. The answer surely is connected to the unpleasant interchange about 'the gospel' and 'the archives' that occurred

Fortress, 1991), 178–86, on p. 186 n. 20; M. D. Goulder, 'Ignatius' "Docetists" ', *VC* 53 (1999), 16–30, on p. 17 n. 4; M. Hengel, *The Four Gospels and the One Gospel of Jesus Christ: An Investigation of the Collection and Origin of the Canonical Gospels* (London: SCM; Harrisburg, Pa.: Trinity Press International, 2000), 64, 134, 248 n. 247. Hengel thinks that Ignatius knew the Gospels of Matthew and John.

[12] See W. R. Schoedel, 'Ignatius and the Archives', *HTR* 71 (1978), 97–106; *idem, Ignatius of Antioch* (Philadelphia: Fortress, 1985), 207.

[13] M. Hengel, *Studies in the Gospel of Mark* (London: SCM Press, 1985), 77–8.

[14] 'als Personen, nicht um Prophetenschriften' (Köster, *Synoptische Überlieferung*, 7).

[15] Schoedel agrees (*Ignatius*, 208 n. 6).

during his journey through Philadelphia,[16] when he was visited by a number of Christians, evidently of varying persuasions. It is this incident that was evidently the catalyst for his use of *εὐαγγέλιον* and the other quasi-canonical terms in *Philadelphians* and *Smyrnaeans*. This does not mean of course that Ignatius did not already know the term or did not approve of it (he at least would have known it from reading Paul). But Ignatius has not used it himself, in *any* sense, in his previous letters; it is as foreign to them as is the term 'archives'. It makes sense, then, to begin with a consideration of this incident before examining each of the other references individually.

THE IGNATIAN PASSAGES

1. The Incident at Philadelphia, Phld. 8. 2

At Philadelphia Ignatius had encountered a problem with a Christian Judaizing faction. During a visit with assorted Christians there, some persons objected to something Ignatius was saying by pointing to 'the archives'. I give here Schoedel's translation.[17]

> I exhort you to do nothing from partisanship but in accordance with Christ's teaching. For I heard some say, 'If I do not find (it) in the archives, I do not believe (it to be) in the gospel'. And when I said, 'It is written', they answered me, 'That is just the question'. But for me the archives are Jesus Christ, the inviolable archives are his cross and death and his resurrection and faith through him—in which, through your prayers, I want to be justified.

This could mean that the Philadelphian detractors accept the gospel, as much as Ignatius does, but do not accept something he had asserted regarding the gospel because they could not find this in the Old Testament.[18] We might then understand Ignatius' reply, 'it is written', as his appeal to some Old Testament text to support his particular understanding of the Christian gospel message. The response of his opponents, 'That is just the question', then, means that they challenge Ignatius' interpretation of the archives. Ignatius, who Schoedel thinks 'was having difficulty in establishing his point' from the archives,[19] can

[16] So also A. and C. Faivre, 'Genèse d'un texte et recourse aux Écritures: Ignace, *aux Ephésiens* 14,1 – 16,2', *RSR* 65 (1991), 173–96, on p. 178.

[17] Other translations from Ignatius' letters are my own.

[18] See C. M. Trevett, *A Study of Ignatius of Antioch in Syria and Asia*, Studies in the Bible and Early Christianity, 29 (Lewiston, Me., Queenston, and Lampeter: Edwin Mellen Press, 1992), 174.

[19] Schoedel, *Ignatius*, 209.

appeal only to the 'higher authority' of Christ himself, his cross, death, and resurrection and faith in him, as the ultimate 'archives'. In Schoedel's view, then, the opponents 'were relatively harmless theologically. They probably represented a threat to the authorities simply because they surpassed them in exegetical expertise.'[20]

This interpretation, though widely accepted, is not without difficulties. First, Schoedel's supplying of an unexpressed 'to be' as part of the object of *πιστεύω*, 'If I do not find (it) in the archives, I do not believe (it to be) in the gospel', has recently been called 'implausible' by Michael Goulder.[21] The opposition of archives to gospel, clear even in Schoedel's translation, is enhanced in the simpler translation: 'unless in the archives I find (it), in the gospel I do not believe (it)'. This translation also preserves the balanced parallel structure of the statement in Greek (*ἐὰν μὴ ἐν τοῖς ἀρχείοις εὕρω ἐν τῷ εὐαγγελίῳ οὐ πιστεύω*). This probably means that his opponents were not objecting to something they thought Ignatius had added to the preached gospel message, but that the element(s) in question, though it be contained 'in the gospel', was not accepted by them because they did not find it in the OT. Accordingly, throughout *Philadelphians* (5. 1; 8. 2; 9. 2) Ignatius asserts the pre-eminence of simply 'the gospel', specifying only the essential points, 'the coming of the Saviour...his passion, and the resurrection' (cf. preface; 8. 2).

Though we cannot be certain, what might have been involved is the interpretation of Christ's death and resurrection as putting an end to the old dispensation and certain practices of the law,[22] like sabbatizing, which, though not mentioned in *Philadelphians*, might have been understood.[23] In any case, the structure of the statement, the polemic of the epistle,[24] and the repeated emphasis on the death and resurrection of Jesus Christ suggest that it was not merely Ignatius' inability to find scriptural support for a peculiar twist on the oral gospel message otherwise held in common,[25] but a more fundamental question of the subordination of 'the gospel' to 'the archives'. In

[20] Schoedel, *Ignatius*, 209; Trevett, *Study of Ignatius*, 175, accepts this view.

[21] Goulder, 'Ignatius' "Docetists" ', 17 n. 4.

[22] Cf. Trevett, *Ignatius*, 176.

[23] Note that he counters the practice in *Magnesians* by an allusion to Christ's death and resurrection: 'no longer sabbatizing, but living according to the Lord's day, on which also our life rose up through him and his death, which some deny!' (*Magn.* 9. 1).

[24] Particularly evident in 6. 1: 'if anyone interpret Judaism to you do not listen to him'; 9. 1: 'The priests likewise are noble, but the High Priest [i.e., Jesus Christ] ... is greater' (note also the *τινων* in 7. 2 and 8. 2).

[25] Taking Schoedel's view would make it hard to understand why Ignatius would want to draw any more attention to an incident in which he had been bested by his opponents in scriptural exegesis, more especially with a comeback which essentially avoided the question.

Ignatius' view, it involved a failure to accord to an objective 'gospel' the 'pre-eminence' it deserved, as containing that to which the prophets themselves had pointed.

Because 'the archives' are written documents of religious authority, the Old Testament, it is possible to read 'the gospel' as a reference to a written authority: as Goulder writes, 'a written *εὐαγγέλιον* to balance the written *ἀρχεία*'.[26] If so, when Ignatius begins his proof with 'it is written', he could be referring not to the archives but to this written gospel. The problem with these Philadelphians, in Goulder's words, is that 'they refused to regard the Gospel as scripture (*γέγραπται*), and gave authority only to the *ἀρχεία*, that is the Old Testament'.[27] Such a use of *γέγραπται* to introduce material from a New Testament writing cannot be paralleled elsewhere in Ignatius' writings (he uses it only to introduce material from Proverbs, *Eph.* 5. 3; *Magn.* 12)—though it would reflect a conception which is not without parallel in Christian writings to about this time (cf. 2 Pet. 3. 16 on Paul's letters; 1 Tim. 5. 18 on Luke 10. 7; Pol. *Phil.* 12. 1 on Eph. 4. 26; *Barn.* 4. 14 on Matt. 20. 16 or 22. 14). Nevertheless, the case for 'the gospel' denoting a written 'gospel' or its content is not dependent upon the question of whether Ignatius' appeal 'it is written' is an appeal to a written gospel.

When Ignatius goes on to say that the true archives are 'Jesus Christ ... his cross, and death, and resurrection, and the faith which is through him', the unexpressed completion of the sentence could be, 'which are just what are contained in the gospel'. Though he is not citing a text *per se*, these subjects might well be seen as the major, or most salient, subjects of any of the written gospels that Ignatius might have known.[28]

Phld. 8. 2 gives us the fundamental occasion for Ignatius' use of *τὸ εὐαγγέλιον*. It is important to note that it appears opposite a reference to the Old Testament scriptures and that the debate concerns a comparison of religious authorities. By itself, this passage seems to favour viewing 'the gospel' either as the name of a written authority or as a summation of the contents of a written authority. On the other hand, many scholars insist that Ignatius' own use, apart from his recollection of the incident in Philadelphia,

[26] Goulder, 'Ignatius' "Docetists" ', 17 n. 4; also Joly, *Le Dossier d'Ignace*, 66; Meier, 'Matthew and Ignatius', 186 n. 20.

[27] Goulder, 'Ignatius' "Docetists" ', 16–17. In 1954 Richard Heard saw it as 'a point of special interest' that certain Judaizing Christians did not respect the written Gospel ('Papias' Quotations from the New Testament', *NTS* 1 (1954), 130–4, at p. 133); the 'point of special interest' for us fifty years later would be that Ignatius did!

[28] *Pace* Schoedel, *Ignatius*, 208 n. 6. A work such as the *Gospel of Thomas* (if it existed) would not have been signified, as it contains none of the elements specified by Ignatius (so B. Metzger, *The Canon of the New Testament: Its Origin, Development, and Significance* (Oxford: Oxford University Press, 1987), 49).

is perceptibly different. We must now briefly examine these other passages, beginning with chapter 5 of *Philadelphians.*

2. *Phld.* 5. 1–2

...that I may attain the lot in which I was shown mercy, having fled to the gospel as to the flesh of Jesus, and to the apostles as to the presbytery of the church.[2] And we also love the prophets, because they also made proclamation pointing to the gospel and set their hope on him and waited for him in whom having believed they were also saved, being in the unity of Jesus Christ, saints worthy of love and worthy of admiration, attested by Jesus Christ and numbered together in the gospel of the common hope.

'Having fled to the gospel' could be understood of an unwritten message. But that the listing of 'gospel' and 'apostles' should have reflexively brought the prophets to mind suggests that his conception of 'the gospel' included writings wherein that 'good news' was set forth authoritatively—particularly since we know that such writings were in circulation by this time. It is conceivable that Ignatius might have appealed to 'the apostles' only as personal authorities, if he had known any of them. But to sustain such an appeal as valid for himself and for the Philadelphians makes more sense if we understand the apostles' teaching to be represented at least in great part by written works which now preserve their teaching and which are the common possession of churches in Syria and Asia Minor—as we know was the case with at least a Pauline corpus.[29] As to 'the prophets', the Köster/Schoedel view would argue, as Charles Thomas Brown has recently written, that 'The OT Prophets function in the Ignatian corpus as authoritative figures and not as texts...figures which announce the gospel in advance'.[30] But this is curious. How did the prophets announce the gospel in advance to Ignatius and the

[29] See Hill, 'Ignatius and the Apostolate'; J. B. Lightfoot, *The Apostolic Fathers: Clement, Ignatius, and Polycarp. Revised Texts with Introductions, Notes, Dissertations, and Translations*, 2nd edn., 2 parts in 5 vols. (Grand Rapids, Mich.: Baker Book House, 1981, repr. of 1889–90 edn.), 2. 2. 260. K. Lake, *The Apostolic Fathers*, LCL (Cambridge, Mass.: Harvard University Press, 1977, repr. of 1912 edn.), i. 243, thinks Ignatius is referring to Christian prophets like the Didachist and Hermas. But this is ruled out by the references to their announcement of the gospel and their waiting for Jesus, and by the pattern of setting the gospel alongside some OT source.

[30] C. T. Brown, *The Gospel and Ignatius of Antioch*, Studies in Biblical Literature, 12 (New York: Peter Lang, 2000), 118; R. Gundry, '*ΕΥΑΓΓΕΛΙΟΝ*: How Soon a Book?', *JBL* 115 (1996), 321–5, on p. 324: 'both *Phld.* 5.2 and 9.2 portray the OT prophets again not as writers of books but...as preachers...In view is not the written record of their preaching, but their preaching itself'; Schoedel, *Ignatius*, 201: 'even when sacred books were known, Ignatius thinks of their authors primarily as people proclaiming a message. The linking of apostles and prophets...need not imply a comparison between classes of documents.'

Asian churches, and where was their preaching encountered, except in their writings? New Testament references to the 'persons' of the prophets, or to their speaking or prophesying, such as Acts 3. 24 or 1 Pet. 1. 10, presuppose the existence of their messages in authoritative scriptural texts. This is surely the case with Ignatius as well.

More tellingly, we must now not fail to consider the context. Ignatius is introducing the word 'gospel' here to the Philadelphians on the heels of the controversy that arose when he was with them. The writings of the prophets certainly belong to the 'archives' which some at Philadelphia had attempted to set against 'the gospel'.[31] Against these erring Philadelphians, Ignatius wants to establish already in chapter 5 that the prophets not only should not be set against the gospel, but that they in fact looked forward to the gospel and are one with us in salvation in Christ. His strong statement of unity between the old and the new is surely aimed at the debate which he is about to recall to their attention in 8. 2. Representing the old are the prophets; representing the new are the gospel and the apostles. In his quest for perfection, Ignatius will take refuge 'in the gospel' and in 'the apostles', while also loving the prophets. Thus a catalogue of 'theological authorities'[32] is certainly supposed. In much the same way as 'the apostles' and 'the prophets' are known through their writings, the good news about Jesus too may be understood as preserved in writings.

Though I think this is reasonably clear, Ignatius goes on to mention 'the gospel' twice more in 5. 2, where the word seems more straightforwardly understood as simply the message of the good news, or the content of that message. For the prophets to have 'made proclamation pointing to the gospel (*εἰς τὸ εὐαγγέλιον κατηγγελκέναι*)' does not immediately suggest a book or set of books. Does this, then, nullify the impression that when listing 'the gospel' along with the apostles and prophets in 5. 1, and in opposition to the archives in 8. 2, Ignatius has in mind written authorities behind the gospel? Not at all. The original Christian meaning of 'the gospel' as the good news about Jesus Christ was current both before and after Ignatius, and continues so to the present moment. But at some point the textual meaning arose. Both meanings occur side by side in several second-century authors,[33] and have done so ever since. At whatever point the textual meaning came into play, presumably its patrons still used the term in its original sense as well. There is thus no

[31] 'The prophets' is often a way of designating the OT as a whole: Justin, *1 Apol.* 67; Irenaeus, *Adv. Haer.* 2. 27. 2; *Muratorian Fragment*, line 79.

[32] Schoedel's term, *Ignatius*, 201.

[33] Irenaeus, in the very same sentence in *Adv. Haer.* 3. 11. 1—albeit an extremely long sentence—uses the term in both senses. Cf. 3. *praef.*; 3. 1. 1; 3. 11. 7.

difficulty in seeing the three instances in *Phld.* 5. 1–2 as an early illustration of the acquired polyvalence of the term.[34]

3. *Phld.* 9. 1–2

Immediately after reporting the 'archives/gospel' incident in *Phld.* 8, Ignatius goes on in 9. 1–2, with probable Johannine allusions, to proclaim Christ as the High Priest entrusted with the Holy of Holies, and as the door of the Father (cf. John 10. 7, 9; 14. 6),

> through which enter Abraham and Isaac and Jacob, and the prophets and the apostles and the Church... but the gospel has something exceptional, the coming of the Saviour, our Lord Jesus Christ, his passion and resurrection. For the beloved prophets made proclamation pointing to him, but the gospel is the perfection of incorruption.

Clearly Ignatius starts out with the persons of the prophets and apostles in view here, along with three named patriarchs and all members of the church. Thus it might be tempting to dismiss entirely any idea of textuality from the word 'gospel' in this passage, as some have done. But, again, we must ask why the patriarchs and prophets, the apostles, and the church, have all come into view. They have come into view because of an alleged superiority of the old over the new, in a carry-over from chapter 8. 'All these things are joined in the unity of God', is Ignatius' rejoinder. The patriarchs, the prophets, just as well as the apostles and all the church, enter through Jesus, the door to the Father. And so the gospel has something distinctive and is in fact superior, for it reveals the coming of the Christ, his passion and resurrection. This is seen from the prophets themselves, 'For the beloved prophets had a message pointing to him (κατήγγειλαν εἰς αὐτόν)'; cf. 5. 2. Here Ignatius has pointedly the *message* of the prophets, not their persons, in mind. Gundry objects that it is still 'not the written record of their preaching, but their preaching itself'[35] which is in view. But, on the contrary, it is not the mere fact that the prophets were preachers which is important, it is the content of their preaching (namely, Christ), and that content is now known only through their writings. 'But the Gospel', asserts Ignatius, 'is the perfection of incorruption.' Earlier in the letter (5. 1–2) Ignatius testified that he was seeking 'perfection' by taking refuge in the gospel and the apostles, while loving also the prophets. The passages belong together. Along with the incident recalled in 8. 2, they suggest

[34] Meier, 'Matthew and Ignatius', 186 n. 20: 'In my view, it may be a mistake to claim that εὐαγγέλιον must *always* mean one thing', admitting 'that there are passages in Ignatius that could argue for "oral kerygma" or "Christ, the content of the kerygma" ', but maintaining that *Phld.* 8. 2 represented the meaning of 'written gospel'.

[35] Gundry, '*ΕΥΑΓΓΕΛΙΟΝ*', 324.

that a sustained comparison is being made between existing religious authorities, the Old Testament (where the stories of the patriarchs are found, but more especially where prophets' *message* about the Christ is found), and the gospel, to which Ignatius even adds 'the apostles'.

In a section in which the authority of 'the gospel' is in view, as compared with the Old Testament, the apparent Johannine allusions to Jesus being the door (*θύρα*, John 10. 7, 9),[36] the only way to the Father (cf. John 14. 6),[37] possibly to Abraham and the patriarchs (John 8. 56, 58),[38] and to the prophets as 'making proclamation unto him' (John 5. 46; 12. 41), are highly significant. They suggest that in Ignatius' mind, either the Gospel of John furnished evidence for the exceptional nature of 'the gospel', or was itself part of what was at issue in his assertion of the gospel's greater ultimacy.[39]

4. *Smyrn.* 5. 1

In Troas Ignatius wrote also to his former hosts in Smyrna, where the threat from Judaizers, so much on his mind when he wrote to the Philadelphians, is all but absent. The immediate threat in Smyrna is from advocates of a docetic view of Jesus Christ. What should convince these people that they are wrong? In *Smyrn.* 5. 1 he laments that 'neither the prophecies nor the law of Moses persuaded them, nor even the gospel until now, nor our own human sufferings'.

Though the presenting problem is different, here, just as in the letter to the Philadelphians, 'the gospel' appears in a list alongside definitely literary, even explicitly scriptural, categories: 'the prophecies', not the prophets as persons or preachers, and Moses, not the man but his law, i.e., the Pentateuch. It is often objected, however, that because Ignatius also appeals here to his own human sufferings, his appeal to 'the gospel' should not be understood as an appeal to a documentary authority. Gundry argues that the strong adversative, *ἀλλά*, just before 'the gospel' distances it from the law and the prophecies and aligns it with 'our human sufferings'. But any distinction intended with

[36] Lightfoot, *Apostolic Fathers*, 2. 2. 275, 'doubtless an allusion to John x. 9'. Inge, *NTAF*, 83, observed a further correspondence between John's *εἰσέλθῃ* and *σωθήσεται* and Ignatius' *εἰσέρχονται* and *σωτῆρος*. See C. E. Hill, *The Johannine Corpus in the Early Church* (Oxford: Oxford University Press, 2003), 438–9.

[37] W. von Loewenich, *Das Johannes-Verständnis im zweiten Jahrhundert* (Giessen: A. Töpelmann, 1932), 35.

[38] Inge, *NTAF*, 83.

[39] Note also that what is usually regarded as the strongest possibility of Johannine borrowing in Ignatius' letters (*Phld.* 7. 1; John 3. 8; 8. 14) occurs in this context, as Ignatius recalls his encounter at Philadelphia with presumably the same opponents.

the adversative is surely temporal (note μέχρι νῦν). It is also clear that in substance the last element is the odd one out, as is proved by its absence from the other four places where 'gospel' appears opposite an Old Testament authority or authorities.[40] It is included here only because of its particular relevance to the specific subject at hand, the Docetist denial of Christ's true, human sufferings. The law of Moses, in which these sufferings are foreshadowed, the prophecies, in which they are foretold, and the gospel, in which they are recorded and proclaimed (*Phld.* 9. 2; *Smyrn.* 7. 2), show an obvious continuity and belong to a promise-fulfilment continuum. Ignatius thinks that his own sufferings also have a place confirming the reality of the sufferings of Christ, but they do not belong to the same continuum. Both the prophecies and the law of Moses are portions of the written 'archives' of *Phld.* 8. 2. In such a context it would be natural for a Christian author to include a reference to Christian writings alongside these portions of the Hebrew Scriptures.

This correlation of the gospel with the prophecies and the law is illuminated when we consider the flow of the epistle to this point. Earlier chapters of *Smyrnaeans* contain some of Ignatius' strongest gospel parallels. In chapter 1, in a semi-credal christological section which looks like an expansion on the 'elements' of the gospel mentioned in *Phld.* 9. 2 and *Smyrn.* 7. 2, Ignatius had used a phrase which must come ultimately from Matthew:[41] 'baptized by John that "all righteousness might be fulfilled by him" ' (1. 1; cf. Matt. 3. 15); he had referred to Herod the Tetrarch's role in the crucifixion, something mentioned only by Luke among the canonical gospels (1. 2; cf. Luke 23. 6–16); and had referred to the crucifixion nails, something mentioned only by John (1. 1, 2; cf. John 20. 25).[42] Then in 3. 2 he seems to have paraphrased the post-resurrection appearance reported in Luke 24. 39.[43] These references to specific

[40] He does appeal to his own captivity in *Trall.* 10. 1, where he does not appeal to the textual authorities.

[41] Because it occurs in a distinctively Matthean redaction, this is the one text which even Schoedel (*Ignatius*, 222) and Köster (*Synoptische Überlieferung*, 57–9) admit comes ultimately from Matthew itself—though still claiming that it does not reflect Ignatius' own use of Matthew, only that he got the language through a 'kerygmatic formula' which was dependent upon Matthew. In the view of J. Smit Sibinga., 'Ignatius and Matthew', *NovT* 8 (1966), 263–83, Ignatius knew only pre-Matthean 'M-material'. Both of these possibilities seem unnecessarily complicated. That an educated Christian bishop in early second-century Antioch would not have known Matthew's Gospel is extremely unlikely. Cf. Köhler, *Rezeption*, 77–9; Meier, 'Matthew and Ignatius', 180–2.

[42] See Hill, *Johannine Corpus*, 440–1.

[43] Jerome (*de vir. ill.* 16) thought that Ignatius must have known the account in the *Gospel of the Hebrews*. The saying 'I am not a bodiless demon' was also, according to Origen (*de Princ.* 1, *prooem.* 8), contained in the *Doctrina Petri* (but see R. M. Grant, 'Scripture and Tradition in St. Ignatius of Antioch', *CBQ* 25 (1963), 322–35, on p. 327). All three works (also cf. *Ep. Apost.* 11) apparently report the same incident, regardless of the question of dependency. The phrase

events in the life of Jesus, his baptism, crucifixion, and appearance in the flesh after the resurrection, seem to show that Ignatius is expanding his elemental definition of 'the gospel' by referring to details contained in 'the gospels'.[44] If this represents a use not of gospels but of unwritten 'Jesus tradition', it at least paves the way for what Christian writers will soon be doing with the written gospels. But because it is unlikely that Ignatius would have had copies of the gospels to hand, there is no convincing reason why he could not be referring here—and indeed elsewhere in his letters—to material in the Gospels of Matthew and Luke, possibly John, from memory.

5. *Smyrn.* 7. 2

It is fitting to avoid such people and not to speak about them in private or in public, but to give heed to the prophets, and especially to the gospel, in which the passion is made clear to us and the resurrection is accomplished.

Once again, the gospel is laid alongside 'the prophets'. That Ignatius refers to the prophets and not to their prophecies, as he had in 5. 1, does not diminish the textual implication, as it was quite impossible for the Smrynaeans to 'give heed to' these long-dead sages in person. The subject again is the suffering and resurrection of Jesus, to which the prophets bore witness beforehand (cf. 1 Pet. 1. 11), and which the gospel records. But the Smrynaeans are to give heed to the gospel 'especially' (ἐξαιρέτως). This again echoes Ignatius' words in *Phld.* 9. 2, where the same two authorities, 'prophets' and 'gospel', are mentioned, with the latter being claimed by Ignatius to be 'exceptional' (ἐξαίρετον). The two texts share something else which they do not share with Pauline usage. In each, Ignatius names explicitly some things contained 'in' that gospel:[45] Christ's passion and resurrection (also his 'coming' in *Phld.* 9. 2). This continues the concern raised in *Phld.* 8. 2, where his opponents

quoted by Ignatius, 'I am not a bodiless demon', corresponds exactly to the reports of Jerome and Origen, but only paraphrases Luke (at least its known manuscript form). Ignatius' reference to Jesus eating and drinking with the disciples after the resurrection, however, corresponds, as far as we know, only to Luke's account. The same applies to his earlier reference to Herod at the time of the crucifixion. Compare, however, the recent treatment in A. Gregory, *The Reception of Luke and Acts in the Period before Irenaeus: Looking for Luke in the Second Century*, WUNT 2.169 (Tübingen: J. C. B. Mohr (Paul Siebeck), 2003), 69–74.

[44] See Hill, 'Ignatius and the Apostolate', 244.

[45] That is, though Paul obviously associates the death and resurrection of Jesus with the preached message of 'the gospel', he never speaks of these or any other topics as being 'in' the gospel. Also, unlike Paul, Ignatius never speaks of anyone hearing or preaching 'the gospel', nor does he use the verb εὐαγγελίζω.

refused to believe something 'in the gospel', where Ignatius writes, 'But to me the archives are Jesus Christ, the inviolable archives are his cross, and his death and resurrection, and the faith which is through him'. The very things which constitute the inviolable archives and which define the gospel are now in *Smyrn.* 7. 2 said to be contained 'in' the gospel. This again sounds like it is referring to a written document or corpus and its major, or most salient, contents.[46]

6. 'The Gospel' as Canonical Category

As we have now seen, the incident in Philadelphia, in which some attempted to pit 'the gospel' against 'the archives', had a formative effect on at least four more passages in Ignatius' letters to the Philadelphians and to the Smyrnaeans. In these passages 'the prophets', or 'the prophecies' and 'the law of Moses', stand in the place of 'the archives' as representing the Old Testament scriptures and appear alongside 'the gospel', or 'the gospel' and 'the apostles'. Here 'the prophets' cannot simply signify the persons of the prophets apart from their textual, scriptural legacy. 'The gospel' is being regarded as a religious authority commensurate with the Old Testament scriptures, but surpassing them in its ultimate significance.[47]

In Appendix I have catalogued expressions used by other second-century authors who, having a textual conception of the gospel, linked it (or 'the Lord') with the law, the prophets, and/or the apostles. The comparison shows an intriguing and suggestive continuity between Ignatius' use and theirs. It now seems more likely that Ignatius is not merely a precursor of this practice, but a contributor to it.

7. Elements 'in the Gospel' as Elements in the Written Gospels

Besides his practice of naming 'the gospel' alongside textual authorities of the Old Testament, another thing which links Ignatius to later writers who give a textual meaning to 'the gospel' is his tendency to specify certain elements of the life of Christ as being 'in' the gospel or as characterizing the gospel

[46] Given the word uttered by Jesus from the cross, τετέλεσται, in John 19. 30, it may be significant that Ignatius uses the word τετελείωται to represent the resurrection's accomplishment, just after mentioning the revelation of the passion, both as 'in' the gospel.

[47] This alone discredits Schoedel's claim (*Ignatius*, 208) that 'there is no convincing evidence that he puts any other source on the same level with' the OT. Quite clearly he does, and those sources are 'the gospel' and 'the apostles' (*Phld.* 5. 1–2).

(*Smyrn.* 7. 2; *Phld.* 8. 2; 9. 2). For instance, in a manner much like Ignatius, the author of the *Muratorian Fragment* will say of the 'gospel books' that 'everything is declared in all: concerning the birth, concerning the passion, concerning the resurrection, concerning the intercourse with his disciples and concerning his two comings' (lines 20–3).[48]

A parallel with Justin is particularly enlightening. Like Ignatius, Justin holds that in the books of the prophets many things about Jesus Christ are foretold (*1 Apol.* 31). But, unlike Ignatius, Justin has both the leisure and the resources on hand to attempt a demonstration of these things from the prophetic writings. Intermittently he refers to more recent written records from which he alleges the emperor can ascertain that these things indeed happened. Citing words about the miraculous birth of Jesus taken from Matthew and Luke, Justin attributes these words to those 'who have recorded (ἀπομνημονεύσαντες) all that concerns our Saviour Jesus Christ' (33. 5)—an obvious reference to plural apostolic 'memoirs', or gospel accounts. For the birth of Jesus in Bethlehem, he actually refers the emperor to 'the registers of the taxing made under Cyrenius, your first procurator in Judea' (34. 2). And for Jesus' being hidden from men until he grew to an adult, and for various details about the crucifixion found in the synoptic gospels and John, Justin encourages the emperor to read these things in 'the acts which took place under Pontius Pilate' (ἐκ τῶν ἐπὶ Ποντίου Πιλάτου γενομένων ἄκτων) (35. 9). He refers again later to certain events in the life of Christ, saying, 'And that He did those things you can learn from the acts which took place under Pontius Pilate (ἐκ τῶν ἐπὶ Ποντίου Πιλάτου γενομένων ἄκτων)' (48. 3). The details attributed to these 'acts'[49] make it impossible to conceive of them as any official Roman document chronicling the events of the procuratorship of Pilate (nor can they be plausibly related to later 'Pilate' literature). In fact, parallels with the Gospels of Matthew, Luke, John, and possibly Mark make plain, I believe, that by 'the acts which took place under Pontius Pilate' Justin is referring to these gospels.[50]

Justin's view of the written gospels as records of 'the acts' of Jesus which took place under Pontius Pilate seems but an amplified echo of Ignatius, who exhorted the Magnesians 'to be convinced of the birth and passion and resurrection which took place at the time of the procuratorship of Pontius Pilate; for these things were truly and certainly done (πραχθέντα) by Jesus

[48] Translation from W. Schneemelcher (ed.), *New Testament Apocrypha*, rev. edn., trans. R. McL. Wilson, 2 vols. (Cambridge: James Clarke & Co.; Louisville, Ky.: Westminster/John Knox Press, 1991), i. 35.

[49] Justin uses an official-sounding Latin loan-word, probably reflecting Greek τὰ πράξεις, πραγμάτα, or πραχθέντα.

[50] For a much fuller demonstration of this see Hill, *Johannine Corpus*, 330–5.

Christ, our hope' (*Magn.* 11. 1). Justin only makes clear that these acts are recorded in written sources.

Somewhere around the time Ignatius wrote, Papias was collecting the sayings of an elder who taught that Mark had written down accurately 'the things either said or done (τὰ ... ἢ λεχθέντα ἢ πραχθέντα) by the Lord' (*HE* 3. 39. 15). In another portion of this elder's teaching, summarized and paraphrased by Eusebius, the aorist or perfect passive participle of πράσσω (τὰ πραχθέντα or τὰ πεπραγμένα) occurs four times, and the noun πράξεις three times, to refer to the acts of Jesus as defining elements of the gospels (*HE* 3. 24. 5–13).[51] This terminology, derived perhaps from Luke 1. 1–2, Acts 1. 1–2, and related to the eventual title for Luke's second volume, confirm that in Ignatius' time, in Asia Minor, the written gospels were regarded as records of 'the acts of Jesus'.

These ways of speaking about the written gospels by Papias's elder, Justin, and the *Muratorian Fragment* show a striking commonality with Ignatius and support the conclusion that he too understood 'the gospel' to be represented in authoritative written form.

8. 'The Gospel' and the 'Decrees of the Lord'

Another relevant aspect of his use of the term is Ignatius' appeal to 'the gospel' as confirming faith. He seeks to 'make the gospel my refuge' (*Phld.* 5. 1), along with the apostles and the prophets. He owns that the gospel, along with the prophecies and the law of Moses ought to convince (ἔπεισαν, *Smyrn.* 5. 1). He tells the Smyrnaeans they ought to pay heed (προσέχειν) to the gospel, also to the prophets (7. 1). These in turn must be compared to two parallel exhortations in which Ignatius does not use the term 'gospel'. In *Magn.* 11. 1, as we have just seen, he exhorts his readers to 'be fully persuaded' (πεπληροφορῆσαι; cf. *Smyrn.* 1. 1) of things he elsewhere identifies with the gospel: the birth, passion, and resurrection under Pontius Pilate, truly and certainly done. Here Ignatius does not subsume these subjects under the word 'gospel', though, as we have seen, he refers to them as the acts or deeds of Jesus. Instead, he goes on in *Magn.* 13. 1, to tell his readers to 'be confirmed (βεβαιωθῆναι) in the decrees of the Lord and of the apostles (ἐν τοῖς δόγμασιν τοῦ κυρίου καὶ τῶν ἀποστόλων)'.[52] Here, being 'confirmed in the decrees of the

[51] See Hill, 'What Papias Said about John', 595–6.

[52] The construction would allow for a single set of decrees 'of the Lord and of the apostles'. This could refer to 'the gospel' as being also the work of apostles, but more likely 'the Lord' alludes to gospels, and 'the apostles' to other apostolic writings. For 'the Lord' see Euseb. *HE* 4. 22. 9; 4. 23; Irenaeus, *Adv. Haer.* 1. 8. 1; 3. 17. 4; Hippolytus, *CD* 4. 49.

Lord and the apostles' (*Magn.* 13. 1) sounds very much like 'taking refuge in' the gospel and the apostles in *Phld.* 5. 1, particularly as it has just followed a reference to 'the birth and passion and resurrection which took place . . . [under] Pontius Pilate—things truly and certainly done by Jesus Christ' (11. 1). It sounds a good deal like 'giving heed' especially to the gospel in *Smyrn.* 7. 2, 'in which the passion has been made clear to us and the resurrection accomplished' (my trans.); and is not unlike being 'persuaded' by the gospel in *Smyrn.* 5. 1. The same underlying structure in fact seems to reveal 'decrees of the Lord and the apostles' in *Magn.* 13. 1[53] to be a fair equivalent of 'the gospel and the apostles' in *Phld.* 5. 1.[54] We are reminded again that at about this time the written Gospels are being spoken of elsewhere as containing 'the Lord's sayings', 'the acts of Jesus', 'things said or done by the Lord'. It is likely, then, that 'decrees of the Lord', since it parallels 'the gospel', and since it assumes content available to Ignatius and to the Asian churches alike, should signify the existence of these 'decrees' in a written gospel or gospels possessed in common.

CONCLUSION

The debate at Philadelphia which threatened to set 'the gospel' against the archives of the Old Testament, forms the critical background for four other listings of 'the gospel' alongside the prophets or the prophecies and the law of Moses (and 'the apostles') as religious authorities in Ignatius' letters. These juxtapositions point both to a textual significance for his use of the term 'gospel' and to his use of these terms as categories of scriptural writings. These conclusions are further supported by Ignatius' parallel reference to 'decrees of the Lord and of the apostles', by Papias's elder's references to the gospels as containing 'the acts', 'the logia', or 'the things said and done by the Lord', by Justin's references to 'the acts which took place under Pontius Pilate', and by the *Muratorian Fragment*'s description of the contents of the 'gospel books'. That 'the gospel' and 'the apostles' should represent scriptural categories of writings in Ignatius receives further corroboration in the way other

[53] Note *Did.* 11. 3–4, which apparently refers to Jesus' instructions in Matt. 10. 40–1 as 'decrees of the gospel' (*τὸ δόγμα τοῦ εὐαγγελίου*). See now J. A. Kelhoffer, ' "How Soon a Book" Revisited: *ΕΥΑΓΓΕΛΙΟΝ* as a Reference to "Gospel" Materials in the First Half of the Second Century', *ZNW* 95 (2004), 1–34.

[54] Cf. 'the ordinances of the apostles' (*Trall.* 7. 1), which must at least include the ordinances preserved in their writings, generally known to Christians of Asia Minor and Syria alike. See Hill, 'Ignatius and the Apostolate', 236–40.

second-century authors use these and similar terms (see Appendix). This means that alongside its original meaning of the good news of salvation in Christ (*Phld.* 5. 2), the word 'gospel' is already being used as a convenient form of reference to the content of an authoritative Christian writing or set of writings containing that good news, the coming, birth, baptism, death, and resurrection of the Lord and faith through him. The familiarity of both Ignatius and the Asian churches with such a use should indicate that it was not coined on the spot by either of them.

Finally, if any of the parallels with Matthew, Luke, and John are judged to represent Ignatius' familiarity with these then-existing gospels in something like their final forms,[55] it then becomes clear that these gospels are being used both in a way similar to the way in which the Philadelphians were using the 'archives' of the Old Testament, and also simply as forming some of Ignatius' thoughts and expressions, much as Pauline and Old Testament materials were functioning for both Ignatius and his contemporaries.

APPENDIX: EARLY EXAMPLES OF 'SCRIPTURAL CATEGORIES'

Ignatius	*Phld.* 5. 1–2	gospel . . . apostles . . . prophets
	Phld. 8. 2	archives . . . gospel
	Phld. 9. 1–2	prophets . . . apostles . . . gospel
	Smyrn. 5. 1	the prophecies . . . the law of Moses . . . the gospel
	Smyrn. 7. 2	prophets . . . gospel
Polycarp	*Phil.* 6. 3	he himself . . . the apostles . . . and the prophets
Marcion		gospel and apostle
Ad Diogn.	11. 6	law . . . prophets . . . gospels . . . apostles
Justin	*1 Apol.* 67. 3	the memoirs of the apostles and the writings of the prophets
	Dial. 119. 6	the voice of God . . . through the apostles of Christ and through the prophets
2 Clement	14. 2	the books (τὰ βιβλία) and the apostles

[55] For John, see Hill, *Johannine Corpus*, 421–43.

Dionysius of Corinth	Euseb. *HE* 4. 23	the scriptures of the Lord[56]
Hegesippus	Euseb. *HE* 4. 22. 9	the law and the prophets and the Lord
Theophilus of Antioch	*Ad Autol.* 3. 12	The law... the prophets... the gospels
Irenaeus	*Adv. Haer.* 1. 3. 6	writings of the evangelists and the apostles... the law and the prophets
	Adv. Haer. 1. 8. 1	the prophets... the Lord... the apostles
	Adv. Haer. 2. 27. 2	the entire scriptures, the prophets and the gospels
	Adv. Haer. 3. 17. 4	the Lord himself, the apostles, and the prophets
Muratorian Fragment	lines 79–80	the prophets... or the apostles
Hippolytus	*CD* 4. 49	the prophets, the Lord, and the apostles
Clement of Alexandria	*Strom.* 7. 16	the prophets, the gospel, and the blessed apostles

[56] On 'the Lord' as a category in Hegesippus, Dionysius of Corinth, Irenaeus, Hippolytus, see also *Apocalypse of Peter* 16, where, 'the book of my Lord Jesus Christ', according to R. J. Bauckham, *The Fate of the Dead: Studies on the Jewish and Christian Apocalypses*, NovTSup 93 (Leiden, Boston, and Cologne: Brill, 1998), 173, is a reference to the Gospel of Matthew.

14

Following in Paul's Footsteps: *Mimēsis* and Power in Ignatius of Antioch

David M. Reis

οὐ γὰρ ἐν λόγῳ ἡ βασιλεία τοῦ θεοῦ ἀλλ' ἐν δυνάμει.

1 Cor. 4. 20

Although it is now a commonplace to acknowledge Ignatius' debt to Pauline thought, scholars continue to debate the precise nature of this relationship. The paucity of direct quotations from the apostle might suggest that Ignatius was not familiar with a collection of letters, and at most had access to one or two. Yet the existence of quotations is not the *sine qua non* for establishing a relationship between authors, and many studies have recognized that the allusions and 'echoes' to Paul demonstrate that Ignatius made use of Pauline ideas at the conceptual level.[1] This realization has unfortunately led to a certain methodological untidiness, as scholars search for a vocabulary for assessing Ignatius' 'Paulinisms'.[2] Recent studies on the art of *mimēsis*, however, have provided a tool that is particularly well suited for evaluating the complex relationship between Ignatius and Paul. Rather than focusing on the existence of direct quotations to establish links between authors, they have instead emphasized the method advised by the ancient rhetoricians.

[1] É. Massaux, *The Influence of the Gospel of Saint Matthew on Christian Literature before Saint Irenaeus*, ed. A. J. Bellinzoni, i (Macon, Ga.: Mercer University Press, 1990), 108: 'the bishop of Antioch knows the apostle's letters so well that he juggles, if I may say so, various Pauline texts to express his own thought'. For summaries of opinions on Ignatius' use of Paul, see W. R. Schoedel, 'Polycarp of Smyrna and Ignatius of Antioch', *ANRW* 2.27.1 (1993), 272–358, at pp. 307–9; C. Munier, 'Où en est la question d'Ignace d'Antioche?: Bilan d'un siècle de recherches 1870–1988', *ANRW* 2. 27. 1 (1993), 359–484, at pp. 391–3. For a list of parallels and allusions to New Testament authors in Ignatius, see Foster, ch. 7 in companion volume.

[2] Even 1 Corinthians, the one Pauline letter that most commentators feel Ignatius knew, is treated in varying ways by Ignatius. As R. M. Grant (*The Apostolic Fathers: A New Translation and Commentary*, i: *An Introduction* (New York: Thomas Nelson and Sons, 1964), 59) concludes, the bishop 'used the letter in several different ways... sometimes he quoted, sometimes he alluded, sometimes he allusively quoted, and sometimes he quotingly alluded. Any idea of exactness in analysing his usage must be read in by the analyst. It does not exist in Ignatius' own writings'.

Specifically, these teachers instructed their students to refrain from simply 'rewriting' earlier texts, but rather, through a creative process of 'internalization' and 're-articulation', to transform them so that they speak to a new situation.[3] By revisiting the Paul–Ignatius question through the lens of *mimēsis*, I will argue that the Ignatian correspondence can be viewed as mimetic productions, and that these letters, like those of Paul, have as their focus a construction of the self that is embedded in ancient notions of power. For Ignatius, this method of self-presentation then becomes the fulcrum for generating a vision of the church based upon hierarchy and unity.

PAUL, *MIMĒSIS*, AND POWER

In *Imitating Paul: A Discourse of Power*, Elizabeth Castelli explores antiquity's understanding of *mimēsis* in order to uncover the rhetorical strategies behind Paul's exhortation to imitation.[4] Through a survey of *mimēsis* language in Greco-Roman literature, Castelli concludes that (1) the model is considered superior to the copy, reflecting a perfection and wholeness for which the latter

Another example of this 'inexactness' is found in Ignatius' understanding of the Jewish scriptures (*Phld.* 8. 2). According to A. Lindemann ('Der Apostel Paulus im 2. Jahrhundert', in J.-M. Sevrin (ed.), *The New Testament in Early Christianity*, BETL 86 (Leuven: Leuven University Press, 1989), 47): 'Solche Argumentation ist näturlich von keinem bestimmten paulinischen Text abhängig. Und doch ist die zugrundeliegende Denkstruktur ohne Paulus kaum vorstellbar.'

[3] See, e.g., Quint. *Inst.* 10. 1. 19; Dion. Hal. *Dinarchus* 7; Seneca, *Ep.* 84. 3–9; [Longinus], *Subl.* 13. 2–3. For modern studies on *mimēsis*, see S. Halliwell, *The Aesthetics of Mimesis: Ancient Texts and Modern Problems* (Princeton: Princeton University Press, 2002); D. R. MacDonald (ed.), *Mimesis and Intertextuality in Antiquity and Christianity* (Harrisburg, Pa.: Trinity Press International, 2001); T. L. Brodie, 'Greco-Roman Imitation of Texts as a Partial Guide to Luke's Use of Sources', in C. H. Talbert (ed.), *Luke–Acts: New Perspectives from the Society of Biblical Literature Seminar* (New York: Crossroad, 1984), 17–46; T. M. Greene, *The Light in Troy: Imitation and Discovery in Renaissance Poetry* (New Haven: Yale University Press, 1982), 54–80; E. Fantham, 'Imitation and Decline: Rhetorical Theory and Practice in the First Century after Christ', *Classical Philology*, 73 (1978), 102–16; *idem*, 'Imitation and Evolution: The Discussion of Rhetorical Imitation in Cicero *De oratore* 2. 87–97 and Some Related Problems of Ciceronian Theory', *Classical Philology*, 73 (1978), 1–16.

[4] E. A. Castelli, *Imitating Paul: A Discourse of Power* (Louisville, Ky.: Westminster/John Knox Press, 1991). Other studies on imitation in Paul include J. A. Brant, 'The Place of *Mimēsis* in Paul's Thought', *Studies in Religion/Sciences Religieuses*, 22 (1993), 285–300; A. Reinhartz, 'On the Meaning of the Pauline Exhortation: "*mimētai mou ginesthe*—become imitators of me" ', *Studies in Religion/Sciences Religieuses*, 16 (1987), 393–403; R. G. Hamerton-Kelly, 'A Girardian Interpretation of Paul: Rivalry, Mimesis and Victimage in the Corinthian Correspondence', *Semeia*, 33 (1985), 65–81; D. M. Stanley, 'Imitation in Paul's Letters: Its Significance for his Relationship to Jesus and his Own Christian Foundations', in P. Richardson and J. C. Hurd (eds.), *From Jesus to Paul* (Waterloo, Ont.: Wilfrid Laurier University Press, 1984), 127–42; *idem*, ' "Become Imitators of Me": The Pauline Conception of Apostolic Tradition', *Bib* 40 (1959), 859–77; B. Sanders, 'Imitating Paul: 1 Cor 4:16', *HTR* 74 (1981), 353–63.

strives; (2) the copy is ultimately unable to attain a 'sameness' with the model, thus leading to the formation of a hierarchy—the model's superiority produces an authority to which the copy submits; (3) a tension develops between model and copy in which (a) any movement toward sameness is linked with unity, harmony, and order, while (b) any movement away from sameness is equated with disunity, discord, and disorder; and (4) reflections of 'sameness' and 'difference' are accorded a soteriological status: the model places those who reflect the values of sameness within the community of believers, while those who do not are marginalized and demonized.[5]

For Castelli, discourse is the field where the expression of these power relations is articulated and contested. Rhetoric thus becomes the primary vehicle for shaping the contours of the social body. Through its expression of power, then, discourse contributes to social formation by constructing what is normative and true, on the one hand, and deviant and false, on the other.[6] Seen through this lens, Paul's use of *mimēsis* terminology[7] seeks to accomplish three interrelated related goals. First, his calls to imitate himself establish his superiority as a model, to which his communities must conform. As the mediator between God/Christ and other Christians, he establishes a hierarchy in which his authority cannot be equalled by other humans. Second, Paul's language of imitation reflects his attempt to create 'sameness', a normative form of social formation based on unity and the eradication of difference. Finally, the normative behaviour that Paul advocates possesses a soteriological function: because salvation is contingent on conforming to his version of Christianity, the apostle makes it clear that dissenting voices will meet an opposite fate.[8]

From the context of the letters in which the calls to imitation are found, it becomes apparent that Paul's understanding of *mimēsis* is connected with the concepts of suffering and unity. Indeed, Paul commends the Thessalonians in his first letter for receiving the word of God 'in much affliction' (ἐν θλίψει πολλῇ, 1. 6), and praises them because they 'suffered' (ἐπάθετε, 2. 14) for the sake of the gospel. In both of these passages, Paul asserts that the Thessalonians' behaviour brings them into the Christian fold: 'their suffering ... ties their experience to that of everyone else in the mimetic system: Paul, the Lord, and the other persecuted communities'.[9] Proper imitation thus rests on receiving the gospel (i.e., Paul's gospel) and suffering on its behalf.

The call to imitation in Phil. 3. 17 is set within the apostle's larger interest in establishing unity within his community. Interpreting this passage as a discourse on power, however, enables Castelli to show that embedded within this

5 Castelli, *Imitating Paul*, 59–87. 6 Ibid. 42–56.

7 1 Thess. 1. 6–7; Phil. 3. 17; 1 Cor. 4. 16; 11. 1. 8 Castelli, *Imitating Paul*, 89–117.

9 Castelli, *Imitating Paul*, 94.

exhortation to unity is an expression of Paul's authority and desire for 'sameness' (one either imitates him or is an enemy of the cross of Christ), a corresponding articulation of hierarchy (with Paul acting as the mediator between Christ and the Philippians), and the contention that unity is contingent upon showing an affinity with the life of Christ (who displayed humility and obedience and gave himself up to death on the cross).[10] The *mimēsis* language in 1 Cor. 4. 16 and 11. 1 represents a further amplification of the interplay between authority, unity, and suffering. In his call to imitation, Paul casts himself as the father of the Corinthians, who asserts authority through his privileged status as the sole mediator between Christ and the community. Adherence to Paul's gospel of the cross thus becomes the litmus test for distinguishing 'insiders' from 'outsiders'. At the same time, he places a burden on the Corinthians to strive for a level of Christian *praxis* that they can never fully attain. This rhetorical ploy has the effect of reinscribing the apostle's authority, while putting the Corinthians in a state of 'perpetual unease' as they attempt to accomplish an impossible task. The result of this rhetoric of coercion is that social harmony can be achieved only through the Corinthians' acceptance of Paul's claims to power and a concomitant obedience to his message.[11]

Castelli's study locates Paul's rhetoric of *mimēsis* within a larger matrix of discourse, power, and social formation. In the contested space of discourse, Paul articulates his claims to authority and a vision of communities united in obedience and harmony to the 'truth' of his message. Furthermore, the rhetorical force of the message apparently hinges on Paul's understanding of his own life, which he has modelled on the life of Christ (1 Cor. 11. 1). If Paul sees himself as a model for other Christians to imitate, what was it about his life that led him to this conclusion and to see in his activities an affinity with Christ?

The autobiographical reminiscences in Galatians suggest that the foundation for Paul's claim to speak authoritatively rests upon the circumstances in which he came to know Christ. Indeed, he is quick to point out to the Galatians that human authorities did not confer upon him the status of apostle, but rather that he received it directly through Jesus and God (Gal. 1. 1). If the conferral of his apostleship bypasses the human sphere, so too does his gospel message: 'For I want you to know... that the gospel that was proclaimed by me was not of human origin (*κατὰ ἄνθρωπον*); for I did not receive it from a human source (*παρὰ ἀνθρώπου*), nor was I taught it, but I received it through a revelation (*ἀποκαλύψεως*) of Jesus Christ' (Gal.

[10] Castelli, *Imitating Paul*, 95–7. [11] Ibid. 97–115.

1. 11–12). Not only did Paul receive the knowledge of the gospel directly from God, but he even claims that this event was pre-ordained as part of God's plan (Gal. 1. 15–16; cf. Rom. 1. 1). Such assertions, which circumvent and undercut the more traditional forms of transmitting knowledge (from teacher to student), serve to elevate Paul's status while simultaneously establishing a uniformity of thought within his churches. With this scheme in place, it is natural to see how Paul could imagine that his gospel was the only true gospel (Gal. 1. 6–9; cf. 2 Cor. 11. 4–5). In essence, because Paul did not learn the gospel from the other apostles (those who knew the human Jesus), but 'received' (*παρέλαβον*) it in an unmediated fashion from the divine teacher, Christ, his message bears an authenticity that his rival missionaries, who are derivative and irrelevant,[12] cannot offer.

This close connection with Christ manifests itself through the reception of divine secrets and the exercise of special gifts. In his 'tearful letter' to Corinth, Paul professes not to boast according to human standards, yet he subsequently recounts the time when he was taken up into the third heaven and received information 'that no mortal is permitted to repeat' (2 Cor. 12. 4). It is this sort of experience that undergirds his claim to speak as one imbued with power. For instance, in 1 Corinthians, Paul recounts how he had come to the Corinthians 'not with plausible words of wisdom, but with a demonstration of the Spirit and of power', which was in turn based on the 'power of God'.[13] Later in this same letter, a case of improper conduct leads the apostle to assert that his spirit is present with the community, and that he has already rendered judgement upon the accused person (1 Cor. 5. 3–4). Likewise, after learning that some within the community are boasting about their abilities to speak in tongues, the apostle reminds them that he surpasses them all in this spiritual gift (1 Cor. 14. 18).

Even though he could match the boastings of others by putting his power on display, Paul states that he has subordinated it for the greater good of concord within the community (e.g., 1 Cor. 9. 19–23; 10. 32; 14. 18–19). He thus sees his missionary journeys as 'labours' and 'work' directed toward that end (1 Thess. 3. 5; 1 Cor. 3. 8; 2 Cor. 10. 15–16; 11. 23; cf. 2 Thess. 3. 7–9). Moreover, the fact that these labours entail suffering testifies to their truth, for it shows that his life is in accord with the sufferings and death of Christ. As he explains to the Philippians, 'I want to know Christ and the power of his resurrection and the sharing of his sufferings by becoming like him in his

[12] Or satanic, according to 2 Cor. 11. 13–15. On Paul's disdain for human authority, see also Gal. 2. 6.

[13] 1 Cor. 2. 4: *οὐκ ἐν πειθοῖ[s] σοφίας [λόγοις] ἀλλ' ἐν ἀποδείξει πνεύματος καὶ δυνάμεως . . . ἐν δυνάμει θεοῦ*. See also 2 Cor. 12. 12.

death'.[14] Because 'power is made perfect in weakness',[15] to become 'afflicted', 'perplexed', 'persecuted', and 'struck down' are all tangible proofs that Paul carries 'the death (νέκρωσιν) of Jesus' in his body.[16] Paradoxically, then, the marks of death inscribed on his body are the very signs that he (and those who imitate him) embodies the life of Christ: 'For while we live, we are always being given up to death for Jesus' sake, so that the life of Jesus may be made visible in our mortal flesh' (2 Cor. 4. 11).[17] Paul can thus tell the Romans that 'suffering produces endurance' (ἡ θλῖψις ὑπομονὴν κατεργάζεται) and a future 'hope' (ἐλπίς) that he will share in God's glory (5. 2–5).[18]

The endurance practised by Paul allows him to claim a spiritual equanimity in the face of the trials of the world (see, e.g., Phil. 4. 11–13). Not surprisingly, then, those who bear the qualities he emphasizes receive commendation for their ability to imitate him. In particular, the apostle singles out the Thessalonians, thanking them for their 'work of faith and labor of love and steadfastness of hope'.[19] Similarly, Paul reassures the Corinthians that they experience comfort when they 'patiently endure the same sufferings that we are also suffering'.[20] The connection that Paul makes between his afflictions and those of his community likewise appears in the letter to the Philippians, as the apostle approvingly remarks that God has given them 'the privilege not only of believing in Christ, but of suffering for him (τὸ ὑπὲρ αὐτοῦ πάσχειν) as well—since you are having the same struggle (ἀγῶνα) that you saw I had and

[14] Phil 3. 10: τοῦ γνῶναι αὐτὸν καὶ τὴν δύναμιν τῆς ἀναστάσεως αὐτοῦ καὶ [τὴν] κοινωνίαν [τῶν] παθημάτων αὐτοῦ, συμμορφιζόμενος τῷ θανάτῳ αὐτοῦ. See also 2 Cor. 1. 5, where Paul states that he and Timothy 'share abundantly in Christ's sufferings' (περισσεύει τὰ παθήματα τοῦ Χριστοῦ).

[15] 2 Cor. 12. 9: ἡ γὰρ δύναμις ἐν ἀσθενείᾳ τελεῖται.

[16] 2 Cor. 4. 8–10; see also 2 Cor. 8. 9; 13. 4–5. For more detailed catalogues of Paul's suffering, see 2 Cor. 6. 3–10; 11. 21–9. Placing these *peristaseis* in a Hellenistic context, Hamerton-Kelly ('Girardian Interpretation', 75) notes that in Stoic and Cynic literature, such lists are designed to 'demonstrate the divine power at work in the missionary by which he is preserved amidst the *peristaseis*'. Likewise, P. B. Duff ('Apostolic Suffering and the Language of Processions in 2 Corinthians 4:7–10', *BTB* 21 (1991), 158–65, on p. 163) concludes that Paul's 'afflictions are a vehicle for God's epiphany in the salvation event. His metaphor suggests that his own suffering can be seen as the very suffering of the Christ... Paul's body has come to function as a visual counterpart to the oral proclamation of the gospel.'

[17] Commenting on Gal. 4. 12–15, Hamerton-Kelly ('Girardian Interpretation', 73–4) shows that the Galatians received Paul as Christ 'not in spite of his affliction, but because of it'.

[18] For a more detailed treatment of ὑπομονή in antiquity, see B. D. Shaw, 'Body/Power/Identity: Passions of the Martyrs', *JECS* 4 (1996), 269–312. D. R. Denton, 'Hope and Perseverance', *SJT* 34 (1981), 313–20, focuses specifically on Paul.

[19] 1 Thess. 1. 3: τοῦ ἔργου τῆς πίστεως καὶ τοῦ κόπου τῆς ἀγάπης καὶ τῆς ὑπομονῆς τῆς ἐλπίδος τοῦ κυρίου ἡμῶν Ἰησοῦ Χριστοῦ. This point has been noticed by Brant, 'Place of *Mimēsis*', 292.

[20] 2 Cor. 1. 6: ἐν ὑπομονῇ τῶν αὐτῶν παθημάτων ὧν καὶ ἡμεῖς πάσχομεν. Continuing this thought, Paul states that 'Our hope for you is unshaken; for we know that as you share in our sufferings (τῶν παθημάτων), so also you share in our comfort' (2 Cor. 1. 7).

now hear that I still have' (Phil. 1. 29–30). In spite of their troubles, the Philippians are nevertheless encouraged to 'Keep on doing the things that you have learned and received and heard and seen in me, and the God of peace will be with you' (Phil. 4. 9). According to the apostle, following this path is proof that the group lives 'with one mind' (Phil. 1. 27; 3. 15; cf. Rom. 12. 16; 15. 5).

While Paul's rhetoric of self-presentation and his prescriptions for his communities are often treated as benign or 'natural', Castelli argues that they are ultimately anchored in a claim for power. Paul's discourse is thus coercive in the sense that it creates an authoritative model for imitation and establishes the conditions for normative belief and practice. In this carefully constructed experiment in social formation, there is no room for dissent; it is, in fact, predicated on the abolition of difference. At the same time, however, Paul's decision to place himself in the position of model and to depict his community as its copy is a shrewd move that secures and reifies his hegemony and a hierarchy of power.

IGNATIUS IMITATING PAUL IMITATING CHRIST

If Pauline thought exercises a strong hold over Ignatius, as most scholars believe, then the question that naturally arises is whether Ignatius' letters display the same tendencies toward establishing power relations. In other words, does the bishop's rhetoric seek to establish authority by emphasizing suffering and unity? And are dissenting voices quashed and placed outside the bounds of the ecclesiastical body? If so, can he then be said to be 'imitating Paul'? Exploring this issue through the lens of ethical and literary *mimēsis* will help make sense of two seemingly irreconcilable tendencies in the letters: on the one hand, Ignatius' extreme humility and deference to Paul and the apostolic age, and on the other hand, his brash claims for authority and the promotion of a 'true' form of Christianity.

Ethical *mimēsis*, well known in Greek philosophical circles, refers to the imitation of a revered figure's dress, mannerisms, and practices by followers who seek to be like their teacher.[21] Less than a century after Paul's death, there is evidence to suggest that he had begun to represent, for some Christians at least, an example worthy of emulation. In *1 Clement*, Paul was 'the greatest

[21] Objects of emulation include figures such as Socrates (Ar. *Aves* 1280–3; Pl. *Apol.* 23C; Xen. *Mem.* 1. 2. 2–3); Heracles (Lucian, *De mort. Peregr.* 21, 24, 36; *Demon.* 1; Ps.-Diog. *Ep.* 10. 1; Philo, *Leg. ad Gaium*, 78–85, 90; Suet. *Ner.* 53; Plut. *De Alex. mag. for.* 1. 10. 332A); and Epicurus (Lucr. *De rer. nat.* 3. 1–13).

example of endurance' for the sufferings he experienced on his journeys.[22] Likewise, Polycarp singles out Paul among the apostles as one whose life of righteousness and endurance is an example for the Philippians.[23] The letters of Ignatius display a similar reverence for the apostle.[24] The most transparent example of Ignatius' recognition of his mimetic relationship to Paul can be found in *Ephesians.* In this letter, the bishop commends the church for being 'a highway for those killed for God's sake' and 'fellow initiates (συμμύσται) of Paul, who was sanctified, approved, worthy of blessing—may I be found in his footsteps when I reach God! (ὑπὸ τὰ ἴχνη εὑρεθῆναι, ὅταν θεοῦ ἐπιτύχω)—who in every letter remembers you' (*Eph.* 12. 2). In this passage the Ephesians are commended for their fidelity to Paul, who himself is identified as an example of proper Christian conduct. Moreover, the close juxtaposition between the Ephesians' role in martyrdom and the apostle signals that Ignatius must have been aware of some martyrological traditions surrounding Paul.[25] It is within this context that Ignatius' personal reflection becomes sensible: just as Paul was sent to Rome to die as a martyr for the faith, so too does the bishop hope to imitate his death.

While Ignatius may see close parallels between his fate and that of Paul, he is clearly uneasy about elevating himself as an equal to the apostle. His letter to the Romans, for example, insists that his authority cannot match that of Peter and Paul: 'they were apostles, I am a convict; they were free, I am even now a slave' (*Rom.* 4. 3). Likewise, when addressing some apparent shortcomings among the Trallians, Ignatius tempers his message in deference to the apostles: 'although I could write more sharply... I did not think myself qualified for this, that I, a convict, should give you orders as though I were an apostle' (ὡς ἀπόστολος ὑμῖν διατάσσωμαι, *Trall.* 3. 3). This sentiment is echoed elsewhere in the letters: while the apostles 'give orders' (δόγματα, διατάγματα, *Magn.* 13. 1) and 'command' (διατάσσειν, *Trall.* 7. 1), Ignatius

[22] *1 Clem.* 5. 7: 'ὑπομονῆς ... μέγιστος ὑπογραμμός'.

[23] Pol. *Phil.* 8–10. The issue of Polycarp's imitation of Paul is addressed in K. Berding, *Polycarp and Paul: An Analysis of their Literary and Theological Relationship in Light of Polycarp's Use of Biblical and Extra-Biblical Literature,* VCSup 62 (Leiden: Brill, 2002), 126–41.

[24] I have consulted two translations of Ignatius' letters: M. W. Holmes (ed.), *The Apostolic Fathers: Greek Texts and English Translations,* 2nd edn. (Grand Rapids, Mich.: Baker Books, 1999); W. R. Schoedel, *Ignatius of Antioch: A Commentary on the Letters of Ignatius of Antioch* (Philadelphia: Fortress, 1985).

[25] For the evidence that early Christian authors knew of oral traditions regarding Paul's death, see D. R. MacDonald, 'Apocryphal and Canonical Narratives about Paul', in W. S. Babcock (ed.), *Paul and the Legacies of Paul* (Dallas: Southern Methodist University Press, 1990), 55–70, at pp. 62–3. R. J. Stoops, Jun., 'If I Suffer... Epistolary Authority in Ignatius of Antioch', *HTR* 80 (1987), 161–178, on p. 166, contends that *Eph.* 12. 2 implies a knowledge of the *totality* of Paul's career, not just his death.

claims only 'to exhort' (παρακαλεῖν, *Rom.* 4. 3).[26] It would appear that the primary characteristic distinguishing the apostles from Ignatius centres on the completion of the Christian life through death. While Peter and Paul have achieved this *telos* and are now 'free' (ἐλεύθεροι), Ignatius remains a 'convict' (κατάκριτος) and a 'slave' (δοῦλος) until his death, at which time he will finally be able to consider himself a 'disciple' (μαθητής).[27] As he categorically states in *Romans* (4. 2), 'I will truly be a disciple of Jesus Christ when the world will no longer see my body.'

The parallel circumstances surrounding the lives of Ignatius and Paul seem to have left a deep impression on the bishop: both were church leaders working in the same community; both composed letters to churches within Asia Minor that emphasized similar theological themes; both were condemned for their work and sentenced to death; and both journeyed to Rome to experience this martyrdom. In a broad sense, then, it may be said that Ignatius 'imitated' Paul through the fulfilment of this journey.[28] In a narrower sense, however, Paul's calls to imitate himself appear to have affected the bishop in precisely the manner that Castelli discovered in her analysis of 1 Corinthians. Specifically, by elevating Paul as a model for emulation, Ignatius seems to have placed himself in the position of a 'copy' of the apostolic 'model'. This phenomenon, as Castelli has shown, not only

The existence of oral traditions surrounding Paul should be added to the material of the historical Paul, the epistolary Paul, and the legendary Paul as evidence that contributes to the complete picture of Paul ('the *Paulusbild*') as available to first- and second-century Christians. For a discussion of this issue, see A. Lindemann, *Paulus im ältesten Christentum: Das Bild des Apostels und die Rezeption der paulinischen Theologie in der frühchristlichen Literatur bis Marcion*, BHT 58 (Tübingen: J. C. B. Mohr, 1979), 36–113; *idem*, 'Paul in the Writings of the Apostolic Fathers', in Babcock (ed.), *Paul and the Legacies of Paul*, 25–45. See also the response to Lindemann's paper by M. C. de Boer, 'Comment: Which Paul?', in Babcock (ed.), *Paul and the Legacies of Paul*, 45–54.

[26] The distinction between the verbs becomes less absolute, however, when it is recognized that in epistolary literature, the verb παρακαλεῖν has the force of a request made by the writer to initiate a plan of action that has yet to be taken; in other words, it is used 'where compliance with the request was obligatory' (Stoops, 'If I Suffer', 169). See also *Trall.* 12. 2, noted below.

[27] Regarding the deaths of Peter and Paul, H. Rathke, *Ignatius von Antiochien und die Paulusbriefe*, TU 99 (Berlin: Akademie-Verlag, 1967), 20, contends that *Rom.* 4. 3 demonstrates that 'Ignatius denkt wahrscheinlich daran, daß beide bereits den Märtyrertod erlitten haben'. See also Stoops, 'If I Suffer', 172: 'Ignatius could be certain of his spiritual freedom only on the other side of death ... Although Ignatius could never become an apostle, he could become similar to Peter and Paul, if he suffered.'

[28] Stoops ('If I Suffer', 167) states that 'The acceptance of suffering and death were seen by Ignatius as part of a larger path leading to God. Paul was viewed as a predecessor, who completed the path. Paul was shown faithful to the end and was therefore approved or attested and worthy of being imitated.' See also Rathke, *Ignatius von Antiochien*, 98, who concludes that Ignatius 'überhaupt in seiner ganzen Haltung Paulus als Vorbild ansah'.

establishes a definitive hierarchy, but it continually forces the imitator into a position of self-examination, in which he constantly seeks but fails to attain a status equal to the model. It is through this technique that the hierarchy is perpetuated and the idea of 'sameness' reified. By constantly drawing attention to his subordinate status and his self-doubts about his Christian status, Ignatius exemplifies the coercive effect of Paul's rhetoric that Castelli has identified.[29]

From the perspective of ethical *mimēsis*, Ignatius appears to cast himself as an imitator of the apostles, a copy that repeatedly tries, but ultimately fails, to attain the level of its model. From the perspective of literary *mimēsis*, however, the bishop's close connection to Pauline vocabulary, ideas, and argumentation have the effect of inviting his readers to identify him with Paul, with all of the associations that such a connection could allow.[30] Ignatius' prologues provide clear evidence of this tendency. For example, the prologue to *Ephesians* is filled with verbal parallels to the opening chapter in the apostle's letter of the same name.[31] Moreover, in *Trallians*, Ignatius begins his salutation by greeting the community 'in apostolic manner' (ἐν ἀποστολικῷ χαρακτῆρι), a rather overt case of Ignatius' conscious identification with Paul (*Trall.* prol.). While less explicit, the greeting found in *Magnesians* captures the sense of a typically Pauline salutation without quoting any one of his letters verbatim.[32] These testimonies, both of which occur at the beginnings of letters (which are themselves likely among the first he wrote),[33] act to frame the rest of the correspondence in an apostolic guise: they are 'signs' that Ignatius places himself squarely within the age of the apostles and encourages his readers to

[29] Ignatius' letter to the Romans provides the clearest and most sustained example of his fears and doubts about his worthiness to be a Christian. See n. 47 below.

[30] This assertion is based on the theory of intertextuality, which asserts that the current of influence between two texts is not linear but multidirectional. Thus, echoes of Paul in the Ignatian correspondence not only transport the apostle into the second century, so to speak; they also take the bishop back to the apostolic age and allow him to speak with that level of authority. For a discussion of this literary-critical approach and a select bibliography, see my article, 'The Areopagus as Echo Chamber: *Mimēsis* and Intertextuality in Acts 17', *Journal of Higher Criticism*, 9 (2002), 259–77. For an extensive list of words found in Ignatius that are either unique to or prevalent in the Pauline corpus, see Massaux, *Influence*, 114–16.

[31] This is not to say, of course, that the historical Paul wrote Ephesians; rather, I am only asserting that at this stage in the development of Christianity, Ignatius would not have known of such a thing as a deutero-Pauline corpus. For a list of the parallels, see Schoedel, *Ignatius of Antioch*, 37; Rathke, *Ignatius von Antiochien*, 45–6.

[32] Compare the salutation in *Magnesians* ('καὶ εὔχομαι ἐν θεῷ πατρὶ καὶ ἐν Ἰησοῦ Χριστῷ πλεῖστα χαίρειν') with those of Rom. 1. 7; 1 Cor. 1. 3; 2 Cor. 1. 2; Gal. 1. 3; Eph. 1. 2; Phil. 1. 2; Col. 1. 2; 1 Thess. 1. 1; 2 Thess. 1. 2.

[33] Stoops ('If I Suffer', 168) argues that Ignatius was 'experimenting' in the prologue of the *Trallians*, and that while 'Ignatius continued to imitate Paul's greetings particularly closely, he never again drew attention to this point' (i.e., the apostolic manner of his letter writing).

think of him as a Paul *redivivus*.[34] With this rhetorical move, Ignatius brings into the foreground the entire body of traditions surrounding the figure of Paul,[35] while elevating his own status as one who speaks with the force of apostolic authority.[36]

The identification of Ignatius with Paul is also strengthened by means of the close connection between the two authors' assertions of authority. Like the apostle, Ignatius is the 'least' of the Syrian Christians and one 'untimely born';[37] yet he claims for himself a spiritual insight that is superior to other Christians. For instance, in *Ephesians* he prepares the community for another letter written under the guidance of divine revelation, and in *Romans* he asserts that he writes not 'according to human standards' (κατὰ σάρκα) but 'according to the purpose of God'.[38] Similarly, the bishop reminds the Philadelphians how he spoke to them 'in a loud voice—the voice of God' and instructed them by means of the Spirit.[39] It is his knowledge of 'heavenly things' (τὰ ἐπουράνια), as well as an insight into 'things invisible and visible' (ὁρατά τε καὶ ἀόρατα, *Trall.* 5. 3; cf. 2 Cor. 12. 4), that allows Ignatius to refer to the Trallians as 'infants' (νηπίοις) who are as yet unable to receive insights into the divine realities that he possesses.[40] By placing himself at the top of the spiritual hierarchy, Ignatius can admonish them to follow his instructions so that his letter will not become a witness against them (*Trall.* 12. 3; see also

[34] This hypothesis softens the boundary between Ignatius and the apostle that Stoops ('If I Suffer', 167–9) has constructed.

[35] Lindemann (*Paulus im ältesten Christentum*, 87) concludes that Ignatius' ' "Paulusbild" enthält jedoch kaum individuelle Züge; das ihm in Ign Eph 12,2 erteilte Lob ist überwältigend, geht aber auf die Person des Apostels selbst praktisch nicht ein'. For this paper, however, the precise nature of Ignatius' knowledge of Paul is less important than is the effect that citing Paul or alluding to Pauline traditions could have had on his readers. This reading, therefore, minimizes the importance of authorial intention, choosing instead to place its emphasis on the rhetorical nature of the letters. For further remarks on this issue, see Castelli, *Imitating Paul*, 120–1.

[36] Rathke, *Ignatius von Antiochien*, 42: 'Ignatius muß wohl selbst empfunden haben, daß die Form und der Ton seiner Briefe den Eindruck erwecken konnten, als ob er sich Rechte und Authorität eines Apostels anmaße.'

[37] Echoing 1 Cor. 15. 8–9, Ignatius writes: 'Remember in your prayers the church in Syria, of which I am not worthy to be considered a member, being as I am the very least of them' (ὢν ἔσχατος ἐκείνων, *Trall.* 13. 1) (see also *Eph.* 21. 2; *Magn.* 14. 1; *Smyrn.* 11. 1); and 'for I am not worthy, since I am the very last of them and one untimely born' (ὢν ἔσχατος αὐτῶν καὶ ἔκτρωμα, *Rom.* 9. 2).

[38] *Eph.* 20. 2; *Rom.* 8. 3: κατὰ γνώμην θεοῦ. Paul uses similar terminology, albeit in different contexts, to distinguish between human and divine standards (Rom. 8. 4–5, 12–13; 2 Cor. 10. 2–5; Gal. 4. 29).

[39] *Phld.* 7. 1–2; see also *Phld.* 5. 1, where Jesus Christ acts through Ignatius on behalf of the Philadelphians. For Pauline parallels, see 1 Cor. 7. 40; 15. 10; Gal. 2. 20.

[40] *Trall.* 5. 1: 'Surely I am not unable to write to write to you about heavenly things? No, but I fear inflicting harm on you who are mere infants. Bear with me, then, lest you be choked by what you are unable to swallow'. Cf. 1 Cor. 3. 1–2.

Phld. 6. 3). Even the bishop Polycarp, who is praised for his 'godly mind', is not immune from Ignatius' criticism, as evidenced by the latter's reprimand that the bishop of Smyrna become 'more diligent' (πλέον σπουδαῖος) in his duties (*Pol.* 3. 2). Finally, Ignatius also employs the Pauline technique of using rhetoric that simultaneously expresses both humility and power. In *Trallians*, for instance, Ignatius' instruction on ecclesiastical authority both subordinates and elevates his personal authority: 'Because I love you I refrain (φείδομαι), though I could write more sharply about this. But I did not think myself qualified for this, that I, a convict (κατάκριτος), should give you orders as though I was an apostle (ἀπόστολος). I have much knowledge in God (Πολλὰ φρονῶ ἐν θεῷ), but I measure myself lest I perish by boasting' (*Trall.* 3. 3–4; cf. *Eph.* 3. 1).[41]

The Pauline echoes found in this passage are particularly revealing in that they demonstrate that Ignatius claimed to subordinate his authority for the benefit of other Christians. In much the same way as Paul, Ignatius thought that his life acquired meaning by following the model of suffering and endurance established by Jesus.[42] Consequently, just as Jesus 'suffered' (παθητόν) and 'endured (ὑπομείναντα) in every way' for the sake of others, (*Smyrn.* 2. 1; *Pol.* 3. 2; cf. *Rom.* 10. 3), so too must Ignatius adhere to the same tenets. In its most general sense, this occurs naturally for all Christians because the world is hostile to them.[43] The only option, then, is to 'endure patiently' (ὑπομένοντες, *Magn.* 1. 2) the abuses that stem from the world, for 'if you endure everything (πάντα ὑπομένοντες) for his sake [i.e. Jesus], you will reach him' (*Smyrn.* 9. 2).[44] Furthermore, like an athlete who is 'bruised, yet still conquers', Christians must 'patiently put up (ὑπομένειν) with all things so that he [i.e. God] may also put up (ὑπομείνῃ) with us' (*Pol.* 3. 1).[45] Those who possess this endurance will, Ignatius proclaims, be recognized as disciples of Jesus, for, like him, these 'imitators of the Lord' strive 'to see who can be the more wronged, who the more cheated, who the more rejected, in order that... with complete purity and self-control [they] may abide in Jesus Christ spiritually and physically' (*Eph.* 10. 3).

Understood more specifically, however, endurance and suffering are closely connected with martyrdom, for according to Ignatius the Christian life is

[41] For similar statements by Paul, see 1 Cor. 2. 6–7; 13. 2; 2 Cor. 12. 6.

[42] W. Rebell, 'Das Leidenverständnis bei Paulus und Ignatius von Antiochien', *NTS* 32 (1986), 457–65.

[43] *Rom.* 3. 3: 'Christianity is greatest when it is hated by the world.' See also *Eph.* 13. 1; *Trall.* 4. 2; 8. 1; *Rom.* 7. 1.

[44] See also *Pol.* 3. 1. In *Eph.* 14. 2, Ignatius likens Christianity to work whose central preoccupation is with 'persevering to the end in the power of faith'. In *Magn.* 9. 1, those who endure will be revealed as disciples of Christ.

[45] Additional passages comparing life to an *agōn* include *Eph.* 3. 2; 4. 1; *Magn.* 7. 2; *Pol.* 6. 1–2.

sealed when the faithful 'voluntarily choose to die into his [Jesus'] suffering' (*Magn.* 5. 2).[46] While he certainly does not suggest that all Christians must choose this path, for him, at least, the journey to Rome represents the fulfilment of his Christian life (*Rom.* 5. 1). Thus he can speak of the Roman guards as leopards whose mistreatment of him makes him more of a disciple, and states that true life will come to him only through suffering: 'if I suffer (*παθῶ*), I will be a freedman in Jesus Christ, and will rise up free in him' (*Rom.* 4. 3).[47] Although Ignatius may view himself as a 'convict' (*κατάκριτος*) and his death as a 'humble sacrifice' (*περίψημα*), such terms conjure up images of both inferiority and lowliness *and* authority and power.[48] Thus, while he contrasts his status as a slave to the freedom of his readers, he can also rather confidently proclaim that his 'spirit and bonds (*δεσμά*) are [an] expiation' for the community of Smyrna (10. 2) and praise those who have not viewed his imprisonment as a sign of weakness (*Pol.* 2. 3).[49] Some Christians along his route, however, appear to have seen Ignatius' discussion of his imprisonment as self-aggrandizing (*Phld.* 6. 3),[50] forcing him to deny that he was attempting to profit from his status: 'I am not commanding you as though I were somebody important. For even though I am in chains for the sake of the Name, I have not yet been perfected in Jesus Christ' (*Eph.* 3. 1); 'even though I am in chains, I cannot be compared to one of you who are at liberty' (*Magn.* 12. 1); and again, 'Not because I am in bonds (*δέδεμαι*) and am able to know heavenly things ... am I already a disciple' (*Trall.* 5. 2).[51]

Yet it might be argued that in his denial of power Ignatius is actually reinforcing it.[52] In any event, he is not always so self-deprecating, and regularly allows himself to appropriate the link between his imprisonment and an authority that ultimately stems from Jesus. For example, Ignatius reminds the Ephesians that he carries around his chains 'in Jesus' (*Eph.* 11. 2), a position restated to the Philadelphians when he defends himself against those who question his honesty (*Phld.* 7.2). In a style of argumentation reminiscent of Paul's defence of the resurrection, Ignatius contends that the death of Jesus justifies the martyrdom of his followers, and that martyrdoms in turn 'prove' (*Smyrn.* 4. 2) that the death of Jesus was a reality: 'For if those things were done by our Lord in appearance only, I too am in bonds in

46 In contrast to Rom. 6. 1–4, this passage makes no reference to baptism.

47 See also *Eph.* 21. 2; *Trall.* 4. 2; *Rom.* 5. 3; 7. 2; 8. 3.

48 Schoedel, *Ignatius of Antioch*, 64, 72.

49 On Ignatius' use of sacrificial imagery, see *Eph.* 8. 1; 18. 1; *Trall.* 13. 3; *Pol.* 6. 1.

50 See the commentary on this passage by Schoedel, *Ignatius of Antioch*, 204. Schoedel (*Ignatius of Antioch*, 11–12) has also explored the theatrical nature of Ignatius' journey to Rome.

51 On this point, see ibid. 49, 129.

52 Compare, e.g., a similar rhetorical strategy in Philem. 8–9.

appearance only' (*Trall.* 10. 1).[53] In an even more striking statement, the bishop claims that it is precisely through his identification with Jesus that he receives his power: 'in the name of Jesus Christ, that I may suffer together (συμπαθεῖν) with him! I endure (ὑπομένω) everything because he himself, who is the perfect human being, empowers (ἐνδυναμοῦντος) me' (*Smyrn.* 4. 2).[54] Embodying divine power enables Ignatius to instruct with authority. This can be detected both in *Magnesians*, when he calls for unity 'in the bonds which I bear', and, more explicitly, in *Trallians*: 'My chains (τὰ δεσμά μου), which I carry around for the sake of Jesus Christ while praying that I might reach God, exhort you (παρακαλεῖ ὑμᾶς): persevere in your unanimity and in prayer with one another' (*Trall.* 12. 2).

IGNATIUS AND THE RHETORIC OF POWER

It is at this point that the purpose behind Ignatius' emulation and literary imitation of Paul and his traditions becomes apparent: they are part of a larger strategy of establishing both a clearly defined hierarchy of power and a vision of ecclesiastical 'sameness'. For Ignatius, it is the recognition of, and submission to, an authoritative hierarchy that naturally leads to unity. Two immediate obstacles threatened to jeopardize this vision: as the bishop of Antioch, he had no direct claim to authority among the churches of Asia Minor, and because his own church was experiencing turmoil, his decision to equate 'godliness' with community concord was a potential stumbling-block. He thus could not simply say, as Paul had done, 'imitate me', for how could he maintain that he was a model for imitation if his leadership over Antioch had not produced *koinōnia*? In this situation, casting himself as a new Paul and evoking the traditions surrounding the apostle was a way to circumvent the immediacy of both of these problems, for not only was he on Paul's (and Jesus') physical journey to die as a martyr, but as one who embodied power through suffering and enduring, he was on their spiritual journey as well.

By identifying himself with the figures of Jesus and Paul, Ignatius stakes a claim for a personal authority that manifests itself in his vision of proper ecclesiastical organization. This topic, which Paul had only touched upon (1 Cor. 12. 28; cf. Eph. 4. 11–12), is treated thoroughly and unequivocally by

[53] Cf. 1 Cor. 15. 12–14. It should be no surprise, then, that the deaths of the martyrs are not enough to convince those who deny Christ's passion (*Smyrn.* 5. 1).

[54] See also *Rom.* 6. 3: 'Allow me to be an imitator of the suffering of my God.' On this aspect of imitation in Ignatius, see W. M. Swartley, 'The *Imitatio Christi* in the Ignatian Letters', *VC* 27 (1973), 81–103, on p. 92.

Ignatius. Indeed, in every letter his understanding of church leadership is either outlined explicitly or assumed. At the head of the church is the bishop, followed by the presbyters and deacons. For Ignatius, each of these three positions has a divine or apostolic analogue. 'Presiding in the place of God' (*Magn.* 6. 1), the bishop is 'a model (τυπόν) of the Father' (*Trall.* 3. 1) whose 'mind' or 'purpose' (γνώμη) closely corresponds with that of his divine exemplar (*Eph.* 3. 2; 4. 1; *Pol.* 8. 1).[55] Representing a lower rung on the hierarchy, the presbyters act 'in the place of the council of the apostles' (*Magn.* 6. 1; see also *Trall.* 3. 1) and 'yield to' the bishop as 'one who is wise in God' (*Magn.* 3. 1). Finally, the deacons occupy a third position: they are 'entrusted with the service of Jesus Christ' and must be 'subject to the bishop as to the grace of God and to the presbytery as to the law of Jesus Christ' (*Magn.* 2).[56] All three offices, then, are invested with a quasi-divine status: they are all 'with' Jesus and 'have been appointed by his purpose' (γνώμη) and 'established by his Holy Spirit' (*Phld.* prol.).

It would appear that the strategy behind such assertions is to elevate the authority of a group of officials who may not always have commanded the respect and obedience that Ignatius felt was appropriate. This is especially true of the bishop, who appears to have been embattled in a few of the Asian communities.[57] To confront this challenge, Ignatius amplifies his rhetoric on behalf of episcopal authority: the bishop's presence is comparable to the presence of Jesus (*Smyrn.* 8. 2); he possesses the 'purpose of God' (*Pol.* 8. 1); and he should be regarded 'as the Lord himself' (*Eph.* 6. 1). The elders display an appropriate attitude toward episcopal leadership when they 'yield to' (συγχωροῦντας) him as if he were God, the divine bishop (*Magn.* 3. 1). As they are superior to ordinary Christians, the implication is that the congregations have an even greater responsibility to submit to the bishop's authority.[58] Furthermore, for those who might not be impressed with Ignatius' pleas 'to do nothing without the bishop' and 'to be subject to the bishop',[59] he recounts how this command, on one occasion at least, did not derive from him, but from a higher power: 'I called out (ἐκραύγασα) when I was with you,

[55] According to Schoedel (*Ignatius of Antioch*, 50), γνώμη is a term 'with widely diffused notions of social and political discipline'.

[56] But see *Trall.* 3. 1, where Ignatius states that the deacons should be given respect 'as (ὡς) Jesus Christ'.

[57] Ignatius is forced on a few occasions to defend the silence of the bishop as a virtue, an indication that some of these leaders suffered from rhetorical deficiencies when confronted with opposing teachings (*Eph.* 6. 1; 15; *Phld.* 1). It appears that some members of the Magnesian community 'took advantage' (συγχρᾶσθαι) of the bishop (*Magn.* 3. 1), forcing Ignatius to reprimand those who 'call a man "bishop" but do everything without regard for him' (*Magn.* 4).

[58] See, e.g., *Pol.* 6. 1: the Smyrneans should 'pay attention to' (προσέχετε) the bishop 'in order that God may pay attention' to them.

[59] *Magn.* 7. 1; 13. 2; *Trall.* 2. 1–2; 7. 1; 13. 2.

I was speaking with a loud voice, God's voice: "Pay attention (προσέχετε) to the bishop and to the presbytery and deacons"... the Spirit itself was preaching (ἐκήρυσσεν), saying these words: "Do nothing without the bishop... Love unity (ἕνωσιν). Flee from divisions. Become imitators of Jesus Christ, just as he is of the Father" ' (*Phld.* 7. 1–2).

This exhortation from *Philadelphians* is notable for two reasons. First, Ignatius states that unity is contingent upon following the dictates of the episcopacy. The bishop must be imitated: just as he displays an 'inexpressible love', so too must the community repay him with love 'in accordance with the standard set by Jesus Christ [so that] all of you will be like him' (πάντας ὑμᾶς αὐτῷ ἐν ὁμοιότητι εἶναι) (*Eph.* 1. 3).[60] Likewise, the Magnesians are instructed that they 'should be united with the bishop and those who lead [because they are] an example (τύπον) and a lesson of incorruptibility' (ἀφθαρσίας) (*Magn.* 6. 2). Second, it appears that Ignatius thinks that this 'oneness' within the earthly community mirrors the unity found in the relationship between Jesus and God. These two features of Ignatius' thought resonate throughout his writings. To the Magnesians he instructs that 'as the Lord did nothing without the Father, either by himself or through the apostles—for he was united with him (ἡνωμένος ὤν)—so you must not do anything without the bishop and the presbyters' (*Magn.* 7. 1; see also *Magn.* 13. 2). Similarly, Ignatius congratulates the Ephesians for being 'united' (ἐνκεκραμένους) with their bishop 'as the church is with Jesus Christ and as Jesus Christ is with the Father, that all things might be harmonious in unity (ἵνα πάντα ἐν ἑνότητι σύμφωνα ᾖ)' (*Eph.* 5. 1). And the Smyrneans, who learn that community division is associated with evil, are all instructed to 'follow (ἀκολουθεῖτε) the bishop, as Jesus Christ followed the Father' (*Smyrn.* 8. 1). To fall dutifully under the aegis of the bishop and his subordinates is thus the primary indication for Ignatius that a church exists in unity and concord; in other words, the 'true' Christian life. Indeed, without these ecclesiastical officials, 'no group can be called a church' (χωρὶς τούτων ἐκκλησία οὐ καλεῖται, *Trall.* 3. 1).

To imitate God or Jesus, as Ignatius counsels, is nothing less than a call to imitate the bishop because of his divine-like status.[61] This perspective allows Ignatius to say 'run together in harmony with the purpose of God' and then two sentences later, "run together with the purpose of the bishop'.[62] When

[60] See also *Smyrn.* 12. 1, where Ignatius commends the Ephesian deacon Burrhus and then offers the wish that 'all were imitators of him (πάντες αὐτὸν ἐμιμοῦντο), for he is a model (ἐξεμπλάριον) of service to God'.

[61] As Swartley ('Imitatio Christi', 92) has shown, the connection between *imitatio* and martyrdom is balanced by the more prevalent tendency for Ignatius to link *mimēsis* to ethical clusters of thought.

[62] *Eph.* 3. 2 (συντρέχητε τῇ γνώμῃ τοῦ θεοῦ); 4. 1 (συντρέχειν τῇ τοῦ ἐπισκόπου γνώμῃ).

community harmony is at issue, it appears that there is very little distinction between the two, a point underscored by the admonition that the Ephesians should 'be careful not to oppose the bishop, in order that we may be obedient to God' (*Eph.* 5. 3; see also *Smyrn.* 9. 1). By anchoring this argument of episcopal dominance to a divine sanction, Ignatius' formulation represents a strengthening of the hierarchy established by Paul, who saw himself only as an intermediary between God/Christ and the church. In Ignatius' view, the bishop represents a divine model that the community, as a copy of the model, should strive to imitate. Yet, as Castelli has shown, *mimēsis* of this sort does not allow for the possibility of equality. Instead, the message of this authoritative voice compels his imitators to engage in constant self-reflection and self-criticism as they pursue their unachievable task. This process ultimately leads to a theological 'sameness', which reveals itself, according to Ignatius, in the unity of the church.

The unity that Ignatius espouses is based upon submission to the episcopate, which in turn is a reflection of God's unity.[63] The opposite is equally true: division appears when the bishop's authority is rejected, a situation that signals a movement away from God. For Ignatius, then, the only two options that life offers are to be with or against God. As he explains, one is either within or outside of the sanctuary; there is no middle ground.[64] Consequently, Ignatius' commands to 'flee from division' (*Phld.* 2. 1; *Smyrn.* 8. 1) and embrace unity are more than simply theoretical commentaries on an ideal social order. Rather, such formulations assume a soteriological quality, for the existence of concord is the primary characteristic of true Christians who have a share in God. As he explains to the Ephesians, 'when no dissention (ἔρις) capable of tormenting you is established among you, then you indeed live according to God's way' (*Eph.* 8. 1). He thus exhorts them to join the bishop and elders, in praising Jesus 'so that by being harmonious in unanimity (σύμφωνοι . . . ἐν ὁμονοίᾳ) and taking your pitch from God you may sing in unison with one voice through Jesus Christ to the Father, in order that he may both hear you and . . . acknowledge that you are members of his Son. It is, therefore, advantageous for you to be in perfect unity (ἑνότητι), in order that you may always have a share in God' (*Eph.* 3. 1–2).[65]

Conversely, divisions within the community reflect a rejection of the Christian 'truth': they are, quite simply, the 'beginning of evils' (ἀρχὴν κακῶν, *Smyrn.* 8. 1). For Ignatius, the divided community does not share

[63] On the unity of God, see *Trall.* 11. 2.

[64] *Eph.* 5. 2; *Trall.* 7. 2; see also *Magn.* 5. 1–2; 10. 1.

[65] See also *Magn.* 7. 1: 'Do not attempt to convince yourselves that anything done apart from the others is right.'

in God,[66] and those who refuse to participate in community life have God for an enemy.[67] Although it appears that Ignatius did not confront widespread factionalism, he does, however, target those who hold 'false' views of Jesus as the source of dissension.[68] These people, whom Ignatius refers to as 'tombstones and graves of the dead' (*Phld.* 6. 1; see also *Smyrn.* 5. 2) disseminate 'an evil teaching' (*Eph.* 9. 1) and 'worthless opinions' (*Magn.* 11) that are 'contrary to the purpose (γνώμῃ) of God' (*Smyrn.* 6. 2; see also *Magn.* 8. 1). Elsewhere they are described as 'wicked offshoots that bear deadly fruit' (*Phld.* 3. 1), so that 'if anyone even tastes it, he dies on the spot' (*Trall.* 6. 1–2; 11. 1).[69] As a result, it is not surprising that Ignatius thinks that in the battle between truth and falsity, the stakes are nothing less than salvation. As he warns the Ephesians, if those who incite divisiveness in earthly matters are cut off from a future with God, it is reasonable to expect that the punishment for those who promote false teachings about Jesus, an even greater sin, is even more assured: 'Do not be misled, my brothers: those who adulterously corrupt households "will not inherit the kingdom of God". Now if those who do such things in the realm of the flesh are put to death, how much more if by evil teaching someone corrupts faith in God, for which Jesus Christ was crucified. Such a person, having polluted himself, will go to the unquenchable fire, as will also the one who listens to him' (*Eph.* 16. 1–2; see also *Eph.* 13. 1; *Smyrn.* 7. 1). This admonition is reinforced in *Philadelphians*: 'if anyone follows a schismatic (σχίζοντι ἀκολουθεῖ), he will not inherit the kingdom of God' (3. 3).

These two passages, the only instances in which Ignatius discusses the kingdom of God, are revealing in their immediate context. Instead of choosing to speak of the kingdom in a positive sense, to elucidate a future existence of peace and righteousness, Ignatius elects to refer to it as a means to condemn and exclude those whom he feels are destined for damnation. Castelli's contention that this type of polemic marginalizes 'otherness' and demonizes 'difference' is clearly apparent, for Ignatius' discourse of power leaves no room for dissension. Moreover, the bishop amplifies his polemic against his opponents by arguing that it is not they who have denied God, but

[66] *Phld.* 8. 1: 'God does not dwell where there is division (μερισμός) and anger.'

[67] *Eph.* 5. 3: 'whoever does not meet with the congregation... demonstrates his arrogance and has separated himself (ὑπερηφανεῖ καὶ ἑαυτὸν διέκρινεν), for it is written, "God opposes the arrogant" '.

[68] To speak of Jesus Christ properly, Ignatius holds that the reality of his incarnation, suffering, death, and resurrection must be affirmed (*Eph.* 18. 2–19. 3; *Magn.* 11; *Trall.* 9. 1–2; *Smyrn.* 2). For a more detailed treatment of the factionalism in the letters, see V. Corwin, *St. Ignatius and Christianity in Antioch* (New Haven: Yale University Press, 1960), 52–87.

[69] See also *Eph.* 7. 1, where false teachers are compared to 'mad dogs that bite by stealth', [whose] 'bite is hard to heal'.

God who has denied *them* (*Smyrn.* 5. 1). Ignatius thinks that they simply reveal God's decision through their teachings: 'their fate will be determined by what they think: they will become disembodied and demonic' (ἀσωμάτοις καὶ δαιμονικοῖς) (*Smyrn.* 2). The bishop therefore advises the communities to sever all contact with these false teachers, so that they may remain 'insiders' and members of God's temple (*Eph.* 9. 1; *Trall.* 6. 1–2; *Smyrn.* 4. 1; 7. 1).

CONCLUSION

In 1 Corinthians, Paul contrasts the wisdom that derives from rhetorical skill with the wisdom of God (1 Cor. 2. 4), and concludes that 'the kingdom of God depends not on talk but on power' (1 Cor. 4. 20). Ignatius concurs with this sentiment, calling Christianity 'the work' (τὸ ἔργον), a way of life that 'is not a matter of persuasive rhetoric' (πεισμονῆς) but of action on behalf of the truth (*Rom.* 3. 3; see also *Eph.* 14. 2). Yet this study would nuance such sentiments, arguing that for Paul and Ignatius, the kingdom does come through power, but that this power is grounded in and expressed through a rhetoric of coercion. The rhetorical strategies that Paul employs—from his claim to speak with authority to his self-effacement, connection with Christ, and calls for imitation—all have parallels in the Ignatian correspondence.

Exploring these letters through the lens of *mimēsis* reveals an 'imitation' that operates in a paradoxical fashion. From an ethical perspective, it reveals that Ignatius saw himself as a 'copy' of the 'model' of behaviour found in the lives and deaths of Paul and Jesus. Yet on the other hand, the literary imitation found in the letters have the effect of elevating Ignatius so that he becomes a 'new' Paul who speaks with a corresponding apostolic authority. The bishop then uses this authoritative voice to promote a vision of theological 'sameness' among the communities of Asia Minor, a vision that is anchored in submission and obedience to the ecclesiastical hierarchy. In this scheme, the community becomes an imitator of the bishop, the divine-like model of Christian identity, and continually seeks to attain his level of perfection. Because this goal cannot be attained, the community must repeatedly re-evaluate its 'Christian-ness' based on its uniform behaviour and attitudes under the bishop's leadership. This becomes the criterion for determining whether a person or group is within the 'true' Christian fold or is a part of the demonic forces of the world. Ignatius' discourse of power thus reinforces and elevates Paul's view that unity comes through a recognition of hierarchy and, furthermore, that the acceptance of this position identifies one's spiritual status, in both this world and the next.

15

The Politics and Rhetoric of Discord and Concord in Paul and Ignatius

Harry O. Maier

'Ignatius was a man of the Greek city and . . . seems to have been relatively at home there. . . . [T]he spirit of popular Hellenistic culture remains more alive in his letters than is generally recognized.'[1] One of the more ground-breaking aspects of William Schoedel's commentary on Ignatius' epistles is its attention to the ways in which the Ignatian corpus echoes the vocabulary and concepts characteristic of contemporary pagan political philosophy and civic culture. Schoedel has urged a reorientation toward politics and rhetoric as indispensable guides for situating Ignatius in his social and theological setting. He has thus sought to do for Ignatius what others have profitably done for *1 Clement* in assessing its indebtedness to political rhetoric, especially that connected with the *topos*, περὶ ὁμόνοιας.[2] With a few exceptions, however, scholars have not followed Schoedel down this path-breaking trail.[3] Almost twenty years after Schoedel's commentary, Ignatius' appropriation of themes common in Hellenistic political culture still awaits detailed exploration.

[1] W. R. Schoedel, *Ignatius of Antioch: A Commentary on the Letters of Ignatius of Antioch*, Hermeneia (Philadelphia: Fortress, 1985), 17.

[2] O. M. Bakke, *'Concord and Peace': A Rhetorical Analysis of the First Letter of Clement with an Emphasis on the Language of Unity and Sedition*, WUNT 2.143 (Tübingen: Mohr Siebeck, 2001), with discussion of earlier treatments.

[3] A noteworthy exception is A. Brent, *The Imperial Cult and the Development of Church Order: Concepts and Images of Authority in Paganism and Early Christianity before the Age of Cyprian*, VCSup 45 (Leiden: Brill, 1999), 210–50; also *idem*, 'Ignatius of Antioch and the Imperial Cult', *VC* 52 (1998), 30–58; see also *idem*, Ch. 16 below, which arrives at a complementary insistence on the importance of attention to concord themes and their ritual connections argued for here. For rhetorical political treatments, S. Carruth, 'Praise for the Churches: The Rhetorical Function of the Opening Sections of the Letters of Ignatius of Antioch', in E. Castelli and H. Taussig (eds.), *Reimagining Christian Origins: A Colloquium Honoring Burton L. Mack* (Valley Forge, Pa.: Trinity, 1996), 295–310; D. L. Sullivan, 'Establishing Orthodoxy: The Letters of Ignatius of Antioch as Epideictic Rhetoric', *Journal of Communication and Religion*, 15 (1992), 71–86; Robert J. Stoops, 'If I Suffer . . . Epistolary Authority in Ignatius of Antioch', *HTR* 80 (1987), 161–78.

This essay seeks to identify the influence of ancient political culture on Ignatius by reading his letters in the light of pagan philosophical and rhetorical commonplaces centring on the motifs of discord and concord. It will be seen that Ignatius borrowed extensively from rhetorical commonplaces associated with these themes in his descriptions of the ideally functioning church in submission to its leaders, and in his vilification of opponents as those whose actions and character have led to division. His extensive use of typical vocabulary and imagery associated with these *topoi* reveals the importance of ancient political and rhetorical culture in the shaping of Ignatius' letters. As we shall see, it also reveals his debt to the apostle Paul and his adaptation of political commonplaces in the representation of conflicts challenging his churches, especially as found in 1 Corinthians.

If the influence of Hellenistic political culture on Ignatius has been largely ignored, in Pauline studies the topic has enjoyed extensive discussion. Especially relevant to this essay is the growing body of scholarship devoted to an investigation of Paul's use of political commonplaces in the Corinthian correspondence. These more politically and rhetorically directed readings of Paul are helpful in reorienting the focus of investigation of Ignatius' letters, since it can be seen that Ignatius takes up and develops motifs he knew from his reading of 1 Corinthians. His use of 1 Corinthians has been well documented. A century ago, the committee formed by the Oxford Society of Historical Theology to investigate the relationship of New Testament writings to the Apostolic Fathers concluded in the case of Ignatius that the language and thought of 1 Corinthians so pervade the Syrian's letters that he 'must have known the Epistle almost by heart'.[4] However, attention to the appearance of political commonplaces in Paul and Ignatius permits a slightly different assessment. While 1 Corinthians was probably known to Ignatius, shared aspects may be better accounted for as a shared adaptation of political commonplaces in their respective representation of discord and communal ideals. Steeped as Ignatius was in the Hellenistic political culture of his day, Paul's uses of political rhetoric would have been immediately recognized by him. Ignatius' creativity may be seen in the way he took these up and developed them in his own letters and thereby offered, as Paul had done before him, a unique theological appropriation of Hellenistic civic ideals.

In recent years several studies have appeared detailing the rhetorical dimensions of the Corinthian correspondence, and their echoing of Hellenistic pagan commonplaces on themes relating to discord and concord.[5] Attention

[4] *The New Testament in the Apostolic Fathers* (Oxford: Clarendon Press, 1905), 67; H. Rathke, *Ignatius von Antiochien und die Paulusbriefe*, TU 99 (Berlin: Akademie-Verlag, 1967), offers systematic support for knowledge of the Corinthian correspondence.

[5] P. Marshall, *Enmity in Corinth: Social Conventions in Paul's Relations with the Corinthians*, WUNT 2.23 (Tübingen: Mohr Siebeck, 1987); L. L. Welborn, 'On the Discord in Corinth:

to parallels with ancient rhetorical and political treatises on civic concord has shown that Paul was clearly drawing on pagan political ideals and vilification in the representation of communal harmony and discord.[6] The patient spadework of these scholars has demonstrated that whatever the theological issues occasioning Paul's rejoinders to the multiple problems dividing the Corinthian church, the apostle responded to them using *topoi*, imagery, and vocabulary drawn from ancient political culture.

The first four chapters of 1 Corinthians represent the most sustained and readily recognizable application of commonplace political themes and vocabulary to the Corinthian situation. In his response to the report from 'Chloe's people' (1 Cor. 1. 11) concerning divisions in Corinth, Paul adopts the vocabulary, metaphors, and *topoi* at home in Hellenistic political rhetoric to describe Corinthian conflicts and ideals. Those problems he casts as 'dissension' (σχίσματα, 1. 10; also 11. 18; 12. 25), factions or strife (ἔριδες, 1. 11; ἔρις, 3. 3), jealousy (ζῆλος, 3. 3), being divided (μερίζειν, 1. 13; also 7. 34; 12. 25 (μεριμνᾶν)), and, in some manuscripts, sedition (διχοστασίαι, 3. 3). Faction has arisen from competing Corinthian claims to apostolic foundation (1. 12, 15; 3. 4, 22). The Corinthian audience hearing Paul's letter would have recognized immediately that the apostle was choosing language typically associated with civic discord to portray a church in crisis. Each of these terms appears regularly in ancient treatises on political themes, and in pagan historical descriptions and representations of στάσις ('civil disorder').[7]

Further, though Paul nowhere uses the term ὕβρις, his audience would have recognized that the apostle was accusing those guilty of faction as suffering from this community-eroding vice and the related shortcoming of arrogance (ἀλαζονεία).[8] The vice of hubris and its associated evils of jealousy leading toward faction and schism were seen by ancients as arising from wealth and

1 Corinthians 1–4 and Ancient Politics', *JBL* 106 (1987), 85–111; *idem*, 'A Conciliatory Principle in 1 Cor. 4:6', *NovT* 29 (1987), 320–46; S. M. Pogoloff, *Logos and Sophia: The Rhetorical Situation of 1 Corinthians*, SBLDS 134 (Atlanta: Scholars Press, 1992); D. B. Martin, *The Corinthian Body* (New Haven: Yale University Press, 1995), 38–68; M. M. Mitchell, *Paul and the Rhetoric of Reconciliation: An Exegetical Investigation of the Language and Composition of 1 Corinthians* (Louisville, Ky.: Westminster/John Knox, 1991).

[6] Thus, e.g., Dio Chrys. *Or.* 38–41; Ael. Arist. *Or.* 23–4; Ps.-Sallust. *Ep.* 2; Thrasymachus, *Peri homonoias*; Antiphon, *Peri homonoias*; Isoc. *Or.* 4; *Ep.* 3, 8, 9; Herodes Atticus, *Peri politeias*, to name only a few examples.

[7] For vocabulary and themes see D. Loenen, *Stasis: Enige aspecten van de begrippen partij-en klassentrijd in oud-Griekenland* (Amsterdam: Noord-Hollandsche Uitgevers Maaschappij, 1953); H. –J. Gehrke, *Stasis: Untersuchungen zu den inneren Kriegen in den griechischen Staaten des 5. und 4. Jahrhunderts v. Chr.*, Vestigia, 35 (Munich: Beck, 1985).

[8] For vocabulary and themes, N. R. E. Fisher, *Hybris: A Study in the Values of Honour and Shame in Ancient Greece* (Warminster: Aris & Phillips, 1992); J. J. Fraenkel, *Hybris* (Utrecht: P. den Boer, 1941).

over-abundance.[9] It is these themes Paul has in mind when he ironically chides the Corinthians as filled and rich (1 Cor. 4. 8). Accusing them of another vice typically associated with discord, he criticizes them as puffed up or self-inflated (φυσιοῦσθαι, 4. 6, 18, 19; also 4. 6; 8. 1; 13. 4). Similarly, they are guilty of that vice most destructive of the political order—boasting (καυχᾶσθαι, 3. 21; 4. 7; see 1. 31; also 13. 3; 5. 6; 9. 15, 16 (καύχημα)), by which is meant the praise of oneself, a vice universally pilloried in antiquity.[10] Thus, when he urges the Corinthians to remember their social origins—that not many of them 'were wise according to worldly standards, not many were powerful, not many were of noble birth' (1. 26), he does so as part of his rhetorical representation of boastful, arrogant, hubristic, factionalist, jealous, and seditious Corinthians. Instead of forming a mature body politic dedicated to the pursuit of a common good, Paul complains—again citing a political commonplace—that the Corinthians are squabbling, jealous children (3. 1–4). They should be adults, but Paul threatens them as though they were adolescents, promising to discipline them with a rod if they do not stop misbehaving (4. 21).[11]

In outlining Corinthian communal ideals, Paul similarly borrows from Graeco-Roman civic commonplaces. Though the term ὁμόνοια nowhere appears in 1 Corinthians, Paul repeatedly invokes terms and commonplaces associated with it.[12] Thus, the apostle periphrastically exhorts his audience to concord when he urges them 'to agree (τὸ αὐτὸ λέγητε)' and 'to be rightly set in the same mind (κατηρτισμένοι ἐν τῷ αὐτῷ νοΐ) and the same judgement (ἐν τῇ αὐτῇ γνώμῃ)' (1. 10). Each of these motifs recurs regularly in ancient political discourse on themes relating to concord.[13] As an antidote to Corinthian invocations of competing apostolic allegiances, he describes his apostolic comrades as συνεργοί (3. 9) and stewards (οἰκονόμοι, 4. 1, 2; see also 9. 17), co-operating in the divinely appointed task of building God's temple on a

[9] See Marshall, *Enmity in Corinth*, 183–218, for discussion of this connection in ancient sources.

[10] See, e.g., Plut. *De laude ipsius; De se ipsum citra invidiam laudando*; E. A. Judge, 'Paul's Boasting in Relation to Contemporary Professional Practice', *ABR* 16 (1968), 37–50; and C. Forbes, 'Comparison, Self-Praise and Irony: Paul's Boasting and the Conventions of Hellenistic Rhetoric', *NTS* 32 (1986), 1–30. What is implicit in 1 Corinthians is explicitly outlined in 2 Cor. 12. 20, where boasting is associated with the typical vices of στάσις : ἔρις, ζῆλος, θυμοί, ἐριθεῖαι, καταλαλιαί, and ἀκαταστασίαι (12. 20).

[11] For στάσις and acting like children, see Dio Chrys. *Or.* 38. 21; Dion. Hal. *Ant. Rom.* 6. 71. 3.

[12] For an overview of typical vocabulary, E. Skard, *Zwei religiös-politische Begriffe: Euergetes-Concordia* (Oslo: Dybwad, 1932); J. de Romilly, 'Vocabulaire et propagande ou les premiers emplois du mot *homonoia*', in F. Bader (ed.), *Mélanges de linguistique et de philologique Grecques offerts à Pierre Chantraine* (Paris: Klincksieck, 1972), 199–209; A. Moulakis, *Homonoia: Eintracht und die Entwicklung eines politischen Bewusstseins* (Munich: List, 1973); K. Thraede, 'Homonoia (Eintracht)', *RAC* 16 (1994), 176–80.

[13] For references, see Mitchell, *Paul*, 74–80.

solid foundation (θεμέλιον, 3. 9–14, 16–17).[14] Further, he studiously avoids taking up individual claims of differing groups, choosing instead to retain a collective focus by carefully addressing his audience 'the church of God which is at Corinth . . . called to be saints with all (σὺν πᾶσιν) those who in every place (ἐν παντὶ τόπῳ) call on the name of the Lord Jesus Christ, both their Lord and ours (αὐτῶν καὶ ἡμῶν)' (1. 2). If suffering schisms and divisions, they nevertheless remain 'brothers (ἀδελφοί)' (1.10, 26; 2.1; 3.1; 4.6), and while the Corinthians divide themselves along the lines of competing apostolic pedigrees, Paul retains a collective focus by referring to himself and his colleagues repeatedly in the first person plural (2. 6, 7, 13; 3. 9; 4. 1, 6, 8–13).

This collective focus on mutual co-operation is reinforced through the use of ὁμόνοια *topoi*. The sacral and household imagery Paul invokes, together with construction terminology (οἰκοδομή, 3. 9; see also οἰκοδομεῖν, 8. 1, 10; 10. 23; 14. 4, 17) are commonplaces in ancient treatments of concord and statecraft.[15] Ancient authors such as Aelius Aristides celebrated the sacral order of the Roman Empire by relating the *Pax romana* to the harmonious construction of local temples and the concord-preserving religious piety and moral order that they promoted.[16] Also recognizably political is Paul's treatment of the church as God's well-governed household or family.[17] Later in 1 Cor. 15. 58, where at the end of his letter Paul echoes the building and labour terms introduced at its start, the apostle exhorts his audience to 'be steadfast (ἑδραῖοι), immovable (ἀμετακίνητοι), always abounding in the work of the Lord, knowing that in the Lord your labour (ὁ κόπος [see 3. 8]) is not in vain.' They are to put into practice the ethos outlined in the letter as a means toward overcoming factionalism and restoring the divinely appointed concord to which the community has been called. Similarly developing concord themes, Paul represents Stephanas and his household (16. 15–16) epideictically as exemplars of community-building ὁμόνοια. Invoking vocabulary associated with ideals of political concord, he describes them as ordering themselves (ἔταξαν ἑαυτούς) for service (διακονία), and urges the Corinthians, again using a politically charged term, to be subject (ὑποτάσσεσθαι)

[14] See A. Fridrichsen, 'Themelios, 1 Kor. 3,11', *TZ* 2 (1946), 316–17; J. Shanor, 'Paul as Master Builder: Construction Terms in 1 Corinthians', *NTS* 34 (1988), 461–71, for ancient political associations.

[15] E.g. Arist. *Pol.* 1. 1 1252a 1–1260b23; Xen. *Mem.* 4. 4. 16; Dio Chrys. *Or.* 24. 241; 38. 15; 48. 14; Ael. Arist. *Or.* 23. 31, 62; 24. 8, 32–3; Philo, *Jos.* 38; *1 Clem.* 21. 7–8. For a systematic discussion, I. Kitzberger, *Bau der Gemeinde: das paulinische Wortfeld oikodome/(ep)oikodomein* (Würzburg: Echter Verlag, 1984), 158–305.

[16] Ael. Arist. *Or.* 27. 40–1.

[17] See Dio. Hal. *Ant. Rom.* 7. 66. 5 for a description of Roman rule likened to a well-governed household with children subject to parents; see also 6. 71. 3; Augustus and his successors capitalized on this *topos*—see Clifford Ando, *Imperial Ideology and Provincial Loyalty in the Roman Empire* (Berkeley: University of California Press, 2000), 398–405.

to such people.[18] These men—picking up the language of 3. 8, 9 used to describe the concord-producing work of Paul and his apostolic associates—are *συνεργοῦντες καὶ κοπιῶντες* (16. 16), the examples to follow to take the Corinthian church out of its faction and discord.

Indeed, such concord-promoting labour is the opposite of the Corinthian arrogance and boasting that leads to *σχίσματα* and *ἔριδες*. In a devastatingly ironical rejoinder to Corinthian boasting and competition over status, Paul represents himself and the apostolic co-founders of Corinth as self-effacing examples (4. 6, 9–13). In contrast to the Corinthians' wisdom, strength, and honour, they are 'fools' (*μωροί*), 'weak' (*ἀσθενεῖς*), and 'dishonoured' (*ἄτιμοι*, v. 11). As impoverished manual labourers (v. 12) they are at the extreme opposite of Corinthian hubristic claims to nobility and royalty; they are 'refuse' and 'off-scouring' (*περικαθάρματα*; *περίψημα*, v. 13). Again, these references have a politically charged application in chapters 1–4 and in the letter as a whole. It was, after all, those inhabiting the extreme opposite end of the social spectrum, the 'rulers of this age (*ἀρχόντες τοῦ αἰῶνος τούτου*)'—the honoured, strong, wise, powerful and nobly born (see 1. 26)—who crucified the Lord of Glory (2. 8). The imperial cult of concord as a celebration of a religiously preserved civil peace thus suffers a direct blow, and falls victim in Paul's burlesque to paradoxical reversals of honour and status considerations.[19]

Later in the letter, invoking the traditional political *topos* of the body, and echoing the paradoxes of 4. 10, traditional considerations of honour and status are again reversed when Paul draws attention to the weaker (*ἀσθενέστερα*, 12. 22), less honourable (*ἀτιμότερα*, 12. 23), inferior (*ὑστερουμένοι*) and unpresentable (v. 24) parts of the body as having greater honour. Paul urges such a reversal, centred in 'care for one another', that 'there may be no discord (*σχίσμα*) in the body' (v. 25). Elsewhere, he undermines appeals to status and honour, again echoing his earlier depictions of congregational faction, by urging stronger members not to be 'puffed up (*φυσιοῦν*)', but 'to build up (*οἰκοδομεῖν*)' (8. 1; see also 10. 23)—thus echoing the themes introduced in the first four chapters—and to care for weaker ones (8. 7–12). He epideictically presents himself (9. 1–27) as one who has given up the rights

[18] For *ὑποτάσσεσθαι* as a term associated with concord, see, e.g., Dio Chrys. *Or.* 32. 37; 36. 21; 40. 35; Ael. Arist. *Or.* 27. 35; Philo, *Jos.* 145. *1 Clement* repeatedly deploys *ὑποτάσσεσθαι* to develop ideals associated with *ὁμόνοια*: 1. 3; 2. 1; 20. 1; 34. 5; 37. 3; 38. 1; 57. 1; 57. 2; 61. 1; see Bakke, '*Concord*', 119–22. For *τάσσειν ἑαυτός* with political connotations, Dio Chrys. *Or.* 34. 21; 36. 31; 40. 35; Ael. Arist. *Or.* 23. 9; 26. 103; 37. 27, where the cognates *τάξις* and *τάγμα* recur; also *1 Clem.* 6. 2; 20. 2; 32. 2; 37. 2, 3; 40. 1; 41. 1; 42. 2. *τάξις* also appears in 1 Cor. 14. 40 to describe a good order enjoined along political lines (see Mitchell, *Paul*, 175).

[19] For imperial devotion to *concordia* and the emperor as embodying her rule, see J. R. Fears, 'The Cult of Virtues and Roman Imperial Ideology', *ANRW* 2. 17. 2 (1987), 828–948, on pp. 893–9.

that go along with his apostolic status, denying himself boasting privileges (9. 15–16) for the sake of the Corinthian community. While the Corinthians are boastful, Paul reminds them that he did not preach the gospel 'in lofty speech or in cleverness (ὑπεροχὴν λόγου ἢ σοφίας),' and that he initially preached 'in weakness (ἀσθενείᾳ)'; his 'speech (ὁ λόγος)' and ... message were not 'in persuasive words of wisdom (ἐν πειθοῖς σοφίας λόγοις)' (2. 1, 3–4). Rhetorical deceit and cleverness were pilloried in antiquity as leading states to warfare and στάσις.[20] Paul thus invokes the 'speech of the cross (ὁ λόγος ... ὁ τοῦ σταυροῦ)' (1. 18), that overturns traditional status considerations based on wisdom, cleverness, and power (1. 19–24, 27–8, 30), a speech he emulates as expressing a concord-preserving ethos that he urges the Corinthians to follow. By the time Paul has concluded the paradoxical treatment of God's weakness and foolishness and status-oriented notions of power and wisdom, Paul the fool (4. 10) is Christ's wisdom; the 'wise' Corinthians are foolish.

A brief survey of the evidence thus shows Paul deploying an array of commonplaces and terms traditionally associated in ancient pagan literature with political themes of discord, and that these themes, while most prevalent in 1 Cor. 1–4, recur repeatedly throughout the letter and bind his exhortations into a rhetorical unity. When we turn to the letters of Ignatius, we discover a similar prevalence of political commonplaces and rhetorical unity. That he uses political terminology has been ably demonstrated by William Schoedel and confirmed by Allen Brent.[21] Ignatius describes the governing institutions of the local Asia Minor churches with the technical vocabulary of pagan civic government.[22] And he carefully produces political vocabulary to promote his hoped-for congratulatory 'embassy' to Antioch to celebrate their recovery of peace.[23] This, however, is only the tip of the iceberg, and hints at larger themes in the corpus as a whole.

[20] Thus, esp. Thuc. 3. 82. 3–7; Thrasymachus, *Peri politeias*, frag. 85 A 1; Arist., *Pol.* 5. 7. 2 1308^{a}1, with the commentary of Welborn, 'Discord', 102–3; further, Pogoloff, *Logos and Sophia*, 99–127.

[21] Schoedel, *Ignatius*, 213; Brent, *Imperial Cult*, 241–8.

[22] Thus, πρεσβυτέριον (*Eph.* 2. 2; 4. 1; 20. 2; *Magn.* 2. 1; 13. 1; *Trall.* 2. 2; 7. 2; 13. 2; *Phld.* 4. 1; 7. 1; 4. 1; 7. 1; *Smyrn.* 8. 1; 12. 2), probably modelled on the συνέδριον τῶν πρεσβυτερῶν (see *Magn.* 6. 1; *Trall.* 3. 1; *Phld.* 5. 1) known in several Asia Minor communities; A. Vilela, 'Le Presbytérion selon saint Ignace de'Antioche', *BLE* 74 (1973), 161–86, on pp. 174–5. Brent, *Imperial Cult*, 190, 202–5, argues that the language was drawn from the imperial cult, in which case one discovers religio-political analogy with Ignatius.

[23] See Schoedel, *Ignatius*, 213; thus, *Phld.* 10. 1, where diplomatic terms for appointing (χειροτονῆσαι) an ambassador (πρεσβεῦσαι ... πρεσβείαν) are deployed; also, Ign. *Pol.* 7. 1–2; *Smyrn.* 11. 2–3. For the vocabulary of civic diplomacy in antiquity, see R. Ragnat, 'Legatio', in C. Daremberg and E. Saglio (eds.), *Dictionnaire des antiquités grecques et romaines* (Paris: Libraire Hachette, 1906), iii. 1025–38. Brent offers further evidence to confirm the importance of this political embassy language in understanding Ignatius as a whole in Ch. 16 below, sect. 4: 'Ambassadors, cult, and Homonoia treaties'.

Concord is a central theme of Ignatius' letters. The frequent appearance of the term ὁμόνοια (eight times: *Eph.* 4. 1, 2; 13. 1; *Magn.* 6. 1; 15. 1; *Trall.* 12. 2; *Phld.* inscr.; 11. 2) hints at the importance of this concept as an organizing principle of the correspondence as a whole. That hunch is confirmed once it is recognized that other terms associated with pagan treatments of concord appear regularly in the letters. Ignatius applies the word ὁμόνοια to celebrate and promote the ideals of a united church, centred around local leaders, especially the bishop (*Eph.* 4. 1; *Magn.* 6. 1), and to express communal ideals of integrity, togetherness, and mutual care (*Eph.* 13. 1; *Magn.* 15. 2; *Phld.* 11. 2; *Trall.* 12. 2). Most importantly for Ignatius, ecclesial harmony manifests, imitates, and arises from divine concord (*Phld.* inscr.; *Magn.* 6. 1; cf. 6. 2, ὁμοήθεια θεοῦ), and in this he echoes a pagan commonplace especially promoted in contemporary imperial propaganda and cultic devotion to *concordia.* Around the central ideals of concord, Ignatius arranges a host of associated concepts, terms, and phrases. In his invocations of ecclesial and theological harmony, he regularly deploys musical (*Eph.* 4. 1; *Rom.* 2. 2; *Phld.* 1. 2), nautical (*Smyrn.* 11. 3; *Pol.* 2. 3), medical (*Eph.* 7. 1–2; 20. 2; *Trall.* 6. 2; *Pol.* 1. 3; 2. 1), body (*Eph.* 4. 2; *Trall.* 11. 2; 4. 2; *Smyrn.* 1. 2), building/temple (*Eph.* 5. 2; 6. 1; 9. 1; 15. 3; 16. 1; *Magn.* 7. 2; *Trall.* 7. 2; *Phld.* 4. 1), athletic (*Pol.* 1. 3; 2. 3; 3. 1), and military imagery (*Pol.* 6. 3)—all of which are recurring *topoi* in ancient political discussions of ὁμόνοια and related ideals.[24] As in contemporary political treatments, such *topoi* are deployed to celebrate or promote the εὐταξία (*Eph.* 6. 2; also πολυεύτακτον—*Magn.* 1. 1) of a community dwelling in concord.[25] In the civic oral culture of Ignatius' audience, the sounding of these metaphors would have been immediately recognizable as echoing cherished political ideals of concord and freedom from faction. Similarly familiar would have been the ideals he urged the Asia Minor churches toward—ταπεινόφρων (*Eph.* 10. 2), ἑδράζειν (with cognates—*Phld.* inscr.; *Smyrn.* 1. 1; 13. 2; *Pol.* 1. 1; *Eph.* 10. 2; *Pol.* 3. 1), ἀσφαλής (*Smyrn.* 8. 2; *Phld.* 5. 1), βεβαιωσύνη (with cognates—*Phld.* inscr.; *Smyrn.* 8. 1, 2; *Magn.* 4. 1;

[24] For musical harmony ὁμόνοια—e.g., Ael. Arist. *Or.* 21. 5; 24. 52; Dio Chrys. *Or.* 48. 7; Them., *Or.* 4. 53b; Lib., *Or.* 59. 172; Plut., *Prae. ger. reip.* 809F; *De frat. amor.* 2. 479A; for political and economic applications, O. Betz, συμφωνέω κτλ., *TDNT* ix. 304–9, at pp. 306, 309; nautical—Plut., *Prae. ger. reip.* 798D, 812C, 815D; Dio Chrys. *Or.* 38. 14; 39. 6; 40. 31; 48. 8; Ael. Arist. *Or.* 24. 54, 55–6; medical—Plut. *Prae. ger. reip.* 815B, 824A–B, 825D–E; Dio Chrys. *Or.* 38. 7, 12; Ael. Arist. *Or.* 24. 16; body—E. Schweizer and F. Baumgärtel, σῶμα κτλ., *TDNT* vii. 1024–94, on pp. 1032–44; Martin, *Corinthian Body,* 3–37; Sen. *Clem.* 2. 2.1; building/ temple—Ael. Arist. *Or.* 23. 31; 24. 8, 32–3; 27. 40–1; Dio Chrys. *Or.* 38. 15; 40. 28–9; athletic—Dio Chrys. *Or.* 41. 28–9; Ael. Arist. *Or.* 23. 79; military—Ael. Arist. *Or.* 23. 34; Epictetus, *Diss.* 3. 24. 31–5; *1 Clem.* 37.

[25] Dio Chrys. *Or.* 40. 35; 36. 31; 44. 10; see also *1 Clem.* 37. 2; 42. 2 (τάγμα, 37. 3; 41. 1; τάξις, 40. 1) and the commentary of Bakke, '*Concord*', 184–8.

11. 1; 13. 1), ἐπιεικεία (*Eph.* 10. 3; *Phld.* 1. 1, 2), ἀκαυχησία (*Pol.* 5. 2). Each belonged to the stock vocabulary of ancient depictions of civil harmony.[26]

The ὁμόνοια *topos* is further presented through circumlocution, where, for example, he congratulates the Ephesians for being 'ever of one mind with the apostles (τοῖς ἀποστόλοις πάντοτε συνῄνεσαν)' (*Eph.* 11. 2), and for obeying their leaders 'with an undisturbed mind' (ἀπερισπάστῳ διανοίᾳ—*Eph.* 20. 2). Similar echoes are heard when he urges the Magnesians to share 'one mind' (εἷς νοῦς—*Magn.* 7. 1), and the Trallians to possess a blameless mind (ἄμωμον διάνοιαν—*Trall.* 1. 1), or when, playing on words, he thanks the Trallians for their κατὰ θεὸν εὔνοιαν via their bishop, Polybius (*Trall.* 1. 2). In a dense application of concord-associated vocabulary, he urges the Philadelphians to 'come all together with undivided heart' (πάντες ἐπὶ τὸ αὐτὸ γίνεσθε ἐν ἀμερίστῳ καρδίᾳ—*Phld.* 6. 2, trans. Lake). Here, alongside the periphrastic exhortation to ὁμόνοια, Ignatius cleverly deploys one of the commonplace antonyms to concord, μερισμός. He joins this with a phrase repeated often in the correspondence and appearing frequently in pagan discussions of concord and political harmony—ἐπὶ τὸ αὐτὸ γίνεσθαι (*Eph.* 13. 1; *Magn.* 7. 2; *Phld.* 10. 1).[27]

A similarly often invoked concept at home in pagan treatments of ὁμόνοια is the celebration of a common or shared (κοίνος) good (*Eph.* 1. 2; 20. 2; 21. 2; *Phld.* 1. 1; 11. 2; cf. *Smyrn.* 7. 2; 12. 2).[28] The Philadelphian bishop, for example, has a ministry 'which makes for the common good (τὸ κοινόν)' (*Phld.* 1. 1, trans. Lake). Ignatius situates 'the common good' in 'our common hope (ἡ κοινὴ ἐλπὶς ἡμῶν)', reinforcing the religious-communal through the pleonastic application of the first person possessive plural (*Eph.* 21. 2; *Phld.* 11. 2; cf. *Phld.* 5. 2 (συνηριθμημένοι ἐν τῷ εὐαγγελίῳ τῆς κοινῆς ἐλπίδος)). Again, as in the case of the direct invocations of ὁμόνοια ideals cited above, the social and the theological are inextricably intertwined, as indeed they are in pagan representations; there are no 'secular' politics in antiquity, and especially not in the imperial period of our author.[29]

[26] For ταπεινόφρων and ἀσφαλής and pagan parallels, see Bakke, '*Concord*', 115–19, 126–36. For ἑδράζειν and βεβαιοσύνη, see Mitchell, *Paul*, 106–9, with reference to 1 Cor. 1. 6, 8, and 15. 58; like Paul and ancient treatments, Ignatius deploys ἑδράζειν with ἀκινήτος to create a commonplace architectural association (*Pol.* 1. 1). For ἐπιεικεία see below; καύχησις n. 10 above.

[27] For verbs associated with τὸ αὐτό as belonging to ὁμόνοια discourse, see Mitchell, *Paul*, 68–70.

[28] For τὸ κοινόν as an expression of concord: e.g., Dio Chrys. *Or.* 38. 46; Ael. Arist. *Or.* 23. 11, 48, 51, 65, 66–9; cf. 46; 24. 37, 42.

[29] For the worship of Concordia as a goddess, see Skard, *Begriffe*, 69, 102–5; Fears, 'Cult of Virtues', 893–9; Brent, Ch. 16 below, sect. 4, draws attention to numismatic evidence to show the interrelation of the political, the religious, and the liturgical in treaties celebrating achievement of ὁμόνοια between cities and offers independent support for the case presented here.

Further, Ignatius deploys a typical term associated with the ideal of concord when he describes his churches as 'coming together / assembling (συνερχέσθαι)' (*Eph.* 13. 1; 20. 2; synonymously also, συντρέχειν—*Eph.* 3. 2; 4. 1; *Magn.* 7. 2; *Pol.* 6. 1; συναθροίζειν—*Magn.* 4. 1).[30] Assembling frequently, Ignatius promises the Ephesians, brings Satan's mischief (i.e., the alleged faction and discord arising from illegitimate meetings orchestrated by docetic false teachers) to nothing 'by the concord (ὁμόνοια) of your faith' (*Eph.* 13. 1). Such coming together results in εἰρήνη and the end of πόλεμος (13. 2; see also *Trall.* inscr.); εἰρήνη regularly appears alongside ὁμόνοια in ancient treatments.[31] The political associations of peace and concord suggest that when Ignatius urges Asia Minor churches to send delegates to Antioch to congratulate them on their 'peace' (*Phld.* 10. 1; *Smyrn.* 11. 2; *Pol.* 7. 1), it is not an end to persecution he celebrates, but an end to faction.[32] Echoing pagan descriptions of concord, Ignatius celebrates and promotes the concord arising from correct assembly through a frequent and sometimes exotic display of nouns and verbs affixed with the prefix συν-.[33] 'Συγκοπιᾶτε ἀλλήλοις, συναθλεῖτε, συντρέχετε, συμπάσχετε, συγκοιμᾶσθε, συνεγείρεσθε', Ignatius urges the Smyrnaeans (*Pol.* 6. 1), piling up concord verbs, and goes on to portray them using ὁμόνοια *topoi* such as οἰκονόμοι καὶ πάρεδροι καὶ ὑπηρέται of God's household, and soldiers in his army (v. 2). He similarly invokes the ideals of concord through repetitious citations of the number one—a recurring characteristic in pagan treatments.[34] Ignatius deftly employs the ὁμόνοια motifs we have been discussing when he urges the Magnesians 'to do nothing "individually (ἰδίᾳ ὑμῖν)'—always linked by Ignatius with the common (see *Smyrn.* 7. 2; 12. 2), that they may possess 'in common (ἐπὶ τὸ αὐτό) one

[30] For συνέρχεσθαι and similar terms as technical political vocabulary used to express concord, see Mitchell, *Paul*, 154–5.

[31] For εἰρήνη καὶ ὁμόνοια as hendiadys, see, e.g., Dio Chrys. *Or.* 39. 2; 40. 26; 49. 6; Ael. Arist. *Or.* 27. 44; Plut. *De garr.* 17; *De Alex. fort.* 1. 9; also *1 Clem.* 20. 3, 10, 11; 60. 4; 61. 1; 63. 2; 65. 1. For faction as war, Ael. Arist. *Or.* 23. 54–7, 65.

[32] Thus also Schoedel, *Ignatius*, 213.

[33] Συνάγειν, *Magn.* 10. 3; συνεγείρειν, *Pol.* 6. 1; συναθροίζειν, *Magn.* 4. 1; συναινείν, *Eph.* 11. 2; συναριθμείν, *Phld.* 5. 2; συναρμόζειν, *Eph.* 4. 1; σύνδουλος, *Eph.* 2. 1; *Magn.* 2. 1; *Phld.* 4. 1; *Smyrn.* 12. 2; συνδιδασκαλίτης, *Eph.* 3. 1; συνδοξάζειν, *Smyrn.* 11. 3; συνεῖναι, *Eph.* 11. 2; συνεσθείν, *Smyrn.* 3. 3; συνευρυθμίζειν, *Phld.* 1. 2; συνήθεια, *Eph.* 5. 1; σύνοδοι, *Eph.* 9. 2; συγχαίρειν, *Eph.* 9. 1; *Trall.* 1. 1; *Phld.* 10. 1; *Smyrn.* 11. 2; συγκοπιείν, *Pol.* 6. 1; συμμύστης, *Eph.* 12. 2; συμπάρειναι, *Trall.* 12. 1; συμπάσχειν, *Smyrn.* 4. 2; *Pol.* 6. 1; σύμφωνος, *Eph.* 4. 1, 2; συμπίνειν, *Smyrn.* 3. 3; see also his repeated use of ἅμα—unique in early Christian literature—*Eph.* 2. 1; *Magn.* 15. 1; *Trall.* 12. 1; *Rom.* 10. 1; *Phld.* 4. 1; *Smyrn.* 12. 1. Ignatius is idiosyncratic, but emphasis on terms with συν- appears in pagan treatments: Dio Chrys. *Or.* 48. 1; Ael. Arist. *Or.* 27. 39.

[34] *Eph.* 2. 2; 4. 2; 7. 2; 11. 2; 15. 1; 20. 2; *Magn.* 7. 1; *Phld.* inscr.; 4. 1; *Smyrn.* 1. 2. See, e.g., Dio Chrys. *Or.* 41. 10; Ael. Arist. *Or.* 23. 62, 77; 24. 31, 37; Plut. *De Alex. fort.* 1. 8–9 330D–E; 1. 6 329B; Epictetus, *Diss.* 3.24. 10; Euseb. *Praep. evang.* 14. 5 citing Numenius; also *1 Clem.* 34. 7; 46. 6. Paul offers similar adaptation: 1 Cor. 12. 12–13; Eph. 4. 34–6.

prayer, one supplication, one mind, one hope in love (μία προσευχή, μία δέησις, εἷς νοῦς, μία ἐλπὶς ἐν ἀγάπῃ)', hastening 'all together (πάντες ... συντρέχετε) as to one temple of God, as to one altar, to one Jesus Christ, who came forth from one Father, and is with one, and departed to one ([ἕνα] ναόν ... θεοῦ, ὡς ἐπὶ ἓν θυσιαστήριον, ἐπὶ ἕνα Ἰησοῦν Χριστόν, τὸν ἀφ' ἑνὸς πατρὸς προελθόντα καὶ εἰς ἕνα ὄντα καὶ χωρήσαντα' (*Magn.* 7. 1, 2). The oneness that Ignatius has in mind, of course, is unity around the bishop, which he represents, deploying the concord-related term, as subjection (ὑποταγή; ὑποτάσσειν).[35] In a densely formulated exhortation, he urges the Ephesians to glorify Jesus, so that they 'may be set in one subjection (ἐν μιᾷ ὑποταγῇ κατηρτίσμενοι), subject to the bishop and the presbytery (ὑποτασσόμενοι τῷ ἐπισκόπῳ καὶ τῷ πρεσβυτερίῳ), and may in all things be sanctified' (*Eph.* 2. 2). By contrast, Ignatius charges (*Eph.* 5. 2–3) that the one who fails to join with the bishop in the common eucharistic assembly (ὁ οὖν μὴ ἐρχόμενος ἐπὶ τὸ αὐτό) is guilty of the faction-associated vice of haughtiness (ὑπερηφανεῖν).[36]

Ignatius further refines language associated with concord by an idiosyncratic application of the term ἕνωσις and the cognates ἑνότης and ἑνόειν.[37] While these terms have often been interpreted as evidence of Gnostic influence, they are best read against a backdrop of civic ideals.[38] It is not *gnosis*, but the ancient *polis* that furnishes us with the closest analogies to Ignatius' ideals centring on unity and concord—though, less frequently, ideals associated with ἕνωσις appear in ancient treatments of concord. Thus, for example, Iamblichus in his *Epistle concerning Concord*, directly links ὁμόνοια and ἕνωσις when he writes, 'Concord (ὁμόνοια), just as the name itself wishes to show, has brought together a gathering of the same mind and partnership and unity (ἕνωσις) in itself.'[39] Further, Ignatius' notion that ecclesial concord expresses divine unity and heavenly peace echoes political ideas celebrating

[35] For ὑποτάσσειν—*Eph.* 2. 2; 5. 3; *Magn.* 2. 1; 13. 2; *Trall.* 2. 1, 2; 13. 2; *Pol.* 2. 1; 6. 1; for parallels in pagan and early Christian literature see n. 18 above.

[36] For ὑπερηφανία as ὕβρις and indicative of στάσις, see my discussion of these themes in '*1 Clement* and the Rhetoric of *hybris*', *StPatr* 31 (1997), 136–42.

[37] Thus, ἕνωσις—*Magn.* 1. 2; 13. 2; *Trall.* 11. 2; *Phld.* 4. 1; 7. 2; 8. 1; *Pol.* 1. 2; 5. 2; ἑνότης—*Eph.* 4. 2; 5. 1; 14. 1; *Phld.* 2. 2; 3. 2; 5, 2; 8. 1; 9. 1; *Smyrn.* 12. 2; *Pol.* 8. 1; ἑνόειν—*Eph.* inscr.; *Magn.* 6. 2; 7. 1; 14. 1; *Smyrn.* 3. 3.

[38] Thus, H. Schlier, *Religionsgeschichtliche Untersuchungen zu den Ignatiusbriefen* (Giessen: Töpelmann, 1929); H.-W. Bartsch, *Gnostisches Gut und Gemeindetradition bei Ignatius von Antiochien* (Gütersloh: Gütersloher Verlag, 1940); V. Corwin, *St. Ignatius and Christianity in Antioch* (New Haven: Yale University Press, 1960), 154–88, 247–71.

[39] H. Diels and W. Kranz (eds.), *Die Fragmente der Vorsokratiker*, 2nd edn. (Berlin: Weidman, 1974–5), ii. 356; similarly, Severianus (fifth century CE), *De pace* 1 (*PG* 52. 425): 'the best of painters, wishing to illustrate unity of spirit (βουλομένοι τῆς ψυχῆς τὴν ἕνωσιν δεῖξαι), place behind kings or brothers who are magistrates Concord (ὁμόνοια), in the form of a woman, embracing with both her arms those who are united'; also Ael. Arist. *Or.* 23. 62; 24. 31.

Roman imperial rule. Just as the imperial *pax* manifests divine concord, so the union of Christians with their leaders, in common worship and devotion to the crucified Jesus, makes visible a transcendent unity.

Attention to this political dimension offers a corrective to interpretations that read Ignatius' treatments of earthly correspondences of ecclesial concord and unity with heavenly images in a too Platonic and mystical fashion, as though Ignatius anticipated the ecclesial hierarchies of Dionysius the Areopagite.[40] Ignatius does not make consistent enough links between earthly ecclesial institutions and heavenly hierarchies to warrant such a Platonizing reading. The application is not so much Platonic as political—earthly concord imitates divine concord.[41] '[I]f imitation of the gods is an act of men of good sense,' counsels Aelius Aristides, 'it would be the part of men of good sense to believe that they are all a unity' (*Or.* 23. 77). Ecclesial union and peace springing forth from legitimate gatherings around the bishop and his co-leaders, especially in united sacred eucharistic assembly (*Phld.* 4. 1; *Smyrn.* 8. 2; *Eph.* 5. 2; *Magn.* 7. 2; *Trall.* 7. 2; *Phld.* 4. 1), imitates heavenly union, and thereby reveals the legitimacy of meetings conducted by 'men of good sense'.[42] This is in sharp contrast to the factionalism and schism that are the by-product of foolish docetic teachers illegitimately meeting apart from the bishop (*Magn.* 4. 1; *Phld.* 7. 2; *Smyrn.* 8. 2; see *Eph.* 6. 2–7. 1; *Trall.* 8. 2). 'Be subject (ὑποταγήτε) to the bishop and to one another,' Ignatius urges, 'as Jesus Christ was subject to the Father, and the Apostles were subject to Christ and to the Father, in order that there may be a union of flesh and of spirit' (*Magn.* 13. 2). The desired goal of unity, springing forth as the fruit of religious devotion, reads like a page from one of Dio Chrysostom's speeches on Concord.[43]

Ignatius' sophistication in drawing together the theological with contemporary political themes associated with concord and union is especially evident in *Eph.* 4. 1–2, where he combines musical and body *topoi* with religious affirmation to exhort his listeners to ὁμόνοια. As Allen Brent has shown, this passage with its imagery of the χορός has direct connection with

[40] Thus, H. Chadwick, 'The Silence of Bishops in Ignatius', *HTR* 43 (1950), 169–72, on p. 170.

[41] Thus, e.g., *Magn.* 3. 1–2; 6. 1; *Eph.* 4. 2. This echoes pagan conceptions likening the ruler's relationship to the state to divine governance of the world—e.g. Ps.-Aristotle, *De mundo* 5.396^{a}32–6.401^{a}11; Ael. Arist. *Or.* 23. 77; Dio Chrys. *Or.* 38. 11; 40. 35; for discussion see G. F. Chesnut, 'The Ruler and the Logos in Neopythagorean, Middle Platonic, and Late Stoic Political Philosophy', *ANRW* 2. 16. 1 (1978), 1310–2.

[42] Ignatius pillories docetic schismatics as ἄφρονας (*Trall.* 8. 2), and those who follow them as 'perishing in folly (μωρός)' (*Eph.* 17. 2); those who submit to the bishop are φρονίμους (*Magn.* 3. 1); Polycarp is to be φρόνιμος (*Pol.* 2. 2).

[43] Thus, *Or.* 39. 8: Chrysostom prays that the gods will 'implant in this city [Nicaea]... a singleness of purpose (μίαν γνώμην), a unity of wish and thought (καὶ βουλέσθαι καὶ φρονεῖν)' (trans. Crosby, LCL); also *Magn.* 1. 2; Ael. Arist. *Or.* 24. 37.

imperial festivals and their associated sacred rites as the sign and preservation of a divinely appointed imperial Concord.[44] Harmony expressed in shared religious ritual is a common *topos* in pagan representations of civic peace.[45] Ignatius has redeployed this politico-religious imagery christologically and ecclesially to urge concord upon a community threatened by faction. Further evidence that Ignatius' deployment of union imagery is best interpreted against the backdrop of contemporary political ideas may be seen in his use of characteristic vocabulary to describe political faction (μερισμός and cognates) as representing the opposite of unity (*Phld.* 2. 2; 3. 2; 8. 1; *Magn.* 6. 2). 'Do nothing without the bishop... love unity (τὴν ἕνωσιν ἀγαπᾶτε), flee divisions (μερισμούς), be imitators of Jesus Christ, as he was also of his Father,' Ignatius exhorts the Philadelphians (7. 2), combining the civic and the theological in a uniquely Christian appropriation of political themes. Ignatius' repeated exhortations to ἕνωσις/ἑνότης play a leading role in his rhetorical treatment of ὁμόνοια; the centrality he gives to these concepts represents his own theological development of the pagan political ideal.

'I did my best as a man who was set (κατηρτισμένος) on unity (ἕνωσιν). But where there is division (μερισμός) and anger (ὀργή), God does not dwell,' Ignatius informs the Philadelphians (8. 1), combining and contrasting terms found regularly in pagan political treatments of ὁμόνοια and στάσις.[46] Indeed, Ignatius throughout his letters is careful to portray his own character as well as that shared by the Asia Minor bishops as possessing qualities that pagan authors celebrated as nurturing concord. Ignatius himself is not boastful, and resists those who would inflate him (*Trall.* 4. 1, φυσιοῦν)—the chief vices leading to faction.[47] On the contrary, he is modest, desires more meekness, and is self-effacing (*Eph.* 3. 1; 12. 1; *Magn.* 12. 1; 14. 1; *Trall.* 3. 2, 3; 4. 2; 5. 2; *Rom.* 4. 3; 9. 2). He carefully portrays himself as a man of moderation who discourages envy—both associated in ancient treatments as essential to concord.[48] As a leader free of boasting, discouraging praise, Ignatius conforms to Plutarch's ideal of the good ruler who has eradicated from himself 'self-love and conceit'.[49] This of course allows him to command without commanding, and paradoxically to deploy self-effacement to advance his cause. Ignatius' representation of himself as enjoying freedom from boasting occasions

[44] Brent, *Imperial Cult*, 216.

[45] E.g., Dio Chrys. *Or.* 38. 22, 46; 40. 28–9; 41. 10; Ael. Arist. *Or.* 23. 66.

[46] For καταρτίζειν (also *Eph.* 2. 2; *Smyrn.* 1. 1) as a technical political term often used to contrast στάσις and μερισμός, see Mitchell, *Paul*, 74–6; cf. 1 Cor. 1. 10 for similar application. Ὀργή is especially associated with στάσις in ancient treatments—e.g., Ael. Arist. *Or.* 24. 32, 37.

[47] See n. 10 above; also Plut. *De se citra invidiam laudando* 547B, where the good citizen resists those who would praise his merits.

[48] E.g., Ael. Arist. *Or.* 24. 39, 48, 59; Plut. *Prae. ger. reip.* 813D, 821A–F.

[49] Plut. *Quomodo adul.* 65F; similarly, *Prae. ger. reip.* 813E–F, 820A–821F.

shrewdly limited self-praise, as well as approval for those who listen to him (*Eph.* 3. 1; 12. 1–2). His exhortations to unity are motivated by love (ἀγάπη *Eph.* 3. 2; *Trall.* 6. 1; 3. 2), and belong to a larger theological framework in which love and ὁμόνοια form a whole (*Phld.* 11. 2). Ἀγάπη as a divine gift and as human expression is the hallmark of unity in Ignatius' letters, as indeed it is in pagan representations of the harmonious community.[50] Further, Ignatius' portrayal of his imprisonment and martyrdom as offering (περίψημα, *Eph.* 8. 1; 18. 1) and sacrifice (ἀντίψυχον—*Eph.* 21. 1; *Smyrn.* 10. 2; *Pol.* 2. 3; 6. 1; see also *Eph.* 1. 2; 11. 2; 12. 2; *Magn.* 1. 2; *Rom.* 2. 2; 4. 1) is at home in the civic ideals of the Hellenistic world, where 'the noble death' of a ruler for his subjects, or a philosopher for his teaching, or as a means of restoring harmony disrupted by faction, is a recurring motif.[51] Comparison with these ideals makes irrelevant the elaborate psychological explanations of Ignatian scholars to account for this language. Ignatius' use of sacrificial language with reference to himself does not reveal a man who has 'experienced a blow to his self-esteem . . . reflected in his dealings with the churches'.[52] Rather, it shows a bishop at home in pagan commonplaces, adept at refashioning them theologically to nurture communal unity and concord.

That adroitness is also revealed in his presentations of, and exhortations to, the leaders of the local churches. Ignatius' descriptions of, and advice to, Polycarp, for example, are at home in contemporary pagan descriptions of good statesmanship. Just as Plutarch urges aspiring rulers to be gentle in the exercise of authority, gently tuning those out of harmony, so Polycarp is to bring the troublesome to subjection through gentleness (πραοτης, *Pol.* 2. 1; see *Trall.* 3. 2).[53] Ignatius borrows from contemporary political discourse athletic

[50] For a thorough discussion of ἀγάπη and civic ideals see, Mitchell, *Paul*, 165–71; Bakke, '*Concord*', 191–6; *1 Clem.* 49–50 offers a similar concord-oriented application.

[51] Cf. *1 Clem.* 55. 1–6 for political self-sacrifice to bring an end to sedition. For the pagan connections with civic virtues, see D. Seeley, *The Noble Death: Graeco-Roman Martyrology and Paul's Conception of Salvation*, JSNTSup 28 (Sheffield: JSOT Press, 1990), 112–41; A. Yarbro Collins, 'From Noble Death to Crucified Messiah' *NTS* 40 (1994), 481–503; also K. Döring, *Exemplum Socratis: Studien zur Sokratesnachwirkung in der kynisch-stoischen Popularphilosophie der frühen Kaiserzeit und im frühen Christentum*, Hermes, 42 (Wiesbaden: Steiner, 1979), esp. 143–62. O. Perler, 'Das vierte Makkabäerbuch, Ignatius von Antiochien und die ältesten Martyrerberichte', *Rivista di archeologia cristiana*, 25 (1949), 47–72, is too restrictive in his argument that Ignatius reveals literary dependence on *4 Macc.* and he does not take up the Hellenistic political dimension. *4 Macc.* itself represents a fascinating application of concord-related themes; see, e.g., 14. 6–8, where ὁμόνοια is joined with chorus imagery to celebrate the union of the seven brothers as a 'sevenfold assembly' mirroring heavenly realities.

[52] Thus Schoedel, *Ignatius*, 13; similarly, B. H. Streeter, *The Primitive Church* (London: Macmillan, 1929), 168; J. Moffatt, 'Ignatius of Antioch: A Study in Personal Religion', *JR* 10 (1930), 169–86, on p. 166.

[53] Plut. *Prae. ger. reip.* 809E; also 800B; see also the closely associated civic ideals of ἐπιεικεία and freedom from wrath in praise of the bishop of Philadelphia (*Phld.* 1. 1, 2); also κολακεύειν (*Pol.* 2. 2); πραυπάθεια, *Trall.* 8. 1.

(*Pol.* 1. 3; 2. 3; 3. 1), medical (*Pol.* 1. 3; 2. 1), and nautical (*Pol.* 2. 3) imagery to illustrate the ideal oversight that Polycarp is to exercise.[54] Correctly applied leadership issues forth in that ancient icon of the harmonious state—the properly ordered household (*Pol.* 5. 1–2), in which there is absence of all boasting and haughtiness (ὑπερηφάνειν, 4. 3; 5. 2; *Smyrn.* 6. 1).[55] Like the virtuous statesman who uses his position to make the lowly born and the poor equal to the noble and the rich, so the ideal bishop is the guardian (φροντιστής) of widows, and is not haughty to slaves (*Pol.* 4. 1, 3).[56] Polycarp is to care for unity (τῆς ἑνώσεως φρόντιζε, 1. 2)—the chief obligation of the ruler committed to the ideals of concord. Elsewhere, Ignatius praises the silence of bishops (*Eph.* 6. 1; *Phld.* 1. 1; 6. 2), which I have argued elsewhere is best interpreted against the backdrop of ideals associated with the self-controlled speech of the ideal ruler.[57] It comes as no surprise that such men as these are praised by their pagan contemporaries (*Trall.* 3. 2)—they are the ideal citizens of a hoped-for community living ideals of concord and freedom from faction.

By contrast, Ignatius' docetic opponents are factionalists, and to them belong the vices associated in pagan political discourse with στάσις. Ignatius borrows from ancient political discourse the technical vocabulary associated with faction to describe ecclesial divisions and the people causing them—ἔρις (*Eph.* 8. 1); ἐριθεία (*Phld.* 8. 2); μερισμός (*Phld.* 2. 1; 3. 1; 7. 2; 8. 1; *Smyrn.* 7. 2); μερίζειν (*Magn.* 6. 2); αἵρεσις (*Eph.* 6. 2; *Trall.* 6. 1); σχίζειν (*Phld.* 3. 3).[58] Alongside this language are commonplace medical and horticultural depictions of his opponents as promoting sickness (*Trall.* 6. 2) and bad growth (*Trall.* 11. 1; *Phld.* 3. 1), reversals of ideal statecraft and the pastoral associations of the ancient utopian imagination.[59] To denounce his opponents, Ignatius makes stock charges borrowed from the Hellenistic moral repertoire of vilification of enemies, especially in political rhetoric dedicated to the themes of concord and faction. His opponents are proud (ὑπερηφάνειν;

[54] See n. 24 above for parallels.

[55] See n. 10 above for parallels and literature. Indeed, the bishop himself is the steward of God's household (*Eph.* 6. 1).

[56] Plut., *Prae. ger. reip.* 821C.

[57] H. O. Maier, 'The Politics of the Silent Bishop: Silence and Persuasion in Ignatius of Antioch', *JTS* 54 (2004), 503–19, for discussion of Plut. *De garr.* 506C, 514E–515A; *Lyc.* 19. 1, 3; additionally, see *Ad princ. inerud.* 780A; *Prae. ger. reip.* 800C, 801C–804B.

[58] For citations, Bakke, '*Concord*', 84–107; Mitchell, *Paul*, 159–57 discussing 1 Cor. 11. 19, cites pagan parallels for αἵρεσις as synonym for σχίσμα, and ibid. (86–9, 157–64), for Paul's treatment of μερίζειν/μεριμνᾶν in 1 Cor. 1. 13 / 12. 25; see also *1 Clem.* 14. 2, where αἵρεσις and στάσις appear together in some manuscripts.

[59] For pastoral utopianism, see A. Demandt, *Der Idealstaat: die politischen Theorien der Antike*, 3rd edn. (Cologne and Vienna: Böhlau, 2000); Plut. *Num.* 16. 3–4; Philo, *Agr.* 1. 1– 6. 26; for husbandry and cultivation of civic virtues, 4. 38–9; also 1 Cor. 3. 6–9; 9. 7.

μεγαλορημοσύνη, *Eph.* 5. 3; 10. 2; see *Trall.* 4. 1), boastful (καύχησις, *Eph.* 18. 1; see *Phld.* 6. 3), foolish (ἄφρων, *Trall.* 8. 2); vainglorious (κενοδοξία, *Phld.* 1. 1), puffed up (φυσιοῦν, *Magn.* 12. 1; *Trall.* 4. 1; 7. 1); deceptive (*Eph.* 8. 1; *Magn.* 3. 2; 4. 1–2; *Phld.* 7. 1); and filled with anger (ὀργή, *Eph.* 10. 2). Corrupters of households (οἰκοφθόροι, *Eph.* 16. 1), they incite war through their mischievous practices and docetism (*Eph.* 13. 1–2). They thus undermine the ὁμόνοια of local churches by encouraging meetings apart from the Asia Minor bishops (*Magn.* 4. 1; *Phld.* 7. 2; *Smyrn.* 8. 2).

The profile that emerges from these descriptions borrows heavily from ancient political treatments of vices leading to στάσις. Ignatius reconfigures these by linking them with false confession. Thus, unlike the disciplined speech of the churches' self-controlled and rightly confessing bishops, his opponents' heterodox confessions reveal them to be vain babblers (μάταια λαλούντων, *Phld.* 1. 1) undermining the common good. Cleverly appropriating pagan criticism of faction arising from the rhetorical abilities of unethical men, he weds that commonplace with notions of social ill arising from false religious teaching, and so presents a fresh synthesis of ideas. The 'prattle' of Ignatius' opponents resides in their wrong christological confession and results in faction, in contrast to the moderated speech of the 'silent' bishops who confess rightly and preserve concord.[60] 'Where is the wise? Where the disputer (συζητητής)? Where is the boasting (καύχησις) of those called prudent (συνετῶν)?', Ignatius asks (*Eph.* 18. 2), echoing 1 Cor. 1. 20, but by the reference to boasting (absent in Paul), relating the questions more directly to the implied charge of στάσις. There is no reason to suppose from these charges that Ignatius was engaged in a struggle against pneumatics taken over by χαρίσμα or Gnostics championing esoteric wisdom.[61] Ignatius was deploying these references as part of a recognizably political profile of communities, with their protagonists and antagonists engaged in typical behaviours associated with concord and faction. In the course of doing so, he offered a series of rhetorically charged representations designed to persuade an audience thoroughly acquainted with the ideals of the Hellenistic city to rally behind a certain set of local leaders. Representing the local situations as concord and discord made his case for unity with the bishop, his associates, and their christological confessions self-evidently true—concord and the social benefits arising from it were amongst the most championed goals of the civic imperial culture of Ignatius' day.

[60] Ignatius directly links christological confession with good order at *Phld.* 4. 1; 8. 1–2; *Smyrn.* 7. 1; 8. 2.

[61] Thus, Corwin, *Ignatius*, 54–65; P. Meinhold, 'Schweigende Bischöfe: die Gegensätze in den kleinasiatischen Gemeinden nach den Ignatianen', in E. Iserloh and P. Manns (eds.), *Glaube und Geschichte* (Baden-Baden: Grimm, 1958), ii. 468–72; Schlier, *Untersuchungen*, 125–74; Bartsch, *Gnostisches Gut*, 11–17, 34–52.

In all this, Ignatius is careful to praise the Asia Minor churches for already possessing the concord, unity, and freedom from faction that he exhorts them to pursue. The inconsistency between Ignatius' high praise for unity with the bishop and descriptions of discord has been one of the more noticed rhetorical features of Ignatius' letters. Shawn Carruth has shown how Ignatius' praise for the Asia Minor churches parallels ancient encomium in which leading citizens are praised along with their cities.[62] Encomium was also a means to nurture concord. Aelius Aristides cites praise for differing cities and their citizens as a chief means of achieving and demonstrating the common bonds of friendship and ὁμόνοια (*Or.* 23. 5–7). Ignatius similarly seeks through encomium to nurture such common bonds of friendship, and is thus careful to include in his letters praise for the various Asia Minor churches, and to commend to one another their leaders and churches (*Magn.* 15. 1; *Trall.* 12. 1; 13. 1; *Rom.* 10. 1; *Phld.* 11. 2; *Smyrn.* 12. 1).

Like Paul, Ignatius borrowed from the political vocabulary and imagery of contemporary civic ideals to achieve a unique theological appropriation of Hellenistic commonplaces oriented around the themes of ὁμόνοια and στάσις. Both writers redeployed the vocabulary and imagery traditionally associated with these motifs to respond to their respective rhetorical situations. Paul responds to Corinthian στάσις and ἔρις by presenting ideals at home in pagan treatments of ὁμόνοια. But a theology of the cross that makes foolish the wisdom of the world, and destabilizes the traditional status considerations on which an imperial civil concord was based (1 Cor. 1. 18–31) refashions pagan ideals and urges them in a new direction. In Ignatius, there is a similar reversal, as the prisoner for Jesus Christ is marched overland to his death by the alleged protectors of civic concord. His anticipated martyrdom becomes the occasion to draw into a startling theological unity the physical incarnation and suffering of Jesus and civic notions of ὁμόνοια. If Ignatius echoes Paul in his application of the ὁμόνοια *topos*, his application is more ritually focused, however. Concordant ἕνωσις in the Eucharist achieves by other means the civil harmony much praised in Hellenistic and imperial civic ideology. In this Ignatius goes much further than the Paul of 1 Corinthians, though there, too, ritual and civic goods are combined (1 Cor. 11. 17–34).[63] Further, what seems with Paul a more occasional device to draw a community riven by multiple quarrels into union, in Ignatius takes on a more central and definitive character. Concord is more than a rhetorical portrait to end division—it expresses a divine reality and mirrors a heavenly ὁμόνοια. Here Ignatius,

[62] S. Carruth, 'Praise for the Churches', 296–8; see also Ael. Arist. *Or.* 22. 1; 26. 4, for the praise of cities and the parallels with *Magn.* 1. 2 observed by Schoedel, *Ignatius*, 104.

[63] The pericope is filled with civic vocabulary, as Mitchell, *Paul*, 149–57, notes.

though bolder and more dramatic in his application, is closer to *1 Clement* (see *1 Clem.* 40. 1; 42. 1–2) than to Paul. However, as in the apostle's adaptation of the concord *topos*, personality looms large in Ignatius' application. In both cases, sustained rhetorical self-example allows for an idiosyncratic and emotive application of concord themes. In both authors, shrewdly deployed autobiography centred in the death of Jesus serves polemical hortatory aims and urges audiences to embrace a theologically reconfigured concord. Ignatius thus finds himself in Paul's footsteps (*Eph.* 12. 2) not only as martyr, but as skilled rhetorician. In portraying docetic Christology as faction, and concord as ritual unity with rightly confessing leaders, Ignatius builds on Paul, especially the epistle he knew 'almost by heart', and offers a striking application of ancient political commonplaces.

16

Ignatius and Polycarp: The Transformation of New Testament Traditions in the Context of Mystery Cults

Allen Brent

The letters of Ignatius of Antioch, written putatively by the bishop of Antioch in Syria,[1] are a key indicator of the provenance of the Gospel of Matthew from that city. Those letters, however, also, make some references, and some tantalizing allusions,[2] to the world of the writer of the Apocalypse, as they do to that of the Fourth Gospel and the Johannine Epistles.[3] If they are genuine, then Polycarp's *Philippians* is uninterpolated, and refers to Ignatius' martyr procession as the cause of their collection by the former into a *corpus Ignatianum*.[4] But in that letter we find, curiously, the church order of the

[1] The Lightfoot–Zahn consensus stands against R. Hübner, 'Thesen zur Echtheit und Datierung der sieben Briefe des Ignatius von Antiochien', *ZAC* 1 (1997), 42–70, and T. Lechner, *Ignatius adversus Valentinianos? Chronologische und theologiegeschichtliche Studien zu den Briefen des Ignatius von Antiochien*, VCSup 47 (Leiden: Brill, 1999); see A. Lindemann, 'Antwort auf die Thesen zur Echtheit und Datierung der sieben Briefe des Ignatius von Antiochien', *ZAC* 1 (1997), 185–94; G. Schöllgen, 'Die Ignatien als pseudepigraphisches Brief-corpus: Anmerkung zu den Thesen von Reinhard M. Hübner', *ZAC* 2 (1998), 16–25; M. J. Edwards, 'Ignatius and the Second Century: An Answer to R. Hübner', *ZAC* 2 (1998), 214–26; H. J. Vogt, 'Bemerkungen zur Echtheit der Ignatiusbriefe', in *ZAC* 3 (1999), 50–63.

[2] I use 'reference' and 'allusion' in the context of the methodological axis set out by Gregory and Tuckett (Ch. 4 in companion volume), on a continuum (direct quotation / citation / allusion / echo / reminiscence). Where the methodological point is critical, I reproduce these terms in italics. My use of the terms holds whether they apply to the oral tradition of the communities in question prior to its appearance in NT texts, or to the written text itself in the fluidity of its early composition; see the defence by Peterson (Ch. 2 in companion volume), of Koester, Ch. 2 in this volume.

[3] For the Johannine parallels with Ignatius, see C. E. Hill, *The Johannine Corpus in the Early Church* (Oxford: Oxford University Press, 2004), 427–46. See also Foster, Ch. 7 in companion volume

[4] For Polycarp's *Philippians* as interpolated by the alleged forger of the Middle Recension, see Lechner, *Ignatius adversus Valentinianos*, 48–65, but see in reply W. Schoedel, 'Polycarp of Smyrna and Ignatius of Antioch', *ANRW* 2. 27. 1 (1993), 272–358, with which cf. P. N. Harrison, *Polycarp's Two Epistles to the Philippians* (Cambridge: Cambridge University Press, 1936).

Pastoral Epistles, but not that of Ignatius' presiding single bishop. Nevertheless Polycarp clearly knows the docetists both of the Johannine Epistles and of Ignatius' letters, even though he does not make even bare allusions to the tradition of the Fourth Gospel found in Ignatius.[5] How are we to account for the differences between Ignatius' distinctive church order and that of Polycarp and the Pastorals? How did Ignatius move from the world of the writer of the Apocalypse into the world of the Johannine shadows, and then beyond?[6]

The answer to both questions we shall find, not in origins of church order in the διαδοχαί of putative philosophical schools, as Irenaeus and Pseudo-Hippolytus have taught us,[7] but in the liturgical forms of pagan mystery processions and in the images borne in them as part of a mystery play, that characterized the central liturgical acts of the religion of the city-states of Asia Minor.[8] Ignatius contextualized his role as martyr-bishop by analogy with a kind of pagan theology of iconography presupposed by such processional rites. It is in the matrix of the mystery cult, expressing sacramentally the ordering of the life of the city-state, that we should understand Ignatius' reshaping of the organization of the community of the Apocalypse, of that of the Johannine community, and of the Pastoral Epistles, in joint response with the community of the Johannine Epistles to early docetism.

1. IGNATIUS AND THE APOCALYPSE

Ignatius addressed three of the churches, Ephesus, Smyrna, and Philadelphia, to which we find letters addressed also in the Apocalypse (Rev. 2. 1–11; 3. 7–13). Here, as elsewhere in this book, we find various parallels.

As *allusions*, we find the cross as the tree of life in the paradise of God, of which the believer will eat (Rev. 2. 7), as will the nations for their healing (Rev. 22. 1–2).[9] For Ignatius true believers are 'branches of the cross (κλάδοι τοῦ

[5] For the possible quotation of 1 John 4. 2–3 in Pol. *Phil.* 7. 1 and other allusions, see Hartog, Ch. 18 below.

[6] For Ignatius' location on such a second-century periphery, see C. P. Hammond Bammel, 'Ignatian Problems', *JTS* 33 (1982), 62–97.

[7] Irenaeus, *Adv. Haer.* 3. 3. 2 and 4. 17. 4–18. For a full discussion of Irenaeus' view of διαδοχή, with bibliography, see A. Brent, 'Diogenes Laertius and the Apostolic Succession', *JEH* 44 (1993), 380–6, and *idem, Hippolytus and the Roman Church in the Third Century: Communities in Tension before the Emergence of a Monarch-Bishop* VCSup 31 (Leiden: Brill, 1995), 446–51, 479–81.

[8] See further A. Brent, 'Ignatius of Antioch and the Second Sophistic', *ZAC*, forthcoming.

[9] Discussed in A. Brent, 'History and Eschatological Mysticism in Ignatius of Antioch', *ETL* 65 (1989), 311–16; *idem, Cultural Episcopacy and Ecumenism*, Studies in Christian Mission, 6 (Leiden: Brill, 1992), 84–5; and *idem, The Imperial Cult and the Development of Church Order*, VCSup 45 (Leiden: Brill, 1999), 213–18.

σταυροῦ)', of which they are the 'imperishing ... fruit (καρπὸς ἄφθαρτος)' (*Trall.* 11. 2). Christ is he 'who was truly nailed for us in flesh (καθηλωμένον ὑπὲρ ἡμῶν ἐν σαρκί) from whom are we the fruit from his divinely blessed passion (ἀφ' οὗ καρποῦ ἡμεῖς ἀπὸ τοῦ θεομακαρίστου αὐτοῦ παθοῦς)' (*Smyrn.* 1. 2).

Ignatius pursues the image of receiving false doctrine in terms of eating poisonous fruits, or drinking drugged wine. The Eucharist is the 'medicine of immortality (φάρμακον ἀθανασίας), the antidote so that one should not die (ἀντίδοτος τοῦ μὴ ἀποθανεῖν)' (*Eph.* 20. 2). Alternatively, those who follow false teaching in their own conventicles are not using 'only Christian food (μόνῃ χριστιανῇ τροφῇ)'. In giving a Christian flavour to their teaching, they are like 'those who administer a deadly drug mixed with honeyed wine (θανάσιμον φάρμακον διδόντες μετὰ οἰνομέλιτος)' (*Trall.* 6. 2). The Trallians should 'keep away from any strange plant which is faction (ἀλλοτρίας δὲ βοτάνης ἀπέχεσθε, ἥτις ἐστὶν αἵρεσις)' (Trall. 6. 1).

The Apocalypse fulfils Rowland's definition of the genre in terms of its primary concern with uncovering the furniture of heaven.[10] Images used are of festivals gathered around altars singing in choirs with white raiment in preparation for participation in a sacrifice. The choirs consist of twenty-four elders, and in addition to an altar there is the throne of God and of the Lamb (Rev. 4. 4; 6. 9; 7. 11–14; 8. 3–6, etc.). Ignatius sees in a highly idealized vision the communities to whom he writes as gathered as a chorus in concord (ὁμόνοια), and as a processional sacrifice whose worshippers can be 'enflamed with blood', around a seated bishop surrounded by a presbyterate (*Eph.* 5. 2; *Magn.* 7. 2; *Phld.* 4). But it is here that we come to a significant difference between the two writers.

The earthly counterpart to the heavenly scene in the Apocalypse is not the present church order but rather the imperial cult, in a counter-cultural relationship: the heavenly imagery is a transformed and sanitized alternative to the earthly.[11] The heavenly church order, with which the members of the sacrificed martyr church on earth are about to join, is the replacement for pagan imperial order: it is 'the kingdom of our God and of his Christ' (Rev. 11. 15). In Ignatius, on the other hand, the present church, if its ecclesial structure is informed by the threefold order, is the counterpart of the heavenly church. In the celebration of the Eucharist the seated bishop, image of the Father, around whom is seated the encircling presbyterate, sends the deacons as representatives of the ministry of Christ. It is here on earth, and not in heaven, that they form a chorus and sing with one voice in harmonious unity to the Father.[12]

[10] C. C. Rowland, *The Open Heaven: A Study of Apocalyptic in Judaism and Early Christianity* (London: SPCK, 1982), 70–2.

[11] Brent, *Imperial Cult*, 213–18.

[12] For an earlier version of this case, see A. Brent, 'The Ignatian Epistles and the Threefold Ecclesiastical Order', *JRH* 17 (1992), 21–3.

The traditionally held view that the angels of the churches were in fact their bishops would, if it were valid, be strong evidence against the view that I have just advanced. But the self-authenticizing claim of the seer as prophet, and not as holder of an ecclesiastical office, would appear to speak against the traditional view.[13] But if the word 'angel' does not refer to a single human individual, it does, nevertheless, refer to the collective personality of the community addressed.

Michael stood as a personification of the kingdom of Persia, and acted as the collectivity acts (Dan. 10. 10–21; 12. 1). So too the collective quality of 'patience (*ὑπομονή*)' of the church of Thyateira (Rev. 2. 21), or of 'lukewarmness (*χλιαρός*)' of Laodicea (Rev. 3. 16) is represented by an angelic personality. Ignatius too has a concept of corporate personality, but this is found not in a heavenly angelic being, but in an earthly bishop: in the clerical representatives of the churches that visit him, he claims to see their corporate character. Here the clear *reference* to the concept of corporate character shows a relation in this regard between the two works.

Polybius, the bishop of Tralles, is described not as an individual personality, but as that of the community. As in the case of Bishop Onesimus of Ephesus, he has such 'converse of mind (*συνήθεια*)' with them that he can see their corporate personality, their *πολυπλήθεια* in both of them (*Eph.* 1. 3; 5. 1). Polybius has revealed to him 'your unwavering and blameless mind (*ἄμωμον διάνοιαν καὶ ἀδιάκριτον*)...so that I saw your whole gathered multitude in him (*ὥστε με τὸ πᾶν πλῆθος ἐν αὐτῷ θεωρῆσαι*)' (*Trall.* 1. 1). Thus Polybius becomes 'an example of your love (*ἐξεμπλάριον τῆς ἀγάπης ὑμῶν*)' (*Trall.* 3. 2). In Damas, bishop of Magnesia, likewise he claims to have seen 'your whole multitude' (*τὸ πᾶν πλῆθος*, *Magn.* 6,1). *Πλῆθος* is the usual word for the gathered church in Ignatius.[14]

The angels of the churches, otherwise the stars of John's initial vision, existed in heaven and thus revealed the corporate character of the communities that they represented before the throne of God. They were the heavenly counterparts to earthly events. But in Ignatius the corporate character of the community is worn by the earthly figure of the bishop. We shall be seeking to argue how this transition has taken place, whether in consequence of a process of historical change over time or whether through a process of dialogue between two early Christian communities at the same time.[15] But first let us look at parallels between Ignatius and the Matthaean and Johannine communities.

[13] A. Satake, *Die Gemeindeordnung in der Johannesapokalypse*, WMANT 21 (Neukirchen: Neukirchener Verlag, 1966).

[14] *Smyrn.* 8. 2; *Trall.* 8. 2 (*ἔνθεον πλῆθος*); cf. W. Schoedel, *Ignatius of Antioch: A Commentary on the Letters of Ignatius of Antioch*, Hermeneia (Philadelphia: Fortress, 1985), 112.

[15] H. Koester, '*ΓΝΩΜΑΙ ΔΙΑΦΟΡΟΙ*: The Origin and Nature of Diversification in the History of the Early Church', *HTR* 58 (1965), 290–306, and W. Bauer, *Rechtgläubigkeit und*

2. IGNATIUS AND THE GOSPELS

Ignatius clearly knew the traditions of the communities of both Matthew[16] and John, despite the highly allusive character of many of the references to both. The clear *reference* to the fulfilment of righteousness at the Baptism, unique to Matthew,[17] anchors his other less direct *allusions* securely to such a tradition. Likewise, Ignatius' references to becoming manifest in the flesh, to the Logos proceeding from God's silence, to Jesus coming from and returning to God are unmistakably Johannine,[18] and anchored firmly to that tradition by more direct quotations.[19]

Ignatius shares with John, in contrast to the Apocalypse, the claim that eschatology is already realized. Ignatius has an *allusion* to the Matthaean tradition of the star of Bethlehem (Matt. 2. 2),[20] but draws Johannine conclusions, when he informs the Ephesians that, following the appearance of the star:

> In consequence all magic was dissolved (ὅθεν ἐλύετο πᾶσα μαγεία), and every bond of wickedness was wiped away (καὶ πᾶς δεσμὸς ἠφανίζετο κακίας); ignorance was removed (ἄγνοια καθῃρεῖτο), and the old kingdom destroyed (παλαιὰ βασιλεία διεφθείρετο), with God appearing humanly (θεοῦ ἀνθρωπίνως φανερουμένου) for the renewal of eternal life (εἰς καινότητα ἀϊδίου ζωῆς)...Here all things were disturbed (ἔνθεν τὰ πάντα συνεκινεῖτο), because the destruction of death had been planned (διὰ τὸ μελετᾶσθαι θανάτου κατάλυσιν) (*Eph.* 19. 1–3).

Ketzerei im ältesten Christentum, BHT 10 (Tübingen: Mohr, 1964). Cf. H. E. W. Turner, *The Pattern of Christian Truth* (London: A. R. Mowbray & Co., 1954); F. W. Norris, 'Ignatius, Polycarp and 1 Clement: Walter Bauer Reconsidered', *VC* 30 (1976), 23–44.

[16] *Smyrn.* 6: ὁ χωρῶν χωρείτω (= Matt. 19. 12: ὁ δυνάμενος χωρεῖν χωρείτω); *Pol.* 2. 2: φρόνιμος γίνου ὡς καὶ ὄφις ἐν ἅπασιν καὶ ἀκέραιος εἰς ἀεὶ ὡς ἡ περιστερά (= Matt. 10. 16: γίνεσθε οὖν φρόνιμοι ὡς οἱ ὄφεις καὶ ἀκέραιοι ὡς αἱ περιστεραί); *Eph.* 14: φανερὸν δὲ τὸ δένδρον ἀπὸ τοῦ καρποῦ (= Matt. 12. 33: ἐκ γὰρ τοῦ καρποῦ τὸ δένδρον γινώσκεται); *Trall.* 11. 1 (cf. *Phld.* 3.1): οὗτοι γὰρ οὔκ εἰσιν φυτεία πατρός (= Matt. 15. 13: πᾶσα φυτεία ἣν οὐκ ἐφύτευσεν ὁ πατήρ μου ...).

[17] *Smyrn.* 1. 1: βεβαπτισμένον ὑπὸ Ἰωάννου ἵνα πληρωθῇ πάσα δικαιοσύνην ὑπ' αὐτοῦ (= Matt 3.15:...πρέπον ἐστὶν ἡμῖν πληρῶσαι πᾶσαν δικαιοσύνην). See also Foster, ch. 7 in companion volume.

[18] *Magn.* 8. 2: εἷς θεός ἐστιν ὁ φανερώσας ἑαυτον διὰ Ἰησοῦ Χριστοῦ τοῦ υἱοῦ αὐτοῦ (= John 17. 6: ἐφανέρωσά σου τὸ ὄνομα τοῖς ἀνθρώποις), ὅς ἐστιν αὐτοῦ λόγος ἀπὸ σιγῆς προελθών (cf. John 1. 14: ὁ λόγος σὰρξ ἐγένετο), ὃς κατὰ πάντα εὐηρέστησεν τῷ πέμψαντι αὐτόν (= John 8. 29: ὁ πέμψας με μετ' ἐμοῦ ἐστιν; ὅτι ἐγὼ τὰ ἀρεστὰ αὐτῷ ποιῶ πάντοτε; 8. 42: ἐγὼ γὰρ ἐκ τοῦ θεοῦ ἐξῆλθον καὶ ἥκω; 16. 28: ἐξῆλθον παρὰ τοῦ πατρὸς ... καὶ πορεύομαι πρὸς τὸν πατέρα). See also n. 3.

[19] *Phld.* 7. 1: τὸ πνεῦμα ... οἶδεν γὰρ πόθεν ἔρχεται καὶ ποῦ ὑπάγει (= John 3. 8: τὸ πνεῦμα ὅπου θέλει πνεῖ ... ἀλλ' οὐκ οἶδας πόθεν ἔρχεται καὶ ποῦ ὑπάγει); *Phld.* 9. 1: ὁ ἀρχιερεὺς ... αὐτὸς ὢν θύρα τοῦ πατρός (= John 10. 9: ἐγὼ εἰμι ἡ θύρα).

[20] Cf. Dio Chrys. *Or.* 36. 22.

The Apocalypse's 'kingdom of our God and of his Christ' are here not future but realized at Bethlehem, just as for John the judgement and the reign begin in the consummation of the history of the Word made flesh on the Cross, through which the devil is cast out and the designs of Judas as son of perdition and Antichrist are thwarted, and the elect are gathered together as on the Last Day.[21] The theme of 'appearing (φανερουμένου)' is also typically Johannine.[22]

The realized kingdom in John continues to be realized in the church through the insufflation of the disciples on the day of the resurrection. The Paraclete will continue these realized eschatological events (John 14. 18; 16. 7–11), and is given when 'he breathed into them (ἐνεφύσησεν) and said to them (καὶ λέγει αὐτοῖς): receive the Holy Spirit (λάβετε πνεῦμα ἅγιον)'. Ignatius makes *reference* to a Matthaean event: 'For this reason the Lord received anointment on his head (διὰ τοῦτο μύρον ἔλαβον ἐπὶ τῆς κεφαλῆς αὐτοῦ ὁ κύριος)', but adds immediately his *allusion* to the Johannine Pentecost: 'in order that he might breath incorruption upon the Church (ἵνα πνέῃ ἀφθαρσίαν τῇ ἐκκλησίᾳ αὐτοῦ)' (*Eph.* 17. 1). For him the incorruption continues to be achieved in the life of the worshipping church at the Eucharist.

But Ignatius now goes beyond such a Johannine tradition in claiming that a valid Eucharist will be marked by the presidency of bishop, presbyters, and deacons performing their assigned liturgical roles (*Smyrn.* 8. 1). The attainment of ἀφθαρσία is the attainment of unity, which can be achieved only by submission to the threefold order:

> Be united with the bishop (ἑνώθητε τῷ ἐπισκόπῳ) and with those who are pre-eminent (καὶ τοῖς προκαθημένοις) in forming an image (εἰς τύπον) of incorruption and (thus) teaching (it) (καὶ διδαχὴν ἀφθαρσίας). (*Magn.* 6. 2)

Eschatology is thus realized through hierarchy, since the latter is necessary to gather and to constitute the ecclesial assembly in which the former is realized:

> Be anxious therefore to assemble frequently (σπουδάζετε οὖν πυκνότερον συνέρχεσθαι) for the Eucharist of God and his glory (εἰς εὐχαριστίαν θεοῦ καὶ εἰς δόξαν), for when you more frequently meet as a Church (ὅταν γὰρ πυκνῶς ἐπὶ τὸ αὐτὸ γίνεσθε), the powers of Satan are destroyed (καθαιροῦνται αἱ δυνάμεις τοῦ Σατανα), and his destruction is unbound (λύεται ὁ ὄλεθρος αὐτοῦ) in the concord of your faith (ἐν τῇ ὁμονοίᾳ ὑμῶν τῆς πίστεως). (*Eph.* 13. 1)

The community of the Fourth Gospel was not a hierarchically governed community. Indeed, it has been argued that it was a charismatic community of equals, which would also account for its later popularity with adherents of the New Prophecy (Montanism). In that respect, its ecclesial order was similar

[21] John 1. 14 (incarnation); 13. 6–7 and 13. 29 (Judas); 12. 31–3 (cross).

[22] e.g. John 2. 1; 17. 6; 21. 1; 1 John 1. 2; 3. 2, etc., cf. n. 18.

to that of the seer's community that we have argued to have been charismatic, as indeed were some forms of Gnosticism.[23] Therefore, just as we needed to ask how the transition could take place from the concept of an angelic being who wore the corporate image of its earthly Christian community to that of an Ignatian bishop on earth with such a role, so too now we are faced with a similar question in the present case.

How, in the case of the Johannine community, concerned with the church as realizing eschatology as the extension of the incarnate life of the Logos made flesh and manifesting incorruption, did what pertained to the community as an undifferentiated, charismatic whole now come in Ignatius to be identified with the threefold hierarchy? What concepts were there in the Hellenistic background of the Greek city-states of Asia Minor that assisted Ignatius' shift to this new position that even Polycarp would have found strange?

3. IMAGE BEARING AND IMAGE WEARING IN THE MYSTERY CULTS

We saw in the last section that Ignatius saw unity, and therefore the attainment of incorruption, in terms of the bishop and the presbyters who formed images (*εἰς τύπον*) of what was to be attained.[24] I shall first show how this was the central concept of the significance both of his martyr procession and of the Sunday Eucharist. We shall then argue that for Ignatius the churches are constituted, like the pagan *ἐκκλησίαι* of the city-states, by means of a hierarchy that bore images in mystery processions, and performed mystery dramas that were expressive of the unity and life of their culture.

3.1 The Eucharist and *προκαθημένος εἰς τύπον*

Ignatius' highly idiosyncratic view of church order was alien to Irenaeus' perspective. For Ignatius the bishop is not the successor of the apostles, nor does he mention any act of ordination performed by bishops forming links in a chain running through secular history.[25]

[23] H. Köster, 'Geschichte und Kultus im Johannesevangelium und bei Ignatius', *ZTK* 54 (1957), 56–69, with which cf. Brent, *Cultural Episcopacy*, ch. 3. For Gnosticism and charismatic church order, see K. Koschorke, 'Eine neugefundene gnostische Gemeindeordnung', *ZTK* 76 (1979), 30–60.

[24] With reference to *Magn.* 6. 2, cf. above, p. 330.

[25] Brent, 'Ignatian Epistles', 18–32.

The bishop is not a successor of the apostles, but rather an image of God the Father, which he projects as he conducts the liturgy. The image of Christ in the performance of the Eucharist is found in the deacons, and that of the apostles in the presbyteral circle or council.[26] As Ignatius says:

Likewise let all revere the deacons (*ὁμοίως πάντες ἐντρεπέσθωσαν τοὺς διακόνους*) as Jesus Christ (*ὡς Ἰησοῦν Χριστόν*), even as they do the bishop who is the image of the Father (*ὡς καὶ τὸν ἐπίσκοπον ὄντα τύπον τοῦ πατρός*), and the presbyters as God's council (*τοὺς δὲ πρεσβυτέρους ὡς συνέδριον θεοῦ*), and as a band of apostles (*καὶ ὡς σύνδεσμον ἀπόστολων*): without these a church cannot be summoned (*χωρὶς τούτων ἐκκλησία οὐ καλεῖται*). (*Trall.* 3. 1)[27]

Similarly, he says:

Be eager to do all things in God's concord (*ἐν ὁμονοίᾳ θεοῦ σπουδάζετε πάντα πράσσειν*), with the bishop presiding as an image of God (*προκαθημένου τοῦ ἐπισκόπου εἰς τύπον θεοῦ*) and the presbyters as an image of the council of the apostles (*καὶ τῶν πρεσβυτέρων εἰς τύπον συνεδρίου τῶν ἀποστόλων*), and of the deacons... entrusted with the ministry of Jesus Christ (*καὶ τῶν διακόνων τῶν ... πεπιστευμένων διακονίαν Ἰησοῦ Χριστοῦ*). (*Magn.* 6. 1)[28]

For Ignatius the public role of the bishop, with his presbyters and deacons, is focused on, and demonstrated by, their role in the liturgical drama.[29] At the Sunday Eucharist the bishop, seated in pre-eminent view (*προκαθημένος*), with his presbyters and deacons, creates the image of God the Father (*εἰς τύπον θεοῦ* or as *ὄντα τύπον τοῦ πατρός*). The image, created by each clerical role in its pre-eminence (*προκαθημένος*), is, as we have seen, *τύπος ἀφθαρσίας*. In Ignatius' liturgical assembly, the Father-bishop has seated around him the circle of the presbyters who create the image of the Spirit-filled apostles at the Johannine Pentecost:

[26] In addition to quotations that follow, see *Trall.* 1. 1–2.

[27] See also *Phld.* 5. 1.

[28] I follow Lightfoot and Zahn in adopting the reading *τύπος* (along with the (abridged) Syriac (S) and Armenian (A)) versions, and not *τόπος* even though the latter is attested by both Greek and Latin versions of the Middle Recension (G and L) as well as the Greek (g) and Latin (l) of the Long Recension. The reading is also supported by Severus of Antioch (c.AD 515). However, the reading *τύπος* in *Trall.*, 3. 1 is secure, which must be a powerful support for not reading *τόπος* instead in this similar passage. Furthermore *Didascalia* 2. 26 attests such an Ignatian usage, which was misunderstood by that writer as type in an exegetical, OT sense, which would explain why Severus and later scribes replaced it with *τόπος*, which by that time described the physical space assigned to the various clerical orders in the architechtural arrangement of the basilicas of Eastern Christendom. But see Schoedel, *Ignatius*, 141. For further discussion, see A. Brent, 'The Relations between Ignatius of Antioch and the *Didascalia Apostolorum*', *SC* 8 (1991), 129–56.

[29] For my discussion of the Ignatian typology, see Brent, 'History and Eschatological Mysticism'; *idem*, *Cultural Episcopacy*, 84–5; *idem*, *Imperial Cult*, 213–23.

Be eager to be confirmed (σπουδάζετε οὖν βεβαιωθῆναι) in the teachings of the Lord and of the apostles (ἐν τοῖς δόγμασιν τοῦ Κυρίου καὶ τῶν ἀποστόλων) . . . together with your worthily esteemed bishop (μετὰ τοῦ ἀξιοπρεπεστάτου ἐπίσκοπου ὑμῶν), and the worthily woven spiritually garlanded presbyterate (καὶ ἀξιοπλόκου πνευματικοῦ στεφάνου τοῦ πρεσβυτερίου), and of the deacons according to God (καὶ τῶν κατὰ θεὸν διακόνων). (*Magn.* 13. 1)

The presbyterate, who sat in a horseshoe circle around the enthroned bishop in the liturgy, thus appeared as an ἀξιοπλόκος πνευματικός στεφάνος. It was πνευματικός, in an Ignatian *allusion* to the Johannine Pentecost,[30] when the risen Christ 'imbreathed (ἐνεφυσήσεν)' the Holy Spirit into the Twelve.

For Ignatius, therefore, the bishop is the human image of God the Father in the drama of replay that is the Eucharist. The presbyterate recalls the Spirit given to the apostolic circle in John on the evening of the resurrection. The deacons, as they take the eucharistic gifts from the Father-bishop and give these to the people, issuing their appropriate eucharistic instructions, thus represent the Christ who comes from the one Father (τὸν ἀφ' ἑνὸς πατρὸς προελθόντα) and returns to him who is one again (καὶ εἰς ἕνα ὄντα καὶ χωρήσαντα).[31]

Ignatius now assimilates the celebration of order in the drama of the redemptive mystery of the Eucharist to that of the pagan mystery cults and their processions in the Greek city-states of Asia Minor of the second century. Because those processions were characterized by a drama of replay involving the bearing or wearing of images, Ignatius was able to attribute to his three Christian orders critical roles in the creation of community through liturgy. Because those images had apotropaic functions, bishops, priests, and deacons by analogy were essential both to gathering the community and to the concept of the gathered community realizing eschatology by the shaking of the demonic powers. Thus the realized eschatology of a Johannine charismatic community became transformed into one whose ecclesial structure was necessarily hierocratic.

Regarding the second transition, which was the grounding of the heavenly church order of the Apocalypse in the church on earth, we shall see that the pagan iconography of mystery cults and their priests also carried over into ambassadorial processions in which the ambassador, like the priest, in carrying the image of his city's deity also bore the corporate personality of his pagan community.

[30] *Eph.* 17. 1; cf. John 21. 22 and n. 26 and related text.

[31] *Magn.* 7. 2: πάντες ὡς εἰς ἕνα ναὸν σύντρέχετε θεοῦ, ὡς ἐπὶ ἓν θυσιαστήριον, ἐπὶ ἕνα Ἰησοῦν Χριστόν, τὸν ἀφ' ἑνὸς πατρὸς προελθόντα καὶ εἰς ἕνα ὄντα καὶ χωρήσαντα.

3.2 θεοφόροι and σεβασταφόροι in the Mystery Cults

Ignatius in his inscription to every letter uses after his name the phrase ὁ καὶ θεοφόρος. Holmes is the most recent to translate this phrase as 'who is also called Theophorus', following Schoedel.[32] Thus the phrase has been understood as a kind of *cognomen* or other kind of second name. But the epigraphic evidence is clear that the term θεοφόρος does not refer to a second name, but in fact to someone who bears an image in a pagan religious procession.

We have an inscription from Oinoanda recording documents relating to a music festival (ἀγών μουσικός) in that city in honour of Julius Demosthenes and recording Hadrian's permission for its observance, given 19 August 124 AD.[33] In the prescribed procession and its ritual we find both θεοφόροι and σεβαστοφόροι, who 'will carry (βαστάσουσι) and lead forward (καὶ προάξουσι) and escort (καὶ προπομπεύσουσι) the images of the emperors and the image of our ancestral god Apollo (τὰς σεβαστικὰς εἰκόνας καὶ τὴν[τοῦ] πατρῴου ἡμῶν θεοῦ Ἀπόλλωνος), and the... holy altar (καὶ τὸν ... ἱερὸν βωμόν'.[34]

Although the portable images carried here are called εἰκόνες, Ignatius' word was τύπος, in terms of what the three orders image. εἰκών is used of Christ in Colossians (1. 15), but never in the Apocalypse, which reserves this term for the image of the beast as the Roman Emperor (Rev. 13. 14–15; 14. 9–11; etc).[35] Ignatius, in the world of second-century Asia Minor, might well have preferred the term τύπος in view of the imperial connotation of εἰκών for some Christian communities who would react negatively to the σεβαστοφόροι in processions celebrating together Hellenic and imperial unity, as in the case of Demosthenes. For Ignatius, as the bishop from the East confronting the Emperor of the West in his arena, the θεός of whom he was the φόρος represented a different ideal.[36]

Nevertheless, τύπος is used of portable images such as those borne in a procession or having apotropaic functions. Josephus uses this term for the

[32] M. W. Holmes, *The Apostolic Fathers: Greek Texts and English Translations* (Grand Rapids, Mich.: Baker Books, 1992/9), 137, 150, 158, 166, 176, 184, 194; Schoedel, *Ignatius*, 35, 103, 140, 165, 195, 219, 257.

[33] *SEG* XXXVIII. 1462.

[34] *SEG* XXXVIII. 1462C.51–4; 56–9; 61–4. For an alternative English translation, see S. Mitchell, 'Festivals, Games, and Civic Life in Roman Asia Minor', *JRS* 80 (1990), 183–7.

[35] Cf. Brent, *Imperial Cult*, 196–7.

[36] *Rom.* 6. 1: 'The furthest ends of the world profit me nothing (οὐδέν με ὠφελήσει τὰ πέρατα τοῦ κόσμου) nor do the kingdoms of this age (οὐδὲ αἱ βασιλεῖαι τοῦ αἰῶνος τούτου): it is better for me to die (καλόν μοι ἀποθανεῖν) for the sake of Jesus Christ (διὰ Ἰησοῦν Χριστόν) than to reign over earth's furthest ends (ἢ βασιλεύειν τῶν περάτων τῆς γῆς).' Cf. Brent, 'Ignatius of Antioch and the Imperial Cult', *VC* 52 (1998), 30–58, and *idem*, *Imperial Cult*, ch. 6.

teraphim of Laban, which he also describes as πατρίοι.[37] They are his *lares et penates*, such as Aeneas carried after the destruction of Troy. Moreover, in Demosthenes' procession τύποι do make their appearance, though they are carried in the sense of 'worn' rather than 'borne'.

The Agonothete who leads that procession wears a golden crown or στέφανος, decorated with embossed images. That these are to be described as τύποι is indicated by their description as ἔκτυπα πρόσωπα (embossed portraits) of a type of which extensive examples remain.[38] We recall that Ignatius used the image of a στέφανος for the presbyterate as τύπος ἀποστόλων (*Magn.* 13. 1).[39] Perhaps the most famous case was Domitian's headdress, when he celebrated the Capitoline games, in which he wore the images of the Capitoline triad: there the *coronae* of the priests contained his own image in addition.[40] In the case of Demosthenes, these ἔκτυπα πρόσωπα were of 'the emperor Nerva Trajan Hadrian Caesar Augustus (Αὐτοκράτορος Νέρουα Τραιανοῦ Ἀδρια[νοῦ] Καίσαρος Σεβαστοῦ) and our Leader the ancestral god Apollo (καὶ τοῦ προκαθη[γέτ]ου ἡ[μῶ]ν πατρῴου θεοῦ Ἀπόλλωνος)'.[41] There is a clear ordering of the life of the city-state within an imperial whole suggested by this interrelationship of the imperial cult with the traditional deity of the city, as there was with Domitian's inclusion of his own image along with those of the Capitoline triad on the *coronae* of Roman priests.

The crown bearing the τύποι was to be worn 'in procession in company with the other magistrates (καὶ συνπομπεύοντα τοῖς ἄλλοις ἄρχουσιν)'.[42] Ignatius, as we have seen, saw the three orders, not simply as τύποι, but as προκαθημένοι εἰς τύπον. We find, when we compare the significance of use of images here with that in other sources, an analogy between his view of ecclesial order and a pagan theology of representation.

The priest who heads the procession, by virtue of the images that he bears, becomes identified with the god or goddess. The priest as προκαθηγέτης, and the god as προκαθηγέτης, are regarded as one in the same. Gods and goddesses are described, like Ignatius' three orders, as προκαθημένοι, which I have translated as 'pre-eminent' rather than 'preside'. Gods and goddesses are quite frequently described as προκαθημένοι/αι, within a semantic field that contains such terms as προκαθηγέτης, προηγέτης, (προ) καθηγεμών, προηγεμών, and

[37] Josephus, *AJ.* 1. 322 (10).

[38] J. Inan and E. Alföldi-Rosenbaum, *Roman and Early Byzantine Portrait Sculpture in Asia Minor* (London: Oxford University Press/British Academy, 1966), 178, cat. no. 228, plate no. CXXVI Geyre (Aphrodisias Depot), Excavation inv. nos. 63–5. Negs. E.R. XXII, 2–3. See also E. Kenan, *Illustrated London News*, Archaeological Section no. 2163, 21 Dec., 1963, fig. 9.

[39] See above, p. 333.

[40] Suet., *Dom.* 4. 4; cf. Brent, *Imperial Cult*, 175–7.

[41] *SEG* XXXVIII. 1462.C.52–3.

[42] *SEG* XXXVIII. 1462.C.58.

θεοὶ πρὸ πόλεως, in a family of concepts that find their overlap, in one of their applications, with the leader of a *θιάσος* of a mystery cult.[43]

Deities are said to be 'pre-eminent' (*προκαθέζομενοι/αι*) in the quite usual, visual and spatial sense of that term, of 'sitting forward', in the only enduringly visible form to humans. We find references to 'Demeter and Kore (*τῇ τε [Δή]μητρι καὶ τῇ Κόρ[ῃ]*), the goddesses who are pre-eminent over city (*ταῖς π]ροκαθημέναις [θε]αῖς τῆς πόλεως ἡμ[ῶν]*)'.[44] In the dedication of P. Aelius Menekrates for Demeter and the god Men, he declares that he has:

> consecrated a silver basket (*καθιερώσαντα κάλαθον περιάργυρον*), which he has left behind for the mystery rites (*τὸν λείποντα τοῖς μυστηρίοις*), and for Men who is pre-eminent before the village (*καὶ τῷ προκαθημένῳ τῆς κώμης Μηνί*).

Here we find that his pre-eminence is expressed quite visually in the form of 'a silver symbol that will process before his mystery rites (*σημήαν περιάργυρον τὴν προπομπεύσασαν τῶν μυστηρίων αὐτοῦς*)'.[45] Finally it is Tateia, priestess of Artemis, who is said herself to be 'pre-eminent before', or to 'head' (*ἡ προκάθηται*) 'the queen's village (*κ[ώμ]ης βασιλητ̈δος*)'.[46]

Ignatius regards the gathering for the Eucharist by analogy with a choir gathering for a pagan festival, as does the Apocalypse:

[43] Robert argued that *προεστώς*, *καθηγεμών*, and *προκαθημένος* are synonymous terms, see: J. and L. Robert, *La Carie: Histoire et Géographie Historique, avec le recueil des inscriptions antiques*, ii: *Le Plateau de Tabai et ses envirions* (Paris: Dépositaire Librarie d'Amérique et d'Orient, 1954), 226 anm. 12. See also, and particularly, L. Robert, *Fouilles d'Amyzon en Carie*, i: *Exploration, Histoire, monnaies et inscriptions*, Commission des fouilles et missions archéologiques au ministèredes relations extérieures (Paris: Diffusion de Boccard, 1983), 172: 'Les inscriptions préciant sa primauté emploient les terms suivants: *εἰς τὸν προε[σ]τῶτα τῆ[ς] π[όλεω]ς ἡμῶν θεὸν Διόνυσον*, ou bien *τοῦ προκαθηγεμ[όνος τῆς πόλεω]ς θεοῦ Διονύσου*, or *τῷ [καθ]ηγεμόνι θεῷ Διονύσῳ*'. See also J. Nollé, *Zur Geschichte der Stadt Etenna in Pisidien, in Asia Minor Studien*, Forschungen in Pisidien, 6 (Bonn: Schwertheim, 1992), 81.

[44] *Syll.*[3] 694.50–4; A. Wilhelm, *Griechische Grabinschriften aus Kleinasien*, SPAW (1932), 792–865; also in *Kleine Schriften*, ii, in W. Peek *et al.* (eds.), *Opuscula: Sammelausgaben seltener und bisher nicht selbständig erschienener wissenschaflicher Abhandlungen*, viii, Akademieschriften zur griechische Inschriftenkunde, Teil 2 (Leipzig: Zentralantiquariat der DDR, 1974), 347. See also Brent, 'Ignatius and the Imperial Cult', 45–7; *idem*, *Imperial Cult*, 224–6. For other references, see (i) *SEG* XXXVII. 1403.20, lines 16–23 (= A. Invernizzi, 'Héraclès a Séleucie du Tigre', *RArc* 1 (1989), 65–113): 'in this temple of the god Apollo (*ἐν ἱερῷ τῷδε θεοῶ Ἀπόλλωνος*), who sits out over the bronze gate (*τοῦ χαλκῆς πύλης προκαθημένου*)'. (ii) J. Nollé, *Side im Altertum: Geschichte und Zeugnisse*, i, Inschriften Griechischer Städte aus Kleinasien, 43, Österreiche Akademie der Wissenschaften, Rheinisch-Westfälische Akademie der Wissenschaften (Bonn: Habelt, 1993), 195, 3.2.1.6–8: Aurelius Mandrianus Longinus (AD 143): 'acted as a priest (*συνιερασάμενον*) . . . for the goddess Athena who is pre-eminent (*τῇ προκαθεζομένῃ θεῷ Ἀθηνᾷ*)'.

[45] *I.Eph.* VII.1.3252.5–9.

[46] Wilhelm, *Griechische Grabinschriflen*, 803/347, prefers *κώμης* to *κούρης*, which I here follow. See also J. G. C. Anderson, 'Explorations in Galatia Cis Halym, Part II', *JHS* 19 (1899), 306 no. 246.

For your worthily named presbytery (*τὸ γὰρ ἀξιονόμαστον ὑμῶν πρεσβυτέριον*) ... is so joined to the bishop (*οὕτως συνήρμοσται τῷ ἐπισκόπῳ*) as cords to a lyre (*ὡς χορδαὶ κιθάρᾳ*), wherefore, in your concord and symphonic love (*διὰ τοῦτο ἐν τῇ ὁμονοίᾳ ὑμῶν καὶ συμφώνῳ ἀγάπῃ/*), Jesus Christ is sung (*'Ιησοῦ Χριστὸς ᾄδεται*). And become those who, as individuals, are a choir (*καὶ οἱ κατ' ἄνδρα δὲ χορὸς γίνεσθε*). (*Eph.* 4. 1)

When Ignatius writes as *θεοφόρος* to those churches, he describes them, as he does the Ephesians, as participants in a mystery cult with ascribed roles in the drama involving the bearing of images: they are 'fellow initiates of Paul (*Παύλου συμμύσται*)'. (*Eph.* 12. 2). The language of *μυστήριον* and *μιμητής* is otherwise used in such a cultic context.[47] The Ephesians, hastening to Ignatius' martyr entourage, as representatives of their churches, are described as *σύνοδοι*.

You are all, therefore (*ἐστὲ οὖν*), fellow cult members (*σύνοδοι πάντες*), God-bearers (*θεοφόροι*), and temple-bearers (*καὶ ναοφόροι*), Christ-bearers (*χριστοφόροι*), bearers of holy things (*ἁγιοφόροι*), in every way adorned with the commandments of Jesus Christ (*κατὰ πάντα κεκοσμημένοι ἐν ἐντολαῖς 'Ιησοῦ Χριστοῦ*). (*Eph.* 9. 2)

The *σύνοδοι* are not merely 'companions', nor even the anachronous 'fellow pilgrims' of recent translations.[48] One of the registers of meaning of this term is 'members of a common cult or guild'. The usual *σύνοδος* appears as a plural here because the churches are joining his martyr procession through their representatives, and therefore each church individually is viewed as its own cult. Furthermore, the term has close associations with mystery cults. We have a letter (AD 147) of Marcus Aurelius and Antoninus Pius, the introduction of which reads:

Greeting ... to the gathering of the followers of the Brysean Dionysus (*συνόδῳ τῶν περὶ τὸν Βρεισέα Διόνυσον*), who are the gathering of those initiated into the mysteries of in Smyrna (*συνόδῳ τῶν ἐν Σμύρνῃ μυστῶν χαίρειν*).[49]

Thus, in terms of the procession, he who as bishop is *θεοφόρος*, bears the *τύπος πατρός* of the suffering Father God, as he gathers the bearers of other images around him as the procession proceeds.

[47] *μιμητής*: *Eph.* 1. 1; *Trall.* 1. 2; *Rom.* 6. 3. *μυστήριον*: *Eph.* 19. 1; *Magn.* 9. 1; *Trall.* 2. 3.

[48] Holmes, *Apostolic Fathers*, 143. Schoedel, *Ignatius*, 65, translates 'companions'; cf. 'compagnons de route' in P. T. Camelot, *Ignace d'Antioche [et] Polycarpe de Smyrne, Lettres: Martyre de Polycarpe*, 4th edn. SC 10 (Paris: Cerf, 1969), 79.

[49] *Syll.*[3] 851.7–9; 26–7 (= *IGROM* 1399). See also Marcus Aurelius to Smyrna (between AD 161 and 166), *IGROM* IV. 1400.9–10 (= *CIG* 3177): 'to the cult gathering (*τῷ συνόδῳ*) of the artists and initiates associated with Brysean Dionysus, greeting (*τῶν περὶ Βρεισέα Διόνυσο[ν τεχνειτῶν καὶ μυστῶν χαίρειν]*)'. The *lacunae* ([]) are supplied from *IGROM* IV. 1399.8. See also Damoteles (Ephesus, 2nd century BC), in *SEG* XLIII. 773.32–3: *πρὸς τὴν σύνοδον 'Αφροδίτῃ πολυαινέτῳ*); Moretti, *IGUR* 246.B.2–9(= *IG* XIV. 253): '*ἡ ἱερὰ ξυστικὴ σύνοδος* of the athletes of the company of Herakles (*τῶν περὶ τὸν 'Ηρακλέα ἀθλητῶν*)'.

The χριστοφόροι and θεοφόροι bear in their human flesh, along with their words and actions, the only image available to a monotheism that disallows plastic representations of deity. But they are nevertheless to be understood by analogy with the image-bearing θεοφόροι and σεβαστοφόροι of Demosthenes' festal procession. In that procession too there was mention of a portable altar in correspondence with Ignatius' ναοφόροι. Apuleius describes in the Isis mysteries how 'the foremost high priests (*antistites sacrorum proceres*) . . . carried before them the distinctive attributes of the most powerful gods (*potentissimorum deum proferebant insignes exuvias*)'. But these θεοφόροι were also accompanied in the goddess's procession by a second group, with a priest who 'carried with both hands an altar (*manibus ambabus gerebat altaria*)'. The altar in question clearly was miniature, and thus we have βωμοφόροι as counterparts to Ignatius's ναοφόροι, or ἁγιοφόροι.[50] Such image bearing and wearing was also part of the Dionysiac mystery procession.[51]

We find one gruesome example of a pagan ἁγιοφόρος in the basket held by a κιστοφόρος that contained the *vires* of Attis. A striking example was found at Rome in a marble relief on a base inscribed in memory of L. Lartius Anthus,[52] who is a κιστοφόρος of the temple of Ma Bellone.[53] Indeed, like Ignatius' θεοφόρος, the title of his position and function in the cultic procession is used almost like a *cognomen.* Lartius is depicted on the relief with a laurel crown decorated with three medallions, with busts of divinities. In his left hand are two double axes, and in his right a laurel twig with which to sprinkle the blood produced by self-mutilation with the axes. On the ground to the right of Lartius is a *cistus,* with closed lid, evidently made of basket work. He wears a crown, possibly originally golden, of laurel leaf design, which is adorned with three medallions (τύποι) of helmeted divinities, the central medallion probably of Bellona, with Mars on the right and Minerva on the left.[54] We note that a *coronatus cistifer,* like Lartius, was of a higher grade than that of ordinary

[50] Apul. *Met.* 11. 10.

[51] See the pillar dedicated to Agrippinilla, Moretti, *IGUR* 160.

[52] *CIL* VI. 2233. See also E. Strong, 'Sepulchral Relief of a Priest of Bellona', *Papers of the British School at Rome,* 9 (1920), 207: 'L. Lartio Antho Cistophoro aedis Bellonae Pulvinensis fecit C. Quinctius Rufinus Fratri et Domino suo pietissimo cui et monumentum fecit interius agro Apollonis Argentei Quinctius Rufinus. (C Quinctius Rufus has made this for L. Lartius Anthus Cistophoros of the Temple of Bellona for his most pious brother, for whom also Quinctius Rufinus made a monument in the neighbourhood of the field of the silver Apollo).'

[53] Ma Bellone was the divine Mother in Cappadocia and Pontus, assimilated to the Roman cult of Bellona from the time of Sulla when introduced at Rome. She was associated nevertheless also with Magna Mater; see Strong, 'Sepulchral Relief', 207.

[54] Ibid., 208–9 and plate XXVI. See also F. Cumont, *Religions orientales dans la paganisme romain* (Paris: Geuthner, 1929), 51 plate II. 2, and, L. Robert, 'Nouvelles remarques sur l' "Édit d'Ériza"', in *OpMinSel,* 2 (1969), 967–968 (= *BCH* (1932), 263).

κιστοφόροι. The *cista* at his feet contained the *vires* of Attis, emblems of his suffering.

Ignatius' martyr procession, too, is a celebration of Christ's death, which can be seen in Ignatius' body. As his procession passes through Ephesus, he speaks of the Ephesians as greeting his procession, and becoming part of it, like Bacchic maenads, or the worshippers of Attis, roused to ecstasy or 'inflamed (ἀναζωπυρήσαντες)' by 'the blood of god (ἐν αἵματι θεοῦ)', in the drama in which they participate through *mimesis*:

> being imitators of God (μιμηταὶ ὄντες θεοῦ), being inflamed by the blood of God (ἀναζωπυρήσαντες ἐν αἵματι θεοῦ) you completed the task that was natural to you (τὸ συγγενικὸν ἔργον τελείως ἀπηρτίσατε)... in order that I might be able to achieve my goal of becoming a disciple (ἵνα διὰ τοῦ ἐπιτυχεῖν δυνηθῶ μαθητὴς εἶναι). (*Eph.* 1. 1)

Thus Ignatius, as θεοφόρος in the procession of the Christian cult, creates the τύπος of the suffering Father God that elicits such a frenzied response (ἀναζωπυρήσαντες).

The bearing or wearing of such portable images also performed an apotropaic function. Philostratus at one point describes Apollonius as criticizing the superstition of those travellers who bear a Δήμητρος ἢ Διονύσου ἄγαλμα in order to avert harm and danger.[55] They are held in the bosom of their garment, or held out in front of them, in order to avert the wrath of the nether gods. Plutarch makes it clear that Sulla, for example, carried a small, portable image (ἀγαλμάτιον), as a protection against his warring enemies.[56]

It is at this point that we discover how Ignatius can regard the church as the extension of the Incarnation in breathing the incorruption of the Johannine Pentecost upon the Church as requiring a hierarchical organization in order to so function. It was their frequent assembling for the Eucharist (συνέρχεσθαι εἰς εὐχαριστίαν) in consequence of which 'the powers of Satan are destroyed' and thus the old kingdom is shaken through 'God appearing humanly (θεοῦ ἀνθρωπίνως φανερουμένου) for the renewal of eternal life (εἰς καινότητα ἀδίου ζωῆς)'. But, as we have seen, the Eucharist required the threefold order to be conducted as a drama of replay by analogy with a mystery procession. The Christian ἐκκλησία is a σύνοδος or a θιάσος. Bishop, presbyterate, and deacons

[55] F. J. Dölger, 'Demeter und Dionysos-Figürchen als Glücksanhänger nach einer Mahnpredigt des Apollonius von Tyana', in *Antike und Christentum*, IV (Münster: Aschendorff, 1934), 277–9; cf. L. Robert, 'Le Serpent Glycon d'Abônouteichos à Athénes et Artémis d'Éphèse à Rome', *OpMinSel*, 5 (1989), 747–69, at pp. 757–762 (= CRAI (1981), 522–8). See also C. A. Faraone, *Talismans and Trojan Horses: Guardian Statues in Ancient Greek Myth and Ritual* (Oxford: Oxford University Press, 1992), Appendix 4, 136–40.

[56] Plut. *Sull.* XXIX. 11.12, cited and discussed in L. Robert, 'Le Serpent Glycon', and F. J. Dölger, 'Das Apollobildchen von Delphi als Kriegsamulett des Sulla', in *Antike und Christentum*, iv. 68–9. See also Apul. *Apol.* 53.

projected the images (τύποι) borne by those office-holders, of divine persons and events. Read in the context, therefore, of Ignatius' pagan background, the bearing of images in the form of patterns in our human flesh has an atropaic function in averting the destructiveness of the heavenly, Satanic powers. The waving as it were of the clerical icons extended the Incarnation, and realized eschatology, because those images had an apotropaic function. Thus the Johannine tradition had become clericalized.

Thus we have answered our first question: namely, how Ignatius has transformed what are nevertheless essentially Johannine themes. Let us now address our second question: namely, how, on my thesis of Ignatius' enculturalization in terms of pagan mystery cult theology, did the angelic corporate personality in the Apocalypse, as heavenly counterpart of the earthly community, come to be located in the earthly figure of the bishop?

4. AMBASSADORS, CULT AND *HOMONOIA* TREATIES

The role of the ambassador as representative of a city was also the role of one who bore the image of the city's god, just like the priest bearing the image of the god at the head of a mystery procession. The pagan representatives of the Alexandrians, in their dispute with their Jewish neighbours, carried the bust of Serapis when their case was heard before the tribunal of Trajan. The *Acts of the Pagan Martyrs* describes such ambassadors as 'each . . . carrying their own gods (ἕκαστοι βαστάζοντες τοὺς ἰδίους θεούς)'.[57] βαστάζειν is a technical term meaning 'to carry in a procession'.[58]

Through their act, the particular tutelary divinity of the city could be said to lead the embassy, just as could the god in the mystery rite by virtue of the priest who bore his image. In Caracalla's letter to Ephesus (AD 200–5), we have the emperor's description of the ambassadors who congratulated him on his Parthian victory. When he says: [ἃ δὲ π]ροεπρέσβευεν ἡ πάτριος ὑμῶν θεὸς Ἄρτεμις, he means that 'your ancestral goddess Artemis heads the embassy', because her image is literally carried at the embassy's head.[59] Furthermore, the city was particularly personified in its deity: the action of the deity was the corporate action of the city itself. It was ambassadors who concluded the ὁμόνοια treaty between city and city. It may therefore have been the case that the ambassadors who concluded the ὁμόνοια treaty carried the coins them-

[57] H. A. Musurillo, *The Acts of the Pagan Martyrs, Acta Alexandrinorum* (Oxford: Oxford University Press, 1954), 8 (= *P Oxy.* 1242). 17–18.

[58] L. Robert, 'Le Serpent Glycon', 764.

[59] *SEG* XXXI. 955; *IEph.* 2026.16.

selves as images of the divine, iconographic representations of the city as part of the ritual of the embassy whose conclusion was a *συνθυσία* in which the altar flames blazed in the presence of such joint images of the two cities.

Ignatius describes the character of the Christian *χόρος* gathered for the Eucharist and shaking the cosmic powers as being *ἐν ὁμονοίᾳ*. Characteristically, the series of *ὁμόνοια* coins show, on their reverse, representations of the deities associated with the two cities between which *ὁμόνοια* has been achieved, honouring each other. For example, we have a commemoration of an agreement between Side and Alexandria, during the reign of Valerian I (253–60), where, on the left side of the image on the obverse of the coin, we have Athena standing with a lance, as the divinity of Side, and, on the right, we have Isis, standing with a *sistrum* in her right hand, and a *sistula* with Nile water in her left, as the divinity of Alexandria.[60] Between them stands a round altar with a burning flame that suggests a festival and a sacrifice cementing the concord between the two representative deities. On the reverse we have *CIΔHTΩN AΛEΞANΔPEΩN OMONOIA*. We thus have portrayed a festival concluding *ὁμόνοια* between Side and Alexandria.[61]

We have a series of such coins with these features.[62] We have coins from both Side and Aspendos from the same reign, showing Athena and Serapis, divinities of their respective cities, with *ὁμόνοια* inscriptions.[63] Athena exemplifies, in various epigraphic examples, the description *προκαθεζόμενη θεός* as sacral representative of her cities, which we have seen to parallel Ignatius' description of a cleric as *προκαθημένος εἰς τύπον*.[64] The ambassadors with their *τύποι* effect the *ὁμόνοια* that for Ignatius it is the function of the community gathered for the Eucharist to both express and secure, in which the powers of Satan are destroyed.

We should remember that the word for such an impressed image on a coin is *τύπος*, but that the coins themselves may have been carried as portable images by the ambassadors. The images on the *στέφανος*, such as that of the Agonothete in Demosthenes procession, are also called *τύποι* or, in his particular instance, *πρόσωπα ἔκτυπα*. And I have now argued that Ignatius,

[60] M. K. Nollé and J. Nollé, 'Vom feinen Spiel städtischer Diplomatie zu Zeremoniell und Sinn kaiserlicher Homonoiafeste', *ZPE* 102 (1994), 244, and Abb. 2, 258; P. R. Franke and M. K. Nollé, *Die Homonoia-Münzen Kleinasiens und der thrakischen Randgebiete*, Saarbrücker Studien zur Archäologie und alten Geschichte, ed. A. Furtwängler, P. R. Franke, and C. Reinsberg, 10 (Saarbrück: Druckerei und Verlag, 1997), 195, nos. 1924–5, and table 89.

[61] Nollé and Nollé, 'Vom feinen Spiel', 241–2.

[62] J. Nollé, 'Side: zur Geschichte einer kleinasiastischen Stadt in der römischen Kaiserzeit im Spiegel ihrer Münzen', *Antike Welt*, 21 (1990), 261, nos. 108–18.

[63] Franke and Nollé, *Homonoia-Münzen*, 15, nos. 82–7.

[64] See also Nollé, *Side im Altertum*, 195, Tep 1. and 200;. See also Nollé, 'Side: zur Geschichte', 251, mentioning a coin (248, nos. 23–4) with the inscription: *CIΔH MYCTIC NEΩKOPOC* ('Side; keeper of the Temple mystery').

in seeing ecclesial order by analogy with the ceremony involving the bearing and wearing of *τύποι*, was drawing on such a pagan background.

In conclusion, therefore, given the character of deity and its imaging as *τύπος* as in one aspect reflecting and embodying the corporate expression of the city community, we can now see how the angelic corporate personality in heaven has been firmly grounded in ecclesial order through its human iconography. Ignatius believed that he could see the corporate character of the churches to whom he wrote in the persons of their bishops, because he believed that they bore or wore, in their flesh, the *τύποι* of divinity that also reflected the divine life of the societies to which they particularly pertained. Thus he was able to effect the transition between the church order of the Apocalypse and the hierarchy that he advocated and reinforced in the communities to whom he wrote.

We are now in a position to consider the relationship between Polycarp and Ignatius against such a background, and the former in relation also to the Pastoral and Johannine Epistles.

5. POLYCARP, THE PASTORAL EPISTLES, AND THE JOHANNINE COMMUNITY

Polycarp's letter, if the forgery thesis fails, must be uninterpolated and unreconstructed. Polycarp was then the collector of the Ignatian corpus on behalf of the Philippian community, who themselves received a letter from Ignatius that has not survived (*Phil.* 13. 1). But if this is the case, there remains the problem of why Polycarp refers neither to Ignatius' theology nor to his practice of church order.

Polycarp knows nothing of an Ignatian single bishop encircled by a presbyteral council and attended by deacons. His church order reflects that of the Pastoral Epistles, to which he makes a reference with several *allusions*.[65] He knows of *πρεσβυτέροι* and *διάκονοι*, for whom he offers moral prescriptions paralleling those demanded by the Pastoral Epistles.[66] Unlike the Pastorals, he uses neither the terms *ἐπίσκοπος* nor *ἐπισκοπή*, although in the former the term appears to be generic and seems to apply to 'the presbyters who preside well (*οἱ καλῶς προεστῶτες πρεσβύτεροι*)'.[67] Titus is to ordain to the office of

[65] *Phil.* 2. 1 (cf. 2 Tim. 4. 1); 4. 1 (cf. 1 Tim. 6. 7 and 10); 5. 2 (cf. 2 Tim. 2. 12). See also n. 5 above.

[66] *Phil.* 5. 2–3; 6. 2; cf. 1 Tim. 3. 8; 6. 1 (cf. Titus 1. 5–6).

[67] 1 Tim. 5. 17: *οἱ καλῶς προεστῶτες πρεσβύτεροι διπλῆς τιμῆς ἀξιούσθωσαν*; cf. 1 Tim. 3. 1–2; Titus 1. 7.

πρεσβύτερος, whose function is described as ἐπισκοπή.[68] Ordination, however, appears as normally the collective act of the presbyterate.[69] We have reference to an order of widows common to both communities (*Phil.* 4. 3; cf. 1 Tim. 5. 3–16).

Polycarp gives no indication that he has any real understanding of Ignatius' threefold typology of order. The subjection to all three orders that Ignatius requires is from the laity, who always function, he thinks, in mutual harmony. Polycarp exhorts submission to the presbyters and deacons alone, which suggests that he did not regard an ἐπίσκοπος as holding a separate office. However, inasmuch as the reason is because submission to the presbyter is 'as to God (ὡς θεῷ)' and to the deacon 'to Christ (Χριστῷ)', that much of Ignatius' claim has rubbed off on his exhortation.[70]

Accepting the genuineness of the Middle Recension, and therefore the integrity of *Philippians*, we must in consequence note that, although he accepts the title given him at the head of Ignatius' personal letter to him (Πολυκάρπῳ ἐπισκόπῳ), he has trouble grasping its precise Ignatian sense.[71] His own preferred self-designation in addressing the Philippians is Πολύκαρπος καὶ οἱ σὺν αὐτῷ πρεσβύτεροι. Polycarp therefore rather regards himself as what his most cited New Testament document, 1 Peter, describes as a συμπρεσβύτερος. Such a presbyter is *primus inter pares*, who has συμπρεσβυτέροι who do not constitute a distinct, Ignatian office characterized by a distinct divine image, even though he will not refer to such an office, as 1 Peter does, by the term ἐπισκοῦντες, in common with the Pastorals, as an exercise of ἐπισκοπή.[72]

It is therefore not only with the subtleties of Ignatian concepts of ἐπισκοπή that Polycarp has problems, but also with the nuances of that term in 1 Peter and the Pastorals, to which works he also makes reference. It is relevant also to observe a further feature of the Pastorals of which Polycarp is quite oblivious, but which illuminates also the Ignatian background. We have, in the former, reference to an embryonic theology of an understanding of God through a *via*

[68] Titus 1. 5: ἵνα . . . καταστήσῃς κατὰ πόλιν πρεσβυτέρους. For ἐπισκοπή as a noun see 1 Tim. 3. 1.

[69] 1 Tim. 4. 11: μὴ ἀμέλει τοῦ ἐν σοὶ χαρίσματος, ὃ ἐδόθη σοι διὰ προφητείας μετὰ ἐπιθέσεως τῶν χειρῶν τοῦ πρεσβυτερίου.

[70] *Phil.* 5. 3: ὑποτασσομένους τοῖς πρεσβυτέροις καὶ διακόνοις ὡς θεῷ καὶ Χριστῷ; cf. 1 Pet. 5. 5: ὁμοίως νεώτεροι ὑποτάγητε πρεσβυτέροις.

[71] Since ἐπίσκοποι is used collectively along with διακόνοι in *Phil.* 1. 1, I cannot accept that there is any suggestion of more than the exercise of a generic ἐπισκοπή in Polycarp's understanding of church order, despite the ingenious suggestion that Polycarp is refusing episcopal jurisdiction in an Ignatian sense over the Philippians; cf. Oakes, Ch. 17 below.

[72] *Phil.* praef.: Πολύκαρπος καὶ οἱ σὺν αὐτῷ πρεσβύτεροι; cf. 1 Pet. 5. 1: πρεσβυτέρους οὖν τούς ἐν ὑμῖν παρακαλῶ ὁ συμπρεσβύτερος: ποιμάνατε τὸ ἐν ὑμῖν ποίμιον τοῦ θεοῦ ἐπισκοῦντες . . . ; cf. 1 Tim. 3. 1. ἐπίσκοπος is used only for God and ἐπισκοπή for his judgement in 1 Pet. 2. 12 and 25.

negativa that is part also of Ignatius' Hellenistic background. God is described as 'he who alone has immortality (ἀθανασία), dwelling in light inapproachable, whom no human being has seen nor is able to see'.[73] ἀθανασία, in the context of the possibility of the direct vision of God, is characteristic of a Hellenistic philosophical theology, and is not found in the earlier books of the New Testament.[74] Similarly, too, the Pastoralist uses the terms ἀφθάρτος and ἀόρατος,[75] but these terms do not occur in Polycarp.

Polycarp is therefore insensitive to this character of documents known to him. We should not be surprised, then, that Polycarp does not enter into Ignatius' reflection of such a milieu when the latter uses of God such terms as ἀόρατος (*Magn.* 3. 2), ἀγέννητος, ἀπαθής (*Eph.* 7. 2; *Pol.* 3. 2), ἄχρονος, or ἀψηλάφητος (*Pol.* 3. 2). That common Asian milieu is also reflected in the sophistical rhetorical juxtapositions of opposites in synthesis, marked both by Ignatius and the Pastorals, but unrepresented in Polycarp.[76] Similarly, though, in contrast with Ignatius, he never refers nor alludes to the Fourth Gospel, he does know the Johannine Epistles, whose anti-docetic message he finds valuable: 'for everyone who does not confess that Jesus Christ has come in flesh is antichrist and whoever does not acknowledge the testimony of the cross is of the devil'.[77]

Here we have a reference to an inaugurated if not a realised eschatology (1 John 2. 19–21), a full-blooded version of which, as we have seen, Ignatius shares in his incarnational view of the church's threefold order. Ignatius too attacks a docetism in a Hellenistic milieu of which, again Polycarp shows little recognition, though he agrees in censuring it as heresy.[78] Ignatius shares with 1 John a theology of deification through *mimesis*, that he nevertheless develops in his own way. 1 John denies accessibility to the direct vision of God in this life: 'No one has ever seen the vision (τεθέαται) of God' (1 John 4. 12). But he nevertheless asserts that deification will take place eschatologically: 'Beloved, now are we children of God, and it has not yet been made manifest (οὔπω ἐφανερώθη) what we shall be. We know that if he should be manifested, we shall be like him (ὅμοιοι αὐτῷ ἐσόμεθα) because we will see him as he is (ὅτι ὀψόμεθα αὐτὸν καθώς ἐστιν)' (1 John 3. 2).

[73] 1 Tim. 6. 16: ὁ μόνος ἔχων ἀθανασίαν, φῶς οἰκῶν ἀπρόσιτον, ὃν εἶδεν οὐδεὶς ἀνθρώπων οὐδὲ ἰδεῖν δύναται.

[74] We have ἀθανασία only in two other places, and this is in the context of the resurrection body of the believer, 1 Cor. 15. 53–4.

[75] 1 Tim. 1. 17: ἀφθάρτῳ ἀοράτῳ μόνῳ θεῷ.

[76] 1 Tim. 3. 16; 2 Tim. 1. 9–10; 2. 11–13; cf. Ign. *Eph.* 7. 2; *Magn.* 5. 1–2.

[77] Poly. *Phil.* 7. 1; cf. 1 John 4. 2–3 and 3. 8. See also nn. 5 and 90.

[78] *Magn.* 11; *Trall.* 9–10; *Smyrn.* 1. 1; 2–3; 4. 2–5.2; 6. 2–7. 1.

The fourth evangelist, in his realized eschatology, equated, rather, Antichrist with Judas Iscariot. Though he will agree that the vision of God is not directly granted, it is nevertheless obtained in this life from the vision of Jesus (John 1. 18; cf. 17. 18, 22–3). Ignatius agrees that union (*ἕνωσις*/*ἑνότης*) with the divine leads to incorruption (*ἀφθαρσία*) in this life, but it is specifically through the divine persons and events, to be seen in the *τύποι ἀφθαρσίας* worn by the three clerical orders (*Magn.* 6. 2).[79]

For as many as are of God and Jesus Christ (*ὅσοι γὰρ θεοῦ εἰσιν καὶ Ἰησοῦ Χριστοῦ*), these are with the bishop (*οὗτοι μετὰ τοῦ ἐπισκόπου εἰσιν*). And as many as having repented (*καὶ ὅσοι ἂν μετανοήσαντες*) come to the unity of the Church (*ἔλθωσιν ἐπὶ τὴν ἑνότητα τῆς ἐκκλησίας*), these also shall be of God (*καὶ οὗτοι θεοῦ ἔσονται*). (*Phld.* 3. 2)

Coming 'to the unity of God (*εἰς ἑνότητα θεοῦ*)' is equivalent to coming to 'the (presbyteral) council of the bishop (*συνέδριον τοῦ ἐπισκόπου*)' (*Phld.* 8. 1).[80] Spiritual and fleshly realms are united in the *τύποι*, so that the redemptive *ἕνωσις* can take place that leads to *ἀφθαρσία*. He prays for 'unity of flesh and spirit (*ἕνωσιν ... σαρκὸς καὶ πνεύματος*)' (*Magn.* 1. 2) in the Churches, which is specifically obtained through subjection 'to the bishop and each other (*τῷ ἐπισκόπῳ καὶ ἀλλήλοις*) ... in order that there may be a spiritual and fleshly unity (*ἵνα ἕνωσις ᾖ σαρκική τε καὶ πνευματική*)' (*Magn.* 13. 2).[81] After the resurrection, the church began with 'those around Peter' touching the risen Christ, and thus 'mingling with his flesh and spirit (*κραθέντες τῇ σαρκὶ αὐτοῦ καὶ τῷ πνεύματι*)' (*Smyrn.* 3. 2). Thus is the 'inbreathing (*ἐνεφύσησεν*)' of the Johannine Pentecost[82] developed into the concept of the church as the extension of the Incarnation, achieving unity with God through the threefold order.

Once again we see Ignatius taking a further step beyond that of both the Johannine Epistles and of the Gospel itself. I have argued in this paper that the clue to this transition lies in his assimilation of the theology of Christian church order with the pagan theology implied by the ceremonial and iconography of the mystery cults. Let us now examine the implication of this transition for Polycarp's relationship with Ignatius.

[79] See above, p. 330.

[80] Cf. the heretics in 2. 2: *ἐν τῇ ἑνότητι ὑμῶν οὐχ ἕξουσιν τόπον.*

[81] See also *Smyrn.* 12. 2: *ἀσπάζομαι τὸν ἀξιόθεον ἐπίσκοπον καὶ θεοπρὲς πρεσβυτέριον καὶ τοὺς συνδούλους μου διακόνους καὶ τοὺς κατ' ἄνδρα καὶ κοινῇ πάντας ἐν ὀνόματι Ἰησοῦ Χριστοῦ καὶ τῇ σαρκὶ αὐτοῦ καὶ τῷ αἵματι, πάθει τε καὶ ἀναστάσει σαρκικῇ τε καὶ πνευματικῇ, ἐν ἑνότητι θεοῦ καὶ ὑμῶν.*

[82] See nn. 26 and 30 and related text.

6. IN CONCLUSION: POLYCARP AND IGNATIUS

Polycarp's meeting with Ignatius was also a meeting of two distinct early Christian worlds. Indeed, there were bridges between Ignatius' world and that of the Pastorals and Johannine Epistles that were in Polycarp's canon, the nature of which the latter failed to grasp. But at all events, Ignatius has gone well beyond such relationships in defining ecclesial order in terms of analogies with pagan mystery cults and the iconographic roles of their priests in a cultic drama. By this means he has made a given church order redemptive.

Accepting the genuineness of Polycarp's references to Ignatius as his contemporary (*Phil.* 1. 1 and 13), Ignatius and his martyr's entourage would have appeared to him strange. Here was a Christian leader claiming that he was a *θεοφόρος* of the Christian cult, with other clerics holding such offices as *ἁγιοφόροι*, *ναοφόροι*, and *χριστοφόροι*, both in his procession and as their own local *σύνοδος* or cult association. Union with the divine nature and the attainment of *ἀφθαρσία* came about in the Christian cult by a process similar to that in the pagan mystery cults: namely, by joining in a sacred drama of replay in which the *μύσται* became what they imitated.[83]

Polycarp made every effort to understand that entourage, but with as little success as with the Pastoral and Johannine Epistles. He regarded Ignatius as regarding rightly the two orders for which he had any real use, presbyters and deacons, as representatives respectively of God and of Christ,[84] and that submission was to both orders: it was not simply a matter of having a presbyter-monarch like the presbyter of the Pastorals or 3 John.[85] Polycarp enters into the spirit of Ignatius' entourage as a procession when he employs the characteristic terms for *προπέμψασιν*, typically used for conducting a pagan procession, as we saw in the case of Demosthenes' procession.[86] His description of what the Philippians did on Ignatius' arrival shows the extent to which he was 'on message' with how Ignatius chose to interpret the theological character of his martyr procession: his use of characteristic Ignatian vocabulary indicates, not a forger's hand, but the visible impression that it had made upon him[87]:

[83] *Eph.* 12. 2 (= *συμμύσται*); *Smyrn.* 12. 1: of a deacon: *πάντες αὐτὸν ἐμιμοῦντο*.

[84] See nn. 26 and 27 and related text.

[85] *ὁ πρεσβύτερος* who writes in the latter case clearly demands obedience against Diotrophes for his letter and presence (3 John 1 and 9–10). In 1 Tim. a *πρεσβύτερος* is described as *προϊστάμενος*, whether as patriarch over his own house (3. 4–5 and 12) or over the church (5. 17).

[86] See nn. 33 and 34 and associated text.

[87] The presence of such Ignatian imagery plays a vital role in all interpolation theories so necessary to removing the pivotal place of this letter as evidence to the authenticity of the Middle Recension.

> I greatly rejoice with you in our Lord Jesus Christ (*συνεχάρην ὑμῖν μεγάλως ἐν τῷ κυρίῳ ἡμῶν Ἰησοῦ Χριστῷ*), since you made welcome the imitations of true love (*δεξαμένοις τὰ μιμήματα τῆς ἀληθοῦς ἀγάπης*), and conducted forward (*καὶ προπέμψασιν*), as opportunity fell to you (*ὡς ἐπέβαλεν ὑμῖν*), those bound with bonds that befit their sanctity (*τοὺς ἐνειλημένους τοῖς ἁγιοπρεπέσιν δεσμοῖς*), which are the diadems of those truly chosen by God and our Lord (*ἅτινα ἐστιν διαδήματα τῶν ἀληθῶς ὑπὸ θεοῦ καὶ τοῦ κυρίου ἡμῶν ἐκλελεγμένων*). (*Phil.* 1. 1)

Polycarp did not like the typology so reminiscent of pagan processions, so he would not use the language of *προκαθημένος εἰς τύπον*. He certainly would have found bewildering the way in which Ignatius has poured his theology of Christian order and cult into such a pagan-shaped mould, as implied by such epithets.

He prefers instead to reinterpret Ignatian theology far more ambiguously, with his reference to *τὰ μιμήματα τῆς ἀληθοῦς ἀγάπης*. For Ignatius to define ecclesial order as specifically threefold—and that because they are *τύποι* of Father, Son, and Spirit-filled apostolic council—is for him a too radical a *rapprochement* with pagan theological culture. With this amendment, Polycarp is prepared to support the procession with elected ambassador-clerics on its way to Rome (see *Phld.* 10. 1; *Smyrn.* 11. 2–3; *Pol.* 7. 1–2).

Indeed, such expressions as *μιμήματα*, *τοῖς ἁγιοπρεπέσιν δεσμοῖς*, and *διαδήματα* are readily comprehensible in the context of the language of processions, even though Polycarp fights shy of Ignatius' precise meaning. *μιμήματα* is a word expressive of a mystery procession, though Ignatius never uses it, even though Polycarp obscured the context by making that of which they are imitations an abstraction (*τῆς ἀληθοῦς ἀγάπης*), and not of the more concrete *τοῦ πάθους θεοῦ μου*.[88] The latter term would have referred to the concrete details of the eucharistic drama of replay, and would therefore have been too close to the pagan background.

Διαδήματα, in the case of Philip of Macedon, were part of a procession involving deification through a processional *ἐνθρόνισμα*. The latter 'sent in procession an image befitting divinity (*ἐπόμπευε θεοπρεπὲς εἴδωλον*)',[89] in which context we should read Polycarp's reference to those that the Philippians 'processed forward, (*καὶ προπέμψασιν*)', as 'those bound with bonds that befit their sanctity (*τοὺς ἐνειλημένους τοῖς ἁγιοπρεπέσιν δεσμοῖς*)'. Unlike Ignatius, who wrote that he was 'bound in bonds most befitting divinity (*δεδεμένος θεοπρεπεστάτοις δεσμοῖς*)', Polycarp will not attribute 'befitting divinity (*θεοπρεπής*)' directly to the martyrs' bonds (*Smyrn.* 11. 1).

[88] *Rom.* 6. 3 : *ἐπιτρέψατέ μοι μιμητὴν εἶναι τοῦ παθους τοῦ θεοῦ μου.*
[89] Diod. Sic. XVI. 92.5.

But why, then, did Polycarp find Ignatius acceptable, and wish to assemble a *corpus* of letters for the martyr? I would suggest that this was for one reason and one reason alone, and that was the anti-docetic message of the choreographed procession that came through Smyrna. It was a dazzling piece of enacted, sophistic rhetoric, and encapsulated a message in more than words that Polycarp found so serviceable to his needs. The message of the martyr-bishop, in his procession to Rome, despite all the semi-pagan cultic imagery, was of

> Jesus Christ ... who was really born (*ὃς ἀληθῶς ἐγεννήθη*), who both ate and drank (*ἔφαγεν τε καὶ ἔπιεν*) ... who really was crucified and died (*ἀληθῶς ἐσταυρώθη καὶ ἀπέθανεν*), who really was raised from the dead (*ὃς καὶ ἀληθῶς ἠγέρθη ἀπὸ νεκρῶν*) ... But if, as some atheists (*εἰ δὲ ὥσπερ τινὲς ἄθεοι ὄντες*), that is unbelievers (*τουτέστιν ἄπιστοι*), say he suffered in appearance only (*λέγουσι τὸ δοκεῖν πεπονθέναι αὐτόν*) ... why am I in chains (*ἐγὼ τί δέδεμαι*), why do I pray that I can fight with wild beasts (*τὶ δὲ εὔχομαι θηριομαχῆσαι*) (*Trall.* 9. 1–2; 10)

The symbolism of the cultic procession was for Polycarp a breath-taking refutation of docetism, in which the eloquent prefigurement of martyrdom in the flesh of Ignatius justified Christ's true birth and sufferings. All other features could be ignored in the light of so visually an enacted refutation of docetism. It was by reason of the martyr procession, the final, spectacular refutation of docetism, and for this reason alone that Polycarp was convinced of the basic soundness of the strange, enigmatic figure who came through. Thus Polycarp's incomprehension was the product of Ignatius' closeness to the pagan culture that Polycarp found as difficult to comprehend in Ignatius as he had in the lesser case of the Pastorals and the Johannine Epistles. He tried to repeat Ignatius' terms in a fashion consistent with his own more conservative, Judaeo-Christian perspective.

Ignatius of Antioch, coming from the Hellenistic shadows, was destined to do for church order what his near-contemporary, Johannine community, also in those same shadows, was to do for later, orthodox theology. Ignatius' conceptualization of church order, in terms of bishop, priests, and deacons was, in a form distorted beyond original recognition, the classical form of the church order of later Christendom. Likewise, the theology of the Fourth Gospel, badly understood, and, until Irenaeus' time, like that of Ignatius, treated circumspectly, was destined to provide the philosophical model, again distorted out of all recognition, for defining theologically the nature and character of the Incarnation.

Polycarp, as we have seen, liked the anti-docetic features of Ignatius' procession, but otherwise shows little comprehension of what for him would have been its semi-pagan typology. The Johannine community perhaps fares even worse with Polycarp, since he never cites the Fourth Gospel, however much he may rely on the anti-docetic texts drawn from the Johannine Epistles.[90] Polycarp clearly justified ideas of which he had little comprehension as orthodox solely on the basis of their writer's position on docetism.

90 1 John 4. 2–3 and 2 John 7, quoted in *Phil.* 7. 1.

Part VII

Polycarp, Letter to the Philippians

17

Leadership and Suffering in the Letters of Polycarp and Paul to the Philippians

Peter Oakes

A comparison of the letters that Paul and Polycarp sent to Philippi suggests some new directions in the study of Polycarp's letter. Two key points of comparison between the letters concern leadership and suffering. Paul and Polycarp present somewhat different models of leadership in the two letters. This difference maps rather well on to the difference in style between the letters, especially in the impression of a certain diffidence on the part of Polycarp. Something has also changed in the leadership of the Philippian church. The ἐπίσκοποι of Paul's day have disappeared. In a context in which Ignatius is a central figure, the issue of episcopal oversight is a crucial one. We will explore the way in which Polycarp's presentation of leadership may be linked with the issues involved in a bishop writing a letter of advice to a bishopless church.

Suffering is present in the context of the letters of both Paul and Polycarp. In Paul's letter it forms a central theme. Consideration of the use of ἀγάπη and δικαιοσύνη in Polycarp's letter suggests that suffering is also a central theme there. Economic suffering is likely to have been an important factor in the Philippian church in both Paul's day and Polycarp's day. This suggests that concern about φιλαργυρία in Polycarp's letter could be linked with the issue of suffering.

Several of the above issues are affected by views on the nature of Polycarp's prior contact with the Philippians. The main evidence for this depends on the Latin of the first sentence of chapter 14, which Lightfoot describes as nonsensical. Freshly accessible evidence allows us to overturn Lightfoot's assertion and to translate the sentence in a way that affirms prior face-to-face contact between Polycarp and the Philippians. This will be handled in an Appendix.

COMPARING THE LETTERS OF POLYCARP AND PAUL

A glance at Polycarp's letter reveals the extent to which he writes under the influence of a range of New Testament texts. This makes comparison of Polycarp's letter with these texts an essential move in the interpretation of the letter. Scholarship has recently benefited from two careful studies in this area, by Paul Hartog[1] and Kenneth Berding.[2] However, the breadth of the range of texts covered by Hartog and Berding allows them little space for going in depth into Polycarp's relationship to any particular New Testament text. Although Paul's letter to the Philippians is not the text most frequently cited by Polycarp, it is a natural text to use for more detailed comparative study, because Polycarp consciously writes in the shadow of that letter.

These things, brethren, I write to you concerning righteousness, not at my own instance, but because you first invited me. For neither am I, nor is any other like me, able to keep pace with the wisdom of the blessed and glorious Paul, who . . . also when he was absent wrote letters to you, from the study of which you will be able to build yourselves up into the faith given you. (Pol. *Phil.* 3. 1–2)[3]

The use of some unusual phrases gives strong evidence of Polycarp's knowledge of Philippians: *πολιτευσώμεθα ἀξίως* (Pol. *Phil.* 5. 2; cf. Phil. 1. 27); *οὐκ εἰς κενὸν ἔδραμον* (Pol. *Phil.* 9. 2; cf. Phil. 2. 16); *inimicis crucis* (Pol. *Phil.* 12. 3; cf. Phil. 3. 18). Berding discusses the evidence in detail, and suggests seven further possible allusions to or reminiscences of passages in Philippians.[4] I would add a further allusion that I think is structurally important. Polycarp's instructions on 'righteousness' seem to reach their climax in the discussion of endurance in the face of martyrdom in chapters 8–9. Here the term *δικαιοσύνη* returns (three times), having been absent since shortly after its introduction in and near 3. 1. The weightiness of the subject-matter in chapters 8–9, the intensity of the rhetoric, and the reintroduction of the martyrs who were probably alluded to in 1. 1, also mark this out as a climactic

[1] P. Hartog, *Polycarp and the New Testament: The Occasion, Rhetoric, Theme, and Unity of the Epistle to the Philippians and its Allusions to New Testament Literature*, WUNT 2.134 (Tübingen: J. C. B. Mohr (Paul Siebeck), 2002).

[2] K. Berding, *Polycarp and Paul: An Analysis of their Literary and Theological Relationship in Light of Polycarp's Use of Biblical and Extra-Biblical Literature*, VCSup 62 (Leiden: Brill, 2002).

[3] The abbreviation Pol. *Phil.* is used to avoid confusion between numerous instances of *Phil.* and Phil. This translation is mainly that of Kirsopp Lake, *The Apostolic Fathers*, i, LCL (Cambridge, Mass.: Harvard University Press, 1912; London: Heinemann, 1925). The expression 'keep pace with' comes from J. B. Lightfoot and J. R. Harmer, *The Apostolic Fathers*, ed. and rev. Michael W. Holmes (Leicester: Apollos, 1990).

[4] Berding, *Polycarp and Paul*, summarized on pp. 200–1. See also Hartog, *Polycarp and the New Testament*, 177.

point in the letter. Polycarp then 'cashes this in' by writing: *in his ergo state et domini exemplar sequimini* (10. 1). The structural parallel to Phil. 4. 1 is striking. Having reached the eschatological climax of his exhortation to the suffering Philippians, Paul concludes, Ὥστε, . . . οὕτως στήκετε ἐν κυρίῳ (Phil. 4. 1). The summarizing use of *state* and στήκετε in the two letters is extremely similar. Moreover, the idea of Christ's example, although unexpressed in Phil. 4. 1, has underlain all Paul's preceding argument, especially Phil. 2. 5.[5]

Another reason for comparing Polycarp's letter with Philippians is that there are actual and perceived continuities in the addressees. Paul had been to Philippi. Polycarp had probably been there too (depending on the reading of Pol. *Phil.* 14). Both had been in repeated contact with the Philippians, so were aware to some extent of their situation. In both Paul's and Polycarp's day, the Philippian church had enough members to have a degree of developed organization, but in neither case is there evidence that the church was very large. The apparent lack of a bishop when Polycarp's letter was written (on which see further below) could be linked to the community being of limited size. In both letters, the Philippians face suffering. When Paul writes, this is unspecified, but generalized to involve the community as a whole (Phil. 1. 29). In Polycarp's letter, some Philippians seem to have been martyred (Pol. *Phil.* 9. 1), and there is a broader sense of danger associated with contact with Christian prisoners taken via Philippi to execution (1. 1).

The nature of the socio-political context in Philippi did not undergo obvious changes between the middle of the first century and the first quarter of the second. It remained a moderate-sized (*c.*10,000–15,000), primarily agricultural town. It was a colony that was particularly firmly under Roman political control. However, the nature of the Roman veteran settlement at Philippi and the typical patterns of Greek peasant behaviour under the Romans suggest that the majority of the population of the town were probably non-Roman (including Greek-speakers from a Thracian cultural background and slaves).[6] If the majority in the town was 'Greek', the same would probably be true to a greater extent in the church. This is supported by the names in Paul's letter and the traditions in Acts 16.[7] Even though Valens, the only name in Polycarp's letter, is Roman, the Philippian church of his day was

[5] For the structure of the argument of Philippians, including some evidence for the integrity of the letter, see P. Oakes, *Philippians: From People to Letter*, SNTSMS 110 (Cambridge: Cambridge University Press, 2001), 103–11.

[6] Ibid. 14–50; P. Pilhofer, *Philippi*, I: *Die erste christliche Gemeinde Europas*, WUNT 87 (Tübingen: J. C. B. Mohr, 1995), 85–92; S. Alcock, *Graecia Capta: The Landscapes of Roman Greece* (Cambridge: Cambridge University Press, 1993), ch. 3.

[7] Oakes, *Philippians*, 55–70.

probably still mainly made up of Greeks, excluded from Roman citizenship and political power at Philippi.

As well as common elements in the actual situations of the first-century and second-century Philippian Christians, there is probably an element of Polycarp envisaging his audience in terms of what Paul writes about the Philippians of his day. This is particularly seen where Polycarp commends the Philippians' faith, both in 1. 2 and especially in 11. 3:

> *Ego autem nihil tale sensi in vobis vel audivi, in quibus laboravit beatus Paulus, qui estis in principio epistulae eius. De vobis etenim gloriatur in omnibus eccelsiis, qui dominum solae tunc cognoverant...*

Notice the way that Polycarp mixes together the two periods in the referents of the pronouns: the *vobis* slides from Polycarp's audience to that of Paul.

In the end, however, the justification for a comparative study must really lie in its ability to shed light on one or both of the letters. The two areas in which the comparison looks potentially to be particularly fruitful are those of leadership and of suffering. For each of these two areas we will look first at factors in the context of each letter, then at the key comparative issues.

LEADERSHIP

Context

Paul founded the church at Philippi. This gave him an element of inherent, long-term authority there. In the Graeco-Roman context, founding a community carried with it patronal implications.[8] This was particularly obvious in the context of Philippi. Its founding as a Roman colony was due to Mark Antony. However, the patronal association that this carried became unsustainable after Antony's defeat at Actium. Moreover, Octavian (soon to be Augustus) wanted to draw all such patronal ties into his own grasp. The colony was 're-founded' and renamed in honour of Augustus and Julius Caesar.[9] Patronal ties[10] gave Paul both authority over the Philippian church

[8] E. Badian, *Foreign Clientelae (264–70BC)* (Oxford: Clarendon Press, 1958), 162.

[9] Oakes, *Philippians*, 13. A wide range of Caesarean, triumviral, or Augustan colonies took titles including Iulia and/or Augusta. See L. Keppie, *Colonisation and Veteran Settlement in Italy, 47–14 BC* (London: British School at Rome, 1983), 15, 63.

[10] Since completing my book on Philippians my view of the nature of patronage has widened. I am now sympathetic to Lukas Bormann's view that Paul stood in what could be called a patronal relationship to the church: L. Bormann, *Philippi: Stadt und Christengemeinde zur Zeit des Paulus*, NovTSup 78 (Leiden: Brill, 1995), 207–24; partly *contra* Oakes, *Philippians*, 132.

and responsibility to show concern for it. For example, his attempt to settle an internal dispute (in the case of Euodia and Syntyche: Phil. 4. 2–3) fits the pattern of behaviour of a Roman patron of a community (in the Republican period at least).[11]

Polycarp did not found the Philippian church, and it is hard to decide whether he had some sort of patronal relationship towards it. His expressions of diffidence about giving them advice (e.g. 3. 1) suggest not. As well as settling internal disputes, Roman patrons of communities were expected to inform them about decrees and laws affecting them.[12] Other types of advice must also have been given. Polycarp's expressions are reminiscent of Paul's diffidence in addressing the Roman Christians, to whom he did not have a patronal link. However, the fact of the Philippians asking Polycarp for such advice implies that the Philippians may have viewed him as their patron. This is especially so if the request centred on dealing with the problem of Valens. If an association had a problem with one of its officers, then appeal for advice to the association's patron would seem a likely course of action. My argument clearly makes several jumps here. Badian's evidence is of patronage by Republican Romans of foreign or colonial communities. I am raising the issue of whether those patterns might shed light in the Imperial period on the relationship between associations and their patrons, and on the behaviour of churches. Further work is needed on these possible links, but it seems worth drawing attention to these patterns, because they show that an act of writing, of the kind that Polycarp engages in, may have weighty implications, in the area of patronage, as well as in relationship to episcopacy. Alternatively, the patterns could suggest that episcopacy, as a concept, had these kinds of links to ideas of patronage.

Paul was in prison. This puts him more on a par with Ignatius than with Polycarp. Suffering grants a measure of authority. Paul was not loath to use it in this way (Philem. 9). In Polycarp's day, this point probably carried yet more weight than in the first century. Certainly Ignatius makes much of his situation (e.g., *Trall.* 5. 2; 10; 12. 2), and Polycarp himself describes martyrs' chains as διαδήματα (Pol. *Phil.* 1. 1). The primary connotation of this must be glory, but this form of glory would seem likely also to imply that martyrs carried a certain authority. On the other hand, it could have the reverse effect. Chaining, and other ways in which prisoners were handled, were part of a Roman system of shaming those who broke the bounds of the social order. Several leading Philippians scholars see Paul's imprisonment as having

[11] Badian, *Foreign Clientelae*, 160, citing various examples; S. N. Eisenstadt and L. Roniger, *Patrons, Clients and Friends: Interpersonal Relations and the Structure of Trust in Society* (Cambridge: Cambridge University Press, 1984), 60.

[12] Badian, *Foreign Clientelae*, 160–1, citing Livy 39. 17. 4.

produced a crisis in the church's perception of his authority. On such a reading, the main theme of the letter is the demonstration that suffering and apostolic authority are compatible.[13] It could even be that, given the difference between the perceptions of Christian suffering in the first and the second centuries, Paul might feel his authority to be endangered by his chains, while Polycarp feels his authority to be endangered by his lack of chains! In fact, even in a single context, both prisoners and non-prisoners could feel compromised by which side of the prison gate they were on.

Ignatius is an important contextual factor in Polycarp's letter. The significance of Ignatius is particularly clear if the letter is a unity. Chapter 13 sees both Polycarp and the Philippians as being strongly interested in the network of correspondence initiated by Ignatius. Polycarp also asks the Philippians to write back to him about Ignatius. However, even if chapter 13 is a separate letter (with or without chapter 14), its content must still indicate what presumably was an abiding interest of both sender and recipients of the rest of Polycarp's letter. This conclusion is strongly reinforced by Ignatius' place as the first in the list of martyrs who had been seen by the Philippians (9. 1), relegating even their own members and Paul. The position of Ignatius in the list makes it likely, in turn, that he and his companions (cf. 13. 2) are the 'representations of the true love'[14] spoken of in 1. 1. In any case, the fact that we know of Ignatius' journey through Philippi, but not the journeys of others, makes it preferable to assume that his is the journey referred to, in the absence of counter-evidence. If chapters 1–12 do date from later than chapter 13, the place of Ignatius in the letter argues in favour of a date reasonably close to his martyrdom. P. N. Harrison's argument for a late date linked to Marcion seems to depend on a degree of anti-Marcionite specificity in the letter that is not actually matched by what the letter says about heresy.[15]

We will now move to the key puzzles about leadership highlighted by a comparative study of the Philippian letters of Paul and Polycarp. Why do the *ἐπίσκοποι* of Philippians disappear by the time of Polycarp's letter, and what are the implications of the lack of the expected *ἐπίσκοπος* in Philippi at that time? Why does the style and content of Polycarp's letter project such a diffident picture of leadership, so different from that projected by Paul or, indeed, Ignatius?

[13] D. Peterlin, *Paul's Letter to the Philippians in the Light of Disunity in the Church*, NovTSup 79 (Leiden: Brill, 1995), esp. 51; R. Jewett, 'Conflicting Movements in the Early Church as Reflected in Philippians', *NovT* 12 (1970), 362–71.

[14] Trans. Lightfoot, Harmer, and Holmes.

[15] Berding, *Polycarp and Paul*, 17–25.

Episkopoi

Peter Pilhofer gives an interesting contextual reading of the surprisingly early appearance of ἐπίσκοποι in the Philippian community (Phil. 1. 1). The markedly Roman context of Philippi has a proliferation of titles for functionaries in many spheres of life. Some of these are unique to Philippi. The church there will thus have felt a cultural inclination to create structures with named posts. The title of the group in question, ἐπίσκοποι, is even rather close to that of certain *procuratores*, who are officials of one of the local cults of the Thracian Rider god.[16] Pilhofer then sees this local nomenclature as having been overtaken by the standardizing of Christian titles in the late first century. The Philippian ἐπίσκοποι become the more standard πρεσβύτεροι. The fact of appeal to Polycarp for advice suggests that there was no ἐπίσκοπος, in the second-century sense, at Philippi at the time of Polycarp's letter.[17]

This seems a reasonable reconstruction of the process that took place, although the tendency of associations everywhere in the Graeco-Roman world to create or adopt a plethora of titles makes me hesitant about linking this to Philippi in particular. What Pilhofer does is to use his knowledge of the inscriptions at Philippi to show how, at Philippi, this would be likely to take place. It is probably demonstrable elsewhere too, but at least it has been demonstrated for the town in question.

However, the disappearance of the ἐπίσκοποι and Polycarp's failure to comment on it seems to me to be part of a broader issue about Polycarp's views on bishops, views that are very striking in the context of the letters and activities of Ignatius. When Ignatius travelled through Philippi, one would imagine that he told them that they needed a bishop (cf. *Phld.* 7. 1). His letters make the place of a bishop central to the healthy functioning of a church (e.g., *Eph.* 6. 1; *Smyrn.* 8). He is deeply worried by the Syrian church being left without a bishop (*Rom.* 9. 1). It might be that, in the absence of a bishop at Philippi, Ignatius suggested that they seek oversight from Polycarp at a distance, in which case their letter to Polycarp (Pol. *Phil.* 3. 1) could even be effectively a request for him to act as a sort of bishop. This speculative line of thought gives a new dynamic to Polycarp's letter. The key question becomes the following: to what extent does the letter imply the acceptance of responsibility for episcopal oversight of the Philippians?

Even assuming that this speculation is wrong, as is likely, the question does not disappear. In a context where Ignatius is a key figure, a letter from a bishop to a church without a bishop, especially when the letter is in response to a request for advice, must involve the issue of the extent to which the

16 Pilhofer, *Philippi I*, 142–7.

17 Ibid. 226–7.

bishop is accepting some sort of episcopal responsibility for the recipients. Polycarp's response to this issue seems to me to be a very careful one. He gives advice, as requested, but he minimizes the exercise of episcopal authority in doing so. Moreover, this response does not seem to be designed to avoid 'treading on the toes' of some other bishop. Polycarp seems to downplay the need for episcopal authority for the Philippians at all.

Polycarp gives himself no title or epithet (Ignatius uses the latter, e.g., *Eph.* heading). Polycarp makes no reference to his episcopal role in Smyrna. He associates the πρεσβύτεροι at Smyrna, as a body, with him in the writing of the letter (1. 1). The simplicity and the collegiality of the opening take away from the impression of the letter being an episcopal pronouncement. Added to this are Polycarp's expressions of diffidence, both in expressing his opinions to the Philippians at all (3. 1) and, curiously, in his scriptural knowledge (12. 1, see below).[18] He is more inclined to send his hearers to the letters of Paul (3. 2) or Ignatius (13. 2) than to assert any authority of his own. Polycarp's protestations of diffidence seem to be carried much more fully into the tone of the letter than are those of Ignatius (such as *Eph.* 3. 1).

The contrast between Polycarp and Ignatius in their calls for submission to church leaders is very striking. Ignatius repeatedly calls for submission to the bishop (e.g., *Trall.* 2), often to the bishop and the presbytery (e.g., *Eph.* 2. 2), and sometimes to bishop, presbytery, and deacons (*Phld.* 7. 1). Ignatius regards submission to the bishop as a defining characteristic of a Christian (*Magn.* 4). Calls for such submission are the most common refrain in Ignatius' letters. Polycarp, on the other hand, despite the literary opportunity presented by his use of a 'household code' form, calls the 'young men' to submission only to church leaders, in this case πρεσβύτεροις (as 1 Pet. 5. 5) and διακόνοις. No mention is made of submission to an episcopal figure, an omission that Ignatius would surely not have contemplated, whatever the current pattern of leadership at Philippi. Moreover, when Polycarp calls all to submission, it is to one another (10. 2).

The closest that Polycarp comes to talking about an ἐπίσκοπος is in using the cognate verb in his instructions to the elders. However, his use of it there is to encourage them to be ἐπισκεπτόμενοι πάντας ἀσθενεῖς (6. 1). The use of the verb in such a specific sense suggests that Polycarp possibly does not commonly use the word-group in its more broad-ranging episcopal sense. The instructions to the presbyters overall seem to be aimed at controlling the use of authority rather than sustaining it (6. 1–2). The emphasis is on mercy. The

[18] On these points see also Berding, *Polycarp and Paul*, 177–8. Berding goes so far as to write that Polycarp 'apparently does not view himself as a singular bishop. He is one of the presbyters of Smyrna' (p. 178). However, such a flat contradiction of Ignatius' description of him (Ign. *Pol.* heading) seems unlikely.

same comes out in the instructions about Valens and his wife (esp. 11. 4), the implementation of which was presumably mainly in the hands of the presbyters. It is notable that the advice to presbyters does not include activities such as teaching.

The placing of the instructions to deacons is unexpected. They seem to be categorized among the congregation (between widows and young men) rather than with the elders. Moreover, the instructions to them seem not to relate particularly to leadership. The overlap between the lists for deacons and for widows is striking.

Polycarp greatly respects Ignatius, as do the Philippians. Polycarp acts on Ignatius' wishes about envoys going to Syria (Pol. *Phil.* 13. 1; Ign. *Pol.* 7). However, Polycarp's letter appears to encourage the Philippians to views on church leadership that differ somewhat from those of Ignatius. The first-century Philippian ἐπίσκοποι have probably become πρεσβύτεροι. Polycarp does not lead them in the direction of seeking an ἐπίσκοπος. And if the Philippians' letter to him was effectively a call for him to take up episcopal oversight at a distance, he seems effectively to have declined the request.

Leadership Styles and Self-sufficiency

These points are taken further by consideration of what Paul and Polycarp convey in their Philippian letters about style of leadership.

The main structure of Philippians is a threefold parallel between Paul, Christ, and the Philippian Christians. The patterns of Paul's action, Christ's action, and the action to which the Philippians are called have important correspondences. The letter is full of signals for the hearers to draw the parallels (1. 7, 30; 2. 5, 17–18; 3. 10, 17; 4. 9). Although a number of recent scholars have argued that the central concern of the letter is the interpretation of Paul's imprisonment, the linking signals imply that the main aim is to encourage the Philippians in facing their own situation.[19]

An implication of such a reading of Philippians is that the main idea of leadership that Paul is conveying is that of leadership by example. The leader undergoes difficulties and demonstrates how the faithful Christian should think and act in such circumstances. Paul can also use his leadership as an example with regard to issues such as missionary self-reliance and integrity (1 Thess. 2. 1–12). Polycarp does not offer himself as an example. In fact, he writes virtually nothing about himself or his activities. This again contrasts with Ignatius, who writes repeatedly about his martyrdom (as one would

[19] Oakes, *Philippians*, 103–23.

expect anyway) and makes a range of points about his attitude in the circumstances he is facing (e.g., *Smyrn.* 4. 2). He clearly expects these to carry lessons for his hearers.

Polycarp's main contention about leadership seems to be that a Christian leader should be gentle. Evidence of this has been cited above, from his own diffidence, from his advice about Valens, and from his instructions to the presbyters. In fact, the links between these three mean that Polycarp is indeed, in a way, a model of leadership. However, in contrast to Paul and Ignatius, he does not present himself as a model in his way of living, only in his way of leading.

Polycarp's gentle leadership in the letter may have a particular point, which brings us back to our earlier discussion. Polycarp's model of leadership may be aimed at encouraging self-sufficiency. Ignatius gives his opinions. Polycarp cites New Testament texts. These are texts accessible to the Philippians. They can use them themselves rather than needing help from him. He ends his letter by pressing this home.

Confido enim vos bene exercitatos esse in sacris litteris et nihil vos latet; mihi autem non est concessum. Modo, ut his scripturis dictum est... (12. 1)

He then cites Eph. 4. 26 (although, as Schoedel argues, the tag 'scripture' may result from Polycarp confusing Eph. 4. 26 with Ps. 4. 5, which it cites[20]), the kind of text to which they seem to have access. Polycarp also turns his hearers to the letters of Ignatius as a source for instruction (13. 2). More forcefully, he turns them to Paul's letter to them. The positioning of that commendation, in counterpoint to Polycarp's expression of diffidence about writing (3. 2), clearly could be a kind of politeness. But it could also aim to draw attention to a key resource that they already have.

From Philippians, and possibly other of Paul's letters, Polycarp also draws commendations of the Philippians' faith (Pol. *Phil.* 1. 2; 11. 3). He sees the commendations of Paul's day as still appropriate now. Again, politeness requires expressions of praise, especially in the letter's opening. However, particularly in the case of Valens, where Polycarp's commendation of the Philippians sits alongside his apparent unwillingness to make any very definite authoritative pronouncement, my impression is that commendation is part of a strategy by Polycarp to put responsibility back on to the Philippians' shoulders.

[20] W. R. Schoedel, *Polycarp, Martyrdom of Polycarp, Fragments of Papias* (London: Thomas Nelson, 1967), 35 n. 12. Schoedel argues that Polycarp's aim here is not to assert inferiority in knowledge of Scripture. Rather, the point is that 'The Philippians are to edify themselves (11. 4b). They know the Old Testament. To instruct them in it is not Polycarp's task. All he will permit himself to do (*modo*) is to draw attention to a few key verses from the Bible.'

Polycarp does give instruction in his letter. But the way in which he does it seems designed to convey the message to the bishopless Philippians that they are able to instruct themselves.

SUFFERING

Scholars have tended to underplay the sense of danger present in the context of both Paul's and Polycarp's letters to Philippi. In each case, the initial impression of a friendly but rather rambling text has led interpreters away from seeing the letter as produced under a threatening cloud. Recent work on Paul's letter has begun to change this, with several scholars seeing suffering as a central issue in the letter.[21] The context of Polycarp's letter seems equally threatening. The theme of suffering probably needs to be more central to study of the letter than has generally been the case so far.

The theme of suffering pervades Paul's letter (Phil. 1. 7, 12–26, 28–30; 2. 6–8, 17–18, 26–30; 3. 10; 4. 12–14). The hearers are described as experiencing suffering (1. 29), and their experience is linked to the sufferings of Paul (1. 30; 2. 17–18), which are, in turn, linked to those of Christ (3. 10).[22] In Polycarp's letter, some Philippians seem to have been martyred (Pol. *Phil.* 9. 1). The letter opens by referring to the journeying martyrs, who are praised as archetypal Christians. The preliminary exhortations end with a reminder that the kingdom of God belongs to the persecuted (2. 3). The theme of righteousness (3. 1) comes to its conclusion in the call to endurance under suffering (chapters 8–9).

Context

In Paul's day the context of Christian suffering was not generally one of martyrdom. Paul may have been facing it, but the Philippians seem not to have been. By a space of at least a couple of years, the letter preceded the Neronian persecutions in Rome, and even these were specific to that city. This means that the suffering 'for the sake of Christ' that the Philippians faced (1. 29) was not an organized attack by the provincial authorities. It was something more piecemeal, more local. The possibilities range from occasional action by

[21] L. G. Bloomquist, *The Function of Suffering in Philippians*, JSNTSup 78 (Sheffield: JSOT Press, 1993); P. Holloway, *Consolation in Philippians*, SNTSMS 112 (Cambridge: Cambridge University Press, 2003); Peterlin, *Paul's Letter.*

[22] Oakes, *Philippians*, 77–89.

city magistrates (judicial beatings, brief imprisonment) to disruption of relationships with family, friends, business associates, or customers. For each of these possibilities, the most tangible long-term effect was likely to be economic. This is true even of magistrates' action, because the continuing effects of one-off punishments would be mainly in the area of reputation, and hence in disruption of economically important relationships.[23]

This reading fits the textual evidence well. Paul writes of the Macedonian churches that

> *ἐν πολλῇ δοκιμῇ θλίψεως ἡ περισσεία τῆς χαρᾶς αὐτῶν καὶ ἡ κατὰ βάθους πτωχεία αὐτῶν ἐπερίσσευσεν εἰς τὸ πλοῦτος τῆς ἁπλότητος αὐτῶν* (2 Cor. 8. 2)

The Philippian or the Thessalonian church, or both, is described as both suffering and poor. (Notice that willingness to give money, as the Philippians did to Paul, is not necessarily an indicator of a relatively wealthy congregation, *contra* many commentators on Philippians.) Moreover, the pattern of argument of Philippians works well in a context of economic suffering. Paul's main call is for standing firm under suffering (1. 27–30). The call is worked out in terms of unity (2. 1–4). This unity is focused on humility and considering the interests of others (2. 3–4). The call is then reinforced by a recounting of the story of Christ in a way that highlights his vast lowering of status, his obedience under suffering, and the universal extent of the authority given to him in response (2. 5–11). In a context of suffering, considering one another's interests must primarily mean the giving of practical help, economic help. Christ's fall in status and obedience under suffering offer an example that provides effective encouragement under the dangers inherent in giving economic help to fellow Christians in trouble. My reading of the statement of authority in 2. 9–11 is that, primarily, it places Christ's imperatives of unity and faithfulness above Philippian society's problematic imperatives, such as those of status-preservation and the avoidance of trouble-makers.[24]

Economic suffering is not a major theme in early Christian texts. Heb. 10. 34 talks of 'plundering of possessions'. The book of Revelation speaks of prevention of trade (Rev. 13. 17). One phase of action against Christians at Lyons was that they were 'excluded from public buildings, baths and markets' (Euseb. *HE* 5. 1). Otherwise the focus is on more dramatic forms of suffering, especially death. Second-, third-, and fourth-generation Christians did not face quite the same issues as the initial groups of converts. The first Christians needed to construct new patterns of economic interaction where some of the prior links with non-Christians had broken down. Later generations inherited an economic *modus vivendi*. However, outbreaks of

[23] Ibid. 89–96. [24] Ibid. 99–102, 175–210.

persecution, as at Lyons, must have tended to disrupt those arrangements, either by breaking more links with non-Christian society or by removing key figures from the Christian community. To take one type of case: the martyrdom of a Christian householder would usually cause long-term economic hardship for that person's dependants.

The event that we know about in Philippi in Polycarp's day is the journey of the martyrs, probably Ignatius and his companions, through the town. This must have been a public event, at least in so far as the magistrates at Philippi would have been aware of it. If the magistrates, and probably a wider group in the town, were aware of, and probably involved in, the transit of Christians who had been condemned to die and were being taken to Rome, then the situation of Christians at Philippi was likely to have been affected. Two factors make this particularly probable. The first is the size of Philippi. In a moderate-sized country town there was not the anonymity that a Christian group might expect to enjoy in Antioch or Corinth. The second is that the Philippian Christians made contact with the prisoners as they passed through Philippi (Pol. *Phil.* 1. 1). By doing so, they forcibly drew to the magistrates' attention their identity of interest with the prisoners.

In fact, by 'receiving' the prisoners and 'sending them on' (1. 1), the Philippians were probably doing what Paul had called *his* generation of Philippians to do: namely, provide practical, probably economic, help to Christians in trouble. The difficulties involved in this may be suggested by Polycarp's note that the Philippians helped the prisoners ὡς ἐπέβαλεν ὑμῖν (1. 1). As a result of drawing this negative attention to themselves, the Philippian Christians must have feared a deterioration in their situation in the town. It is likely that some such deterioration occurred and that Polycarp writes in that context.

Martyrdom would be a danger facing the second-century Philippian Christians. However, there was no likelihood of wholesale killing. That hardly ever happened. There would be specific danger to church leaders. More generally, a deterioration in the situation of Christians in the town probably meant harassment, either in dealings with officials or in encounters with others, or the breaking of some of the relationships that must have still existed between Christians and non-Christians. The most obvious implications of this would, as in the first-century context, be economic.

Polycarp wrote in a context where the aftermath of the martyrs' journey through Philippi must have engendered fear in the Philippian church. The fact that martyrdom was likely to be prominent in the Philippians' minds is reinforced by their request for the letters of Ignatius (13. 2), in which martyrdom is a central theme. It was also no doubt in their minds because Philippians appear, at some point, to have been martyred (9. 1). As well as increased fear, the letter implies that the Philippians are also likely to have been facing worsening relations in the town. Current persecution is suggested by 2. 3 and 12. 3. The most likely effects of persecution would again be economic. Reading Polycarp's letter in a context of economic suffering has a significant effect on its interpretation.

Love, Righteousness, and Suffering

The context of Polycarp's letter means that one would expect suffering to be a leading theme, or even the main theme. However, scholars tend to see the main focus of the letter as lying elsewhere, in ethical teaching or the issue of heresy or the problem over Valens. The reason for this is probably that suffering seems not to have a place in the letter that is structurally important: Valens (at the end) or the Household Code (in the centre) look better placed. Yet all would agree that 'righteousness' has a crucial place in the letter. I would argue that 'love' also has a crucial place, and that the co-ordination of the two terms forms the most important structure in the letter, a structure which focuses on suffering and martyrdom.

The letter opens by describing the martyrs as *τὰ μιμήματα τῆς ἀληθοῦς ἀγάπης*, 'the representations of the true love' (1. 1).[25] Elsewhere in the letter, *ἀγάπη* is generally a human action (first of two occurrences in 2. 2; 3. 3; 4. 2; 9. 2), and it seems likely that that is the case in 1. 1 as well. The acts of the martyrs in 1. 1 demonstrate their love (whether or not they also demonstrate God's love). This then fits Polycarp's conclusion to his call in chapter 9 for the Philippians to follow the martyrs in endurance. They suffered with Christ, *οὐ γὰρ τὸν νῦν ἠγάπησαν αἰῶνα, ἀλλὰ τὸν ὑπὲρ ἡμῶν ἀποθανόντα* (9. 2). The martyrs' love brackets a major section of the letter.

This structure is complicated by the introduction of *δικαιοσύνη* in 2. 3–4. 1. After noting that *δικαιοσύνη* is that for which Christians are persecuted (2. 3), Polycarp sets the term up as a theme for his letter (3. 1). He adverts to Paul, then to faith, which brings him to *ἀγάπη* for God, Christ, and neighbour (3. 2–3). This leads him to characterize *δικαιοσύνη* as a command which is fulfilled by *ἀγάπη* (which, in turn, protects from sin, 3. 3). *Φιλαργυρία* is then described as the beginning of all troubles (*χαλεπῶν*). The armour of *δικαιοσύνη* is commended, and the first thing to be taught is to walk in the 'command of the Lord' (4. 1), presumably the 'command of *δικαιοσύνη*' of 3. 3, which was fulfilled by *ἀγάπη*.

As noted above, except in a description relating to deacons (5. 2), the *δικαιοσύνη* terminology does not return until chapters 8–9. Then it returns

[25] Following Lightfoot, Harmer, and Holmes, *contra* Lake.

insistently, and with a very specific focus. The suffering Christ is the ἀρραβὼν τῆς δικαιοσύνης ἡμῶν (8. 1). The Philippians are called to imitate his endurance (8. 2). Polycarp sums up his call as being for all of them πειθαρχεῖν τῷ λόγῳ τῆς δικαιοσύνης καὶ ἀσκεῖν πᾶσαν ὑπομονήν (9. 1), imitating the martyrs who 'ran' ἐν πίστει καὶ δικαιοσύνῃ and, as noted above, did not love the world but loved Christ (9. 2).

The explicit application of the δικαιοσύνη theme, announced in 3. 1, lies in encouraging the Philippians to ὑπομονή under suffering, following the λόγον τῆς δικαιοσύνης in imitation of the ἀρραβὼν τῆς δικαιοσύνης and of those who ran ἐν δικαιοσύνῃ. This makes the issue of suffering central to the structure of the letter. This is particularly so since it also maps on to the main use of ἀγάπη. The ἐντολὴ δικαιοσύνης is fulfilled by love. The paradigms of love are the martyrs of 1. 1 and 9. 2.

Chapters 1–9 thus form a structure beginning and ending with the martyrs and their love. The theme of righteousness, introduced in the context of persecution at the end of chapter 2, may have many ramifications in issues of behaviour and belief (chapters 4–7). However, when it returns explicitly, in chapters 8–9, it, like love, concerns endurance in the face of suffering and martyrdom. My suggestion is that Polycarp, like Paul, is particularly aiming to encourage the Philippian Christians to stand firm under the threat of suffering: στήκετε ἐν κυρίῳ: *in his ergo state* (Phil. 4. 1; Pol. *Phil.* 10. 1).

Suffering and the Love of Money

Polycarp does not only stress the need to love. He also stresses the need not to love. The martyrs οὐ . . . τὸν νῦν ἠγάπησαν αἰῶνα (9. 2). The letter's first call to love specifies that only certain things should be loved, ἀγαπῶμεν ἃ ἠγάπησεν (2. 2). This fits with Polycarp's repeated calls for people to distance themselves from certain things. The first call to action, δουλεύσατε τῷ θεῷ ἐν φόβῳ καὶ ἀληθείᾳ (2. 1), continues, ἀπολιπόντες. . . . The call to love in 2. 2 continues, ἀπεχόμενοι. The person having love μακράν ἐστιν πάσης ἁμαρτίας (3. 3). The widows are called to μακρὰν οὔσας (4. 3), the young men ἀνακόπτεσθαι (5. 3), the presbyters to be ἀπεχόμενοι (6. 1), all to be ἀπολιπόντες (7. 2). One explanation for the concentration of this kind of language could be that Polycarp was reinforcing the sharpness of the community boundaries as a way of strengthening the community as it faces suffering.[26] However, some of

[26] Harry Maier sets out the evidence on Polycarp's concern with group boundaries. Maier sees this as a strategy for handling 'the "social chaos" which resulted from the avarice of the presbyter Valens': H. O. Maier, 'Purity and Danger in Polycarp's Epistle to the Philippians:

the things that he calls the Philippians to avoid may be seen by him as posing more specific threats to the community.

The avoidance of *φιλαργυρία* is the most striking motif in the letter. *Πλεονεξία* and *φιλαργυρία* are the first specific terms in the first list of behaviour to avoid (2. 2). As noted above, the main ethical discourse begins with a condemnation of *φιλαργυρία* as the beginning of all *χαλεπῶν* (4. 1). After sins of speech, the widows are warned against *φιλαργυρία* (4. 3). The same pattern is followed for the deacons. Elders are called to *μακρὰν ὄντες πάσης φιλαργυρίας* (6. 1), a wording that somewhat highlights this prohibition in the midst of a list of other things. Finally, the section on Valens includes emphatic instructions for the Philippians to avoid *avaritia* (11. 1–2), which is the word consistently used in the letter to translate *φιλαργυρία*.[27]

Φιλαργυρία is frequent enough to stick out to the hearer as a key issue. However, it is not allowed to become the overriding issue. Other matters often overshadow it. The two main scholarly approaches on *φιλαργυρία* have been to see it as primarily relating to heresy[28] or as being about Valens.[29] Although other early Christian evidence suggests the possibility of a link with heresy,[30] the issue of *φιλαργυρία* markedly disappears when Polycarp actually writes about heresy (chapter 7). The theory that the topic essentially relates to Valens clearly carries some weight. However, the distribution of the word suggests that *φιλαργυρία* also has wider ramifications in the Philippian community. Moreover, such theories tend to see Valens as the central issue in the letter. In that case *φιλαργυρία* would probably need to be visible as the overriding topic, which it is not.

What the martyrs loved was Christ and not *τὸν νῦν . . . αἰῶνα* (9. 2). In practice that meant, above all, willingness to lose life. However, not loving the present age must also have meant the martyrs not loving other goods such as prestige and wealth. As Polycarp calls the Philippians to imitate the endurance of the martyrs, he would probably expect that, for the Philippians, 'not loving this age' would particularly be lived out in terms of issues such as reputation and wealth. The need for such a warning in a context of suffering is clear. The main route to apostasy was probably through being drawn back into relational networks, economic networks, that involved some Graeco-Roman religious practice or other activity anathema to the Christians. If, as I have argued above, the main long-term form of widespread suffering in the

The Sin of Valens in Social Perspective', *JECS* 1 (1993), 229–47. The place of the martyrs in Polycarp's letter prevents me from seeing Valens as the letter's overriding focus.

[27] J. B. Lightfoot, *The Apostolic Fathers* (London: Macmillan, 1889 edn.), 2. 3. 340–1.

[28] Meinhold, P., 'Polykarpos', *PRE* 21. 2, 1686–7.

[29] Maier, 'Purity and Danger'.

[30] See the helpful discussion in Hartog, *Polycarp and the New Testament*, 106–8.

Philippian church was economic, then a call to avoid φιλαργυρία would be an important element of a call for the Christians to stand firm under suffering.[31]

Such a theory would account for the prominent, but not overwhelmingly dominant, place of φιλαργυρία in the letter. Other issues also needed to be addressed as part of Polycarp's call to stand firm, but φιλαργυρία was the one that seems to have struck him most often. The problem over Valens must have contributed to this, but it did not determine it. One possibility about Valens is that he had compromised his Christianity to escape economic suffering. In Paul's letter, my preference for interpreting those ὧν ὁ θεὸς ἡ κοιλία (Phil. 3. 19) is in this direction. Such people could also be the 'enemies of the cross' (Phil. 3. 18 and Pol. *Phil.* 12. 3).[32]

Both Paul and Polycarp call the Philippian Christians to 'stand firm'. Both do this in a context of suffering. In each case, economic suffering, which is a likely component of the situation, would relate in a specific way to prominent features of the letter.

CONCLUSIONS

Comparison of the Philippian letters of Paul and Polycarp raises surprising issues. The disappearance of the Philippian ἐπίσκοποι between the two letters becomes a major issue given the Ignatian context of Polycarp's writing. Contrasting Polycarp's leadership style with the styles of both Paul and Ignatius sharpens the issue. Polycarp's explicit encouragement of the Philippians to study Paul's letter, and the way in which his use of New Testament and other texts implicitly calls them to use the resources that they have available, suggests that Polycarp wants the bishopless Philippian community to be self-sufficient and not to seek oversight from elsewhere, including him.

The two letters share a context of suffering. Consideration of the structure of each letter suggests that suffering was, in each case, a major theme. Study of the historical context of Paul's day suggests that, where Christians were suffering for their faith, the main long-term effects of this were economic. Indications in Paul's letter to Philippi fit this scenario. Although second-century Christianity

[31] Hartog has an interesting alternative route to link φιλαργυρία and suffering. He sees Polycarp's main concern as being to discourage revenge against Valens, whose φιλαργυρία has brought them suffering: they are called to patient endurance and non-retaliation in this situation (ibid. 138–45). I agree that this is an important aim for Polycarp. However, much of the retaliation and endurance material in the letter is in the context of persecution and martyrdom, rather than in relation to problems caused by Valens.

[32] Oakes, *Philippians*, 106, 111.

had a more developed economic system than did the first generation, the crisis relating to the martyrs' journey through Philippi means that the Philippian church probably faced fresh difficulties. Again, the most widespread component of this was likely to be economic. Such a context makes sense of the interaction between the themes of love, righteousness, and martyrdom in Polycarp's letter. It also offers an explanation for the surprisingly prominent, but not dominant, place of φιλαργυρία in the letter.

APPENDIX: DID POLYCARP VISIT PHILIPPI? THE TRANSLATION OF *IN PRAESENTI* (POL. *PHIL.* 14)

For a contextual reading of Polycarp's letter, it is clearly important to consider the nature of his prior contact with the Philippian church. His letter shows that there had been some previous interaction.[33] This certainly could have included face-to-face contact, either through a Philippian deputation going to Smyrna or through a visit by Polycarp to Philippi. Whether the letter gives positive evidence of such face-to-face contact depends on the solution to one of the most long-standing puzzles in the interpretation of the letter. The crux is the first sentence of chapter 14: *Haec vobis scripsi per Crescentem, quem in praesenti commendavi vobis et nunc commendo.* J. B. Lightfoot is very forthright about this: 'Looking at the authorities, there can be no doubt that this should be adopted as the reading of the Latin Version. But as it makes no sense it must be a mistranslation.'[34] Hartog expresses the issue succinctly: 'If the Latin were correct, we would read, "I have written this to you by Crescens, whom I commended to you *now*, and now commend again" '.[35]

Lightfoot and Schoedel each offer a solution to this by arguing that the Latin translator has misrepresented the Greek. They then give translations of the suggested underlying Greek. Lightfoot suggests ἄρτι, to be rendered as 'recently'.[36] Schoedel suggests ἐν τῷ παρέλθοντι, to be rendered as 'in the past', with the Latin translator having misread the Greek as ἐν τῷ πάροντι.[37] As well as the great uncertainties involved in working back to the Greek (especially in Schoedel's case), each of these solutions has the problem of still leaving the Latin translator producing what is, in their eyes, nonsensical Latin. Walter Bauer is less dogmatic about the incomprehen-

[33] Hartog, *Polycarp and the New Testament*, 78–81.
[34] Lightfoot, *Apostolic Fathers*, 2. 3. 349.
[35] Hartog, *Polycarp and the New Testament*, 79, emphasis original.
[36] Lightfoot, *Apostolic Fathers*, 2. 3. 349–50, 476.
[37] Schoedel, *Polycarp*, 41.

sibility of the Latin, merely describing *in praesenti* as 'dunkel'. However, he follows the same route of translating a supposed underlying Greek phrase, in this case not a temporal one (as Lightfoot and Schoedel) but a locative one, which Lake follows in rendering the clause as 'Crescens, whom I commended to you when present, and now commend again'.[38]

The tradition of scholarship on the word *praesens* is helpfully set out in the *Oxford Latin Dictionary*.[39] The main meanings of the word are locative, about being at the scene in question. Presumably by extension, there are a range of further meanings, especially temporal ones. The phrase *in praesenti* occurs under three categories. Cicero uses it to mean 'imminent': *in praesenti metu mortis* (Cic. *Caec.* 31). Scribonius Largus uses it to mean 'at the scene of action', 'on the spot': *compositiones non solum quas desiderasti, verum etiam si quas alias expertas in praesenti habui, in hunc librum contuli* (Scribonius Largus, pr. p. 5, l. 18). This is categorized as a version of the commoner expression, *in re praesenti.* Finally, a number of textually disputed passages use *in praesenti* to mean 'for the present', 'temporarily', e.g., *hoc et in praesenti tollit dolorem et in futurem remediat* (Scribonius Largus, 162). Of these options, neither of the temporal ones could work in Pol. *Phil.* 14. Only the locative sense, 'on the spot', looks possible. However, the unusual example from Scribonius Largus does not provide a substantial basis for a judgement about the Polycarp passage. The evidence is very scanty.

The online availability of Duke University's *Databank of Documentary Papyri*[40] has recently opened up the early medieval evidence for easier scrutiny. The Duke databank provides a searchable text of J.-O. Tjäder's *Die nichtliterarischen lateinischen Papyri Italiens aus der Zeit 445–700.*[41] In these papyri, *in praesenti* is a very common technical phrase used in the formal witnessing of transactions

... *vendatoribus, ipsis praesentibus testis superscripsi, et suprascriptum pretium [a]uri s[olidos] centum decem et in praesenti adnumeratos et traditos vidi.* (*P. Ital.* 30, ll. 90–1, Ravenna, AD 539)

... *pretium quadraginta solidos ei in praesenti traditos vidi, et mei praesentia signum fecit.* (*P. Ital.* 31, l. 15, Ravenna, AD 540)

Iulianus, forensis civitatis Ravennatis, scriptor huius documenti sex unciarum fundi Geniciani cum casale, sicut superius legitur, a testibus roboratum et traditum in praesenti complevi et absolvi. (*P. Ital.* 36, ll. 59–61, Ravenna, AD 575–91)

Ioannes, domesticus numeri Dacorum, huic chartulae a die praesenti donationis de suprascripta omnia immobilia praedia, quae sunt territorio Agubio, seu intro civitate seu [f]oris

[38] Lake, following W. Bauer, *Die Briefe des Ignatius von Antiochia und der Polykarpbrief*, HNT, Die Apostolischen Väter, 2 (Tübingen: Mohr Siebeck, 1920), 298. Bauer does not specify the underlying Greek.

[39] P. G. W. Glare (ed.), *Oxford Latin Dictionary*, vi: *Pactus–Qualitercumque* (Oxford: Clarendon Press, 1977), 1439–40.

[40] This is now available for searching by means of the Perseus web-site.

[41] J.-O. Tjäder (ed.), *Die nichtliterarischen lateinischen Papyri Italiens aus der Zeit 445–700*, Pt. 1 (Lund: Gleerup, 1955), Pt. 2 (Stockholm: Gleerup, 1982). Some of the Latin spelling below has been normalized.

civitate, ubi ubi ei competit, factae ab Istefano magn[ifico] graeco illustrio in sancta subscripsit, ipso praesente testis subscripsi, et hanc donationem in praesenti [ac]toribus sanctae ecclesiae Ravennatis traditam vidi. (*P. Ital.* 18–19, fr. B, ll. 28–34, Rome, ? seventh century)

The texts are official evidence of purchases or donations. The thirty-seven instances of *in praesenti* span most of the period of Tjäder's collection. The main group are from Ravenna, but others are from as far away as Syracuse (*P. Ital.* 10–11). The function of *in praesenti* in these documents is clear. It is a phrase recording the fact that the transaction took place with the parties to the transaction, and the scribe, present.[42] It was a face-to-face transaction.

The meaning is further clarified in an important current project edited by O. Weijers and M. Gumbert-Hepp, the *Lexicon Latinitatis Nederlandicae Medii Aevi*. The Dutch manuscripts use *in praesenti* in either of two senses. One is temporal: 'of the time', 'now', 'in this life'. The other is the locative one that we saw in the Italian manuscripts. The editors give this as *in eigen persoon, aanwezig* or, in Latin, *praesens (ipse), personaliter.* They give examples from witnessed documents. They also quote a manuscript from Utrecht (AD 937): *consiliantibus nobis episcopis, qui tunc in praesenti erant.*[43] The *tunc* clearly shows that, in this case, *in praesenti* is locative rather than temporal.

Writers such as Lightfoot knew medieval Latin texts. A glance through the many occurrences of *in praesenti* in the *Cetedoc CD-Rom Library of Christian Latin Texts*[44] shows that, overwhelmingly, the use of the phrase is to describe the present, in contrast to the future. It is no surprise that Lightfoot saw this as the sense of the word even if he considered medieval evidence. Most dictionaries of medieval Latin go down this kind of temporal route.[45] However, Souter does spot the locative possibility, and even offers a suggested Greek equivalent, *κατὰ πρόσωπον*.[46]

Since a locative meaning of *in praesenti* is quite possible in the early medieval period, this looks to be the sense in Pol. *Phil.* 14. (It is also a piece of evidence for an

[42] Tjäder's translations vary rather more than is helpful for what is clearly a technical term. *In praesenti* is represented by *bar* ('in cash':... *und ich habe gesehen, dass der obengenannte Preis vierzig Solidi ihm bar übergeben worden ist; P. Ital.* 31) or *vor meinen Augen* ('before my eyes':... *in seiner Gegenwart als Zeuge unterschreiben und ich habe vor meinen Augen gesehen, dass diese Schenkung an die Vertreter der heiligen ravennatischen Kirche übergeben worden ist; P. Ital.* 18–19), or even *sofort* ('at once':... *wie oben zu lesen ist, habe ich nach der Bekräftigung durch die Zeugen und nach der Übergabe sofort gefertigt und ausgehändigt; P. Ital.* 36). However, the point in each case is that the scribe witnessed the transaction with the parties present. I am grateful to my colleague, Michael Hoelzl, for a helpful discussion on this.

[43] Chart. *Trai.* 102 p. 106 = *Oorkonkendboek van het sticht Utrecht tot 1301*, ed. S. Muller Fzn, A. C. Bouman, K. Heeringa, and F. Ketner (The Hague, 1920–59), cited in O. Weijers and M. Gumbert-Hepp, *Lexicon Latinitatis Nederlandicae Medii Aevi*, vi: 'P' (Leiden: Brill, 1998), 842–3.

[44] P. Tombeur (ed.), *Cetedoc Library of Christian Latin Texts*, 4th edn. (Turnholt: Brepols, 2000).

[45] A. Blaise, *Lexicon Latinitatis Medii Aevi* (Turnholt: Brepols, 1975); J. F. Niermayer, *Mediae Latinitatis Lexicon Minus* (Leiden: Brill, 1976).

[46] A. Souter, *A Glossary of Later Latin to 600 AD* (Oxford: Clarendon Press, 1949), citing *Corp. Scr. Eccl. Lat.* 31 (1), 198–9.

early medieval date for the Latin translation of the letter.) It seems that Polycarp commended Crescens when Polycarp was with the Philippian Christians. I would suggest translating the key words as 'Crescens, whom I commended to you face to face'. This might have happened on a visit by a representative group of Philippians to Smyrna. However, since Polycarp's letter is to the church as a whole, the commendation probably took place during a visit by him to Philippi.

18

The Opponents of Polycarp, *Philippians*, and 1 John

Paul A. Hartog

The 1905 Oxford Society of Historical Theology classified the possible use of 1 John in Polycarp's *Philippians* with a 'C' rating, meaning that they thought there was a 'lower degree of probability' that Polycarp's letter to the Philippians used 1 John.[1] Some scholars have expressed similar uncertainty.[2] For example, S. E. Johnson labelled the possibility of dependence as 'doubtful',[3] and H. F. von Campenhausen dismissed the parallels between 1 John and Polycarp's letter as a typical 'kirchliche Parole im Kampf gegen die kleinasiatische Gnosis'.[4] However, many other scholars have disagreed with the Oxford Society's assessment.[5] G. Strecker asserted that Polycarp 'no doubt' uses 1 John 4. 2–3.[6] J. Painter agreed that Polycarp's letter is 'almost certainly' dependent

[1] A Committee of the Oxford Society of Historical Theology, *The New Testament in the Apostolic Fathers* (Oxford: Clarendon Press, 1905), pp. iii, 100, 137.

[2] Kleist expressed some uncertainty (J. A. Kleist, *The Didache; The Epistle of Barnabas; The Epistles and the Martyrdom of St. Polycarp; The Fragments of Papias; The Epistle to Diognetus*, ACW (Westminster: Newman Press, 1948), 192 n. 53). Schoedel maintained that parallels did 'not necessarily point to a literary relationship' (W. R. Schoedel, 'Polycarp, Epistle of', in *ABD* v. 390–2). See also F. X. Gokey, *The Terminology for the Devil and Evil Spirits in the Apostolic Fathers* (Washington: The Catholic University of America Press, 1961), 90–2.

[3] S. E. Johnson, 'Parallels between the Letters of Ignatius and the Johannine Epistles', in E. W. Conrad and E. G. Newing (eds.), *Perspectives in Language and Text* (Winona Lake, Ind.: Eisenbrauns, 1987), 327–38, on p. 329. Cf. ibid. 338.

[4] H. F. von Campenhausen, *Polykarp von Smyrna und die Pastoralbriefe* (Heidelberg: C. Winter, 1951), 40–1.

[5] B. Dehandschutter, 'Polycarp's Epistle to the Philippians: An Early Example of "Reception"', in J.-M. Sevrin (ed.), *The New Testament in Early Christianity*, BETL 86 (Leuven: Leuven University Press, 1989), 275–91, on p. 284. W. von Loewenich, *Das Johannes-Verständnis im zweiten Jahrhundert* (Gießen: A. Töpelmann, 1932), 23. É. Massaux considered 'literary contact' to be 'beyond doubt' (É. Massaux, *The Influence of the Gospel of Saint Matthew on Christian Literature before Saint Irenaeus*, ed. A. J. Bellinzoni (Macon, Ga.: Mercer University Press, 1990), i. 34). Cf. B. M. Metzger, *The Canon of the New Testament* (Oxford: Clarendon Press, 1987), 62.

[6] G. Strecker, *The Johannine Epistles*, Hermeneia (Minneapolis: Fortress, 1996), p. xxix.

on the Johannine Epistles.[7] P. N. Harrison concluded that dependence is 'highly probable' and 'practically certain'.[8] The question of Polycarp's use of 1 John centres on Pol *Phil.* 7, a passage that discusses theological opponents. This present study will examine Pol. *Phil.* 7 in its context, address the issue of possible dependence, draw some textual conclusions, and sound an important word of caution.

SETTING THE STAGE

Polycarp's letter to the Philippians is a paraenetic letter.[9] The prescript contains the epistolary address, and 1. 1–3 includes a thanksgiving. The exordium is found in 2. 1 and states: 'Therefore prepare for action and serve God in fear and truth, leaving behind (ἀπολιπόντες) the empty and meaningless talk of the error of the crowd (τῶν πολλῶν).'[10] The credal material that follows probably contrasts 'the error of the crowd' with true belief. True belief concerns the resurrection and exaltation of the Lord Jesus Christ, who is returning as Judge. The theme of the letter ('righteousness') is introduced in chapter 3.[11] Pol. *Phil.* 4. 2–6. 1 includes a series of *Haustafeln*.

Polycarp stresses the certainty of future judgement within his moral paraenesis. In fact, A. Bovon-Thurneysen argues that eschatological judgement has become the basis of Polycarp's ethics.[12] Immediately after the exordium, Pol. *Phil.* 2. 1 asserts that all things in heaven and on earth have been subjected to the risen Jesus Christ, 'who is coming as Judge of the living and the dead'.[13]

[7] J. Painter, *1, 2, and 3 John* (Collegeville, Minn.: Liturgical Press, 2002), 41. See also J. B. Bauer, *Die Polykarpbriefe*, KAV 5 (Göttingen: Vandenhoeck & Ruprecht, 1995), 57; W. Bauer, *Die Briefe des Ignatius von Antiochia und der Polykarpbrief*, HNT, Die Apostolischen Väter, 2 (Tübingen: Mohr Siebeck, 1920), 290–1.

[8] P. N. Harrison, *Polycarp's Two Epistles to the Philippians* (Cambridge: Cambridge University Press, 1936), 300.

[9] In a forthcoming volume, M. W. Holmes contends that Pol. *Phil.* combines elements from the paraenetic letter, the letter of advice, and the letter of admonition. He agrees, though, that the primary genre is the paraenetic letter.

[10] Translations come from M. W. Holmes, *The Apostolic Fathers: Greek Texts and English Translations*, rev. edn. (Grand Rapids, Mich.: Baker Books, 1999). Although 'vanity and error' could be used by Christian writers to refer to idolatry or worldliness, in other places (including here) they refer to heresy (see W. R. Schoedel, *Polycarp, Martydom of Polycarp, Fragments of Papias* (London: Thomas Nelson, 1967), 11–12; cf. Pol. *Phil.* 7. 2).

[11] Polycarp himself states that the theme of his epistle is 'righteousness', and that he was asked to write about 'righteousness' (3. 1). Berding goes further and repeatedly claims that Polycarp was asked to write 'as Paul did': K. Berding, *Polycarp and Paul*, VCSup 62 (Leiden: Brill, 2002).

[12] A. Bovon-Thurneysen, 'Ethik und Eschatologie im Philipperbrief des Polykarp von Smyrna', *TZ* 29 (1973), 241–56.

[13] Polycarp's emphasis upon resurrection and judgement in 2. 1–2 suggests that the opponents denied these (Schoedel, *Polycarp*, 11; cf. Pol. *Phil.* 7. 1–2).

In the remainder of Pol. *Phil.* 2, Polycarp transforms the theme of judgement into a warning not to judge others (2. 3; cf. 6. 1).

Within the *Haustafeln* series, Polycarp reminds the widows that God is omniscient, and 'nothing escapes him, whether thoughts or intentions or secrets of the heart' (4. 3). Polycarp's moral rationale is succinctly stated in 5. 1. The omniscient character of God becomes his basis: 'Knowing, therefore, that God is not mocked'.[14] The application follows logically: 'we ought to live in a manner that is worthy of his commandment and glory.' On the positive side, 'If we please him in this present world, we will receive the world to come' and will reign with him (5. 2). On the negative side, those who practise various iniquities will not inherit the kingdom of God (5. 3).[15] Polycarp's argument continues: 'Therefore (διό), one must keep away from all these things' (5. 3).

Polycarp returns to the theme of the omniscient God in 6. 2: 'For we are in full view of the eyes of the Lord and God' (cf. 7. 2). The subtext of future judgement then comes to the fore again: 'And we must all stand before the judgment seat of Christ, and each one must give an account of himself.' Pol. *Phil.* 6. 3 exhorts the readers to serve God 'with fear and all reverence'.[16] This duty was proclaimed by the prophets, the apostles, and the Lord himself (6. 3). Readers were to avoid those who tempt others to sin (σκανδάλων) and 'false brothers who bear the name of the Lord hypocritically'. These false brothers 'lead foolish men astray' (6. 3). One notices that Polycarp responds more strongly to the false teachers who lead others astray (ἀποπλανῶσι in 6. 3) than to those followers who have been led astray (ἀποπεπλανημένα in 6. 1).

Pol. *Phil.* 7. 1 gets to the heart of the issue. We find that Polycarp is worried about 'the many' who may attempt to deny true belief, including the return of Jesus Christ as Judge (7. 1). Of course, such a denial of future judgement would undermine Polycarp's moral exhortation. The passage is structured around three statements and three labels. An opponent is one who (1) does not confess that Jesus Christ has come in the flesh; (2) does not acknowledge the testimony of the cross; and (3) twists the sayings of the Lord to suit his own desires and claims that there is neither resurrection nor judgement. Such a one is labelled as (1) 'antichrist', (2) 'of the devil', and (3) 'the first-born of Satan'.

Pol. *Phil.* 7. 2 returns to the same language as the exordium. 'Therefore let us leave behind (ἀπολιπόντες) the worthless speculation of the crowd

[14] Cf. Gal. 6. 7. Polycarp introduces various traditional materials with 'knowing (therefore) that' (εἰδότες (οὖν) ὅτι). See 1. 3; 4. 1; 5. 1; 6. 1.

[15] Berding finds a dependence on 1. Cor 6. 9–10 alone in this statement (Berding, *Polycarp and Paul*, 78–80). But having just alluded to Gal. 5. 17, Polycarp may employ Gal. 5. 19–21 as a bridge to 1 Cor. 6. 9–10.

[16] Cf. the exhortation to serve God with 'fear and truth' in the exordium of 2. 1.

(τῶν πολλῶν) and their false teachings.' One recognizes the repetition of the thought of 2. 1: 'Leaving behind (ἀπολιπόντες) the empty and meaningless talk and error of the crowd (τῶν πολλῶν)'. Instead, readers are to 'return' (ἐπιστρέψωμεν) unto the 'word delivered to us from the beginning' (7. 2).[17] Polycarp exhorted the Philippians to 'be self-controlled with respect to prayer and persevere in fasting' (7. 2). They are to 'hold steadfastly and unceasingly to our hope and the guarantee of our righteousness, who is Christ Jesus' (8. 1).

POLYCARP'S CONCERN ABOUT JUDGEMENT

Based upon this overview, I would argue that a key point of contention with the opponents is found in the last of the three statements in 7. 1. The false teachers denied a future resurrection and judgement. In the context of Polycarp's letter this was a crucial flaw, since Polycarp's moral exhortation was founded largely upon such eschatological judgement (including the central case of Valens in 11. 1–2). In Polycarp's mind, their denials opened the door to sinful desires.

Polycarp accuses the opponents of 'twisting' the Lord's λόγια to fit their own ἐπιθυμίαι. Some have questioned whether Polycarp refers to 'sinful lusts' or more neutral 'wishes'.[18] However, Polycarp clearly uses ἐπιθυμία in the sense of 'sinful desire' earlier in 5. 3, a passage addressed to the younger men. They were 'to be cut off from the sinful desires (ἐπιθυμιῶν) in the world, because every sinful desire (ἐπιθυμία) wages war against the spirit'.[19] The context of 7. 1 also indicates unrighteous desires.

What might 'twisting the sayings of the Lord' mean in 7. 1? These 'sayings' (λόγια) of the Lord may be dominical oracles or gospel traditions.[20] Although some have seen a Marcionite removal of texts in the verb μεθοδεύειν,[21]

17 Polycarp had earlier urged the presbyters to turn back (ἐπιστρέφοντες) those who had gone astray (ἀποπεπλανημένα) (*Phil.* 6. 1).

18 M. Staniforth translates ἐπιθυμία as 'wishes' in Pol. *Phil.* 7. 1 (*Early Christian Writings* (London: Penguin, 1968), 121). The verb ἐπιθυμοῦσιν is used in a positive way in Pol. *Phil.* 1. 3.

19 Cf. the use of ἐπιθυμίαι for 'sinful desires' in Ign. *Pol.* 4–5.

20 Schoedel, *Polycarp*, 24.

21 Koester believes that Pol. *Phil.* 7. 1 refers to Marcion's revised edition of Luke (H. Koester, *An Introduction to the New Testament*, ii (Philadelphia: Fortress, 1982), 307). Harrison hypothesized that Marcion 'twisted' Scripture before arriving in Rome (based upon Pol. *Phil.* 7. 1), but later excised texts (*Polycarp's Two Epistles*, 180). For a rebuttal of the view that Marcion is addressed here, see P. Hartog, *Polycarp and the New Testament*, WUNT 2.134 (Tübingen: J. C. B. Mohr (Paul Siebeck), 2002), 89–105.

W. R. Schoedel argues for the common meaning of 'twisting' or 'manipulating'.[22] According to Polycarp, the opponents misused the materials in order to please their own ἐπιθυμίαι or 'lusts' and claimed that 'there is neither resurrection nor judgment'.[23] Perhaps the opponents believed in an 'over-realized' eschatology that denied any future resurrection and judgement.[24]

Judgement, then, serves as a link between the ethical exhortation in Polycarp's letter (including Valens's greed in 11. 1–2) and the denouncement of the false teachers (7. 1–2). Maier sees no 'explicit connection' (if any) between these two topics: 'the twin problems of heresy and avarice stand side by side with no attempt at integration'.[25] On the other hand, P. Meinhold viewed the two as closely connected, since he conjectured that Valens had accepted a donation from the heretic Marcion.[26] Schoedel postulated a looser connection, believing that 'the two issues were more or less separate in the letter from the Philippians'. He suggested that Valens was an 'embarrassment to the orthodox cause'.[27] Previously I adopted and modified Schoedel's view, asserting that the Valens case manifested a communal weakness which might also be vulnerable to false teaching.[28] But this current study stresses a further connection: the moral exhortation (including the Valens affair) is largely founded upon the incentive of a future judgement, and this

[22] Schoedel, *Polycarp*, 24. 'Die Worte des Herrn "verdrehen, umbiegen" bedeutet sicher, Jesusworte der Evangelien umdeuten' (J. B. Bauer, *Die Polykarpbriefe*, 59; cf. Irenaeus, *Adv. Haer.* 3. 3. 6; Clem. *Strom.* 3. 4. 39. 2). Tertullian speaks of those like Valentinus and Marcion, who corrupt Scripture *detractione, vel adiectione vel transmutatione* (Tert., *De praescr. haeret.* 38). See C. E. Hill, 'The *Epistula Apostolorum*: An Asian Tract from the Time of Polycarp', *JECS* 7 (1999), 1–53, on pp. 25–9. Hill believes that the logia in Pol. *Phil.* 7.1 were most likely written Scriptures, and he asserts that Cerinthus is the opponent who best fits the passage.

[23] The connection between wrong belief and immoral ethics was a common manoeuvre in early Christian polemics. See L. T. Johnson, 'The New Testament's Anti-Jewish Slander and the Conventions of Ancient Polemic', *JBL* 108 (1989), 419–41, on pp. 428–34.

[24] Cf. 2 Tim. 2. 18. *2 Clem.* 9. 1 succinctly exhorts: 'And let none of you say that the flesh is not judged and does not rise again.' Cf. J. B. Bauer, *Die Polykarpbriefe*, 59: 'Wenn die Gnostiker beispielsweise vom Gericht sprechen, stellt dieses für sie nur das Vorhandensein des rettenden Lichtfunkens fest und bringt die Vernichtung der Finsternis. . . . Solche gnostische Christen behaupteten, daß die Auferstehung schon geschehen sei, insofern nämlich die "Befreiung der Seele" durch die Erkenntnis als ein Akt der "Auferstehung von den Toten" (= Unwissenden) interpretiert wurde.'

[25] H. O. Maier, 'Purity and Danger in Polycarp's Epistle to the Philippians: The Sin of Valens in Social Perspective', *JECS* 1 (1993), 229–47, on p. 229.

[26] P. Meinhold, 'Polykarpos,' in *PE* 21.2. 1662–93, on pp. 1686–7.

[27] Schoedel, *Polycarp*, 17.

[28] 'Even as the leaders had failed to refrain from avarice, there was the possibility that they might refrain from combating heresy. (Notice the flow of thought in *Phil* 6. 1–7. 2). The failure of leadership at Philippi led to social chaos, and the social chaos created a vulnerability to false teaching' (Hartog, *Polycarp and the New Testament*, 108).

judgement is denied by the false teachers. This position brings the material against the doctrinal opponents more into the main thrust of the paraenetic letter.[29]

THE POSSIBLE USE OF 1 JOHN

We now return to the opening considerations of the 1905 Oxford Society. Does Pol. *Phil.* use 1 John?[30] The first sentence in Pol. *Phil.* 7 .1 states: *Πᾶς γὰρ ὃς ἂν μὴ ὁμολογῇ Ἰησοῦν Χριστὸν ἐν σαρκὶ ἐληλυθέναι ἀντίχριστός ἐστιν.* The language of this sentence is similar to 1 John 4. 2b–3a: *Πᾶν πνεῦμα ὃ ὁμολογεῖ Ἰησοῦν Χριστὸν ἐν σαρκὶ ἐληλυθότα ἐκ τοῦ Θεοῦ ἐστιν, καὶ πᾶν πνεῦμα ὃ μὴ ὁμολογεῖ τὸν Ἰησοῦν ἐκ τοῦ θεοῦ οὐκ ἔστιν. Καὶ τοῦτό ἐστιν τὸ του ἀντιχρίστου.*[31] The Johannine Epistles are the only New Testament documents that employ the label 'antichrist' (1 John 2. 18; 2. 22; 4. 3; 2 John 7), and Polycarp is the only other early Christian author to use it as well.[32] Pol. *Phil.* 7. 1a appears to be a 'compressed citation' of 1 John 4. 2–3.[33] D. R. Stuckwisch

[29] Pol. *Phil.* 2. 1 already (briefly) opposed false teachers within a context of future resurrection and judgement. 'Deshalb muß er auch gegen den Doketismus Front machen, der durch die Leugnung der Realität des Leidens und Sterbens Jesu seiner Auffassung der Gerechtigkeit die Grundlage entzieht' (P. Steinmetz, 'Polykarp von Smyrna über die Gerechtigkeit', *Hermes*, 100 (1972), 63–75, on p. 74). One could add that the 'future judgment' was a key ingredient of Polycarp's exhortation on righteousness that the opponents denied.

[30] Stuckwisch compares Polycarp's frequent comments about the 'Truth' with 1 John 3. 18–19 (Pol. *Phil.* 1. 1; 2. 1; 3. 2; 4. 2; 5. 2). He also compares 'walking in the truth' in 1 John 4–6 with Pol. *Phil.* 2. 2; 4. 1; 5. 2; and states that Pol. *Phil.* 1. 1 is reminiscent of 3 John 5–8 (D. R. Stuckwisch, 'Saint Polycarp of Smyrna: Johannine or Pauline Figure', *CTQ* 61 (1997), 113–25, on p. 120). But these parallels are rather ordinary in the first case and inexact and tenuous in the latter cases. Harrison lists various parallels between 1 John and Polycarp's letter apart from these in 7. 1 (*Polycarp's Two Epistles*, 300). I find Harrison's other parallels to be inconsequentially weak. The footnotes in Schoedel's translation highlight the following possible parallels (though Schoedel does not argue that they necessarily reveal any dependency): 1 John 4. 6 and 2 John 7 (Pol. *Phil.* 2. 1); 1 John 2. 17 (2. 2); 1 John 1. 7; 2. 29; 3. 9–11 (3. 3); 1 John 2. 6, 4. 11; 2 John 6 (5. 1); 3 John 4 (5. 2); 1 John 2. 16 (5. 3); 1 John 3. 8; 4. 3; 2 John 7 (7. 1); 1 John 4. 9 (8. 1); 3 John 8 (10. 1).

[31] The 1905 Oxford Society rated the use of 1 John 4. 2–3; 3. 8; and 2 John 7 in Pol. *Phil.* 7. 1 as 'c'. The only other parallel they discussed was the possible use of 1 John 4. 8, 16, in Pol. *Phil.* 1. 1, which they rated as 'd' (*NTAF*, 100). I would consider this latter dependence unlikely.

[32] For brief reviews of *ἀντίχριστος* in early Christianity, see Strecker, *Johannine Epistles*, 236–41; Painter, *1, 2, and 3 John*, 210–11.

[33] Berding, *Polycarp and Paul*, 91. Strecker calls it an 'indirect citation' (*Johannine Epistles*, p. xxix). Harrison refers to it as a 'conscious allusion' (*Polycarp's Two Epistles*, 300). J. B. Bauer labels it 'eine vereinfachte Textform von 1 Joh 4,2f.' (*Die Polykarpbriefe*, 57). The repetition of 'spirit' is key in the context of 1 John 3. 24–4. 6, but it is unnecessary and therefore missing in Pol. *Phil.* 7.

labels this passage 'The most remarkable "quotation" of any book of the New Testament in Polycarp's epistle'.[34]

The formulation of Pol. *Phil.* 7. 1 is also similar to 2 John 7: ὅτι πολλοὶ πλάνοι ἐξῆλθον εἰς τὸν κόσμον, οἱ μὴ ὁμολογοῦντες Ἰησοῦν Χριστὸν ἐρχόμενον ἐν σαρκί. Οὗτός ἐστιν ὁ πλάνος καὶ ὁ ἀντίχριστος. But Polycarp's placement of the phrase ἐν σαρκί before the verb ἐληλυθέναι may point to 1 John 4. 2 rather than 2 John 7. The use of the perfect tense in ἐληλυθέναι would also tend to lead one toward 1 John 4. 2–3 (ἐληλυθότα) rather than 2 John 7 (ἐρχόμενον).[35] If one concedes that Polycarp uses 1 John 4. 2–3, then the use of 2 John 7 seems unnecessary.[36]

The second statement asserts: Καὶ ὃς ἂν μὴ ὁμολογῇ τὸ μαρτύριον τοῦ σταυροῦ ἐκ τοῦ διαβόλου ἐστίν. The phrase ἐκ τοῦ διαβόλου is found in 1 John 3. 8, and this would appear to be a probable allusion.[37] K. Berding further notes that 'the testimony of the cross' may be reminiscent of 1 John 5. 6–9.[38] However, he acknowledges that because of 'the lack of closer verbal links', the reminiscence 'cannot be considered more than possible'.[39] Direct dependence is difficult to prove, especially since it is possible that Polycarp is combining Johannine and Ignatian thought.[40]

The third statement affirms: 'and whoever twists the sayings of the Lord to suit his own sinful desires and claims that there is neither resurrection nor

[34] Stuckwisch, 'Saint Polycarp', 120.

[35] Strecker, *Johannine Epistles*, p. xxix.

[36] See R. M. Grant, *The Formation of the New Testament* (New York: Harper & Row, 1965), 104–5; K. Lake, *The Apostolic Fathers*, LCL (London: William Heinemann, 1912), i. 292; Harrison, *Polycarp's Two Epistles*, 173. H-J. Klauck, *Der erste Johannesbrief*, EKK 23.1 (Zürich: Benziger Verlag, 1991), 17. Harrison concluded that the possible echoes of 2 and 3 John in Pol. *Phil.* were 'faint and inconclusive' (*Polycarp's Two Epistles*, 300–1). But cf. R. E. Brown, *The Epistles of John*, AB 30 (Garden City, NY: Doubleday, 1982), 9: 'Overall Polycarp is closer to II John, although the word order of the phrase "in the flesh" is closer to I John.' Campenhausen believed that the language in Pol. *Phil.* and the Johannine Epistles derives from a common anti-Gnostic tradition (Campenhausen, *Polykarp*).

[37] Strecker, *Johannine Epistles*, p. xxix; Dehandschutter, 'Polycarp's Epistle', 284; H. J. Bardsley, 'The Testimony of Ignatius and Polycarp to the Writings of St. John', *JTS* 14 (1913), 218; Berding, *Polycarp and Paul*, 90–1; cf. J. B. Bauer, *Die Polykarpbriefe*, 59. For the full sense of τοῦ διαβόλου as parentage, see 1 John 3. 8–10.

[38] Berding, *Polycarp and Paul*, 90; S. E. Johnson, 'Parallels', 332. Schoedel refers to the 'tenuous parallel' (*Polycarp*, 23).

[39] Berding, *Polycarp and Paul*, 90.

[40] Cf. the 'cross' in Ign. *Smyrn.* 1; *Phld.* 8; *Eph.* 18. Ignatius refers to the 'blood' in *Trall.* 8. 1; *Phld.* praescr.; *Smyrn.* 1. 1; 6. 1; 12. 2. Carson categorizes six views of the 'water' and the 'blood' in 1 John 5. 6–8 (D. A. Carson, 'The Three Witnesses and the Eschatology of 1 John', in T. E. Schmidt and M. Silva (eds.), *To Tell the Mystery*, JSNTSup 100 (Sheffield: Sheffield Academic Press, 1994), 216–32). See additional possibilities in M. C. de Boer, 'Jesus the Baptizer: 1 John 5:5–8 and the Gospel of John', *JBL* 107 (1988), 87–106; R. Winterbotham, 'The Spirit, and the Water, and the Blood', *Expositor*, 8 (1911), 62–71; M. Miguens, 'Tres Testigos: Espiritu, Agua, Sangre', *SBFLA* 22 (1972), 74–94.

judgment—well, that person is the first-born of Satan'. Strecker states that the word ἐπιθυμίας seems to be borrowed from 1 John.[41] However, Polycarp uses the term elsewhere in the letter, and a direct literary dependence is not necessary. Berding argues that the phrase 'first-born of Satan' may have come from 1 John 3. 12, since that text mentions Cain being 'of the evil one'.[42] However, direct reliance is difficult to prove because the verbal similarity is inexact. N. A. Dahl demonstrates that the label 'firstborn of Satan' probably originated in Jewish sources as an application to Cain (cf. Gen. 4. 1). It was later applied in various polemical contexts.[43]

Although Berding's references to 1 John in Pol. *Phil.* 7 end at 7. 1, one may continue into 7. 2. The next sentence refers to 'the word delivered to us from the beginning'. Berding compares this phrase with Jude 3 and *1 Clem.* 19. 2. In light of Berding's inclination toward 'clusters', one wonders if 1 John 1. 1–3 may be a more likely possible source.[44] Painter notes that the 'Word' that is from the beginning in *Pol. Phil.* 7. 2 'echoes' 1 John.[45] 'From the beginning' may also be compared with 1 John 2. 7, 24; 3. 11.[46] Thus, Pol. *Phil.* 7. 2 may be a final possible reminiscence of 1 John, especially 1 John 1. 1–3.

Berding accuses the Oxford Society of inconsistency.[47] They rated Polycarp's use of 1 John as 'C' ('lower degree of probability'); yet they added: 'The numerous coincidences of language render it probable that Polycarp either used 1 John or was personally acquainted with its author.'[48] Berding finds inconsistency between the 'lower degree of probability' of the 'C' rating and the word 'probable' in the Society's latter statement. Yet the crux of the latter quote is that it is 'probable' that Polycarp '*either* used 1 John *or* was personally acquainted with its author' (italics added). In other words, the Oxford Society was open to the possibility of an oral/personal dependency rather than a

[41] Strecker, *Johannine Epistles*, p. xxix.

[42] Berding, *Polycarp and Paul*, 91: 'It is possible that since Polycarp's first label is drawn from 1 John 4:3 and his second label is probably drawn from 1 John 3:8 that 1 John 3:12 provides the link to his first <sic: third> label'. See also Klauck, *Der erste Johannesbrief*, 200.

[43] N. A. Dahl, 'Der erstgeborene Satans und der Väter des Teufels (Polyk 7:1 und Joh 8:44)', in W. Eltester and F. H. Kettler (eds.), *Apophoreta: Festschrift für Ernst Haenchen*, BZNW 30 (Berlin: A. Töpelmann, 1964), 70–84. Dahl thinks the label lies behind John 8. 44 as well.

[44] Cf. Berding, *Polycarp and Paul*, ch. 4. Berding seems to downplay the non-Pauline clusters. The cluster of 1 Peter material in Pol. *Phil.* 8. 1–2 is not addressed in the chapter, and 1 Pet. 2. 24 does not appear in the foundational chart on p. 148 (cf. pp. 94–5).

[45] Painter, *1, 2, and 3 John*, 41. Staniforth translates λόγος in 7. 2 as a personified 'Word' (*Early Christian Writings*, 122). Clearly 'Hope' and 'Pledge' are personalized in Pol. *Phil.* 8 (cf. Ign. *Trall.* prescript, 2; Ign. *Smyrn.* 10; 1 Tim. 1. 1).

[46] Stuckwisch, 'Saint Polycarp', 120. Cf. the 'faith' which 'has been delivered' in Pol. *Phil.* 3. 2 and 4. 2. Brown draws attention to the difference of prepositions between 1 John and Pol. *Phil.* (Brown, *Epistles of John*, 9), but Polycarp regularly changed prepositions in his allusions.

[47] Berding, *Polycarp and Paul*, 89 n. 195.

[48] *NTAF*, 100.

literary dependency. Berding's stated methodology would appear to favour literary dependencies.[49] Yet one should not dismiss the possibility of oral dependence out of hand.[50] For example, the question of oral transmission versus literary reliance is well known in the case of Gospel traditions and materials.[51]

Nevertheless, literary dependence on 1 John should be rated as 'almost certain'.[52] First, the quantity of verbal similarities between Pol. *Phil.* 7. 1 and 1 John 4. 2–3 warrants this conclusion: *πᾶς* with the relative pronoun, *ὁμολογῇ Ἰησοῦν Χριστὸν, ἐν σαρκί*, the perfect tense *ἐληλυθέναι*, and *ἀντίχριστος*.[53] Second, the distinctive nature of *ἀντίχριστος* (found only in the Johannine Epistles and Polycarp's letter within early Christian literature) points to reliance. Third, the density of parallels clustered in Pol. *Phil.* 7 leans one toward dependence on 1 John. The passage includes an almost certain condensed citation of 1 John 4. 2–3, a probable allusion to 1 John 3. 8, and a possible reminiscence of 1 John 1. 1–3 (see also 1 John 5. 6–8).[54]

Some may wonder if these similarities might actually reveal a reliance of 1 John upon Polycarp. However, the evidence points in the opposite direction. Although 1 John and Polycarp's epistle contain some of the same phrases and labels, they are listed in close succession in Pol. *Phil.* 7, while they are embedded within broader contexts in 1 John.[55] Comparing the two, it seems more likely that Pol. *Phil.* strung these locutions together from 1 John, rather than 1 John diffusing Polycarp's expressions into larger discourses. This seems to be confirmed by the pastiche-like character of Polycarp's letter, which gleans phrases and allusions from many sources (and often

[49] Berding, *Polycarp and Paul*, 28–9.

[50] Although Strecker states that there is 'no doubt' that Pol. *Phil.* borrows from 1 John 4. 2–3, he believes that Polycarp's use of *ἀντίχριστου* can be explained 'either on the basis of the letter itself or from oral tradition' (*Johannine Epistles*, pp. xxix and 63).

[51] Cf. the Oxford Society's discussion of the synoptics in Polycarp (*NTAF*, 103).

[52] In my previous work, I labelled the use of 1 John as 'probable' (Hartog, *Polycarp and the New Testament*, 195). The rating options in that work were 'certain', 'probable', 'possible', and 'unprovable'. Berding used 'almost certain', 'probable', 'possible', and 'unlikely'. In the end, all these labels concern our ability to verify dependence rather than actual dependence. For example, in his own mind, Polycarp may have 'certainly' taken even a commonplace phrase from a specific text. But since the phrase is so conventional, we as interpreters cannot necessarily prove this is so.

[53] See Berding, *Polycarp and Paul*, 88–90. Bardsley comments that Pol. *Phil.* 'is as near to 1 John iv 2–3 as any early citation can be expected to be' ('Testimony', 207–20).

[54] Berding adds the 'possible reminiscences' of 1 John 5. 6–8 and 1 John 3. 12. These uses may be possible, given the clustering of Johannine materials in the passage. Definitely the language fits a Johannine milieu. But the examples seem more tenuous and difficult to prove as literary dependences, especially the latter (see the discussions above). Berding himself acknowledges that the use of 1 John 3. 12 is 'somewhat tenuous' (Berding, *Polycarp and Paul*, 91).

[55] Cf. the context of testing spirits in 1 John 3. 24–4. 6 and the use of 'antichrist' in the context of the secession found in 1 John 2. 18–23.

in clusters, as in chapter 7).[56] In other words, we know that Polycarp habitually treats other materials in a similar manner. Furthermore, 1 John 2. 18 reminds readers, 'you heard that antichrist is coming' (cf. 4. 3). But in fact the current secessionists were already 'antichrists' (cf. 2. 22; 4. 3). Polycarp does not imply any future arrival of 'antichrist'. Everyone who does not confess that Jesus Christ has come in the flesh is already 'antichrist'. The purely contemporary emphasis fits a Polycarpian reliance on 1 John, but not vice versa.[57]

Some scholars have further noted that Polycarp's knowledge of 1 John 'is supported by the evidence of Eusebius concerning Papias'.[58] The material in Polycarp's letter certainly fits Eusebius' assertion that Papias (a contemporary of Polycarp) referred to both 1 John and 1 Peter.[59] But the case should rest on the internal evidence found in Pol. *Phil.* 7. 1–2 itself. Our extant materials from Papias do not include any references or allusions to 1 John, so Polycarp stands as the earliest external witness to the epistle.[60]

TEXTUAL QUESTIONS

There is a textual question whether the opponents' treatment of Jesus Christ in 1 John 4. 3 should read *λύει* or *μὴ ὁμολογεῖ*. Can Polycarp's letter assist with this textual issue, since 7. 1 has *μὴ ὁμολογῇ*? H.-J. Klauck acknowledges that Polycarp is the 'ältester Zeuge', but 'gelegentlich geäußerten Zweifeln an der Kenntnis des 1Joh durch Polykarp erschweren es, diese Selle vorbehaltlos als schlagenden Beweis für *μὴ ὁμολογεῖ* als älteste Lesart in 1Joh 4,3 zu werten'.[61] This investigation may at least help remove some of those 'occasionally voiced doubts' about Polycarp's knowledge of 1 John.

Zahn, Westcott, Harnack, Brooke, Büchsel, Bultmann, Schnackenburg, and R. E. Brown all agree with the reading of *λύει* in 1 John 4. 3.[62] Brown contends

[56] See Berding, *Polycarp and Paul*, 145–52.

[57] The insertion of an introductory *γάρ* in Pol. *Phil.* 7. 1 (cf. 1 John 4. 2–3) may further indicate the use of previous materials.

[58] Painter, *1, 2, and 3 John*, 41; Berding, *Polycarp and Paul*, 89. R. E. Brown, *Epistles of John*, 9, argues similarly. Cf. W. R. Schoedel, 'Papias', in *ANRW* 2.27.1 (1993), 235–70, on pp. 236, 254–5.

[59] Euseb. *HE* 3. 39. 17; cf. Euseb. *HE* 3. 39. 3 and 1 John 2. 3. Polycarp repeatedly quotes or alludes to 1 Peter.

[60] See Strecker, *Johannine Epistles*, p. xxxix; Painter, *1, 2, and 3 John*, 40–1; and esp. R. E. Brown, *Epistles of John*, 6–9. Brown considers Pol. *Phil.* to be the only 'probative' early witness (ibid. 7).

[61] Klauck, *Der erste Johannesbrief*, 234–5.

[62] For a discussion in support of *λύει*, see R. E. Brown, *Epistles of John*, 494–6; R. Schnackenburg, Die Johannesbriefe, HTKNT 13 (Freiburg: Herder, 1953); ET *The Johannine Epistles*:

that the text was changed to μὴ ὁμολογεῖ in order to parallel the positive confession in 1 John 4. 2 (ὁμολογεῖ). He maintains that the μή before the verb form ὁμολογεῖ is 'dubious grammar', but arose from 'a slavish imitation' of 2 John 7.[63] In 2 John 7, μή is used before the participle ὁμολογοῦντες. While the participle was transferred to 1 John and changed to the indicative, the negative μή was not changed. For Brown, Pol. *Phil.* 7 serves as a parallel example of 'this process of harmonization already at work'.[64]

But, as I argued earlier, Pol. *Phil.* 7. 1 can be explained without recourse to 2 John 7.[65] Furthermore, Brown does not clarify that the Greek texts of 1 John 4. 3 read μὴ ὁμολογεῖ, while Pol. *Phil.* 7. 1 has μὴ ὁμολογῇ.[66] This distinction is important, because μή with the indicative can be seen as a 'difficult reading' due to its grammatical irregularity.[67] The theory of Brown (and Harnack) relies on the questionable hypothesis that the entire Greek manuscript tradition abandoned λύει and merged 2 John 7 with 1 John 4. 3 to form the μὴ ὁμολογεῖ without changing the unusual grammar.[68] If one accepts the alternative case of a μὴ ὁμολογεῖ original, Polycarp's μὴ ὁμολογῇ is an early witness to a grammatical polishing of the text.

Another textual question surrounds the variants ἐληλυθέναι and ἐληλυθότα in 1 John 4. 2. Like Polycarp's letter, Vaticanus also contains the perfect infinitive ἐληλυθέναι. Most early witnesses (including Codices Sinaiticus, Alexandrinus, and Ephraemi Rescriptus), however, contain the perfect participle ἐληλυθότα. Brown claims that both Polycarp and Vaticanus performed a

A Commentary (Tunbridge Wells: Burns and Oates, 1992), 201–2; R. Bultmann, *The Johannine Epistles*, Hermeneia (ET Philadelphia: Fortress, 1973), 62. Bultmann believes that μὴ ὁμολογεῖ 'was a correction very probably occasioned by v 2'.

[63] R. E. Brown, *Epistles of John*, 495. Here Brown follows Harnack. Cf. F. Blass, A. Debrunner, and R. W. Funk, *A Greek Grammar of the New Testament and Other Early Christian Literature* (Chicago: University of Chicago Press, 1961), 428 n. 4.

[64] R. E. Brown, *Epistles of John*, 495.

[65] See also Metzger, *Canon*, 61–2.

[66] See the similar simplification by I. H. Marshall, *The Epistles of John* (Grand Rapids, Mich.: Eerdmans, 1978), 207 n. 11.

[67] See other examples in B. D. Ehrman, '1 John 4.3 and the Orthodox Corruption of Scripture', *ZNW* 79 (1988), 221–43, on p. 223 n. 8. Cf. J. H. Moulton, *A Grammar of New Testament Greek* (Edinburgh: T. & T. Clark, 1908), i. 169–71.

[68] Ehrman argues convincingly for μὴ ὁμολογεῖ rather than λύει. If λύει is the original reading, then either μὴ ὁμολογεῖ was found in a very early archetype which affected the entire Greek tradition; or μὴ ὁμολογεῖ was created independently by various very early scribes and took over the tradition. Otherwise, μὴ ὁμολογεῖ is original (Ehrman, '1 John 4.3', 224). See also Ehrman's critique of the implausibility of 2 John 7 affecting the textual transmission of 1 John 4. 3 (ibid. 227). Ehrman further contends that λύει τὸν Ἰησοῦν 'represents a second-century corruption of the text generated precisely *by* the context in which it is still preserved: orthodox Christological polemics' (ibid. 222). Cf. J. Denney, 'He that Came by Water and Blood', *Expositor*, 7 (1908), 416–28, on p. 420.

'scribal "improvement" ' of the 'somewhat awkward' perfect participle.[69] Since the perfect infinitive can be seen as a 'stylistic improvement' rather than a grammatical irregularity (such as μὴ ὁμολογεῖ), the hypothesis seems reasonable.[70] Schnackenburg further asserts that the context in Polycarp reveals that his reading can be explained as a 'free rendition'.[71]

A CAUTIONARY NOTE

Now a question naturally arises: can we use Polycarp to help reconstruct the opponents in 1 John? Both dealt with 'many' opponents (1 John 2. 18; 4. 1; Pol. *Phil.* 2. 1; 7. 2) who 'lead astray' (1 John 2. 26; Pol. *Phil.* 6. 3), using the same polemical language ('antichrist' and 'of the devil' in 1 John 2. 18, 22; 3. 8; 4. 3; Pol. *Phil.* 7. 1). Some scholars have understandably compared the opponents in Polycarp with those in 1 John.[72]

The difficulty of 'reconstructing' the secessionists of 1 John is a well-known puzzle.[73] The opponents deny that 'Jesus is the Christ' (2. 22; 5. 1). They deny that 'Jesus is the Son of God' (4. 15; 5. 5).[74] They deny that 'Jesus Christ come in the flesh' (4. 2; 2 John 7). They apparently deny that he came by both water and blood (5. 6).[75] Various identifications of these adversaries have been

[69] R. E. Brown, *Epistles of John*, 492. Cf. the aorist participle in 1 John 5. 6 and the present participle in 2 John 7.

[70] Painter, *1, 2, and 3 John*, 254.

[71] Schnackenburg, *Johannine Epistles*, 200 n. 11; cf. 202 n. 17.

[72] H.-C. Puech, 'Review of *Polycarp's Two Epistles to the Philippians*', *RHR* 119 (1939), 96–102, on p. 102; Harrison, *Polycarp's Two Epistles*, 173. Stuckwisch, 'Saint Polycarp', 115. Schoedel, *Polycarp*, 23. See also S. E. Johnson, 'Parallels'.

[73] Schnackenburg listed four points on which 'there is general agreement': (1) 1 John opposes a single group; (2) they espoused both christological error and a false ethic; (3) they manifested a 'gnostic' tendency; and (4) they arose in a Gentile Christian milieu (Schnackenburg, *Johannine Epistles*, 17–18). But not even these four points hold a complete consensus: e.g., Vorster questions the 'false ethic' (W. S. Vorster, 'Heterodoxy in 1 John', *Neot* 9 (1975), 87–97, on p. 92). Lieu and Edwards believe that the 'moral debate' is not related to the secessionists (J. M. Lieu, *The Theology of the Johannine Epistles* (Cambridge: Cambridge University Press, 1991), 15–16; R. B. Edwards, *The Johannine Epistles* (Sheffield: Sheffield Academic Press, 1996), 64–67). Smalley denies that there was only one schismatic group (S. S. Smalley, *1, 2, 3 John* (Waco, Tex.: Word, 1984), pp. xiii–xv). Various commentators question the 'gnostic' tendencies of the false teachers.

[74] Many interpreters agree that 'Son of God' is interchangeable with 'Christ' in 1 John (Schnackenburg, *Johannine Epistles*, 232; Ehrman, '1 John 4.3', 234 n. 45; cf. 1 John 5. 1–5). The use of the article demonstrates that the formulae answer the question 'Who *is* the Christ (or the Son of God)?' (Ehrman, '1 Joh 4.3', 234 n. 45; de Boer, 'Jesus the Baptizer', 87).

[75] These four denials represent a more 'minimalist' reconstruction of the adversaries in 1 John. For a more 'maximalist' approach which includes the evidences of the boasts, the

set forth,[76] including Jewish-Christians,[77] Docetists,[78] Cerinthians,[79] heretical perfectionists,[80] and pneumatic/charismatic prophets.[81]

Scholars have proposed various ways in which the opponents could have made Christ's death only 'appear' to have salvific importance. In its 'narrower' sense, the term 'docetism' refers to the belief that the humanity and sufferings of the earthly Jesus were 'apparent' (in some phantasmal manner) rather than real.[82] Another view ('Cerinthian') would allow for a 'real' human Jesus, but hold that the connection between 'Christ' and the human 'Jesus' was not a personal unity (but, in a sense, a deceptive appearance). A further explanation would claim that another individual was mistakenly crucified in Jesus' place on the cross, yet it 'appeared' that it was really him. A final category would include any other belief that downplayed the actual salvific importance of the

denials, the discussion of the role of the Spirit, the antitheses, and the lack of dependence on the Old Testament, see J. Painter, 'The "Opponents" in 1 John', *NTS* 32 (1986), 48–71. Painter agrees with those who view the conflict with the schismatics as the interpretive key to 1 John (ibid. 48). Lieu, however, warns against 'over-reading' the opponents' role (and anti-opponent material) in 1 John (*Theology*, 13–16). See also B. Childs, *The New Testament as Canon: An Introduction* (Valley Forge, Pa.: Trinity, 1994), 482–3; Edwards, *Johannine Epistles*, 57–68; P. Perkins, *The Johannine Epistles* (Wilmington, Del.: Michael Glazier, 1979), pp. xxi–xxiii.

76 For a brief summary of views up to 1999, see G. Strecker, 'Johannine Letters', in J. H. Hayes (ed.), *Dictionary of Biblical Interpretation* (Nashville: Abingdon Press, 1999), 603–9, on pp. 605–6; cf. R. E. Brown, *Epistles of John*, 47–68; J. Blank, 'Die Irrlehrer des ersten Johannesbriefes', *Kairos*, 26 (1984), 166–93. See also K. Weiss, 'Orthodoxie und Heterodoxie im 1. Johannesbriefe', *ZNW* 58 (1967), 247–55; A. Wurm, *Die Irrlehrer im ersten Johannesbrief* (St Louis: Herder, 1903).

77 J. C. O'Neill, *The Puzzle of 1 John* (London: SPCK, 1966). Cf. also one of the two schismatic groups proposed by Smalley, *1, 2, 3 John*, pp. xiii–xv.

78 G. Strecker, 'Chiliasm and Docetism in the Johannine School', *ABR* 38 (1990), 45–61; in German as 'Chiliasmus und Doketismus in der Johanneischen Schule', *KD* 38 (1992), 30–46. Vorster, 'Heterodoxy', 88–90. S. E. Johnson, 'Parallels', 331. B. Witherington III, 'The Waters of Birth: John 3.5 and 1 John 5.6–8', *NTS* 35 (1989), 155–60, on p. 160. Bultmann, *Johannine Epistles*, 62. E. M. Yamauchi, 'The Crucifixion and Docetic Christology', *CTQ* 46 (1982), 1–20, on p. 6. Ehrman, '1 Joh 4.3', 241.

79 K. Wengst, *Häresie und Orthodoxie im Spiegel des ersten Johannesbriefes* (Gütersloh: Mohn, 1976). S. E. Johnson, 'Parallels', 332. Schnackenburg, who opposes the Cerinthian hypothesis, lists past adherents and opponents of it (*Johannine Epistles*, 21 n. 56).

80 J. Bogart, *Orthodox and Heretical Perfectionism in the Johannine Community as Evident in the First Epistle of John* (Missoula, Mont.: Scholars Press, 1976), 138.

81 F. Büchsel, *Die Johannesbriefe* (Leipzig: Deichert, 1970), 4–5.

82 On possible definitions of 'docetism', see J. M. Lieu, 'Authority to Become Children of God', *NovT* 23 (1981), 210–28, on p. 211; Ehrman, '1 John 4.3', 236–7; P. Weigandt, 'Der Doketismus im Urchristentum und in der theologischen Entwicklung des zweiten Jahrhunderts' (diss. theol. Heidelberg, 1961); M. Slusser, 'Docetism: A Historical Definition', *SC* 1 (1981), 163–71; N. Brox, ' "Doketismus'—eine Problemanzeige', *ZKG* 95 (1984), 301–14; G. Salmon, 'Docetism', in W. Smith and H. Wace (eds.), *Dictionary of the Christian Bible* (London: J. Murray, 1911), 867–70.

death of Jesus.[83] For example, U. B. Müller maintained that the opponents in 1 John considered Jesus to be a glorious figure, but not a saviour. He did not suffer and die to save men; therefore, his sufferings were merely 'apparent' and not real.[84] Brown argued that the 'secessionists' relativized the salvific importance of the earthly life of Jesus.[85]

Can Polycarp help us identify the Johannine schismatics? I would caution that the natural inclination to use Polycarp's dependence on 1 John to reconstruct the exact identity and theology of the Johannine opponents may go beyond the evidence. First, Polycarp alters the wording of 1 John. One recalls that Polycarp seems to have changed the perfect participle in 1 John 4. 2 into a perfect infinitive. 1 John 4. 2 can be translated as 'confessing Jesus Christ come in the flesh', where the verb 'confesses' has only one object—the entire phrase taken as a unity. Or it could be translated with 'Jesus' as the direct object and 'Christ having come in the flesh' as the predicate. Or 'Jesus Christ' may be seen as the direct object and 'having come in the flesh' as the predicate.[86] On the other hand, Polycarp's substitution of the perfect infinitive more clearly renders 'confesses that Jesus Christ has come in the flesh'. It is possible to interpret 1 John 4. 2–3 against opponents who broadly denigrate the soteriological significance of Jesus Christ, rather than against the metaphysical views of docetic opponents *per se*.[87] But Polycarp's language is more definite in its anti-docetic import. Even if one believes that 1 John is also anti-docetic in its polemic, one must acknowledge that Polycarp's construction is even more distinctly so.[88]

Second, Polycarp's third disagreement with the adversaries in Pol. *Phil.* 7 goes beyond the emphases of 1 John. This third denial seems to include a crucial issue for Polycarp, the denial of future judgement. 1 John does not address a denial of eschatological judgement by the secessionists, and an

[83] 'They all play down the historic person of Jesus Christ as the unique and true savior. They all deny the way of salvation through his flesh and blood. In their precise christological interpretation of the figure of Jesus, these dangerous heretics, dissolving as they did the substance of the Christian faith, evidently went off in different directions' (Schnackenburg, *Johannine Epistles*, 23).

[84] U. B. Müller, *Die Geschichte der Christologie in der johanneischen Gemeinde* (Stuttgart: Katholisches Bibelwerk, 1975), 53–79.

[85] R. E. Brown, *Epistles of John*. See also R. E. Brown, 'The Relationship to the Fourth Gospel Shared by the Author of 1 John and by his Opponents', in E. Best and R. McL. Wilson (eds.), *Text and Interpretation: Festschrift for M. Black* (Cambridge: Cambridge University Press, 1979), 57–68, on pp. 62–4.

[86] Lieu, 'Authority', 217.

[87] Schnackenburg, *Johannine Epistles*, 201. R. E. Brown believes, 'This text gives little support to those scholars who have assumed that the secessionists denied that there was a real incarnation' (*Epistles of John*, 494).

[88] Of course, Ignatius is even more specific in his condemnation of docetism (S. E. Johnson, 'Parallels', 332, 336, 338).

emphasis on judgement as a basis for moral exhortation is not prevalent in the epistle.[89] Certainly 'judgment' is mentioned explicitly in 1 John 4. 17, but the verse simply affirms: 'By this love has been perfected among us, in order that we may have confidence in the day of judgment; because as that one is, we are also in the world.' 1 John 2. 28–3. 3 comes closest to an eschatological basis for moral exhortation, but the passage does not mention 'judgment' explicitly: 'And now, little children, remain in him; so that, when he appears, we may have confidence and not be ashamed before him in his coming.' Everyone who has the 'hope' of becoming like him in his appearing 'purifies himself, even as he is pure'. 1 John does not accentuate a heretical denial of judgement in the same manner as Polycarp.[90]

Third, it is unclear whether Polycarp himself is addressing a specific, well-defined 'system'. H.-C. Puech describes the heretical opposition in Polycarp as 'assez banale', 'insaisissable pour nous sous des traits si généraux'.[91] R. Joly agrees: 'en général, les traits polémiques sont vagues'.[92] J. B. Bauer asserts that 'Eine nähere Bestimmung der von Polykarp ins Auge gefaßten Doketen ist nicht möglich'.[93] H. Maier concludes that 'The most the evidence allows one to conclude is that Polycarp like Ignatius was opposing a form of docetism',[94] since the polemical language of Polycarp shares some similarities with Ignatius' letters to the Smyrnaeans and Polycarp.[95] Furthermore, the language may

[89] Like Pol. *Phil.* 7. 1, 1 John may link ἐπιθυμίαι with the false teachers (but only indirectly so). 1 John condemns the ἐπιθυμίαι found in the κόσμος in 2. 15–17. This section leads into the introduction of the 'antichrists' who left the Johannine community (2. 18–19). Perhaps the tie between the two adjoining paragraphs is the fact that when the adversaries left the community, they went out into the κόσμος (stated explicitly in 4. 1). The false teachers apostasized and entered the world with all of its sinful desires. Painter mentions the ἐπιθυμίαι in Pol. *Phil.* 5. 3 in his discussion of 1 John 2. 15–17 (*1, 2, and 3 John*, 191; cf. R. E. Brown, *Epistles of John*, 325). As in Pol. *Phil.* 5, the context in 1 John may especially stress the dangers of ἐπιθυμίαι to the young men (2. 14–17).

[90] Ignatius repeatedly castigates docetic opponents, but only brings up 'judgment' against them in *Smyrn.* 6. 1 (for their unbelief).

[91] Puech, 'Review', 102.

[92] R. Joly, *Le Dossier d'Ignace d'Antioche* (Brussels: Éditions de l'Université de Bruxelles, 1979), 35.

[93] J. B. Bauer, *Die Polykarpbriefe*, 58.

[94] Maier, 'Purity and Danger', 231 n. 8. For a recent discussion of the opponents in Ignatius' letters, see J. L. Sumney, 'Those Who "Ignorantly Deny Him": The Opponents of Ignatius of Antioch', *JECS* 1 (1993), 345–65. Ignatius seems to oppose some form of 'judaizing' Christianity in *Magn.* 8–11 and *Phld.* 6–9. Docetic teachers seem to be in view in *Eph.* 7; *Trall.* 8–11; and *Smyrn.* 1–6. *Magn.* 9–11 discusses both traits. In a rhetorical ploy, Ignatius refused to name his docetic adversaries (*Smyrn.* 5. 3).

[95] Some scholars have wondered if Ignatius' polemics reflect more of the situation 'back home' in Antioch than the communities being addressed in Asia Minor. See V. Corwin, *St. Ignatius and Christianity in Antioch* (New Haven: Yale University Press, 1960). See also D. L. Hoffman's cautions ('Ignatius and Early Anti-Docetic Realism in the Eucharist', *Fides et Historia*, 30 (1998), 74–88). For Ignatius, the problem of 'docetism' was primarily its soteriological

even warn against more of a 'possible' threat in Philippi than a present enemy.[96]

Fourth, Polycarp's use of 'the enemies of the cross' in 12. 3 demonstrates that he can cite traditional polemical labels with new implications. Berding notes that the phrase is found only here and in Phil. 3. 18 within the New Testament and the Apostolic Fathers.[97] Philippians 3 begins with a censure of 'judaizing' opponents and continues with autobiographical material. The description 'enemies of the cross' in 3. 18–19 is probably a reference to the same antagonists as earlier in the chapter, although it may refer to others who 'mind earthly things' (3. 19).[98] Polycarp, however, uses the label in a context concerning political authorities and persecutors: 'Pray for all the saints. Pray also for kings and powers and rulers, and for those who persecute and hate you, and for the enemies of the cross, in order that your fruit may be evident among all people, that you may be perfect in him.' Berding believes that 'the enemies of the cross' in Pol. *Phil.* 12. 3 are docetists.[99] But the context links them with rulers and persecutors, and it does not seem likely that Polycarp would have encouraged intercessory prayer for 'docetic' opponents within this passage. If Polycarp could use 'the enemies of the cross' with new implications, one must acknowledge the possibility that labels such as 'antichrist', 'of the devil', and 'firstborn of Satan' could be used in new ways as well.

Fifth, the later ecclesiastical utilization of both Polycarp and John further manifests the flexible and malleable nature of polemical language. Irenaeus asserted that the Gospel of John countered the Nicolaitans, while Jerome

ramifications: an annulment of the salvific work of Christ (I. A. Saliba, 'The Bishop of Antioch and the Heretics: A Study of a Primitive Christology', *EQ* 54 (1982), 65–76). In Pol. *Phil.*, an important part of the threat appears to have been the ethical ramifications.

[96] Ignatius warned against adversaries before their actual arrival (*Magn.* 11; *Phld.* 3; and *Smyrn.* 4). In personal correspondence, M. W. Holmes argues that it is 'likely' that the target(s) of Polycarp's polemic actually reside in or around Smyrna, not Philippi. Definitely, Polycarp does not seem to be in a 'crisis' mode, as Harrison incorrectly pictured (see L. W. Barnard, 'The Problem of St. Polycarp's Epistle to the Philippians', in *idem*, *Studies in the Apostolic Fathers and their Background* (New York: Schocken Books; Oxford: Basil Blackwell, 1966), 31–40, on pp. 34–5).

[97] Berding, *Polycarp and Paul*, 123. For a history of the label 'enemies of the cross' in early Christianity, see S. Heid, 'Die Frühkirchliche Beurteilung der Häretiker als "Feinde des Kreuzes" ', in M. Hutter, W. Klein, and U. Vollmer (eds.), *Haireses* (Münster: Aschendorff, 2002), 107–39.

[98] Oakes proposes that Phil. 3. 18–19 refers to those who had compromised their Christian commitment in order to avoid economic suffering (P. Oakes, *Philippians: From People to Letter*, SNTSMS 110 (Cambridge: Cambridge University Press, 2001), 106, 111). Fee theorizes that they were self-serving itinerant preachers (G. D. Fee, *Paul's Letter to the Philippians*, NICNT (Grand Rapids, Mich.: Eerdmans, 1995), 366–75). A complete discussion of the identification of the adversaries in Phil. 3 would take us beyond the scope of this paper. For an example, see C. Mearns, 'The Identity of Paul's Opponents at Philippi', *NTS* 33 (1987), 194–204.

[99] Berding, *Polycarp and Paul*, 183.

claimed that it was directed 'adversus Cerinthum aliosque haereticos'.[100] Irenaeus related an anecdote about the apostle John running from a bath-house with Cerinthus inside (*Adv. Haer.* 3. 3), but Epiphanius' version changed the adversary to Ebion (*Pan.* 30. 24). A later story was also told of John confronting the Gnostic Basilides. Tertullian declared that the Johannine Epistles opposed those 'whom the Apostle John pronounced to be antichrists, because they denied that Christ had come in the flesh', who are 'a sort of premature and abortive Marcionites' (*Marc.* 3. 8). The 'anti-Marcionite' prologues claimed that John condemned Marcion in person.[101] Irenaeus asserted that Polycarp also personally confronted Marcion, calling him 'the firstborn of Satan' (*Adv. Haer.* 3. 3).[102] Obviously, the same materials from previous traditions could be directed against a variety of adversaries.

CONCLUSION

In conclusion, Polycarp warns against the threat of false teachings in Pol. *Phil.* 7. A crucial issue is the denial of a future judgement, since this undermines his moral exhortation. Polycarp's literary dependence upon 1 John is 'almost certain'. Pol. *Phil.* 7. 1 should not be utilized to support the reading of λύει over μὴ ὁμολογεῖ in 1 John 4. 3. (In fact, probably the reverse is true.) Finally, many factors cause us to be prudently cautious in any attempt to use Polycarp's letter to reconstruct the opponents of 1 John and their exact tenets.

100 See Schnackenburg, *Johannine Epistles*, 21.

101 The 'anti-Marcionite' prologue of the Gospel of John (in the Toletan and other codices).

102 See Hartog, *Polycarp and the New Testament*, 90–94. Cf. the claim that Ignatius labelled Simon Magus as the 'firstborn' of the devil in Ps.-Ign., *Trall.* 10–11.

Part VIII

The *Martyrdom of Polycarp*

19

The New Testament and the *Martyrdom of Polycarp*

Boudewijn Dehandschutter

When in 1905 a 'Committee of the Oxford Society of Historical Theology' published *The New Testament in the Apostolic Fathers*, the *Martyrdom of Polycarp*, or *Martyrium Polycarpi* (= *Mart. Pol.*) was not included. The Committee may have had good reasons for restricting the corpus of 'Apostolic Fathers', but this should not mean that the question about the New Testament and the *Martyrdom of Polycarp* has to be neglected in a volume that marks the centenary of the publication of the committee's conclusions. For whatever reasons, the *Martyrdom* has been printed in editions of the Apostolic Fathers from Cotelier to the present.[1] It is my conviction, moreover, that further research on the theme of the present contribution can lead to a better understanding of the general theme 'The New Testament and the Apostolic Fathers'. My contribution will therefore take into consideration some elements of the history of research on the *Martyrdom* in the hope that this will clarify some of the problems that arise when dealing with 'The New Testament and the Apostolic Fathers'.

In the history of research on the *Martyrdom* we can easily discern several 'contexts' in which the relationship with New Testament texts (mainly the Gospels) is taken up:

1. The nineteenth-century controversy over the Quartodeciman tradition.
2. The defence of the authenticity of the *Martyrdom*.

[1] On ancient editions , see B. Dehandschutter, *Martyrium Polycarpi: Een literair-kritische Studie*, BETL 52 (Leuven: Universitaire Presse, 1979), 57–9; on Cotelier, *idem*, 'The Text of the *Martyrdom of Polycarp* again (with a note on the Greek Text of Polycarp, ad Phil.)', in F. Garcia Martinez and G. P. Luttikhuizen (eds.), *Jerusalem, Alexandria, Rome: Studies in Ancient Cultural Interaction in Honour of A. Hilhorst* (Leiden: Brill, 2003), 101–6. A restrictive view regarding the Apostolic Fathers has been put forward in recent times by J. A. Fischer, *Die Apostolischen Väter griechisch und deutsch* (Munich: Kösel Verlag, 1956), p. xi: 'Auch die Berichte über die Martyrien Apostolischer Väter (Klemens, Ignatius, Polykarp) gehören nicht hierher. Überdies ist nur das Martyrium Polycarpi . . . als relativ echt und zuverlässig anzusprechen; doch ist dieses nicht Schrift eines Apostolischen Väters.'

3. Interpolation theories.
4. The question of vocabulary.
5. The theology of martyrdom.

1. THE QUESTION OF THE QUARTODECIMAN CHARACTER OF THE *MARTYRDOM* AND ITS BACKGROUND

The nineteenth-century debates about the authenticity of the Gospel of John seem far removed from our concerns today.[2] But it might be helpful to concentrate for a moment on this debate, as it poses the problem of the 'nature' of the parallels between the gospels and the *Martyrdom*. The focus of the debate, one recalls, was about the early ecclesiastical tradition of Polycarp as a disciple of John (see Irenaeus, in Euseb. *HE* 5. 20. 4) and the fact that neither Polycarp's *Epistle* nor the *Martyrdom* shows any acquaintance with the Fourth Gospel. It is in this context that A. Hilgenfeld published his 1860 book on *Der Paschastreit der alten Kirche*,[3] in which he argued that the synoptic chronology of the passion story is the basis of the Quartodeciman tradition, and that the *Martyrdom* gives evidence of this. Central to Hilgenfeld's argument is the identification of the 'great Sabbath' in *Mart. Pol.* 8 with the sabbath of Nisan 15; this is in agreement with the synoptic chronology. Moreover, all this fits with the presentation of Polycarp's martyrdom as parallel with Jesus' passion according to the synoptics! Among many other parallels, Hilgenfeld refers to the predictions of Matt. 26. 2 and *Mart. Pol.* 5. 2, the betrayal of the domestic servants, the irenarch Herodes, etc.[4] Hilgenfeld was contradicted by G. E. Steitz,[5] who had been a target of his polemics. Steitz rejects the idea of a synoptic chronology, and makes every effort to prove that there are also

[2] Recent studies about the Quartodeciman tradition in the context of *Martyrdom* are R. Cacitti, *Grande Sabato: Il contesto pasquale quartodecimano nella formazione della teologia del martirio* (Milan: Vita e pensiero, 1994); A. Stewart-Sykes, *The Lamb's High Feast: Melito, Peri Pascha and the Quartodeciman Paschal Liturgy at Sardis*, VCSup 42 (Leiden: Brill, 1998). For earlier studies, see Dehandschutter, *Martyrium Polycarpi*, 131 n. 302. On the 'Johannine Quest', see M. Hengel, *Die johanneische Frage: Ein Lösungsversuch*, WUNT 67 (Tübingen: Mohr, 1993); it is my pleasure to read on pp. 25–6 that Hengel considers my position to be 'too cautious'. But see now on the whole question B. Mutschler, *Irenäus als johanneischer Theologe: Studien zur Schriftauslegung bei Irenäus von Lyon* (Tübingen: Mohr, 2004).

[3] A. Hilgenfeld, *Der Paschastreit der alten Kirche nach seiner Bedeutung für die Kirchengeschichte und für die Evangelienforschung urkundlich dargestellt* (Halle: Pfeffer, 1860). For further details on the history of research, see my *Martyrium Polycarpi*, 131–4, 234–7.

[4] Hilgenfeld, *Paschastreit*, 245–6.

[5] G. E. Steitz, 'Der Charakter der kleinasiatischen Kirche und Festsitte um die Mitte des zweiten Jahrhunderts', *Jahrbuch für deutsche Theologie*, 6 (1861), 102–41, on pp. 117–20.

reminiscences of Johannine and Pauline literature in the *Martyrdom*. The voice from heaven in *Mart. Pol.* 9. 1 is comparable with John 12. 28, 29; and the blood flowing in *Mart. Pol.* 16. 1 corresponds with John 19. 34. According to Steitz, there is no reason to accept that the 'martyrdom according to the gospel' (*Mart. Pol.* 1) would refer only to the synoptics. According to him, it is all about 'die eine, in allen Evangelien mit sich selbst einig gedachte Ueberlieferung des evangelischen Geschichtsstoffes'. Hilgenfeld immediately rebuked Steitz:[6] apart from earlier arguments, he shows that *Mart. Pol.* 4 goes beyond indeterminate 'evangelische Geschichtsstoff'; rather, the Gospel of Matthew is used here! And with other examples Hilgenfeld demonstrates that the Johannine parallels are 'mit den Haaren herbeigezogen'.

2. THE DEFENCE OF THE AUTHENTICITY OF THE *MARTYRDOM*

Hilgenfeld continued to defend his position, first against R. A. Lipsius, and later against T. Keim.[7] But both scholars, together with H. J. Holtzmann, brought another aspect of the question into the debate.[8] Holtzmann offers a long list of parallels between the *Martyrdom* and the New Testament, but connects this with a later date for the *Martyrdom*. Along the same line as Lipsius and Keim, Holtzmann proposes a date during the Decian persecution for the actual text of the *Martyrdom*. The latter has to be dissociated from the historical period of the facts, and in that way the authority of the gospels, including the Fourth Gospel, is no longer a problem. Keim in turn insists again on the parallels with the whole New Testament, in order to show that the *Martyrdom* is a 'katholisches Produkt', accepting all the apostles.[9] It is clear that with Keim and the others the authenticity of the *Martyrdom* is called into question, but it might be interesting to point for one moment to Hilgenfeld's reaction: the latter firmly rejects the idea that the parallels with the gospels threaten the authenticity of the *Martyrdom*. Again he argues against the use of John and observes here an important difference between the *Martyrdom* and a

[6] A. Hilgenfeld, 'Das neueste Steitzianum über den Paschastreit', *ZWT* 4 (1861), 106–10; *idem*, 'Der Quartodecimanismus Kleinasiens und die kanonischen Evangelien', *ZWT* 4 (1861), 285–318.

[7] R. A. Lipsius, 'Der Märtyrertod Polykarps', *ZWT* 17 (1874), 188–214; T. Keim, *Aus dem Urchristenthum* (Zürich: Füssl, 1878).

[8] H. J. Holtzmann, 'Das Verhältnis des Johannes zu Ignatius und Polykarp', *ZWT* 20 (1877), 187–214.

[9] For other writings of Keim with the same criticism of the authenticity of *Martyrdom*, see my *Martyrium Polycarpi*, 133 n. 316.

text such as the *Martyrdom of Lyons and Vienne* (177 CE): this latter text, unlike the former, clearly knows *John.*[10]

The questioning of authenticity provoked a long reaction (mainly against Keim) in the unrivalled magisterial work of J. B. Lightfoot on the Apostolic Fathers. For the bishop of Durham, the Quartodeciman character of the *Martyrdom* is no longer a matter of discussion—all the more reason why the real meaning of the gospel parallels has to be evaluated correctly. Lightfoot again gives the list of references, considering their authenticity as interpreted by the introduction of the *Martyrdom* which speaks about a martyrdom 'according to the gospel'. This may mean that there are more obvious parallels and more indirect ones; but his final judgement would influence scholarship for a long time: 'the violence of the parallelism is a guarantee of the accuracy of the facts'.[11]

Thus, at the end of the nineteenth century one can observe a shift between two tendencies: from discussion of the authenticity of the Johannine Gospel and its position in early Christianity to an appreciation of the New Testament parallels with regard to the authenticity of the text of the *Martyrdom.*

3. THE INTERPOLATION THEORY WITH REGARD TO *THE MARTYRDOM*

Lightfoot's analysis did not have that much effect on German 'Literarkritik'. Following observations of Lipsius and others, H. Müller reconsidered the case of the *Martyrdom.*[12] In Müller's opinion, the parallels with the passion story could not belong to a simple historical narrative as offered by the letter to the Smyrneans. But instead of rejecting the text of the *Martyrdom* as a later literary fiction, Müller wanted to maintain the 'main' text. In comparison with the latter, the gospel parallels are later additions, and this can be seen as well by the version of the *Martyrdom* in Eusebius' *Church History.* This interpolation theory, also sustained by E. Schwartz,[13] leads directly to the well-known thesis

[10] A. Hilgenfeld, 'Polykarp von Smyrna', *ZWT* 17 (1874), 305–45; *idem*, 'Das Martyrium Polykarp's von Smyrna', *ZWT* 22 (1879), 145–70. Hilgenfeld was later supported by E. Egli who, approaching *Martyrdom* from the point of view of hagiography, nevertheless accepted Hilgenfeld's parallels. But Egli added the influence of the book of Acts, especially the 'way of suffering' of Paul, to the possible sources of inspiration of *Mart. Pol.*; cf. E. Egli, *Altchristliche Studien: Martyrien und Martyrologien ältester Zeit* (Zürich, 1887); cf. Dehandschutter, *Martyrium Polycarpi*, 134–5, 236–7.

[11] J. B. Lightfoot, *The Apostolic Fathers*, Part II: *S. Ignatius, S. Polycarp* (London: Macmillan, 1889), i. 614. As such it became a common assumption among scholars, that if the parallels had been introduced by a later editor, they would have been more elaborated.

[12] H. Müller, 'Das Martyrium Polykarps', *Römische Quartalschrift*, 22 (1908), 1–16; cf. *idem*, *Aus der Überlieferungsgeschichte des Polykarpmartyriums: Eine hagiographische Studie* (Paderborn: Schöningh, 1908).

[13] E. Schwartz, *De Pionio et Polycarpo* (Göttingen: Akademie, 1905).

of H. von Campenhausen, and is at the basis of many considerations of the *Martyrdom* as a (later) hagiographic document: the text has a historical nucleus but 'suffered' (inevitably) from later expansions.

It is instructive, however, to follow for a moment the criticisms levelled against Müller. In their studies on the *Martyrdom*, B. Sepp and W. Reuning[14] pointed out that the case for gospel parallels should not be overestimated. The mistake of Müller lay in seeing contacts between the *Martyrdom* and the gospels where there are only very general similarities. Both authors want to save the historicity of the story (as too would Lightfoot) by minimizing the phenomenon of the similarities. Fundamentally, H. von Campenhausen wants the same. But in his famous study of 1957, he elaborates this by a theory of interpolations among which the 'Evangelien-Redaktor' plays a crucial role.[15] The German church historian is quite certain in identifying what had been the initial 'simple' story of Polycarp on the basis of a comparison with Eusebius; and as a result he can identify later additions where the parallels with the gospels are not infrequently laborious constructions. His theory has been very influential, as I tried to show in my earlier contributions.[16] However, it is possible today to argue that the so-called gospel parallels could belong to the original document, and that it is certainly not correct to use Eusebius as a criterion for the contents of that document.[17] It has to be recognized that Christian hagiography is an early phenomenon, and so that there is nothing against the influence of it on the earliest redaction of the story of Polycarp's death.[18]

[14] B. Sepp, *Das Martyrium Polycarpi nebst Anhang über die Afralegende* (Regensburg: Akademische Buchdruckerei von F. Straub in München, 1911), 5–14; W. Reuning, *Zur Erklärung des Polykarpmaryriums* (Darmstadt: Wintersche Buchdruckerei, 1917), 10–20.

[15] H. von Campenhausen, 'Bearbeitungen und Interpolationen des Polykarpmartyriums', *Sitzungsberichte Akademie Heidelberg* (1957), 5–48; also in *idem, Aus der Frühzeit des Christentums: Studien zur Kirchengeschichte des ersten und zweiten Jahrhunderts* (Tübingen: Mohr, 1963), 253–301.

[16] Dehandschutter, *Martyrium Polycarpi*, 139–40, 238–9; cf. *idem*, 'The *Martyrium Polycarpi*: A Century of Research', *ANRW* 2. 27. 1 (1993), 485–522; *idem*, 'The Martyrdom of Polycarp and the Outbreak of Montanism', *ETL* 75 (1999), 430–7, cf. 431 n. 8. The most striking example of support for von Campenhausen's theory is H. Conzelmann, 'Bemerkungen zum Martyrium Polykarps', in *Sitzungsberichte Akademie Göttingen* (Göttingen: Vandenhoeck & Ruprecht, 1978), who renewed the view that a text such as *Mart. Pol.* contains a 'historical' nucleus, later adapted and enlarged for theological or hagiographical reasons.

[17] This has been seen clearly already by L. W. Barnard, 'In Defence of Pseudo-Pionius' Account of Saint Polycarp's Martyrdom', in P. Granfield and J. A. Jungmann (eds.), *Kyriakon: Festschrift für J. Quasten* (Münster: Verlag Aschendorff, 1970), 192–204; = *idem, Studies in Church History and Patristics* (Thessaloniki: Patriarchal Institute for Patristic Studies, 1978), 224–41; most recently the major commentary of G. Buschmann has again been critical of von Campenhausen: G. Buschmann, *Das Martyrium des Polykarp*, KAV 6 (Göttingen: Vandenhoeck & Ruprecht, 1998), 91–2.

[18] See my 'Hagiographie et histoire: à propos des Actes et Passions des Martyrs', in M. Lamberigts and P. van Deun (eds.), *Martyrium in Multidisciplinary Perspective*, Mémorial

4. THE QUESTION OF VOCABULARY

Preceding von Campenhausen's essay by a few years, the magisterial study by É. Massaux on the influence of the Gospel of Matthew on early Christian literature before Irenaeus posed again the problem of the impact of the (canonical) gospels,[19] but tried to arrive at conclusions on the basis of a careful textual comparison.

According to Massaux, the *Martyrdom* does not show any interest in a particular gospel text. The author of the martyr story follows only the important moments of the passion which are reflected in Polycarp's death. Strikingly, Massaux is quite cautious about a direct literary influence of New Testament texts on the *Martyrdom*. Even the case of *Martyrdom* 2. 3 with what appears to be a very direct reference to 1 Cor. 2. 9 is not decisive: it might be that the *Martyrdom* is using the same tradition as was available to Paul, so there is no necessary literary contact.[20] As for the prayer in *Mart. Pol.* 14, one must take into consideration the possibility that the many biblical reminiscences in the prayer are borrowing from an early Christian liturgical prayer.[21] If Massaux's inquiry remains rather undecided about literary influences on the *Martyrdom*, it has brought an important methodical issue again to the fore: what can be regarded as real literary influence? The Louvain scholar observed that this is a question not only of 'quotation', but also of the phrasing of a text, a certain

L. Reekmans (Leuven: Peeters, 1995), 295–301; see now also R. H. Seeliger, 'Märtyrerakten', and his concept of 'hagiographischer Diskurs', in S. Döpp and W. Geerlings (eds.), *Lexikon der antiken christlichen Literatur* (Freiburg: Herder, 1997), 411–19, on p. 413.

[19] É. Massaux, *Influence de l'Evangile de saint Matthieu sur la littérature chrétienne avant saint Irénée* (Louvain: Publications Universitaires de Louvain, 1950; réimpression anastatique, BETL 65 (Leuven: Peeters, 1986)); Massaux preceded also the well-known study by H. Köster, *Synoptische Überlieferung bei den Apostolischen Vätern*, TU 65 (Berlin: Akademie Verlag, 1957) but the latter does not take *Martyrdom* into account; see also F. Neirynck, 'Introduction à la réimpression', pp. x–xi; the book of Massaux has been translated into English: *The Influence of the Gospel of Saint Matthew on Christian Literature before Saint Irenaeus* (Macon, Ga.: Mercer University Press, 1990); on the *Martyrdom*, cf. *Book 2: The Later Christian Writings*, 45–53.

[20] However, the use of 1 Cor. 2. 9 in other early Christian texts might point to the contrary. Also the next case of the prayer of Polycarp gives us the impression that, for Massaux, *Mart. Pol.* 14 is in the first place to be discussed from the point of view of liturgical traditions. But the question of liturgical traditions is seldom unequivocal. In the case of the famous prayer of *1 Clem.* 59. 2– 61. 3, it has been argued by Lona that the prayer is redactional! Cf. H. E. Lona, *Der erste Clemensbrief*, KAV 2 (Göttingen: Vandenhoeck & Ruprecht, 1998), 583–623; a recent study by Löhr places the prayer again in a liturgical context: H. Löhr, *Studien zum frühchristlichen und frühjüdischen Gebet: Untersuchungen zu 1 Clem 59 bis 61 in seinem literarischen, historischen und theologischen Kontext*, WUNT 160 (Tübingen: Mohr Siebeck, 2003).

[21] See previous note; the question of the tradition behind the prayer has been studied fully by Buschmann, *Das Martyrium*, 226–57.

terminology making some vocabulary visible. This was reiterated by M. L. Guillaumin in a short study preparatory to the first volume of the *Biblia Patristica*.[22] This study tried to identify a peculiar vocabulary and the combination of expressions as parallels between the *Martyrdom* and biblical texts. In this way one may discover a lot of 'rapprochements', but only those which reflect the intention of the author should be retained, and this reduces, for example, the real references to the passion story. Guillaumin, however, demonstrates that small correspondences can also be meaningful, and that New Testament texts other than the gospels may have played a role in the formulation of the author.

The fact that we find in the *Martyrdom* more reminiscences, rather than exact borrowings or citations, is what I tried to explain in my dissertation of 1977, comparing the phenomenon with what we find elsewhere during the first half of the second century in writings such as *1 Clement*: namely, earlier Christian documents being 'received' in the form not of quotations but of allusions, implying the common basis of a written text but without 'scriptural' authority. It must be added that the *Martyrdom* shows some evolution to a certain 'authority' in the sense that it refers to the 'example of the Lord' (1. 2) and 'the gospel' (1. 1, 4; 19. 1).

In the meantime W. D. Köhler took up the problem, especially in relation to Matthew. Although he refines the analysis of the materials parallel to the gospels, he does not achieve a conclusive position. Köhler sees no instance of literary dependence on Matthew on the part of the *Martyrdom*, only a possibility ('gut möglich') for a text such as *Mart. Pol.* 6. 2. Positively, he reformulates the question whether the notion of *euaggelion* may point to a written gospel in the *Martyrdom*. But for Köhler all this is valid only at the level on which the 'Evangelienredaktor' was formulating! This reduces very much the impact of his judgement.[23]

Almost simultaneously, V. Saxer published an inquiry on the Bible and hagiography, about the use of the Bible in early Christian Acts of Martyrdom.[24] For the *Martyrdom*, Saxer shows the importance of the theme of imitation

[22] M. L. Guillaumin, 'En marge du "Martyre de Polycarpe": le discernement des allusions scripturaires', in *Forma Futuri: Studi in onore del Cardinale M. Pellegrino* (Turin: Bottega d'Erasmo, 1975), 462–9; cf. *Biblia Patristica: Index des citations et allusions bibliques dans la littérature patristique*, i: *Des origines à Clément d'Alexandrie et Tertullien* (Paris: Éditions du Centre National de la Recherche Scientifique, 1975).

[23] W.-D. Köhler, *Die Rezeption des Matthäusevangeliums in der Zeit vor Irenäus*, WUNT 2.24 (Tübingen: Mohr Siebeck, 1987), 487–9.

[24] V. Saxer, *Bible et Hagiographie: Textes et thèmes bibliques dans les Actes des martyrs authentiques des premiers siècles* (Bern: Lang, 1986), 27–35; cf. *idem*, 'The Influence of the Bible in Early Christian Martyrology', in P. M. Blowers (ed.), *The Bible in Greek Christian Antiquity* (Notre Dame, Ind.: University of Notre Dame Press, 1997), 342–74.

as a clear purpose in the use of the Bible, but leaves undecided whether this implies reference to a particular gospel. Apart from other reminiscences, Saxer discusses the prayer of Polycarp (*Mart. Pol.* 14). Emphasizing the density of scriptural reminiscences, Saxer believes in the influence of liturgical tradition as many others before (and after him) have done.

As a summary, we can observe that the discussion of the authors presented in this section points to the need for careful attention to the exact nature of the biblical references in the *Martyrdom*: these references are more allusive than 'quoting'. Above all, this kind of 'appropriation' does not exclude reference to a written text; on the contrary, the 'martyrdom according to the gospel' implies the written gospel(s).[25]

5. THE THEOLOGY OF MARTYRDOM

Buschmann's impressive commentary returned to the question of 'the *Martyrdom of Polycarp* and the New Testament', treating the issue wholly from the side of a theological interpretation of the idea of martyrdom according to the gospel. In a way that he had already anticipated in his 1994 monograph,[26] Buschmann interprets the *κατὰ τὸ εὐαγγέλιον* intention of *Mart. Pol.* as 'katholisch-normativ und anti-enthusiastisch'.[27] The question of the use of a particular gospel text is present only marginally; the emphasis is on the theological meaning of the parallel. As the normative intention of the text is dominant for Buschmann, he continuously risks overestimating the nature of the parallels. And this certainly is nothing new, but can be discovered more than once when the early theology of Christian martyrdom is at stake. So, if one can agree with Buschmann's presentation of *Mart. Pol.* 5 (the flight of Polycarp) and his description of the terminological parallels of this passage with the gospels, one should at the same time disagree about the perspective: 'Die zahlreichen Anspielungen an die Passion Christi werden zur ethischen Umsetzung benutzt.'[28] Are these 'Anspielungen' really so numerous? And if they are

[25] And not a general idea of the (oral) gospel message. Buschmann, *Martyrium des Polykarp*, 127–8, develops this again, in comparison with the use of 'euaggelion' in *2 Clement* and the *Didache*. Certainly the latter text shows in my opinion that the matter of interpretation has little to do with 'earlier' or 'later'. Unfortunately, *Martyrdom* is not discussed by D. A. Hagner, 'The Sayings of Jesus in the Apostolic Fathers and in Justin Martyr', in D. Wenham (ed.), *The Jesus Tradition outside the Gospels*, Gospel Perspectives, 5 (Sheffield: JSOT Press, 1985), 233–68, cf. 260 n. 5.

[26] G. Buschmann, *Martyrium Polycarpi: Eine formkritische Studie. Ein Beitrag zur Frage nach der Entstehung der Gattung Märtyrerakte* (Berlin and New York: De Gruyter, 1994), 321–7.

[27] Buschmann, *Martyrium des Polykarp*, 51.

[28] Ibid. 127.

only 'Anspielungen', can they really have been so normative? Another example of the perspective of (omnipresent) normativity is Buschmann's exaggeration of the meaning of the parallelism between the vision of Polycarp and the 'Leidensankündigung' (Mark 8. 31 par.). That such a presentation risks being too generalizing, I have tried to show on other occasions.[29] It is, however, true that Buschmann's commentary invites us to summarize some methodical aspects of the question of the relationship between the *Martyrdom* and the New Testament, which I want to do by way of conclusion.

CONCLUSIONS

1. The notion of 'gospel' in the expression 'martyrdom according to the gospel' can be taken in the sense of written gospel (so also Buschmann). It remains undecided, however, whether this implies one or more gospels. The author of the *Martyrdom* can be considered as having not one particular gospel in mind, although he might have known more than one gospel, as we do nowadays. The trouble remains to find something more (cf. Köhler): it is true that Quintus' conduct in *Mart. Pol.* 4 is not praised, in contradiction to what the gospel teaches. Editions and commentaries refer here as a rule to Matt. 10. 23 and John 7. 1; 8. 59; 10. 39 (cf. Bihlmeyer), but in the end these texts shed little light on the case of Quintus. On the other hand, the reference ὡς ἐπὶ λῃστὴν τρέχοντες is much closer to a specific text such as Matt. 26. 55, although another synoptic gospel might be implied.

2. There remains little support for the 'Gospel Redactor'. A certain parallelism with the passion story must be admitted, but Lightfoot's warning about the 'violence' of the parallelism remains: it makes little sense to maintain this phenomenon outside the passage where the author of *Martyrdom* himself indicates it (*Mart. Pol.* 6. 2). There is all the more reason to doubt the existence of any parallelism in the case of Polycarp being put on a donkey (8. 1)!

3. It appears that much description of the 'use' of the New Testament in the *Martyrdom* has been governed by ideas about the theological tendencies in

[29] I have commented elsewhere sufficiently on this; cf. 'Martyrdom of Polycarp and the Outbreak of Montanism'. That it is possible to integrate *Martyrdom* into a wider perspective of early theology of Christian martyrdom, without exaggerations of the kind made by Buschmann, has been shown by T. Baumeister, *Die Anfänge der Theologie des Martyriums* (Münster: Aschendorff, 1980), 295–306, cf. p. 302; and my article 'Le Martyre de Polycarpe et *le* développement de la conception du martyre au deuxième siècle', in E. A. Livingstone (ed.), *St Patr* 17, 2 (Oxford and New York: Pergamon Press, 1982), 659–68; and the reaction by W. R. Schoedel.

relation to martyrdom. But the difficulty remains that we cannot speak about formal 'quotation'. The statement in *Mart. Pol.* 7. 1, 'God's will be done'—most crucial in my opinion for the understanding of the entire document—can be linked to Acts 21. 14 as well as to Matt. 6. 10 (the Lord's Prayer), and only indirectly to the context it evokes: namely, the Gethsemane scene in Matt. 26. 39 par.

Thus it seems that New Testament references and reminiscences in the *Martyrdom* are embedded within a view of the meaning of martyrdom without it being appropriate to overdo the idea 'according to the gospel' in the sense of an anti-Montanist statement, or as an idea that implies a strict parallelism with the passion story. That we should become 'imitators of the Lord' is given expression with a Pauline reference (Phil. 2. 4; see *Mart. Pol.* 1. 2 and 17. 3). The most recognizable Pauline 'quotation', 1 Cor. 2. 9, is adapted to a context about the heavenly reward for the martyrs (*Mart. Pol.* 2. 3). As I have tried to show in earlier contributions, all this implies a 'free' reception of early Christian texts, including what were later to become the canonical gospels, the authority of which is not questioned, although they are neither formally used nor normatively exploited.

One important remark remains after this brief discussion of the history of research. It is not superfluous to restore expressions such as 'Evangelien-Redaktor' or 'martyrdom according to the gospels' to their proper proportions. Only this can lead to a correct evaluation of the appropriation of earlier Christian literature in the *Martyrdom*. It is possible to illustrate this by another example of early Christian literature: the *Martyrium of Lyons and Vienne* (Euseb. *HE* 5. 1–3 = *Mart. Lugd.*). In this text too we can find a 'use' of early Christian literature that is more 'integrating' than formally 'quoting'.[30] There are, however, two exceptions: in *Mart. Lugd.* 1. 15, the fulfilment of the saying of our Lord in John 16. 2, and the fulfilment of the *graphe* in Rev. 22. 11, which is an adapted version of Dan. 12. 10. One sees here a process whereby a text gets 'authority': as fulfilment, without being in contradiction with other less formal 'quotations'. But with the *Martyrium Lugdunensium* we are getting close to the situation of an Irenaeus of Lyons, for whom formal quotation became an instrument in building up his refutation against Gnostics and Marcionites. And Irenaeus knows the four gospels. In my view, it might remain a riddle how this could be possible, and be functioning in a

[30] Cf. Rom. 8. 18 in *Mart. Lugd.* 1. 6; Rev. 14. 4 in *Mart. Lugd.* 1. 10; 1 Cor. 4. 9 in *Mart. Lugd.* 1. 40; Phil. 2. 6 in *Mart. Lugd.* 2. 2; Rev. 3. 14 in *Mart. Lugd.* 2. 3. More recently the monograph of Nagel on the Gospel of John does not treat *Martyrdom* or *Martyrdom Lugdunensium*; cf T. Nagel, *Die Rezeption des Johannesevangeliums im 2. Jahrhundert: Studien zur vorirenaischen Aneignung und Auslegung des vierten Evangeliums in christlicher und christlich-gnostischer Literatur* (Leipzig: Evangelische Verlagsanstadt, 2000).

polemical writing, had the gospels not been disseminated and read decades earlier, exercising some authority not only on the field of the transmission of the *logia Iesou* in the early Christian communities, but also on the field of the story of Jesus' life and passion. The case of the *Martyrdom* contains at least the warning that this was not necessarily a matter of explicit quotation, as if only the latter could guarantee real literary influence.

20

The *Martyrdom of Polycarp* and the New Testament Passion Narratives

Michael W. Holmes

A surprising feature of the *Martyrdom of Polycarp*, a document that explicitly declares its intention to describe a 'martyrdom in accord with the gospel' (*Mart. Pol.* 1. 1; cf. 19. 1), is that nowhere in the course of its narrative does it ever quote a gospel or a saying of Jesus. At the same time, there are numerous apparent parallels and allusions to gospel tradition, which in the opinion of many provide the key to understanding Polycarp's martyrdom as an *imitation* of the passion of Jesus. This unusual circumstance—the seemingly central role of gospel parallels in a document that never cites a gospel—calls for further investigation. I propose to look first at the relationship (if any) between the *Martyrdom of Polycarp* and the gospels,[1] and second at the relationship between the meaning of a martyrdom 'according to the gospel' and the parallels with the gospel tradition, and its significance for understanding the *Martyrdom.*

THE GOSPELS IN THE *MARTYRDOM OF POLYCARP*

In this section, the focal question is relatively straightforward: *is there any demonstrable evidence that the author of the* Martyrdom of Polycarp *has made use of any of the written gospels now included in the canonical New Testament?* The question is limited to the gospels for the moment, because features intrinsic to the *Martyrdom of Polycarp* (noted in the preceding paragraph) direct particular attention to the gospels.[2]

[1] It will be noticed that *The New Testament in the Apostolic Fathers* (Oxford: Clarendon Press, 1905) did not include the *Martyrdom of Polycarp* in its purview.

[2] The rest of the New Testament is discussed in an appendix at the end of this essay.

The simplicity of the question masks, of course, substantial methodological and procedural difficulties. These have been well articulated by Andrew Gregory, whose general approach and perspective will be adopted.[3] In what follows I will proceed through the *Martyrdom of Polycarp* in the order of its text, assessing those instances where there is some possibility that the document may draw upon material from a (now canonical) gospel text. There is no attempt to list all possible parallels between the gospels and the *Martyrdom of Polycarp*, since Dehandschutter has compiled a very detailed list of verbal links, similarities, or parallels.[4] Instead, the investigation will focus on those instances which seem most likely (or which have been claimed) to offer probative evidence of the knowledge or use of *specific* gospel texts or documents.[5]

Mart. Pol. 4

'We do not praise', says the narrator near the end of §4, 'those who hand themselves over' (Quintus, of course, being the prime example of one who did), 'since the gospel does not so teach.' Massaux observes that 'commentators have wondered where such a teaching of the gospel is read. They generally go back to Mt. 10. 23; Jn. 7. 1; 8. 59; 10. 39, where the teaching of Christ and his example show that persecutors can be fled from and that it is not necessary to wait for them.'[6] But this is an odd line of interpretation to propose: the

[3] Andrew Gregory, *The Reception of Luke and Acts in the Period before Irenaeus: Looking for Luke in the Second Century*, WUNT 2.169 (Tübingen: J. C. B. Mohr (Paul Siebeck), 2003), 5–20. See also the introductory essay on this topic by Andrew Gregory and Christopher Tuckett in the companion volume.

[4] See B. Dehandschutter, *Martyrium Polycarpi: Een literair-kritische studie*, BETL 52 (Leuven: Universitaire Presse, 1979), 241–54. See also the commentary by Gerd Buschmann, which on individual passages typically offers extensive lists of parallels: *Das Martyrium des Polykarp*, KAV 6 (Göttingen: Vandenhoeck & Ruprecht, 1998). For surveys of previous research, consult Dehandschutter, *Martyrium Polycarpi*, 231–41; B. Dehandschutter, 'The *Martyrium Polycarpi*: A Century of Research', *ANRW* 2.27.1 (1993), 485–522, on pp. 503–7; Buschmann, *Das Martyrium*, 49–58; cf. also M.-L. Guillaumin, 'En marge du "Martyre de Polycarpe": Le discernement des allusions scripturaires', in *Forma Futuri: Studi in onore del Cardinale Michele Pellegrino* (Turin: Bottega d'Erasmo, 1975), 462–9.

[5] This means that a number of 'obvious' parallels, such as those to material occurring in the Triple Tradition, will not be listed, since there is no way the parallel can be linked to a specific gospel text.

[6] Édouard Massaux, *The Influence of the Gospel of Saint Matthew on Christian Literature before Saint Irenaeus*, ii: *The Later Christian Writings*, ed. A. J. Bellinzoni (Louvain: Peeters; Macon, Ga.: Mercer University Press, 1992), 48; his list of possible references follows J. B. Lightfoot, *The Apostolic Fathers*, Part 2: *S. Ignatius, S. Polycarp*, 2nd edn., 3 vols. (London: Macmillan, 1889; repr. Grand Rapids, Mich.: Baker Book House, 1981), 3. 370. Cf. also Dehandschutter, *Martyrium Polycarpi*, 244; Buschmann, *Das Martyrium*, 126–8.

(uniquely Matthean) directive in Matt. 10. 23 to *flee* persecution contradicts the explicit behaviour for which Polycarp is commended in 1. 2: 'he *waited* to be betrayed, just as the Lord did.' Moreover, it is rather odd to propose parallels in the gospels for something that, according to the *Martyrdom*, the 'gospel' does *not* teach. Köhler's claim that dependence on Matt. 10. 23 is 'gut möglich'[7] would appear to overstate the matter considerably.

Mart. Pol. 5. 2a

Lightfoot suggests that there is in 5. 2 an allusion to Matt. 26. 2: 'As Christ prophecies his betrayal "after two days" (Matt. xxvi. 2), so Polycarp "three days before he was apprehended" foretold the fate that awaited him (§ 5).'[8] But Polycarp, unlike Jesus, did *not* predict the timing of his betrayal (nor of his fate): the mention of 'three days before he was apprehended' is the report of the document's author, not a prediction by Polycarp. There is here no parallel to the gospel account, and thus no allusion to Matt. 26. 2.

Mart. Pol. 5. 2b

Both Jesus and Polycarp are, however, reported to have predicted the manner of their death, the one by crucifixion and the other by fire (5. 2; cf. 12. 3)—an action which, in Polycarp's case at least, hardly required any unusual foresight, in view of Roman custom and practice. So here there is a firm parallel between the gospel tradition and the *Martyrdom*.[9] It cannot, however, be linked to a specific gospel, inasmuch as Jesus' prediction is reported in both Matthew and John. The latter might be thought to be the closer parallel, since it mentions, like the *Martyrdom*, both the prediction (12. 32–3) and its fulfilment (18. 32). On the other hand, Matthew twice portrays Jesus as specifying in advance death by crucifixion (20. 19;[10] 26. 2; cf. 23. 34), and thus both offer a possible source of the parallel (as also, we must not forget, oral tradition likely does). In short, this is a parallel to gospel tradition, but it cannot be linked with a specific gospel.

[7] W.-D. Köhler, *Die Rezeption des Matthäusevangeliums in der Zeit vor Irenäus*, WUNT 2.24 (Tübingen: Mohr Siebeck, 1987), 489.

[8] Lightfoot, *Apostolic Fathers*, 2. 1. 610.

[9] Cf. ibid. 2. 3. 385; 2. 1. 611; Dehandschutter, *Martyrium Polycarpi*, 251.

[10] The synoptic parallels (Mark 10. 34; Luke 18. 33) to this third passion prediction retain the less specific 'kill' (ἀποκτείνω) of the two earlier predictions (Matt. 16. 21 // Mark 8. 31 // Luke 9. 22; Matt. 17. 23 // Mark 9. 31).

Mart. Pol. 6. 2a

The narrative indicates that Polycarp's arrest was inevitable, inasmuch as 'the very persons who betrayed him were people of his own household' (οἰκεῖοι). Citing Matt. 10. 36, a passage unique to the first gospel (echoing Mic. 7. 6[11])—'and a man's foes will be those of his own household' (οἰκιακοί)—Lightfoot suggests that 'Here again the martyrdom of Polycarp was κατὰ τὸ εὐαγγέλιον . . . for Christ likewise was betrayed by one of His own household (John xiii. 18)'.[12] The similarity between οἰκεῖοι and οἰκιακοί (elsewhere in the NT only at Matt. 10. 25) is the primary reason for linking 6. 2a with Matt. 10. 36, whose context is otherwise rather different. Köhler rates this as no more than 'gut möglich', and Massaux only raises a question ('Is the author perhaps making a casual reference to this saying?').[13] The one-word connection is much too slender a basis to demonstrate use of Matthew.

Mart. Pol. 6. 2b

In a remarkable coincidence (which for the writer was probably not a 'coincidence' at all), Herod, the police captain responsible for the arrest of Polycarp, bore the same name as the tetrarch of Galilee and Perea in office when Jesus was arrested and tried, Herod Antipas. This (grammatically somewhat awkward) reference is clearly one of the most intentional allusions to the gospel narrative in the *Martrydom*. But not even here can one reliably relate it to a specific gospel text, for whereas the confrontation between Herod and Jesus is narrated only in Luke 23. 6–12, Acts 4. 27 ('For truly in this city there were gathered together against Your holy servant Jesus, whom You anointed, both Herod and Pontius Pilate, along with the Gentiles and the peoples of Israel') and Ignatius (*Smyrn.* 1. 2, 'truly nailed in the flesh . . . under Pontius Pilate and Herod') remind us that Herod's name was part of the larger tradition about Jesus. The bare reference to Herod's name, given the absence of any mention of (or allusion to) distinctive Lucan material, is insufficient to justify any higher rating than 'possible' in regard to a link with the third gospel.

[11] Mic. 7. 6 LXX: ἐχθροὶ ἀνδρὸς πάντες οἱ ἄνδρες οἱ ἐν τῷ οἴκῳ αὐτοῦ.

[12] Lightfoot, *Apostolic Fathers*, 2. 3. 370–1; cf. Buschmann, *Das Martyrium*, 146; P. T. Camelot, *Ignace d'Antioche [et] Polycarpe de Smyrne, Lettres. Martyre de Polycarpe*, 4th edn., SC 10 (Paris: Cerf, 1969), 217 n. 4; Dehandschutter, *Martyrium Polycarpi*, 246.

[13] Köhler, *Die Rezeption*, 489; Massaux, *Influence*, ii. 48–9.

Mart. Pol. 6. 2c

The narrator states that those who betrayed Polycarp 'received the punishment of Judas himself', and Köhler thinks that here dependence on Matt. 27. 5 is 'gut möglich'.[14] But Matt. 27. 5 is one of at least three extant accounts of the fate of Judas, each one different; the other two are reported in Acts (1. 18) and by Papias.[15] Since the narrator does not mention what the specific 'punishment of Judas' was, there is no way to determine which of the three accounts—indeed, if any of them—is the referent of the author's comment.

Mart. Pol. 7.1a

Here the author reports that those pursuing Polycarp came after him 'as though chasing after an armed rebel' (ὡς ἐπὶ λῃστὴν τρέχοντες). A search of the *Thesaurus Linguae Graecae* for 'ὡς ἐπὶ λῃστὴν' in centuries 2 BCE–2 CE turns up only five instances: one here in *Mart. Pol.* 7. 1, three in the synoptics (Matt. 26. 55 = Mark 14. 48 = Luke 22. 52), and one in Origen (*Comm. Jo.* 28. 14. 113, clearly citing synoptic gospel material). Therefore in this instance we may with some confidence label this a virtually certain allusion to the gospel narrative. But there is no way to determine whether the allusion is to an oral or a written version of that narrative; moreover, even if it could be determined that it was from a written gospel, it is impossible, in view of the verbal identity of the phrase in all three synoptic gospels, to connect the allusion to any one gospel.[16]

Mart. Pol. 7.1b

Massaux lists Matt. 6. 10; 26. 42; Luke 22. 42; and Acts 21. 14 as possible sources for the phrase τὸ θέλημα τοῦ θεοῦ γενέσθω in 7. 1, and then declares, with no explanation, that 'Only Matt 26: 42 and L. 22: 42 can be considered' (even though the wording of 26. 42 is identical to that of Matt. 6. 10).[17] But in key respects, the wording and form of 7. 1 is most like that of Acts 21. 14 (τοῦ κυρίου τὸ θέλημα γινέσθω), though certainly not close enough to demonstrate

[14] Köhler, *Die Rezeption*, 489.

[15] For Papias's account (cited in an excerpt attributed to Apollinaris of Laodicaea), see Michael W. Holmes, *The Apostolic Fathers: Greek Texts and English Translations*, rev. edn. (Grand Rapids, Mich.: Baker Books, 1999), 582–5.

[16] Similarly, Massaux (*Influence*, ii. 47), contra Köhler, *Die Rezeption*, 489.

[17] Massaux, *Influence*, ii. 47.

anything more than a possible link. A prayer such as this surely was a common feature of early Christian experience; texts such as εὐχόμεθα καὶ ἐπὶ γῆς γενέσθαι τὸ θέλημα τοῦ θεοῦ ὡς ἐν οὐρανῷ (Clem. Al. *Strom.* 4. 8. 66)[18] show how easily the second person address of the Lord's Prayer could become a third person statement such as we find in *Mart. Pol.* 7. 1. Moreover, the distinction between θεοῦ and κυρίου is not insignificant: in the New Testament, references to the 'will of God' outnumber those to the 'will of the Lord' eleven to three, a ratio that holds as well for the rest of first- and second-century Christian literature. Finally, it may be suggested that if the phrase in 7. 1 is an allusion, the most likely reference is to be found in the *Martyrdom* itself: namely, 2. 1 ('all the martyrdoms that have taken place in accordance with the will of God', ... τὸ θέλημα τοῦ θεοῦ γεγονότα).

Mart. Pol. 8.1a

The narrative indicates that when Polycarp had finished his prayer, 'the hour having come to depart', his captors led him into town. The phrase τῆς ὥρας ἐλθούσης may be a Johannine echo (cf. John 17. 1 and 13. 1),[19] but Mark 14. 41 (ἦλθεν ἡ ὥρα) may equally be in view[20]—if one assumes that a parallel is intended and that the phrase is more than a simple indication of time.

Mart. Pol. 8. 1b

Polycarp's captors seat him on a donkey (ὄνῳ) before leading him into town. In the canonical gospels the substantive ὄνος occurs only in Matt. 21. 2, 7; again, Köhler thinks dependence on Matthew 'gut möglich'.[21] But the related diminutive ὀνάριον occurs in the Johannine version of the episode (12. 12), and Massaux is right to conclude that a single shared word is 'too thin a clue, however, to conclude in favor of a literary dependence'[22]—especially if the possibility of influence from oral tradition is kept in mind.

[18] Cf. also Origen, *De or.* 26. 1; *AJ* 18. 12.

[19] Cf. Judith M. Lieu, *Image and Reality* (Edinburgh: T. & T. Clark, 1996), 71 ('Johannine echoes are hard to avoid'); Charles E. Hill, *The Johannine Corpus in the Early Church* (Oxford: Oxford University Press, 2004), 358.

[20] The Matthean parallel, 26. 45, has ἤγγικεν rather than a form of ἔρχομαι.

[21] Köhler, *Die Rezeption*, 489.

[22] Massaux, *Influence*, ii. 47.

Mart. Pol. 8. 1c

At first glance the remark in 8. 1 that Polycarp's captors 'brought him into the city, it being a great Sabbath' (ὄντος σαββάτου μεγάλου) is an evident allusion to John 19. 31 (ἦν γὰρ μεγάλη ἡ ἡμέρα ἐκείνου τοῦ σαββάτου).[23] An immediate difficulty for this claim is the lack of synchronicity: in John (and the synoptics as well) Jesus dies the day *before* a 'great Sabbath', whereas Polycarp dies *on* a 'great Sabbath'. Thus it is possible that the reference to a 'great Sabbath' here is, like the other reference (in ch. 21, the 'chronological appendix' to the main narrative, where a 'great Sabbath' is part of a complex dating formula[24]), nothing more than a chronological marker.[25] In view, however, of the context of the reference—'the long sentence which it closes, as a genitive absolute, is loaded with deeper significance'[26]—it is not surprising that many have sought a literary or theological explanation of the phrase. Despite all the discussion, there is certainly no consensus, or much clarity, regarding the possible meaning(s) of the phrase.[27] This reference is certainly a possible allusion to the Gospel of John, but it is difficult to find any firm ground that would justify raising it to a more certain category.

Mart. Pol. 9. 1

Lightfoot claims that 'the parallel to John xii. 28, where likewise a voice comes from heaven to Christ at the supreme crisis . . . is manifest'.[28] However, in all there are three instances of a voice from heaven in the gospel tradition: not only John 12. 28, but also at the Baptism and the Transfiguration (which is in its own right nearly as climactic a moment—coming as it does just after the

[23] E.g., most recently, Hill, *Johannine Corpus*, 358.

[24] Whether ch. 21 is supplementary or secondary is for the moment immaterial; for the former view cf. Lightfoot, *Apostolic Fathers*, 2. 1. 626–38; for the latter, W. R. Schoedel, *Polycarp, Martyrdom of Polycarp, Fragments of Papias* (London: Thomas Nelson, 1967), 77–8.

[25] Perhaps indicating, e.g., the day of the week (cf. W. Rordorf, 'Zum Problem des "grossen Sabbats" im Polykarp- und Pioniusmartyrium', in E. Dassmann and K. S. Frank (eds.), *Pietas: Festschrift für B. Kötting* (Münster: 1980), 245–9).

[26] Lieu, *Image and Reality*, 71. Her correct observation that 'against this background it is natural to look for a symbolical, "Gospel" significance in the mention of "a great sabbath" ' does not, however, constitute evidence that such significance is (or need be) present.

[27] For discussions (with bibliography) see Remo Cacitti, *Grande Sabato: Il contesto pasquale quartodecimano nella formazione della teologia del martirio*, 19 (Milan: Vita e Pensiero, 1994); Lieu, *Image and Reality*, 70–9; Buschmann, *Das Martyrium*, 166–9; Dehandschutter, 'Century of Research', 498–501.

[28] Lightfoot, *Apostolic Fathers*, 2. 1. 611.

first passion prediction and not long before his final ascent to Jerusalem—as John 12. 28). Moreover, in John 12. 30 Jesus indicates that the voice has not come for his sake, but for that of the crowd around him—a distinctive *functional* difference from *Mart. Pol.* 9. 1, where the voice is clearly intended to encourage the martyr himself.[29] Indeed, in terms of *function*, Luke 22. 43 offers a closer parallel in certain respects (as would Acts 18. 9–10 and 23. 11, were we not so predisposed by *Mart. Pol.* 1. 1 to confine our search to gospel tradition). Nor should it be overlooked that the closest parallels with regard to the *content* of the heavenly voice are in LXX Joshua (1. 6, 7, 9, 18). In short, while John 12. 28 may be an obvious parallel, it is clearly not the only possible parallel, or perhaps, even the most probable one. In short, once again we find the *Martyrdom of Polycarp* echoing gospel tradition, without being able to relate that echo (at least with any degree of probability) to a specific gospel.[30]

Mart. Pol. 11. 2

Without providing details, Köhler asserts as 'gut möglich' dependence of 11. 2 on Matt. 25. 46 (unique to Matthew); he apparently has in mind the two-word phrase *αἰωνίου κολάσεως* (reversed from Matthew).[31] While the term *κόλασις* occurs only twice in the New Testament (1 John 4. 18 is the other place), there are ten instances in the Apostolic Fathers—three of which occur in *Mart. Pol.* 2. 3–4—and over twenty instances in Justin Martyr.[32] In short, the term is not uncommon in the vocabulary of Christian writers in the second century, and thus is of little value for the question at hand.

Mart. Pol. 12. 3 (see on 5. 2b above)

Mart. Pol. 14. 2a

The prayer recorded in *Mart. Pol.* 14 bristles with allusions and echoes of scriptural and early Christian texts, here pulled together in a clearly liturgical context. One such allusion or echo is the reference in 14. 2 to the 'cup of Christ'. Once again Köhler thinks that dependence on Matthew (in this

[29] Notice the second person address, which occurs in the canonical narratives only in the Marcan and Lucan versions of the Baptism.

[30] Cf. Dehandschutter, *Martyrium Polycarpi*, 249.

[31] Köhler, *Die Rezeption*, 489.

[32] The two-word combination (disregarding the order) also occurs in *2 Clem.* 6. 7; Justin Martyr, *1 Apol.* 8. 4; 12. 1; 18. 2; *Dial.* 117. 3.

instance, 20. 22–3) is 'gut möglich'.[33] But the phrase is so short and non-specific that it could be linked with any number of passages (e.g., Matt. 20. 22–3 // Mark 10. 38–9; Matt. 26. 39 // Mark 14. 36 // Luke 22. 42), and thus is of no value for tracing a connection to any specific document.

Mart. Pol. 14. 2b

The phrase *εἰς ἀνάστασιν ζωῆς αἰωνίου* occurs only here in Christian literature of the first two centuries CE.[34] The first part of the phrase (*εἰς ἀνάστασιν ζωῆς*) occurs elsewhere in the same corpus only at John 5. 29, while the second part (*ζωῆς αἰωνίου*) occurs fifty-two times in the New Testament and Apostolic Fathers (including John 5. 24). It is difficult not to see here the influence of the Fourth Gospel. What is indeterminable, however, is how this influence was exerted. Does this reflect direct knowledge of a written gospel, or indirect influence via the language of prayer and worship (especially in eucharistic contexts)? The phrase is simply too short to do more than suggest the possibility of direct dependence.[35]

Mart. Pol. 15. 1

In Lightfoot's opinion, the eyewitnesses of the events surrounding Polycarp's death 'lay stress on their providential preservation that they might relate the incidents to others (§15), just as the evangelist emphasizes in similar language the fact of his presence as witness' in John 19. 35 (cf. 21. 24).[36] But Buschmann[37] thinks that the emphasis is on the testimony to the 'wonders'

[33] Köhler, *Die Rezeption*, 489; cf. Bruce M. Metzger, *The Canon of the New Testament* (Oxford: Clarendon Press, 1987), 121 (the phrase 'is a reminiscence of Matt. xx. 22 and xxvi. 39').

[34] To be more precise, 'Christian literature of the first two centuries that is included in the *TLG* data base'.

[35] Cf. Massaux, *Influence*, ii. 49 ('The words...recall Jn. 5:29, which does not have the adjective *αἰωνίου*; the context is different.... To be sure, the author of the *Martyrdom of Polycarp* may have taken the expression ready made from Jn., but there is no element in the text to suggest it. On the contrary, the words which follow, "of soul and body in the incorruptibility of the Holy Spirit," do not lead to Jn. 5:29'); differently Hill, *Johannine Corpus*, 358–9. For liturgical (especially eucharistic) parallels, cf. Buschmann, *Das Martyrium*, 282–4.

[36] Lightfoot, *Apostolic Fathers*, 2. 1. 611; also Hermann Müller, 'Das Martyrium Polycarpi: Ein Beitrag zur altchristlichen Heiligengeschichte', *Römische Quartalschrift*, 22 (1908), 1–16, at p. 11; L. W. Barnard, 'In Defence of Pseudo-Pionius' Account of Saint Polycarp's Martyrdom', in P. Granfield and J. A. Jungmann (eds.), *Kyriakon: Festschrift Johannes Quasten*, 2 vols. (Münster: Aschendorff, 1970), i. 192–204, at p. 195.

[37] Buschmann, *Das Martyrium*, 298.

attending his death, with Mark 15. 33–9 // Matt. 27. 45–54 // Luke 23. 44–8 being the more comparable texts; from this perspective one might suggest Matt. 27. 54 // Luke 23. 47–8 as an even closer parallel. Dehandschutter offers, however, the key assessment: that 15. 1 reflects the general idea rather than direct knowledge of John 19. 35.[38] But if we are dealing only with the general idea, we can no longer distinguish between gospel tradition and gospel text. Once again, there is no more than a possibility of dependence on a specific gospel.

Mart. Pol. 16. 1

With regard to the administration of the *coup de grâce* by means of a short sword (ξιφίδιον), Lightfoot expresses a widely followed opinion: 'The incident doubtless presents itself to the mind of the writers as a parallel to John xix. 34...In both cases the act of piercing with the spear or sword was an exceptional act, which could not have been foreseen from the mode of execution.'[39] In the estimation of Schoedel (and similarly Dehandschutter), however, 'No parallelism with John 19. 34 is intended (we are not even told that the dagger pierced his side as we would expect if John were imitated).'[40] Such sharp disagreement over how to read the *Martyrdom* only increases the difficulty of determining whether the author here alludes to the Fourth Gospel.

Nevertheless, we should not let this disagreement regarding the intent of the author of the *Martyrdom* obscure its effect: the passage brings to mind, for virtually all its scholarly readers, the Johannine episode.

Or is it also a Matthean episode? To the end of Matt. 27. 49, a not-insignificant group of witnesses—ℵ B C L (Γ), 34 minuscule MSS, vg^{mss} mae—add αλλος δε λαβων λογχην ενυξεν αυτου την πλευραν και εξηλθεν υδωρ και αιμα, a phrase reminiscent of, but not identical to, John 19. 34 (ἀλλ' εἷς τῶν στρατιωτῶν λόγχῃ αὐτοῦ τὴν πλευρὰν ἔνυξεν καὶ ἐξῆλθεν εὐθὺς αἷμα καὶ ὕδωρ). This phrase is typically dismissed as a harmonizing addition from John 19.[41] But the wording of the phrase is distinctive enough to raise a

[38] Dehandschutter, *Martyrium Polycarpi*, 253.

[39] Lightfoot, *Apostolic Fathers*, 2. 3. 390; Müller, 'Martyrium', 11; Barnard, 'Defence', 195; Lieu, *Image and Reality*, 65 ('an unmistakable Gospel echo'); cf. Buschmann, *Das Martyrium*, 312.

[40] Schoedel, *Polycarp*, 72; Dehandschutter, *Martyrium*, 253. Earlier W. Reuning, *Zur Eklärung des Polykarpmartyriums* (Darmstadt: Wintersche Buchdruckerei, 1917), 20; also W. C. Weinrich, *Spirit and Martyrdom: A Study of the Work of the Holy Spirit in Contexts of Persecution and Martyrdom in the New Testament and Early Christian Literature* (Washington: University Press of America, 1981), 183 n. 34.

[41] So Bruce M. Metzger, *A Textual Commentary on the Greek New Testament*, 2nd edn. (Stuttgart: Deutsche Bibelgesellschaft and United Bible Societies, 1994), 59.

question against this consensus. Moreover, this combination of external support is intriguing, especially as none of the minuscule MSS are known for any Alexandrian affinities, and the uniformity of the wording of this phrase in the witnesses supporting it suggests the possibility of a common ancestor. Finally, its placement in the Matthean passion narrative—before the death of Jesus, when the stab of the lance would have been quite painful, rather than after—makes it a 'difficult' reading. In the words of Davies and Allison, 'we are almost moved to think the line original.'[42] Westcott and Hort placed double brackets around the words in question, but 'did not feel justified in removing them from the text'; they note that 'two suppositions alone are compatible with the whole evidence': either the words 'may belong to the genuine text of the extant form of Mt', or they comprise 'a *very early* interpolation'.[43] Either option raises the possibility that the author of the *Martyrdom* knew the phrase from a source (written or oral) other than the Johannine gospel.

In short, while here the possibility of dependence on John is clear, I am disinclined to raise this to the level of probability, particularly in view of the possibility of continuing influence of oral tradition.

Summary

This section of the investigation has focused on a single question: is there any demonstrable evidence that the author of the *Martyrdom of Polycarp* has made use of any of the gospels now included in the canonical New Testament? On the basis of the preceding investigation, a clear answer emerges, one that is entirely negative: in not a single instance have we been able to observe more than the possibility of dependence on a specific written gospel. To be sure, there are many verbal and conceptual parallels between the *Martyrdom of Polycarp* and the canonical gospels, but in none of these many instances does the evidence lead to any stronger conclusion. This does not mean that the writer did not know any of these documents (as Gregory points out, an inability to demonstrate use of a document does not prove non-use or ignorance of a document[44]), merely that we are unable to demonstrate such knowledge on the part of the author. The author of *Martyrdom* clearly knows and is deeply indebted to gospel tradition; the evidence leaves us unable, however, to demonstrate any use of a specific written version of it.

[42] W. D. Davies and D. C. Allison, *A Critical and Exegetical Commentary on Matthew*, 3 vols., ICC (Edinburgh: T. & T. Clark, 1997), iii. 627.

[43] B. F. Westcott and F. J. A. Hort, *The New Testament in the Original Greek: Introduction* [and] *Appendix*, 2nd edn. (London and New York: Macmillan, 1896), 21–2, emphasis added.

[44] Gregory, *Reception of Luke*, 5.

This conclusion is, admittedly, to a large extent shaped by the methodological approach adopted at the start: rather than assume the existence and availability of a corpus of documents, we looked, following the approach adopted by Gregory, for probative evidence of use of specific written documents. This 'strict', or 'minimalist', approach is required by the history of the canon. Even after the time of Irenaeus (in whose writings there are clear indications of an emerging core canon that includes four specific gospels), one cannot assume that citations or allusions to gospel material necessarily derive from the four canonical gospel narratives. Prior to Irenaeus, to use a less rigorous approach runs the risk of assuming the existence of that for which one is looking.

This negative conclusion to a very precise, targeted question is hardly, of course, the whole story. The absence of explicit citations has not hindered scholarship from drawing attention to the seemingly extensive parallels between the passion narratives as reported in the canonical gospel accounts and the report of the martyrdom of Polycarp of Smyrna.[45] Indeed, so extensive and explicit are these parallels, in the opinion of some, that they have been attributed to the work of a later, theologically motivated redactor who reworked an earlier briefer account by exaggerating existing parallels and introducing others.[46] But even though these proposals should be rejected—as I am persuaded that all the 'gospel parallels' are in fact part of the very warp and woof of the narrative—they serve none the less to spotlight a fundamental feature of the narrative: its desire to present 'a martyrdom in accord with the gospel' (*Mart. Pol.* 1. 1; cf. 19. 1).

But just what is it about Polycarp's martyrdom that is κατὰ τὸ εὐαγγέλιον? To that question I now turn.

GOSPEL TRADITION AND THE *MARTYRDOM OF POLYCARP*: THE *MARTYRDOM* AS INTERPRETATION OF GOSPEL TRADITION

Martyrdom κατὰ τὸ εὐαγγέλιον

The author of the *Martyrdom* clearly wishes to persuade his correspondents in Philomelium that Polycarp's martyrdom was κατὰ τὸ εὐαγγέλιον (1. 1; cf.

[45] For typical lists consult Lightfoot, *Apostolic Fathers*, 2. 1. 610–12 (essentially repeated in Barnard, 'Defence,' 194–5); Müller, 'Martyrium', 6–12; Camelot, *Martyre*, 200–2.

[46] E.g., Müller, 'Martyrium' 1–16; H. von Campenhausen, 'Bearbeitungen und Interpolationen des Polykarpmartyriums', SHAW 1957, repr. in *idem*, *Aus der Frühzeit des Christentums* (Tubingen: Mohr, 1963), 253–301.

19. 1, κατὰ τὸ εὐαγγέλιον Χριστοῦ). But what, precisely, does it mean for a martyrdom to be 'in accord with the gospel'? As Dehandschutter notes, many interpreters have understood this as indicating that it is a martyrdom that *imitates* the episodes and events in the passion of Jesus, one that *repeats* in its own time the things that happened to Jesus as he went to his death at the hands of the Romans.[47] But this sort of approach, emphasizing as it does the parallels with the gospel tradition as the key to both the meaning of the phrase κατὰ τὸ εὐαγγέλιον and the document in which it occurs, goes seriously astray in two significant respects.[48] First, it does not give sufficient weight to the explicit definition of a martyrdom κατὰ τὸ εὐαγγέλιον provided by the document; and secondly (as a consequence), it confuses a literary feature of the narrative with the meaning of the narrative.

With regard to the first point, defining a 'martyrdom according to the gospel', we may begin by noticing that in its initial occurrence the phrase 'a martyrdom according to the gospel' (τὸ κατὰ τὸ εὐαγγέλιον μαρτύριον) in 1. 1 is practically synonymous with a martyrdom 'according to the will of God' (cf. τὰ μαρτύρια πάντα τὰ κατὰ τὸ θέλημα τοῦ θεοῦ γεγονότα) in 2. 1. The close association of these two phrases is strengthened by the correlation of the other instance of the phrase, in 19. 1 (τὸ μαρτύριον . . . κατὰ τὸ εὐαγγέλιον Χριστοῦ γενόμενον), with the idea of 'the Lord, who makes the choice from among his own servants' (τὸν κύριον τὸν ἐκλογὰς ποιούμενον τῶν ἰδίων δούλων) in 20. 2. One may also note a fundamental point made in 1. 2a: namely, that Polycarp 'waited to be betrayed, just as the Lord did'. That is, Polycarp did not court or pursue arrest (in sharp contrast to Quintus, who went forward on his own—something which 'the gospel does not teach'); instead, 'as the Lord did' (ὡς καὶ ὁ κύριος), Polycarp waited for his pursuers to come to him.[49] In short,

[47] B. Dehandschutter, 'Le Martyre de Polycarpe et le développement de la conception du martyre au deuxième siècle', in E. A. Livingstone (ed.), *StPatr* 17, 2 (Oxford and New York: Pergamon, 1982), 659–68, at pp. 660–1; also *idem*, 'Century of Research', 505, 512–13. Examples include scholars as different in their approaches as Lightfoot (*Apostolic Fathers*, 2. 1. 610–12, 2. 3. 365) and H. von Campenhausen (*Die Idee des Martyriums in der alten Kirche* (Göttingen: Vandenhoeck & Ruprecht, 1936), 82–5, esp. p. 84: Polycarp's martyrdom is 'das ideale Vorbild aller Martyrien, die Passion Jesu selbst, wiederholt habe'); see also Camelot, *Martyre*, 200–1; Victor Saxer, *Bible et Hagiographie: Textes et thèmes bibliques dans les Actes des martyrs authentiques des premiers siècles* (Berne: Peter Lang, 1986), 27–9; cf. H. D. Betz, *Nachfolge und Nachahmung Jesu Christi im Neuen Testament*, BHT 37 (Tübingen: Mohr (Siebeck), 1967), 181–2.

[48] One could add a third, lesser respect: the inherent implausibility of many of the alleged 'parallels' (e.g., Polycarp's retreat to a farm not far from town as somehow parallel to Jesus going out to Gethsemane).

[49] Lightfoot (*Apostolic Fathers*, 2. 1. 619 n. 1) argues that περιέμενεν γὰρ ἵνα παραδοθῇ means 'he lingered *about* so as to be *in the way* of his captors', and that the later incident in mind is not ch. 5 (Polycarp fled from town to a country estate) but ch. 7 ('though he could have escaped from there to another place, he refused, saying, "May God's will be done"'), with the true gospel

rather than forcing matters, he allowed events to unfold according to God's will and timing.[50]

A second characteristic of a martyrdom *κατὰ τὸ εὐαγγέλιον* is indicated in 1. 2b: waiting to be betrayed in some way exemplifies 'not looking only to that which concerns ourselves, but also to that which concerns our neighbors'.[51] This concern for others is then characterized in 1. 2c as 'the mark of true and steadfast love', a love that seeks not just the salvation (*σώζεσθαι*) of oneself but of 'all the brothers and sisters as well'. Note further how in 3. 1 Germanicus is praised for defeating the devil by encouraging those condemned with him—that is, by showing concern for others. Perhaps a contrast is intended with Quintus, whose behaviour put at risk not only himself but apparently also those whom he forced to come forward with him (§4).

A third characteristic of a martyrdom *κατὰ τὸ εὐαγγέλιον* is endurance. Though this third point is not mentioned in 1. 2 as are the other two, it is none the less interesting to observe where the 'endurance' language turns up in the narrative:

1. After stating (in 2. 1) that 'blessed and noble' are 'all the martyrdoms that have taken place in accordance with the will of God', the narrative then continues: 'for who could fail to admire their nobility and patient endurance and loyalty to the Master?' (2. 2). Of these three terms, it is 'endurance' (*ὑπομονητικόν*) that is immediately picked up in the narrative: the martyrs 'endured' (*ὑπέμειναν*, 2. 2), wringing pity from the bystanders; they are 'those who endure' (*τοῖς ὑπομείνασιν*, 2. 3); they 'endured' (*ὑπέμειναν*, 2. 4) without denying their faith; and Germanicus encouraged others by his own 'endurance' (*ὑπομονῆς*, 3. 1).
2. In 13. 3, Polycarp asks to be tied rather than nailed to the post, 'for he who enables me to endure (*ὑπομεῖναι*) the fire will also enable me to remain (*ἐπιμεῖναι*) on the pyre'.
3. In 19. 1b–2a, the narrative informs us that Polycarp's martyrdom 'was in accord with the gospel of Christ. By his endurance (*διὰ τῆς ὑπομονῆς*) he defeated the unrighteous magistrate and so received the crown of immortality...'

parallels being Jesus' going up to Jerusalem for the last time in spite of the warnings of his disciples and thereby placing himself in danger, and his 'lingering in the garden when He knew the fate that awaited Him'. But the reference in §4 to those like Quintus who *προδιδόντας ἑαυτους* indicates that the emphasis in 1. 2 is indeed on the *παραδοθῇ* rather than the *περιέμενεν* (cf. Weinrich, *Spirit and Martyrdom*, 167).

[50] Cf. further 5. 2, the 'it is necessary' (*δεῖ*; also 12. 3); 6. 2, 'that he might fulfill his appointed destiny'; 7. 1, 'May God's will be done'.

[51] On the possible relationship of this phrase to Phil. 2. 4, see the discussion of *Mart. Pol.* 1. 2 in the Appendix below.

In short, at the beginning and end, precisely where the 'martyrdom according to the gospel' is being defined (1. 1–2. 1) or summarized (19), and in between at a critical moment in the narrative (13. 3), it is precisely 'endurance' that is being spotlighted.

To summarize the definition: as set out in the opening paragraphs of the narrative, a martyrdom *κατὰ τὸ εὐαγγέλιον*:

(1) is a matter of divine calling rather than human accomplishment or initiative;
(2) demonstrates a concern for the salvation or well-being of others (a point supported by an allusion to Pauline tradition[52]); and
(3) displays endurance in the midst of suffering.[53]

These characteristics—not the repetition, imitation, or recapitulation of events and details from the passion of Jesus—are the key elements, according to the narrative, of a martyrdom *κατὰ τὸ εὐαγγέλιον*.

To put the matter a bit differently, a gospel-shaped martyrdom is not one that merely recapitulates or imitates events of the passion of Jesus, but rather one that (regardless of whether it parallels any of the events of the passion) reflects a particular approach to (one might even say a theology of) martyrdom: one that reacts rather than initiates (thus permitting the divine will to be accomplished), one that demonstrates the concern for others exemplified by Jesus, and one that is characterized by endurance in the face of trials.

Defining a 'martyrdom according to the gospel' in this manner has an immediate effect on how one understands the parallels between the passion narrative and the martyrdom.

First, negatively, it means that the meaning of a martyrdom in accord with the gospel does not lie in the many alleged parallels (real or otherwise) between it and the passion of Jesus (the meaning, as we have just noted, lies elsewhere).

Second, positively, it suggests that the gospel parallels are simply a feature of the narrative genre.[54] That is, parallels with the gospel narratives are a

[52] None the less, while the phrasing is Pauline (see the discussion of 1. 2 below), the concept itself is not without roots in the gospel narrative; cf. Matt. 20. 28 // Mark 10. 45; Luke 22. 27; John 13. 14–17.

[53] This formulation is my modification of the definition given by Weinrich (*Spirit and Martyrdom*, 168) and adopted by Buschmann (*Das Martyrium*, 83): 'A martyrdom "according to the gospel", therefore, has three essential elements: 1) it is in obedience to a divine call and not a voluntary quest for suffering; 2) it serves to promote faithful endurance on the part of the brethren and thus their salvation; and 3) the martyr himself endures steadfastly his own suffering and death.'

[54] Cf. similarly Dehandschutter, 'Le Martyre', 662. Perhaps the parallels in the *Martyrdom of Polycarp* have been emphasized by scholarship more than those in other extant martyrdoms

widely shared feature of early Christian martyriological accounts; there is nothing unique or even particularly distinctive about this feature of the *Martyrdom of Polycarp.*[55] It is a mistake, therefore, to elevate a feature of the genre to the level of an interpretive key.

The *Martyrdom* as Interpretation

This recognition that the parallels are a feature of the genre, and not central to the meaning of the text, requires that we reconceptualize the relationship between the *Martyrdom* and the gospel tradition. A claim made by the document at the end of §4 offers a useful starting-point for doing so.

There the narrative specifically states that in regard to the model offered by Quintus—that of forcing the matter by going forward on one's own initiative—'the gospel does not so teach' (§4, *οὐκ οὕτως διδάσκει τὸ εὐαγγέλιον*). To state that the 'gospel does not teach' *X* would imply that it does teach something else—presumably the pattern of behaviour modelled by Polycarp. But with respect to the gospel narratives (at least as they are preserved in the canonical gospels), it is difficult to find any (even semi-explicit) 'teaching' upon which to base the central claim of the *Martyrdom of Polycarp*: namely, that the first, and primary, aspect of a martyrdom according to the gospel is to 'wait to be betrayed'. It is certainly possible to infer this from the narrative—for example, while Judas was executing his plot with the Jewish leaders, Jesus went about his own business, and his followers should do likewise—but it nowhere approaches the level of explicit or obvious 'teaching'.

The realization that one cannot identify a text or passage that 'teaches' the main point which the *Martyrdom* seeks to inculcate offers an important clue to understanding the relationship between the *Martyrdom* and the passion narrative: it is the fruit of an act of interpretation. In an incident that the gospel tradition *narrates*—namely, Jesus' betrayal and arrest in Gethsemane—the author of the *Martyrdom* discerns a foundational principle: namely, that a martyrdom according to the gospel is one in which the potential martyr *waits to be betrayed*, 'just as the Lord' (1. 2). In the polemical

because it 'bedeutet den Anfang einer Literaturgattung' (H. W. Surkau, *Martyrien in jüdischer und frühchristlicher Zeit* (Göttingen: Vandenhoeck & Ruprecht, 1938), 134).

[55] Cf. H. Delehaye, *Les Passions des martyrs et les genres littéraires* (Brussels: Bollandistes, 1921, 2nd edn. 1966), 20–2, esp. 21 ('Toute l'antiquité est pénétrée de cette pensée que le martyr souffre avec le Sauveur et reproduit sa passion en lui. On la retrouve un peu plus tard dans la lettre des Églises de Vienne et de Lyon, dans Hégésippe à propos de Jacques le Juste, dans la Passion de Perpétue et Félicité, et dans beaucoup d'autres textes'); earlier (and with more detail), Lightfoot, *Apostolic Fathers*, 2. 1. 612–13. For the accounts see H. A. Musurillo, *The Acts of the Christian Martyrs* (Oxford: Clarendon Press, 1972).

context of a debate about the proper understanding of martyrdom, the narrative identifies a specific and seemingly circumstantial element of the gospel tradition and elevates it to the status of a fundamental guideline. This manner of treating the passion narrative is not a matter of simple imitation: it involves reflection and interpretation. The author does not simply repeat the narrative as received, but instead offers a 'reading' of it (if one may be permitted to speak of a 'reading' of what may have been an oral account!) to support a particular understanding of martyrdom.

Recognizing the hermeneutical intent of the author frees us to think about the significance and function of these 'parallels' in their own right within the context of the narrative about Polycarp. Instead of viewing them as attempts, sometimes simplistic, awkward, or overreaching, to draw attention to (or even create, if necessary) parallels between the experience of Polycarp and the passion of Jesus, they can now be analysed with respect to their function and effect, first within the narrative and second within the larger politico-social context in which the narrative was written.

When we do so, we find that many of the incidents which may 'parallel' the gospel narratives serve much more fully the author's goal of establishing the character of Polycarp: first, as a charismatic and prophetic bishop who models in his approach to martyrdom obedience to the divine will, and second, as a figure who embodies many of the heroic and/or athletic virtues and characteristics idealized by Graeco-Roman culture. In comparison to these fundamental concerns, the bulk of the 'gospel parallels', while not insignificant as such, are secondary features of a narrative whose central emphases fall elsewhere.

I conclude this section by offering a few quick sketches of what it might look like to interpret some of the supposed 'parallels' (or, in one case, a 'non-parallel') in their own right within the narrative. Though only sketches, they are suggestive of the possibilities that the different approach to the matter proposed here might open up.

1. The observation in *Mart. Pol.* 6. 2a (discussed above) that 'it was really impossible for him to remain hidden, since the very persons who betrayed him were people of his own household' (*οἰκεῖοι*) is often understood as a parallel to Matt. 10. 36 ('and a man's foes will be those of his own household', *οἰκιακοί*), and thus an instance where the martyrdom of Polycarp is allegedly *κατὰ τὸ εὐαγγέλιον*.

But to focus only on this aspect draws attention away from the significance of this particular sentence in the author's narrative. The assertion that 'it was really impossible for him to remain hidden' (6. 2a) functions apologetically to explain why Polycarp did not, as Matt. 10. 23 advises, continue to flee his pursuers, especially as he had the opportunity to do so (cf. 7. 1, 'he still could have escaped'). The narrator has a tricky problem here: he wants to demonstrate that Polycarp's martyrdom was indeed in accord with the gospel, in that Polycarp 'waited to be betrayed' (in sharp contrast to Quintus), but at this particular point Polycarp's actions seem *not* to accord with the teaching of Matt. 10. 23, or the example of Jesus as portrayed in John 7. 1; 8. 59; 10. 39. Stressing the 'inevitability' of capture enables the author to downplay this point by highlighting Polycarp's submission to the divine will (7. 1, 'may God's will be done').

2. Both Jesus and Polycarp are reported to have accurately predicted the manner of their death, the one by crucifixion and the other by fire; the key passage is *Mart. Pol.* 5. 2, 'It is necessary that I be burned alive' (discussed above). So here there is a firm parallel between the gospel tradition and the *Martyrdom.*

The gospel parallel, however, should not be permitted to overshadow the function and importance of this prediction in the *Martyrdom*, which has more to do with the narrative's characterization of Polycarp than the establishment of one more parallel between him and Jesus. Notice that when the fulfilment of the prophecy in 5. 2 is later reported in 12. 3, the narrator goes out of his way to emphasize that Polycarp spoke 'prophetically' (προφητικῶς) on that earlier occasion—thus establishing the basis for the important claim that will be made in 16. 2: namely, that Polycarp proved to be a 'prophetic teacher in our own time...for every word which came from his mouth was accomplished'. Any parallel to the gospel tradition is at best secondary to the author's goal of characterizing Polycarp as the model catholic bishop.[56]

3. A third example may be drawn from a 'non-parallel': the manner in which Polycarp goes to his execution. In a sharp contrast, Polycarp does not recapitulate the pre-execution suffering of Jesus and many other martyrs (including, apparently, all the others martyred in Smyrna at that time); indeed, he goes to his death virtually unmarked at all.[57] Also, unlike some other martyrs whose outstretched arms mimicked the cross,[58] Polycarp is neither nailed nor stretched out; instead, he is tied to a stake. In this latter instance, the contrast serves the author's agenda: in this particular case, to reinforce the *difference* between the suffering Christ and his disciples (cf. 17. 2–3).

4. In *Mart. Pol.* 7. 2, when Polycarp's pursuers (fully 'armed...as though chasing after an armed rebel') finally arrive late at night at the farm where Polycarp is staying, the old man 'immediately ordered that a table be set for

[56] If one reads καθολικης with bspE (mL read αγιας).

[57] He suffers only an accidental bruise to his shin as he is made to dismount from Herod's carriage (8. 3).

[58] E.g., Blandina, one of the martyrs of Lyons and Vienne (Euseb. *HE* 5. 1. 41).

them to eat and drink as much as they wished at that hour'. This meal is not, as is sometimes claimed, a parallel to the 'last supper';[59] instead, we see Polycarp filling the function of a gracious and generous host, solicitous of the well-being of his 'guests'. Thus not only does Polycarp fulfil secular social expectations and models of an ideal host,[60] but he also thereby shames those who pursued him—so much so that 'many regretted that they had come after such a godly old man' (7. 3). Thus they become, almost against their will, witnesses to the godly character of Polycarp. If there is a gospel parallel involved here, the centurion's declaration as Jesus died (Matt. 27. 54 // Mark 15. 39 // Luke 23. 47) would seem to be the more likely one. In any case, this particular scene involves no superficial parallel to the gospel tradition, but rather plays a key role in the narrative's developing characterization of Polycarp.

5. As a final example, let us consider the cumulative effect of a number of seemingly unrelated incidents in the story:

In 7. 1, Polycarp's pursuers are able to capture him only because *he* chooses to stop running ('Though he still could have escaped from there to another place, he refused, saying, "May God's will be done".').

In 7. 2, he orders a table to be set for the newly arrived 'guests' (that is, his pursuers) as *he* fills the role of the gracious host, the social superior extending hospitality to visitors.

In 8. 1, the entourage departs for town with their prisoner only after *he* has finished praying for an extended length of time: effectively he, not they, determines when events unfold.[61]

In 8. 2–3, it is Polycarp who exhibits dispassionate self-control, in contrast to Herod and Nicetes, the designated representatives of imperial power, who embarrass themselves by their manner of questioning, their failure to persuade him, and their lack of self-control.

In 9. 2–12. 1, at the hearing in the arena (that symbol of Roman power and control), it is the proconsul who behaves in a womanly fashion by threatening, pleading, insisting;[62] it is Polycarp who again demonstrates self-mastery and

[59] So Müller ('Martyrium', 9): 'Es ist die Parallele zum Abendmahl und zur Einsetzung der Eucharistie.'

[60] Moreover, it should not be missed that by emphasizing Polycarp's commitment to prayer (cf. 7. 3; 8. 1; also 14), the narrator presents Polycarp as fulfilling another characteristic of idealized Graeco-Roman heroes.

[61] Cf. Lieu, who (reading the text in light of John 17, however) observes, 'As there, the effect is to stress that Polycarp, like Jesus, is not the victim of events but is in control both of them and of himself' (*Image and Reality*, 71).

[62] L. S. Cobb, ' "Be A Man": The Rhetoric and Politics of Masculinity in Early Christian Martyrologies', paper presented at the Annual Meeting of the SBL, Denver, Colo., 19 Nov. 2001.

philosophical detachment, who by his steadfastness effectively controls the direction and outcome of the hearing. It is Polycarp who delivers the closest thing there is to a verdict in this narrative, when he brings the hearing to a climax (and effectively to a close) by declaring boldy, *Χριστιανός εἰμι*.

In 13. 2–15. 1, it is Polycarp who with quiet dignity undresses himself before the stake; who instructs the executioners in proper procedure (tied but not nailed); who compels them to wait to start the fire until he has finished praying.

Who's in charge here? In a situation intended to display Roman power and authority, to remind everyone who is in control, the author of the *Martyrdom* presents a subversive narrative that mocks Roman pretensions. Rome's agents—the *διωγμῖται*, Herod, the proconsul—only think they are in charge. In the world of the narrative, they all bend to the will of a determined 86-year-old bishop, who himself is merely an obedient instrument of the divine will of the Christian God (cf. 2. 1; 1. 2). The declaration in §21 (regardless of whether it is supplementary or secondary[63]) catches the point clearly: Polycarp 'was arrested by Herod, when Philip of Tralles was high priest during the proconsulship of Statius Quadratus, but while Jesus Christ was reigning as king forever'.

The several instances in this last example typically are not details that are seen as 'gospel parallels'; indeed, in some respects the comportment and unmarked appearance of Polycarp stand in sharp contrast to the mocked and beaten Jesus. Yet, taken together, they comprise a strong parallel to John 19. 11 (where Jesus answers Pilate, 'You would have no power over me unless it had been given you from above'): God, not Rome, is really in control. This is the level at which the passion narratives shape the narrative of Polycarp's martyrdom.

Summary

These few examples have tried to demonstrate some of the implications of my main point, to which it is time to return. The relationship of the *Martyrdom of Polycarp* to the passion narratives of the gospel tradition is more complex than at first appears. The *Martyrdom* does not merely (or simplistically) imitate or repeat the gospel; it interprets it. For the author of the *Martyrdom*, the passion narrative is not a guide or map or movie script for retracing the steps of Jesus from Gethsemane to Golgotha. The more significant parallels

[63] For the former view cf. Lightfoot, *Apostolic Fathers*, 2. 1. 626–38; for the latter, Schoedel, *Polycarp*, 77–8.

between the passion narratives and the *Martyrdom* are to be found at a deeper level, where the passion narrative serves as a 'master paradigm' in terms of modelling a foundational theological perspective or even world-view. The document offers a not-unsophisticated example of a contemporizing 'reading' of an authoritative narrative. We should therefore add the name of Marcianus[64] of Smyrna (20. 1) to our list of those who in the second century struggled to maintain a faithful understanding (from their perspective, at least) of the gospel narratives by interpreting them for, and in a different and rapidly-changing, socio-political and theological context.

APPENDIX: THE REST OF THE NEW TESTAMENT IN THE *MARTYRDOM OF POLYCARP*

The gospels having been covered above, the same focal question will now be directed to the rest of the New Testament: *is there any demonstrable evidence that the author of the* Martyrdom of Polycarp *has made use of any of the other texts now included in the canonical New Testament?* The same procedures and methodologies that were followed for the gospels will be employed here. As before, there is no attempt to list all possible parallels between the rest of the New Testament and the *Martyrdom of Polycarp*, since Dehandschutter has compiled a very detailed list of verbal similarities or parallels.[65] Proceeding through the *Martyrdom* in the order of its text, this survey will focus on those instances which seem most likely (or which have been claimed to be so) to offer probative evidence of the knowledge or use of *specific* texts or documents.

Mart. Pol. Inscr.

Saxer claims that the stereotypical salutation with which the address concludes ('may mercy and peace, and love of God the Father and our Lord Jesus Christ be multiplied', *ἔλεος καὶ εἰρήνη καὶ ἀγάπη θεοῦ πατρὸς καὶ τοῦ κυρίου ἡμῶν Ἰησοῦ Χριστοῦ πληθυνθείη*) 'contient une citation de l'Epître de Jude' (*ἔλεος ὑμῖν καὶ εἰρήνη καὶ*

[64] Or is it 'Marcion'? *Marcianum* L] *Μαρκιωνος* m; *Μαρκου* bpsa. Lightfoot (*Apostolic Fathers*, 2. 3. 398–9), followed by Holmes (*Apostolic Fathers*, 242–3) adopt the reading of the Latin, whereas Dehandschutter (*Martyrium Polycarpi*, 126, 187–9) and now Buschmann (*Das Martyrium*, 356–7) make a persuasive case for reading 'Marcion'.

[65] See Dehandschutter, *Martyrium Polycarpi*, 241–54; also Buschmann, *Das Martyrium*.

ἀγάπη πληθυνθείη).[66] Equally similar, however, are a number of other texts, including 1 Tim. 1. 2 and 2 Tim. 1. 2 (*χάρις ἔλεος εἰρήνη ἀπὸ θεοῦ πατρὸς καὶ Χριστοῦ Ἰησοῦ τοῦ κυρίου ἡμῶν*), *1 Clem.* prescript. (*χάρις ὑμῖν καὶ εἰρήνη ἀπὸ παντοκράτορος θεοῦ διὰ Ἰησοῦ Χριστοῦ πληθυνθείη*), and Pol. *Phil.* prescript. (*ἔλεος ὑμῖν καὶ εἰρήνη παρὰ θεοῦ παντοκράτορος καὶ Ἰησοῦ Χριστοῦ τοῦ σωτῆρος ἡμῶν πληθυνθείη*). In short, Jude 2 is only one of a number of texts to which the author may be alluding.

Mart. Pol. 1. 2

In *Mart. Pol.* 1. 2 the phrase 'not looking only to that which concerns ourselves, but also to that which concerns our neighbors' (*μὴ μόνον σκοποῦντες τὸ καθ' ἑαυτοὺς ἀλλὰ καὶ τὸ κατὰ τοὺς πέλας*) is often said to be a quotation of Phil. 2. 4 (*μὴ τὰ ἑαυτῶν ἕκαστος σκοποῦντες ἀλλὰ καὶ τὰ ἑτέρων ἕκαστοι*).[67] But the conceptual link between the two texts is stronger than the verbal link. The closest connection between the two texts is the presence of *σκοπέω*, which in early Christian literature is largely a Pauline term (Phil. 2. 4, 3. 17; Rom. 16. 17; 2 Cor. 4. 18; Gal. 6. 1; elsewhere Luke 11. 35; *1 Clem.* 51. 1). For the plural *τά* in Philippians, *Martyrdom* has the singular *τό* (as in 1 Cor. 10. 24, 33), and the use of *πέλας* in *Martyrdom* is the only instance in either the New Testament or the Apostolic Fathers. Furthermore, the conceptual link is not limited to Phil. 2. 4, but is shared with 1 Cor. 10. 23 and 10. 33, the latter of which expresses, like the concluding sentence of 1. 2, the concern that others might be saved (note the occurrence of the passive of *σῴζω* in both). In short, we quite likely have here a definite allusion, but one which cannot be linked confidently to a specific text or document.[68]

Mart. Pol. 2. 3a

A *TLG* search of 3 BCE–CE 2 for the phrase 'eyes of the heart' produces only Eph. 1. 18 (*τοὺς ὀφθαλμοὺς τῆς καρδίας*), *1 Clem.* 36. 2 (*οἱ ὀφθαλμοὶ τῆς καρδίας*) and 59. 3 (*τοὺς ὀφθαλμοὺς τῆς καρδίας*), *Corpus Herm.* 4. 11 (*τοῖς τῆς καρδίας ὀφθαλμοῖς*) and 7. 1 (*τοῖς ὀφθαλμοῖς τῆς καρδίας*), and *Mart. Pol.* 2. 3 (*τοῖς τῆς καρδίας ὀφθαλμοῖς*). Hagner thinks it is 'very probable' that *1 Clem.* 59. 3 is dependent on Eph. 1. 18.[69] Either one—or neither—could be the source of *Mart. Pol.* 2. 3. The phrase is probably allusive, but we have no way of identifying a specific source or target of the allusion.

[66] Saxer, *Bible et Hagiographie*, 27; cf. Metzger, *Canon*, 121 ('an expansion of the salutation of Jude 2').

[67] E.g., F. X. Funk, K. Bihlmeyer, and W. Schneemelcher (eds.), *Die Apostolischen Väter*, 3rd edn. (Tübingen: Mohr Siebeck, 1970), 121; Holmes, *Apostolic Fathers*, 226–7 (regrettably).

[68] Cf. similarly Dehandschutter, *Martyrium*, 242; Massaux, *Influence*, ii. 50.

[69] D. A. Hagner, *The Use of the Old and New Testaments in Clement of Rome*, NovTSup 34 (Leiden: Brill, 1973), 223–4 (he mentions but does not discuss 36. 2).

Mart. Pol. 2. 3b

Here we encounter what Dehandschutter terms 'de meest directe verwijzing naar een nieuwtestamentische tekst' to be found in *Martyrdom*.[70] The text and its most relevant parallels read as follows.[71]

1 Cor. 2. 9: *καθὼς γέγραπται· ἃ ὀφθαλμὸς οὐκ εἶδεν καὶ οὖς οὐκ ἤκουσεν καὶ ἐπὶ καρδίαν ἀνθρώπου οὐκ ἀνέβη, ἃ/ὅσα ἡτοίμασεν ὁ Θεὸς τοῖς ἀγαπῶσιν αὐτόν.*[72]

1 Clem. 34. 8: *λέγει γάρ· ὀφθαλμὸς οὐκ εἶδεν καὶ οὖς οὐκ ἤκουσεν, καὶ ἐπὶ καρδίαν ἀνθρώπου οὐκ ἀνέβη, ὅσα ἡτοίμασεν τοῖς ὑπομένουσιν αὐτόν.*[73]

Mart. Pol. 2. 3: . . . *τὰ τηρούμενα τοῖς ὑπομείνασιν ἀγαθά, ἃ οὔτε οὖς ἤκουσεν οὔτε ὀφθαλμὸς εἶδεν, οὔτε ἐπὶ καρδίαν ἀνθρώπου ἀνέβη, ἐκείνοις δὲ ὑπεδείκνυτο ὑπὸ τοῦ κυρίου,*[74]

2 Clem. 11. 7: *ληψόμεθα τὰς ἐπαγγελίας ἃς οὖς οὐκ ἤκουσεν οὐδὲ ὀφθαλμὸς εἶδεν οὐδὲ ἐπὶ καρδίαν ἀνθρώπου ἀνέβη.*

The problem of the identity of Paul's source in 1 Cor. 2. 9 is well known.[75] *1 Clem.* 34. 8 is probably dependent on 1 Cor. 2. 9.[76] What about *Mart. Pol.* 2. 3? That *Martyrdom* and *1 Clement* both have a participial form of *ὑπομείνω* suggests a link in that direction; on the other hand, the statement in *Martyrdom* that the Lord has shown these things to the martyrs could echo Paul's declaration in 1 Cor. 2. 10, 'but to us God revealed' (*ἡμῖν δὲ ἀπεκάλυψεν ὁ θεός*).[77] Against both these texts stands the reversed order 'ear . . . eye' in *Martyrdom*, which it shares with *2 Clement*; against all three is the distinctive *οὔτε . . . οὔτε . . . οὔτε* construction in *Martyrdom*. The author of the martyrdom is almost certainly citing or alluding to a saying well known to his

70 Dehandschutter, *Martyrium*, 243; cf. *idem*, 'Century of Research', 507.

71 For other parallels—the statement occurs widely in Jewish and early Christian literature, including the *Gospel of Thomas* 17—see Buschmann, *Das Martyrium*, 106 n. 94; Weinrich, *Spirit and Martyrdom*, 184 n. 40.

72 Re the variation: *α* p[46] ℵ D F G 33,1739 *rel* ClemAlex] *οσα* p[11vid] A B C[vid] *pc* Didymus.

73 This is the text of *Alexandrinus*; the variations in the other witnesses (C L S ClemAlex) are all in the direction of 1 Cor. 2. 9.

74 Minor textual variations in some witnesses (see Dehandschutter, *Martyrium*, 113, for details) are all in the direction of 1 Cor. 2. 9.

75 See Anthony C. Thiselton, *The First Epistle to the Corinthians* (Grand Rapids, Mich., and Cambridge: Eerdmans, 2000), 249–52.

76 Hagner, *Use*, 76, 204–8; A. Lindemann, *Paulus im ältesten Christentum: Das Bild des Apostels und die Rezeption der paulinischen Theologie in der frühchristlichen Literatur bis Marcion*, BHT 58 (Tübingen: J. C. B. Mohr, 1979), 187–8; cf. *idem*, *Die Clemensbriefe*, HNT 17 (Tübingen: Mohr Siebeck, 1992), 107.

77 So T. Zahn, *Geschichte des neutestamentlichen Kanons*, i (Erlangen and Leipzig, 1889), 790–1 (as cited by Dehandschutter, *Martyrium*, 243 n. 638). Differently Massaux (*Influence*, ii. 50): 'no element of the text and context leads to 1 Cor. 2:9.'

readers, but the source of the saying (or text to which he is alluding) is clearly indeterminable.

Mart. Pol. 7. 1b

For the possibility that the reference in 7. 1b to 'the will of God' is an allusion to Acts 21. 14, see the discussion of this passage in the analysis of gospel parallels above.

Mart. Pol. 9. 1

For possible references to Acts 18. 9–10 and 23. 11, see the discussion of this passage in the analysis of gospel parallels above.

Mart. Pol. 10. 2

In response to a request from the proconsul, Polycarp is reported to have replied: 'You I might have considered worthy of a reply, *for we have been taught to pay proper respect to rulers and authorities appointed by God*, as is fitting, as long as it does us no harm' (*δεδιδάγμεθα γὰρ ἀρχαῖς καὶ ἐξουσίαις ὑπὸ θεοῦ τε ταγμέναις τιμὴν ... ἀπονέμειν*). Lightfoot proposes that 'the reference in *δεδιδάγμεθα* is especially to Rom. xiii. 1 sq, I Pet. ii. 13 sq', while Metzger suggests that the passage 'seems to be a recollection' of Rom 13:1, 7 and Titus 3:1'.[78] The relevant texts run as follows: Rom. 13. 1: *ἐξουσίαις ... ὑποτασσέσθω. οὐ γὰρ ἔστιν ἐξουσία εἰ μὴ ὑπὸ θεοῦ, αἱ δὲ οὖσαι ὑπό θεοῦ τεταγμέναι εἰσιν*; 13. 7: *τῷ τὴν τιμὴν τὴν τιμήν*; Titus 3. 1: *ἀρχαῖς ἐξουσίαις ὑποτάσσεσθαι, πειθαρχεῖν*; 1 Pet. 2. 13–14: *ὑποτάγητε ... εἴτε βασιλεῖ ὡς ὑπερέχοντι, εἴτε ἡγεμόσιν*. Any link to 1 Pet. 2 is clearly a conceptual one only. The reference to *ἀρχαῖς καὶ ἐξουσίαις* (the only instance in the Apostolic Fathers) could echo Titus 3 (where the large majority of MSS read the *καί*), while the strongest verbal link is to Rom. 13 (esp. *ὑπὸ θεοῦ τεταγμέναι* and *τιμήν*). The discordant element is the absence of the verb common to Rom. 13, Titus 3, and 1 Pet. 2, *ὑποτάσσω*; instead, *Martyrdom* has *ἀπονέμειν*, a relatively uncommon term (cf. 1 Pet. 3. 7; *1 Clem.* 1. 3; Ign. *Magn.* 3. 1; Justin, *Dial.* 103. 4; 130. 4). It seems reasonable to see *Mart. Pol.* 10. 2 as part of a tradition or stream of teaching arising out of texts like Romans, Titus, and perhaps 1 Peter; but whether this came to the author via textual or oral transmission is a more uncertain judgement. The possibility of a link to Romans is evident; there is not, however, sufficient evidence to indicate probability of textual dependence.

[78] Lightfoot, *Apostolic Fathers*, 2. 3. 381; Metzger, *Canon*, 121; cf. Dehandschutter, *Martyrium*, 250.

Mart. Pol. 14. 1

The phrase κύριε ὁ θεὸς ὁ παντοκράτωρ (14. 1, cf. 19. 2) occurs also at Rev. 11. 17; 15. 3; and 16. 7, while in 4. 8 and 21. 22 the nominative replaces the vocative (cf. also 1. 8 and 19. 6). The shorter κύριος παντοκράτωρ occurs in an allusion to 2 Sam. 7. 8, LXX, in 2 Cor. 6. 18, and (ὁ) παντοκράτωρ Θεός (in various cases) in *1 Clement* (inscr.; 2. 3; 32. 4; 62. 2). Buschmann notes that the phrase is the common stuff of Jewish prayer,[79] while Massaux notes the possibility of liturgical influence on this part of the *Martyrdom.*[80] It is indeed possible that the *Martyrdom* is here dependent on Revelation,[81] but it is equally possible that both Revelation and the *Martyrdom* reflect a common tradition, influence, or source.

Mart. Pol. 17. 2

Metzger suggests that 'the phrase "Christ... the blameless One for sinners" ' in 17. 2 'may be reminiscent of' 1 Pet. 3. 18; Dehandschutter adds 1 Pet. 1. 19.[82] The connection, however, is more conceptual than verbal, and is insufficient to serve as probative evidence of a knowledge of 1 Peter.

Summary

Here, as in the discussion of the gospels earlier, a clear answer emerges to the question of whether there is any *demonstrable* evidence that the author of the *Martyrdom* has made use of any of the non-gospel material now included in the canonical New Testament. In not a single instance have we been able to observe more than the possibility of dependence on a specific written text. The kind of evidence one finds, for example, in the report about the martyrs in Lyons and Vienne—for example, a twelve-word verbally exact match to Phil. 2. 6[83]—is simply not to be found in the *Martyrdom of Polycarp.* To be sure, there are many verbal and conceptual parallels between the *Martyrdom* and the documents in question, but in none of these many instances does the evidence lead to any stronger conclusion than mere possibility. This does not mean that the writer did not know any of these documents (Gregory's point is worth repeating: an inability to demonstrate use of a document does not prove non-use or ignorance of a document[84]), merely that we are unable to demonstrate such knowledge on the part of the author.

[79] Buschmann, *Das Martyrium,* 274; see 273–4 n. 111 for a full list of parallels (many Septuagintal). Cf. also David Aune, *Revelation,* i, Word Bible Commentary 52a (Dallas: Word, 1997), 306; ii, Word Bible Commentary 52b (Nashville: Thomas Nelson, 1998), 642.

[80] Massaux, *Influence,* ii. 50.

[81] So Hill, *Johannine Corpus,* 358.

[82] Metzger, *Canon,* 121; Dehandschutter, *Martyrium,* 254.

[83] Euseb., *HE* 5. 2. 2 (... μιμηταὶ Χριστοῦ ἐγένοντο, ὃς ἐν μορφῇ θεοῦ ὑπάρχων οὐχ ἁρπαγμὸν ἡγήσατο τὸ εἶναι ἴσα θεῷ, ὥστε ...).

[84] Gregory, *Reception of Luke,* 5.

Once again, this negative conclusion to a very precise and targeted question is hardly the whole story. If, for example, one were to ask whether it is probable that the church in Smyrna possessed copies of at least some of the documents now found in the canonical New Testament, the evidence supplied by the letter that the congregation's bishop wrote some years earlier to the church in Philippi suggests that the answer would be an assured 'yes'.[85] It is not possible, however, to confirm that hypothesis on the basis of evidence supplied by the *Martyrdom of Polycarp.*

[85] See the discussion in Ch. 8 of companion volume of the use of the New Testament in Polycarp's *Letter to the Philippians.*

Bibliography

A Committee of the Oxford Society of Historical Theology, *The New Testament in the Apostolic Fathers* (Oxford: Clarendon Press, 1905).

Aland, K., *Did the Early Church Baptize Infants?* (London: SCM Press, 1963).

Alcock, S., *Graecia Capta: The Landscapes of Roman Greece* (Cambridge: Cambridge University Press, 1993).

Alexander, L. C. A., 'The Living Voice: Scepticism towards the Written Word in Early Christianity and Graeco-Roman Texts', in D. J. A. Clines, S. E. Fowl, and S. E. Porter (eds.), *The Bible in Three Dimensions*, JSOTSup 87 (Sheffield: JSOT Press, 1990), 221–47.

Alon, G., 'Halakah in the Teaching of the Twelve Apostles (*Didache*)', in Draper (ed.), Didache *in Modern Research*, 165–94.

—— , *The Jews in their Land in the Talmudic Age (70–640 CE)* (ET Cambridge, Mass.: Harvard University Press, 1989).

Anderson, J. G. C., 'Explorations in Galatia Cis Halym, Part II', *JHS* 19 (1899), 280 ff.

Anderson, P. N., *The Christology of the Fourth Gospel: Its Unity and Disunity in the Light of John 6* (Valley Forge, Pa.: Trinity Press International, 1997).

—— , 'The *Sitz im Leben* of the Johannine Bread of Life Discourse and its Evolving Context', in R. A. Culpepper (ed.), *Critical Readings of John 6*, Biblical Interpretation Series (Leiden: Brill, 1997), 1–59.

Ando, Clifford, *Imperial Ideology and Provincial Loyalty in the Roman Empire* (Berkeley: University of California Press, 2000).

Attridge, H. W., 'Appendix: The Greek Fragments', in B. Layton (ed.), *Nag Hammadi Codex II, 2–7*, NHS 20 (Leiden: Brill, 1989), 95–128.

—— (ed.), *Nag Hammadi Codex I (The Jung Codex)*, 2 vols., NHS 22–3 (Leiden: Brill, 1985).

Audet, J.-P., *La Didachè: Instructions des Apôtres*, ÉBib (Paris: Gabalda, 1958).

Aune, *Revelation*, i, Word Bible Commentary 52a (Dallas: Word, 1997); ii, Word Bible Commentary 52b (Nashville: Thomas Nelson, 1998).

Badian, E., *Foreign Clientelae (264–70BC)* (Oxford: Clarendon Press, 1958).

Baker, W. R., *Personal Speech-Ethics: A Study of the Epistle of James against its Background*, WUNT 2.68 (Tübingen: J. C. B. Mohr (Paul Siebeck), 1995).

Bakke, O. M., *'Concord and Peace': A Rhetorical Analysis of the First Letter of Clement with an Emphasis on the Language of Unity and Sedition*, WUNT 2.143 (Tübingen: Mohr Siebeck, 2001).

Balabanski, V., *Eschatology in the Making: Mark, Matthew and the Didache*, SNTSMS 97 (Cambridge: Cambridge University Press, 1997).

Bammel, E., 'Schema und Vorlage von *Didache* 16', in F. L. Cross (ed.), *StPatr* 4, TU 79 (Berlin: Akademie-Verlag, 1961), 253–62.

Baptism, Eucharist and Ministry, Faith and Order Paper, 111 (Geneva: World Council of Churches, 1982).

Bardsley, H. J., 'The Testimony of Ignatius and Polycarp to the Writings of St. John', *JTS* 14 (1913), 207–20, 489–500.

Barnard, L. W., 'The Dead Sea Scrolls, Barnabas, the *Didache* and the Later History of the "Two Ways" ', in *Studies in the Apostolic Fathers and their Background* (New York: Schocken Books; Oxford: Basil Blackwell, 1966), 87–108.

—— , 'The Problem of St. Polycarp's Epistle to the Philippians', in *idem, Studies in the Apostolic Fathers and their Background* (New York: Schocken Books; Oxford: Basil Blackwell, 1966), 31–40.

—— , 'In Defence of Pseudo-Pionius' Account of Saint Polycarp's Martyrdom', in P. Granfield and J. A. Jungmann (eds.), *Kyriakon: Festschrift Johannes Quasten*, 2 vols. (Münster: Aschendorff, 1970), i. 192–204 = *idem, Studies in Church History and Patristics* (Thessaloniki: Patriarchal Institute for Patristic Studies, 1978), 224–41.

Barth, G., 'Matthew's Understanding of the Law', in G. Bornkamm, G. Barth, and H. J. Held, *Tradition and Interpretation in Matthew* (ET Philadelphia: Westminster; London: SCM Press, 1963), 58–164.

Bartlett, D. L., *Ministry in the New Testament* (Minneapolis: Fortress, 1993).

Barton, S. C., 'Gospel Wisdom', in *idem* (ed.), *Where shall Wisdom be Found?* (Edinburgh: T. & T. Clark, 1999), 93–110.

Bartsch, H.-W., *Gnostisches Gut und Gemeindetradition bei Ignatius von Antiochien* (Gütersloh: Gütersloher Verlag, 1940).

Bauckham, R. J., *The Fate of the Dead: Studies on the Jewish and Christian Apocalypses*, NovTSup 93 (Leiden, Boston, and Cologne: Brill, 1998).

—— , *James: Wisdom of James, Disciple of Jesus the Sage* (London and New York: Routledge, 1999).

Bauer, J. B., *Die Polykarpbriefe*, KAV 5 (Göttingen: Vandenhoeck & Ruprecht, 1995).

Bauer, W., *Die Briefe des Ignatius von Antiochia und der Polykarpbrief*, HNT, Die Apostolischen Väter, 2 (Tübingen: Mohr Siebeck, 1920).

—— , *Rechtgläubigkeit und Ketzerei im ältesten Christentum*, BHT 10 (Tübingen: Mohr, 1964).

Baumeister, T., *Die Anfänge der Theologie des Martyriums* (Münster: Aschendorff, 1980).

Bell, H. I., and Skeat, T. C., *Fragments of an Unknown Gospel* (London: British Museum, 1935).

—— —— , *The New Gospel Fragments* (London: British Museum, 1935).

Bellinzoni, A. J., *The Sayings of Jesus in the Writings of Justin Martyr*, NovTSup 17 (Leiden: Brill, 1967).

—— , 'The Gospel of Matthew in the Second Century', *SC* 9 (1992), 197–259.

—— , 'The Gospel of Luke in the Second Century CE', in R. P. Thompson and T. E. Phillips (eds.), *Literary Studies in Luke–Acts: Essays in Honor of Joseph B. Tyson* (Macon, Ga.: Mercer University Press, 1998), 56–76.

Benoît, A., *Le Baptême chrétien au second siècle: la théologie des pères*, Études d'histoire et de philosophie religieuses, 43 (Paris: Presses Universitaires de France, 1953).

Berding, K., *Polycarp and Paul: An Analysis of their Literary and Theological Relationship in Light of Polycarp's Use of Biblical and Extra-Biblical Literature*, VCSup 62 (Leiden: Brill, 2002).

Berger, K., *Die Gesetzesauslegung Jesu: ihr historischer Hintergrund im Judentum und im Alten Testament*, WMANT 40 (Neukirchen-Vluyn: Neukirchener Verlag, 1972).

—— , 'Hellenistische Gattungen im Neuen Testament', *ANRW* 2. 25. 2 (1984), 1149–71.

—— , *Im Anfang war Johannes: Datierung und Theologie des vierten Evangeliums* (Stuttgart: Quell Verlag, 1997).

Betz, H. D., *Nachfolge und Nachahmung Jesu Christi im Neuen Testament*, BHT 37 (Tübingen: Mohr Siebeck, 1967).

—— , *Galatians: A Commentary on Paul's Letter to the Churches in Galatia*, Hermeneia (Philadelphia: Fortress, 1979).

Betz, J., 'Die Eucharistie in der Didache', *Archiv für Liturgiewissenschaft*, 11 (1969), 10–39.

—— , 'The Eucharist in the *Didache*', in Draper (ed.), *The* Didache *in Modern Research*, 244–75.

Betz, O., *συμφωνέω κτλ*, *TDNT* ix. 304–9.

Beyschlag, K., *Clemens Romanus und der Frühkatholizismus: Untersuchungen zu I Clemens 1–7*, BHT 35 (Tübingen: Mohr Siebeck, 1966).

Bhaldraithe, E. de, 'The Christology of Ignatius of Antioch', in M. Wiles and E. Yarnold (eds.), *StPatr* 36 (Leuven: Peeters, 2001), 200–6.

Biblia Patristica: Index des citations et allusions bibliques dans la littérature patristique. i: *Des origines à Clément d'Alexandrie et Tertullien*, ed. J. Allenbach (Paris: Éditions du Centre National de la Recherche Scientifique, 1975).

Bigg, C., 'Notes on the Didache', *JTS* 6 (1905), 411–15.

Binder, D. D., *Into the Temple Courts: The Place of the Synagogue in the Second Temple Period* (Atlanta: Society of Biblical Literature, 1999).

Blaise, A., *Lexicon Latinitatis Medii Aevi* (Turnholt: Brepols, 1975).

Blank, J., 'Die Irrlehrer des ersten Johannesbriefes', *Kairos*, 26 (1984), 166–93.

Blass, F., Debrunner, A., and Funk, R. W., *A Greek Grammar of the New Testament and Other Early Christian Literature* (Chicago: University of Chicago Press, 1961).

Bloomquist, L. G., *The Function of Suffering in Philippians*, JSNTSup 78 (Sheffield: JSOT Press, 1993).

Bogart, J., *Orthodox and Heretical Perfectionism in the Johannine Community as Evident in the First Epistle of John* (Missoula, Mont.: Scholars Press, 1976).

Bormann, L., *Philippi: Stadt und Christengemeinde zur Zeit des Paulus*, NovTSup 78 (Leiden: Brill, 1995).

Bornkamm, G., 'Das Doppelgebot der Liebe', in W. Eltester (ed.), *Neutestamentliche Studien für Rudolf Bultmann*, BZNW 21 (Berlin: Töpelmann, 1954), 85–93; repr. in *idem*, *Geschichte und Glaube*, i: *Gesammelte Aufsätze* 3 (Munich: Kaiser, 1968), 37–45.

—— , 'Die eucharistische Rede im Johannesevangelium', *ZNW* 47 (1956), 161–9, repr. in *idem*, *Geschichte und Glaube, Erster Teil: Gesammelte Aufsätze* 3 (Munich: Kaiser, 1968), 60–7.

Bouriant, U., 'Fragments du texte grec du livre d'Énoch et de quelques écrits attribués à saint Pierre', in *Mémoirs publiés par les members de la mission archéologique française au Caire*, 12,1 (Paris, 1892).

Bousset, W., *Die Evangelienzitate Justins des Märtyrers* (Göttingen: Vandenhoeck & Ruprecht, 1891).

Bouyer, L., 'Les sacraments dans l'évangile johannique', *BVC* 1 (1953), 121–2.

Bovon, F., *Luke 1: A Commentary on the Gospel of Luke 1:1–9:50*, Hermeneia (Minneapolis: Fortress, 2002).

Bovon-Thurneysen, A., 'Ethik und Eschatologie im Philipperbrief des Polykarp von Smyrna', *TZ* 29 (1973), 241–56.

Bowe, B. E., *A Church in Crisis* (Minneapolis: Fortress, 1988).

Bradshaw, P. F., *The Search for the Origins of Christian Worship: Sources and Methods for the Study of Early Liturgy*, 2nd edn. (New York and Oxford: Oxford University Press, 2002).

Brant, J. A., 'The Place of *Mimēsis* in Paul's Thought', *Studies in Religion/Sciences Religieuses*, 22 (1993), 285–300.

Brent, A., 'Pseudonymity and Charisma in the Ministry of the Early Church', *Augustinianum*, 27 (1987), 347–76.

—— , 'History and Eschatological Mysticism in Ignatius of Antioch', *ETL* 65 (1989), 311–16.

—— , 'The Relations between Ignatius of Antioch and the *Didascalia Apostolorum*', *SC* 8 (1991), 129–56.

—— , *Cultural Episcopacy and Ecumenism*, Studies in Christian Mission, 6 (Leiden: Brill, 1992).

—— , 'The Ignatian Epistles and the Threefold Ecclesiastical Order', *JRH* 17 (1992), 18–32.

—— , 'Diogenes Laertius and the Apostolic Succession', *JEH* 44 (1993), 367–89.

—— , *Hippolytus and the Roman Church in the Third Century: Communities in Tension before the Emergence of a Monarch-Bishop*, VCSup 31 (Leiden: Brill, 1995).

—— , 'Ignatius of Antioch and the Imperial Cult', *VC* 52 (1998), 30–58.

—— , *The Imperial Cult and the Development of Church Order Concepts and Images of Authority in Paganism and Early Christianty before the Age of Cyprian*, VCSup 45 (Leiden: Brill, 1999).

—— , 'Ignatius of Antioch and the Second Sophistic', *ZAC*, forthcoming.

Brockhaus, U., *Charisma und Amt: die paulinische Charismenlehre auf dem Hintergrund der frühchristlichen Gemeindefunktionen* (Wuppertal: Rolf Brockhaus, 1972).

Brodie, T. L., 'Greco-Roman Imitation of Texts as a Partial Guide to Luke's Use of Sources', in C. H. Talbert (ed.), *Luke–Acts: New Perspectives from the Society of Biblical Literature Seminar* (New York: Crossroad, 1984), 17–46.

Brooks, S. H., *Matthew's Community: The Evidence of his Special Sayings Material*, JSNTSup 16 (Sheffield: Sheffield Academic Press, 1987).

Brown, C. T., *The Gospel and Ignatius of Antioch*, Studies in Biblical Literature, 12 (New York: Peter Lang, 2000).

Brown, M. P., *The Authentic Writings of Ignatius* (Durham, NC: Duke University Press, 1963).
—— , *The Epistles of John*, AB 30 (Garden City, NY: Doubleday, 1982).
Brown, R. E., 'The Johannine Sacramentary Reconsidered', *TS* 23 (1962), 183–206.
—— , *The Gospel according to John*, 2 vols., AB 29–29A (Garden City, NY: Doubleday, 1966, 1970).
—— , 'The relationship to the Fourth Gospel shared by the author of 1 John and by his opponents', in E. Best and R. McL. Wilson (eds.), *Text and Interpretation* (Cambridge: Cambridge University Press, 1979), 57–68.
—— , *An Introduction to New Testament Christology* (New York: Paulist Press, 1994).
—— , *An Introduction to the New Testament* (New York: Doubleday, 1997).
Brox, N., ' "Doketismus"—eine Problemanzeige', *ZKG* 95 (1984), 301–14.
Brückner, W., 'Zur Kritik des Jakobusbriefes', *ZWT* 17 (1874), 530–41.
Bryennios, P., *Διδαχὴ τῶν δώδεκα ἀποστόλων* (Constantinople: S. I. Boutura, 1883).
Büchsel, F., *Die Johannesbriefe* (Leipzig: Deichert, 1970).
Bultmann, R., *The History of the Synoptic Tradition* (ET Oxford: Basil Blackwell, 1963).
—— , 'Ignatius und Paulus', in E. Dinkler (ed.), *Exegetica: Aufsätze zur Erforschung des Neuen Testaments* (Tübingen: Mohr Siebeck, 1967), 400–11.
—— , *The Gospel of John: A Commentary* (ET Philadelphia: Westminster, 1971).
—— , *The Johannine Epistles*, Hermeneia (ET Philadelphia: Fortress, 1973).
—— , *Theologie des Neuen Testaments*, UTB 630, 9th edn. (Tübingen: Mohr Siebeck, 1984).
Bumpus, H. B., *The Christological Awareness of Clement of Rome and its Sources* (University Press of Cambridge, 1972).
Bunge, W. F., 'The Christology of Ignatius of Antioch' (Th. D. diss., Harvard University, 1966).
Burchard, C., *Der Jakobusbrief*, HNT 15.1 (Tübingen: J. C. B. Mohr (Paul Siebeck), 2000).
Burghart, W., 'Did Saint Ignatius of Antioch Know the Fourth Gospel?', *TS* 1 (1940), 130–56.
Burtchaell, J. T., *From Synagogue to Church: Public Services and Offices in the Earliest Christian Communities* (Cambridge: Cambridge University Press, 1992).
Buschmann, G., *Martyrium Polycarpi: Eine formkritische Studie. Ein Beitrag zur Frage nach der Entstehung der Gattung Märtyrerakte* (Berlin and New York: De Gruyter, 1994).
—— , *Das Martyrium des Polykarp*, KAV 6 (Göttingen: Vandenhoeck & Ruprecht, 1998).
Butler, B. C., 'The Literary Relations of *Didache*, Ch. XVI', *JTS* 11 (1960), 265–83.
—— , 'The "Two Ways" in the *Didache*', *JTS* 12 (1961), 27–38.
Cacitti, R., *Grande Sabato: Il contesto pasquale quartodecimano nella formazione della teologia del martirio* (Milan: Vita e pensiero, 1994).
Camelot, P. T., *Ignace d'Antioche [et] Polycarpe de Smyrne, Lettres: Martyre de Polycarpe*, 4th edn., SC 10 (Paris: Cerf, 1969).

Cameron, R., *Sayings Traditions in the Apocryphon of James*, HTS 34 (Philadelphia: Trinity Press International, 1984).

Campbell, R. A., *The Elders* (Edinburgh: T. & T. Clark, 1994).

Campenhausen, H. von, *Die Idee des Martyriums in der alten Kirche* (Göttingen: Vandenhoeck & Ruprecht, 1936).

—— , *Polykarp von Smyrna und die Pastoralbriefe* (Heidelberg: C. Winter, 1951).

—— , 'Bearbeitungen und Interpolationen des Polykarpmartyriums', *Sitzungsberichte Akademie Heidelberg* (1957), 5–48; also in *idem*, *Aus der Frühzeit des Christentums: Studien zur Kirchengeschichte des ersten und zweiten Jahrhunderts* (Tübingen: Mohr, 1963), 253–301.

—— , *Ecclesiastical Authority and Spiritual Power in the Church of the First Three Centuries* (ET Stanford, Calif.: Stanford University Press, 1969).

Carruth, S., 'Praise for the Churches: The Rhetorical Function of the Opening Sections of the Letters of Ignatius of Antioch', in E. Castelli and H. Taussig (eds.), *Reimagining Christian Origins: A Colloquium Honoring Burton L. Mack* (Valley Forge, Pa.: Trinity, 1996), 295–310.

Carson, D. A., 'The Three Witnesses and the Eschatology of 1 John', in T. E. Schmidt and M. Silva (eds.), *To Tell the Mystery*, JSNTSup 100 (Sheffield: Sheffield Academic Press, 1994), 216–32.

Castelli, E. A., *Imitating Paul: A Discourse of Power* (Louisville, Ky.: Westminster/John Knox Press, 1991).

Catechism of the Catholic Church (London: Geoffrey Chapman, 1994).

Cerfaux, L., 'La multiplication des pains dans la liturgie de la Didachè', *Bib* 40 (1959), 943–58.

Chadwick, H., 'The Silence of Bishops in Ignatius', *HTR* 43 (1950), 169–72.

—— , *The Sentences of Sextus*, TS 5 (Cambridge: Cambridge University Press, 1959).

Chesnut, G. F., 'The Ruler and the Logos in Neopythagorean, Middle Platonic, and Late Stoic Political Philosophy', *ANRW* 2. 16. 1 (1978), 1310–32.

Childs, B., *The New Testament as Canon: An Introduction* (Valley Forge, Pa.: Trinity, 1994).

Chow, J. K., *Patronage and Power: A Study of Social Networks at Corinth*, JSNTSup 75 (Sheffield: JSOT Press, 1992).

Claußen, C., *Versammlung, Gemeinde, Synagoge: Das hellenistisch-jüdische Umfeld der frühchristlichen Gemeinden*, SUNT 27 (Göttingen: Vandenhoeck & Ruprecht, 2002).

Clerici, L., *Einsammlung der Zerstreuten: Liturgiegeschichtliche Untersuchung zur Vor- und Nachgeschichte der Fürbitte für die Kirche in Didache 9,4 und 10,5*, Liturgiewissenschaftliche Quellen und Forschungen, 44 (Münster: Aschendorffsche Verlagsbuchhandlung, 1966).

Cobb, L. S., ' "Be A Man": The Rhetoric and Politics of Masculinity in Early Christian Martyrologies' (paper presented at the Annual Meeting of the SBL, Denver, 19 Nov. 2001).

Cody, A., 'The *Didache*: An English Translation', in C. N. Jefford (ed.), *The* Didache *in Context: Essays on its Text, History and Transmission*, NovTSup 77 (Leiden: Brill, 1995), 3–14.

Collins, A. Y., 'From Noble Death to Crucified Messiah', *NTS* 40 (1994), 481–503.

Connolly, R. H., 'The Didache in Relation to the Epistle of Barnabas', *JTS* 33 (1932), 237–53.

—— , 'Agape and Eucharist in the Didache', *DR* 55 (1937), 477–89.

Conzelmann, H., 'Bemerkungen zum Martyrium Polykarps', in *Sitzungsberichte Akademie Göttingen* (Göttingen: Vandenhoeck & Ruprecht, 1978).

—— , '*εὐχαριστέω κτλ*', *TDNT* ix. 407–15.

—— , A. Lindemann, *Arbeitsbuch zum Neuen Testament*, 14th edn., UTB 52 (Tübingen: Mohr Siebeck, 2004).

Corell, A., *Eschatology and Church in the Gospel of St John* (London: SPCK, 1958); translation of *Consummatum est: Eskatologi och kyrka i Johannesevangeliet* (Stockholm: Svenska kyrkans diakonistyrelses bokförlag, 1950).

Corwin, V., *St. Ignatius and Christianity in Antioch* (New Haven: Yale University Press, 1960).

Countryman, L. W., 'The Intellectual Role of the Early Catholic Episcopate', *Church History*, 48 (1979), 261–8.

Court, J. M., 'The Didache and St. Matthew's Gospel', *SJT* 34 (1981), 109–20.

Credner, K. A., *Beiträge zur Einleitung in die biblischen Schriften* (Halle, 1832).

Cross, F. L. (ed.), *Oxford Dictionary of the Christian Church*, 3rd edn., ed. E. A. Livingstone (Oxford: Oxford University Press, 1997).

Crossan, J. D., *The Birth of Christianity* (New York: HarperSanFrancisco, 1998).

Cullmann, O., *Baptism in the New Testament*, SBT 1 (London: SCM Press, 1950).

—— , *Early Christian Worship*, SBT 10 (London: SCM Press, 1953).

—— , 'The Meaning of the Lord's Supper in Primitive Christianity', in *idem* and F. J. Leenhardt (eds.), *Essays on the Lord's Supper* (Atlanta: John Knox, 1958), 5–23.

Culpepper, R. A. (ed.), *Critical Readings of John 6*, Biblical Interpretation Series 22 (Leiden: Brill, 1997).

Cumont, F., *Religions orientales dans la paganisme romain* (Paris: Geuthner, 1929).

Dahl, N. A., 'Der erstgeborene Satans und der Vater des Teufels (Polyk 7:1 und Joh 8:44)', in W. Eltester and F. H. Kettler (eds.), *Apophoreta: Festschrift für Ernst Haenchen*, BZNW 30 (Berlin: A. Töpelmann, 1964), 70–84.

Danby, H., *The Mishnah Translated from the Hebrew with Introduction and Brief Explanatory Notes* (Oxford: Oxford University Press, 1933).

Daniélou, J., *The Theology of Jewish Christianity* (ET London: Darton, Longman and Todd, 1964).

Davids, P. H., *The Epistle of James: A Commentary on the Greek Text*, NIGTC (Grand Rapids, Mich.: Eerdmans, 1982).

Davies, W. D., *The Setting of the Sermon on the Mount* (Cambridge: Cambridge University Press, 1966).

—— and Allison, D. C., *A Critical and Exegetical Commentary on Matthew*, 3 vols. ICC (Edinburgh: T. & T. Clark, 1988–97).

Davila, J. R., *Liturgical Works*, Eerdmans Commentaries on the Dead Sea Scrolls, 6 (Grand Rapids, Mich.: Eerdmans, 2000).

De Boer, M. C., 'Jesus the Baptizer: 1 John 5:5–8 and the Gospel of John', *JBL* 107 (1988), 87–106.

—— , 'Comment: Which Paul?', in W. S. Babcock (ed.), *Paul and the Legacies of Paul* (Dallas: Southern Methodist University Press, 1990), 45–54.

Dehandschutter, B., *Martyrium Polycarpi: een literair-kritische Studie*, BETL 52 (Leuven: Universitaire Presse, 1979).

—— 'Le Martyre de Polycarpe et le développement de la conception du martyre au deuxième siècle', in E. A. Livingstone (ed.), *StPatr* 17/2 (Oxford and New York: Pergamon, 1982), 659–68.

—— , 'Polycarp's Epistle to the Philippians: An Early Example of "Reception" ', in J.-M. Sevrin (ed.), *The New Testament in Early Christianity*, BETL 86 (Leuven: Leuven University Press, 1989), 275–91.

—— , 'The *Martyrium Polycarpi*: A Century of Research', *ANRW* 2.27.1 (1993), 485–522.

—— , 'Hagiographie et histoire: à propos des Actes et Passions des Martyrs', in M. Lamberigts and P. van Deun (eds.), *Martyrium in Multidisciplinary Perspective: Mémorial L. Reekmans* (Leuven: Peeters, 1995), 295–301.

—— , 'The Martyrdom of Polycarp and the Outbreak of Montanism', *ETL* 75 (1999), 430–7.

—— , 'The Text of the *Martyrdom of Polycarp* again (with a note on the Greek Text of Polycarp, ad Phil.)', in F. Garcia Martinez and G. P. Luttikhuizen (eds.), *Jerusalem, Alexandria, Rome: Studies in Ancient Cultural Interaction in Honour of A. Hilhorst* (Leiden: Brill, 2003), 101–6.

Delehaye, H., *Les Passions des martyrs et les genres littéraires* (Brussels: Bollandistes, 1921; 2nd edn. 1966).

Demandt, A., *Der Idealstaat: die politischen Theorien der Antike*, 3rd edn. (Cologne and Vienna: Böhlau, 2000).

Denney, J., 'He that Came by Water and Blood', *Expositor*, 7 (1908), 416–28.

Denton, D. R., 'Hope and Perseverance', *SJT* 34 (1981), 313–20.

Deppe, D. B., *The Sayings of Jesus in the Epistle of James* (D.Th. dissertation, Free University of Amsterdam; Ann Arbor: Bookcrafters, 1989).

Deutsch, C., *Hidden Wisdom and the Easy Yoke: Wisdom, Torah and Discipleship in Matthew 11.25–30*, JSNTSup 18 (Sheffield: JSOT Press, 1987).

Dibelius, M. 'Die Mahl-Gebete der Didache', *ZNW* 37 (1938), 32–41, 126–7.

—— , and Conzelmann, H., *The Pastoral Epistles: A Commentary*, Hermeneia (Philadelphia: Fortress, 1972).

—— , *James: A Commentary*, ET Hermeneia (Philadelphia: Fortress, 1976).

Diels, H., and W. Kranz (eds.), *Die Fragmente der Vorsokratiker*, 6th edn. (Berlin: Weidman, 1974–5).

Dillman, C. N., 'A Study of Some Theological and Literary Comparisons of the Gospel of Matthew and the Epistle of James' (Ph.D. diss., University of Edinburgh, 1978).

Dix, G., *The Shape of the Liturgy* (Westminster: Dacre, 1945).

Dölger, F. J., 'Das Apollobildchen von Delphi als Kriegsamulett des Sulla', in *Antike und Christentum*, iv (Münster: Aschendorff, 1934), 68–9.

—— , 'Demeter und Dionysos-Figürchen als Glücksanhänger nach einer Mahnpredigt des Apollonius von Tyana', in *Antike und Christentum*, iv (Münster: Aschendorff, 1934), 277–9.

Döpp, S., and W. Geerlings (eds.), *Dictionary of Early Christian Literature* (New York: Crossroad, 2000).

Döring, K., *Exemplum Socratis: Studien zur Sokratesnachwirkung in der kynisch-stoischen Popularphilosophie der frühen Kaiserzeit und im frühen Christentum*, Hermes 42 (Wiesbaden: Steiner, 1979).

Draper, J .A., 'A Commentary on the Didache in the Light of the Dead Sea Scrolls and Related Documents' (Ph.D. diss., Cambridge University, 1983).

—— , 'Torah and Troublesome Apostles in the *Didache* Community', *NovT* 33 (1991), 347–72.

—— , 'Christian Self-Definition against the "Hypocrites" in *Didache* 8', in E. H. Lovering (ed.), *Society of Biblical Literature 1992 Seminar Papers* (Atlanta: Scholars Press, 1992), 362–77.

—— , 'Weber, Theissen and the Wandering Charismatics of the Didache', *JECS* 6 (1998), 541–76.

—— , 'The Didache in Modern Research: An Overview', in Draper (ed.), *The* Didache *in Modern Research*, 1–42.

—— , 'Ritual Process and Ritual Symbol in Didache 7–10', *VC* 54 (2000), 121–58.

—— , 'Social Ambiguity and the Production of Text: Prophets, Teachers, Bishops, and Deacons and the Development of the Jesus Tradition in the Community of the *Didache*', in Jefford (ed.), *The* Didache *in Context*, 284–312.

—— , 'A Continuing Enigma: The "Yoke of the Lord" in *Didache* 6:2–3 and Early Jewish–Christian Relations', in P. J. Tomson and D. Lambers-Petry (eds.), *The Image of Judaeo-Christians in Ancient Jewish and Christian Literature*, WUNT 158 (Tübingen: Mohr Siebeck, 2003), 106–23.

—— , 'Does the (Final) Version of the Didache and Matthew Reflect an "Irrevocable Parting of the Ways" with Judaism?', in H. van de Sandt (ed.), *The Didache and Matthew: Two Documents from the same Jewish-Christian Milieu?* (Assen: van Gorcum Press, 2004), 217–41.

—— (ed.), *The* Didache *in Modern Research*, AGAJU 37 (Leiden: Brill, 1996).

Drews, P., 'Untersuchungen zur Didache', *ZNW* 5 (1904), 53–79.

Duff, P. B., 'Apostolic Suffering and the Language of Processions in 2 Corinthians 4:7–10', *BTB* 21 (1991), 158–65.

Dunn, J. D. G., 'Jesus: Teacher of Wisdom or Wisdom Incarnate?', in S. C. Barton (ed.), *Where shall Wisdom be Found?* (Edinburgh: T. & T. Clark, 1999), 75–92.

Easton, B. S., 'New Testament Ethical Lists', *JBL* 51 (1932), 1–12.

Edwards, M. J., 'Ignatius and the Second Century: An Answer to R. Hübner', *ZAC* 2 (1998), 214–26.

Edwards, R. B., *The Johannine Epistles* (Sheffield: Sheffield Academic Press, 1996).

Egli, E., *Altchristliche Studien: Martyrien und Martyrologien ältester Zeit* (Zürich, 1887).

Ehrhard, A., *Die altchristliche Literatur und ihre Erforschung von 1884–1900*, i: *Die vornicäische Literatur*, Straßburger Theologische Studien, Supplementband 1 (Freiburg im Breslau: Herdersche Verlagshandlung, 1900).

Ehrman, B. D., '1 John 4.3 and the Orthodox Corruption of Scripture', *ZNW* 79 (1988), 221–43.

—— (ed.), *The Apostolic Fathers, i and ii*, LCL 24 (Cambridge, Mass.: Harvard University Press, 2003).

Eisenstadt, S. N., and Roniger, L., *Patrons, Clients and Friends: Interpersonal Relations and the Structure of Trust in Society* (Cambridge: Cambridge University Press, 1984).

Elbogen, I., *Der jüdische Gottesdienst in seiner geschichtlichen Entwicklung*, 3rd edn. (Frankfurt am Main: J. Kauffmann, 1931).

Elliott, J. H., 'Elders as Honored Household Heads and not Holders of "Office" in Earliest Christianity: A Review Article', *BTB* 33 (2003), 77–82.

Emmel, S. (ed.), *Nag Hammadi Codex III,5: The Dialogue of the Savior*, NHS 26 (Leiden: Brill, 1984).

Everding, H. E., Jun., 'A Response to Arthur J. Bellinzoni', *SC* 9 (1992), 259–60.

Faivre, A., and Faivre, C., 'Genèse d'un texte et recourse aux Écritures: Ignace, *aux Ephésiens* 14,1–16,2', *RSR* 65 (1991), 173–96.

Falk, D. K., 'Prayer in the Qumran Texts', in W. Horbury, W. D. Davies, and J. Sturdy (eds.), *The Cambridge History of Judaism*, iii: *The Early Roman Period* (Cambridge: Cambridge University Press, 1999), 852–76.

Fantham, E., 'Imitation and Decline: Rhetorical Theory and Practice in the First Century after Christ', *Classical Philology*, 73 (1978), 102–16.

——, 'Imitation and Evolution: The Discussion of Rhetorical Imitation in Cicero *De oratore* 2. 87–97 and Some Related Problems of Ciceronian Theory', *Classical Philology*, 73 (1978), 1–16.

Faraone, C. A., *Talismans and Trojan Horses: Guardian Statues in Ancient Greek Myth and Ritual* (Oxford: Oxford University Press, 1992).

Farrar, F. W., 'The Bearing of the "Teaching" on the Canon', *Expositor*, 8 (1884), 81–91.

Fears, J. R., 'The Cult of Virtues and Roman Imperial Ideology', *ANRW* 2.17.2 (1987), 828–948.

Fee, G. D., *Paul's Letter to the Philippians*, NICNT (Grand Rapids, Mich.: Eerdmans, 1995).

Ferguson, E., 'Christian and Jewish Baptism according to the *Epistle of Barnabas*', in S. E. Porter and A. R. Cross (eds.), *Dimensions of Baptism: Biblical and Theological Studies*, JSNTSup 234 (Sheffield: Sheffield Academic Press, 2002), 207–23.

Finkelstein, L., 'The Birkat-Ha-Mazon', *JQR* 19 (1928/9), 211–62.

Fiorenza, E. Schüssler, *In Memory of Her: A Feminist Reconstruction of Christian Origins* (New York: Crossroad, 1989).

Fischer, J. A., *Die Apostolischen Väter griechisch und deutsch* (Munich: Kösel Verlag, 1956).

Fisher, N. R. E., *Hybris: A Study in the Values of Honour and Shame in Ancient Greece* (Warminster: Aris & Phillips, 1992).

Fitzmyer, J. A., *The Gospel of Luke (I–IX)*, AB 28 (Garden City, NY: Doubleday, 1981).

Flusser, D., 'Paul's Jewish-Christian Opponents in the *Didache*', in S. Shaked, D. Shulman, and G. G. Stroumsa (eds.), *Gilgul: Essays on Transformation, Revolution and Permanence in the History of Religions, Dedicated to R. J. Zwi Werblowsky*, Studies in the History of Religions, Supplements to Numen, 50 (Leiden: Brill, 1987), 71–90; repr. in Draper (ed.), *The* Didache *in Modern Research*, 195–211.

Forbes, C., 'Comparison, Self-Praise and Irony: Paul's Boasting and the Conventions of Hellenistic Rhetoric', *NTS* 32(1986), 1–30.

Fraenkel, J. J., *Hybris* (Utrecht: P. den Boer, 1941).

Franke, P. R., and Nollé, M. K., *Die Homonoia-Münzen Kleinasiens und der thrakischen Randgebiete*, Saarbrücker Studien zur Archäologie und alten Geschichte, 10, ed. A. Furtwängler, P. R. Franke, and C. Reinsberg (Saarbrück: Druckerei und Verlag, 1997).

Frankemölle, H., *Der Brief des Jakobus*, ÖTKNT 17 (Gütersloh: Gütersloher Verlag-Haus; Würzburg: Echter Verlag, 1994).

Frey, J., *Die johanneische Eschatologie*, i: *Ihre Probleme im Spiegel der Forschung seit Reimarus*, WUNT 96 (Tübingen: J. C. B. Mohr (Paul Siebeck), 1997).

—— , 'Das vierte Evangelium auf dem Hintergrund der älteren Evangelientradition: Zum Problem: Johannes und die Synoptiker', in T. Söding (ed.), *Johannesevangelium—Mitte oder Rand des Kanons? Neue Standortbestimmungen*, QD 203 (Freiburg: Herder, 2003), 60–118.

Freyne, S., *Galilee from Alexander the Great to Hadrian 323 BCE to 135 CE: A Study of Second Temple Judaism* (Edinburgh: T. & T. Clark, 1980).

Fridrichsen, A., 'Themelios, 1 Kor. 3,11', *TZ* 2 (1946), 316–17.

Funk, F. X., K. Bihlmeyer, and W. Schneemelcher (eds.), *Die Apostolischen Väter*, 3rd edn. (Tübingen: Mohr Siebeck, 1970).

Gärtner, B., *The Temple and the Community in Qumran and the New Testament*, SNTSMS 1 (Cambridge: Cambridge University Press, 1965).

Garrow, A. J. P., *The Gospel of Matthew's Dependence on the* Didache, JSNTSup 254 (London: T. & T. Clark International, 2004).

Gehrke, H.-J., *Stasis: Untersuchungen zu den inneren Kriegen in den griechischen Staaten des 5. und 4. Jahrhunderts v. Chr.*, Vestigia, 35 (Munich: Beck, 1985).

Gelston, A., *The Eucharistic Prayer of Addai and Mari* (Oxford: Clarendon Press, 1992).

Giet, S., 'Coutume, évolution, droit canon, à propos de deux passages de la "Didachè" ', *RDC* 16 (1966), 118–32.

—— , *L'Énigme de la Didachè*, Publications de la faculté des lettres de l'université de Strasbourg, 149 (Paris: Éditions Ophrys, 1970).

Glare, P. G. W. (ed.), *Oxford Latin Dictionary*, vi: *Pactus–Qualitercumque* (Oxford: Clarendon Press, 1977).

Glover, R., 'The Didache's Quotations and the Synoptic Gospels', *NTS* 5 (1958), 12–29.

Gokey, F. X., *The Terminology for the Devil and Evil Spirits in the Apostolic Fathers* (Washington: The Catholic University of America Press, 1961).

Goltz, E. A., *Das Gebet in der ältesten Christenheit* (Leipzig: J. C. Hinrichs'sche Buchhandlung, 1901).

——, *Tischgebete und Abendmahlsgebete in der altchristlichen und in der griechischen Kirche*, TU n.s. 14 (Leipzig: Hinrichs, 1905).

Goodenough, E. R., 'John a Primitive Gospel', *JBL* 64 (1945), 145–82.

Goodspeed, E. J., *The Meaning of Ephesians* (Chicago: University of Chicago Press, 1933).

——, 'The Didache, Barnabas and the Doctrina', *ATR* 27 (1945), 228–47.

Gordon, M. M., *Assimilation in American Life: The Role of Race, Religion, and National Origins* (New York: Oxford University Press, 1973 [1964]).

Goulder, M. D., 'Ignatius' "Docetists" ', *VC* 53 (1999), 16–30.

——, 'A Poor Man's Christology', *NTS* 45 (1999), 332–48.

Grant, R. M., 'The Decalogue in Early Christianity', *HTR* 40 (1947), 1–18.

——, 'Scripture and Tradition in St. Ignatius of Antioch', *CBQ* 25 (1963), 322–35.

——, *The Apostolic Fathers: A New Translation and Commentary*, i: *An Introduction* (New York: Thomas Nelson and Sons, 1964).

——, *The Formation of the New Testament* (New York: Harper & Row, 1965).

——, *The Apostolic Fathers*, iv: *Ignatius of Antioch* (London: Thomas Nelson & Sons, 1966).

Greene, T. M., *The Light in Troy: Imitation and Discovery in Renaissance Poetry* (New Haven: Yale University Press, 1982).

Gregory, A., *The Reception of Luke and Acts in the Period before Irenaeus: Looking for Luke in the Second Century*, WUNT 2.169 (Tübingen: Mohr Siebeck, 2003).

Greiff, A., *Das älteste Pascharituale der Kirche, Did. 1–10 und das Johannesevangelium*, Johanneische Studien, 1 (Paderborn: Schöningh, 1929).

Grillmeier, A., *Christ in Christian Tradition*, i (London: Mowbrays, 1975).

Gronewald, M., 'Unbekanntes Evangelium oder Evangelienharmonie (Fragment aus dem "Evangelium Egerton")', *Kölner Papyri*, 6 (PapyCol, 7) (Cologne, 1987), 136–45.

Gryglewicz, F., 'L'Épitre de St. Jacques et l'Évangile de St. Matthieu', *Roczniki Theologicano-Kanoniczne*, 8 (1961), 33–55.

Guillaumin, M. L., 'En marge du "Martyre de Polycarpe": le discernement des allusions scripturaires', in *Forma Futuri: Studi in onore del Cardinale M. Pellegrino* (Turin Bottega d'Erasmo, 1975), 462–9.

Gundry, R., '*ΕΥΑΓΓΕΛΙΟΝ*: How Soon a Book?', *JBL* 115 (1996), 321–5.

Hagner, D. A., *The Use of the Old and New Testaments in Clement of Rome*, NovTSup 34 (Leiden: Brill, 1973).

——, 'The Sayings of Jesus in the Apostolic Fathers and in Justin Martyr', in D. Wenham (ed.), *The Jesus Tradition outside the Gospels*, Gospel Perspectives, 5 (Sheffield: JSOT Press, 1985), 233–68.

Hahnemann, G., *The Muratorian Fragment and the Development of the Canon* (Oxford: Clarendon Press, 1992).

Halleux, A. de, 'Ministers in the *Didache*', in Draper (ed.), *The* Didache *in Modern Research*, 300–20.

Halliwell, S., *The Aesthetics of Mimesis: Ancient Texts and Modern Problems* (Princeton: Princeton University Press, 2002).

Hamerton-Kelly, R. G., 'A Girardian Interpretation of Paul: Rivalry, Mimesis and Victimage in the Corinthian Correspondence', *Semeia*, 33 (1985), 65–81.

Hammond Bammel, C. P., 'Ignatian Problems', *JTS* 33 (1982), 62–97.

Hanson, K. C., and Oakman, D. E., *Palestine in the Time of Jesus: Social Structures and Social Conflicts* (Minneapolis: Fortress, 1998).

Haraguchi, T., 'Das Unterhaltsrecht des frühchristlichen Verkündigers', *ZNW* 84 (1993), 178–95.

Harnack, A. von, *Die Lehre der zwölf Apostel nebst Untersuchungen zur ältesten Geschichte der Kirchenverfassung und des Kirchenrechts*, TU 2 (Leipzig: Hinrichs'che Buchhandlung, 1884).

—— , *The Constitution and Law of the Church in the First Two Centuries* (ET London: Williams and Norgate, 1910).

Harrington, D. J., *Wisdom Texts from Qumran* (London and New York: Routledge, 1996).

Harrison, C., 'Augustine, Wisdom and Classical Culture', in S. C. Barton (ed.), *Where shall Wisdom be Found?* (Edinburgh: T. & T. Clark, 1999), 125–37.

Harrison, P. N., *Polycarp's Two Epistles to the Philippians* (Cambridge: Cambridge University Press, 1936).

Hartin, P. J., *James and the 'Q' Sayings of Jesus*, JSNTSup 47 (Sheffield: Sheffield Academic Press, 1991).

—— , *James*, Sacra Pagina, 14 (Collegeville, Minn.: Liturgical Press, 2003).

Hartog, P., *Polycarp and the New Testament: The Occasion, Rhetoric, Theme, and Unity of the Epistle to the Philippians and its Allusions to New Testament Literature*, WUNT 2.134 (Tübingen: J. C. B. Mohr (Paul Siebeck), 2002).

Hays, R. B., 'Wisdom according to Paul', in S. C. Barton (ed.), *Where shall Wisdom be Found?* (Edinburgh: T. & T. Clark, 1999), 111–23.

Heard, R., 'Papias' Quotations from the New Testament', *NTS* 1 (1954), 130–4.

Hedrick, C. W., Stroumsa, G. G., and Ehrman, B. D., 'The Secret Gospel of Mark: A Discussion', *JECS* 11 (2003), 133–63.

Heid, S., 'Die frühkirchliche Beurteilung der Häretiker als "Feinde des Kreuzes" ', in M. Hutter, W. Klein, and U. Vollmer (eds.), *Hairesis* (Münster: Aschendorff, 2002), 107–39.

Heinemann, J., and J. J. Petuchowski, *Literature of the Synagogue* (New York: Behrman, 1975).

—— , *ha-Tefilah bi-tekufat-ha-Tana'im veha-Amora'im*: (= *Prayer in the Period of the Tanna'im and the Amora'im*) (Jerusalem: Hebrew University Press, 1964; 2nd edn. 1966; ET: *Prayer in the Talmud: Forms and Patterns*, Studia Judaica, 9 (Berlin and New York: Walter de Gruyter, 1977).

Hempel, C., Lange, A., and Lichtenberger, H. (eds.), *The Wisdom Texts from Qumran and the Development of Sapiential Thought*, BETL 159 (Leuven: Peeters, 2002).

Henderson, I. H., '*Didache* and Orality in Synoptic Comparison', *JBL* 111 (1992), 283–306.

——, 'Style-Switching in the *Didache*: Fingerprint or Argument?', in Jefford (ed.), *The* Didache *in Context*, 177–209.

Hengel, M., *Die Evangelienüberschriften*, SHAW, Philosophisch-Historische Klasse (Heidelberg: Winter, 1984).

——, *Studies in the Gospel of Mark* (London: SCM Press, 1985).

——, *Die johanneische Frage: Ein Lösungsversuch*, WUNT 67 (Tübingen: Mohr, 1993).

——, *The Four Gospels and the One Gospel of Jesus Christ: An Investigation of the Collection and Origin of the Canonical Gospels* (London: SCM Press; Harrisburg, Pa.: Trinity Press International, 2000).

——, and Schwemer, A. M., *Paul between Damascus and Antioch: The Unknown Years* (London: SCM Press, 1997).

Héring, J., 'Un texte oublié: Matthieu 18:10. A propos des controversies récentes sur le pédobaptisme', in *Aux sources de la tradition chrétienne: Mélanges offerts à M. M. Goguel* (Neuchâtel and Paris: Delachaux & Niestlé, 1950), 95–102.

Hilgenfeld, A., *Der Paschastreit der alten Kirche nach seiner Bedeutung für die Kirchengeschichte und für die Evangelienforschung urkundlich dargestellt* (Halle: Pfeffer, 1860).

——, 'Das neueste Steitzianum über den Paschastreit', *ZWT* 4 (1861), 106–10.

——, 'Der Quartodecimanismus Kleinasiens und die kanonischen Evangelien', *ZWT* 4 (1861), 285–318.

——, 'Polykarp von Smyrna', *ZWT* 17 (1874), 305–45.

——, 'Das Martyrium Polykarps von Smyrna', *ZWT* 22 (1879), 145–70.

Hill, C. E., 'What Papias Said about John (and Luke): A "New" Papian Fragment', *JTS* 49 (1998), 582–629.

——, 'The *Epistula Apostolorum*: An Asian Tract from the Time of Polycarp', *JECS* 7 (1999), 1–53.

——, 'Ignatius and the Apostolate: The Witness of Ignatius to the Emergence of Christian Scripture', in M. F. Wiles and E. J. Yarnold (eds.) *StPatr* 36 (Leuven: Peeters, 2001), 226–48.

——, *The Johannine Corpus in the Early Church* (Oxford: Oxford University Press, 2004).

Hoehner, H., *Ephesians—An Exegetical Commentary*, BECNT (Grand Rapids, Mich.: Baker Academic, 2002).

Hoffman, D. L., 'The Authority of Scripture and Apostolic Doctrine in Ignatius of Antioch', *JETS* 28 (1985), 71–9.

——, 'Ignatius and Early Anti-Docetic Realism in the Eucharist', *Fides et Historia*, 30 (1998), 74–88.

Holloway, P., *Consolation in Philippians*, SNTSMS 112 (Cambridge: Cambridge University Press, 2003).

Holmes, M. W., *The Apostolic Fathers: Greek Texts and English Translations* (Grand Rapids, Mich.: Baker Books, 1992; rev. edn. 1999).

Holtzmann, H. J., 'Das Verhältnis des Johannes zu Ignatius und Polykarp', *ZWT* 20 (1877), 187–214.

Hooker, M. D., 'Where is Wisdom to be Found? Colossians 1. 15–20 (1),' in D. F. Ford and G. N. Stanton (eds.), *Reading Texts, Seeking Wisdom* (London: SCM Press, 2003), 116–28.

Hoppe, R., *Jakobusbrief*, Stuttgarter kleiner Kommentar. Neues Testament, n.s. 15 (Stuttgart: Verlag Katholisches Bibelwerk, 1989).

Horsley, R. A., and Draper, J. A., *Whoever Hears You Hears Me: Prophets, Performance, and Tradition in Q* (Harrisburg, Pa.: Trinity Press International, 1999).

Hruby, K., 'La "Birkat Ha-Mazon" ', in *Mélanges liturgiques offerts au R. P. Dom B. Botte O.S.B. de l'Abbaye du Mont César à l'occasion du cinquantième anniversaire de son ordination sacerdotale (4 Juin 1972)* (Louvain: Abbaye du Mont César, 1972), 205–22.

Hübner, H., *Law in Paul's Thought: A Contribution to the Development of Pauline Theology*, SNTW (Edinburgh: T. & T. Clark, 1984).

Hübner, R., 'Thesen zur Echtheit und Datierung der sieben Briefe des Ignatius von Antiochien', *ZAC* 1 (1997), 44–72.

Humphrey, E., *The Ladies and the Cities*, JSPS 17 (Sheffield: Sheffield Academic Press, 1995).

Hurtado, L. W., *Lord Jesus Christ: Devotion to Jesus in Earliest Christianity* (Grand Rapids, Mich.: Eerdmans, 2003).

Inan, J., and Alföldi-Rosenbaum, E., *Roman and Early Byzantine Portrait Sculpture in Asia Minor* (London: Oxford University Press/British Academy, 1966).

Invernizzi, A., 'Héraclès a Séleucie du Tigre', *RArc* 1 (1989), 65–113.

Jackson-McCabe, M. A., *Logos and Law in the Letter of James: The Law of Nature, the Law of Moses, and the Law of Freedom*, NovTSup 100 (Leiden: Brill, 2001).

Jeffers, J. S., *Conflict at Rome: Social Order and Hierarchy in Early Christianity* (Minneapolis: Fortress, 1991).

Jefford, C. N., *The Sayings of Jesus in the Teaching of the Twelve Apostles*, VCSup 11 (Leiden: Brill, 1989).

—— , 'Tradition and Witness in Antioch: Acts 15 and Didache 6', in E. V. McKnight (ed.), *Perspectives on Contemporary New Testament Questions: Essays in Honour of T. C. Smith* (Lewiston, Me.: Edwin Mellen Press, 1992), 409–19.

—— (ed.), *The* Didache *in Context: Essays on its Text, History and Transmission*, NovTSup 77 (Leiden: Brill, 1995).

—— , 'Reflections on the Role of Jewish Christianity in Second-Century Antioch', in S. C. Mimouni and F. S. Jones (eds.), *Actes du colloque international: Le judéo-christianisme dans tous ses états* (Paris: Éditions du Cerf, 2001), 146–67.

—— , 'The Milieu of Matthew, the Didache, and Ignatius of Antioch: Agreements and Differences', in H. van de Sandt (ed.), *Matthew and the Didache: Two Documents from the Same Jewish-Christian Milieu?* (Assen: Van Gorcum, 2005), 35–47.

—— , with Harder, K. J., and Amezaga, L. D., Jun., *Reading the Apostolic Fathers: An Introduction* (Peabody, Mass.; Hendrickson, 1996).

Jeremias, J., *Hat die Urkirche der Kindertaufe geübt?*, 2nd edn. (Göttingen: Vandenhoeck & Ruprecht, 1949).

—— , *Infant Baptism in the First Four Centuries* (London: SCM Press, 1960).

Jeremias, J., *The Origins of Infant Baptism* (London: SCM Press, 1963).

—— , *The Eucharistic Words of Jesus* (London: SCM Press, 1966).

Jewett, R., 'Conflicting Movements in the Early Church as Reflected in Philippians', *NovT* 12 (1970), 362–71.

Johnson, L. T., 'The Use of Leviticus 19 in the Letter of James', *JBL* 101 (1982), 391–401.

Johnson, S. E., 'A Subsidiary Motive for the Writing of the Didache', in M. H. Shepherd and S. E. Johnson (eds.), *Munera Studiosa: Studies Presented to W. H. P. Hatch on the Occasion of his Seventieth Birthday* (Cambridge, Mass.: Episcopal Theological School, 1946), 107–22.

—— , 'Parallels between the Letters of Ignatius and the Johannine Epistles', in E. W. Conrad and E. G. Newing (eds.), *Perspectives in Language and Text* (Winona Lake, Ind.: Eisenbrauns, 1987), 327–38.

—— , 'The New Testament's Anti-Jewish Slander and the Conventions of Ancient Polemic', *JBL* 108 (1989), 419–41.

—— , *The Letter of James: A New Translation with Introduction and Commentary*, AB 37A (Garden City, NY: Doubleday, 1995).

—— , 'Baptism 1: Early Christianity', in P. Bradshaw (ed.), *The New SCM Dictionary of Liturgy and Worship* (London: SCM Press, 2002), 35–7.

Joly, R., *Le Dossier d'Ignace d'Antioche* (Brussels: Éditions de l'Université de Bruxelles, 1979).

Judge, E. A., 'Paul's Boasting in Relation to Contemporary Professional Practice', *ABR* 16 (1968), 37–50.

Käsemann, E., 'Ministry and Community in the New Testament', in *idem*, *Essays on New Testament Themes* (ET London: SCM Press, 1964), 63–94.

Kee, H. C., 'The Ethical Dimensions of the Testaments of the XII as a Clue to Provenance', *NTS* 24 (1978), 259–70.

Keim, T., *Aus dem Urchristenthum* (Zürich: Füssl, 1878).

Kelber, W. H., *The Oral and the Written Gospel* (Philadelphia: Fortress, 1983).

Kelhoffer, J. A., ' "How Soon a Book" Revisited: *ΕΥΑΓΓΕΛΙΟΝ* as a Reference to "Gospel" Materials in the First Half of the Second Century', *ZNW* 95 (2004), 1–34.

Kenan, E., *Illustrated London News*, Archaeological Section no. 2163, 21 Dec. 1963.

Kennedy, G. A., *Progymnasmata: Greek Textbooks of Prose Composition and Rhetoric* (Atlanta: Society of Biblical Literature, 2003).

Keppie, L., *Colonisation and Veteran Settlement in Italy, 47–14 BC* (London: British School at Rome, 1983).

King, K. L., *The Gospel of Mary of Magdala: Jesus and the First Woman Apostle* (Santa Rosa, Calif.: Polebridge, 2003).

Kirk, J. A., 'Did "Officials" in the New Testament Church Receive a Salary?', *ExpT* 84 (1973), 105–8.

Kitzberger, I., *Bau der Gemeinde: das paulinische Wortfeld oikodome/(ep)oikodomein* (Würzburg: Echter Verlag, 1984).

Klauck, H.-J., *Der erste Johannesbrief*, EKK 23.1 (Zürich: Benziger Verlag, 1991).

Klein, G., 'Die Gebete in der Didache', *ZNW* 9 (1908), 132–46.

——, *Der älteste christliche Katechismus und die jüdische Propaganda-Literatur* (Berlin: Reimer, 1909).

Kleist, J. A., *The Didache; The Epistle of Barnabas; The Epistles and the Martyrdom of St. Polycarp; The Fragments of Papias; The Epistle to Diognetus*, ACW (Westminster: Newman Press, 1948).

Klinghardt, M., *Gemeinschaftsmahl und Mahlgemeinschaft: Soziologie und Liturgie frühchristlicher Mahlfeiern*, TANZ 13 (Tübingen and Basel: A. Francke Verlag, 1996).

Kloppenborg, J. S., 'Didache 16:6–8 and Special Matthean Tradition', *ZNW* 70 (1979), 54–67.

——, 'Patronage Avoidance in the Epistle of James', *HTS* 55, no. 4 (1999), 755–94.

——, 'The Reception of the Jesus Tradition in James', in J. Schlosser (ed.), *The Catholic Epistles and the Tradition*, BETL 176 (Leuven: Peeters, 2004), 93–141.

——, 'The Transformation of Moral Exhortation in *Didache* 1–5', in Jefford (ed.), *The* Didache *in Context*, 88–109.

——, 'The Use of the Synoptics or Q in Did. 1.3b–2.1', in H. van de Sandt (ed.), *The Didache and Matthew: Two Documents from the Same Jewish-Christian Milieu?* (Assen: Van Gorcum; Minneapolis: Fortress, 2005), 105–29.

Klos, H., *Die Sakramente im Johannesevangelium*, SBS 46 (Stuttgart: Katholisches Bibelwerk, 1970).

Knopf, R., *Die Lehre der zwölf Apostel; Die zwei Clemensbriefe*, HNT (Tübingen: Mohr, 1920).

Knox, J., *Philemon among the Letters of Paul* (Chicago: University of Chicago Press, 1935).

Köhler, W.-D., *Die Rezeption des Matthäusevangeliums in der Zeit vor Irenäus*, WUNT 2.24 (Tübingen: Mohr Siebeck, 1987).

Koester, H., 'Geschichte und Kultus im Johannesevangelium und bei Ignatius', *ZTK* 54 (1957), 56–69; ET 'History and Cult in the Gospel of John and in Ignatius of Antioch', *JTC* 1 (1965), 111–23.

——, '*ΓΝΩΜΑΙ ΔΙΑΦΟΡΟΙ*: The Origin and Nature of Diversification in the History of the Early Church', *HTR* 58 (1965), 290–306.

——, *An Introduction to the New Testament*, ii (Philadelphia: Fortress, 1982).

——, 'History and Development of Mark's Gospel (From Mark to *Secret Mark* and "Canonical" Mark)', in Bruce Corley (ed.), *Colloquy on the New Testament* (Macon Ga.: Mercer University Press, 1983), 35–57.

——, 'From the Kerygma-Gospel to Written Gospels', *NTS* 35 (1989), 361–81.

——, 'The Text of the Synoptic Gospels in the Second Century', in W. L. Petersen (ed.), *Gospel Traditions in the Second Century: Origins, Recensions, Text, and Transmission*, Christianity and Judaism in Antiquity, 3 (Notre Dame, Ind.: University of Notre Dame Press, 1989), 19–37.

——, *Ancient Christian Gospels: Their History and Development* (London: SCM Press; Harrisburg, Pa.: Trinity Press International, 1990).

——, *History and Literature of Early Christianity*, 2nd edn. (New York: De Gruyter, 2000).

Köster, H., *Synoptische Überlieferung bei den Apostolischen Vätern*, TU 65 (Berlin: Akademie-Verlag, 1957).

Koschorke, K., 'Eine neugefundene gnostische Gemeindeordnung', *ZTK* 76 (1979), 30–60.

Kraft, R. A., *Barnabas and the Didache: The Apostolic Fathers, A New Translation and Commentary*, iii (New York: Thomas Nelson, 1965).

—— , 'Didache', *ABD* ii. 19–8.

Kuhn, H.-W., 'The Qumran Meal and the Lord's Supper in Paul in the Context of the Graeco-Roman World', in A. Christophersen, C. Claussen, J. Frey, and B. Longenecker (eds.), *Paul, Luke and the Graeco-Roman World: Essays in Honour of Alexander J. M. Wedderburn*, JSNTSup 217 (Sheffield: Sheffield Academic Press, 2002), 221–48.

Lake, K., *The Apostolic Fathers*, LCL (Cambridge, Mass.: Harvard University Press, 1912; London: Heinemann, 1925).

Lang, M., *Johannes und die Synoptiker: Eine redaktiongeschichtliche Analyse von Joh 18–20 vor dem markinischen und lukanischen Hintergrund*, FRLANT 182 (Göttingen: Vandenhoeck & Ruprecht, 1999).

Laporte, J., *Eucharistia in Philo* (New York: Mellen, 1983).

Lautenschlager, M., 'Abschied vom Disputierer: zur Bedeutung von *συζητητής* in 1 Kor 1,20', *ZNW* 83 (1992), 276–85.

Laws, S., *A Commentary on the Epistle of James*, BNTC (London: A. & C. Black, 1980).

Layton, B., 'The Sources, Date and Transmission of *Didache* 1.3b–2.1', *HTR* 61 (1968), 343–83.

Lechner, T., *Ignatius adversus Valentinianos? Chronologische und theologiegeschichtliche Studien zu den Briefen des Ignatius von Antiochien*, VCSup 47 (Leiden: Brill, 1999).

Ledogar, R. J., 'Zur altchristlichen Verfasssungsgeschichte', in *Kleine Schriften*, i, TU 67 (Berlin: Akademic, 1958), 141–85.

—— , *Praise Verbs in the Early Greek Anaphoras* (Rome: Herder, 1968).

Leonhardt, J., *Jewish Worship in Philo of Alexandria*, TSAJ 84 (Tübingen: Mohr Siebeck, 2001).

Leutzsch, M., *Die Wahrnehmung sozialer Wirklichkeit im Hirten des Hermas* (Göttingen: Vandenhoeck & Ruprecht, 1989).

Lietzmann, H., *Mass and Lord's Supper: A Study in the History of the Liturgy: With Introduction and Further Inquiry by Robert Douglas Richardson* (ET Leiden: Brill, 1979); German original of part 1, i.e. pp. xxv–xxvi, 1–215: *Messe und Herrenmahl—Eine Studie zur Geschichte der Liturgie* (Berlin: Walter de Gruyter, 1926).

Lieu, J. M., 'Authority to Become Children of God', *NovT* 23 (1981), 210–28.

—— , *The Theology of the Johannine Epistles* (Cambridge: Cambridge University Press, 1991).

—— , *Image and Reality* (Edinburgh: T. & T. Clark, 1996).

Lightfoot, J. B., *The Apostolic Fathers: Clement, Ignatius, and Polycarp. Revised Texts with Introductions, Notes, Dissertations, and Translations*, 2nd edn., 2 parts in 5 vols. (London: Macmillan, 1891; Grand Rapids, Mich.: Baker Book House, 1981, repr. of 1889–90 edn.; rev. edn. 1999).

——, and Harmer, J. R. (eds.), *The Apostolic Fathers: Greek Texts and English Translations of the Writings*, ed. and rev. M. W. Holmes (Leicester: Apollos, 1990; 2nd edn. Grand Rapids, Mich.: Baker Book House, 1992).

Lindemann, A., *Paulus im ältesten Christentum: Das Bild des Apostels und die Rezeption der paulinischen Theologie in der frühchristlichen Literatur bis Marcion*, BHT 58 (Tübingen: J. C. B. Mohr, 1979).

——, 'Der Apostel Paulus im 2. Jahrhundert', in J.-M. Sevrin (ed.), *The New Testament in Early Christianity*, BETL 86 (Leuven: Leuven University Press, 1989), 39–67.

——, 'Paul in the Writings of the Apostolic Fathers', in William S. Babcock (ed.), *Paul and the Legacies of Paul* (Dallas: Southern Methodist University Press, 1990), 25–45.

——, *Die Clemensbriefe*, HNT 17 (Tübingen: Mohr Siebeck, 1992).

——, 'Antwort auf die "Thesen zur Echtheit und Datierung der sieben Briefe des Ignatius von Antiochien" ', *ZAC* 1 (1997), 185–94.

——, 'Die Gemeinde von "Kolossä": Erwägungen zum 'Sitz im Leben' eines pseudopaulinischen Briefes', in *idem Paulus, Apostel und Lehrer der Kirche: Studien zu Paulus und zum frühen Paulusverständnis* (Tübingen: Mohr Siebeck, 1999), 187–210.

——, 'Die Kirche als Leib: Beobachtungen zur "demokratischen" Ekklesiologie bei Paulus', in *idem*, *Paulus, Apostel und Lehrer der Kirche: Studien zu Paulus und zum frühen Paulusverständnis* (Tübingen: Mohr Siebeck, 1999), 132–57.

——, *Der erste Korintherbrief*, HNT 9.1 (Tübingen: Mohr Siebeck, 2000).

——, Review of T. Lechner, *Ignatius adversus Valentinianos? Chronologische und theologiegeschichtliche Studien zu den Briefen des Ignatius von Antiochien*, VCSup 47 (Leiden: Brill, 1999), *ZAC* 6 (2002), 157–61.

——, 'Die Sammlung der Paulusbriefe im 1. und 2. Jahrhundert', in J.-M. Auwers and H. J. de Jonge (eds.), *The Biblical Canons*, BETL 153 (Leuven: Peeters, 2003), 321–51.

—— and Paulsen H. (eds.), *Die apostolischen Väter: Griechisch–deutsche Parallelausgabe auf der Grundlage der Ausgaben von F. X. Funk, K. Bihlmeyer und M. Whittaker, mit Übersetzungen von M. Dibelius und D.-A. Koch* (Tübingen: Mohr Siebeck, 1992).

Lipsius, R. A., 'Der Märtyrertod Polykarps', *ZWT* 17 (1874), 188–214.

Löhr, H., *Studien zum frühchristlichen und frühjüdischen Gebet: Untersuchungen zu 1 Clem 59 bis 61 in seinem literarischen, historischen und theologischen Kontext*, WUNT 160 (Tübingen: Mohr Siebeck, 2003).

Loenen, D., *Stasis: Einige aspecten van de begrippen partij-en klassentrijd in oud-Griekenland* (Amsterdam: Noord-Hollandsche Uitgevers Maatschappij, 1953).

Loewenich, W. von, *Das Johannes-Verständnis im zweiten Jahrhundert* (Giessen: A. Töpelmann, 1932).

Lohse, E., 'Wort und Sakrament im Johannesevangelium', *NTS* 7 (1960), 110–25.

——, 'Die Entstehung des Bischofamtes in der frühen Christenheit', *ZNW* 71 (1980), 58–73.

——, *Der Brief an die Römer*, KEK 4 (Göttingen: Vandenhoeck & Ruprecht, 2003).

Lona, H. E., *Der erste Clemensbrief*, KAV 2 (Göttingen: Vandenhoeck & Ruprecht, 1998).

Lugmayr, P. M., 'Anaphoren ohne "direkte" Wandlungsworte bereits unter Pius XI (1922–1939): ein Beitrag zu einer aktuellen Diskussion', *Una Voce-Korrespondenz*, 33 (2003), 227–44.

——, 'Die "Anaphora von Addai und Mari" und die Dogmatik', *Una Voce-Korrespondenz*, 33 (2003), 30–47.

Lührmann, D., *Das Offenbarungsverständnis bei Paulus und in paulinischen Gemeinden*, WMANT 16 (Neukirchen-Vluyn: Neukirchener Verlag, 1965).

——, 'Das Bruchstück aus dem Hebräerevangelium bei Didymus von Alexandrien', *NovT* 29 (1987), 265–79.

——, *Die apokryph gewordenen Evangelien: Studien zu neuen Texten und zu neuen Fragen*, NovTSup 112 (Leiden: Brill, 2004).

Luz, U., *Matthew 1–7: A Continental Commentary* (ET Minneapolis: Fortress, 1989).

MacDonald, D. R., 'Apocryphal and Canonical Narratives about Paul', in W. S. Babcock (ed.), *Paul and the Legacies of Paul* (Dallas: Southern Methodist University Press, 1990), 55–70.

—— (ed.), *Mimesis and Intertextuality in Antiquity and Christianity* (Harrisburg, Pa.: Trinity Press International, 2001).

MacDonald, M. Y., 'The Ideal of the Christian Couple: Ign. *Pol.* 5.1–2 Looking Back to Paul', *NTS* 40 (1994), 105–25.

Magne, J., 'Klasma, sperma, poimnion: le vœu pour le rassemblement de Didachè IX,4', in *Mélanges d'histoire des religions offerts à Henri-Charles Puech* (Paris: Presses universitaires de France, 1974), 197–208.

Maier, H. O., *The Social Setting of the Ministry as Reflected in the Writings of Hermas, Clement and Ignatius* (Waterloo, Ont.: Wilfred Laurier University Press, 1991)

——, 'Purity and Danger in Polycarp's Epistle to the Philippians: The Sin of Valens in Social Perspective', *JECS* 1 (1993), 229–47.

——, '*1 Clement* and the Rhetoric of *hybris*', *StPatr* 31 (1997), 136–42.

——, 'The Politics of the Silent Bishop: Silence and Persuasion in Ignatius of Antioch', *JTS* 54 (2004), 503–19.

Main, E., 'For King Joshua or Against? The Use of the Bible in 4Q448', in M. Stone and E. G. Chazon (eds.), *Biblical Perspectives: Early Use and Interpretation of the Bible in Light of the Dead Sea Scrolls: Proceedings of the First International Symposium of the Orion Center for the Study of the Dead Sea Scrolls and Associated Literature, 12–14 May 1996*, STDJ 28 (Leiden, Boston, and Cologne: Brill, 1998), 113–35.

Malina, B., 'Patron and Client: The Analogy behind Synoptic Theology', *Forum*, 4 (1988), 2–32.

——, 'Was Jesus a Charismatic Leader?', in *idem*, *The Social World of the Gospels* (London: Routledge, 1996), 123–42.

Marshall, I. H., *The Epistles of John* (Grand Rapids, Mich.: Eerdmans, 1978).

Marshall, P., *Enmity in Corinth: Social Conventions in Paul's Relations with the Corinthians*, WUNT 2.23 (Tübingen: Mohr Siebeck, 1987).

Marshall, S. S. C., '*Δίψυχος*': A Local Term?', *SE* 6 (1973), 348–51.

Martin, D. B., *The Corinthian Body* (New Haven: Yale University Press, 1995).

Martin, R. P., *James*, Word Biblical Commentary 48 (Waco, Tex.: Word Books, 1988).

Massaux, É., *Influence de l'Evangile de saint Matthieu sur la littérature chrétienne avant saint Irénée* (Louvain: Publications Universitaires de Louvain, 1950; réimpression anastatique, BETL 65; Leuven: Peeters, 1986); ET *The Influence of the Gospel of Saint Matthew on Christian Literature before Saint Irenaeus*, 3 vols., ed. A. J. Bellinzoni (Macon, Ga.: Mercer University Press, 1990).

Mazza, E., 'Didaché IX–X: Elementi per una interpretazione Eucaristica', *Ephemerides Liturgicae*, 92 (1979), 393–419.

—— , 'Didache 9–10: Elements of a Eucharistic Interpretation', in Draper (ed.), *The* Didache *in Modern Research*, 276–99.

—— , *The Origins of the Eucharistic Prayer* (Collegeville, Minn.: Liturgical Press, 1995).

Mearns, C., 'The Identity of Paul's Opponents at Philippi', *NTS* 33 (1987), 194–204.

Meier, J. P., 'Matthew and Ignatius: A Response to William R. Schoedel', in D. L. Balch (ed.), *Social History of the Matthean Community: Cross-Disciplinary Approaches* (Minneapolis: Fortress, 1991), 178–86.

Meinhold, P., 'Geschehen und Deutung im ersten Clemensbrief', *ZKG* 58 (1939), 82–129.

—— , 'Polykarpos', in *PRE* 21.2., 1662–93.

—— , 'Schweigende Bischöfe: die Gegensätze in den kleinasiatischen Gemeinden nach den Ignatianen', in E. Iserloh and P. Manns (eds.), *Glaube und Geschichte* (Baden-Baden: Grimm, 1958), ii. 468–72.

—— , *Studien zu Ignatius von Antiochen* (Wiesbaden: Franz Steiner, 1979).

Menken, M. J. J., 'John 6:51c–58: Eucharist or Christology', in R. A. Culpepper (ed.), *Critical Readings of John 6*, Biblical Interpretation Series 22 (Leiden: Brill, 1997), 183–204.

Merz, A., *Die fiktive Selbstauslegung des Paulus: intertextuelle Studien zur Intention und Rezeption der Pastoralbriefe*, NTOA 52 (Göttingen: Vandenhoeck & Ruprecht; Fribourg: Academic Press, 2004).

Metzger, B. M., *The Canon of the New Testament: Its Origin, Development, and Significance* (Oxford: Clarendon Press, 1987).

—— , *A Textual Commentary on the Greek New Testament*, 2nd edn. (Stuttgart: Deutsche Bibelgesellschaft & United Bible Societies, 1994).

Michaelis, W., *Pastoralbriefe und Gefanenschaftsbriefe: zur Echtheitsfrage der Pastoralbriefe* (Gütersloh: Bertelsmann, 1930).

Middleton, R. D., 'The Eucharistic Prayers of the Didache', *JTS* 36 (1935), 259–67.

Miguens, M., 'Tres Testigos: Espiritu, Agua, Sangre', *SBFLA* 22 (1972), 74–94.

Milavec, A., *The Didache: Faith, Hope, and Life of the Earliest Christian Communities, 50–70 C.E.* (New York and Mahwah, NJ: Newman Press, 2003).

—— , 'The Purifying Confession of Failings Required by the Didache's Eucharistic Sacrifice', *BTB* 33 (2003), 64–76.

—— , 'Synoptic Tradition in the *Didache* Revisited', *JECS* 11 (2003), 443–80.

Mitchell, M. M., *Paul and the Rhetoric of Reconciliation: An Exegetical Investigation of the Language and Composition of 1 Corinthians* (Louisville, Ky.: Westminster/John Knox, 1991).

Mitchell, N., 'Baptism in the *Didache*', in Jefford (ed.), *The* Didache *in Context*, 226–55.

Mitchell, S., 'Festivals, Games, and Civic Life in Roman Asia Minor', *JRS* 80 (1990), 183–7.

Moffatt, J., 'Ignatius of Antioch: A Study in Personal Religion', *JR* 10 (1930), 169–86.

Morgan, R., 'Jesus Christ, the Wisdom of God (2)', in D. F. Ford and G. N. Stanton (eds.), *Reading Texts, Seeking Wisdom* (London: SCM Press, 2003), 22–37.

Moulakis, A., *Homonoia: Eintracht und die Entwicklung eines politischen Bewusstseins* (Munich: List, 1973).

Moule, C. F. D., 'A Note on Didache IX,4', *JTS* 6 (1955), 240–3.

Moulton, J. H., *A Grammar of New Testament Greek* (Edinburgh: T. & T. Clark, 1908).

Moulton, W. F., and Geden, A. S. (eds.), *A Concordance to the Greek Testament according to the Texts of Westcott and Hort, Tischendorf and the English Revisers* (Edinburgh: T. & T. Clark, 1957).

Muddiman, J., *The Epistle to the Ephesians*, BNTC (London: Continuum, 2001).

Müller, H., *Aus der Überlieferungsgeschichte des Polykarpmartyriums: Eine hagiographische Studie* (Paderborn: Schöningh, 1908).

—— , 'Das Martyrium Polycarpi: Ein Beitrag zur altchristlichen Heiligengeschichte', *Römische Quartalschrift*, 22 (1908), 1–16.

—— , 'Das Martyrium Polykarpi', *Römische Quartalschrift*, 22 (1908), 1–16.

Müller, U. B., *Die Geschichte der Christologie in der johanneischen Gemeinde* (Stuttgart: Katholisches Bibelwerk, 1975).

Munier, C., 'Où en est la question d'Ignace d'Antioche?: Bilan d'un siècle de recherches 1870–1988', *ANRW* 2.27.1 (1993), 359–484.

Mussner, F., *Der Jakobusbrief: Auslegung*, HTKNT 13.1, 3rd edn. (Freiburg, Basel, and Vienna: Verlag Herder, 1975).

Musurillo, H. A., *The Acts of the Pagan Martyrs, Acta Alexandrinorum* (Oxford: Oxford University Press, 1954).

—— , *The Acts of the Christian Martyrs* (Oxford: Clarendon Press, 1972).

Mutschler, B., *Irenäus als johanneischer Theologe: Studien zur Schriftauslegung bei Irenäus von Lyon* (Tübingen: Mohr Siebeck, 2004).

Nagel, T., *Die Rezeption des Johannesevangeliums im 2. Jahrhundert: Studien zur vorirenaischen Aneignung und Auslegung des vierten Evangeliums in christlicher und christlich-gnostischer Literatur* (Leipzig: Evangelische Verlagsanstalt, 2000).

Neijenhuis, J., *Das Eucharistiegebet—Struktur und Opferverständnis: Untersucht am Beispiel des Projekts der Erneuerten Agende*, Arbeiten zur Praktischen Theologie, 15 (Leipzig: Evangelische Verlagsanstalt, 1999).

Neirynck, F., *The Minor Agreements of Matthew and Luke against Mark*, BETL 37 (Leuven: Leuven University Press, 1979).

—— , 'Introduction à la réimpression', in Massaux, *Influence de l'Évangile de Saint Matthieu* (1986 edn.), pp. vii–xv; ET in Massaux, *The Influence of the Gospel of Saint Matthew*, pp. xi–xix.

Neusner, J., *A History of Jews in Babylonia*, i (Leiden: Brill, 1965).

Neymeyr, U., *Die christlichen Lehrer im zweiten Jahrhundert*, VCSup 4 (Leiden: Brill, 1989).

Niederwimmer, K., 'Der Didachist und seine Quellen', in Jefford (ed.), *The* Didache *in Context*, 15–36.

——, *The Didache: A Commentary*, Hermeneia (ET Minneapolis: Fortress, 1998).

Niermayer, J. F., *Mediae Latinitatis Lexicon Minus* (Leiden: Brill, 1976).

Nock, A. D., 'Liturgical Notes', *JTS* 30 (1929), 381–95.

Nollé, J., 'Side: zur Geschichte einer kleinasiastischen Stadt in der römischen Kaiserzeit im Spiegel ihrer Münzen', *Antike Welt*, 21 (1990), 261.

——, *Zur Geschichte der Stadt Etenna in Pisidien, in Asia Minor Studien*, Forschungen in Pisidien 6 (Bonn: Schwertheim, 1992).

——, *Side im Altertum: Geschichte und Zeugnisse*, i (Bonn: Habelt GMBH, 1993).

Nollé, M. K., and Nollé, J., 'Vom feinen Spiel städtischer Diplomatie zu Zeremoniell und Sinn kaiserlicher Homonoiafeste', *ZPE* 102 (1994), 241–61.

Norris, F. W., 'Ignatius, Polycarp and 1 Clement: Walter Bauer Reconsidered', *VC* 30 (1976), 23–44.

Oakes, P., *Philippians: From People to Letter*, SNTSMS 110 (Cambridge: Cambridge University Press, 2001).

O'Neill, J. C., *The Puzzle of 1 John* (London: SPCK, 1966).

Opitz, H., *Ursprünge frühkatholischer Pneumatologie* (Berlin: Evangelische Verlaganstalt, 1960).

Osiek, C., *The Shepherd of Hermas*, Hermeneia (Minneapolis: Fortress, 1999).

Painter, J., 'The "Opponents" in 1 John', *NTS* 32 (1986), 48–71.

——, *1, 2, and 3 John* (Collegeville, Minn.: Liturgical Press, 2002).

Paulsen, H., *Die Briefe des Ignatius von Antiochia und der Brief des Polykarp von Smyrna: zweite, neubearbeitete Auflage der Auslegung von Walter Bauer*, HNT 18 (Tübingen: Mohr Siebeck, 1985).

Perkins, P., *The Johannine Epistles* (Wilmington, Del.: Michael Glazier, 1979).

Perler, O., 'Das vierte Makkabäerbuch, Ignatius von Antiochien und die ältesten Martyrerberichte', *Rivista di archeologia cristiana*, 25 (1949), 47–72.

Pernveden, L., *The Concept of the Church in the Shepherd of Hermas*, STL 27 (Lund: Gleerup, 1966).

Perry, J. M., 'The Evolution of the Johannine Eucharist', *NTS* 39 (1993), 22–35.

Peterlin, D., *Paul's Letter to the Philippians in the Light of Disunity in the Church*, NovTSup 79 (Leiden: Brill, 1995).

Peterson, E., '*Μερίς*—Hostienpartikel und Opferanteil', in *Frühkirche, Judentum und Gnosis: Studien und Untersuchungen* (Rome: Herder, 1959), 97–106.

Pilhofer, P., *Philippi, I: Die erste christliche Gemeinde Europas*, WUNT 87 (Tübingen: J. C. B. Mohr, 1995).

Pogoloff, S. M., *Logos and Sophia: The Rhetorical Situation of 1 Corinthians*, SBLDS 134 (Atlanta: Scholars Press, 1992).

Porter, S. E., 'Is *Dipsuchos* (James 1,8; 4,8) a "Christian" Word?', *Bib* 71 (1991), 469–98.

Puech, H.-C., Review of *Polycarp's Two Epistles to the Philippians*, *RHR* 119 (1939), 96–102.

Quasten, J., *Patrology*, i (Westminster, Md.: Newman Press, 1950).

Rackl, M., *Die Christologie des heiligen Ignatius von Antiochien*, Freiburger Theologische Studien 14 (Freiburg im Breisgau: Herdersche Verlagshandlung, 1914).

Räisänen, H., *Paul and the Law* (Philadelphia: Fortress, 1986).

Ragnat, R., 'Legatio', in C. Daremberg and E. Saglio (eds.), *Dictionnaire des antiquités grecques et romains* (Paris: Libraire Hachette, 1906), iii. 1025–38.

Ratcliff, E. C., 'The Original Form of the Anaphora of Addai and Mari: A Suggestion', *JTS* 30 (1928), 23–32.

Rathke, H., *Ignatius von Antiochien und die Paulusbriefe*, TU 99 (Berlin: Akademie-Verlag, 1967).

Rebell, W., 'Das Leidenverständnis bei Paulus und Ignatius von Antiochien', *NTS* 32 (1986), 457–65.

Reinhartz, A., 'On the Meaning of the Pauline Exhortation: "*mimētai mou ginesthe*—become imitators of me" ', *Studies in Religion/Sciences Religieuses*, 16 (1987), 393–403.

Reis, D. M., 'The Areopagus as Echo Chamber: *Mimēsis* and Intertextuality in Acts 17', *Journal of Higher Criticism*, 9 (2002), 259–77.

Resch, A., *Agrapha: Außerkanonische Schriftfragmente gesammelt und untersucht*, 2nd edn., TU 15,3–4 (Leipzig, 1906); repr. Darmstadt: Wissenschaftliche Buchgesellschaft, 1967; 1st edn. published in 1889 as *Agrapha: Außerkanonische Evangelienfragmente*, TU 5,4).

Reuning, W., *Zur Erklärung des Polykarpmartyriums* (Darmstadt: Wintersche Buchdruckerei, 1917).

Richardson, C. C., *The Christianity of Ignatius of Antioch* (New York: AMS Press, 1935).

—— , *Early Christian Fathers*, The Library of Christian Classics 1 (Philadelphia: Westminster Press, 1953).

Riesenfeld, H., 'Das Brot von den Bergen: zu Did. 9, 4', *Eranos*, 54 (1956), 142–50.

Riggs, J. W., 'From Gracious Table to Sacramental Elements: The Tradition-History of Didache 9 and 10', *SC* 4 (1984), 83–101.

Roberge, M., 'Le discours sur le pain de vie, Jean 6,22–59: problèmes d'interpretation', *LTP* 38 (1982), 265–99.

Robert, J., and Robert, L., *La Carie: Histoire et Géographie Historique, avec le recueil des inscriptions antiques*, ii: *Le Plateau de Tabai et ses envirions* (Paris: Dépositaire Librarie d'Amérique et d'Orient, 1954).

Robert, L., 'Nouvelles remarques sur l'" "Édit d'Ériza" ', *OpMinSel*, 2 (1969), 967–8 (= *BCH* (1932), 263).

—— , 'Le Serpent Glycon d'Abônouteichos à Athénes et Artémis d'Éphèse à Rome', *OpMinSel*, vs (1989), 747–69 (= CRAI (1981), 513–35).

—— , *Fouilles d'Amyzon en Carie*, i: *Exploration, Histoire, monnaies et inscriptions*, Commission des fouilles et missions archéologiques au ministère des relations extérieures (Paris: Diffusion de Boccard, 1983).

Robillard, E., 'Christologie d'Ignace d'Antioche', in R. Laflamme and M. Gervais (eds.), *Le Christ hier, aujourd'hui et demain* (Québec: Les Presses de L'Université, 1976), 479–87.

Robinson, J. A., 'The Problem of the Didache', *JTS* 13 (1912), 339–56.

—— , *Barnabas, Hermas and the Didache* (London: SPCK; New York: Macmillan, 1920).

Robinson, J. M., 'Die Hodajot-Formel in Gebet und Hymnus des Frühchristentums', in *Apophoreta Festschrift für E. Haenchen*, BZNW 30 (Berlin: Alfred Töpelmann, 1964), 194–235.

—— , 'Introduction', in *The Nag Hammadi Library in English* (Leiden: Brill, 1977), 1–25.

—— , Hoffmann, P., and Kloppenborg, J. S. (eds.), *The Critical Edition of Q*, Hermeneia Supplements (Minneapolis: Fortress, 2000).

—— —— —— , (eds.), *The Sayings Gospel Q in Greek and English with Parallels from Mark and Thomas* (Minneapolis: Fortress, 2002).

Romilly, J. de, 'Vocabulaire et propagande ou les premiers emplois du mot *homonoia*', in F. Bader (ed.), *Mélanges de linguistique et de philologique Grecques offerts à Pierre Chantraine* (Paris: Klincksieck, 1972), 199–209.

Ropes, J. H., *Die Sprüche Jesu, die in den kanonischen Evangelien nicht überliefert sind: eine kritische Bearbeitung des von D. Alfred Resch gesammelten Materials*, TU 14, 1 (Leipzig: Hinrichs, 1896).

—— , *A Critical and Exegetical Commentary on the Epistle of St. James*, ICC (New York: Charles Scribner's Sons, 1916).

Rordorf, W., 'Le Baptême selon la *Didachè*', in *Mélanges liturgiques offerts au R. P. Dom Bernard Botte O.S.B.* (Louvain: Abbaye du Mont César, 1972), 499–509; ET 'Baptism according to the Didache', in Draper (ed.), *The* Didache *in Modern Research*, 212–22.

—— , 'L'eucharistie selon la *Didachè*', in *idem et al.* (eds.), *L'eucharistie des premiers chrétiens*, Le point théologique, 17 (Paris: Beauchesne, 1976), 7–28.

—— , 'Zum Problem des "grossen Sabbats" im Polykarp- und Pioniusmartyrium', in E. Dassmann and K. S. Frank (eds.), *Pietas: Festschrift für B. Kötting* (Münster: Aschendorff, 1980), 245–9.

—— , 'Does the Didache Contain Jesus Tradition Independently of the Synoptic Gospels?', in H. Wansbrough (ed.), *Jesus and the Oral Gospel Tradition*, JSNTSup 64 (Sheffield: JSOT Press, 1991), 394–423.

—— and Tuilier, A., *La Doctrine des douze apôtres (Didachè): introduction, texte, traduction, notes, appendice et index*, 2nd edn. revue et augmentée, SC 248 (Paris: Cerf, 1998).

Rouwhorst, G., 'Jewish Liturgical Traditions in Early Syriac Christianity', *VC* 51 (1991), 72–93.

Rowland, C. C., *The Open Heaven: A Study of Apocalyptic in Judaism and Early Christianity* (London: SPCK, 1982).

—— ' "Sweet Science Reigns": Divine and Human Wisdom in the Apocalyptic Tradition', in S. C. Barton (ed.), *Where shall Wisdom be Found?* (Edinburgh: T. & T. Clark, 1999), 61–74.

Sabatier, P., *La Didachè, ou l'Enseignement des douze apôtres, texte grec retrouvé par Mgr Philotheos Bryennios,... publié pour la première fois en France, avec un commentaire et des notes* (Paris: Fischbacher, 1885).

Safrai, S., and Stern, M., *The Jewish People in the First Century: Historical Geography, Political History, Social, Cultural and Religious Life and Institutions* (Assen: Von Gorcum; Philadelphia: Fortress, 1976).

Saldarini, A. J., *Matthew's Christian-Jewish Community* (Chicago and London: University of Chicago Press, 1994).

Saliba, I. A., 'The Bishop of Antioch and the Heretics: A Study of a Primitive Christology', *EQ* 54 (1982), 65–76.

Salmon, G., 'Docetism', in W. Smith and H. Wace (eds.), *Dictionary of the Christian Bible* (London: J. Murray, 1911), 867–70.

Sandelin, K.-G., *Wisdom as Nourisher: A Study of an Old Testament Theme, its Development within Early Judaism and its Impact on Early Christianity*, Acta Academia Aboensis, ser. A, 64/3 (Åbo: Åbo Akademi, 1986).

Sanders, B., 'Imitating Paul: 1 Cor 4:16', *HTR* 74 (1981), 353–63.

Sanders, E. P., *Paul, the Law, and the Jewish People* (Philadelphia: Fortress, 1983).

—— , *Judaism: Practice and Belief 63 BCE–66 CE* (London: SCM Press; Philadelphia: Trinity Press International, 1992).

Sandt, H. van de, ' "Do not give what is holy to dogs" (Did 9:5d and Matt 7:6a): The Eucharistic Food of the Didache in its Jewish Purity Setting', *VC* 56 (2003), 223–46.

—— , and Flusser, D., *The Didache: Its Jewish Sources and its Place in Early Judaism and Christianity*, CRINT 3.5 (Assen: Royal Van Gorcum; Minneapolis: Fortress, 2002).

Satake, A., *Die Gemeindeordnung in der Johannesapokalypse*, WMANT 21 (Neukirchen: Neukirchener Verlag, 1966).

Saxer, V., *Bible et Hagiographie: Textes et thèmes bibliques dans les Actes des martyrs authentiques des premiers siècles* (Bern: Lang, 1986).

—— , 'The Influence of the Bible in Early Christian Martyrology', in P. M. Blowers (ed.), *The Bible in Greek Christian Antiquity* (Notre Dame, Ind.: University of Notre Dame Press, 1997), 342–74.

Schiffman, L. H., *Texts and Traditions: A Source Reader for the Study of Second Temple and Rabbinic Judaism* (Hoboken, NJ: KTAV Publishing House, 1998).

Schille, G., 'Das Recht der Propheten und Apostel—gemeinderechtliche Beobachtungen zu Didache Kapitel 11–13', in P. Wätzel and G. Schille (eds.), *Theologische Versuche*, i (Berlin: Evangelische Verlag-Anstalt, 1966), 84–103.

Schlier, H., *Religionsgeschichtliche Untersuchungen zu den Ignatiusbriefen* (Giessen: Töpelmann, 1929).

Schmid, J., 'Didache', *RAC* iii. 1009–13.

Schmitt, T., *Paroikie und Oikoumene: Sozial- und mentalitätsgeschichtliche Untersuchungen zum 1. Clemensbrief*, BZNW 110 (Berlin and New York: Walter de Gruyter, 2002).

Schnackenburg, R., *Das Johannesevangelium: Dritter Teil: Kommentar zu Kapitel 13–21*, HTKNT 4/3 (Freiburg: Herder, 1957).

—— , *Die Johannesbriefe*, HTKNT 13 (Freiburg: Herder, 1953); ET *The Johannine Epistles: A Commentary* (Tunbridge Wells: Burns and Dates, 1992).

Schneemelcher, W. (ed.), *New Testament Apocrypha*, rev. edn, trans. R. McL. Wilson: 2 vols. (Cambridge: James Clarke & Co., Louisville, Ky.: Westminster/John Knox, 1991).

Schnelle, U., *Das Evangelium nach Johannes*, THKNT 4, 2nd edn. (Leipzig: Evangelische Verlagsanstalt, 2000).

Schoedel, W. R., *Polycarp, Martydom of Polycarp, Fragments of Papias* (London: Thomas Nelson, 1967).

——, 'Ignatius and the Archives', *HTR* 71 (1978), 97–106.

——, *Ignatius of Antioch: A Commentary on the Letters of Ignatius of Antioch*, Hermeneia (Philadelphia: Fortress, 1985).

——, 'Papias', *ANRW* 2.27.1 (1993), 235–70.

——, 'Polycarp, Epistle of', in *ABD* v. 390–2.

——, 'Polycarp of Smyrna and Ignatius of Antioch', *ANRW* 2.27.1 (1993), 272–358.

Schöllgen, G., 'The *Didache* as a Church Order: An Examination of the Purpose for the Composition of the *Didache* and its Consequences for its Interpretation', in Draper (ed.), *The* Didache *in Modern Research*, 43–71.

——, 'Didache: Zwölf-Apostel-Lehre: Einleitung, Übersetzung und Kommentar', in *idem* and W. Geerlings, *Zwölf-Apostel-Lehre: Apostolische Überlieferung: Lateinisch, Griechisch, Deutsch*, FC 1 (Freiburg: Herder, 1991), 23–139.

——, 'Die Ignatien als pseudepigraphisches Brief-corpus: Anmerkung zu den Thesen von Reinhard M. Hübner', *ZAC* 2 (1998), 16–25.

Schürer, E., Vermes, G., Millar, F., and Black, M., *The History of the Jewish People in the Age of Jesus Christ (175 B.C.–A.D. 135)*, ii (Edinburgh: T. & T. Clark, 1979).

Schwartz, E., *De Pionio et Polycarpo* (Göttingen: Akademie, 1905).

Schweizer, E., 'Das johanneische Zeugnis vom Herrenmahl', *EvTh* 12 (1953), 341–63; repr. in *idem*, *Neotestamentica: deutsche und englische Aufsätze 1951–1963* (Zürich: Zwingli Verlag, 1963), 371–96.

——, *Matthäus und seine Gemeinde*, SBS 71 (Stuttgart: Verlag Katholisches Bibelwerk, 1974).

—— and Baumgärtel, F., σῶμα κτλ. *TDNT* vii. 1024–94.

Seeley, D., *The Noble Death: Graeco-Roman Martyrology and Paul's Conception of Salvation*, JSNTSup 28 (Sheffield: JSOT Press, 1990).

Seeliger, R. H., 'Märtyrerakten', in S. Döpp and W. Geerlings (eds.), *Lexikon der antiken christlichen Literatur* (Freiburg: Herder, 1997), 411–19.

Seidensticker, P., *Die Gemeinschaftsform der religiösen Gruppen des Spätjudentums und der Urkirche* (Jerusalem: Studium Biblicum Franciscanorum Liber Annus, 1959).

Sepp, B., *Das Martyrium Polycarpi nebst Anhang über die Afralegende* (Regensburg: Akademische Buchdruckerei von. F. Straub in München, 1911).

Shanor, J., 'Paul as Master Builder: Construction Terms in 1 Corinthians', *NTS* 34 (1988), 461–71.

Shaw, B. D., 'Body/Power/Identity: Passions of the Martyrs', *JECS* 4 (1996), 269–312.

Shepherd, M. H., 'The Epistle of James and the Gospel of Matthew', *JBL* 75 (1956), 40–51.

Sim, D. C., *The Gospel of Matthew and Christian Judaism: The History and Social Setting of the Matthean Community* (Edinburgh: T. & T. Clark, 1998).

Skard, E., *Zwei religiös-politische Begriffe: Euergetes-Concordia* (Oslo: Dybwad, 1932).

Skehan, P. W., and Di Lella A. A., *The Wisdom of Ben Sira: A New Translation with Notes*, AB 39 (Garden City, NY: Doubleday, 1987).

Slee, M., *The Church in Antioch in the First Century CE: Communion and Conflict*, JSNTSup 244 (London: T. & T. Clark International, 2003).
Slusser, M., 'Docetism: A Historical Definition', *SC* 1 (1981), 163–71.
Smalley, S. S., *1, 2, 3 John* (Waco, Tex.: Word, 1984).
Smallwood, E. M., *The Jews under Roman Rule*, SJLA 20 (Leiden: Brill, 1981).
Smit Sibinga, J., 'Ignatius and Matthew', *NovT* 8 (1966), 263–83.
Smith, M., *Clement of Alexandria and a Secret Gospel of Mark* (Cambridge, Mass.: Harvard University Press, 1973).
—— , *The Secret Gospel: The Discovery and Interpretation of the Secret Gospel of Mark* (New York: Harper & Row, 1973).
Snyder, G. F., 'Hermas' The Shepherd', in *ABD* 3. 148.
—— , 'The Historical Jesus in the Letters of Ignatius of Antioch', *BR* 8 (1963), 3–12.
Sordi, M., *The Christians and the Roman Empire* (ET London and Norman, Okla.: University of Oklahoma Press, 1986).
Souter, A., *A Glossary of Later Latin to 600 AD* (Oxford: Clarendon Press, 1949).
Spinks, B., 'Beware the Liturgical Horses! An English Interjection on Anaphoral Evolution', *Worship*, 59 (1985), 211–19.
Staniforth, M., *Early Christian Writings* (London: Penguin, 1968).
Stanley, D. M., ' "Become Imitators of Me": The Pauline Conception of Apostolic Tradition', *Bib* 40 (1959), 859–77.
—— , 'Imitation in Paul's Letters: Its Significance for his Relationship to Jesus and his Own Christian Foundations', in P. Richardson and J. C. Hurd (eds.), *From Jesus to Paul* (Waterloo, Ont.: Wilfrid Laurier University Press, 1984), 127–42.
Steinmetz, P., 'Polykarp von Smyrna über die Gerechtigkeit', *Hermes*, 100 (1972), 63–75.
Steitz, G. E., 'Der Charakter der kleinasiatischen Kirche und Festsitte um die Mitte des zweiten Jahrhunderts', *Jahrbuch für deutsche Theologie*, 6 (1861), 102–41.
Stempel, H.-A., 'Der Lehrer in der "Lehre der zwölf Apostel" ', *VC* 34 (1980), 209–17.
Stewart-Sykes, A., *The Lamb's High Feast: Melito, Peri Pascha and the Quartodeciman Paschal Liturgy at Sardis*, VCSup 42 (Leiden: Brill, 1998).
—— , *From Prophecy to Preaching*, VCSup 59 (Leiden: Brill, 2001).
Stoops, R. J., Jun., 'If I Suffer... Epistolary Authority in Ignatius of Antioch', *HTR* 80 (1987), 161–78.
Story, C., 'The Christology of Ignatius of Antioch', *EQ* 56 (1984), 173–82.
Strecker, G., 'Chiliasm and Docetism in the Johannine School', *ABR* 38 (1990), 45–61; in German as 'Chiliasmus und Doketismus in der Johanneischen Schule', *KD* 38 (1992), 30–46.
—— , *The Johannine Epistles*, Hermeneia (Minneapolis: Fortress, 1996).
—— , 'Johannine Letters', in J. H. Hayes (ed.), *Dictionary of Biblical Interpretation* (Nashville: Abingdon Press, 1999), 603–9.
Streeter, B. H., *The Primitive Church* (London: Macmillan, 1929).
Strong, E., 'Sepulchral Relief of a Priest of Bellona', *Papers of the British School at Rome*, 9 (1920), 205–13.

Stuckwisch, D. R., 'Saint Polycarp of Smyrna: Johannine or Pauline Figure', *CTQ* 61 (1997), 113–25.

Sullivan, D. L., 'Establishing Orthodoxy: The Letters of Ignatius of Antioch as Epideictic Rhetoric', *Journal of Communication and Religion*, 15 (1992), 71–86.

Sumney, J. L., 'Those Who "Ignorantly Deny Him": The Opponents of Ignatius of Antioch', *JECS* 1 (1993), 345–65.

Surkau, H. W., *Martyrien in jüdischer und frühchristlicher Zeit* (Göttingen: Vandenhoeck & Ruprecht, 1938).

Swartley, W. M., 'The *Imitatio Christi* in the Ignatian Letters', *VC* 27 (1973), 81–103.

Swete, H. B., *The Gospel of Peter: The Akhmim Fragment of the Apocryphal Gospel of St Peter*, 2nd edn. (London: Macmillan, 1893).

Talley, T., 'The Eucharistic Prayer of the Ancient Church according to Recent Research: Results and Reflections', *SL* 11 (1976), 138–58.

—— , 'The Eucharistic Prayer: Tradition and Development', in K. Stevenson (ed.), *Liturgy Reshaped* (London: SPCK, 1982), 48–64.

—— , 'The Literary Structure of Eucharistic Prayer', *Worship*, 58 (1984), 404–20.

—— , 'From Berakah to Eucharistia: A Reopening Question', *Worship*, 50 (1976), 115–37; repr. in K. Seasoltz (ed.), *Living Bread, Saving Cup: Readings on the Eucharist* (Collegeville, Minn.: Liturgical Press, 1987), 80–101.

Taylor, C., *The Teaching of the Twelve Apostles: With Illustrations from the Talmud* (Cambridge: Deighton Bell, 1886).

Theissen, G., 'Legitimation und Lebensunterhalt: ein Beitrag zur Soziologie urchristlicher Missionäre', *NTS* 21 (1975), 192–221.

—— , *The First Followers of Jesus: A Sociological Analysis of Earliest Christianity* (London: SCM Press; Philadelphia: Fortress, 1978).

—— , *The Social Setting of Pauline Christianity* (ET Philadelphia: Fortress, 1982).

Thiselton, A. C., *The First Epistle to the Corinthians* (Grand Rapids, Mich., and Cambridge: Eerdmans, 2000).

Thraede, K., 'Homonoia (Eintracht)', *RAC* 16 (1994), 176–80.

Thrall, M., *The Second Epistle to the Corinthians*, 2 vols., ICC (Edinburgh: T. & T. Clark, 1994, 2000).

Till, W. C., *Die gnostischen Schriften des koptischen Papyrus Berolinensis 8502*, TU 60 (Berlin: Akademie-Verlag, 1955; 2nd edn. by H.-M. Schenke, 1972).

Tjäder, J.-O. (ed.), *Die nichtliterarischen lateinischen Papyri Italiens aus der Zeit 445–700*, Pt. i (Lund: Gleerup, 1955), Pt. 2 (Stockholm: Gleerup, 1982).

Tombeur, P. (ed.), *Cetedoc Library of Christian Latin Texts*, 4th edn. (Turnholt: Brepols, 2000).

Tomson, P., *Paul and the Jewish Law: Halakah in the Letters of the Apostle to the Gentiles*, CRINT 3.1 (Assen and Maastricht: Van Gorcum; Minneapolis: Fortress, 1990).

—— , 'Halakhic Elements in Didache 8 and Matthew 6', in H. van de Sandt (ed.), *The Didache and Matthew: Two Documents from the Same Jewish-Christian Milieu?* (Assen: Van Gorcum; Minneapolis: Fortress, 2004), 131–41.

Trakatellis, D., 'God Language in Ignatius of Antioch', in B. A. Pearson (ed.), *The Future of Early Christianity: Essays in Honour of Helmut Koester* (Minneapolis: Fortress, 1991), 422–30.

Treat, J. C., 'Barnabas, Epistle of', *ABD* i. 611–14.

Trevett, C. M., 'Prophecy and Anti-Episcopal Activity: A Third Error Combatted by Ignatius?', *JEH* 34 (1983), 1–18.

——, 'Approaching Matthew from the Second Century: The Under-Used Ignatian Correspondence', *JSNT* 20 (1984), 59–67.

——, *A Study of Ignatius, of Antioch in Syria and Asia*, Studies in the Bible and Early Christianity, 29 (Lewiston, Me., Queenston, and Lampeter: Edwin Mellen Press, 1992).

Tsuji, M., *Glaube zwischen Vollkommenheit und Verweltlichung: Eine Untersuchung zur literarischen Gestalt und zur inhaltlichen Kohärenz des Jakobusbriefes*, WUNT 2.93 (Tübingen: J. C. B. Mohr (Paul Siebeck), 1997).

Tuckett, C. M., 'Synoptic Tradition in the *Didache*', in J.-M. Sevrin (ed.), *The New Testament in Early Christianity: La Réception des Écrits Néotestamentaires dans le christianisme primitif*, BETL 86 (Leuven: Peeters, 1989), 197–230.

Turner, H. E. W., *The Pattern of Christian Truth* (London: A. R. Mowbray & Co., 1954).

Tyson, J. B., 'Source Criticism of the Gospel of Luke', in C. H. Talbert (ed.), *Perspectives on Luke–Acts* (Macon, Ga.: Mercer University Press, 1978), 24–39.

Van der Horst, P. W., *The Sentences of Pseudo-Phocylides: With Introduction and Commentary*, SVTP 4 (Leiden: Brill, 1978).

Vawter, B., 'The Johannine Sacramentary', *TS* 17 (1956), 151–66.

Verme, M. del, 'The Didache and Judaism: The ἀπαρχή of *Didache* 13:3–7', *SP* 26 (1993), 113–39.

Vielhauer, P., *Geschichte der urchristlichen Literatur*, DGL (Berlin: De Gruyter, 1975).

Vilela, A., 'Le Presbytérion selon saint Ignace de'Antioche', *BLE* 74 (1973), 161–86.

Vitringa, C., *De synagoga vetere libri tres: quibus tum de nominibus, structurā, origine, præfectis, ministris, & sacris synagogarum, agitur; tum præcipue, formam regiminis & ministerii earum in ecclesiam christianam translatam esse, demonstratur: cum prolegomenis* (Franeker: Typis & impensis J. Gyzelaar, 1696); abbreviated translation by J. L. Bernard, *The Synagogue and the Church: Being an Attempt to Show that the Government, Ministers and Services of the Church were Derived from those of the Synagogue* (London: B. Fellowes, 1842).

Vööbus, A., *Liturgical Traditions in the Didache*, Papers of the Estonian Theological Society in Exile, 16 (Stockholm: Estonian Theological Society in Exile, 1968).

Vogt, H. J., 'Bemerkungen zur Echtheit der Ignatiusbriefe', *ZAC* 3 (1999), 50–63.

Vokes, F. E., *The Riddle of the Didache: Fact or Fiction, Heresy or Catholicism?* (London: SPCK, 1938).

Vorster, W. S., 'Heterodoxy in 1 John', *Neot* 9 (1975), 87–97.

Wachob, W. H., *The Voice of Jesus in the Social Rhetoric of James*, SNTSMS 106 (Cambridge and New York: Cambridge University Press, 2000).

Wall, R. W., *The Community of the Wise* (Valley Forge, Pa.: Trinity Press International, 1997).

Wall, W., *The History of Infant Baptism*, 3 vols., 4th edn. (London: Griffith, Farran, Browne & Co., 1819).

Wallace, A. F. C., 'Revitalization Movements', *American Anthropologist*, 58 (1956), 264–81.

Weber, M., *Economy and Society*, i (ET Berkeley: University of California Press, 1978).

Weeks, S., 'Wisdom in the Old Testament', in S. C. Barton (ed.), *Where shall Wisdom be Found?* (Edinburgh: T. & T. Clark, 1999), 19–30.

Wehr, L., *Arznei der Unsterblichkeit: Die Eucharistie bei Ignatius von Antiochien und im Johannesevangelium*, NTAbh, n. s. 18 (Münster: Aschendorff, 1987).

Weigandt, P., 'Der Doketismus im Urchristentum und in der theologischen Entwicklung des zweiten Jahrhunderst' (diss. theol. Heidelberg, 1961).

Weijers, O., and Gumbert-Hepp, M., *Lexicon Latinitatis Nederlandicae Medii Aevi*, vi: 'P' (Leiden: Brill, 1998).

Weinandy, T., *Does God Suffer?* (Edinburgh: T. & T. Clark, 2000).

—— , 'Cyril and the Mystery of the Incarnation', in T. Weinandy and D. Keating (eds.), *The Theology of St. Cyril of Alexandria: A Critical Appreciation* (London: T. & T. Clark/Continuum, 2003), 23–54.

Weinfeld, M., 'Grace after Meals in Qumran', *JBL* 111 (1992), 427–40.

Weinrich, W. C., *Spirit and Martyrdom: A Study of the Work of the Holy Spirit in Contexts of Persecution and Martyrdom in the New Testament and Early Christian Literature* (Washington: University Press of America, 1981).

Weiß, H.-F., *Der Brief an die Hebräer*, KEK 13 (Göttingen: Vandenhoeck & Ruprecht, 1991).

Weiss, K., 'Orthodoxie und Heterodoxie im 1. Johannesbriefe', *ZNW* 58 (1967), 247–55.

Welborn, L. L., 'Clement, First Epistle of', *ABD* 2. 1055–60.

—— , 'A Conciliatory Principle in 1 Cor. 4:6', *NovT* 29 (1987), 320–46.

—— , 'On the Discord in Corinth: 1 Corinthians 1–4 and Ancient Politics', *JBL* 106 (1987), 85–111.

—— , 'The Preface to *1 Clement*: The Rhetorical Situation and the Traditional Date', in C. Breytenbach and L. L. Welborn (eds.), *Encounters with Hellenism: Studies on the First Letter of Clement*, AGAJU 53 (Leiden and Boston: Brill, 2004), 197–216.

Wengst, K., *Häresie und Orthodoxie im Spiegel des ersten Johannesbriefes* (Gütersloh: Mohn, 1976).

—— , *Didache (Apostellehre), Barnabasbrief, Zweiter Klemensbrief, Schrift an Diognet, eingeleitet, herausgegeben, übertragen und erläutert*, SUC 2 (Darmstadt: Wissenschaftliche Buchgesellschaft, 1984).

Weren, W., 'The History and Social Setting of the Matthean Community', in H. van de Sandt (ed.), *The Didache and Matthew: Two Documents from the Same Jewish Christian Milieu?* (Assen: Van Gorcum, 2005), 51–62.

Westcott, B. F., and F. J. A. Hort, *The New Testament in the Original Greek: Introduction* [and] *Appendix*, 2nd. edn. (London and New York: Macmillan, 1896).

Whittaker, J., 'The Value of Indirect Tradition in the Establishment of Greek Philosophical Texts or the Art of Misquotation', in John N. Grant (ed.), *Editing Greek and Latin Texts* (New York: AMS Press, 1989), 63–95.

Wilhelm, A., *Griechische Grabinschriften aus Kleinasien*, Sitzungberichte der Preussischen Akademie der Wissenschaften, philos.-histor. Klasse (1932), 792–865; = *Kleine Schriften*, ii, in W. Peek, R. Fischer, and R. Grose (eds.), *Opuscula: Sammelausgaben seltener und bisher nicht selbständig erschienener wissenschaflicher Abhandlungen*, viii, Akademieschriften zur griechische Inschriftenkunde, Teil 2 (Leipzig: Zentralantiquariat der DDR, 1974).

Wilken, R. L., 'Wisdom and Philosophy in Early Christianity', in *idem* (ed.), *Aspects of Wisdom in Judaism and Early Christianity* (Notre Dame, Ind.: University of Notre Dame Press, 1975), 143–68.

Wilkens, W., 'Das Abendmahlszeugnis im vierten Evangelium', *EvTh* 18 (1958), 354–70.

Wilson, St. B., 'The Anaphora of the Apostles Addai and Mari', in P. F. Bradshaw (ed.), *Essays on Early Eastern Eucharistic Prayers* (Collegeville, Minn.: Liturgical Press, 1997), 19–37.

Winslow, D. F., 'The Idea of Redemption in the Epistles of St. Ignatius of Antioch', *GOTR* 11 (1965), 119–31.

Winterbotham, R., 'The Spirit, and the Water, and the Blood', *Expositor*, 8 (1911), 62–71.

Wintermute, O. S., 'Jubilees: A New Translation and Introduction', in J. H. Charlesworth (ed.), *The Old Testament Pseudepigrapha*, ii (New York: Doubleday, 1985), 35–142.

Wire, A., *The Corinthian Women Prophets: A Reconstruction through Paul's Rhetoric* (Minneapolis: Fortress, 1991).

Witherington, B.,'The Waters of Birth: John 3.5 and 1 John 5.6–8', *NTS* 35 (1989), 155–60.

—— , III, *Jesus the Sage* (Minneapolis: Fortress, 1994).

—— , *Jesus the Seer* (Peabody, Mass.: Hendrickson, 1999).

Wright, D. F., 'Baptism', in Nigel M. de S. Cameron *et al.* (eds.), *Dictionary of Scottish Church History and Theology* (Edinburgh: T. & T. Clark, 1993), 56–8.

—— , 'Infant Dedication in the Early Church', in S. E. Porter and A. R. Cross (eds.), *Baptism, the New Testament and the Church: Historical and Contemporary Studies in Honour of R. E. O. White*, JSNTSup 171 (Sheffield: Sheffield Academic Press, 1999), 352–78.

—— , 'Out, In, Out: Jesus' Blessing of the Children and Infant Baptism', in S. E. Porter and A. R. Cross (eds.), *Dimensions of Baptism: Biblical and Theological Studies*, JSNTSup 234 (Sheffield: Sheffield Academic Press, 2002), 188–206.

Wurm, A., *Die Irrlehrer im ersten Johannesbrief* (St Louis: Herder, 1903).

Yamauchi, E. M., 'The Crucifixion and Docetic Christology', *CTQ* 46 (1982), 1–20.

Young, F., 'Proverbs 8 in Interpretation (2): Wisdom Personified. Fourth Century Readings: Assumptions and Debates', in D. F. Ford and G. N. Stanton (eds.), *Reading Texts, Seeking Wisdom* (London: SCM Press, 2003), 102–15.

—— , 'Wisdom in Augustine's *De Doctrina Christiana*', forthcoming in *StPatr.*

Young, R. D., 'Ignatius of Antioch, "Attaining the Father" ', *Comm* 26 (1999), 333–43.

Young, S., 'Being a Man: The Pursuit of Manliness in the Shepherd of Hermas', *JECS* 2 (1994), 237–55.

Zahavy, T., *Studies in Jewish Prayer* (Lanham, Md.: University Press of America, 1990).

Zahn, T., *Forschungen zur Geschichte des neutestamentlichen Kanons und der altkirchlichen Literatur,* iii: *Supplementum Clementinum* (Erlangen: A. Deichert, 1884).

—— , *Geschichte des neutestamentlichen Kanons,* i (Erlangen and Leipzig, 1889).

Zandee, J., *'The Teachings of Silvanus' and Clement of Alexandria: A New Document of Alexandrian Theology* (Leiden: Ex Oriente Lux, 1977).

Zetterholm, M., *The Formation of Christianity in Antioch* (London and New York: Routledge, 2003).

Zunz, L., *Die gottesdienstlichen Vorträge der Juden, historisch entwickelt: ein Beitrag zur Alterthumskunde und biblischen Kritik, zur Literatur- und Religionsgeschichte* (Berlin: Asher, 1832; 2nd edn. von Nehemias Brüll nach dem Handexemplar des Verfassers berichtigte und mit einem Register vermehrte Auflage, Frankfurt am Main: J. Kauffmann, 1892; repr. Hildesheim: Olms, 1966).

Index of Citations

Old Testament and Apocrypha

New Testament

Apostolic Fathers

Other non-biblical Christian literature

Pseudepigrapha and other extra-biblical Jewish literature

Classical sources

Index of Subjects

Note: Page references in italics indicate tables.

Index of Modern Authors

CONCORDIA UNIVERSITY LIBRARIES
SIR GEORGE WILLIAMS CAMPUS
WEBSTER LIBRARY